DATE DUE

DE 18 '03			
FE 11 '04			
MR 3 1 '09			

DEMCO 38-296

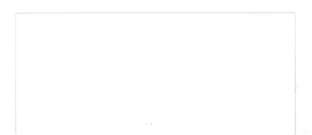

LANDS AND PEOPLES

LANDS AND PEOPLES
ASIA · AUSTRALIA
NEW ZEALAND · OCEANIA

Volume 2

GROLIER
INCORPORATED
DANBURY, CONN.

LANDS AND PEOPLES

HOW TO USE THIS VOLUME

This volume of LANDS AND PEOPLES consists of three main parts. The first and longest part, from page 1 to page 472, covers the nations of Asia. These nations are grouped into five regions: Southwest Asia, South Asia, Southeast Asia, Central and North Asia, and East Asia. Each regional section opens with an introductory essay that serves as a brief overview of the nations, peoples, and geography of that region.

The second part, which runs from page 473 to page 518, examines Australia and New Zealand. Both nations have important indigenous populations—the Aborigines in Australia and the Maoris in New Zealand. However, the dominant culture in each nation has roots that trace back to a single source, the United Kingdom. For this reason it seemed advisable to deal with these nations together and not with the rest of Oceania's nations, all of whose dominant ethnic groups are rooted in the Pacific region.

The third part, on Oceania, runs from page 519 to page 576. Its nations are grouped into three ethnographic regions: Micronesia, Melanesia, and Polynesia. Brief introductory essays are designed to orient the reader to each of these regions.

Many articles in this volume are accompanied by sidebars—short, related items set apart from the main text in a box. Sidebar topics include everything from important river and mountain systems to rare animals, unusual customs, and exotic cultures. The subjects discussed within sidebars, as well as those discussed within the main articles, are listed in the general index found in Volume 6.

CONTENTS

ASIA · AUSTRALIA
NEW ZEALAND · OCEANIA
Volume 2

FLAGS OF ASIA, AUSTRALIA, NEW ZEALAND, OCEANIA

TURKEY

CYPRUS

ARMENIA

GEORGIA

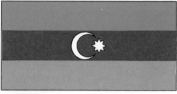

AZERBAIJAN

SYRIA

LEBANON

ISRAEL

JORDAN

SAUDI ARABIA

YEMEN

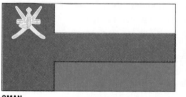

OMAN

UNITED ARAB EMIRATES

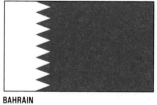

BAHRAIN

QATAR

KUWAIT

IRAQ

IRAN

AFGHANISTAN

PAKISTAN

INDIA

NEPAL

BHUTAN

BANGLADESH

SRI LANKA

MALDIVES

MYANMAR

THAILAND

LAOS

CAMBODIA

VIETNAM

MALAYSIA

SINGAPORE

INDONESIA

BRUNEI

FLAGS OF ASIA, AUSTRALIA, NEW ZEALAND, OCEANIA (continued)

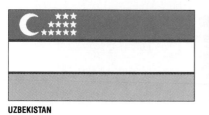

PHILIPPINES

KAZAKHSTAN

UZBEKISTAN

KYRGYZSTAN

TURKMENISTAN

TAJIKISTAN

MONGOLIA

CHINA, PEOPLE'S REPUBLIC OF

CHINA, REPUBLIC OF (TAIWAN)

KOREA, NORTH

KOREA, SOUTH

JAPAN

AUSTRALIA

NEW ZEALAND

PALAU

FEDERATED STATES OF MICRONESIA

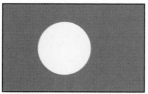

MARSHALL ISLANDS

FLAGS OF ASIA, AUSTRALIA, NEW ZEALAND, OCEANIA (continued)

NAURU

KIRIBATI

PAPUA NEW GUINEA

SOLOMON ISLANDS

VANUATU

FIJI

TONGA

WESTERN SAMOA

TUVALU

Mt. Everest (at left), the highest point on Earth, rises in Asia's tallest mountain range, the Himalayas.

ASIA

In June 1990, an earthquake measuring 7.3 to 7.8 on the Richter scale struck northern Iran. Within seconds, dozens of villages disappeared. Tens of thousands of people died. Two months later, in an apparently unrelated event, scientists 3,000 mi. (4,828 km.) east of Iran made an astounding discovery. They found that the crust beneath Lake Baikal, the world's oldest, deepest lake, is splitting apart at the rate of an inch a year. The scientists suggested that a new ocean is starting to form in the heart of Asia.

The first event was sudden and cataclysmic. The second may take millions of years to unfold. But both point to the powerful natural forces that constantly mold and reshape Asia, the world's largest continent.

Asia periodically endures floods, *tsunamis* (tidal waves), violent quakes, typhoons, and droughts. The June disaster was only one of 10 such big quakes to hit Iran since 1970.

From their earliest known history, Asians have been deeply conscious of the impact of natural forces on their lives. One of the oldest myths in the Yellow (Hwang Ho) River valley in China told of how Yu, a protective dragon, had to defeat the god of floods, Gonggong. While modern-day Chinese and other Asians look to dams and canals to check seasonal floods, their cultural philosophies still reflect a deep respect for the forces of the natural world.

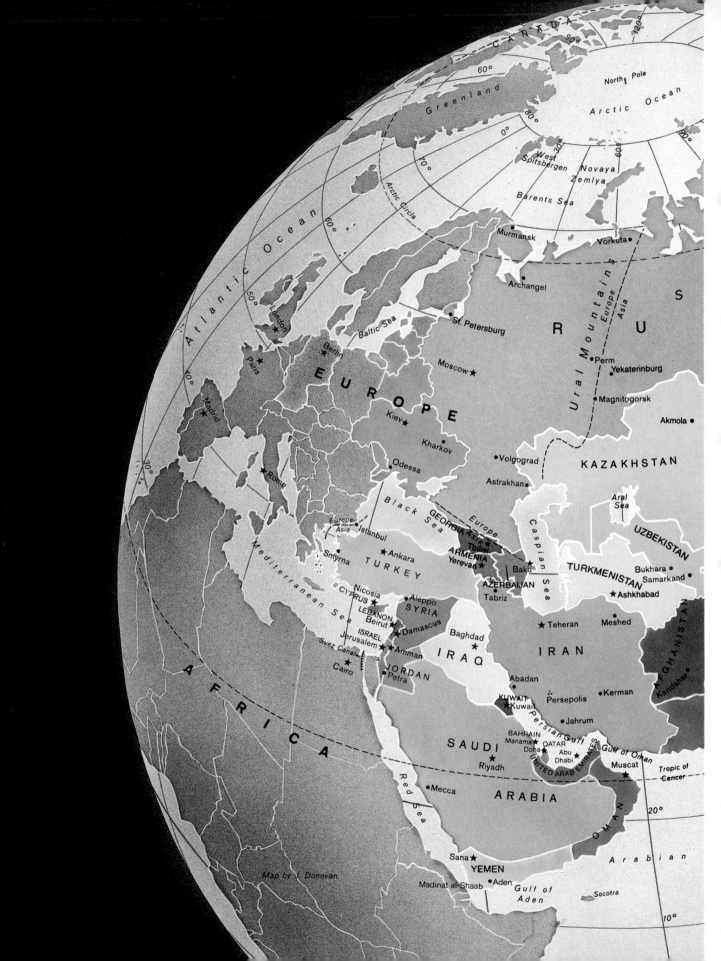

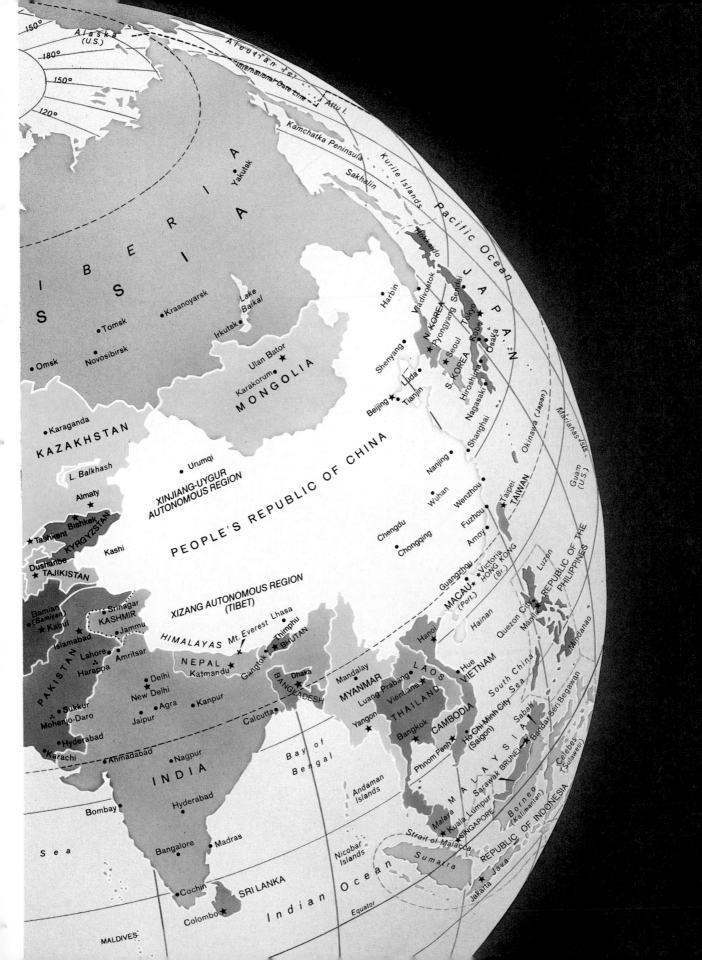

FACTS AND FIGURES

LOCATION: Mainland Asia extends from: **Latitude—** 1°16′ N to 77°41′ N. **Longitude—**26°04′ E to 169°40′ W.

AREA: Approximately 17,000,000 sq. mi. (44,000,000 sq. km.).

POPULATION: 3,501,000,000 (1996 est.; annual growth 1.6%).

PHYSICAL FEATURES: Highest point—Mount Everest (29,028 ft.; 8,848 m.). **Lowest point—**Dead Sea (about 1,300 ft.; 396 m.) below sea level. **Chief rivers—**Chang Jiang (Yangtze), Huang He (Yellow), Amur, Lena, Mekong, Yenisey, Ob, Irtysh, Brahmaputra, Salween, Euphrates, Amu Darya, Ganges, Kolyma, Syr Darya, Irrawaddy, Tarim, Tigris.

THE COUNTRIES OF ASIA

COUNTRY	AREA (sq. mi.)	AREA (sq. km.)	POPULATION (1996 estimate)	CAPITAL
Afghanistan	250,000	647,497	21,500,000	Kabul
Armenia	11,500	29,785	3,800,000	Yerevan
Azerbaijan	33,400	86,506	7,600,000	Baku
Bahrain	260	673	600,000	Manama
Bangladesh	55,598	143,998	119,800,000	Dhaka
Bhutan	18,147	47,001	800,000	Thimphu
Brunei	2,230	5,776	300,000	Bandar Seri Begawan
Cambodia	68,898	178,445	10,900,000	Phnom Penh
China, People's Republic of	3,705,390	9,596,916	1,217,600,000	Beijing
Cyprus	3,572	9,251	700,000	Nicosia
Georgia	26,900	69,671	5,400,000	Tbilisi
India	1,269,340	3,287,575	949,600,000	New Delhi
Indonesia	751,276	1,945,796	201,400,000	Jakarta
Iran	636,293	1,647,991	63,100,000	Teheran
Iraq	167,923	434,919	21,400,000	Baghdad
Israel	8,019	20,769	5,800,000	Jerusalem
Japan	143,749	372,308	125,800,000	Tokyo
Jordan	35,267	91,341	4,200,000	Amman
Kazakhstan	1,049,200	2,717,415	16,500,000	Akmola
Korea (North)	46,541	120,541	23,900,000	Pyongyang
Korea (South)	38,028	98,492	45,300,000	Seoul
Kuwait	6,880	17,819	1,800,000	Kuwait
Kyrgyzstan	76,600	198,393	4,600,000	Bishkek
Laos	91,429	236,800	5,000,000	Vientiane
Lebanon	4,015	10,399	3,800,000	Beirut
Malaysia	128,400	332,554	20,600,000	Kuala Lumpur
Maldives	115	298	300,000	Male
Mongolia	604,103	1,564,620	2,300,000	Ulan Bator
Myanmar	261,217	676,549	46,000,000	Yangon
Nepal	56,827	147,181	23,200,000	Kathmandu
Oman	82,025	212,444	2,300,000	Muscat
Pakistan	310,402	803,937	133,500,000	Islamabad
Philippines	115,830	299,998	72,000,000	Manila
Qatar	4,247	11,000	700,000	Doha
Saudi Arabia	829,996	2,149,680	19,400,000	Riyadh
Singapore	239	619	3,000,000	Singapore
Sri Lanka	25,332	65,610	18,400,000	Colombo
Syria	71,499	185,182	15,600,000	Damascus
Taiwan	13,892	35,980	21,400,000	Taipei
Tajikistan	55,250	143,097	5,900,000	Dushanbe
Thailand	198,456	513,999	60,700,000	Bangkok
Turkey	301,382	780,576	63,900,000	Ankara
Turkmenistan	188,500	488,213	4,600,000	Ashkhabad
United Arab Emirates	32,276	83,594	1,900,000	Abu Dhabi
Uzbekistan	172,700	447,291	23,200,000	Tashkent
Vietnam	129,806	336,196	76,600,000	Hanoi
Yemen	203,849	527,966	14,700,000	Sana

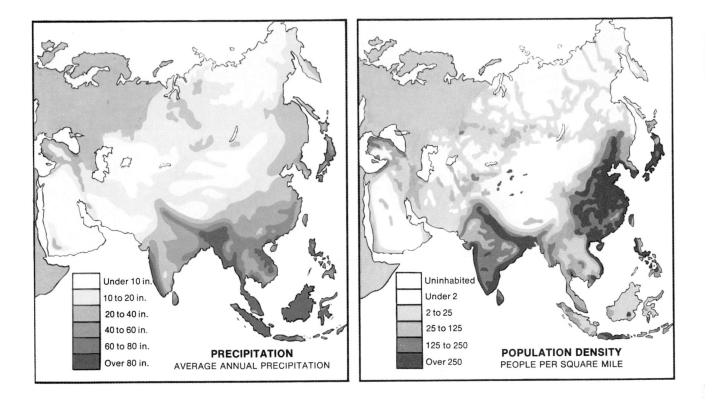

PRECIPITATION
AVERAGE ANNUAL PRECIPITATION

Under 10 in.
10 to 20 in.
20 to 40 in.
40 to 60 in.
60 to 80 in.
Over 80 in.

POPULATION DENSITY
PEOPLE PER SQUARE MILE

Uninhabited
Under 2
2 to 25
25 to 125
125 to 250
Over 250

Separate Continents. Although it is described as the largest continent, Asia is, in fact, the eastern section of an even greater landmass called Eurasia. The Ural Mountains, which lie within Russia and Kazakhstan, are the chief natural boundary between Asia and Europe. The Black Sea, the Bosporus Strait, and the Mediterranean Sea form similar boundaries.

None of these features, however, is as impassable as some of the landforms within Asia, such as the Himalayan Mountains. What that tells us is that the modern-day distinction between the two continents is more the result of separate cultural histories than of geographic barriers.

In fact, Southwest Asia was an ancient crossroads for trade and other contacts between Europe and the rest of Asia. Asia's very name is a reminder of such early contacts. The ancient Greeks, who were among the founders of European civilization, named the land to their immediate east "Asia." The term, which meant the "region of the rising sun," gradually came to apply to all lands between Europe and the Pacific Ocean.

Regions within Asia. For purposes of study, Asia itself is typically divided into six regions. Each is identified by a combination of geographic landforms and distinct cultural traditions. This volume of LANDS AND PEOPLES includes an introductory essay on each region, as well as a detailed article on each country within each region.

Southwest Asia, where the first known human civilization emerged thousands of years ago, has been at the center of world attention for the past several decades. This is the region that produces one-third of the world's oil. Coincidentally, it has been the stage for a long, unresolved conflict between Israel and the Arab world.

Once a strategic and cultural prize coveted by warring empires, Southwest Asia today includes 18 nations: Turkey, Cyprus, Syria, Lebanon, Israel, Jordan, Saudi Arabia, Yemen, Iraq, Iran, Oman, the United Arab Emirates (UAE), Bahrain, Qatar, and Kuwait. Three new independent countries—Armenia, Azerbaijan, and Georgia—emerged in the historic region of Transcaucasia after the collapse of the Soviet Union in December 1991.

South Asia is a peninsula, roughly triangular in shape, separated from the rest of the continent by the Himalayas and several other imposing mountain ranges. The region is dominated by India, which has the second-largest population in the world—more than 900 million in the mid-1990s. Pakistan, Afghanistan, Nepal, Bhutan, Bangladesh, Sri Lanka, and the Maldives also belong to this region.

Southeast Asia embraces a peninsula, sometimes referred to as Indochina, and several major island nations. The region includes Myanmar (formerly Burma), Thailand, Laos, Cambodia, Vietnam, Malaysia, Singapore, Indonesia, Brunei, and the Philippines.

East Asia is home to five nations and two colonies. The global impact of two of these nations is enormous. China has more than 1 billion people—roughly one-fifth of the human race. Japan, with the world's second-largest gross national product (GNP), is by far the continent's most economically successful member. In addition to Taiwan, North

The vast desert land in Southwest Asia contains one-third of the world's oil.

Korea, and South Korea, East Asia includes the British colony of Hong Kong and the Portuguese colony of Macau, both to be returned to China by the end of this century.

Central and **North Asia.** For centuries this huge expanse has been dominated by Russia, which spans land in both Europe and Asia. When the Soviet Union disintegrated in late 1991, five new independent countries replaced the central Asian Soviet republics: Kazakhstan, Uzbekistan, Turkmenistan, Kyrgyzstan, and Tajikistan. Another country in the

The mighty rivers of South Asia serve as the main avenues of trade and transportation.

region is Mongolia. Northern Asia, generally known as Siberia, remains part of the European-centered Russia.

Asia's Population. Altogether, Asia has more than 3.5 billion inhabitants. In the mid-1990s, this number represented about 61 percent of all humankind.

The size of Asia's population has less to do with the continent's habitability (much of Asia's landscape is harsh and forbidding and the climate quite extreme) than with a long history of civilized life among its many peoples. As a matter of fact, the world's first human civilizations—the first city-states, kingdoms, and empires—developed on this continent. Ruins of cities that flourished thousands of years ago are not an uncommon sight in many parts of Asia.

THE LAND

Including both mainland and island nations, Asia covers more than 17 million sq. mi. (44 million sq. km.). Measured along the 40th parallel —from Istanbul, Turkey, to a point north of Tokyo, Japan—Asia spans over 6,000 mi. (9,656 km.), west to east. The distance from its northernmost tip to the southern coast of Indonesia is just about the same.

Topography. Obviously, no single feature could dominate so vast an area as Asia. The most awe-inspiring landforms are the great mountain ranges that radiate from the Pamir highlands of Central Asia, extending eastward through China and as far west as Turkey. To climbers, the best known of these ranges is the Himalayas. Its towering peaks are topped

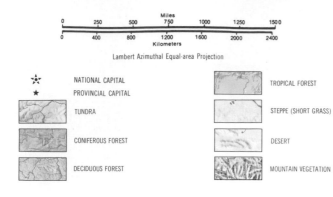

Miles
0 250 500 750 1000 1250 1500

Kilometers
0 400 800 1200 1600 2000 2400

Lambert Azimuthal Equal-area Projection

☆ NATIONAL CAPITAL
★ PROVINCIAL CAPITAL

TUNDRA

CONIFEROUS FOREST

DECIDUOUS FOREST

TROPICAL FOREST

STEPPE (SHORT GRASS)

DESERT

MOUNTAIN VEGETATION

INDEX TO ASIA MAP

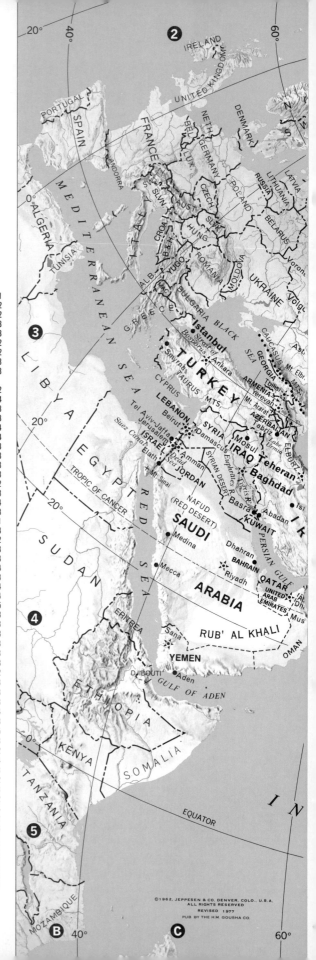

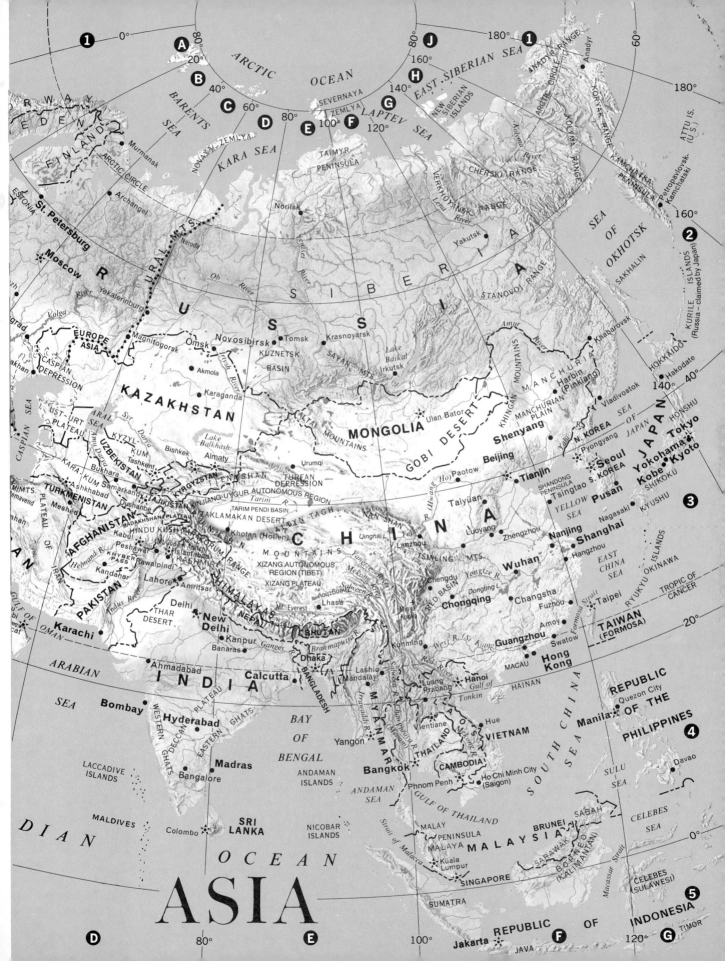

ASIA

OCEAN

Southeast Asia's fertile soil and abundant rainfall favor the growing of rice, the region's staple food.

by Mount Everest, which—at 29,028 ft. (8,850 m.)—is the highest mountain in the world.

Other Asian ranges include the Hindu Kush, which extends west of the Pamirs, through Afghanistan; the Tien Shan and Altai, which thrust into China and North Asia; and the Karakoram and Altyn Tagh, close neighbors of the Himalayas.

Associated with these ranges are the great plateaus of Mongolia, Xizang (Tibet), and India. Xizang, an autonomous region of China, is sometimes referred to as the "roof of the world," a reference to its elevations of more than 3 mi. (4.8 km.).

As Asia's terrain spreads northward, it unfolds in successive belts of deserts, steppes, dark forests, and frozen tundra. Northern Asia, which encompasses almost a third of the continent's area, is known as Siberia.

Of Asia's many desert regions, the largest are the Thar, in India and Pakistan; the Taklamakan, in China; the Syrian and Rub' al-Khali, in Southwest Asia; and the vast Gobi, in Mongolia. The Gobi is particularly well known to modern-day paleontologists for its treasures of massive dinosaur skeletons.

Climate. Spreading from the Arctic Ocean to the equator, Asia includes every major type of climate zone. Yet, despite its vast size and varied climes, much of Asia (particularly in the center and in the north) is not hospitable to human life. Furthermore, it has been estimated that only 10 percent of the continent is capable of supporting crop growth.

Over much of Asia, the annual average rainfall is too slight to permit dry farming—the growing of crops without artificial irrigation. Thus, for centuries, dams, canals, and devices to raise water from rivers and wells have been vital necessities.

On the other hand, tropical rainfall is abundant in many parts of South and Southeast Asia, especially where the rain-laden summer monsoon winds prevail. When the monsoon fails to bring rain, farmers can be wiped out. This fact lends urgency to plans for new irrigation projects along the many great rivers that course through these regions.

Rivers. Asia has more than a third of the world's principal rivers. Among the longest are the Yangtze and Yellow (Hwang Ho) rivers in East Asia; the Ob, Yenisey, Irtysh, Amur, and Lena in North Asia; the Mekong and Irrawaddy in Southeast Asia; the Brahmaputra, Indus, and Ganges in South Asia; and the Tigris-Euphrates rivers in Southwest Asia.

Except for North Asia, where bitter winter temperatures freeze many rivers right down to their beds, Asia's waterways have always been vital to the economies of its various peoples. Indeed, rivers are the key to Asia's past.

EARLY RIVER CIVILIZATIONS

The ancestors of modern-day Asians were Stone Age hunters, whose own forebears had probably emigrated from Africa. Archaeological evidence suggests that tens, and perhaps hundreds, of thousands of years ago, people lived in small clusters in Asia's mountain caves. They hunted, gathered food, and spent a great deal of time making stone tools with which they killed prey, scraped animal skins, and pounded grain.

About 10,000 years ago, the supply of wild animals in Asia's highlands probably began to thin. Whatever the cause, groups of hunters migrated toward the lower valleys of some of the continent's great rivers. Here, in a sequence of steps that is not yet completely clear, they learned to cultivate grains, domesticate animals, and develop practices we now associate with civilized society.

A significant step in the emergence of civilization was the discovery of how to make clay pottery, which could be used for storing water and food. Equally important were the evolution of trade routes, systems of accounting, and the invention of written communication. Communities learned to build permanent relations with one another and, eventually, to unite into what the modern world calls a "state."

The earliest known civilizations in Asia developed near the mouths of the Tigris-Euphrates rivers in Southwest Asia, the Indus River in South Asia, and the Yellow (Hwang Ho) River in East Asia. On these flat, well-watered lowlands, people developed arts, literature, and laws with a wisdom and skill that astonish and inform us today.

Tigris-Euphrates Civilizations

The first civilization to arise was Sumeria, a kingdom between the converging Tigris and Euphrates rivers in what is now Iraq, in Southwest Asia. The Sumerians, who arrived from the Iranian plateau, were not the first people to populate this fertile watershed. But they were the first to develop a permanent state.

The Sumerians' greatest cultural invention may well have been their system of cuneiform (wedge-shaped) writing, which was in use at least

Nearly 4,000 years ago, an ancient people called the Babylonians flourished in the lands between the Tigris and Euphrates rivers, in present-day Iraq. One of their kings, Hammurabi (depicted at left receiving the insignia of royal office), compiled a collection of laws known as the Code of Hammurabi. The ancient sculpture below sets out the laws in cuneiform, the earliest system of writing known.

as early as 3500 B.C. With sharpened marsh reeds, they inscribed clay tablets with messages, prayers, business accounts, royal edicts, legends about their gods, and descriptions of daily life. To their neighbors, the development of written communication must have been as startling as the first television broadcast, thousands of years later.

Their success bred rivals. In about 1900 B.C., political power passed from the Sumerians to the Babylonians, a Semitic people who had migrated north from the Arabian Peninsula. The Babylonians were in turn absorbed by the Assyrians. And thus was set the pattern that would characterize Southwest Asia for thousands of years to come—indeed, into modern times.

One after another, rulers of different empires arose, laying claim to the valley of the Tigris-Euphrates and to other lands within the region. Assyrians, Medes, Persians, Greeks, Romans, Arabs, and Turks swept through Southwest Asia, each absorbing the riches of the previous empire while at the same time often erasing its predecessor's religion, language, and customs. The Greeks gave the Tigris-Euphrates Valley a name—Mesopotamia, ''land between rivers.''

Indus River Civilization

Unlike Southwest Asia, the southern region of the continent has a mysterious past. There is some evidence that the earliest known inhabitants of South Asia arrived from Africa. Thousands of years ago, they were apparently displaced by a later, more dominant group, the Dravidians. The newcomers pushed the original inhabitants southward, forcing many to leave India for the islands off its coast.

By about 2500 B.C., the Dravidians had built an astonishing civilization along a 1,000-mi. (1,609-km.) swath of the fertile Indus River valley, in what is now Pakistan. The remains of two splendid cities, Harappa and Mohenjo-Daro, reveal that the Dravidians understood the concept of urban planning. Ivory, copper, silver, and bronze artifacts testify to their advances in the arts. And there is evidence that they worshiped a mother goddess, as well as sacred animals.

A thousand years later, the more warlike Aryans overpowered the Dravidians and shattered their culture. The Aryans, Indo-Europeans from Central Asia, would influence the future of the region in profound ways. They streamed through mountain passes into the Indian subcontinent at about the same time that other Central Asians were migrating to the Iranian plateau in Southwest Asia.

At first, the Aryans had a nomadic life-style. They seized what they needed as they moved through the land, herding animals as they went. But between the 4th and 6th centuries A.D., their descendants were settled throughout India, and they had created a culture known for its poetry, science, and high moral values.

The great city of Mohenjo-Daro flourished in the Indus Valley thousands of years ago.

Dramatic stone lions guard the gate outside the Forbidden City in Beijing, China.

Among the Aryans' contributions to the subcontinent were a rigid class system and Hinduism, a religion in which life is perceived as a cycle of suffering and rebirth. Buddhism, a religion based on meditation and the observance of moral precepts, also arose in India, but it eventually declined there, flourishing instead among other Asian peoples.

Like Southwest Asia, the Indian peninsula endured a succession of invaders through the ages—Persians, Greeks, Huns, Arabs, and, most notably, Turks. But unlike the region to its west, South Asia remained essentially a multistate region. Accurate or not, the report by a Chinese visitor during the seventh century—that India was divided into 70 kingdoms—had the ring of truth.

The Yellow River Civilization

Although culturally rich societies appeared earlier in other Asian regions, China, in East Asia, boasts the longest continuous civilization.

The language, philosophy, and cultural outlook—but not the politics—of today's Chinese people can be traced back, uninterrupted, to ancestors who lived thousands of years ago.

As with other Asian regions, East Asia was home to humans long before historical records began to be kept. It is clear, for example, that primitive villages were clustered around the "big knee" of the Yellow (Hwang Ho) River, in northern China, as early as 5000 B.C.—many centuries before the ancient Egyptians built the pyramids.

But the first known documents of life in China did not emerge until 3,500 years later. These records are from the Shang dynasty, which governed a civilized state on the banks of the Yellow River between the 16th and 11th centuries B.C.

The Shang state was small, but its people were skilled in silk weaving and the use of bronze, and they considered their way of life superior to that of their neighbors. Border peoples who did not acknowledge the Shang king as the "Son of Heaven" were considered barbarians. This early attitude of Chinese people toward themselves and outsiders became embedded within their tradition.

With few lapses, China was governed by a series of dynasties for the next 30 centuries. The Zhou (Chou) dynasty (c. 1066–256 B.C.) presided over the "classical" age of Chinese culture. It was marked in literature by excellent prose and poetry, in art by the crafting of bronze vessels that are museum pieces today, and in religion and ethics by the teachings of Confucius and other philosophers.

The Han dynasty, which lasted for four centuries (202 B.C.-A.D. 220), was marked by the introduction of Buddhism, the crafting of beautiful

Animals and processions decorate a stairway in Persepolis, an ancient city in modern-day Iran.

THE PEOPLES OF ASIA

An Arab from Kuwait (above right), a girl from Turkey (below right), and a Nepalese girl of Indian descent (near right) are all of Caucasoid stock, as are most of the peoples who live in Southwest and South Asia.

porcelains, the standardization of a written language, and the development of an encyclopedia. By then, the written language of the Chinese contained thousands of separate characters, each of which had to be memorized for use in reading and writing.

During succeeding dynasties, China's government expanded its territory though, in the 13th century A.D., its northern sectors were overrun by Mongols from North Asia, under Genghis Khan. Other Mongols at the time were advancing as far west as the Arabian Peninsula and Central Europe.

It was during the Mongol period, in A.D. 1271, that Marco Polo set out from Venice, Italy, to travel the length of Asia. His written account of his journey, with its descriptions of Chinese silks, paintings, lacquerware, and jade carvings, fascinated Europeans (although some thought his account too fantastic to be true) and made some of them eager to acquire all they read about. In their eagerness for China's goods, however, many Europeans would overlook the other marks of China's civilization, including its highly developed philosophy and literature.

Spread of Civilization

Migrations, trade, and other cultural contacts spread the early cultural achievements of India and China to neighboring parts of Asia. Japan and Southeast Asia provide contrasting examples of how this spread occurred.

Japan. Although no longer thought to be the first to settle in Japan, the Ainu are Japan's earliest known inhabitants. Today, the Ainu number only a few thousand. The people who were to evolve into the dominant Japanese culture arrived from North Asia and other parts of the continent, as well as from nearby Pacific islands.

By the early 400s, Japan had the semblance of a centralized imperial government. Among accounts of this period is the legend of the first

Peoples of East and Southeast Asia include an Indonesian woman (left), an Ainu from Japan (above), Chinese children from Taiwan (near right), and a Boy Scout (far right) from Myanmar.

Japanese emperor, who, the legend held, was directly descended from the sun goddess Amaterasu. (In fact, this belief persisted into the 1900s. Until shortly after World War II, the Japanese ruling family was publicly honored as divine.)

The Japanese adapted the Chinese form of writing to create a written language of their own. This was just one of Japan's many borrowings from the more advanced culture on the Asian mainland. The Japanese also imitated Chinese painting and textile making and adopted Buddhism.

Despite the powerful influence of Chinese thought and culture, the Japanese developed a distinctive culture of their own. The teachings of Buddhism, for example, were merged with the Shinto animist beliefs of the Japanese people. And, unlike China, Japan went through a long period of government by shoguns (military warriors) during the 1100s.

Southeast Asia. Throughout the early human history of Southeast Asia, one group after another was displaced and pushed southward by successive waves of immigrants from China and Xizang (Tibet). Only the inhabitants of the highlands retained their traditional culture.

By the 1st century A.D., traders from India and China were vying for a foothold in the region, drawn there by its rich abundance of minerals, spices, and forest products. For the next 13 to 14 centuries, India's influence dominated, except in what is now Vietnam. China maintained a political foothold there for 1,000 years. Even after it lost control over the area during the 900s, Chinese migrants and merchants continued to make a strong impact on the region.

Throughout this long period, local kingdoms, such as the Khmer empire, rose and fell, but the peoples of the region were never unified culturally. Frequently, they were caught up in savage wars with one another. Even today, there is a legacy of distrust among groups of differing ancestries in Southeast Asia.

The multiethnic character of the peninsula's population is reflected in its religious history. Hinduism (from India) made an early inroad into Southeast Asia. Buddhism eventually became a much more powerful influence. Then, as the ships of Arab traders reached Malaysia and Indonesia during the 1200s, Islam began a heavy penetration of the region, which still has many Muslims.

SHARED CULTURAL OUTLOOK

By the time that Arab traders were plying their vessels eastward across the Indian Ocean, several distinct characteristics had become part of the legacy of most Asian peoples.

Religious and Philosophic Teachings. Without exception, all the great religions of the modern world evolved in Asia. The coincidence has a lot to do with the early emergence of Asian civilization. But it also comes from the deep curiosity about the origins and meaning of life that prevailed among Asian peoples during the time of their ancient history.

The shocking effects of typhoons and floods and earthquakes imprinted a fear and awe of nature on early Asians, as it did on peoples of other continents. By the time they developed civilized societies and the ability to write, Asian peoples had learned to assign the cause of such disasters to all-powerful spirits. Such legends and myths, perpetuated in writing, became the forerunners of organized religions.

Judaism evolved in the second millennium B.C. among the Hebrews, who lived along the Mediterranean coast of Southwest Asia. The He-

Most of the people of mainland Southeast Asia are devout Buddhists.

Islam is the religion of most Southwest Asians. In some areas, notably Iran, Islamic fundamentalists have gained great power. During the prolonged Iran-Iraq War of the 1980s, captured Iraqi troops (above) were forced to display photographs of Iran's leader, the Ayatollah Khomeini.

The Dalai Lama (left) is the spiritual leader of Lamaism, the system of Buddhist teaching and practices developed in Tibet, now the Chinese province of Xizang. He won the 1989 Nobel Peace Prize for his nonviolent campaign to preserve Tibetan culture.

brews rejected the notion that many gods exist, in favor of belief in one deity who made the world and determined its destiny. Exiled from their homeland many times by invading conquerors, the Hebrews, or Jews, eventually migrated to Europe and other continents.

Hinduism, which evolved 4,000 years ago, is an elaborate and difficult religion to define. Most Hindus believe in the existence of many gods, in a cycle of rebirth, and in the wisdom contained in the Vedas, a collection of writings associated with the history of their faith.

During the 6th century B.C., an Indian prince, Siddhartha Gautama, gave up material pleasures for a life of meditation and teaching. In the eyes of his disciples, Gautama attained the status of "the enlightened one," and the faith known as **Buddhism** was born.

In China, the philosopher Confucius taught such values as love, compassion, and justice tempered with mercy. During his lifetime (551–479 B.C.), he placed great emphasis on the importance of observing proper relationships among family members and within the larger community. **Confucianism** became embedded in the attitudes and customs of the Chinese and other Asians.

To the Hebrew belief in one god, the early Christians of Southwest Asia added the notion of an eternal struggle between good and evil and a belief that Jesus Christ was the Son of God, risen from the dead. **Chris-**

Polo originated in Persia (Iran) centuries ago, and eventually spread to China, Pakistan (above), and finally India, where British cavalry officers discovered the game and introduced it to the West.

tianity soon spread to Europe and Africa, though it did not immediately attract as many followers in Asia.

To the monotheism of Jews and Christians, **Islam** in the 7th century added a striking call for social equality. Within a few decades of the summons to faith by the prophet Muhammad, hundreds of thousands converted to Islam. The new religion, carried by Arab merchants and tribal leaders, spread rapidly across Southwest Asia and Africa. To the east, it penetrated Central Asia, India, and Southeast Asia.

Admiration of Strong, Charismatic Leaders. To many early Asians, the ruler of their state, kingdom, or empire had the qualities of a demigod. He was, alternately, high priest or (as in Japan) an offspring of the gods. In real life, he very often was a conqueror, whose victories seemed to confer glory on his people.

The most renowned of Southwest Asian rulers in the 2nd millennium B.C. was **Hammurabi,** ruler of Babylon. His proclamation of standard-setting, permanent laws made him famous throughout the region. More than a thousand years later, during the 5th century B.C., **Darius I** brought glory to the Persians when he united an empire that stretched across Southwest and South Asia. He and his successors bore the impressive title "Great King."

A different kind of leader was **Asoka**, an Indian ruler in the 3rd century B.C. After uniting almost all of India, he grew tired of war and turned to Buddhism for guidance. He dispatched Buddhist missionaries to countries as far away as Egypt and is sometimes credited with having made Buddhism a world religion.

From Mesopotamia, in the 12th century A.D., arose a great Muslim leader. During his lifetime, the warrior **Saladin** elated his followers by twice defeating European armies that were trying to gain a foothold for Christendom on the eastern shore of the Mediterranean. (In 1990, Iraqi leader Saddam Hussein sought to link his name with Saladin's, after Iraq invaded Kuwait, and both Arab and non-Arab leaders throughout the world condemned the move.)

Accepting One's "Proper Place." In every organized Asian society in early times, there was a privileged elite, in which membership was the result of birth, appointment, or victory in war. The rest of the population worked hard for a meager living, and there was little to break up the daily cycle of work, meals, and sleep.

In India, a special form of class distinction, the caste system, emerged with the arrival of the Aryans. The four major categories of castes included Brahmans, or priests (the highest level); Kshatriyas, or warriors; Vaisyas, or bankers and merchants; and Sudras, or farmers, artisans, and laborers. Below the Sudras were the "Untouchables"—a group whose members performed tasks that others despised and who were not allowed social contacts with anyone outside their number.

Loyalty to One's Family Group and Tribe. In ancient Asia, the vast majority of people were members of an agricultural community or a nomadic tribe. Nomads followed a code based on loyalty to other tribal members. In such places as Iran, Arabia, and Mongolia, nomads were completely dependent on what nature provided for the survival of their animal herds and themselves. The location of pasturage, for example, determined where they would next pitch their tents. A nomad owned only as much as animals on the move could carry.

With such a life-style, the ever-present threat of disaster—a drought, a contagious disease, or a raid by enemies—bound the members of each tribe or village to one another in hard work and mutual help. At the very heart of every social group was the family unit, whose responsibility was to instill and reward community loyalty and punish disloyalty.

One of the outcomes of such cultural experiences was a strong tendency to seek group consensus before acting. This goal nurtured habits of long discussion, patient listening, and attention to courtesies that still persist among many Asians today.

Technological Excellence. Despite the harsh daily working conditions that Asians faced in early times, the civilizations they were a part of often flourished for long periods. In such circumstances, skilled craftwork became a cultural legacy. For centuries, anonymous Asians created great works of artistic value—brilliant handwoven silks, vessels of gleaming metal and fine pottery, jewelry encrusted with gems, and breathtaking works of architecture. Among the latter, several "wonders of the ancient world" stand out.

Persepolis, in southern Iran, was the spiritual heart of the empire of the Medes and the Persians, who conquered much of Asia. Set upon a rock and rising from a vast plain, its ruins reveal an amazing array of buildings from the 6th to 5th centuries B.C. Persepolis boasts carved stone reliefs showing people bearing gifts for their rulers—animals, weapons, vessels of metal and stone, and jewelry. The site was destroyed by the Greeks in 330 B.C.

Angkor Wat, a temple complex, lies within what was the ancient capital of Cambodia. In about A.D. 1100, great stone towers were erected on the site, each carved with figures and faces of Brahma and other

An old painting depicts an unsuccessful invasion of Korea by the Japanese.

Hindu gods. The magnificence of Angkor Wat lies in its great size and architectural complexity.

The church of **Hagia Sophia,** or "divine wisdom," was constructed at Constantinople (now Istanbul, Turkey) in the 6th century A.D. Hagia Sophia covers an enormous area and was the outstanding monument of the Byzantine, or Eastern Roman, Empire. After the capture of Constantinople by the Turks in 1453, the church became a Muslim mosque. It now serves as a museum.

ASIAN HISTORY SINCE THE 1400s

The Muslim Turks who captured Constantinople in the middle of the 1400s developed the last great empire in Southwest Asia before modern times. In its early stages, the Ottoman Empire embodied all the trappings of a traditional Asian society, with autocratic rulers, conquering armies, and the unquestioned loyalty of its peoples to religion, tribe, and leader.

Southwest Asia was not alone in its ascendancy in the mid-1400s. In East Asia, the Chinese had driven out the Mongol invaders and, under the Ming dynasty, were making great achievements in trade, architecture, and literature. The Indians in South Asia were just a few decades away from the establishment of a powerful Mogul Empire, under Muslim rulers. And in Southeast Asia, the new state of Malacca on the Malay Peninsula was becoming that region's major trading center.

Democracy and capitalism as the modern world knows them did not exist in Asia in the mid-1400s. But within a few years, the voyages to Asia of a handful of Europeans would lead to the development of both great institutions of the modern world and, simultaneously, to the decline of Asia's empires.

Advance of the Europeans

In 1498, the Portuguese navigator Vasco da Gama reached India by sailing around the southern tip of Africa. The report of his crew's success electrified western Europeans, who had been seeking a route, other than the overland passage used by Italian merchants, to the lucrative trading ports of Asia.

Da Gama was followed by Portuguese traders, who set up commercial contacts along the coasts of India, Ceylon (now Sri Lanka), and Malaya (now Malaysia). During the latter half of the 1500s, Spain established a trading post in the Philippine Islands. The Dutch began to colonize Indonesia, then known as the Dutch East Indies, during the 1600s.

Marco Polo's 13th-century travels across Asia introduced Europe to the wonders of the East.

Rivalry for the pepper, cloves, nutmeg, camphor, sandalwood, pearls, musk, and other riches of the "Far East" intensified among European trading companies. This was particularly true in India.

During the 1600s, the English East India Company set up trading posts at Madras, Bombay, and Calcutta. But as the British moved inland, their advance was blocked by both French rivals and local Indian rulers. A series of wars resulted, and, by the end of the 1700s, the British emerged as the dominant colonial power in India. From India, they expanded south and east, taking Ceylon from the Dutch (who had earlier taken it from the Portuguese) and conquering Myanmar (Burma).

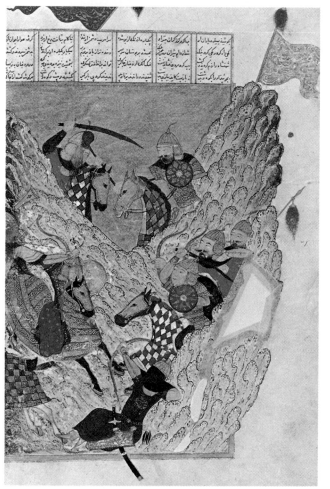

In 1260, the victory of the Mongol armies of the Chinese brought Kublai Khan to the throne of China as the first emperor of the Yuan, or Mongol, dynasty.

While the British were active in India, the French carved out an empire in Southeast Asia. In 1862, they gained control of three provinces in what is now Vietnam. Eventually they took over the eastern part of the Southeast Asian peninsula. French Indochina, as it came to be called, included the present states of Vietnam, Cambodia, and Laos.

Meanwhile, the northern part of Asia—known as Siberia—was gradually being claimed by Russia. The first expansions east of the Urals began at the end of the 1500s; by the early 1800s Russia controlled a huge territory as far east as Kamchatka and as far south as Kazakhstan. The region remained only sparsely inhabited, but Siberian furs and minerals became important export items of the Russian Empire.

Two-way trade with China had long been a goal of European powers, but the Chinese wanted only half the opportunity. Chinese emperors were willing to allow the sale of porcelain, silk, and other goods to foreign merchants but saw no reason to buy from "barbarians." As a result of a war in the early 1800s, however, the British acquired Hong Kong and gained special trading rights in Chinese port cities. Other nations claimed "spheres of influence" along China's coast. Chinese nationalists reacted strongly to this foreign intervention. In 1900, a nationalist group known as the Boxers attacked the foreign legations in Beijing

(Peking), but a combined military force from the colonizing nations defeated them.

Japan. Japan was long open to the influence of China, but it deliberately refused almost all Western contacts, beginning in the early 1600s. By 1853, however, it reversed that policy. During a visit by an American naval squadron, the Japanese were pressured into establishing trade relations with the United States, whose interest in Asia would grow still greater when it acquired the Philippines in 1898.

Realizing that their country would remain a third-rate power if they continued to rely on agriculture alone, the Japanese agreed. In addition, they soon began an enormous and successful effort to catch up with Western industrialization. The Japanese adoption of a constitutional monarchy in 1889 only served to spur this effort.

A few years later, when the Russians attempted to move into Korea, the Japanese strongly opposed them, resulting in the Russo-Japanese War (1904–5). Japan, which had adopted Western methods and military techniques, defeated the Russians. This was the first time that an Asian nation had defeated a European colonial power in a major war.

Asia in the 20th Century

The Japanese victory against the troops of the Russian czars gave hope to other Asians who wished to end European colonialism and establish independent governments. In addition, many young Asians who had studied in Europe and the United States felt inspired to agitate for political independence in their homelands. Added to this, the upheavals of World War I and World War II shattered many of the old-world underpinnings of imperialism and colonialism.

East Asia. The first major success of a nationalist movement in Asia occurred in China, where Sun Yat-sen and his Guomindang (Kuomin-

In 1853, U.S. warships forced Japan to open itself to trade with the West.

tang), or Nationalist Party, established a republic in 1912 after the collapse of the Qing (Ch'ing or Manchu) dynasty. For the next few decades, the Chinese were caught up in a civil war, a struggle between Nationalist and Communist factions, and an invasion by the Japanese. The conflict with the Japanese pulled China into World War II.

China was on the winning side of that war. But the Communist government, which came to power in China in 1949, undertook a disastrous effort to impose unity and uniformity throughout China. It also tried to cope with the country's economic problems through national, rather than provincially focused, programs. In the process, the government created much turmoil when it tampered with many of the old values of Chinese society, including customs that supported its traditional, tight-knit family units.

Korea, which Japan had annexed in 1910, was divided at the end of World War II in a conflict of influence between the Soviet Union and the United States. By the mid-1990s, Communist North Korea and the Republic of Korea in the south were still separated, but the mutual hostility had diminished and they were beginning to communicate.

Southwest Asia.   The breakup of the Ottoman Empire in 1918, following World War I, seemed an opportune moment for the victorious allies to establish their presence in Southwest Asia. Armed with mandates from the newly formed League of Nations, Great Britain and France began

Jerusalem remains an important holy city to Jews, Muslims, and Christians.

In many Asian countries, religious minorities agitate against discrimination. In India, the Sikhs' militant campaign to establish their own homeland in the state of Punjab has not been well received by the Indian government.

to control the region, but in the following decades each state in Southwest Asia achieved independence. A bitter conflict arose after World War II between Israel and the surrounding Arab nations, and even though peace negotiations began in late 1993, real peace is still far away.

South Asia. During the 1920s and 1930s, Mohandas K. Gandhi developed the tactics of nonviolent opposition to authority as a weapon against the British presence in India. When India gained independence from the British Empire in 1947, it split into two states—predominantly Hindu India and predominantly Muslim Pakistan. Bangladesh, formerly East Pakistan, came into existence in 1971. Bhutan and Sri Lanka gained independence in the late 1940s, and Nepal's king established a cabinet government in 1951. In the mid-1960s, Maldives proclaimed independence, and in the early 1970s, Afghanistan became a republic.

Southeast Asia. The period after World War II saw an intensification in nationalist feeling and movements for independence in many Southeast Asian nations. The Philippines, Myanmar (formerly Burma), Laos, Cambodia, Malaysia, Singapore, and Indonesia all became sovereign states in the decades following World War II.

In 1954, after drawn-out fighting with France, Vietnam won its independence. Yet, by agreement with the French, it remained divided temporarily at the 17th parallel. Antagonisms between northerners and southerners flared into a civil war that did not end until 1975 with a victory for the Communist north. Vietnam was united in 1976.

Transcaucasia and Central Asia. In early 1992, eight new Asian states emerged from the ruins of the defunct Soviet Union: Armenia, Azerbaijan, and Georgia in Transcaucasia; and Kazakhstan, Uzbekistan, Turkmenistan, Kyrgyzstan, and Tajikistan in Central Asia. A series of fierce ethnic wars in Transcaucasia and a civil and religious war in Tajikistan brought these countries close to economic and social collapse.

Asian Languages: Profile of a Continent

The diversity of peoples in modern-day Asia is no more apparent than in a survey of the languages they speak. These languages are classified as "families," or groups of languages related by common ancestry, and as distinct tongues that are native to specific places.

In 1989, a brief but dramatic movement for greater democracy in China was crushed by the government.

Language Families. In Asia, the major language group is **Sino-Tibetan,** which includes languages spoken in China and throughout Southeast Asia. **Indo-European** languages comprise the second-largest group of languages spoken in Asia; they are prevalent throughout India and in countries to its west, and they include Russian, which is spoken in Central and North Asia.

Other language families in Asia include **Hamito-Semitic** languages, such as Arabic and Israeli Hebrew, in Southwest Asia; **Dravidian,** heard in South Asia—especially in southern India and northern Sri Lanka; **Malayo-Polynesian,** spoken throughout Southeast and East Asia, from the Malay Peninsula to Taiwan; and **Altaic,** heard in such far-apart places as Mongolia (in North Asia) and Turkey (in Southwest Asia).

Asia's Most Widespread Languages. In China alone, 836 million people speak Mandarin. In India, more than 333 million speak Hindi. Arabic is the native tongue of more than 186 million people. Bengali, Malay-Indonesian, and Japanese are each spoken by more than 100 million Asian people.

More than 20 other languages—Punjabi, Korean, Tamil, Wu, Javanese, and Farsi, for example—are each the native language of more than 20 million people. In the majority of Asian countries, the most widely spoken second language is English.

ASIA TODAY

By the late 1990s, colonialism in Asia was a thing of the past. But several major problems, some of which predated the arrival of the Portuguese in 1498, still held Asia in their grip.

Finding a Workable Form of Government

Probably the most far-reaching impact of the Western world on Asia was the introduction of its political theories and institutions. All Asian nations now have constitutions and claim to be democratic, but full multiparty democracy is in place in very few countries. Japan may be closest to a Western political model, but it has preserved many of its traditional characteristics. India, which has been democratic for decades, is plagued by its enormous social, religious, and ethnic problems. In nations such as South Korea, Taiwan, or Indonesia, the opposition parties have much less clout than do their counterparts in the West.

Communism was also a European import, and it took hold in many Asian countries, particularly in the east and southeast. The first Asian country to adopt Communism was Mongolia, in 1924, followed by China and others after World War II. The collapse of Communist rule in Eastern Europe and the Soviet Union has had repercussions in Asia as well. Mongolia and the former Soviet republics in Central Asia have shed Communist ideology (albeit not Communist practices), and Afghanistan's Communist government was defeated in early 1992. China, Laos, and Vietnam remain Communist, but are becoming economically more open. Even North Korean leaders are now somewhat less hostile in their dealings with non-Communist countries.

Beyond these conflicts, however, general political instability has troubled many Asian nations. After Indonesia gained its independence in 1949, for example, divisiveness and antagonism among some 30 political parties prevented needed legislation from being passed. In other cases—Myanmar after 1962 and Iran during the 1980s and early 1990s, for instance—authoritarian leaders have managed to dominate all elements

In South Korea, civil unrest has moved the government to make numerous reforms.

of legitimate government. The possibility of a military coup is also a continual threat in some states, as it was in the Philippines during the late 1980s and early 1990s.

Addressing Minority Rights

Other forces in Asia today tend to hinder national unity. One such hindrance is the resistance of minority groups that have been thrust together with unrelated peoples within national boundaries set by colonial powers to intermingle peacefully. Other minorities strive to rid themselves of the second-class status they experience in lands to which they migrated centuries ago. And still others suffer the double indignity of being unwelcome refugees in lands already poor.

Moves for Self-determination. Various groups throughout Asia—the Kurds in Southwest Asia, for example—have agitated for autonomy, or self-government, based on language or ethnic distinctiveness. Their goal is not without precedent. In 1971, the East Bengalis won their independence in a civil war, from which the new nation of Bangladesh emerged.

Unwelcome Minorities. Another problem facing a number of Asian governments arises from tensions between ethnic minorities and the predominant culture group in a country. The status of Koreans in Japan, who feel treated as second-class citizens, is one such example. Sizable Chinese and Indian minorities in several Southeast Asian states have similar complaints. These groups sometimes dominate small business and banking, and for these reasons majority populations often look on them with a mixture of envy and resentment.

In 1990, the Iraqi invasion of Kuwait produced hundreds of thousands of new refugees.

After the 1990 Iraqi invasion of Kuwait, U.S. troops were sent to the region to repel further aggression.

Refugees. The world in the mid-1990s contained more than 16 million refugees, slightly less than half of them in Asia. Nearly 6 million people fled from Afghanistan during the Soviet occupation and subsequent civil war. More than 2 million refugees were Palestinians, including several generations of families displaced during Arab-Israeli wars.

Many more were voluntary economic refugees, migrants from poor countries who had taken temporary jobs in such places as the oil-rich states of the Persian Gulf. The crisis provoked by Iraq's invasion of Kuwait in 1990 put hundreds of thousands of such workers to flight. Most had to leave behind all their money and possessions. After the 1991 Gulf War, Kuwait expelled most of its substantial Palestinian population from the emirate.

After the end of the Vietnam War, thousands of so-called boat people fled Vietnam in fishing boats in hopes of eventually reaching the United States. Many of them continue to languish in Asian refugee camps, while others have been turned back from Hong Kong and other Asian ports for fear that temporary asylum might turn them into permanent settlers.

Resolving Border Disputes

Asia is not the only continent that is heir to border disputes and other causes of friction between neighbors. But some of these conflicts are long-lived and especially volatile, and a few have had a global impact.

Cambodia disputes at least three points on its border with Vietnam, a traditional enemy. China has had border disagreements with India, North Korea, and Russia. And Japan has a territorial conflict with Russia, which occupied the northern Kuril Islands at the end of World War II.

In Southwest Asia, boundary disputes between Iran and Iraq had been a factor in a long (1980–88) war between the two countries. In 1990, Iraq invaded Kuwait, claiming—among other things—that Kuwait was stealing Iraqi oil. A swift defeat of Iraq in the 1991 Gulf War was followed by talks aimed at a broad peace settlement in the Middle East.

The most intractable dispute in the region has been the warring between Israel and its Arab neighbors. The 1996 election of a Palestinian self-rule authority in the West Bank and Gaza Strip was a sign of progress toward peace, although violence by Palestinian extremists continued.

A deadly conflict that emerged in the late 1980s between Armenians and Azerbaijani over the Armenian-inhabited enclave of Nagorno-Karabakh within Azerbaijan continued into the late 1990s, although the Armenian government renounced its formal claim to the region in 1992.

Building a Workable Economy

The top long-term goal of most Asian nations is the development of a stable, independent economy. Though most Asian countries have not yet recovered from the economic drain imposed by colonialism and recent wars, a few have enjoyed enormous economic success. Foremost among the success stories are the oil-rich states of the Persian Gulf in Southwest Asia; Japan in East Asia; and several smaller but rapidly advancing market economies throughout the continent.

U.S. weaponry, such as the Patriot missile below, led to an Iraqi defeat in the Persian Gulf War.

Armed forces from both western and Arab countries worked together to liberate Kuwait.

Oil Economies. During the 1980s, Saudi Arabia, Kuwait, Iraq, Iran, and other Gulf states produced and sold enormous quantities of petroleum and natural gas. Much of the great wealth from such sales was used to build roads and other infrastructure and to provide social benefits for the people. Before the 1990 Iraqi invasion, tiny Kuwait had one of the highest per-capita incomes in the world. Kuwait's oil installations were damaged during the Iraqi occupation, and a total international embargo of Iraqi oil exports continued until May 1996.

The Japanese Model. After defeat in World War II, Japan regained and then surpassed the industrial might it had achieved during the 1920s and 1930s. With early support from the government, Japanese industrialists first built an export market in textiles, then switched to steel, cars, and other manufactures, and finally turned to electronics. By the beginning of the 1990s, the value of Japan's annual output of goods and services was surpassed only by the individual output of the United States.

Taiwan and Other Asian "Tigers." The lesson taught by Japan was not lost on some of its neighbors. Taiwan, the island refuge of Nationalist Chinese who fled Communism in 1949, was the first to adopt the Japanese economic model. The country followed a similar export path—from agricultural products, to textiles, to electrical machinery. The standard of living in Taiwan is now among the highest in all Asia.

During the 1970s, the economies of South Korea, Hong Kong, and Singapore also made enormous strides. Together, these four nations won the world's admiring title "Asia's Tigers."

Newly Industrialized Economies (NIEs). Like impatient cubs, still other Asian countries—Thailand, Malaysia, the Philippines, and Indonesia—are following the path opened by the four tigers. Differences exist, however. Most capital investments for Asian industry once came from the United States and Europe. But today's NIEs draw most of their investments from Japan and Taiwan. One assessment of Japan's extensive investments, in *Forbes* magazine, suggested that Japan was creating a sort of "economic colony" in other parts of Asia.

Another difference for the newer NIEs lies in their strategy for attracting investment. When Asian economies, such as Singapore's, began to expand in the 1960s, they relied on being entrepôts—points at which exports from country "A" were unloaded for reshipment to country "B." But today, NIEs urge foreign companies to locate plants within their borders, offering low-salaried workers as an attraction.

The strategy is paying off. Thailand entered the 1990s as the world's number-one exporter of canned tuna. Its economy is growing at an annual rate of more than 7 percent, and Malaysia's growth rate is about 9 percent.

Communist and Formerly Communist Countries. China, the major Communist nation of Asia, has moved toward a "mixed" economy—that is, a combination of state-owned and privately owned businesses and industries. Private farming was introduced in the late 1970s: farmers lease land from the government and are allowed to make a profit from the sale of all produce beyond the amount they contract to deliver to the state.

Japan and other affluent Asian countries have embraced many aspects of Western culture.

Poverty and overpopulation present seemingly insurmountable problems for many Asian countries.

The new system has been very successful, and Chinese farm products now account for a large part of the country's export income. The Chinese government also encourages small and medium-sized industries, but heavy industry remains under the control of the national government. Another country that has also reopened the door to free enterprise is Vietnam: by 1990, one-third of its people's income came from privately owned, profit-making farms and businesses.

Mongolia and the former Soviet republics in Central Asia and Transcaucasia are all struggling with the legacy of decades of centrally managed economies, as they experiment with free-market systems. In addition, their economic progress is hampered by political and ethnic conflict. The economies of two former Communist countries, Afghanistan and Cambodia, have been ravaged by protracted civil wars, and it will take years for them to heal.

Overcoming Obstacles to Growth

Despite China's enthusiastic goals and the success of Japan and the NIEs, the transition to industrialization in many Asian countries faces big obstacles. In order to industrialize, many Asian countries must import machinery, iron and steel, electrical equipment, cars, trucks, and hundreds of other start-up materials. But to pay for such goods, they must have something to sell.

With few exceptions, Asia's major resources are raw materials, such as jute, rice, tea, rubber, oil, tin, and timber. These products must compete for markets with similar goods from other parts of the world, in a global economy in which the selling prices of raw materials often fluctuate. One result is that many Asian countries cannot overcome an unfavorable balance of trade. The sale of their goods overseas earns them far less than they need to buy goods abroad. They face a number of other obstacles as well.

Rapid Urban Growth. In many Asian countries, urban growth is occurring at a faster rate than growth in rural areas, where electrification and other basic services are still in short supply. In addition, the pressure for housing and jobs is so intense for poor rural families that younger Asians simply leave their villages and head for the nearest large city, such as Calcutta, in India; Jakarta, in Indonesia; and Karachi, in Pakistan. At least 15 Asian cities have populations of 5 million or more.

At least two nations have tried to temper this rush to the cities. In China, no one can move to a city without permission. Moreover, agricultural reforms have raised living standards in rural areas, reducing the desire to move to big cities. In addition, jobless farm workers can often find employment in small towns and medium-sized cities in the country's interior. India's government, also, is steering new industries into provinces with a high rate of joblessness and giving small-scale enterprises favored treatment.

Persistent Poverty. The average per capita income of two-thirds of all Asians falls below the 1990 World Bank's poverty line of $370. At issue is not only the lack of good jobs and money. Riding the coattails of poverty

Members of the growing Asian middle class often run retail shops and other small businesses.

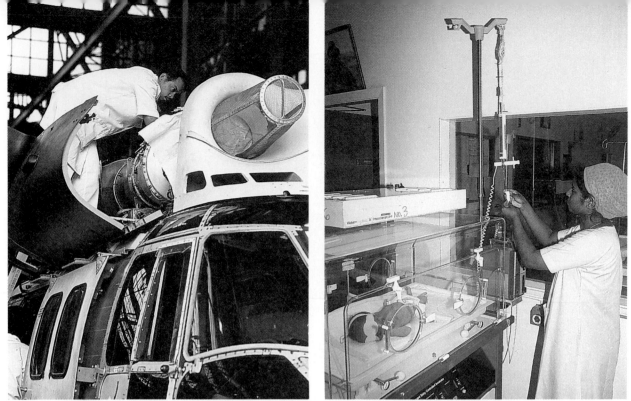
State-of-the-art technology has contributed to the swift industrialization of Indonesia (left) and other countries. Modern medicine has dramatically lowered the infant mortality rate (right).

are other problems that only governments can address—widespread hunger, disease, and illiteracy, to name a few. In at least six Asian nations, for example—Afghanistan, Bhutan, Nepal, Cambodia, Bangladesh, and Yemen—the infant mortality rate in the mid-1990s was higher than 10 percent.

Virtually every country in Asia, rich and poor, has defined its citizens' rights to a job, to adequate food and lodging, free medical care, and various social-security benefits. But in the majority of countries, limited financial resources make such promises meaningful only as distant goals.

Energy Needs. Asia's thirst for energy to fuel its factories sometimes seems insatiable. South Korea's oil use increased by 20 percent during the 1980s. Thailand's need for electricity rose 10 percent a year during the same decade. Fuels (mostly oil) constitute the first or second most important import of the majority of Asian nations. In India, the substantial consumer interest in home washing machines is offset by the unavailability of electricity, despite the fact that India has the fourth-largest reserves of coal in the world.

China has a good deal of petroleum and more than enough coal to supply its needs. But it lacks railways and roads to ship coal from its western mines to the industrial centers in its east. Only Japan, which practices intense conservation measures and which derives more than a third of its power from nuclear-power plants, entered the 1990s confident that it could meet any temporary fuel shortage.

The remedy may lie with Asia's many great rivers and their huge potential for hydroelectric power. Studies have already been completed for an ambitious project to develop the resources and water supply of

Rapid modernization has not diminished the central role played by the family in Asian life.

the Mekong River valley, which separates Thailand from Laos and crosses through Cambodia and Vietnam.

Absorbing Social Change

The end of colonialism, the advent of democracy, and the new directions of Asian economies have caused enormous changes in some aspects of Asian society. The most dramatic changes are occurring in the lives of women—and, for that reason, in family life as well.

In the eyes of Westerners, the situation of women in some Asian countries is oppressive. One of the clues to women's status within a Muslim community is the prevalence—or absence—of the *purdah* (complete veil) or *tudong* (half veil) on women seen in public. Such customs are the community's signal that the woman's place is in her home, where her role is to teach children obedience and loyalty to religion, family, and the community.

Some Muslim women in Asia argue that, far from making women second-class citizens, Islam teaches the equality of the sexes. They hold that prohibitions concerning the dress and out-of-home occupations of women are merely ancient customs, dating from times before the advent of Islam. The fact that women are encouraged to pursue higher education and to work outside their homes in such Islamic nations as the United Arab Emirates and Kuwait bolsters their argument.

In fact, women throughout Asia are increasingly entering the workplace. In Hong Kong and Taiwan, 55 percent of all women between the ages of 15 and 64 were employed outside the home during the early 1990s. In Pakistan, India, Nepal, and Bangladesh, poor rural women have all they can do caring for their large families. But even here, a village

The presence of Asian women at universities has grown significantly in recent years.

woman who manages to develop a small handicraft, such as embroidery, may market her goods and gain a major increase in income and status.

As Asian women become more literate and begin to participate in democratic government, their role—and that of men as well—will undoubtedly change. The promise is already there. The 1987 Philippine constitution declared that "the state recognizes the role of women in nation-building and shall ensure the fundamental equality before the law of men and women."

ASIA TOMORROW

As Asian nations face the 21st century, they are confronted with several challenges. At the top of the list is finding ways to cope with rapid population growth. After 1750, it took 150 years for the continent's population to double. Currently, doubling occurs about every 30 years—more quickly in nations such as Bangladesh, Mongolia, and Pakistan.

Population Control

In many Asian countries, the problem of overpopulation is being tackled through family planning and birth control. However, the governments of some countries with large Catholic constituencies, such as the Philippines, face the objections of church leaders to the recommendation of contraceptives for family planning.

India's middle class—about one-eighth of its population—has been able to reduce its birthrate, but traditional rural populations continue to resist birth-control measures. India's total population, increasing by 2 percent a year, is expected to outstrip China's sometime during the early decades of the next century.

Japan was one of the first countries to establish goals for population growth, and, as a result, its population is increasing at less than 1 percent a year. China's government adopted a strong birth-control policy during the 1970s, demanding that married couples limit their families to one child each. The campaign involved offers of economic rewards, such as job bonuses and free education, to one-child families. The policy has come under considerable criticism, however, for being too extreme.

Ethnic Strife

The conflicts between Israel and its Arab neighbors, the striving of Kurds for autonomy, the war between Armenians and Azerbaijani, and many other ethnic hostilities will not be resolved quickly. With the end of the Cold War, however, greater international cooperation and good-will may eventually bring solutions. The almost unanimous world response condemning Iraq's aggression against Kuwait, international efforts to stop hostilities in Transcaucasia, the holding of elections in Cambodia under United Nations supervision, and international pressures to create peace in the Middle East could be harbingers of the future.

The Reconciliation of Old and New Values

Another challenge confronting Asians is finding ways to sustain traditional cultures in a world that tends to measure progress by access to Western fast food, pop music, and appliances. Among Asia's young, especially, the spread of television, with its depictions of luxurious lifestyles enjoyed by the privileged few, has raised the level of economic expectation—and, in some cases, resentment.

As in many Western countries, television has had an enormous impact on Asians. In China, millions watched the 1988 television presentation of the *River Elegy* series, which dealt with China's past and future. Millions more have watched the Sunday-morning episodes of Hindu epics, such as the *Ramayana* and the *Mahabharata,* in India. Indian television carries advertisements for products that the vast majority of viewers will never be able to afford.

Despite such changes, traditional values are still strong among modern-day Asians. For example, the Confucian values of dedication to one's family and a readiness to postpone pleasure in the face of obligation are surely major factors in East Asia, where workers routinely put in 10-hour-per-day, six-day workweeks.

Elsewhere on the continent, many Muslims believe that the teachings of Islam should govern the social, political, and economic conduct of all community members. During the 1980s and 1990s, calls for a return to the "pure" Muslim community were heard with increasing frequency in places such as Pakistan and especially Iran, which now is ruled by a government that is essentially an Islamic theocracy.

The conflict between new and old values will undoubtedly engage Asians well into the 21st century. The conflict has the potential to overturn governments, as it did in Iran in 1979, when a call to traditional values scuttled a dynasty that promoted Western ways. And Asia will certainly have its share of turmoil in the coming years. Yet as Asians build their future, it may also turn out that they will once more offer the world a new vision of what truly civilized life can be.

DONALD N. WILBER, Editor, *The Nations of Asia*

The countries of Southwest Asia produce more than one-third of the world's oil.

SOUTHWEST ASIA

About 5,000 years ago, Enmerkar, priest-king of the Sumerian city of Uruk, decided to send a warning to his enemy, the lord of Aratta. Enmerkar summoned his envoy. But as he ticked off his demands, the envoy grew uneasy: the message was detailed and difficult to remember.

Realizing this, Enmerkar had a flash of inspiration. He took damp clay, states a legend from the time, "smoothed [it] with his hand, and set down his words on it, in the manner of a tablet." This is the first recorded instance of a special-delivery letter—the invention of a Sumerian king.

The story of Enmerkar's innovation reminds us that there was once a time when such simple methods of communication as writing, which we now take for granted, had to be established. For taking many of the first steps in creating a civilization, the Sumerians will be honored forever. They and other peoples of Southwest Asia produced the world's first city-states and its first written communications and codified laws. They also created Judaism, Christianity, and Islam, the three great monotheistic (single-god) religions that continue to shape our world.

The land once ruled by Sumerians is now part of Iraq, a modern republic. Seventeen other nations are located in Southwest Asia. They include the republics of Cyprus, Iran, Israel, Lebanon, Syria, Turkey, and Yemen; the monarchies of Bahrain, Jordan, Kuwait, Oman, Qatar, and Saudi Arabia; the federation of the United Arab Emirates (UAE); and three new independent states in Transcaucasia—Armenia, Azerbaijan, and Georgia—that until late 1991 formed part of the former Soviet Union. These 18 nations are part of a larger region that is often referred to as the Middle East. (See sidebar, page 43.)

Religion plays an important role in Southwest Asia. Most of the countries in the region are overwhelmingly Muslim (left); Georgia, Armenia, and the island country of Cyprus are mostly Christian, while Israel is primarily Jewish.

THE LAND

Southwest Asia covers a region of roughly 2,494,800 sq. mi. (6,461,532 sq. km.), about one-seventh the size of all Asia. It is separated from the rest of the continent by the Elburz Mountains, the western Hindu Kush, and the Caspian Sea.

The region is bounded on the north by the Caspian and Black seas and by Russia and Turkmenistan, successor states of the defunct Soviet Union. Its eastern boundaries are Afghanistan and Pakistan. To the south lie the Arabian Sea and the Gulf of Aden, and to the west the Red and Mediterranean seas.

Geographically, Southwest Asia comprises four major areas. One area includes the mountains and plateaus of Turkey, Transcaucasia, and Iran. A second area is the fertile coastal strip along the eastern Mediterranean. The floodplains and delta of the Tigris-Euphrates river system constitute a third region. The fourth is the desert that extends southward from Syria through the Arabian Peninsula.

About 70 to 80 percent of the region is arid. But the lower valleys of the Tigris and Euphrates rivers, plus the strip of land along the eastern Mediterranean, form part of a valuable arc of land known as the "Fertile Crescent." (The western part of the crescent lies along Africa's Nile River, in Egypt.)

Climate. Southwest Asia is typified by a hot, dry climate, with temperatures rising to well over 100° F. (38° C.) in many places during the summer months. But significant variations in the climate occur from one area to the next.

Cyprus, Lebanon, the coastal areas of Turkey, and some lower-lying parts of Transcaucasia enjoy typical Mediterranean weather—normally hot, dry summers and cool, wet winters. The same climate mantles the shores of Syria and Israel and a small strip of western Jordan. However, the inland areas of these three countries are mostly dry and arid.

Farther east, Iran and Iraq also have a mostly desert climate—one marked by low rainfall, as little as 4 in. (10 cm.) a year. Both have extremely hot summers and cold winters. The exception to this pattern occurs in low-lying areas near the Persian Gulf, where the climate is subtropical.

MAKING SENSE OF THE TERM "MIDDLE EAST"

As a natural land bridge between Africa, Asia, and Europe, Southwest Asia has long been a crossroads for trade between the continents. Over the course of Western history, this strategically located region has been known by several names. Most of the names reflected the geographic perspective of the merchants and politicians who used them.

To medieval Europeans, who thought of themselves as being at the center of the known world, Asia was the East, or Orient. Following this tradition, Southwest Asia has variously been called the Levant, the Near East, and the Middle East.

Levant, a term that derives from Italian, also means East, or Orient. For centuries, Italian sea merchants carried goods from one port to another on the shores of the Mediterranean. To them, the Levant was the eastern Mediterranean—and, by extension, the entire coastal area between Italy and Syria.

During the 1800s, Europeans used the term *Far East* to refer to the lands of China, Japan, and their neighbors. The term *Near East* embraced the area controlled by the Ottoman Turks in Southwest Asia, Africa, and Europe. The term *Middle East,* coined in 1902, referred to the remaining countries of southern Asia, located between Arabia and India. But this neat division of the world soon fell apart.

With the breakup of the Ottoman Empire at the end of World War I, the term *Near East* began to fall into disuse, although it still finds some use in referring to another geographic entity—Asia Minor. By the 1940s, *Middle East* had largely replaced both terms, although its use—then as now—was inconsistent. Today, people sometimes use *Middle East* to refer to a huge swatch of land—those parts of northern Africa and Southwest Asia where Islamic culture predominates. The term is more commonly used, however, to designate Southwest Asia plus Egypt and Libya.

To the Western eye, the countries of Southwest Asia lie to the east, giving rise to the term "Middle East" for the region. In its common usage, the term also includes the African countries of Egypt and Libya, two nations that share Southwest Asia's Islamic culture.

MIDDLE EAST

In Beirut, Lebanon, an entire generation came of age amid a protracted civil war.

Along the Gulf's west coast, Kuwait, Bahrain, Qatar, Oman, and the UAE are hot for most of the year and endure intense humidity during the summer. The only cool breezes to be found in this part of the world are in the mountains of Oman. Saudi Arabia—the kingdom that fills most of the Arabian Peninsula—and neighboring Yemen are in the same climate zone as the Gulf states. Some of the highest temperatures in Southwest Asia have been recorded in the vast Saudi desert called the Rub' al-Khali ("Empty Quarter").

THE PEOPLE

About 240 million people live in Southwest Asia. Roughly half of these inhabitants are Arabic-speaking peoples known as Arabs. (Although the great majority of Arabs are Muslims, there are significant numbers of Christian Arabs in Lebanon, Syria, and elsewhere.) Southwest Asia contains seven nations outside the Arab world—Cyprus, Iran, Israel, Turkey, and the three Transcaucasian republics. Jews, Kurds, and other minorities also comprise a substantial portion of the region's population.

Languages. Among Arabic-speaking peoples in this part of the world, distinct dialects can be heard, including Palestinian, Syrian, Iraqi, and Yemeni. The Turks speak Turkish; Iranians speak Farsi, a Persian language; and Israelis speak Hebrew, which, like Arabic, is a Semitic language. French and English are commonly spoken throughout the region and are taught in many schools.

The isthmus of Caucasus is noted for a complex linguistic mosaic. About 40 languages are still spoken, and they belong to three separate families. The Indo-European group includes Armenian and several languages of the Iranian branch—and, of course, Russian, which continues to be used throughout the former Soviet republics. Turkic is spoken by the Azerbaijani and some smaller ethnic groups, such as the Kumyk and the Nogay. Finally, Caucasus is the ancestral home of the Caucasian language family, whose most prominent member is Georgian.

Religions. Today, most of the peoples in the region are followers of Islam. The two predominantly Christian countries are Georgia and Armenia; the majority of people on Cyprus are also Christians. Lebanon is almost equally populated by Christians and Muslims, and Israel is mostly Jewish. Smaller groups of Christians and Jews live in almost all the other countries of Southwest Asia.

Muslims themselves are divided between the minority Shi'ites, who tend to be fundamentalists, and the majority Sunnis. The historic split between the branches originated in a disagreement over the line of succession to the prophet Muhammad. Among the 20 to 30 percent of Southwest Asians who are Shi'ites, most live in Iran, although sizable numbers are in Iraq, Yemen, and other countries.

Way of Life

Southwest Asians are sufficiently diverse to prevent generalizations about the region's life-style. Wealthy Saudi Arabians live quite differently than their poorer neighbors in Iraq, for example. Israel, a nation settled in part by more than 1 million European immigrants, differs from Yemen in its social institutions. In recent years, many Muslim Turks have become "Europeanized" in their outlook, tastes, and laws. Nevertheless, Southwest Asia bears the stamp of the traditional Arab culture more than any other.

Social Organization. Among Arabs, the extended family is a basic feature of social structure. Typically, such a family group is headed by an older man and includes his wife and their children—unmarried daughters, and both married and unmarried sons.

Most such families live in a village with a mosque, an outdoor marketplace, and small, walled houses made of brick or stone. Except in the wealthy oil states, people in such villages earn, per person, the equivalent of only $1,000 to $2,000 a year.

To Western eyes, the Arab Muslim world is clearly a man's world. Boys are taught that the interests of their parents' family must always come first, while girls eventually leave their parents' homes to join the family groups of their husbands. The man is the only one who can initiate a divorce. He merely says "I divorce you" in the presence of witnesses, and it is done.

Recent Changes. As a result of increasing contacts with Europeans and Americans, the way of life in Southwest Asia is taking on some of the external trappings of Western culture. Urban dwellers now have television and home furnishings typical of the West. Depending on local religious custom, they may also abandon the region's traditional flowing garments for Western styles of clothing. The Muslim custom of having women veil most of their faces in public is disappearing, although it is still enforced wherever strict forms of Islam are observed, as in Iran.

A rapid rise in the level of education has also led to some changes in the attitudes of Southwest Asians toward women. Many women in the region now attend universities and have jobs, though there are still more restrictions on their mobility than exist for men.

Transcaucasia. Until the disintegration of the Soviet Union, Transcaucasia belonged politically to Europe. Historically and culturally, however, it has always straddled the two continents, while maintaining a special character of its own. Most of the 50 or so ethnic groups living in the region are noted for their fierce national and tribal loyalties (which have led to recent ethnic wars), and a patriarchal way of life. The inhabitants of Caucasus are also known for their longevity, with many of them living more than 100 years.

Cities

Since ancient times, the cities of Southwest Asia have been important centers of commerce and culture. Today, almost 20 percent of the region's people live in more than a dozen cities with upwards of 1 million inhabitants each.

Teheran, a name derived from Persian that means "warm place," is Iran's capital and its most important industrial, communications, and cultural center. With a population of more than 6 million, it is the second largest city in Southwest Asia. **Mashhad** (1.5 million), **Tabriz** (1 million), and **Isfahan** (1 million) are other major cities in Iran.

Istanbul, in Turkey, has the region's largest population (over 6.5 million). Istanbul has always been important as the port that commands the water passage between the Mediterranean and the Black seas. Originally the Greek city of Byzantium, it was renamed Constantinople in A.D. 330 by the Roman emperor Constantine. It gained its current name in 1930. Other key Turkish cities include **Ankara** (2.6 million), **Izmir** (1.8 million), **Adana** (0.9 million), and **Bursa** (0.8 million).

Baghdad, the capital of Iraq, has a population of between 3.4 million and 4.6 million. Founded in A.D. 762 during the sweep of Muslim armies

Jerusalem has been an important religious center for thousands of years. The city is revered by Christians (left), Jews, and Muslims alike. Each of these groups has its own individual sacred sites within the city.

JERUSALEM: HOLY CITY

Almost 4,000 years old, Jerusalem, according to one historian, was 17 times destroyed and 17 times reborn. Today the capital of Israel, it has been a holy city to Jews, Christians, and Muslims throughout the history of their faiths.

Historic Holy Places. The religious history of Jerusalem began when King David captured it from the Jebusites in about 1000 B.C. David made Jerusalem the capital of the Kingdom of Israel. King Solomon, his son, built a temple there to honor Yahweh (God). But over time, as peoples of different faiths gained control of Jerusalem, they constructed their own places of worship. Most are in the section now known as the "Old City."

Today, Judaism's most revered site is the Western Wall, or Wailing Wall. This wall is the last remnant of a temple erected in 516 B.C. on the ruins of Solomon's temple. The most sacred Christian site is the Church of the Holy Sepulcher, built around A.D. 335 by Emperor Constantine. The church marks the place of Jesus' burial, the site from which Christians believe he rose again to life.

across Southwest Asia, Baghdad quickly became a center of Islamic art and commerce.

Riyadh (1.25 million) is Saudi Arabia's capital; **Jidda,** with approximately the same population, is its largest commercial center. **Mecca** (Makkah) contains the Kaaba, Islam's holiest shrine, and the city of **Medina** is the site of the prophet Muhammad's tomb.

Both **Damascus** (1.55 million), the capital of Syria, and **Aleppo** (1.6 million) are at least 4,000 years old. Today, they are Syria's leading industrial and business communities.

The capitals of the three new independent countries in Transcaucasia are all historic cities. **Baku**, the capital of Azerbaijan and the largest of the three, has a population of 1.1 million. Settled since about the fifth century, it quickly expanded after the beginnings of industrial oil extraction in the 1870s. **Tbilisi**, the capital of Georgia, with 1.3 million people, dates from the 5th century. Formerly the liveliest Soviet city, it was badly damaged in the civil war of the early 1990s. Armenia's capital, **Yerevan** (1.2 million), stands on the site of a settlement from 782 B.C.

Other key cities in Southwest Asia include **Amman** (1 million), the capital of Jordan; **Beirut** (1.67 million), the capital of Lebanon; and **Jerusalem** (500,000), Israel's capital. (See sidebar, beginning on facing page.)

HISTORY

The history of Southwest Asia is a tale of the rise and fall of one great civilization after another. First on the scene was Sumeria.

Muslims consider Jerusalem the third-holiest city in Islam, after Mecca and Medina. Muslims believe that the prophet Muhammad ascended to Heaven from a rock close to the Western Wall. Today a gold-domed mosque, the Dome of the Rock, shelters this holy Muslim site.

Jerusalem in the 1900s. After the defeat of the Ottomans in World War I, Jerusalem became the capital of the British mandate of Palestine. The mandate was marked by clashes between Arab and Jewish nationalist groups, each of whom wanted Jerusalem as their capital in a new, independent state. Eventually, the United Kingdom referred the matter to the United Nations.

In 1947, a U.N. proposal recommended that Palestine be divided into an Arab and a Jewish state and that Jerusalem be established as a separate international city under U.N. control. But in 1948, war broke out between the new state of Israel and its Arab neighbors, and the recommendation concerning Jerusalem was never acted on.

After the war, Jerusalem lay divided between Israel and Jordan. It remained so until the war of 1967, when Israeli forces captured the Jordanian-controlled sector. Israel then integrated this sector into the part of Jerusalem that already served as its capital. Israel's claim to all of Jerusalem was not recognized by most nations and remains a source of friction between Israel and the Arabs.

A Modern City. Today, Jerusalem is a modern metropolis with a cosmopolitan culture. Signs in its shop windows reflect the three languages—Hebrew, Arabic, and English—prevalent among its citizens. Similarly, three Sabbaths are honored within Jerusalem: Friday (Muslims), Saturday (Jews), and Sunday (Christians).

The city's economy supports major industries, such as chemical production, diamond polishing, and food processing. It also includes small handicraft businesses, such as pottery making. Israel's second-largest campus, Hebrew University, is just a short walk from the Old City.

The ancient ruins found throughout Southwest Asia attest to the region's glorious history.

Earliest Civilizations

The Sumerian kingdom developed in the lower valleys of the Tigris and Euphrates rivers. (See sidebar, page 50.) The Greeks, in later years, named the area with these valleys in mind. They called it Mesopotamia, "the land between two rivers."

Sumerians. The Sumerians immigrated to this region from the east coast of the Persian Gulf in the 6th or 5th millennium B.C. Colonizing an area the size of New Jersey, they created many basic features of civilization still in use today. For instance, they were the first to develop a system of irrigation canals and they succeeded in cultivating dates and barley.

They invented a calendar based on farming seasons and perfected a wheel for making pottery. The Sumerians also laid out trade routes for exporting food, textiles, weapons, and jewelry, and they constructed beautiful temples and walled cities. Eventually, they arrived at the concept of embracing several such cities in one kingdom.

Around 3500 B.C., the Sumerians invented a system of cuneiform (wedge-shaped) writing. Their poetry, among other writings, includes epic narratives, prayers to their gods, and the story of such priest-kings as Enmerkar.

Akkadians and Babylonians. As Sumerians were building a kingdom, Semitic migrants from the Arabian Peninsula settled to their north. Centered around the city of Akkad, they became the Sumerians' rivals. Under the rule of Sargon I, the Akkadians absorbed the Sumerians—and some of their other neighbors, too. Sargon ruled an empire that stretched from the Persian Gulf to the Mediterranean.

After 1900 B.C., however, supremacy in Mesopotamia passed to the Semitic Babylonians. Between about 1792 and 1750 B.C., Hammurabi, one of their rulers, issued a code of laws to which modern-day scholars have attached his name. The Babylonians also compiled dictionaries, contributed to the science of mathematics, and began to plot the movements of the heavens.

Conquerors in Mesopotamia

Babylonia, too, fell before challengers. More than 700 years after its heyday, newcomers were chipping away at its power.

Assyrians. Assyrian power first developed around the city of Ashur, on the upper Tigris. As ancient Babylon crumbled, the Semitic Assyrians filled the vacuum, at one point extending their empire as far as Egypt. Excavations of Assyrian palaces have uncovered hundreds of scenes carved on great stone walls, showing Assyrian kings hunting lions and engaged in warfare.

In a turn of the tide, the Babylonians revived their power and destroyed the Assyrians in 625 B.C., but their prosperity did not endure. Babylon fell to Cyrus the Great, king of the Medes and Persians, in the 6th century B.C.

Persians. When the Persians, who were not Semites, first reached the plateaus of Iran, they were a nomadic people. By the 7th century B.C., they occupied Fars, a part of Iran controlled by the Assyrians. By the middle of the next century, they were at the height of their power, ruling not only Iran, but also an empire that stretched from Afghanistan in Asia to the Danube River in Europe.

The Persians built a vast network of roads to connect the cities of this large empire. Messengers traveled hundreds of miles in a matter of days by changing horses at way stations along the route.

Greeks and Romans. The great empire of the Persians was finally split about 330 B.C. by Alexander the Great, fresh from his triumphs in Greece. The Greeks ruled Mesopotamia for the next two centuries, until the Romans established their authority in Southwest Asia. After the Roman Empire split in two in A.D. 395, the Eastern, or Byzantine, Empire continued to rule most of Southwest Asia.

Developments in the Eastern Mediterranean

Sometime after the Sumerian kingdom emerged in Mesopotamia, the Egyptians developed another great civilization along the banks of the Nile River in Africa. After 1500 B.C., they and other peoples began making forays along the Mediterranean coast of Southwest Asia. The conflicts of this period were heightened by the widespread use of armored horses, chariots, and bows and arrows.

Hittites and Phoenicians. The Hittites, an Indo-European people, entered Southwest Asia in the area now known as Turkey. Gradually, they extended their influence southward to the Syrian Desert and the Mediterranean coast, becoming the major cultural influence in this part of the world between 1400 and 1200 B.C. The Phoenicians, a Semitic people who settled in what is now Lebanon, concentrated on maritime trade with far-flung Mediterranean seaports. Between about 1250 and 450 B.C., they expanded the worldview of Southwest Asians, through reports of their voyages to the West. They also invented the predecessor of our alphabet —an improvement over the symbol writing used by Mesopotamians and Egyptians.

Hebrews. The Hebrews, another Semitic people on the eastern coast of the Mediterranean, emerged in history in the 2nd millennium B.C. According to their tradition, Yahweh (God) made a covenant with the people of Abraham, promising that the pastoral Hebrews would become a great nation. The Hebrews thus developed the first religion based on belief in one God.

The Hebrews built a kingdom that reached its height with the reign of King Solomon. After his death around 925 B.C., the kingdom split into

This 4,500-year-old tablet comes from Lagash, a once-thriving ancient city that lay between the Tigris and Euphrates rivers.

THE TIGRIS AND EUPHRATES RIVERS

According to tradition, the Garden of Eden was located in Southwest Asia, someplace in the area washed by the Tigris and Euphrates rivers. Whatever truth may lie behind the legend, this is the region that witnessed civilization's start.

The convergence of the two great rivers on a flat plain near the Persian Gulf—called Mesopotamia by the ancient Greeks—formed an ideal setting for the development of structured human society. Both rivers provided water for life, as well as avenues for transportation and trade. Their lower valleys had rich alluvial soil, good for producing several crops of grain a year.

River Geography. From its source in eastern Turkey, the Tigris River flows southward for nearly 1,150 mi. (1,851 km.). Below the Iraqi city of Mosul, it is joined by its two main tributaries, the Great and the Little Zab. The river then continues past Baghdad, Iraq's capital city. From there, it flows southeast of Al Qurna, where it joins the Euphrates River to form a single waterway, the Shatt-al-Arab. About 120 mi. (193 km.) farther south, the mingled waters enter the Persian Gulf.

two parts—Israel and Judah. Eventually, the Hebrews were overcome by armies from Assyria and new Babylonia. During this time, large segments of their population went into exile. When Babylon was conquered by Persians, the Hebrews were allowed to return to their land, but they were again exiled by Roman conquerors in A.D. 70.

Christians. A few decades before the Romans exiled the Hebrews, Jesus of Nazareth, a Judean, began to preach a message of redemption through filial love for God and fraternal love for one's neighbor. His message eventually led him to be crucified in Jerusalem. After his death, his disciples spread his teachings throughout the Roman Empire. During the 4th century A.D., the emperor Constantine made Christianity a state religion.

Early History of Transcaucasia

Settled since the prehistoric era, Caucasus served from the earliest times as a connecting link between Asia and Europe and as a gateway for nomads, settlers, invaders, and conquerors. The precursor of Armenia, the 6th century B.C. kingdom of Urartu was centered around Lake Van in eastern Turkey. The area was later dominated by Persians, who were in turn replaced by Greeks. From 95 to 55 B.C., Armenian king Tigranes the Great ruled over a territory stretching from the Caspian Sea to present-day Turkey, Iran, and Iraq. After his death, the area came under the hegemony of Romans and, later, Byzantines. In the early A.D. 300s, Ar-

The Euphrates is the region's longest river. It rises in the highlands of eastern Turkey and from there meanders in a southeastern direction for 1,700 mi. (2,736 km.). It courses through Syria, where it is joined by its principal tributary, the Khabur River, and then heads for the plains of Iraq. On its way, the river rolls past the ancient sites of Babylon, Uruk, and other once-great cities.

History through Excavations. For centuries, the ruins of early civilizations lay buried or forgotten in Southwest Asia. Not until the 1800s did archaeologists begin to turn up objects associated with the first organized societies in the region.

A recent excavation in a place called Tell Abu Hureyra in northern Syria supports the theory that such societies in Southwest Asia took thousands of years to emerge. For example, the people of Tell Abu Hureyra, near the Euphrates, engaged in farming as early as 9500 B.C.

But they also continued to rely on hunting and gathering. Only gradually did the tending of domesticated plants and animals become their most important economic activities.

By the 4th millennium B.C., the more prosperous villages had grown into city-states. Their inhabitants had houses made of sun-dried bricks or stone. They worked as weavers, potters, and silversmiths and traded the products they made for food. Usually, these cities were built around temples, where priests sought the favor of the gods by making offerings of silver and other precious goods.

The city of Ur, on the Euphrates, is believed by excavators to have had a population of several hundred thousand in its prime. Amazing treasure—including musical instruments of rare wood and ivory and delicate gold jewelry—has been recovered from the tombs of its kings. Other great civilizations in the region included the Babylonian and Assyrian empires. They are glowing reminders of the achievements of early human life in a region justly called the "cradle of civilization."

menia became the first state to adopt Christianity as a state religion. Georgia followed its lead soon after.

The Muslim World

The parts of Southwest Asia claimed by the Eastern Roman Empire and by a remnant of the Persian Empire eventually fell to a great force.

Arabs. In A.D. 622, the Arab prophet Muhammad set up a religious community at Medina, on the Arabian Peninsula. Muhammad preached total submission to the will of Allah (God), a practice that united believers in a new religion, Islam. Islam was based on lengthy revelations from Allah, which were collected in a sacred book, the Koran.

After Muhammad's death in 632, his followers spread the teachings of Islam throughout Southwest Asia, across North Africa to Spain, and east to the borders of China and India. Muslims preserved the literary heritage of Greece and Rome, works that were then banned in Christian Europe. They spread the Chinese art of papermaking and the Indian system of numerals throughout the rest of the known world.

Turks. Toward the end of the 11th century, Seljuk Turks who had embraced Islam conquered part of Southwest Asia. European Crusaders, eager to return Jerusalem to Christian rule, invaded the "Holy Land," too. Although they failed to hold on to their conquests, the Crusaders did help to expose Europeans to the cultures of Southwest Asia. By the 1500s, Ottoman Turks ruled most of Southwest Asia.

Beginning of Modern Times

From the 17th century on, a powerful state was growing in the north. The Russians had had previous contacts with the Caucasus, but in the 1700s they challenged Persian rule there. By the early 1800s, present-day Georgia, Armenia, and Azerbaijan were part of the Russian Empire.

By the late 1800s, the Ottoman Empire was crumbling. When the Suez Canal opened a strategic passageway between the Mediterranean and the Far East in 1869, Europeans made fresh attempts to influence the region. In 1882, the British seized Egypt from the Ottomans, to guarantee their access to the canal.

Aftermath of World War I. By the end of World War I, the Ottoman Empire was dead. With the approval of the League of Nations, Europeans divided parts of Southwest Asia into new states, over which they exercised political influence.

France established a protectorate over Syria and Lebanon. The United Kingdom exercised a mandate over Iraq and Jordan, and it had protectorates over Cyprus, Kuwait, and several neighboring states. But the inhabitants resisted and gradually won their independence.

After briefly shaking off Russian rule between 1918 and 1920, following the Bolshevik takeover, Transcaucasia again came under the sway of Moscow. During the next seven decades, Communist ideology submerged all national aspirations, but they violently resurfaced when the system unraveled in the late 1980s.

A major turning point in the region's politics occurred when the state of Israel was created. In 1948, a U.N. resolution suggested that the former British mandate of Palestine be divided into separate Jewish and Arab states. Both Jews and Arabs had historical claims to Palestine. But when the new state of Israel proclaimed its existence, Arabs regarded its establishment as a theft of their land.

On May 15, 1948, Arab armies moved into the area in support of Palestinian Arabs. As war broke out, many Palestinian civilians left the scene of conflict. After seven months, the Arab forces were defeated, and most Palestinian Arabs were stateless.

In 1956, 1967, and 1973, war erupted between Israel and its Arab neighbors. Egypt and Israel signed a peace accord in 1979, and Jordan and Israel ended their formal state war in 1994. A 1993 accord between Israel and the Palestine Liberation Organization (PLO) on self-rule for Palestinian Arabs in Jericho and the Gaza Strip also became effective in 1994, although progress toward a comprehensive regional peace settlement stalled after the Likud victory in the 1996 Israeli elections.

ECONOMIES

As the 20th century neared its end, the economies of the states of Southwest Asia were in sharp variance with one another. The oil states were prosperous, though the economies of Iran and Iraq were depleted by war. Except for Israel—and, perhaps, Turkey and Cyprus—the other states' economies were fragile.

Oil Boom. As a region, Southwest Asia produces more than one-third of the world's crude oil. Saudi Arabia is the leading oil producer. The region exports millions of barrels of oil daily to Europe, the United States, Japan, and elsewhere. Money from the sale of this oil has enabled most of the producing states to raise their people's standard of living

This Saudi Arabian airport terminal combines both traditional and contemporary architecture.

through public works, improved education, and the development of new industries.

Agriculture. Although oil is the most important source of income, farming is the main occupation in Southwest Asia, as it has been for thousands of years. About 35 to 40 percent of the region's people are farmers. (In the mid-1990s, Turkey, Yemen, and Oman reported that more than 40 percent of their workforces engaged in farming.) Cereal grains and fruits are among the region's principal crops.

Because of the shortage of water in Southwest Asia, only 10 to 15 percent of the region is cultivated. Simple, ancient devices for lifting water from rivers to fields are still in use in many places. Desalinization plants have helped solve the water shortage in some places.

Other Nonoil Industries. Laborers who are not involved in farming or the oil industry in Southwest Asia work mainly in crafts and light industries. Since earliest times, the people of Southwest Asia have been noted for their skill in producing fine textiles, leather goods, woodwork and metalwork, jewelry, and ivory carvings.

A small but increasing number of trained professionals in the region work in health care, education, communications, and other service industries. Many such positions have been created as the region's governments expand domestic programs for their citizens.

Transcaucasian Republics. The former Soviet republics in Transcaucasia—Georgia, Armenia, and Azerbaijan—all developed diversified industries under Soviet rule and, thanks to native entrepreneurship, were relatively prosperous. Their economies virtually collapsed in the early 1990s because of ethnic conflicts, and energy shortages brought many factories to a standstill. By 1996, however, prospects for economic revival had improved, particularly in connection with huge oil reserves in Azerbaijan and a projected pipeline through Georgia.

The prolonged *intifada* uprising against Israeli occupation of the West Bank and Gaza Strip caused much death and destruction and devastated the economy of the area.

Future Prospects.   Apart from oil, natural gas, and fertile soil in a few areas, Southwest Asia does not have a strong resource base for the economic support of its fast-growing population. In the mid-1990s, the average annual growth rate for the 10 largest countries in the region was less than 2 percent. Since the average urban growth rate was almost 4 percent, the pressure for more nonfarm jobs will be especially urgent in coming years. Most nations in the region hope to improve their industrial strength. Even the oil states are aware that their economies need a broader base than one dependent on a single resource. If a substitute energy source were to capture the world's interest, the price of oil—and the economies depending on its sale—could plummet.

SOUTHWEST ASIA AND THE WORLD

As Southwest Asians face the 21st century, four issues grip the region's member states and peoples. First is the successful settlement of the Arab-Israeli dispute. Next is a debate over control of the production and sale of Southwest Asia's oil. Third is the new issue of ethnic conflict in the successor states in Transcaucasia. The fourth issue concerns the tension that persists in regard to Islamic fundamentalism and the notion of one "Arab Nation," along with the influence exerted on the region by Western powers.

Arabs and Israelis.   In 1979, Egypt became the first nation to sign a peace treaty with Israel in the wake of the Arab-Israeli wars. But other efforts toward regional peace were mired in disagreements over the fate of the Palestinian Arabs.

Even the question of who should represent Palestinians in peace talks caused dissent. Israel objected to the Palestine Liberation Organization (PLO), which made the strongest claim to this role. During the 1980s, the conflict between Israel and the PLO erupted in Lebanon. From late 1987, Israeli Palestinians were locked with the authorities in an *inti-*

fada, or uprising, that contributed to historic accords on Palestinian self-rule between Israel and the PLO in 1993, 1994, and 1995. For their contributions to changing the face of Mideast diplomacy, Israeli leaders Yitzhak Rabin and Shimon Peres and PLO leader Yasir Arafat shared the 1994 Nobel Peace Prize. Jordan and Israel ended their state of war on July 25, 1994. The two nations signed a peace treaty on October 26.

Control of Oil. In 1960, six nations in Southwest Asia joined other oil-producing nations to form the Organization of Petroleum Exporting Countries (OPEC). OPEC drove up world oil prices in the 1970s, and a 1973 Arab boycott of oil shipments to nations friendly to Israel used oil as a political weapon.

Oil also led to conflicts within Southwest Asia. During the 1980s the Gulf states were criticized for producing too much oil, thus depressing world prices. Iraq invaded Kuwait in 1990 to gain control of the Kuwaiti oil fields.

Ethnic Strife. From 1988 to 1994, Armenians and Azerbaijani warred over the enclave of Nagorno-Karabakh, and in the early 1990s, Georgia was convulsed by civil and ethnic conflicts. By 1996, however, the region was calm, and peace seemed close at hand. The price has been greater Russian influence in the area, including a Russian military presence in Georgia and Armenia.

Islamic Fundamentalists, "Arab Nation." Increasingly, the peoples of Southwest Asia have sought to reduce the intervention of Western powers in their region. Muslim fundamentalists want to restore a strict observance of Islam and to overcome what they call

Arab activists hope to repair the damage caused by the Persian Gulf War while gaining greater local control over Southwest Asian affairs.

the "contamination" of Muslims' lives by Western influence. In a parallel movement, supporters of the concept of an "Arab Nation" dream of unity among Arab states. The short-lived United Arab Republic (1958–61), which linked Egypt and Syria, was an expression of such a desire.

Passionate talk of the need for Arab unity and Arab control of Southwest Asian affairs followed Iraq's invasion of Kuwait. The stridency of Muslim fundamentalism temporarily subsided in the aftermath of Iraq's spectacular defeat by a U.S.-led coalition that included most of the Arab states. Violence by radical Islamic groups later threatened the growing rapprochement between Israel and its Arab neighbors.

Reviewed by RICHARD W. BULLIET, Middle East Institute, Columbia University

The Suleymaniye Mosque is one of many architectural treasures found in the European section of Istanbul.

 TURKEY

"Whoever is the master of Constantinople is the master of the world." These words were spoken by Napoleon Bonaparte of France in the late 1700s. In Napoleon's day, Constantinople was the capital of the Ottoman Empire, the predecessor of modern Turkey. But the great empire of the Ottomans is long gone. Constantinople, known since 1930 by its Turkish name, Istanbul, remains a great city. But it is no longer Turkey's capital, and Turkey has no interest in controlling the world's destiny.

Nevertheless, Turkey remains one of the most important sites on the globe. It is a gateway to Southwest Asia, and it controls the vital straits that link the Black Sea with the Mediterranean.

Straddling Europe and Asia, the land that is now Turkey has been important since the beginning of recorded history. Around 1600 B.C., one of the world's earliest civilizations, that of the Hittites, flourished in Anatolia, the part of Turkey that is in Asia. The Hittites were among the first people to work iron and use a form of writing. The partly legendary city of Troy was located on the Aegean coast of Turkey, and along this same coast the genius of ancient Greece flourished. The region has been a battleground of empires. Alexander the Great made it the pivot of his vast conquests. The Romans, already masters of most of Europe, made Constantinople their capital in the East.

The first Turks, among them the Seljuks, migrated to Turkey from beyond the Ural Mountains, acquiring the Muslim religion along the way. The empire of the Seljuks was besieged from the west by the Crusaders and from the east by the Mongols of Genghis Khan. Finally, the region fell to another branch of the Turks, the Osmanlis, or Ottomans, ancestors of the present-day Turks. The Ottomans captured Constantinople and built an empire that became one of the great powers of the world.

Like all empires, that of the Ottomans declined, too. It lost most of its European possessions in the late 1800s and early 1900s. It lost its Arab possessions after its defeat in World War I. The empire collapsed in 1923, and out of the ruins the Republic of Turkey was born. Today, Turkey is one of Southwest Asia's most developed nations, and it has strong military and economic ties with the West.

THE LAND

Modern Turkey, covering some 301,380 sq. mi. (780,580 sq. km.), is about twice the size of California. Ninety-seven percent of it is in Asia. The Asian part, the huge peninsula of Anatolia, also called Asia Minor, and the European part, called Thrace, are separated by a series of three interlinked waterways—the Strait of Bosporus, the Sea of Marmara, and the Strait of the Dardanelles—connecting the Black Sea with the Mediterranean.

The coastal regions of Turkey enjoy warm summers and mild winters with sufficient rainfall to permit intense cultivation. Along the northern coast, on the Black Sea, the principal crops include world-famous Turkish tobacco, hazelnuts, and tea. One of Turkey's most prosperous areas is found in the west, along the coast of the Aegean Sea, an arm of the Mediterranean. The Aegean has some of the best harbors; its cities are

For centuries, people have hollowed out homes in the bizarre volcanic formations found in Cappadocia.

centers of trade and finance; and the sun-drenched soil provides rich crops of cotton, tobacco, grapes, and figs. The southern, or Mediterranean, coast produces cotton and citrus fruits and has several attractive resort beaches.

Most of Turkey's land area consists of the Anatolian Plateau, a vast highland region framed by mountain ranges. Summers there are hot and dry. Winters are severely cold. Much of the soil is barren, and rainfall is limited. Although most of Turkey's large cities are located in the coastal regions, Ankara, the capital, is on the Anatolian Plateau.

Pasture and prairie cover most of the plateau. About 30 percent of it is cultivated, and another 25 percent is forest. The chief crops are wheat, barley, maize (corn), potatoes, and sugar beets. Some of the land is devoted to vineyards and olive groves. Sheep and goats are raised both for food and for their wool and hair.

The Anatolian Plateau is rich in mineral resources, with large deposits of chromite (chromium oxide), copper, and iron ore. Turkey also has rich seams of coal and some petroleum. Much of the country's mineral wealth has yet to be fully explored and utilized.

FACTS AND FIGURES

OFFICIAL NAME: Republic of Turkey.

NATIONALITY: Turk(s).

CAPITAL: Ankara.

LOCATION: Southeastern Europe and southwestern Asia. **Boundaries**—Black Sea, Georgia, Armenia, Azerbaijan, Iran, Iraq, Syria, Mediterranean Sea, Aegean Sea, Greece, Bulgaria.

AREA: 301,380 sq. mi. (780,580 sq. km.).

PHYSICAL FEATURES: Highest point—Mount Ararat (16,945 ft.; 5,164 m.). **Lowest point**—sea level. **Chief rivers**—Kizil Irmak, Menderes, Seyhan, Ceyhan, Gediz, Orontes. **Major lakes**—Van, Tuz.

POPULATION: 63,900,000 (1996; annual growth 1.6%).

MAJOR LANGUAGES: Turkish (official), Kurdish, Arabic.

MAJOR RELIGIONS: Islam, Christianity, Judaism.

GOVERNMENT: Republic. **Head of state**—president. **Head of government**—prime minister. **Legislature**—unicameral Grand National Assembly.

CHIEF CITIES: Istanbul, Ankara, Izmir, Adana.

ECONOMY: Chief minerals—antimony, coal, chromium, mercury, copper. **Chief agricultural products**—cotton, tobacco, cereals, sugar beets, fruits, olives. **Industries and products**—textiles, food processing, mining, steel, petroleum. **Chief exports**—cotton, tobacco, fruits, nuts, metals, livestock products. **Chief imports**—crude oil, machinery, transportation equipment, metals, pharmaceuticals.

MONETARY UNIT: 1 lira = 100 kurus.

NATIONAL HOLIDAY: October 29 (Anniversary of the Declaration of the Republic).

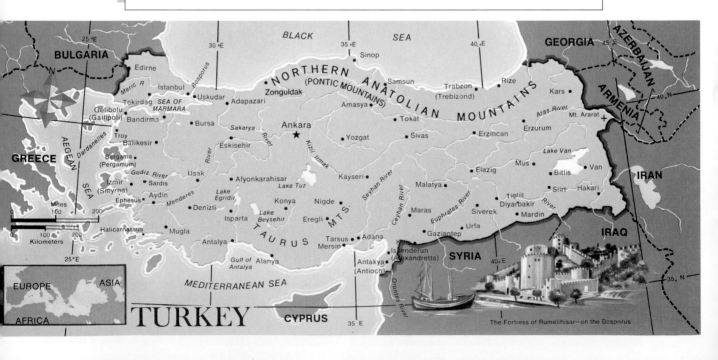

The Fortress of Rumelihisar—on the Bosporus

The "whirling dervish" order, now banned, is allowed to perform its ritual dance only once a year.

THE PEOPLE

Throughout history, the land that is now Turkey has had a diverse population. About 85 percent of the people are Turks today. The next-largest group consists of about 6.6 million Kurds, amounting to 12 percent of the population. Most Kurds live in the southeastern mountains near the borders of Iraq, Iran, and Syria. During the late 1980s and early 1990s, their demands for more freedom to run their own affairs flared into civil war. The remaining 3 percent of the population consists of about 1 million Arabs and smaller numbers of Circassians, Greeks, Armenians, Georgians, and Jews.

While 98 percent of the population is Muslim, Turkey is not officially a Muslim country. The Turkish Republic has been a secular nation since 1923. Many Turks look, dress, and think of themselves as southeastern Europeans.

Language.   The Turkish language, however, differs from most of the languages of Europe. Turkish does not belong to the Indo-European family. It belongs to the Altaic group, which derived its name from the Altai Mountain region in the heart of Asia. Other languages in the group include Mongolian, Uzbek, and Turkic. Though Turkish is the official language, Kurds and Arabs speak Kurdish and Arabic in their respective communities.

Way of Life

Village Life.   About 55 percent of all Turks now live in cities. Of the remaining 45 percent, most are farmers living in traditional villages. Some are herders who raise sheep and goats.

The traditional Turkish farm village consists of houses built of sun-dried mud brick without any adornment. Because Anatolia was a major invasion route over the centuries, villagers often built their homes between hills or in depressions in the land so that they could not be easily seen. The houses are usually austere and functional inside and out. They

Wrestling is a popular sport among Turks. By tradition, the contestants are oiled before a match.

contain a few cooking utensils, the traditional *mangal,* or charcoal grill, and essential furniture and bedding. The lively colors of Turkish carpets brighten the rooms.

Nearly every village usually has a few larger houses of stone. These may include the homes of locally eminent families, a separate village house used for social occasions, and perhaps a coffeehouse where the men can gather in the twilight hours after the day's work. Larger villages —usually those with access to roads—have a *sinema,* or movie theater. Visits of dancing bears are a popular folk entertainment. Wrestling is a favorite sport with men, while *futbol* (soccer) is very popular with boys as well as men. The monotony of everyday life is also broken by feasts of circumcision in Muslim communities and by weddings in Christian and Muslim communities.

Life in the Cities.   Life in the large towns and in the cities is, of course, quite different. Such major cities as Istanbul, Ankara, and Izmir have a variety of social, educational, and cultural institutions—theaters, orchestras, museums, universities, art exhibits—as do large cities almost everywhere. The difference between town and country is noticeable in the dress of the people. Western clothes are usually worn by city people. In the traditional rural areas, women wear pajamalike bloomers, usually while working in the fields. Although the wearing of veils by women has been prohibited, country women often still cover their faces with loose-hanging scarves at the approach of unfamiliar male adults.

Food and Drink.   Except for pork, which is forbidden by Islamic law, meat is usually a basic part of Turkish meals. Turks are not fond of American turkey, which they call *hindi* because they believe it originated in India. Instead, they prefer mutton, lamb, and beef. Shish kabob—

pieces of lamb broiled on skewers, with onion and green pepper—is very popular. *Döner-kabob*—slices from the side of a lamb cooked on a spit—is also a favorite. Another popular food is *pilaw*, which is a rice dish made with meat or fish. Some of the Turkish sweets are famous in many parts of the world, particularly halvah (made with crushed sesame seeds) and baklava (a pastry usually filled with nuts and honey). Turkish coffee also has acquired well-earned fame, and tea is a popular drink.

MAJOR CITIES

Istanbul. Turkey's largest and best-known city is located at the narrowest part of a series of straits—the Dardanelles, the Sea of Marmara, and the Bosporus—linking the Mediterranean and the Black seas. For over 1,600 years, the strategic city, the only one in the world to span two continents, was known as Constantinople. Before that, it was called Byzantium, the name given to it by its Greek founders in 667 B.C. From A.D. 330 to 1453, it was the capital of the Eastern Roman (Byzantine) Empire and was one of the world's wealthiest and most magnificent cities. Over the ages, its strong walls enabled the fabled city to withstand many sieges. But it finally fell to the Ottoman Turks in 1453, and it served as the capital of the Ottoman Empire until 1923.

Many splendors from its Byzantine and Ottoman past can be seen in modern Istanbul. These include a Roman aqueduct built by the Emperor Valens in A.D. 378, and the earthen walls, built around 413, that withstood numerous sieges. The Sancta Sophia (or Hagia Sophia, which means "holy wisdom" in Greek), a cathedral of colossal proportions, is considered the greatest example of Byzantine architecture. Completed in 537, it was turned into a mosque by the Turks and converted into a

The Bosporus, a body of water that separates European and Asian Turkey, is spanned by a bridge at Istanbul, Turkey's largest city (left). Ankara (right) is the nation's capital.

Bodrum and its fortress (above) were the last of the Christian strongholds on the Aegean coast to fall to the Ottomans. Ankara (left) and other large Turkish cities continue to expand beyond their borders as new housing is built to accommodate a growing middle class.

museum in the 1930s. The city's second most renowned structure is the magnificent Blue Mosque. Istanbul's hundreds of mosques remind visitors that they are in a Muslim land. The seraglios (palaces and harems) of the former sultans recall the days of the Ottoman Empire.

Modern Istanbul is divided by water into three distinct sectors: Stamboul and Beyeglou on the European side of the Bosporus, and Uskudar on the Asian side. Stamboul is the oldest part of the city. Most of the city's buildings and monuments of the Byzantine period are there, and so are the older mosques, palaces, and bazaars of the Ottoman period. Stamboul is separated from Beyeglou to the north by the Golden Horn, a wide inlet of the Bosporus. Beyeglou, once a Genoese trading outpost, is now a center of trade and commerce. It contains communities of Greeks, Armenians, Jews, and other minorities. Stamboul and Beyeglou are linked by three bridges spanning the Golden Horn.

Uskudar, on the Asian side of the Bosporus, is Istanbul's newest sector. A sprawling district that developed during the 1800s and 1900s, it was remote from the heart of the city until 1973, when a bridge was completed across the Bosporus. Now roads link all three sectors of this great city of more than 6 million inhabitants. Istanbul is Turkey's chief port and the nation's commercial, financial, and cultural center.

Ankara is Turkey's capital and its second-largest city, with nearly 4 million residents. Although the city goes back to ancient times, modern Ankara dates from its establishment as the capital in 1923. The older part of the city has meandering lanes and crowded bazaars, while the newer part has modern buildings and wide boulevards. As well as being the seat of government, Ankara is an important industrial city and the heart of the region that produces the famed Angora goat, whose long, silky hair is known as mohair.

Izmir. A seaport on the Aegean coast, Izmir (formerly known as Smyrna) is one of Turkey's most important commercial cities. It was one of the ancient Greek cities along the eastern Aegean and is said to be the birthplace of the poet Homer. Izmir, with about 2.5 million residents, is particularly popular with tourists. Other important Turkish cities include Adana, Bursa, Zonguldak, Samsun, and Trabzon.

ECONOMY

Until the 1980s, most Turks were employed in agriculture and food processing. Much of the country's industrial output was provided by state-owned and state-controlled enterprises. Oil-price increases and a widespread economic recession during the 1970s forced many of these enterprises to scale down their operations. Thousands of Turks went to Western Europe in search of jobs.

The arid climate of the central Anatolian Plateau is well suited for herding.

Textile manufacturing is out-ranked only by food processing as Turkey's chief industry. A textile factory in Adana in southern Turkey (left) processes the cotton grown in the vicinity.

During the early 1980s, Turkey put a greater emphasis on the growth of privately owned businesses. The government ended some major restrictions on imports, reformed the banking system, cut taxes and agricultural subsidies, lifted price controls, and sold off many state-owned enterprises. As a result, Turkey's manufacturing and mining industries grew rapidly, and so did exports, including tobacco, cotton, textiles, cement, raisins, nuts, leather, glass, and ceramics.

One of the country's goals is to reduce the economic gap between Turkey and Western Europe. Although Turkey's application for full membership in the European Community (EC) was rebuffed in 1989, the EC said it was merely postponing a final decision because of concerns over Turkey's population growth of more than 2 percent a year, its comparatively undeveloped economy, and human-rights violations. Turkey finally was admitted to the European Union (formerly the EC) in January 1996.

HISTORY AND GOVERNMENT

The Ottoman Empire. The Ottomans were members of a Turkish tribe from Central Asia named for the legendary founder of their dynasty, Othman, or Osman. In the centuries following their arrival in Turkey, they expanded rapidly, crossed the Bosporus into Europe, and conquered most of the territory of the decaying Byzantine Empire. Only Constantinople, behind its strong fortifications, held out. In 1453, after a siege during which the Turks moved part of their fleet overland to the Golden Horn, the city fell and the Ottoman Turks made it the capital of their empire. From Constantinople's strategic location on the straits, the Ottoman Turks pushed westward into Europe, southward into Africa, and eastward toward the Indian Ocean.

The Ottoman Turks were successful in the 1400s and 1500s because they were a military people, rigidly regimented and accustomed to hardship. Above all, they were united. Their foes often were not. In their forays into Europe, the Turks forced strong, bright Christian boys into their army. These boys were given special training, converted to the Muslim faith, and became the nucleus of the *yeniçeri* ("new troops"), or Janissaries, the shock troops of the Ottoman army.

The Ottomans reached the height of their power during the reign of Suleiman the Magnificent (1520–66). At that time, the empire stretched from the walls of Vienna to the Caspian Sea, and from southern Russia to North Africa. Following Suleiman's death in 1566, the Ottoman Empire slowly declined. Several factors contributed to the decline. One was the growing power of nearby European Christian nations. This culminated in the crushing defeat of the Ottoman navy by a combined Christian fleet at Lepanto in 1571. A second factor was the rise of nationalism among the non-Turkish peoples of the empire. This caused disunity in the empire. A third, most important, factor was the rule of several corrupt, inefficient sultans.

Jealousies, conspiracies, and suspicions plagued the Ottoman government and army in the 1700s and 1800s. The once-elite Janissaries devoted more time to palace intrigues than to fighting the empire's external enemies. Finally, in 1826, Sultan Mahmud II ordered the massacre of 6,000 Janissaries. By that time, the Ottoman empire was facing bankruptcy. Its northern neighbor, Russia, was pressing hard to gain control of the Bosporus-Dardanelles straits, and thus access for the Russian fleet to the Mediterranean. Only intervention by Great Britain and France, who feared Russian power, thwarted this ambition. Nevertheless, during the 1800s and early 1900s, the Ottomans lost most of their European territory.

In 1909, reform-minded army officers known as the Young Turks deposed Sultan Abdul Hamid II and forced his successor, Mohammed V, to accept constitutional government and modern reforms. This slowed the decline, but failed to stop it.

The Creation of the Republic. The final breakup of the Ottoman Empire came after World War I. During the war, the Turks had been allied with the defeated Central Powers—Germany, Austria, and Bulgaria. Victorious British and French forces occupied Constantinople and

In 1516, the Ottomans defeated Christian forces and took possession of the city of Antioch.

The ruins in Ephesus date from Roman times, although the city played a role in ancient Greece as well.

imposed the punitive Treaty of Sèvres on the defeated sultan. As a result, the Ottoman Empire lost all its remaining non-Turkish territory, including the Arab lands of Southwest Asia. The straits were placed under international control, and Izmir and its surrounding region were occupied by Greek troops. The treaty also called for an independent Armenia and an independent Kurdistan.

Turkish nationalists led by General Mustafa Kemal opposed the treaty and rallied Turkish army units in the highlands of Anatolia. Kemal's forces defeated the Armenians and Kurds in the east and the Greeks in the west. The Allies were forced out, and Mohammed VI, the last Ottoman sultan, was deposed. In 1923, the Republic of Turkey was founded with Kemal as its first president. The Treaty of Sèvres was replaced by the Treaty of Lausanne (1923), which set Turkey's present boundaries.

The Reforms of Kemal Atatürk. The Turkey that Kemal took over was a backward state, afflicted with disease, poverty, and ignorance. Only 10 percent of the people could read. He immediately launched a series of reforms that covered the entire spectrum of Turkish life. A crash program in sanitation and education was begun. Bright children barely out of primary school were installed as teachers. Land was taken from religious foundations and large estates and distributed among the peasants. An ambitious program of industrialization was started.

Under the Ottoman system, the chief of state, the sultan, was also the religious head, or caliph. Kemal separated church and state, making Turkey a secular nation. He replaced the turban and the fez, which were associated with the old regime, with Western-style hats. He made having more than one wife at a time illegal and gave women the same rights as men. Under Ottoman rule, many of the laws of the land were based on the Koran, the holy book of Islam. Kemal changed that by introducing a legal system based on the most progressive laws of European countries.

The Ottoman Empire had used the Arabic alphabet, which Kemal decided was hard to learn. To encourage literacy and to bring his country closer to the West—one of his primary goals—he had the Roman alphabet adopted. As a political forum for the country, Kemal earlier had established the Grand National Assembly. His party, the Republican People's Party, ruled into 1950.

Kemal ordered all Turks to adopt family names, something they did not have under the Ottomans. He took the name Atatürk—"father of the Turks." "Atatürkism" became the label for the way of thinking that Kemal introduced through his reforms. Atatürkism espouses secularism, nationalism, and a largely state-run economy, and it urges Turks to look to the West for inspiration and support. Though the subject of much debate, it still guides much decision making in Turkey today.

Turkey Since World War II. Kemal Atatürk died in 1938, a year before the start of World War II. Turkey was neutral during most of the war, but joined the Allies in 1945. After the war, when the old Russian threat reasserted itself, U.S. President Harry Truman offered Turkey aid under the Truman Doctrine. Later, Turkey became a member of the North Atlantic Treaty Organization. In late 1974, Turkey revived hostilities with Greece and invaded the nearby island nation of Cyprus, occupying the northern half of the island.

Inflation, corruption, and rising factionalism were rampant in the 1960s and led to a military coup in 1971. Democratic government was restored in 1973, and a series of weak coalition governments followed until 1980, when the armed forces again staged a coup. The coup suspended the 1961 constitution, banned political parties, and put thousands of political activists in prison.

In November 1982, Turkish voters approved a new constitution that preserves a secular, democratic, parliamentary form of government with a unicameral parliament, the Grand National Assembly (GNA), and a strengthened presidency. Executive power is shared by the president and the prime minister. The 450-member GNA chooses the president, who holds office for seven years. The prime minister, head of the GNA's largest voting bloc, administers the government. Candidates for the GNA can be seated only if their parties win 10 percent of the national vote.

The Motherland Party dominated the elections of 1983 and 1987. In 1989, Turgut Özal, then prime minister and leader of the Motherland Party, was elected to the presidency. Özal was only the second president of Turkey since 1923 to come from a civilian rather than a military background. After Özal died in April 1993, Prime Minister Suleyman Demirel of the True Path Party (TPP) was chosen president. Demirel, a moderate political veteran, had become prime minister after the Motherland Party lost its parliamentary majority in the 1991 elections. Tansu Ciller of the TPP became Turkey's first woman prime minister in June 1993. The Islamic Welfare Party (Rafeh) won the largest number of seats in the December 1995 elections, but not enough to govern on its own. In July 1996, after a coalition government formed by the Motherland Party and the TPP collapsed, Islamic Welfare Party leader Necmettin Erbakan became Turkey's first Islamist prime minister since independence.

Reviewed by RICHARD W. BULLIET, Middle East Institute, Columbia University

The flagpole in the background marks the "Green Line" that separates Nicosia, the capital of Cyprus, into Greek and Turkish sectors.

CYPRUS

Cyprus, the easternmost island in the Mediterranean Sea, is an outpost of European culture in the shadow of Asia. Though Cyprus is 40 mi. (64 km.) from Turkey and 65 mi. (104 km.) from Syria, about 78 percent of all Cypriots are of Greek origin, with roots that date back more than 3,000 years. Just 18 percent of all Cypriots are ethnic Turks, a reminder that Turkey controlled the island from 1571 until 1878, when it yielded control to Britain.

Cyprus became independent in 1960. Since then, anger and distrust have marked the relationship between the Greek and Turkish communities. Fearing that the Greek majority planned to unite Cyprus with Greece, the Turkish army partitioned the nation in 1974.

THE LAND

Smaller than the state of Connecticut, Cyprus has three distinct geographical regions: the Kyrenia Mountains in the north; the Troodos Mountains in the south; and the Messaoria plain in between, where most

Cypriots live. Winters are generally mild, with rainfall occurring between November and March. Summers can be hot and dry in the intensively farmed central plain. In recent years, dams and irrigation projects have helped ease the periodic droughts and increase farm yields there. Restoration of ancient hillside forests of pine, oak, and cypress is also easing the drought problem and helping improve river flows.

Almost all rivers in Cyprus rise in the Troodos Mountains. Some of the smaller ones flow directly south into the Mediterranean Sea. A few flow west. The two largest ones, the Pedias and the Yialias, flow north and then east before merging to enter Famagusta Bay.

The island's many rulers have left their marks on the land. Greek temples, Roman amphitheaters, Byzantine churches, Crusader castles, Venetian forts, Turkish mosques, and British post offices can be seen throughout the country. They all add to the charm of the rugged island.

THE PEOPLE

Until recently, Greek and Turkish Cypriots lived similar lives in their separate villages and farms. In both communities, people farmed in traditional ways and cherished their male-dominated, extended-family structures. Generally, women were kept secluded. Children in Turkish villages studied in the Turkish language and acquired Muslim values. Children in Greek villages studied in Greek and acquired Greek Orthodox values. There were few contacts between the two groups.

This way of life had started to change when Cyprus became independent in 1960. The emphasis on education increased. Young Cypriots from both communities learned English as a second language in secondary schools, technical colleges, and universities. Western music, movies, styles, and literature became increasingly popular, particularly among Greek Cypriots. The nuclear family—parents and children—started to replace the extended family as the basic social unit. Women began en-

Hand-painted religious images called icons decorate many Greek Orthodox churches on Cyprus.

tering college, business, the professions, and even politics. Today, women can join the Greek Cypriot armed forces.

The pattern of change was sharply accelerated by the Turkish invasion in July 1974. The Turkish army occupied 40 percent of the country, including the entire Kyrenia mountain region, the upper part of the Messaoria plain, the northern suburbs of Nicosia, and the leading port of Famagusta. The Turkish army drove more than 200,000 Greek Cypriots from their homes and forced them to move south. In the south, a few thousand Turkish Cypriots were forced to move north.

In a nation of about 700,000 people, this double exodus had an enormous impact. City populations swelled. Traditional values were abandoned. The Cypriot government had to raise taxes in the Greek area to aid refugees, and at the same time, it had to expand the southern ports of Limassol and Larnaca to make up for the loss of Famagusta.

Although talks sponsored by the United Nations to promote the reunification of Cyprus occur regularly, the two communities remain divided by increased bitterness and by a U.N. buffer zone stretching across the country from Morphou Bay in the west to Famagusta Bay in the east.

ECONOMY

The 1974 Turkish invasion that forced thousands of Greek Cypriots into the cities at first caused considerable unemployment and hardship. But the 1980s and early 1990s saw gains in tourism and in the export of farm and manufactured goods, which alleviated these problems.

With 14 percent of the workforce engaged in farming, agriculture remains important. The country's major exports include citrus fruit, potatoes, grapes, olives, and wine.

Nearly a third of all Cypriot workers are employed in light industries, where they make shoes, clothes, pharmaceuticals, and cigarettes for export. A rapidly growing part of the economy involves banking, trading,

FACTS AND FIGURES

OFFICIAL NAME: Republic of Cyprus. The northeast declared itself the **Turkish Republic of Northern Cyprus** in 1983, but only Turkey recognized its independence.

NATIONALITY: Cypriot(s).

CAPITAL: Nicosia.

LOCATION: Island in the eastern Mediterranean Sea.

AREA: 3,572 sq. mi. (9,251 sq. km.).

PHYSICAL FEATURES: Highest point—Mount Olympus (6,406 ft.; 1,953 m.). **Lowest point**—sea level. **Chief river**—Pedias.

POPULATION: 700,000 (1996; annual growth 0.9%).

MAJOR LANGUAGES: Greek, Turkish (both official), English.

MAJOR RELIGIONS: Greek Orthodox Christianity, Islam.

GOVERNMENT: Republic. **Head of state and government**—president. **Legislature**—unicameral House of Representatives.

ECONOMY: Chief minerals—iron and copper pyrites, gypsum. **Chief agricultural products**—potatoes, vegetables, grains, grapes. **Industries and products**—foodstuffs, beverages, textiles, chemicals. **Chief exports**—wine, potatoes, citrus fruits, grapes, raisins. **Chief imports**—fuel, food, machinery.

MONETARY UNIT: 1 Cypriot pound = 100 cents.

NATIONAL HOLIDAY: October 1 (Independence Day).

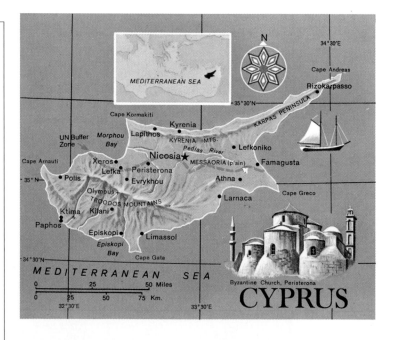

Byzantine Church, Peristerona

CYPRUS

Many city dwellers in Cyprus live in multistory, European-style apartment buildings.

currency exchange, and international communications. Turmoil in Lebanon forced many businesses to move to Nicosia from Beirut, which used to be the trading capital of the Middle East.

Cyprus has no heavy industries, and its only energy resources are hydroelectric plants in the Troodos Mountains. As a result, the country has to import petroleum products, machinery, and transportation vehicles.

Both sectors of Cyprus are working hard to revive tourism, which declined during the 1970s. Now, increasing numbers of Northern Europeans travel to the sunny beaches and scenic mountains of Cyprus.

In times past, Cyprus was rich in metals. Its most important one, copper, was coveted throughout the ancient world. The scientific name for copper, *cuprum*, comes from the Latin word, *cyprium* (Cyprian metal). Cyprus still exports copper and a few other metals, including asbestos, but in dwindling amounts each year.

CITIES

Nicosia, the capital and largest city of Cyprus, is located in the middle of the Messaoria plain. Cyprus's other important cities are on the coast. The Green Line separating the Turkish-controlled region from the rest of Cyprus runs through the northern fringe of the city.

Famagusta, the capital of Cyprus during the period of Venetian rule in the 15th and 16th centuries, contains many historic sites. Before July 1974, it was the leading port of Cyprus. The Turkish assault on Famagusta in August 1974 caused widespread damage and forced two-thirds of the population to flee. Under Turkish control, port traffic is only a fraction of its pre-1974 level.

Limassol's large natural port on the south coast has been greatly improved and expanded since 1974. It is now the nation's leading port.

Larnaca, a port city on the site of ancient Citium, was mainly used for local trade until 1974. Since then, modernized and expanded, its port has become second only to Limassol in international trade.

HISTORY

Archaeological excavations show that Cyprus has been inhabited by humans for at least 6,000 years. But we know very little about the early cultures. There is evidence that Greek settlers moved to the island around 1500 B.C. Since then, Cyprus has had a dominant Greek culture that has survived many foreign invasions and rulers.

Phoenicians set up trading colonies in Cyprus around 800 B.C. Later, the island was in turn ruled by Assyria, Egypt, and Persia. Alexander the Great restored Greek rule from 333 to 323 B.C. After his death, the island reverted to Egyptian control. When Egypt fell under Roman influence, Cyprus became a Roman colony in 58 B.C.

The split of the Roman Empire into two parts in the 4th century A.D. placed Cyprus in the Eastern, or Byzantine, Empire. Throughout the long period of Byzantine rule, Cyprus was attacked several times by Muslims from Asia and North Africa. In 1191, Christian Crusaders led by King Richard I of England occupied Cyprus and used it as a base for their campaign in the Holy Land (Palestine). Crusaders ruled Cyprus until 1489, when they passed control to the Italian city-state of Venice. The Turks conquered Cyprus in 1571 and remained for 300 years. It was during this period that many Turks moved to the island.

At the Congress of Berlin in 1878, Turkey ceded administration of Cyprus to Britain in exchange for British support against Russia. Britain made Cyprus part of the British Empire at the start of World War I in 1914, when Turkey sided with Germany and Austria-Hungary.

The ruins that dot the Cypriot countryside range from ancient temples to medieval castles.

For years the UN has tried to negotiate peace between Cyprus's Greek and Turkish communities.

MODERN CYPRUS

Despite the wishes of Greek Cypriots, Britain never allowed Cyprus to reunite with Greece. First, they feared fierce resistance from the Turkish Cypriot community and Turkey. Second, they valued Cyprus as a base from which to protect British interests in the Middle East.

Greek Cypriot frustration with the British position led to violence during the 1950s. A Greek Cypriot underground movement, known as EOKA, waged a guerrilla campaign against the British to gain *enosis* (union with Greece). The Turkish community, in opposing the drive for *enosis*, also resorted to violence. In 1959, a compromise solution to the conflict was worked out by Britain, Greece, Turkey, and the two Cypriot communities. The agreement forbade *enosis* and the partition of Cyprus into Greek and Turkish sectors. Cyprus became an independent nation in 1960, with a constitution that spelled out a power-sharing arrangement between Greek and Turkish Cypriots and guaranteed the rights of the Turkish community. The arrangement called for the president to be a Greek Cypriot and the prime minister to be a Turkish Cypriot.

Conflict did not end, however. In 1963, the United Nations sent a force to restore peace. An uneasy peace was maintained for 11 years.

In 1974, Greek Cypriot forces led by Greek army officers overthrew the government of Cypriot President Archbishop Makarios. Fearing that *enosis* was the reason behind the coup, Turkey sent 20,000 troops to Cyprus and seized the northern part of the country.

In 1975, an Autonomous Turkish Cypriot Administration was set up in the 40 percent of Cyprus occupied by the Turkish army, and the small island nation was effectively divided. In 1983, the area was proclaimed the Turkish Republic of Northern Cyprus. Most nations consider the administration of the Greek Cypriot president to be the legitimate government of all Cyprus. U.N. efforts to negotiate a solution and to reunite the island continue.

Reviewed by RICHARD W. BULLIET, Middle East Institute, Columbia University

Yerevan, Armenia's capital, has many broad avenues lined with stately apartment buildings.

ARMENIA

Armenia is heir to a long and proud history. Present-day Armenia arose out of the ashes of the Soviet Union, which disintegrated in December 1991. The current borders of the country encompass only a small portion of the historic Armenian homeland. Part of Russia from the early 19th century, Armenia was from 1936 to 1991 the smallest of the 15 constituent republics of the Union of Soviet Socialist Republics.

From 1988 until a cease-fire in May 1994, Armenia was embroiled in a bloody conflict with neighboring Azerbaijan over the province of Nagorno-Karabakh, which lies within Azerbaijan but is inhabited mainly by Armenians. About 18,000 people were killed and 25,000 wounded in the war. Thanks to international mediation efforts, hopes for a permanent peace settlement were running high during 1996. Russia continues to consider Armenia within its sphere of influence.

THE LAND

Landlocked Armenia lies in Transcaucasia, just south of the Caucasus mountain range. Most of the country is mountainous and lies at elevations of 3,300 ft. (1,000 m.) or more; the only lowland, the site of Armenia's capital, Yerevan, is a narrow strip of the Ararat Plain adjoining the border of Turkey.

Lake Sevan, which lies at an altitude of about 6,200 ft. (1,900 m.), is one of the world's largest mountain lakes. Irrigation works on the lake's only outlet, the Razdan River, shrank Sevan's surface by about one-third, revealing a number of buildings more than 2,000 years old.

Armenia's climate is dry and sunny. Winters, particularly in higher locations, are quite severe: the lowest temperature ever recorded was −51° F. (−46° C.). Armenia lies in a zone of geological instability; in December 1988, it was hit by an earthquake that caused an estimated 25,000 deaths and massive property destruction. This was the first time in Soviet history that a natural disaster was given worldwide publicity; previously, the Soviet style was to permit as little publicity as possible for such occurrences, as if even natural catastrophes were incompatible with the glorious goal of Communism.

THE PEOPLE

Armenians are an ancient people with a tragic sense of history and a fiercely felt patriotism. For centuries, they suffered under the domination of conquerors and overlords—from the Persians in the 6th century B.C. to the Russians in the present era. Still, Armenians have preserved their special identity and are ready to fight for it. The Byzantine emperor Maurice called them an "unruly nation, which stirs up trouble." Armenians are also sometimes referred to as "the Jews of the Caucasus" because they are found in many countries of the world. In 1992–93, some 700,000 Armenians emigrated because of the war with Azerbaijan. In the United States, the Armenian Church of America claimed 414,000 members in 1995, and several hundred thousand ethnic Armenians live in various countries of the Middle East.

Within Armenia proper, Armenians represent about 93 percent of the population; the country is one of the most ethnically homogeneous of the former Soviet republics. The remaining 7 percent include Azerbaijani, Russians, and Kurds. The number of Azerbaijani within Armenia has decreased in recent years, however, as a result of the conflict over the enclave of Nagorno-Karabakh.

FACTS AND FIGURES

OFFICIAL NAME: Republic of Armenia.

NATIONALITY: Armenian(s).

CAPITAL AND CHIEF CITY: Yerevan.

LOCATION: Southwestern Asia, south of the Caucasus mountain range; landlocked. **Boundaries**—Georgia, Azerbaijan, Iran, Turkey.

AREA: 11,500 sq. mi. (29,785 sq. km.).

PHYSICAL FEATURES: Highest point—Mt. Aragats (13,418 ft.; 4,090 m.), near the border with Turkey. **Lowest point**—gorges of Debed and Araks rivers (1,150 1,300 ft.; 350–400 m.). **Chief rivers**—Araks, Arpa, Razdan. **Major lake**—Sevan.

POPULATION: 3,800,000 (1996; annual growth 0.7%).

MAJOR LANGUAGES: Armenian, Russian.

MAJOR RELIGION: Christianity.

GOVERNMENT: Republic. **Head of state**—president. **Head of government**—prime minister. **Legislature**—Supreme Soviet.

ECONOMY: Chief minerals—copper, molybdenum. **Chief agricultural products**—peaches, apricots, tobacco. **Industries and products**—chemicals, precision instruments, machinery, textiles, essential oils. **Chief exports**—brandy, wines. **Chief imports**—fuel, chemicals, textiles, clothing.

MONETARY UNIT: 1 dram = 100 luna.

NATIONAL HOLIDAY: September 21 (Referendum Day).

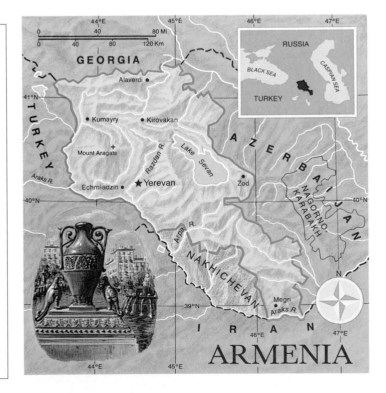

ARMENIA

During the Soviet era, Armenia became a predominantly urban country. More than two-thirds of the population now live in cities, the largest of which is Yerevan, with about 1.2 million people. A village in the 1920s, Yerevan has become a bustling metropolis with a distinctly Middle Eastern flavor. The city is surrounded by mountains: the four peaks of Mount Aragats rise in the northwest; the two peaks of Mount Ararat are 32 mi. (51 km.) to the southwest.

Language. Armenian, an Indo-European tongue, is the only surviving member language of the Thracian branch. According to a historical work from the 5th century A.D., an Armenian monk named Mesrop Mastoc created the 36 symbols of the Armenian alphabet in 404–406. The striking rounded letters were probably based on the Greek alphabet. There are two distinct forms of written Armenian: one, called *grabar,* is the scholarly, liturgical language dating from the 5th century; the other, known as *ashkharabar,* is the modern Armenian that developed in the 15th century and is still used today in literature and newspapers.

Religion. Most churchgoing Armenians belong to the Armenian Apostolic Church, which has about 1.6 million members worldwide; about 1 million of them live in Armenia and Nagorno-Karabakh. Armenia was the first country to introduce Christianity as a state religion, in about A.D. 300. The Armenian Apostolic Church has been on its own since 451 and recognizes no foreign affiliation. It is also the only ancient Christian church that does not celebrate Christmas. Throughout the tortuous history of Armenia, the church has helped Armenians maintain a sense of national identity and often has exercised leadership.

Education and Culture. During the Soviet era, most Armenians learned Russian in addition to their own language. Eight years of schooling is compulsory, and there are numerous trade schools, secondary schools, and colleges. Yerevan State University, which was founded in 1923, and several other institutes of higher learning (polytechnical, medical, agricultural, pedagogical, theatrical, and musical) provide higher education. The Yerevan Ancient Manuscript Library contains more than 12,000 Armenian manuscripts, the oldest from the 9th century. Many of them are beautifully illuminated.

Armenian literature dates to the 5th century and boasts a long line of writers. The earliest Armenian historian known by name is Moses of Khoren (Moses Khorenatsi), whose 5th-century history of Armenia is the primary source for our knowledge of the distant past of the country. The 10th-century poet St. Grigor Narekatsi (Gregory of Narek) wrote religious hymns and meditations, which he called "conversations with God from the depth of the heart." The most popular modern author is Hagop Melik-Agopias, known as "Raffi," who wrote romantic novels in the 19th century and is a favorite with young Armenian patriots.

In music the best-known Armenian composer is Aram Khachaturian, whose *Saber Dance* is one of the most popular classical compositions for orchestra.

Armenia is particularly noted for its architecture, which has been preserved mostly in churches and fortresses. The oldest surviving church is at Echmiadzin, about 16 mi. (26 km.) west of Yerevan. It is the site of the ancient capital of Armenia (from about A.D. 184 to 340), and is a holy place for most Armenians because it is the residence of the Apostolic Church's leader, the Supreme Catholicos.

Women in Armenia make up more than half of the country's labor force. They work in a wide range of occupations, and are well represented in farmwork (above) and factory machine operations (left).

ECONOMY

During the Soviet era, Armenia became an industrial country, one of the most rapidly developing republics within the Soviet Union. Armenian industry became very diversified and included production of electrical equipment, chemicals, textiles, precision instruments, and clothing. Armenia has small deposits of copper, molybdenum, and gold. Cultivation of fruits, potatoes, and vegetables is the main agricultural activity.

The war with Azerbaijan badly disrupted the economy. During three successive winters in the early 1990s, Armenians had to do without heat or light for long periods of time. Western economists, however, have been praising the government of President Levon Ter-Petrosyan for its handling of the economic crisis, particularly its discipline in financial matters. The economic-reform program, including privatization, has gathered speed recently. The forthcoming foreign credits should help the economic revival.

HISTORY

Armenia has a very convoluted history, made more complex by innumerable shifts of its borders. Historical Armenia extended over a much larger territory than the area contained within the present borders, and included portions of modern Georgia, Azerbaijan, Iran, and Turkey. The region around Lake Van in easternmost Turkey played an important role in Armenian history, and the most sacred mountain of Armenia, Mount Ararat (legendary site of the landing of Noah's ark), is also now in Turkey.

Armenia entered history as a satrapy (province) of the Persian Empire in the 6th century B.C., and, in 311 B.C., the region became part of the Macedonian Empire created by Alexander the Great. About 150 years later, there arose two independent Armenian kingdoms. In the 2nd century B.C., ancient Armenia, under King Tigranes the Great, stretched from present-day Georgia in the north to Syria on the Mediterranean Sea.

After adopting Christianity at the beginning of the 4th century A.D., Armenia plunged into a long conflict with Persia and was finally partitioned in A.D. 387, with its western part being absorbed by the Byzantine Empire and its eastern part by Persia. In the 7th century, Persia fell to the Arabs, and Armenia came under Arab rule. During the centuries of Persian and Arab rule, the country was administered by local princes known as *nakharars*.

The dynasty of Bagratuni ruled Armenia from 884. Under King Gagik Bagratuni I (A.D. 989–1020), the country experienced a golden age, with flourishing arts, culture, and commerce. In 1071, however, Seljuk Turks came from the east and incorporated Armenia into their lands. Less than 200 years later, they were replaced by Mongol Tatars.

In the 16th century, Ottoman Turks conquered the original Armenian homeland and ruled it for the next 400 years. In 1828 Armenia became part of Russia.

To this day, Armenians worldwide remember with sadness a major tragedy of modern Armenian history. In the late 19th century, Turkish persecutions of Christians led to wholesale massacres of Armenians, which culminated in massive deportations of Armenians from Anatolia during World War I. It is estimated that between 600,000 and 1 million people died in this "first genocide of modern times."

In 1918 an independent republic of Armenia was established within the present borders, but in 1920 the ruling party of Dashnak turned the government over to Russian Communists rather than surrender to Turks. In 1922 Armenia became part of the Soviet Union.

The mountains surrounding Yerevan are dotted with ancient caves of great archaeological interest.

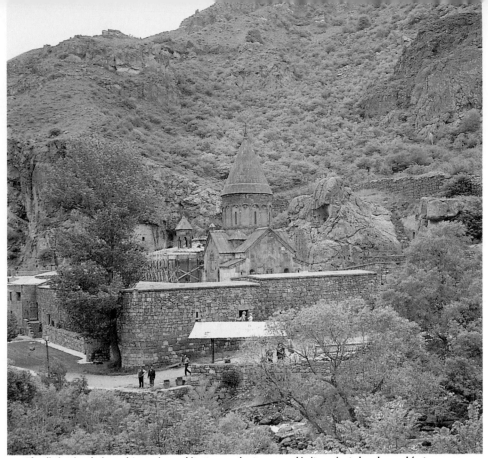

The distinctive designs of Armenian architecture are best preserved in its ancient churches and fortresses.

For the following seven decades, Armenian national consciousness was repressed by the Soviet state. Soon after Mikhail Gorbachev introduced his political reforms in the late 1980s, Armenia became embroiled in a violent conflict with neighboring Azerbaijan over the enclave of Nagorno-Karabakh. The conflict first came to the world's attention in February 1988, when dozens of Armenians were massacred in the Azerbaijani city of Sumgait.

Initially, international sympathies were with the Armenians, but a massacre of Azerbaijani civilians in February 1992 showed that violent acts were being perpetrated by both sides. In 1993, Armenian forces captured more than one-fourth of Azerbaijani territory.

International mediators led by the United States (within the Organization of Security and Cooperation in Europe) have put pressure on both countries to resolve the conflict. A cease-fire was signed in May 1994, and although sporadic clashes continued for some time, it seemed in 1996 that a settlement was finally within sight.

GOVERNMENT

Armenia is a republic with a strong presidency. Levon Ter-Petrosyan was elected to his second term in September 1996. Several opposition parties were banned in the mid-1990s, but others continue their activities. Armenia is a member of the Commonwealth of Independent States, a loose alliance that replaced the Soviet Union in 1991.

IRINA RYBACEK / Reviewed by EDWARD W. WALKER, Ph.D., Columbia University

GEORGIA

Georgia, located in the picturesque mountainous area where Europe meets the Middle East, is renowned for its strong nationalistic fervor and lively, colorful culture.

The Republic of Georgia is a small country in the Caucasus region of what was formerly the Soviet Union. Endowed with beautiful scenery, a pleasant climate, and vivacious and hospitable people, the country is located at the juncture of two adjoining but disparate cultures, those of Europe and the Middle East. Even though the uniqueness of Georgian culture was largely suppressed during the decades of harsh Communist rule, the country nevertheless stood out as the most colorful and lively Soviet republic.

In the early 1990s, Georgia became a battlefield. A war between supporters and opponents of Zviad Gamsakhurdia, the first freely elected Georgian president, was followed by two ethnic conflicts, with the Ossetians in the north and the Abkhazians in the west. The fighting in the autonomous region of Abkhazia was the worst, leaving 30,000 dead and more than 200,000 refugees. By the mid-1990s, peace had been restored, and Georgia began to rebuild its shattered economy.

THE LAND

Georgia lies just to the south of the Great Caucasus mountain range, bordering the easternmost coast of the Black Sea. To the north the republic adjoins Russia; to the south it shares borders with Azerbaijan, Armenia, and Turkey. Most of the country is mountainous, except for the Kolkhida Plain around the delta of the Rioni River. The Lesser Caucasus mountain system stretches to the south, and the country is divided into its eastern and western parts by the Surami Range.

The road connecting Tbilisi, the capital, and Vladikavkaz (formerly Ordzhonikidze) in Russia, built in 1799 and known since then as the Georgian Military Highway, passes through one of the most spectacular regions of the former Soviet Union. Only 130 mi. (208 km.) long, it is the shortest route crossing the Caucasus. The famous novel by the great Russian poet Mikhail Lermontov, *A Hero of Our Times* (first published in 1840), opens at Krestovy Pass, one of the landmarks of this route.

Georgia's climate ranges from subtropical along the Black Sea coast to more continental in the east, but it is generally very pleasant, with few extremes. About one-third of the country is covered by forests; the higher reaches of the mountains are capped by snow year-round. Fruit and nut trees abound, and vineyards exist that have had their beginnings traced to prehistory.

THE PEOPLE

The Georgians, a proud and temperamental people, can be very charming but very fierce. They call themselves Kartvelians. Georgians belong to a separate ethnic branch of Caucasian peoples, different from the Indo-European and Turkic stock of their neighbors. It is likely that their ancestors lived in the region from prehistoric times. Georgians tend to be tall, wiry, and long-lived, and the women are known for their beauty.

The Georgian tongue is part of the Caucasian language family. It is written in a distinct alphabet created in the early 5th century A.D. that is somewhat similar to Armenian script. Two different forms of the Georgian alphabet exist today: one, called *khutsuri,* is reserved for liturgical purposes; the modern version, known as *mkhedruli,* is used in all other communication.

After decades of persecution, Orthodox Christian Georgians are now free to worship as they please.

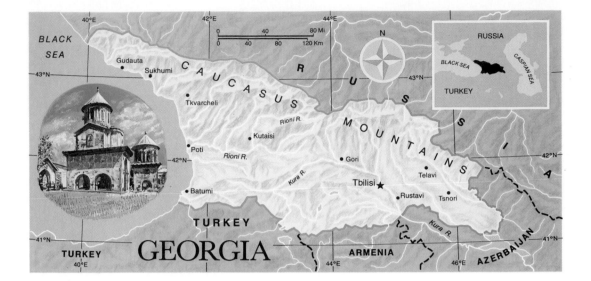

FACTS AND FIGURES

OFFICIAL NAME: Republic of Georgia.

NATIONALITY: Georgian(s).

CAPITAL AND CHIEF CITY: Tbilisi.

LOCATION: South of the Caucasus Mountains, bordering the Black Sea. **Boundaries**—Russia, Azerbaijan, Armenia, Turkey.

AREA: 26,900 sq. mi. (69,670 sq. km.).

PHYSICAL FEATURES: Highest point—Shkhara (16,627 ft.; 5,070 m.), on the border with Russia. **Lowest point**—Kolkhida Lowlands near the Black Sea. **Chief rivers**—Inguri, Rioni, Kura.

POPULATION: 5,400,000 (1996; annual growth 0.2%).

MAJOR LANGUAGES: Georgian (official), Russian.

MAJOR RELIGION: Eastern Orthodox Christianity.

GOVERNMENT: Republic. **Head of state**—president. **Head of government**—prime minister. **Legislature**—unicameral Parliament.

ECONOMY: Chief minerals—coal, petroleum, manganese. **Chief agricultural products**—wine, tea, citrus fruits. **Industries and products**—production of hydroelectricity, mineral extraction, machinery. **Chief exports**—machines, chemicals, wines, cognac. **Chief imports**—fuel, wheat, foodstuffs, light manufactures.

MONETARY UNIT: lari.

NATIONAL HOLIDAY: May 26 (Independence Day).

Most Georgians belong to the national Orthodox Church, which is close to the Russian Orthodox Church. Many inhabitants of Adzharia and Abkhazia are Muslims.

Minorities. Georgians constitute only about 70 percent of the republic's population; minorities include Armenians, Russians, Azerbaijani, Ossetians, and Abkhazians, with the latter two having autonomous regions within Georgia. The Ossetians, who live in central-north Georgia, speak an Indo-European language of the Iranian branch and are thought to be the descendants of Sarmatians, who were pushed into the Caucasus by the Huns in the 6th century A.D. The Abkhazians, a Caucasian people, have their autonomous region in the northwestern corner of Georgia. The Adzhar autonomous region in the southwest, around Batumi, is inhabited by Turkicized Georgians, Russians, and Armenians.

Way of Life. Georgians are known for their quick-witted resourcefulness, their ability to negotiate, their hospitality, and their enjoyment of food and drink. Under the old Soviet regime, many Georgian farmers even managed to travel to Moscow to sell fresh produce.

Georgians love social gatherings and celebrations. One traditional feast is called *tamada;* its main purpose is the reconciliation of enemies. Georgian food is spicy, with lots of herbs and garlic. Chicken and mutton are the favorites. Some Georgian specialties, such as shashlik and chicken tabaka, are served in restaurants worldwide.

Two Native Sons. Two Georgians played major roles in the history of the Soviet empire. The first is the infamous Iosif Vissarionovich Dzhugashvili, better known as Joseph Stalin (the surname means "of steel"). Born in a small town outside the Georgian capital, Stalin never lost his Georgian accent. After succeeding Lenin as head of the Communist Party and Soviet leader, Stalin initiated a series of devastating purges that led to the deaths of millions. It is ironic that this vicious and paranoid dictator managed to charm some staunch Western anti-Communists and persuade them of his good intentions and responsible statesmanship.

Another Georgian was prominent during the unraveling of the empire: Eduard Shevardnadze, the last Soviet foreign minister. Shevardnadze headed the Georgian Communist Party from 1972 to 1985, and was noted for his crackdown on corruption and support of Georgian culture. In his position as the last Soviet foreign minister, from 1985 to 1991, he helped end the Cold War. He returned to Georgia in March 1992 and has led the country since that time.

Education and Culture. During the Soviet era, illiteracy was virtually eliminated. Tbilisi State University dates from 1918, and there is also an Academy of Sciences.

In the early years of *glasnost* ("openness," "loosening of censorship"), one film by a well-known Georgian director, T. J. Abuladze, was seen by millions of people in many countries. Called *Repentance,* it is a powerful condemnation of political tyranny and at the same time a fascinating portrait of Georgian life.

Georgia has an ancient culture; the medieval monasteries at Ikalto and Gelati were important educational centers. The greatest medieval writer is Shota Rustaveli, whose heroic poem, *The Man in the Tiger's Skin* (written about A.D. 1200), is one of the country's national treasures.

People have lived nestled against Georgia's Caucasus Mountains since prehistoric times.

ECONOMY

Georgia is home to the world's largest manganese mines; coal is also plentiful, and forests provide timber. Until the early 1990s, industry focused on the production of wood, textiles, iron, steel, and automobiles.

The country has always concentrated on crops that do not require great expanses of land. Georgian tea supplied about 95 percent of all the tea consumed in the Soviet Union. Vineyards have traditionally been very important: after centuries of cultivation, there are about 500 varieties of grapes. Other crops include citrus fruits and tobacco.

After World War II, Georgian resorts, such as Batumi and Sukhumi on the Black Sea, became popular vacation spots. Despite government restrictions during the Communist era, a black-market underground economy flourished in Georgia, and individual Georgian entrepreneurs would regularly bring planeloads of fresh fruit to Moscow.

During the fighting in the first years of independence, Georgia's economy was almost completely destroyed. Factories were bombed out and prices rose astronomically. A turnaround came in mid-1994 when the government agreed to the Russian demand to set up military bases in the country in return for economic assistance. Yet Russia's aid is no longer paramount: in 1995, the largest trading partner of Georgia was Turkey. As a result, the pace of economic reform, including privatization, has quickened.

HISTORY

Ancient Greeks set up colonies in western Georgia from the 6th century B.C. onward. The plain by the Rioni River on the Black Sea coast was immortalized as the fabulously rich Colchis region, home of the Princess Medea and the dragon from whom Jason stole the Golden Fleece. The Romans, led by Pompey, established their hegemony over the region in 65 B.C. In the early 4th century A.D., eastern Georgia, known as Iberia, adopted Christianity; and in the course of the next three centuries, the country was enmeshed in the conflict between Byzantium and Persia.

In the 7th century came the Arabs, who set up an emirate in Tbilisi. Georgia's Golden Age started in the late 8th century, when the dynasty of Bagratids began to unite all lands inhabited by the Iberians, and reached its highest point during the reign of Queen Tamara (A.D. 1184–1213). Tamara's kingdom included parts of modern Azerbaijan and Circassia, north of the Caucasus Range.

The Mongol Tatars swept over Transcaucasia from A.D. 1236 to 1242, and Georgia splintered into small, quarreling kingdoms. Tamerlane invaded next, to be replaced by Turks and Persians, and, in the 19th century, by Russians. Despite this succession of foreign rulers, however, Georgia maintained its unique identity. Russification efforts by the czars only led to the rise of a strong Georgian nationalist movement.

In May 1918, Georgia proclaimed independence, but it was cut short by the arrival of the Russian Red Army in April 1920. The suppression of nationalist groups was particularly fierce: hundreds of people were killed and 100,000 were deported to Siberia. Ironically, this brutal campaign was led by three Georgian Communists who came to play leading roles in the new Soviet state: Stalin and two of his comrades, Sergo Ordzhonikidze and Lavrenti Beria. In 1936, Georgia became one of the 15 constituent republics of the Soviet Union.

The cliff dwellings in Vardzia, Georgia, were used in the 12th century as a hideaway from invading armies.

Independent Georgia. The long-suppressed Georgian yearning for independence intensified after April 1989, when Soviet troops fired into peaceful crowds of nationalists in Tbilisi and killed about 20 people. In April 1991, Georgia declared independence, and in May a former dissident, Zviad Gamsakhurdia, was elected president of the country, becoming the first freely elected leader in any Soviet republic.

Authoritarian and erratic, Gamsakhurdia soon alienated large parts of the population. He was run out of Tbilisi in December 1991, and for the next two years he and his followers battled their fellow Georgians in a fierce civil war. In late 1993, he committed suicide.

Meanwhile, ethnic strife erupted in Ossetia and in Abkhazia, claiming lives, displacing thousands of people, and causing an almost complete economic collapse. Russia apparently fanned these conflicts in order to be able to step in later and regain some influence in the area. After much hesitation, Eduard Shevardnadze called in the Russian troops in late 1993 and agreed to allow Russian military bases to be set up. Reluctantly, Georgia also joined the Commonwealth of Independent States (CIS) in December 1993. Russians then helped calm the fighting and promised economic help.

GOVERNMENT

The anti-Gamsakhurdia forces that took power in 1992 restored Georgia's 1921 constitution. Eduard Shevardnadze, head of the country since March 1992, was elected president by more than 70 percent of the vote in November 1995. His Union of Georgia Citizens is not a regular political party, but an alliance of clan-based groups. Three other parties are represented in the Parliament. Compared with Armenia and Azerbaijan, Georgia is clearly a freer and more democratic state.

IRINA RYBACEK / Reviewed by EDWARD W. WALKER, Ph.D., Columbia University

Oil production quickly transformed Baku into one of the largest cosmopolitan centers in Azerbaijan.

AZERBAIJAN

The Republic of Azerbaijan is a small country located in the eastern part of the Isthmus of Caucasus and inhabited mostly by Turkic-speaking Muslim Azerbaijani. The region belonged for centuries to Persia, but became part of the Russian Empire in the early 1800s.

After a brief period of independence during the Russian civil war, Azerbaijan was occupied by the Red Army in 1920. It was then incorporated into the Soviet Union in 1922, and remained a part of the Soviet Union for almost 70 years. Following a failed coup attempt in Moscow in August 1991, Azerbaijan declared independence, and when the Soviet Union finally split in December 1991, the country entered a new era.

Between 1988 and 1994, Azerbaijani were locked in a war with their neighbors and traditional enemies, the Christian Armenians, over the enclave of Nagorno-Karabakh. This small area within Azerbaijan—only 70 mi. (112 km.) across at its widest—is inhabited mainly by Armenians, but both nations claim historical right to it. More than 18,000 people perished in the conflict and about 1 million became refugees. By 1996, prospects for a final peaceful settlement looked promising.

THE LAND

Azerbaijan lies south of the Great Caucasus mountain range, bordering on Armenia and Georgia to the west, Russia to the north, the Caspian Sea to the east, and Iran to the south. It is a country of varied scenery, with lowlands and steppes taking up about half of its area. The Great Caucasus ridges in the north are noted for their rugged beauty.

Two autonomous regions are part of Azerbaijan. The predominantly Armenian-inhabited Nagorno-Karabakh ("Nagorno" means "Upper," indicating its mountainous character) is located in southwestern Azerbaijan, and only a narrow strip of land separates it from Armenia.

The other autonomous region is Nakhichevan, which lies sandwiched between Armenia and Iran. There is also a large territory called Azerbaijan in northwestern Iran, which is separated from the Azerbaijan Republic by the Araks River.

The climate of Azerbaijan is subtropical in the center and east, and moderately cold in the north and west. The capital of the country, Baku, has a very pleasant, dry climate for most of the year.

THE PEOPLE

Azerbaijani are a proud and ancient people of Turkic stock. They speak Azeri Turkish, a language whose script uses the Cyrillic alphabet. Azerbaijani are predominantly Shi'ite Muslims, but decades of official Soviet atheism have contributed to a decline in religious fervor.

In the mid-1990s, the population included 3 percent Dagestani, 3 percent Russians, 2 percent Armenians, and smaller numbers of other Caucasian peoples. The percentage of Armenians has decreased in recent years as a result of the prolonged conflict with Armenia, which has resulted in hundreds of deaths and destruction of property.

Education and Cultural Life. Illiteracy was substantially reduced during the Soviet era. There are almost 20 institutes of higher learning, the largest being the Azerbaijan Institute of Petroleum and Chemistry. In 1989, a higher Islamic school, a *madrassa,* was opened in Baku for Shi'ite Muslims. It was the first such institution permitted since 1920, when all religious schools were closed down.

Azerbaijani trace the beginning of their literature to the 7th century, when the area came under Arab influence. The greatest medieval literary flourishing took place in the 11th and 12th centuries, after Azerbaijan became part of the Persian Empire. Following the Russian conquest in the early 1800s, Azerbaijani culture was influenced by Europe.

FACTS AND FIGURES

OFFICIAL NAME: Republic of Azerbaijan.

NATIONALITY: Azerbaijani(s).

CAPITAL: Baku.

LOCATION: Southwestern Asia, south of the Caucasus mountain range, bordering the Caspian Sea. **Boundaries**—Iran, Armenia, Georgia, Russia. The Nakhichevan autonomous area, separated from Azerbaijan by Armenia, borders on Turkey, Armenia, and Iran.

AREA: 33,400 sq. mi. (86,506 sq. km.).

PHYSICAL FEATURES: Highest point—Bazar Dyuzi (14,652 ft.; 4,466 m.), on the northern border. **Lowest point**—sea level. **Chief rivers**—Kura, Araks. **Major lakes**—Adzhinour, Alagyel, Akgyel.

POPULATION: 7,600,000 (1996; annual growth 1.4%).

MAJOR LANGUAGES: Azerbaijani, Russian.

MAJOR RELIGION: Islam.

GOVERNMENT: Republic. **Head of state**—president. **Head of government**—prime minister. **Legislature**—unicameral National Assembly.

CHIEF CITIES: Baku, Gyandzha, Sumgait.

ECONOMY: Chief minerals—oil, gas, zinc, iron. **Chief agricultural products**—cotton, tobacco. **Industries and products**—electrical equipment, chemicals. **Chief exports**—petroleum products, textiles, cotton. **Chief imports**—machinery, light manufactures.

MONETARY UNIT: 1 manat = 100 gopik.

NATIONAL HOLIDAY: May 28 (Independence Day).

88

Azerbaijan's rapidly expanding oil-refining industry (above) utilizes state-of-the-art technology. By contrast, ancient farming techniques are still used to produce high-quality cotton, silk, and tobacco.

ECONOMY

In the early years of this century, Azerbaijan produced more oil than the United States, and was the birthplace of the oil-refining industry. Azerbaijan's other minerals are zinc, cobalt, and molybdenum; there are also limestone and marble quarries.

The city of **Baku** grew into a large industrial metropolis only during the 20th century, when its oil fields began to be exploited on a massive scale. With 1.2 million people, Baku is one of the largest cities in the region. Located on a natural harbor, the city descends in gently sloping terraces to a bay.

During the Soviet era, the economy of Azerbaijan became very diversified. The chemical industry and metallurgy works are located at **Sumgait**; **Gyandzha** (formerly Kirovabad) is one of the centers of light industry, mostly textiles. The Kura Valley is a fertile agricultural area. The major crops include cotton, silk, tobacco, and tea. Fishing is also important, and a lucrative export item is caviar, harvested from the Caspian Sea.

The present economic situation in Azerbaijan is in disarray, however. The disruption of economic ties with the former Soviet republics, efforts to introduce a market economy, and ethnic strife all led to a sharp downturn in production, and hardship for the Azerbaijani people. Turkey has become the major foreign-aid donor to Azerbaijan. Economic prospects had improved by the mid-1990s, however, because of an expected increase in oil production. New oil is scheduled to begin flowing in 1997.

HISTORY

The area of present-day Azerbaijan was known in ancient times as Albania. It had a similar social structure to neighboring Armenia and Iberia (present-day Georgia), but was for most of its early history a vassal of Iran. In A.D. 643 the region came under Arab control. Widespread conversions to Islam gradually displaced the Christian population by 821.

From the 11th century until the early 1800s, Azerbaijan was part of the Persian Empire. In 1813, however, after protracted warfare, Russia acquired the area north of the River Araks.

A century later an independent Azerbaijan arose briefly during the civil war in Russia. Proclaimed independent in May 1918 and recognized by the Allied powers in January 1920, the republic survived only until April 1920, when it was invaded by the Red Army. Two years later Azerbaijan was incorporated into the Transcaucasian Soviet Federated Socialist Republic; in 1936 it became a union republic.

Submerged for decades in the uniformity of Soviet life, Azerbaijan was the site of one of the first series of ethnic clashes that occurred when the huge Soviet empire began unraveling in the late 1980s. The Armenian population of Nagorno-Karabakh voted for unification with Armenia in early 1988, claiming discrimination at the hands of Azerbaijani authorities. This led to a pogrom in the city of Sumgait in February 1988, in which dozens of Armenians were killed.

The violence escalated during the following years, growing into a widespread war with Armenia. Soviet troops intervened in Baku in January 1990 to regain control, killing hundreds of people during the onslaught. This brutality was widely criticized, both within the Soviet Union and internationally.

The following year brought the demise of the Soviet Union and a new independence for Azerbaijan, but ethnic bloodshed continued. The first president of the country was Ayaz Mutalibov, a former Communist Party boss, who was elected in September 1991. In March 1992, he was forced to resign in the wake of nationalist demonstrations led by the opposition Popular Front, which accused Mutalibov of being too soft in the war with Armenia. Abulfaz Elchibey, a charismatic former dissident, assumed the presidency in June 1992.

Defeats in the war with Armenia led to Elchibey's ouster in June 1993 and his replacement by Heydar Aliyev, a onetime Communist hard-liner and KGB general. Under Russian pressure, a cease-fire was concluded in May 1994, and fighting gradually subsided. In 1996, hopes were running high that a permanent settlement of the status of Nagorno-Karabakh was close at hand.

In September 1994, the Azerbaijani government signed a "contract of the century" with an international oil consortium, and since then, Aliyev has been promising to turn Azerbaijan into a "new Kuwait." The renewed oil production should begin in mid-1997.

GOVERNMENT

The first legislative elections since independence took place in several rounds of voting between November 1995 and February 1996, but international observers claimed that there were numerous irregularities. After the elections, President Aliyev increased his persecution of opposition members.

A new constitution was approved in a referendum in November 1995, defining Azerbaijan as a republic with a strong executive presidency. Legislative power is exercised by a 125-member parliament.

IRINA RYBACEK / Reviewed by EDWARD W. WALKER, Ph.D., Columbia University

A poster of President Assad adorns a building in Damascus, Syria's capital and largest city.

SYRIA

Syria, a mostly Arab land in the heart of the Middle East, has been a center of commerce for more than 5,000 years. Its capital, Damascus, is the world's oldest continuously inhabited city. Syria's strategic location, linking Asia with Africa and Europe, attracted traders and conquerors through the ages. They included Egyptians, Phoenicians, Greeks, Romans, Arabs, Mongols, Turks, and French. Syria became an independent nation in 1946.

THE LAND

In ancient and medieval times, Syria was the geographical term for the entire northwestern part of the region once known as the Fertile Crescent. This landmass, stretching from the Euphrates and Tigris rivers in the east to the Mediterranean Sea in the west, now contains Lebanon, Israel, Jordan, and part of Iraq as well as modern Syria.

Syria is divided into two main geographic zones. The western zone consists of two mountain ranges—the Anti-Lebanon and the Jebel Ansariyah—with a valley between. The mountain ranges and valley run parallel to the Mediterranean Sea. The eastern zone is much larger. It consists of a semiarid plateau sloping toward the Euphrates River valley.

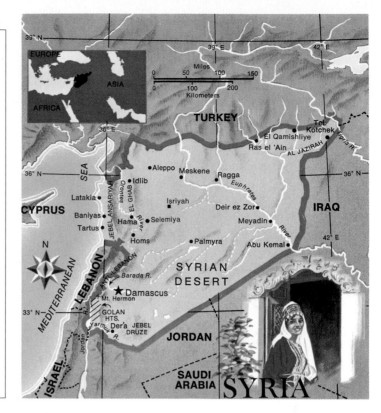

Summers are hot and dry throughout Syria. A cool rainy season prevails from November to April, with an average annual rainfall of 30 in. (76 cm.) in the western mountains and valley, and about 10 in. (25.4 cm.) in the eastern plateau.

About 30 percent of Syria's total land area is arable. Most of this arable land is located in the valley between the Jebel Ansariyah and the Anti-Lebanon ranges in the west and the broad valley of the Euphrates River in the east. Much of the area in between is semidesert. Most Syrians live in the western part of the country, which contains the largest cities —**Damascus**, **Aleppo**, **Homs**, **Latakia**, and **Hama**.

THE PEOPLE

Family, ethnic, and religious loyalties are extremely important values in Syria. From early childhood, a Syrian is expected to work for the good of the family and for the group to which the family belongs. Independence and individuality are viewed as undesirable, selfish qualities. Strong family and group loyalties highlight ethnic and religious differences and influence all aspects of Syrian society. Leaders of government and business tend to give top priority to relatives when it comes to jobs and benefits.

Syria's population consists of four major ethnic groups and several minor ones. Arabs make up about 90 percent of the population. Kurds constitute 6 percent, Armenians 3 percent, and Turkic peoples 1.5 percent. There are also several smaller groups.

Religion. About 75 percent of Syrians are Sunni Muslims, 12 percent are Alawites, and 3 percent are Druzes. The Druzes are a religious offshoot of Shi'a Islam and came to Syria in the 11th century from Egypt.

The second-largest Muslim group, the Alawites, are another off-shoot of Shi'ism, dating from the 9th and 10th centuries. The Alawites lived close to Christian groups for centuries. As a result, the Alawites' beliefs, festivals, and customs have been influenced by Christianity.

Persecution by the Sunni Muslim majority and geographical seclusion in the mountainous region of northwestern Syria led to great social cohesion among the Alawites. This social cohesion enabled the Alawites to gain control of the Baath (Arab Socialist Renaissance) Party and the Syrian government in the 1960s.

More than 10 different Christian groups make up about 12 percent of Syria's population. Historic association with the Christian West led to greater emphasis on education and the study of foreign languages in the Christian community than in the Muslim community. It also led to doubts about the Arab nationalism of Syrian Christians.

WAY OF LIFE

In traditional and modern Syria, religious association is the most important part of a person's identity. Position in society also is determined by family and group connections. Success as a merchant, religious leader, soldier, or politician depends on family ties and personal friends.

Village Life. At the end of World War I, 80 percent of Syria's population was rural. Most rural peasants were landless. They lived in some 4,000 scattered villages. Up to 80 percent of the land under cultivation was owned by large landlords, who often took more than half of the crop. Some landlords owned entire villages. Most of the villages were isolated, and the roads that connected them were inadequate. Mortality rates were high, disease rampant, and drinking water polluted.

Such isolated villages and towns had to be self-sufficient. Village life was communal, and villagers had to depend on one another to survive. Marriages, funerals, holidays, and festivals were all celebrated in the village.

In urban areas, Syrians often opt to wear Western-style clothes instead of traditional garb.

Life was not easy. Farming was primitive, and the ability to grow enough food in a year depended on the annual rainfall. In 1934, Syria produced about 250,000 metric tons of wheat. By 1993, wheat production was up to 3,625,000 metric tons. In the 1930s, fewer than half the males and very few females could read or write. By 1990, the literacy rate was up to 78 percent for males and 51 percent for females. These and other gains were the result of many often painful social and political changes.

Social and Cultural Change

Syria, like most Middle Eastern countries, has undergone dramatic urbanization during the last half of the 20th century. By the 1970s, nearly all of Syria's towns had expanded far beyond their medieval walls. The nation's urban population swelled to 60 percent of the total. Multistoried concrete apartment blocks and office buildings mushroomed. Most Syrians now live in apartment buildings rather than houses. Unable to buy automobiles, many urban dwellers live close to city centers in order to use public transportation.

Education. In 1938, predominantly agricultural Syria had approximately 100,000 elementary students, 7,000 high-school pupils, and 350 university students. Over the past three decades, rapid urbanization and the rise of industry and commerce placed a new emphasis on education. By 1993, school enrollment was up to 2.8 million elementary students, 845,000 high-school pupils, and over 178,000 university students.

Women are still largely secluded in Syrian society, but the government policy of secularism and socialism has enabled more than 100,000 women to graduate from college, and engage in most professions.

ECONOMY

Since independence in 1946, Syria's economic and industrial development has been hampered by several factors: wars with Israel in 1948, 1967, 1973, and 1982; and disputes with its Arab neighbors of Lebanon, Jordan, and Iraq. Political conflict with Iraq over Baathist socialist ideology led to several closings of the pipeline carrying Iraqi crude oil across Syria to Mediterranean ports. Political instability in the 1960s and 1970s resulted in many economic decisions being based on political needs.

The Syrian government's rigid control of production and trade in the 1970s and early 1980s was poorly managed and inefficient. As a result, the economy was severely hurt. Socialist policies were eased in the late 1980s, and Syria experienced a mild economic revival in the 1990s.

HISTORY

Syria's geographical location between the Nile Valley, Mesopotamia, and the Iranian plateau has made it a highway for caravans and armies. The Canaanites and Phoenicians came in 3000 B.C. Recent excavations southwest of Aleppo indicate that a major state existed in Syria between 3000 and 2500 B.C. The Egyptians conquered the southern part of Syria in 1600 B.C., while their rivals, the Hittites, controlled the northern part. In succeeding centuries, the Babylonians, Assyrians, and Aramaeans fought over the area, with the Aramaeans winning control by 1200 B.C. They established their capital at Damascus, which had been settled first in 2000 B.C. Syria derives its name from Syriac, the Aramaean dialect that was spoken around Damascus.

The way of life in isolated villages has changed little over the centuries.

Ancient Syria made great cultural contributions to the civilization of the Western world. One of these was the alphabet employed by the Phoenicians and subsequently adopted by many other peoples. In the 6th century B.C., Syria became part of the far-flung Persian Empire. Two centuries later, Alexander the Great destroyed Persian power, took the region, and paved the way for the Roman conquest of Syria.

Roman ruins still dot the Syrian landscape. Christianity, which was born in Palestine as an offshoot of Judaism, flourished in Roman-ruled Syria. Saint Paul was converted on the road to Damascus, and founded Christian communities throughout Syria. When the Roman Empire split into eastern and western sections in the 4th century A.D., Syria became part of the eastern, Byzantine Empire, headquartered in Constantinople (Istanbul) in modern-day Turkey.

Muslim Rule. Syria was conquered by Arab Muslims in 634–36. The Arabs gave Syria two of its unifying national characteristics: the Arabic language and the Islamic religion. But until the late 1200s, the western part of Syria along the Mediterranean (which at that time included Lebanon) remained more than 50 percent Christian, with a Hellenistic and Western-oriented culture.

From 661 to 750, Syria was the center of the Islamic world. Damascus served as the capital of the Omayyad dynasty, which ruled an empire stretching from Spain to India. Syria's marketplaces were full of jewels, silk, spices, and perfumes from the East, and textiles, wines, and glassware from Europe. The artisans of Damascus and Aleppo were world-famous for their skill, especially with silver, gold, brass, and copper products. Aleppo, with its imposing citadel, controlled the northern caravan and military routes. It was the passageway from the Persian Gulf and the Indian Ocean to the Mediterranean.

The disintegration of the Abbasid caliphate in the 11th century contributed to the conquest of Syria by the Seljuk Turks, who captured Damascus in 1075. In 1091, Western Europeans launched the first of several Crusades, which resulted in nearly a century of European rule over much of Syria. By the end of the 1100s, Syria was recaptured by Muslim Arabs under the leadership of Saladin.

In 1516, Syria was conquered by the Ottoman Turks, and for most of the next four centuries, Syria was part of the Ottoman Empire. By the late 1700s, however, much of Syria outside the cities was under the control of local warlords, called *pashas*.

Modern History. By the late 19th century, the Ottoman Empire was weak. Local Ottoman officials in Syria and Lebanon were often unwilling or unable to curb fighting among the various ethnic and religious groups in the area. Massacres of Christians by Muslims in the Levant States (Syria and Lebanon) brought threats of European intervention. France in particular seemed ready to send troops. Ottoman weakness and the constant threat of European intervention contributed to the rise of Syrian Arab nationalism, which was quite strong by 1914.

The Ottoman Empire entered World War I on the side of Germany and Austria, mostly for the chance to get even with its old enemy, Russia. Early in the war, Britain and France tried to knock out Turkey with a direct attack. Failing that, they worked on the discontent and nationalism of Arabs under Ottoman rule to trigger a revolt. Led by T. E. Lawrence, an English scholar turned soldier, and Faisal Ibn Hussein, a desert prince, an Arab army waged guerrilla warfare against the Turks and captured Damascus in 1918.

A Syrian nationalist congress made Faisal king of independent Syria. However, the British and French had already agreed to split control of the region between them. France was given mandates, or administrative

In Damascus (right) and other large Syrian cities, the streets and shops of the bazaar spread over many blocks.

Legend holds that King Solomon founded Palmyra, an ancient city of which only ruins remain.

power, over Syria and Lebanon. Britain was given control of Palestine, Iraq, and Jordan.

To enforce their mandate, the French defeated the Syrian Arab army in 1920 and forced out Faisal. The British compensated him by making him king of Iraq. From 1920 to 1946, French administrators exploited the divisions that had always existed in Syria by passing laws and enforcing policies to favor the various ethnic and religious minorities. This outraged Arab nationalists, who mounted a long, bitter campaign against French rule. They finally won. Syria became independent in 1946.

Following independence, Syria was ruled by a series of unstable governments. In an attempt to foster Arab solidarity and identity, Syria joined Egypt in 1958 to form the United Arab Republic. The union ended violently in 1961 with a military coup in Syria. Two years later, leftist Syrian army officers helped the Baath Party seize power. Baathist Hafiz al-Assad seized the premiership in a 1970 coup.

Feeling isolated and exposed by Egypt's peace accords with Israel, Syria intervened in Lebanon's civil war to counter an Israeli presence there. In 1989, Syria finally brokered a peace accord. Despite its strained relations with other Arab nations because of Syria's support for non-Arab Iran in its war against Iraq (1980–88), Syria had been able to count on the Soviet Union and Eastern Europe for military and diplomatic support until the breakup of the Soviet Union in the early 1990s.

In the 1990s, Syria struggled to improve its economy, strengthen relations with other Arab countries, and appear as a stabilizing force in the Middle East. It therefore joined the anti-Iraq military coalition in the 1991 Gulf War. Syria opposed the 1993 Israeli-PLO and the 1994 Israeli-Jordanian accords. As a condition for peace with Israel, Syria demanded the immediate return of the Golan Heights, which Israel had occupied in the 1967 Arab-Israeli War and formally annexed in 1981.

Reviewed by RICHARD W. BULLIETT, Middle East Institute, Columbia University

Beirut, once a fashionable, cosmopolitan city, was ravaged by a brutal 15-year civil war.

LEBANON

Although it is a small nation, Lebanon has played a major role in world affairs since ancient times. Carved on a cliff at the mouth of Dog River north of Beirut are the names of 18 great men of history who passed through the country to conquer or be conquered. Among the names are those of Ramses II of Egypt, Nebuchadnezzar of Babylon, Alexander the Great of Macedon, and Caracalla, the Roman emperor. The 19th and final inscription, carved in 1946, commemorates Lebanon's independence.

Under the Phoenicians, Lebanon's early inhabitants, the country held a unique position as a trading and seafaring nation. Modern Lebanon also gained a unique position because of its commerce, its generally high standards of living and education, and its role in world affairs. An intermittent civil war, which erupted in 1975, splintered the country, caused great destruction and loss of life, and endangered the peace of the region. The war finally ended in 1990.

THE LAND
Lebanon stretches along the eastern shore of the Mediterranean Sea from northern Israel to coastal Syria. Unlike most countries in the Middle East, Lebanon has no desert. Parallel mountain ranges run the length of the country. The western range, the Lebanon Mountains, rises close to the sea, leaving only a narrow coastal plain. The Lebanon Mountains reach a height of more than 10,000 ft. (3,000 m.). The eastern range, the Anti-Lebanon, is almost as high. Between them is the Bekaa, a fertile plateau.

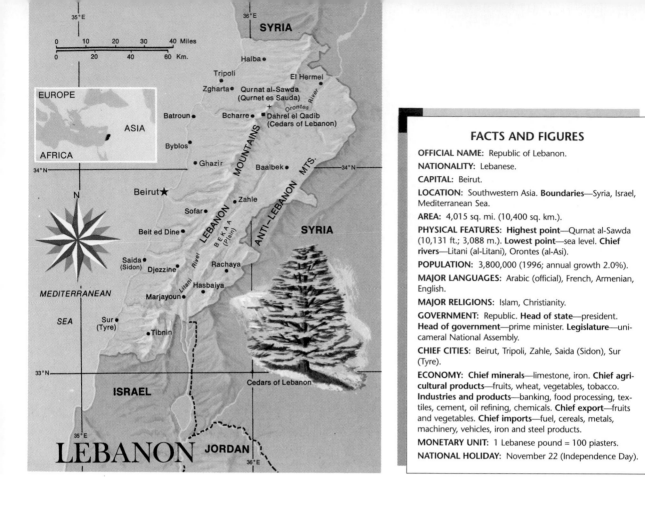

Lebanon's landscape is varied and scenic. The coastline is dotted with deep bays and broad beaches. In several places the mountains reach the sea. In northern Lebanon, on Mount al-Mukammal, a single grove remains of the majestic ancient cedars of Lebanon. The Phoenicians built their galleys with wide beams of cedar. Today, the cedar remains the symbol of Lebanon. The tree appears on the nation's flag and on its coins and stamps.

Reminders of past invaders decorate the landscape. The ruins of ancient Baalbek in northwestern Lebanon provide evidence of several civilizations. It was probably built by Canaanite worshipers of the Sun God, Baal. The Greeks, who named the city Heliopolis, added modest temples. The city reached its peak under Roman rule. The ruins of huge temples of Jupiter and Bacchus can be seen there today. Along the Lebanese coast, several hills are crowned by mighty Crusader castles.

Economy. Lebanon has few natural resources. Before the outbreak of civil war in 1975, the energy and industry of its people compensated for that shortcoming, giving it one of the highest standards of living in the Middle East. Trade and tourism, along with insurance, real estate, and banking firms, brought in most of the national income.

Agriculture was also economically important, especially in the fertile Bekaa. From the air, the plateau looks like a vast carpet of varying shades of green, each shade representing a different crop—wheat, barley, corn, alfalfa, and potatoes. In recent years, fruit orchards and chicken and dairy farming have been introduced to the area. Farmers have patiently

Some Lebanese make a living herding sheep in the country's grassy mountainous areas.

terraced the steep hillsides and lower foothills and planted them with fig trees and grapevines. The lower hills and coastal plain are dotted with groves of date palms and of olive, orange, and lemon trees.

Lebanon's industrial activity is among the most advanced in the Middle East, despite the scars and disruptions of the civil war. Leading industrial products include processed food, textiles and yarns, furniture, cement, ceramics, and pharmaceuticals.

THE PEOPLE

People from all over the Middle East have left cultural imprints on Lebanon. Recent immigrants include Palestinian refugees and Syrians. The national language is Arabic, but French and English are widely spo-

The centuries-old port of Byblos was a great city-state in ancient Phoenician times.

ken. Within the two main religious groups, Muslims and Christians, there are many recognized communities. Most Muslims belong to either the Sunni or the Shi'ite (Shi'a) branch of Islam. Druzes, whose religion combines elements of Islam and other faiths, form a large, militant minority. Most Lebanese Christians belong to the Maronite Church, one of the Eastern Catholic churches. The remaining Christians mostly belong to the Eastern Orthodox Church.

It is generally conceded that Muslims are now in the majority in Lebanon. But no census has been taken since 1932. At that time, Christians were in the majority and were thus allocated most seats in the Chamber of Deputies (now called the National Assembly). For a long time, Lebanese Muslims have felt cheated of their fair share of political power. For their part, Lebanese Christians say that they made the country the modern showplace of the Middle East and that they are now in danger of becoming a persecuted minority. In recent years, many wealthy Christians have left Lebanon. Many poorer ones have gone from the war-torn cities to ancestral villages in the hills.

The civil war in Lebanon was triggered by political rivalries between Christians and Muslims, but it was never just a straightforward struggle between the two major religions. Christians have fought Christians, and Muslims have fought Muslims. Strange alliances have been frequently made and broken. Foreign troops—Palestinians, Israelis, and Syrians—have been often involved.

Beirut. Before Lebanon's capital was devastated by civil war, it was the financial center of the Middle East. Many American and European business firms had offices there. To help transact business, a large number of local banks operated alongside foreign ones. People from the Lebanese mountains and plains rubbed shoulders with business tycoons, Beirut intellectuals, and tourists on Beirut's crowded sidewalks. The city's broad beaches were lined with ultramodern luxury hotels. The narrow streets of the old city were crammed with cars from every country. Many urban Lebanese dream and hope that that time will come again.

Life in the Villages. Life in the many mountain villages of Lebanon is a world apart from that of the cities. Villages perch on mountain ridges or nestle in narrow valleys, depending on the location of springs. Each village has its own identity, based on religion, size, and distance from Beirut.

Before the civil war, life-styles in the isolated Druze and Muslim settlements in eastern Lebanon differed greatly from those of the mountain villages near Beirut. The eastern isolated villages are family-centered, with strong attachments to the traditions, styles, and customs of the past. Constructed of local limestone, the traditional village houses are small and flat-roofed. In contrast, several of the villages near Beirut had modern villas, hotels, nightclubs, swimming pools, and television to attract summer vacationers. Western dress could be seen in such villages, particularly in the Christian ones. The war curbed the tourist trade and cut communities off from each other, putting many of these attractions out of business.

Education. Many schools have been destroyed or occupied, and many foreign teachers have been forced to leave. Nonetheless, the Lebanese still have a high literacy rate and a deep respect for education. All children must have at least five years of primary schooling, in either a government school or a private school. Large numbers of Lebanese boys and girls, especially in the Christian communities, manage to go on to secondary schools and universities.

HISTORY AND GOVERNMENT

The earliest civilization in Lebanon was that of the Phoenicians, who developed the first alphabetical system of writing. In the golden days of the Phoenicians (from the 12th to the 9th century B.C.), great city-states grew up—Arwad, Byblos, Sidon, and Tyre. From these city-states, the

The Roman occupation of present-day Lebanon began in 64 B.C. and lasted several centuries. Ruins of a temple built by the Romans still stand at Baalbek (above). According to legend, disappointed lovers leaped to their deaths from Beirut's Pigeon Rock (left).

During the long civil war, Lebanese teachers strove to provide their students an uninterrupted education.

Phoenicians sailed westward in their double-deck ships, carrying products to trade—fruits, glass, jewelry, and purple-dyed wool and linen.

Later, a succession of powers—the Assyrians, the Persians, and the Greeks under Alexander the Great—dominated the Phoenician city-states. Lebanon came under Roman rule in 64 B.C. and enjoyed several centuries of peace and prosperity. By A.D. 300, Christianity had become the prevailing religion. During the 600s, invaders from the Arabian Peninsula brought the new religion of Islam. Christian Crusaders ruled the country during the 1100s and 1200s.

Lebanon became part of the Ottoman (Turkish) Empire in 1516 and remained under Muslim rule for almost 400 years. But with its own capable princes, Lebanon managed its political and economic affairs independently. Trouble between the Christians and the Druzes led to a civil war in 1860. European powers intervened and guaranteed that Lebanon would be self-governing.

Independence. After World War I, Lebanon became a French mandate under the League of Nations. It became an independent republic in 1943, although French troops didn't leave the country until 1946. Following independence, it was agreed that the president of Lebanon was to be a Maronite Christian, the prime minister a Sunni Muslim, and the speaker of the legislature a Shi'ite Muslim. Under the same agreement, six seats in the legislature were allocated to the then-majority Christians, and five to the minority non-Christians.

This delicate balance between Christians and Muslims was upset within a few years by the rapid growth of the Muslim population and an influx of Palestinian refugees following the creation of Israel in 1948. In 1958, a likely Muslim revolution threatened to end the delicate balance, but peace was restored when the United States sent in troops. Lebanon's Christian-dominated government tried to maintain a moderate Arab po-

Much of once-stylish Beirut became a wasteland during Lebanon's long civil war. In the early 1990s, war-weary citizens began to rebuild, and much progress had been made by 1996.

sition in the Arab-Israeli wars of 1956, 1967, and 1973. But this policy was increasingly opposed by Lebanon's Muslims, now in the majority. Complicating the Christian-Muslim power struggle was the presence of the Palestine Liberation Organization (PLO).

Civil War.   Full-scale civil war erupted between Lebanese Christians and Muslims in 1975. One year later, Syrian troops intervened to separate the two groups. They remained to serve Syrian interests in Lebanon. Israel attacked PLO guerrilla bases in Lebanon in 1978, withdrew, then invaded the country in 1982. Israeli troops occupied south Lebanon, including Beirut, and forced out the PLO. A Christian leader, Bashir Gemayel, who was elected president of Lebanon in 1982, was assassinated the same year. In retaliation, Christian militia attacked two Palestinian refugee camps, killing hundreds of civilians.

In 1983, a multinational force of U.S., French, and Italian troops landed in Beirut to restore peace and stability and to speed the withdrawal of Israeli, Syrian, and Palestinian forces. The peacekeepers soon became targets, as Muslim terrorists inflicted heavy casualties on U.S. and French troops. The multinational force withdrew from Beirut in 1984.

After the last Israeli troops left Lebanon in 1985, Syria attempted to end the civil war. The collapse of Lebanon's weak central government in 1988 led to the formation of rival Muslim and Christian governments. A 1989 Arab-brokered peace accord granting political parity to Muslims and Christians finally seemed to take hold after the October 1990 surrender of Christian prime minister Gen. Michel Aoun. Syria and Lebanon signed a cooperation accord in May 1991. In 1992 Lebanon held its first legislative elections in 20 years. Syrian forces remained, however, and Israel continued its air raids against Muslim guerrillas in southern Lebanon. Pro-Syrian candidates won a legislative majority in the 1996 elections.

VIOLA H. WINDER, Author, *The Land and People of Lebanon*

Tel Aviv-Jaffa, Israel's largest city, dominates the country's commercial and cultural life.

 ISRAEL

Modern Israel was founded in 1948 as a homeland for Jews from around the world. This national rebirth occurred almost 2,000 years after Jews were driven from the land of Israel by the Romans and scattered throughout the world.

Three important factors shape the policies and outlook of modern Israel. First is the memory of World War II, in which the Nazis deliberately and systematically murdered 6 million Jews. This horror, which has become known as the Holocaust, convinced Israelis that Jews can be truly safe only in their own nation, and that for this reason, Israel must be preserved and defended at all costs. The second factor that influences Israeli decision making is the reality that the nation is surrounded and outnumbered by hostile Arab countries. The third factor is the existence of special political and economic ties between the U.S. and Israel.

THE LAND

Israel is a relatively small country located at the crossroads of three continents—Asia, Africa, and Europe. The land Israel occupies—called Canaan, Israel, Judea, and Palestine at various times in history—has played an important role in the development of three great religions: Judaism, Christianity, and Islam. All consider Jerusalem, Israel's capital city, a holy place.

Within frontiers established by cease-fire agreements with the Arab nations in 1949, Israel has an area of 8,017 sq. mi. (20,764 sq. km.). As a result of Israel's victory in the Six-Day War in 1967, it occupied an additional three territories, totaling about 2,500 sq. mi. (6,475 sq. km.): the West Bank, which was captured from Jordan; the Gaza Strip, taken from Egypt; the Golan Heights, taken from Syria; plus the Sinai peninsula, returned to Egypt in 1982. The Palestinian Arabs of the West Bank and Gaza Strip gained limited self-rule in 1994 under accords signed by Israel and the Palestine Liberation Organization in 1993 and 1994. The future status of East Jerusalem, captured from Jordan in 1967 and formally annexed by Israel in 1980, is a major issue in Israeli-Arab relations.

Israel is bordered on the north by Lebanon, on the east by Jordan and Syria, on the south by the Gulf of Aqaba, and on the west by Egypt and the Mediterranean Sea. The Sea of Galilee (also called Lake Tiberias and Yam Kinneret), out of which the Jordan River flows, is of great historic interest. The Dead Sea, a salt lake, is the lowest point on the earth's surface—about 1,300 ft. (400 m.) below sea level. The principal rivers of Israel are the Jordan, the Kishon, and the Yarkon.

Physical Geography.   Israel has four geographic regions. The Negev Desert, a triangle-shaped region in the south that occupies more than half of the country, has low-lying hills that become more and more barren toward the south. The Mediterranean coastal plain, where the majority of the population lives, varies in width from 9.5 to 16 mi. (15 to 25 km.). To the east of the coastal plain, stretching the length of the country, is a central range of hills, with an average height of 2,000 ft. (600 m.), known in the north as the Galilean Hills. The Plain of Esdraelon forms the southern boundary of the Galilee and is a showplace of Israeli agriculture. To the south of the plain, the central range forms an upland plateau in the area of the West Bank. To the east of the central hills lies the Jordan River valley.

Climate.   Much of Israel has a Mediterranean climate, with cool, wet winters and warm, dry summers. Both temperature and rainfall change dramatically from north to south. In the northern hills, January temperatures often drop to 40° F. (4° C.); average annual rainfall often exceeds 40 in. (102 cm.). In contrast, the Negev receives no rain in the summer and occasional sudden showers in the winter. August temperatures in the southern Negev frequently exceed 100° F. (38° C.).

THE PEOPLE

About 82 percent of Israel's people are Jews. Most of the other 18 percent are Arabs. About 85 percent of Israel's Arab citizens are Muslims, and the remainder are Christians. The Druzes, a small sect that split from Islam in the 11th century, account for about 1.5 percent of the population. Many of the more than 2.1 million Arabs who live in the West Bank and the Gaza Strip commute to work in Israel. (About 11 percent of the people in the West Bank and Gaza Strip are Israeli settlers.)

Israel's Jewish population is united by a common religious-ethnic background and a common history of persecution. Yet it is made up of people from some 70 different countries, and they represent a multitude of cultures and languages.

There are two major groups within the Jewish population. Ashkenazi Jews immigrated to Israel from Europe (except Spain and Portugal) and North America. Sephardi Jews come from the Arab countries of the Middle East and North Africa, Spain, Portugal, and parts of Asia. Today, the

FACTS AND FIGURES

OFFICIAL NAME: State of Israel.

NATIONALITY: Israeli(s).

CAPITAL: Jerusalem.

LOCATION: Southwestern Asia. **Boundaries**—Lebanon, Syria, Jordan, Gulf of Aqaba, Egypt, Mediterranean Sea.

AREA: 8,019 sq. mi. (20,770 sq. km.).

PHYSICAL FEATURES: Highest point—Mount Meron (3,963 ft.; 1,208 m.). **Lowest point**—Dead Sea, about 1,300 ft. (400 m.) below sea level. **Chief rivers**—Jordan, Kishon, Yarkon. **Major lakes**—Sea of Galilee, Dead Sea.

POPULATION: 5,800,000 (1996; annual growth 1.5%).

MAJOR LANGUAGES: Hebrew (official), Arabic, English.

MAJOR RELIGIONS: Judaism, Islam, Christianity.

GOVERNMENT: Republic. **Head of state**—president. **Head of government**—prime minister. **Legislature**—unicameral parliament (Knesset).

CHIEF CITIES: Jerusalem, Tel Aviv-Jaffa, Haifa.

ECONOMY: Chief minerals—copper, phosphates, bromide, potash, clay, sand, sulfur, bitumen, manganese. **Chief agricultural products**—fruits and vegetables, cotton, livestock products. **Industries and products**—food processing, diamond cutting and polishing, textiles, chemicals. **Chief exports**—polished diamonds, fruits, textiles, metals and machinery, processed foods, fertilizer. **Chief imports**—military equipment, rough diamonds, oil, chemicals, machinery.

MONETARY UNIT: 1 new shekel = 100 new agorot.

NATIONAL HOLIDAY: May 14 (Independence Day).

Sephardi Jews and their descendants form the majority of the population, but Ashkenazi Jews from industrialized Western societies control much of the economy and government.

A number of forces are working to erase the differences between the two major Jewish communities. These include rising educational levels among Sephardi Jews, joint military service, and increasing intermarriage between the two groups. From 1989 on, a flood of Jewish immigrants from the former Soviet Union has increased the Ashkenazi element of the population. At the same time, however, this new immigration is straining Israel's social services, housing stock, and economy.

The 700,000 Arabs living in Israel are full citizens under the law. (Another 1.7 million Arabs live in the occupied territories.) Arabs sit

Jerusalem, Israel's capital city, contains sites sacred to Jews, Muslims, and Christians.

in the Israeli parliament, called the Knesset. The Arabs who reside in Israel tend to have a higher standard of living than Arabs in the occupied territories and in many of Israel's neighboring countries. Nonetheless, many Israeli Arabs complain that they are treated as second-class citizens in their own land. Since the beginning of the uprising of Palestinian Arabs in the occupied territories in 1988, Israeli Arabs have become increasingly conscious of their Palestinian heritage and sympathies.

Way of Life

Israeli society is the most democratic in the Middle East. Its press is free, except for censorship of military operations. There are strong opposition political parties and freely expressed public criticism of the government.

Israelis lead a varied life. They dress very much like Europeans or Americans, but with emphasis on informal styles. Families usually eat some kind of boiled or roasted meat daily, although poorer Israelis eat meat less frequently. On holidays, chicken is a common dish. Generally there is an ample supply of fresh fruits and vegetables, and salads are eaten even at breakfast. One of the most popular dishes is eggplant, cooked in dozens of ways.

On holidays, Israelis often visit the many beautiful natural settings and ancient archaeological sites that abound in the country. It is said that every Israeli is an amateur archaeologist, and people of all ages display a deep attachment to the past.

Although Israel is a Jewish state, only a minority of its Jewish population is religious in an orthodox, or strict, way. Nevertheless, the Jewish character of the country is expressed in the observance of Saturday as the weekly day of rest and worship, and in religious holidays, particularly the New Year (Rosh Hashanah) and the Day of Atonement (Yom Kippur).

Education

Education is compulsory until age 16 and free until age 18. Israel's educational system attempts to teach national, social, and religious values, with emphasis on Jewish studies and programs to promote democratic values and understanding among ethnic groups. Wishing to preserve their own culture, religion, and identity, most Israeli Arabs attend separate schools in which Arabic is the language of instruction. Students in Hebrew-language schools study Arabic, and those in Arabic-language schools study Hebrew. Students in both systems study English as a foreign language. The largest institutions of higher learning are the Hebrew University in Jerusalem and Tel Aviv University.

Culture and the Arts

Since its establishment, Israel has placed great emphasis on developing Hebrew language and culture. Singing and folk-dancing groups attract large numbers of participants. Israel has achieved a solid reputation in classical music, due to the high level of performance of the Israel Philharmonic Orchestra. Israel has about 250 cultural institutions that are active in theater, music, dance, literature, film, visual arts, and folklore.

Many of Israel's Jewish immigrants maintain cultural ties with their countries of origin.

Much of Israel's heavy industry is centered in Haifa, a port in the northern part of the country.

Cities

About 89 percent of Israel's people live in cities or large towns, making Israel one of the world's most urbanized countries. About 8 percent live in rural settlements such as cooperatives and farm villages. Nearly 3 percent live in collective settlements (kibbutzim). Fewer than 1 percent of the people are Arab Bedouin, nomadic and seminomadic people who raise sheep, goats, and camels. More than two-thirds of the Jewish population is concentrated in the three metropolitan areas of Tel Aviv–Jaffa, Haifa, and Jerusalem.

Tel Aviv–Jaffa.   The largest of the metropolitan areas, Tel Aviv–Jaffa lies on the thin coastal plain along the Mediterranean Sea. There is evidence of continuous settlement at Jaffa for the past 7,000 to 10,000 years. Increasing numbers of Jews began to settle the area in the late 1800s, founding Tel Aviv in 1909 on the barren sand dunes to the north of Jaffa. Tel Aviv is today the center of Israel's commerce, light industry, and entertainment. It has beaches, modern hotels, shops, cafés, theaters, concert halls, museums, and universities.

Jerusalem.   Jerusalem is the capital of modern Israel, just as it was the capital of the two ancient Jewish states. Located high in the Judean hills, the "old city" contains holy places of Judaism, Christianity, and Islam. (For a discussion of JERUSALEM, see page 46.)

Haifa.   The beautiful port city of Haifa in northern Israel is located on a small peninsula that juts out into the Mediterranean, where it rises from its harbor up the green slopes of Mount Carmel. Haifa is Israel's busiest port and major industrial center, and it is the home of the Israel Institute of Technology (the Technion). On Mount Carmel is the world center of the Baha'i faith.

Other Cities.   Other important cities include **Beersheba,** the regional center of the Negev; **Eilat,** the southern port providing access to the Red Sea and the Indian Ocean; and the port cities of **Ascalon** and **Acre.**

Only about 3 percent of the Israeli population lives on kibbutzim, collective settlements that concentrate on agriculture (above) or industry, or a combination of the two. Residents own most of the property in common, share the work, and eat meals together. On or off the kibbutz, Israeli farmers have been quite successful. Through irrigation, they have transformed much arid land into highly productive orange groves (left).

ECONOMY

The largest proportion (almost 30 percent) of the work force is employed in public and community services. About 22 percent of Israel's workers are employed in mining and manufacturing, 10 percent in finance and business, 7 percent in transport and communications, and about 6.5 percent in construction and public works. Only about 5.5 percent of the labor force are involved in farming, fishing, and forestry.

Israel has over 200 collective settlements called kibbutzim, but they are home to fewer than 3 percent of the population. A kibbutz is a settlement in which most property is owned collectively and decisions are made by elected representatives. In most of these settlements, members eat in a common dining hall, and children are cared for during the day in collective nurseries and schools. Kibbutzim have been in the forefront of agricultural, social, and industrial development in Israel.

Israel's principal crops of citrus fruits and vegetables are popular on the European market in winter. Wheat and barley are also important. Poultry is the most widely raised livestock. The only natural resources of importance are potash and phosphates. Israeli industry includes food processing, diamond polishing, and chemical, textile, cement, ceramic, and machinery production. Petroleum, rough diamonds, and machinery are major imports, while polished diamonds, weapons, fruits, and vegetables are key exports. In recent years, Israel has developed a solid reputation in computers and other high-technology products, including advanced weaponry.

Despite its continual state of war, Israel has developed a relatively high standard of living. In the early 1980s, this living standard was severely eroded by annual price rises of more than 1,000 percent. Government economic policies eventually brought the problem under control, and as the 1990s began, inflation, though worrisome, was no longer a major economic threat.

Israel has a mixed economy: privately owned plants employ about 75 percent of the labor force; state-owned industries and those owned by the Histadrut (the General Federation of Labor) employ the remainder. Israel's development has been greatly assisted by United States foreign aid and financial contributions from the world Jewish community.

GOVERNMENT

Israel has a parliamentary system of government consisting of a single legislative assembly of 120 members called the Knesset. The prime minister, who is the head of the cabinet, is the leader of the ruling political party. The president, elected by the Knesset, holds a mostly ceremonial post. Laws passed by the Knesset cannot be vetoed by the president or overturned by any court.

Israeli elections differ from those of the United States in several ways. Members of the Knesset do not represent regions of the country. Each political party puts forward a slate of candidates. Depending on how many votes a party receives nationwide, it is given a certain number of seats to fill in the Knesset. No party in Israeli history has been able to receive enough votes to gain an absolute majority (61 seats). Thus, the party with the most seats is usually asked by the president to try to form a coalition with other (usually small) parties.

HISTORY

The modern State of Israel was proclaimed on May 14, 1948, with these words: "The Land of Israel was the birthplace of the Jewish people. Here their spiritual, religious, and national identity was formed. Here they achieved independence and created a culture of national and universal significance. Here they wrote and gave the Bible to the world."

Biblical Roots. According to the Bible, Abraham led his family from Ur to Canaan, the land that is now Israel, about 4,000 years ago. Abraham, his son Isaac, and his grandson Jacob are considered ancestors of the Jewish people. Over the centuries, the Jewish people were conquered several times and exiled at least three times. But they continued to survive and flourish.

Starting around 63 B.C., Roman rule was gradually extended over the land of Israel, which was renamed Palestine by the Romans. In time, the Romans tried to control all aspects of Jewish life. This led to several revolts. The most determined of these was crushed in A.D. 70. Jerusalem was destroyed, and Jews were dispersed throughout the world.

During centuries of dispersal, or Diaspora, to numerous countries, Jews were often persecuted, and for them the Land of Israel—Zion—was a symbol of their nationhood and religious heritage. On the important holy days of Passover and Yom Kippur (Day of Atonement), exiled Jews intoned the hopeful prayer, "Next year in Jerusalem. . . ." In the 1800s, influential leaders in various countries urged their fellow Jews to return to the Land of Israel, rebuild it, restore Jewish national life, and revive the Hebrew language. The Zionist movement, as it was called, gained popularity, and many European Jews immigrated to Palestine, which at the time was ruled by the Ottoman Turks. By the outbreak of World War I in 1914, there were about 85,000 Jews in Palestine, making up about 20 percent of the population.

Palestine under the British Mandate. During World War I, Britain, which was fighting the Germans and Turks, tried to gain worldwide Jewish support by issuing the Balfour Declaration. This stated that the British government would "view with favor" the establishment "of a national home for the Jewish people in Palestine," provided it would not prejudice "civil and religious rights of existing non-Jewish communities in Palestine, or the rights or political status enjoyed by Jews in any other country." At the same time, the British promised the Arabs independence in territories taken from the Ottoman Empire, while they also secretly made an agreement with France to divide control of the region between them.

Masada, an ancient fortress near the Dead Sea, has become a symbol of Israeli resistance to foreign rule.

לְכָל מָקוֹם אֵלָיו אֲנִי הוֹלֵךְ, הוֹלֵךְ אֲנִי לְאֶרֶץ-יִשְׂרָאֵל

Language classes and other orientation programs help new immigrants adjust to life in Israel.

After World War I, victorious Britain was given a mandate over Palestine by the League of Nations. Part of the terms of this mandate required the British to implement the Balfour Declaration. Some Arab leaders welcomed Jewish immigrants at the time. This attitude changed with the rise of nationalism, religious fervor, and frustration with British rule among Palestinian Arabs. Zionist aspirations and demands by Arabs for independence met head-on, leading to three-way violence. The British attempted compromises, but all were rejected by either the Jews or the Arabs.

Between the two world wars, the Jewish population increased until Jews formed about one-third (more than 600,000) of Palestine's total population.

After World War II, Zionist demands for independence grew. Jewish underground groups began to attack the British administration in Palestine. As a result, the situation was presented to the United Nations. The United Nations voted for partition of Palestine into a Jewish state and an Arab state joined in an economic union, with Jerusalem as an international city. Arabs who lived in areas assigned to the Jewish state could become citizens of the Arab state without moving. Likewise, Jews who lived in areas assigned to the Arab state could become citizens of the Jewish state without moving.

Palestine's Arab neighbors refused to accept partition. On May 14, 1948, as the last British troops were about to leave, the Jewish leaders of Palestine declared independence. Israel was attacked by five Arab armies. As a result of this war, Jordan annexed the West Bank, which was to have been the heart of the Palestinian Arab state; Egypt took control of the Gaza Strip; and Israel captured the Galilee region.

The Continuing State of War. At the conclusion of Israel's war for independence in 1949, Egypt, Lebanon, Syria, and Jordan signed armi-

LANDS IN DISPUTE:
THE WEST BANK AND GAZA

Two of the areas that ended up in Israeli hands after the Six-Day War of 1967 became a major cause of friction between Israel and Arab nations. The West Bank is the larger of the two areas, covering 2,270 sq. mi. (5,879 sq. km.). The smaller area is the Gaza Strip, covering 270 sq. mi. (699 sq. km.) along the Egyptian-Israeli border.

The West Bank. With a population of about 1.4 million, 97 percent of them Arabs, the West Bank is a densely populated area of rolling hills and fertile valleys. It contains several cities of historic significance for Arabs and Jews. These include Jericho, Nablus, Bethlehem, Ramallah, and Hebron. Because the territory was part of biblical Israel, modern Israelis call it Judea and Samaria. Many Israelis consider it to be strategically important for their country's security, because its hills dominate Israel's narrow, densely populated coastal plain.

Gaza. Not nearly as scenic or as prosperous as the West Bank, the dusty, narrow Gaza Strip, 21 mi. (34 km.) long, sits between Israel and Egypt. A large proportion of its 700,000 people live in overcrowded, squalid refugee camps. With less to lose than the residents of the West Bank, the people of Gaza were more defiant of Israeli authorities. When Israeli troops broke up a 1988 march to honor the Palestine Liberation Organization (PLO), Gaza residents responded angrily. Their uprising, known as the *intifada,* spread to the West Bank.

Source of Turmoil. In 1947, when the United Nations voted to partition Palestine into Jewish and Arab states, the area now known as the West Bank was the heart of

stice agreements with United Nations assistance. The Arab states refused to negotiate directly with Israel and pledged continuing hostility.

In 1956, a second war broke out over access to the Suez Canal. Egypt closed the Strait of Tiran to Israeli shipping by blocking access to the Red Sea and the Indian Ocean from the port of Eilat. It also nationalized the Suez Canal and refused Israeli ships passage through this international waterway. In concert with Britain and France, Israel attacked Egypt and occupied the Gaza Strip and the Sinai Peninsula. Pressure from the United States and the United Nations forced the Israelis to withdraw from the occupied areas. A United Nations peacekeeping force was stationed in the Sinai. The Strait of Tiran was opened, but Egypt continued to deny Israel access to the Suez Canal.

In 1967, war broke out again. At Egyptian insistence, United Nations forces had been withdrawn; the blockade of the Strait of Tiran was reimposed; and Egyptian troops moved into the Sinai. Israel reacted to these actions by attacking Egypt. Syria and Jordan attacked Israel. Within six days, Israeli forces defeated all three Arab countries and occupied large parts of their territory.

A fourth war (the Yom Kippur War) broke out in 1973 when Egypt and Syria attacked Israeli forces in the occupied areas. After this war, the United Nations asked Israel to withdraw from the Suez Canal region, and a series of disengagement agreements was negotiated by U.S. Secretary of State Henry Kissinger. In 1977, President Anwar el-Sadat of Egypt accepted Israeli Prime Minister Menachem Begin's invitation to visit Jeru-

the intended Arab Palestine state. Jews supported the partition plan, but most Arabs within and outside Palestine opposed it. During the war that followed Israel's declaration of independence in 1948, Jordan captured East Jerusalem and held on to the West Bank. Cease-fire agreements in 1949 put Arab East Jerusalem and the West Bank under Jordanian control, and the Gaza Strip under Egyptian rule. Both areas contained large camps of Arab refugees who had fled or been expelled from those parts of Palestine that were made part of Israel. The minority of Arabs who remained in Israel became Israeli citizens. In 1950, Jordan annexed the West Bank and East Jerusalem.

Sticking Points. After Israeli forces captured the West Bank and Gaza Strip in 1967, Israeli administrators continued to apply Jordanian civil and criminal law in the West Bank, and Egyptian military law in Gaza. However, the residents of the areas continued to think of themselves as Palestinians rather than as Jordanians or Egyptians, and to view the exiled PLO as their representative.

On July 31, 1988, King Hussein of Jordan gave up all claims to the West Bank and recognized the PLO as the "sole legitimate representative of the Palestinian people." On September 13, 1993, Israel and the PLO signed an accord on Palestinian self-rule in Jericho and the Gaza Strip. For this, PLO leader Yasir Arafat and Israeli leaders Yitzhak Rabin and Shimon Peres shared the 1994 Nobel Peace Prize. A more detailed five-year interim accord was signed in May 1994. An elected Palestinian authority took office in July and soon gained control of local services in most of the West Bank. By 1996, however, attacks by Palestinian militants opposed to the accords, Israeli retaliations, and the resumption of Israeli settlement on the West Bank threatened the fragile peace.

salem. These diplomatic moves led to accords hammered out in 1978 by President Sadat and Prime Minister Begin at Camp David, the U.S. president's retreat in Maryland, and to a 1979 peace treaty. In return for Egypt's recognition of Israel as a sovereign state, Israel returned the Sinai Peninsula to Egypt and agreed to discuss Palestinian self-determination.

Attacks by Lebanese-based elements of the Palestine Liberation Organization (PLO) prompted a 1982 invasion of Lebanon by Israeli troops. Before they withdrew in 1985, thousands of PLO supporters were dispersed from Lebanon to locations throughout the Middle East. In 1988, Palestinian Arabs in the West Bank and Gaza launched an *intifada* (uprising) to protest Israeli military occupation and the spread of Jewish settlements in the occupied areas. The *intifada* continued into the 1990s.

A new round of peace talks between Israel and its Arab neighbors was initiated after the 1991 Gulf War, and the Labor-led government that took office in 1992 signed an accord with the PLO in 1993 providing for a transfer of power in the Gaza Strip and Jericho to an elected Palestinian administration. This took place in 1994, when Israel also signed a peace treaty with Jordan. Israeli prime minister Yitzhak Rabin was assassinated on November 4, 1995, by a right-wing Israeli. Likud leader Benjamin Netanyahu, who became prime minister in 1996, took a much harder line against the PLO and against Hizbollah attacks on Israeli targets from southern Lebanon, and peace negotiations stalled.

Reviewed by RICHARD W. BULLIET
Middle East Institute, Columbia University

Religious life in Amman, the capital of Jordan, centers around the Hussein mosque.

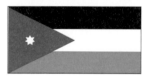

JORDAN

The Hashemite Kingdom of Jordan is an Arab land of rocky deserts and rugged hills east of the Jordan River. Its western border has been fluid since the Arab-Israeli War of 1948–49, when Jordanian forces captured East Jerusalem and an area of east-central Palestine which became known as the West Bank. In 1950, Jordan formally annexed the West Bank, adding 2,270 sq. mi. (5,879 sq. km.) to its territory. This addition greatly increased Jordan's population, national wealth, urban areas, and arable land.

In the Six-Day War of 1967, Israeli troops captured the West Bank, and they have occupied it ever since. Israel annexed East Jerusalem, which it also took in 1967, but it continued to treat the West Bank as Jordanian territory. Jordan did, too, continuing to provide funds to West Bank towns and to pay officials and teachers who had been Jordanian employees in 1967. In 1988, however, Jordan's King Hussein I did an about-face and cut all administrative and legal ties to the West Bank. Jordan's territory was again officially limited to land east of the Jordan River, as it had been before 1950.

THE LAND

Jordan is bordered by Syria on the north, Iraq on the east, Saudi Arabia on the east and south, and Israel and the occupied Palestinian West Bank on the west. It has a 10-mile stretch of coastline on the Red Sea, which includes the port of Aqaba.

Most of Jordan's 37,537-sq.-mi. (97,226-sq.-km.) area covers a semi-arid plateau that becomes increasingly desertlike toward the east and south. Just 6 percent of the land supports crops, pastures, or woodlands, and most of it is located along the east bank of the Jordan River. The Jordan River, separating Jordan from Israel and the Palestinian West Bank, occupies a deep depression—below sea level in places—and flows southward into the Dead Sea, which is shared by Jordan and Israel.

Jordan's climate is similar to that of other eastern Mediterranean lands. Winters are rainy and relatively cold, particularly in the highlands, while the other seasons are extremely hot and dry. In the Jordan Valley, summer temperatures rise to 120° F. (49° C.). Rainfall in the eastern plains is approximately 8 in. (20 cm.) a year. This makes the land fertile enough for desert nomads to graze their flocks. In the western portion of the country, annual rainfall is about 15 to 25 in. (38 to 64 cm.).

THE PEOPLE

Jordan's population is 98 percent Arab. Those who are descended from nomadic Bedouin Arabs constitute the traditional ruling elite. But their political control has been challenged in recent years by a rapidly expanding population of former Palestinians. Large numbers of Palestinian Arabs fled to Jordan during the Arab-Israeli Wars of 1948, 1967, and 1973. Many of these refugees live in camps built and supported by the United Nations. The 1.3 million to 1.6 million Jordanian citizens of Palestinian origin were unaffected by King Hussein's decision in 1988 to end Jordan's claim to the West Bank.

In addition to Arabs, Jordan has small communities of Circassians and Kurds. The Circassians are European Muslims who immigrated to

FACTS AND FIGURES

OFFICIAL NAME: Hashemite Kingdom of Jordan.

NATIONALITY: Jordanian(s).

CAPITAL: Amman.

LOCATION: Southwestern Asia. **Boundaries**—Syria, Iraq, Saudi Arabia, Gulf of Aqaba, Israel.

AREA: 35,267 sq. mi. (91,347 sq. km.), excluding West Bank (2,270 sq. mi.; 5,879 sq. km.).

PHYSICAL FEATURES: Highest point—5,755 ft. (1,754 m.). **Lowest point**—about 1,300 ft. (400 m.) below sea level. **Chief river**—Jordan.

POPULATION: 4,200,000 (1996; annual growth 2.6%).

MAJOR LANGUAGE: Arabic (official).

MAJOR RELIGIONS: Islam (Sunni), Christianity.

GOVERNMENT: Constitutional monarchy. **Head of state**—king. **Head of government**—prime minister. **Legislature**—bicameral National Assembly.

CHIEF CITIES: Amman, El Zerqa, Irbid.

ECONOMY: Chief mineral—phosphates. **Chief agricultural products**—vegetables, fruits, olive oil, vinegar, livestock (sheep, goats, cattle, camels). **Industries and products**—tourism, phosphates, fishing, textiles, soap, cement, tobacco and cigarettes, handicrafts. **Chief exports**—phosphates, vegetables and plants, phosphate rock. **Chief imports**—motor vehicles, petroleum products, textiles, machinery, foodstuffs, fuel.

MONETARY UNIT: 1 Jordanian dinar = 1,000 fils.

NATIONAL HOLIDAY: May 25 (Independence Day).

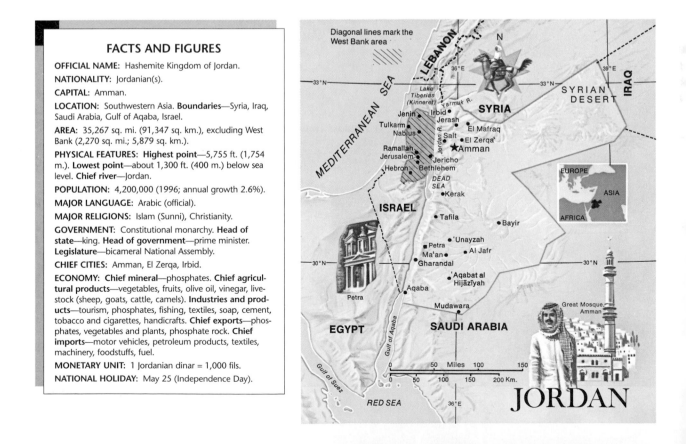

Jordan from the Russian Caucasus in the 1800s. The Kurds are non-Arab pastoral people related to the ancient Persians.

About 94 percent of Jordan's people are Sunni Muslims, and 5 percent are Christians. Arabic is the official language. Many educated Jordanians also speak English. More than 70 percent of the population now live in urban areas. Most of the rest live in rural villages. Fewer than 5 percent are nomads. **Amman,** the capital, is the country's largest city, with some 833,000 people. Other cities include El Zerqa, Irbid, and the port of Aqaba.

Way of Life. Despite differences among city dwellers, villagers, and nomadic Bedouin tribesmen, Jordanians are united by their religion, language, and historic traditions. Certain traditional values and customs, including hospitality, personal honor, and loyalty to kin, are still important. Many of Jordan's leading families, even those several generations removed from the traditional nomadic herding life in the desert, take pride in their Bedouin origins and connections.

About one in four Jordanians live in small farming villages. The villagers' homes are flat-roofed buildings made of stone or baked-earth bricks. One room in the house is used for livestock and farm tools. Most villages have one or more small squares, or *sahah,* where open markets and social events are held. Large apartment houses have been built in the bigger towns, but most city people live in small family dwellings. Jordan's small Bedouin minority still lead a nomadic life, herding sheep, goats, camels, and horses. Bedouin live in tents in temporary desert encampments.

Jordanian dress varies from Western-style clothes in the cities to traditional Arab costume in the villages and the desert encampments of the Bedouin nomads. Arab male dress consists of a black or brown cape called an *abayyah,* and the *kafiyyah,* a folded cloth headdress. Loose, flowing white and black robes are worn by the desert-roaming Bedouin. Most Jordanian women wear colorful shawls, gaily embroidered jackets, and long skirts. Many men in the cities wear the traditional *kafiyyah* along with Western-style suits.

In parts of Jordan, Bedouin Arabs roam the desert in search of pastureland for their flocks.

Many Palestinian refugees live in Jordan in camps built by the United Nations.

The food Jordanians eat is similar to what is eaten in other Arab lands. Appetizers are made from mashed chick-peas or eggplant mixed with sesame oil, lemon juice, and spices. Main courses often consist of lamb or chicken, which is combined with squash, eggplant, or okra and served with rice and pine nuts. A flat, round bread is eaten with these dishes. The favorite desserts are honeyed baklava and *katayif* pastries.

Education.   Nearly three out of four Jordanians can read. Jordanian children are required to attend school for a minimum of nine years. The nation's institutions of higher learning include teachers colleges, technical schools, the University of Jordan, and Yarmouk University.

ECONOMY

Jordan is poor in natural resources. Its developing economy was hurt by Israel's occupation of the West Bank, which was Jordan's most productive region from 1949 to 1967. To support the large Palestinian refugee population and to fund economic expansion, Jordan requires large amounts of foreign aid. Aid from the oil-rich Arab nations was cut off when Jordan refused to join the anti-Iraq military alliance in the 1991 Gulf War. During the Gulf crisis, the Jordanian economy was devastated by an influx of refugees, the aid cutoff, and an international embargo on trade with Kuwait and Iraq (Jordan's chief trade partners).

About 20 percent of the labor force is engaged in farming. The most productive farmlands are in the Jordan Valley, where thousands of acres have been brought under irrigation since 1967. Some farming without irrigation also occurs in upland areas favored with sufficient rainfall. Chief crops are wheat, barley, lentils, and various fruits and vegetables. About 94 percent of the land is given over to nomadic pastoral grazing.

Another 20 percent of the Jordanian labor force is engaged in mining and manufacturing. Phosphate is the chief mineral resource. It is widely used, together with potash, in the manufacture of fertilizers, and it accounts for much of Jordan's income from exports. Other manufacturing is on a small scale, with an emphasis on soap, tobacco products, cement, textiles, shoes, and other consumer items. Amman, El Zerqa, and Irbid are the chief manufacturing centers. Aqaba is the only seaport.

GOVERNMENT

Jordan is a constitutional monarchy in which the monarch holds the balance of power. The king has the power to dissolve the two-house National Assembly, which consists of an appointed Senate and a popularly elected Chamber of Deputies. Until 1988, the lower house included members representing the Israeli-occupied West Bank. Executive power is exercised by the king and a Council of Ministers, which he appoints. The king signs all laws, appoints judges, approves amendments to the constitution, and commands the armed forces. He can also veto laws, but his veto can be overturned by a two-thirds majority of both legislative houses. A national charter approved in 1991 reintroduced a multiparty system; the nation's first multiparty elections since 1958 were held in 1993.

HISTORY

In biblical times, the area that Jordan covers today contained the Semitic kingdoms of Moab, Edom, Ammon, and Gilead. Later, both the Greeks (in the 4th century B.C.) and the Romans (from the 1st to the 4th century A.D.) ruled this land. During the 700s, the area was conquered by the Arab followers of the prophet Muhammad and became a part of the Muslim empire. The Arab invaders introduced Islam to the people of the region. Jordan was dominated by the Ottoman Turks from 1516 to 1918.

The ruins of tombs carved out of the rock at Petra recall the region's colorful ancient past.

Palestine Mandate. The land that is now Jordan was part of the Ottoman Turkish empire up through World War I. Near the end of the war, it was liberated by a British-led Arab army and became part of the short-lived Kingdom of Syria. In 1920, the League of Nations gave Britain a mandate to administer the lands on both sides of the Jordan River. The British soon realized, however, that the lands and people on the two sides of the river were different. So they split the mandated territory in 1922. The relatively fertile land on the western side of the Jordan, with a population of village and city Arabs and Jewish settlers, became British-administered Palestine. The mostly barren land on the eastern side, with a population of desert Arabs and wandering Bedouin, became the semi-independent Emirate of Transjordan ("beyond the Jordan"), under the rule of Emir Abdullah ibn Hussein. Hussein was a member of the Hashemite family, which claims descent from Muhammad.

Independence. Transjordan gained full independence in 1946 and joined in the Arab attack to crush the new State of Israel. During the 1948–49 Arab-Israeli War, the Transjordanian army captured the West Bank region. The West Bank was made part of Transjordan in 1950. Shortly after that, the country's name was changed to the Hashemite Kingdom of Jordan, to reflect the fact that it existed not just beyond the Jordan River but on both sides of it.

King Abdullah was assassinated in 1951. After a brief reign by Abdullah's son, Talal, King Hussein I (Talal's son)—the present monarch—came to Jordan's throne. King Hussein, who assumed full power at the age of 18, has faced many problems. Israel's occupation of the West Bank of the Jordan River—after the 1967 Arab-Israeli War—resulted in severe economic losses. Additional burdens were imposed by thousands of new refugees and the emergence of strong Palestinian nationalism.

Since 1967, King Hussein has tried to end Israeli occupation of the West Bank and to find a just solution to the "Palestinian problem." He has also struggled to retain control of his kingdom. This has not been easy, because Palestinians form a large part of the population.

Dealing with the PLO. Hussein's relations with the Palestine Liberation Organization (PLO) have ranged from cooperation to hostility. In 1970, faced with growing Palestinian unrest, the Jordanian army put down a Palestinian uprising and drove PLO leaders from the country. But in 1974, under Arab pressure, the king agreed to recognize the PLO as the sole spokesman for Palestinian rights. In effect, his severing of Jordan's ties with the West Bank in 1988 acknowledged that West Bank residents considered the PLO their true representative. Elections for a new legislature that no longer included West Bank members were held in 1989.

Over the years, Jordan followed a generally pro-Western policy, although it suffered economic hardships for failing to condemn the August 1990 Iraqi invasion of Kuwait. The 1993 Israeli-PLO accord freed Hussein from his responsibility for the fate of the Palestinian people. On July 25, 1994, Jordan and Israel formally ended their 46-year state of war; on October 26, they signed a formal peace treaty. The following year, Jordan and the PLO signed a cooperation pact. The peace process failed to produce the expected economic dividends for Jordan, causing domestic unrest. Following the Likud victory in Israel's 1996 elections, the peace process stalled, sparking criticism from Hussein.

Reviewed by RICHARD W. BULLIET, Middle East Institute, Columbia University

Life in Riyadh, Saudi Arabia's capital and largest city, still revolves around the mosque.

SAUDI ARABIA

Under cover of darkness one night in 1902, a young Arab prince and 40 to 50 friends moved silently across the desert toward Riyadh, a walled town in the interior of the Arabian Peninsula. A few hours later, in a dramatic dawn raid, they captured Riyadh, the place from which the prince's family had been exiled years before.

Abdul Aziz Al-Saud's victory was the first in a chain of conquests by which he united four-fifths of the Arabian Peninsula. He and his successors created the Kingdom of Saudi Arabia, based its government on Islamic religious teachings, and made it the biggest oil-exporting nation in the world. In the process, the Sauds led a traditional, nomadic people into the technological world of the 1900s.

THE LAND

More than three times the size of Texas, Saudi Arabia is often pictured in Western novels and films as a vast, mysterious desert. Actually, the kingdom has a varied topography, including fertile highlands and coastal plains, as well as deserts.

Topography. On the western edge of the kingdom, a thin strip of lowland borders the Red Sea, becoming a coastal plain (the Tihamah) toward the south. Tall mountains, some more than 9,000 ft. (2,700 m.) high, rise abruptly to the east of this strip. On the inland side of the mountains, the surface slopes gently downward, merges with an interior plateau, then reaches sea level again at the Persian (or Arabian) Gulf. Saudi Arabia has no permanent rivers or lakes.

Climate. Saudi Arabia is in the same latitudes as northern Africa and the Gulf of Mexico. During summer, the heat is intense in most parts of the country, often topping 120° F. (48° C.), even in the shade. Winter temperatures are less extreme. Though both coastal areas are quite humid, most of the country receives only 2 to 4 in. (5 to 10 cm.) of rain annually.

Regions.   Two of the kingdom's six major regions are in the west. The **Hijaz,** home to 34 percent of the total population, includes several of the peninsula's oldest cities—Mecca (Makkah) and Taif, for example. South of the Hijaz, the **Asir** receives more rain than any other region— up to 30 in. (75 cm.) in the summer. About 70 percent of the Asir's inhabitants live in farming villages.

The central region of Saudi Arabia is **Najd** (Nejd), a great rocky plateau. Najd is the Saudis' heartland, the place where Riyadh, their capital and diplomatic center, is located. Though years may elapse between rainfalls, Najd holds 25 percent of the kingdom's population.

The fourth and fifth regions are deserts. The **Nafud** lies to the north of Najd and is home to many nomadic herders. To the south of Najd, the **Rub' al Khali** ("Empty Quarter") is a forbidding desert, covering about a third of Saudi Arabia. A sea of sand sheets and dunes, the Rub' al Khali is totally waterless, uninhabited except for a few nomads. Both deserts are connected by Dahna, a thin band of sand mountains.

The **Eastern Province** (or Hasa) borders the Persian Gulf. Though it contains Saudi Arabia's greatest natural resource, its oil reserves, this region has only 13 percent of the Saudi population.

Resources.   Apart from vast deposits of oil, a few other minerals, and fishing banks along both coasts, the kingdom has no other major resources. Less than 1 percent of the land is fertile.

THE PEOPLE

Arabic is the official language, and Islam is the state religion in Saudi Arabia. Nearly all citizens are Muslims of the Sunni sect of Islam, although there is a small Shi'ite (Shi'a) Islamic minority.

Saudi Arabia does not report an exact census of its people. But estimates suggest there are about 7 million to 8 million Saudis—half of whom are under 15—plus 3.5 million to 4 million foreign-born workers.

Saudi Arabia's gigantic oil reserves form the entire basis of the kingdom's economy.

The Bedouin have traditionally lived a nomadic life in the desert. In recent years, however, their way of life has changed rapidly, with many Bedouin now living in settled areas.

FACTS AND FIGURES

OFFICIAL NAME: Kingdom of Saudi Arabia.

NATIONALITY: Saudi(s) or Saudi Arabian(s).

CAPITAL: Riyadh.

LOCATION: Arabian Peninsula in Southwestern Asia. **Boundaries**—Jordan, Iraq, Kuwait, Persian Gulf, Bahrain, Qatar, United Arab Emirates, Oman, Yemen, Red Sea, Gulf of Aqaba.

AREA: 829,996 sq. mi. (2,149,690 sq. km.).

PHYSICAL FEATURES: Highest point—Mount Razih (11,999 ft.; 3,657 m.). **Lowest point**—sea level.

POPULATION: 19,400,000 (1996; annual growth 3.2%).

MAJOR LANGUAGE: Arabic (official).

MAJOR RELIGION: Islam (official).

GOVERNMENT: Monarchy. **Head of state and government**—king. **Legislature**—Consultative Council.

CHIEF CITIES: Riyadh, Jidda, Mecca, Taif, Dammam, Medina.

ECONOMY: Chief minerals—oil, natural gas, iron ore, gold, copper. **Chief agricultural products**—dates, grains, livestock. **Industries and products**—crude oil production, petrochemicals, petroleum refining, cement. **Chief exports**—petroleum and petroleum products. **Chief imports**—manufactured goods, transportation equipment, construction materials, processed foods, textiles.

MONETARY UNIT: 1 Saudi riyal = 100 halalas.

NATIONAL HOLIDAY: September 23 (Unification of the Kingdom).

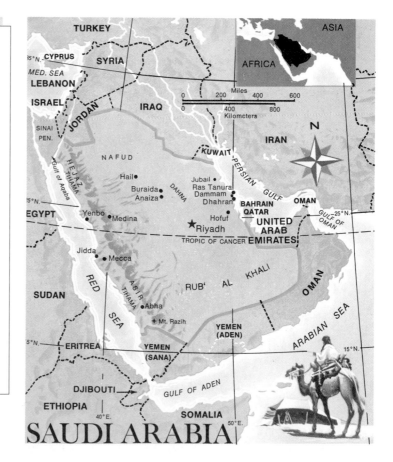

SAUDI ARABIA

The proportion of non-Saudis in the total labor force is high, having risen from 28 percent in 1975 to 60 percent by 1985. Increasingly, the kingdom's people have moved to its cities or settled in oasis communities. Only 5 percent still lead a nomadic life.

Cities. Saudi Arabia's largest city is **Riyadh,** the capital. Once a small oasis settlement, Riyadh now has a population of 1.5 million. The traditional old quarters of Riyadh have recently been replaced by new boulevards, offices, and government buildings. **Jiddah,** Saudi Arabia's most cosmopolitan city, is a major cargo port on the Red Sea, with a population of 1.4 million.

Urban centers on the eastern coast of the kingdom—**Dammam, Dhahran,** and **Jubail**—have grown with the nation's oil industry. Jubail, a government-planned industrial center and port, has 12 major industries (petrochemicals, fertilizers, steel, plastics, and gas) and more than 60 light industries. It is linked by cross-country pipeline to another new industrial center, **Yanbu,** on the Red Sea.

Not far inland from the Red Sea are **Mecca** (also spelled Makkah) and **Medina,** the holiest cities in the Islamic world. Mecca's permanent population (837,000) more than doubles during the hajj, a religious pilgrimage. (See sidebar, page 126.) In Mecca, the pilgrims' main goal is the Kaaba, a structure that Muslims believe was built by the prophet Abraham. Medina was the home of Muhammad, Islam's founder, during the last years of his life.

Way of Life. Though Arabians are economically advanced, the influence of Islamic and other traditional customs on their daily life is still enormous. The nationwide practice of interrupting all activity five times a day for public prayer is just one example of this influence. Others include a total ban on the sale or use of alcohol, and the segregation of women at public events.

The strength of tradition can also be seen in Saudi clothing. In general, most Saudis still wear traditional ankle-length robes in public, even though they may wear Western-style outfits at home. Most men also wear a head covering *(ghoutra)* bound by a cord *(agal)*, and women must be veiled when in public areas.

To Western eyes, the role of Saudi women in public life is sharply limited. An unaccompanied Saudi woman does not usually meet any man unless he is a close relative. As a result, dating is unknown, and marriages are often arranged by families. Women may not drive cars, and must obtain the permission of their husbands or other male relatives before traveling any distance. And while Saudi women have recently become doctors, engineers, teachers, and bank officers, they are still obliged to work in segregated places.

Education. Just a few decades ago, practically all Saudis were educated at home and in religious assemblies. Even today, public school education is not compulsory, though the government is opening many free schools. About 80 percent of all Saudi boys and 70 percent of all Saudi girls are now enrolled, a factor that should improve the country's 35 to 50 percent literacy rate. Saudi Arabia has seven modern universities, and quite a few Saudis study abroad.

Leisure. Through contacts with foreign schools, writers, politicians, and entrepreneurs, Saudi Arabians have begun to experience some cultural changes. They still enjoy traditional forms of leisure—poetry, horse racing, and falconry. But playing soccer, reading novels, and watching television have become popular, too. As Saudis increasingly watch television and videos from other parts of the world, their social customs are bound to be further affected.

HISTORY

Archaeologists confirm that civilizations flourished in the Arabian Peninsula at least 7,000 years ago. At that time, Arabia was a fertile land; but, by 3,000 B.C., the climate had changed, and much of the interior turned to desert. Nomadic desert dwellers, the tribal Bedouin, then developed an economy based on animals and plants—camels, sheep, and dates—that could survive around the peninsula's scattered oases. They also developed thriving trade routes with coastal settlements.

Muhammad and Islam.   In A.D. 570, a child who was to become one of the great religious leaders of all time was born in the trading town of Mecca. Muhammad was 40 when he first announced that he had received revelations from God. Meccan leaders rejected him as a prophet, however, and Muhammad fled to Yathrib (Medina) in 622. He gathered followers rapidly after that, and eventually won over Mecca and most of Arabia. (Muhammad's flight to Medina, the *hijrah,* marks the first year of the Muslim calendar.)

Muhammad died in 632, but Islam continued to gain followers. Within the next century, the new religion spread—often by way of conquest—across the Middle East and to lands as far-flung as Spain and China. Gradually, the seat of power within the Muslim world shifted northward from the peninsula, which itself came under outside attack.

THE FIVE PILLARS OF ISLAM

For Muslims the world over, Islam (or submission to the will of God) is manifested by five basic practices: a profession of faith, daily prayer, sharing wealth with the needy (*zakat*), fasting, and—for those who are able—a pilgrimage (or *hajj*) to Mecca.

Faith.   Muslims believe that there is only one God, whose name is Allah, and that Muhammad is his prophet. They recite this belief daily in a simple formula.

Prayer.   No matter where they may be, Muslims are obliged to pray at five specific times each day—at dawn, noon, midafternoon, sunset, and nightfall. Prayers may be said in a field, factory, or university, as well as at home or in a mosque. There is no priesthood in Islam, so prayers are led by a learned person who knows the Koran, the sacred book of Islam.

Zakat.   Believing that all things belong to God and are only held in trust by individuals, Muslims set aside some of their possessions for those in need. In most cases, the *zakat* equals 2.5 percent of the money a person has not committed to necessities, such as rent and food.

Fasting.   Every year, during the month of Ramadan, all Muslims who are physically able observe a fast from first light until sundown. By abstaining from food, drink, and sexual relations during daylight hours, Muslims strive to purify themselves from worldly comforts.

Pilgrimage.   The pilgrimage to Mecca, the *hajj,* is an obligation only for Muslims who are physically and financially able to make it. About 2 million pilgrims from all corners of the world make the *hajj* each year. The king of Saudi Arabia, who prefers the title "Custodian of the Holy Places," spends heavily to provide pilgrims with up-to-date transportation and health facilities.

The Kaaba in Mecca, the holiest city in Islam, draws Muslim pilgrims from all over the world.

By the 1500s, the Ottoman Turkish Empire had conquered the eastern and western coasts of Arabia, though much of the peninsula's desert interior still remained in the hands of Bedouin tribes.

The Saud Family. By the 1700s, observance of Islam had become corrupted in Arabia. A religious reformer, Muhammad Bin Abd al-Wahhab, began a movement to restore Islam to its original spirit. With the material help of princes of the Saud family, this movement, known as Wahhabism, rapidly gained followers. The Ottomans saw Wahhabism as a threat to their control of Mecca, and sent armies to crush the Sauds. Though defeated, the Sauds held onto their reformist ambitions.

In 1902, Abdul Aziz Al-Saud ("Ibn Saud") recaptured Riyadh, his family's traditional seat in Najd. In the years following, he drove the Ottomans from Hasa and conquered the Hijaz and the Asir. By 1926, he controlled more than three-fourths of the Arabian Peninsula. All such conquests were unified in 1932, when the name Kingdom of Saudi Arabia was given to the new country. After his death in 1953, Ibn Saud was succeeded as king by four of his sons: Saud (1953), Faisal (1964), Khalid (1975), and Fahd (1982). In 1995, Fahd briefly turned over power to his brother, Crown Prince Abdullah, due to ill health.

Saudi Government. The kingdom of Saudi Arabia functions as an absolute monarchy. The king and his family make all key decisions. There are no political parties, elections, or legislature, although the king announced a new constitution and bill of rights in 1992 in response to

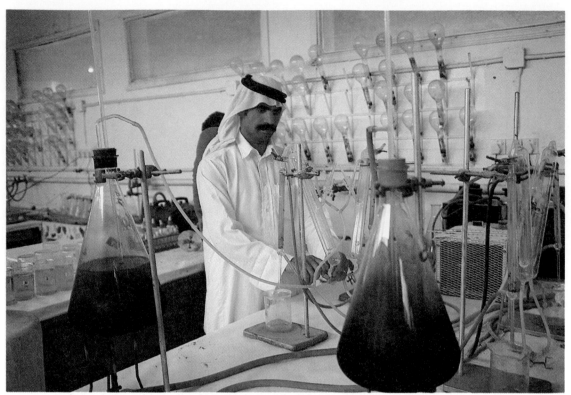

Students train for work in Saudi Arabia's oil industry at the University of Petroleum in Dhahran.

demands for political reform following the Gulf War. In 1993, he inaugurated an advisory Consultative Council. Members of the cabinet and this council are appointed by the king, who is also the prime minister. The monarchy is restrained, however, by the religious law of Islam, which the courts administer as the law of the land. This law, *sharia,* is based on the Koran, the book containing God's revelations to Muhammad, and on the *hadith,* traditions and sayings attributed to Muhammad himself.

ECONOMY

Oil was discovered in Saudi Arabia in 1938. As monarchs, the Sauds receive all of the kingdom's income from the development of this resource, although their wealth grew slowly at first. It was not until the 1970s that billions of "oil dollars" began to flow into the government's treasury. Oil revenues form the basis for the entire economy and have been used to build roads, hospitals, airports, schools, and industrial sites and to provide Saudi citizens with the benefits of modern society.

Oil Industry.   The kingdom's proven oil reserves equal about 257.8 billion barrels, or about 25 percent of the world's reserves. Production is centered on 14 major oil fields, mostly in the Eastern Province. Among the most important are Ghawar (believed to be the world's largest oil field) and Safaniyah (the largest offshore field).

By the mid-1990s, petroleum and petroleum products accounted for more than 90 percent of the kingdom's exports, by value. Oil dollars make it possible for Saudi Arabia to import goods it does not produce, including passenger cars, barley, consumer goods, industrial machinery, and telecommunications, construction, and farming equipment.

Oil Politics. In 1960, Saudi Arabia and other Third World oil producers formed a price-setting cartel known as the Organization of Petroleum Exporting Countries (OPEC). King Faisal played a large role in building cooperation among OPEC members, who engineered a sharp increase in the price of oil during the 1970s.

A price slump in the mid-1980s, however, alarmed Saudi leaders. They grew convinced of the need to diversify their economy, so that the country could reduce its dependence on oil exports. Private enterprise was encouraged and government spending was deemphasized. The 1990s saw successful efforts to expand the petrochemical industry and businesses producing goods for markets in neighboring Gulf states. The 1995 five-year plan called for eliminating Saudi Arabia's budget deficit.

Agriculture. Saudi planners are intent on making the kingdom self-sufficient in food production. To do so, they must deal with the country's water shortage. The government has dug deep wells to tap aquifers, ancient deposits of water far below the surface. Desalination plants convert seawater to fresh water, which is pumped to farms—and cities and industries—hundreds of miles inland. Farmers use drip irrigation systems to conserve water. Since 1970, the kingdom has spent enormous sums to reclaim the desert and improve irrigation.

By the end of the 1980s, these combined efforts were showing some payoff. Saudi farmers were able to provide 35 percent of the population's food needs—up from 15 percent in 1984. Agricultural products with the largest output in tons included wheat, milk, dates, watermelons, tomatoes, and poultry. Wheat production was so high in 1989 (3 million tons) that Saudi Arabia was able to export a surplus.

Such success has created its own problems. At the present rate of water consumption, Saudi Arabia faces the prospect of exhausting its natural water supply by the year 2010. And, despite the nation's success in producing surplus crops, the cost of doing so is punishing. Saudi Arabians spend eight times as much to produce their wheat crop as it would cost them to import the wheat they need.

SAUDI ARABIA AND THE WORLD

Saudi Arabia's oil wealth and its religious importance for Muslims have allowed it to play a large role in international matters. In addition to its membership in OPEC, the kingdom is a member of the United Nations, the Arab League, and the Gulf Cooperation Council (GCC).

Saudi Arabia has long considered the United States a major friend; nonetheless, before 1990, Saudis also were among the principal financial backers of the Palestine Liberation Organization (PLO) and consistently opposed Israel, a U.S. ally. Fearful of the spread of Islamic fundamentalism, the Saudi government aided Iraq during the Iran-Iraq War (1980–88). Its support for Iraq and the PLO quickly evaporated, however, when Iraq invaded neighboring Kuwait in August 1990 (a move supported by the PLO). When Iraqi troops moved toward Saudi Arabia's border, American troops were invited to Saudi Arabia to prevent further Iraqi aggression. Saudi forces joined the multinational coalition that defeated Iraq in the 1991 Gulf War. After the war, Saudi Arabia strengthened its ties to the United States and supported efforts to reach a broad Middle East peace settlement while providing funds to Arab Islamist groups.

WILLIAM OCHSENWALD, Virginia Polytechnic Institute and State University

In 1990, North and South Yemen combined to form a new nation, the Republic of Yemen, with the ancient city of Sana as its capital.

YEMEN

The merger of North and South Yemen in 1990 gave birth to a new nation, the Republic of Yemen, on the southern tip of the Arabian Peninsula. As a result, all Yemenis are joined under a single government for the first time in three centuries. The two separate nations, among the world's poorest, united in hopes of reaching a level of prosperity together that they failed to achieve apart.

Yemenis in the north and south have much in common, including their Arab roots and their Muslim religion. They also share a heritage that includes Saba, the biblical Sheba—one of many kingdoms that flourished from the 10th to the 2nd century B.C.

THE LAND

Yemen borders the Red Sea on the west, Saudi Arabia on the north, Oman on the east, and the Gulf of Aden on the south. Yemen's possessions include the 1,400-sq.-mi. (3,636-sq.-km.) island of Socotra in the Gulf of Aden; the islands of Perim, Al Hanish al Kabar, Jazirat Jabal Zuqar, and Kamaran in the Red Sea; and smaller islands in the Arabian Sea.

Yemen's geography played a key role in its economic and political development and in the formation of the hardy, independent Yemenis. The nation's location at the entrance to the Red Sea made it an inviting target for invaders from several nations. Its rugged landscape, especially in its mountainous interior, enabled Yemeni traditions to survive long periods of foreign occupation. These same mountains helped keep Yemenis in the north isolated from advances going on nearby.

The western region that was once North Yemen contains most of the nation's fertile land. Alongside the Red Sea is a strip of semidesert plain called the **Tihama**. About 40 mi. (64 km.) wide, the Tihama is a hot, sandy region with sparse vegetation and an occasional oasis. Wadis, dry waterways that flood during the rainy season, run from the mountains to the sea. Irrigation schemes along the wadis have enabled farmers there to produce an abundance of vegetables, fruits, and cotton. The old port of Mocha, which gave Yemeni coffee its name, is located in the Tihama. Today, the region's main port is **Hodeida**.

East of the coastal strip, the land rises into highlands that reach 4,000 to 12,000 ft. (1,200 to 3,600 m.). More than 15 in. (38 cm.) of rain fall during the summer, when monsoon winds blow off the Indian Ocean. The average July temperature is 70° F. (21° C.).

Farmers in the highlands cultivate crops on terraces. The 1970s and 1980s saw an increasing number of these terraces turned over to the cultivation of khat, a shrub whose leaves Yemenis chew for its mild narcotic effect. Expanded khat production puts more money in farmers' pockets but adds to the nation's food woes. Yemen relies on imports of sugar, grain, and flour to meet its food needs.

The nation's capital, **Sana**, situated more than 7,120 ft. (2,170 m.) above sea level, is the former capital of North Yemen. A mud-brick, gated wall surrounds this ancient city. Within the walls are some of the high-rise buildings typical of Yemen. These rectangular houses of stone and mud brick are often more than five stories high. Their windows are decorated with delicately designed tracery. **Taizz**, 4,600 ft. (1,402 m.) above sea level, is a major city in the southwest.

FACTS AND FIGURES

OFFICIAL NAME: Republic of Yemen.

NATIONALITY: Yemeni(s).

CAPITAL: Sana.

LOCATION: Arabian Peninsula's southern tip.

AREA: 203,849 sq. mi. (527,968 sq. km.).

PHYSICAL FEATURES: Highest point—Jebel Hadur (12,336 ft.; 3,760 m.). Lowest point—sea level.

POPULATION: 14,700,000 (1996; annual growth 3.2%).

MAJOR LANGUAGE: Arabic.

MAJOR RELIGION: Islam (57% Sunni, 43% Shi'ite).

GOVERNMENT: Republic. **Head of state**—president. **Head of government**—prime minister. **Legislature**—unicameral House of Representatives.

CHIEF CITIES: Sana, Aden, Taizz, Hodeida.

ECONOMY: **Chief minerals**—crude oil, rock salt, marble, coal, nickel, copper, gold, lead. **Chief agricultural products**—khat, cereals (durra, wheat, barley, corn, rice, oats, millet, sorghum), fruits and vegetables. **Industries and products**—mining, petroleum refining, food processing, building materials, textiles, ship refueling. **Chief exports**—refined oil products, agricultural products, dried/salted fish, cotton, hides, skins. **Chief imports**—crude oil, machinery, transportation equipment, manufactured products, grains, sugar, edible oils.

MONETARY UNIT: 1 Yemeni rial = 1,000 fils.

NATIONAL HOLIDAY: May 22 (Proclamation of the Republic).

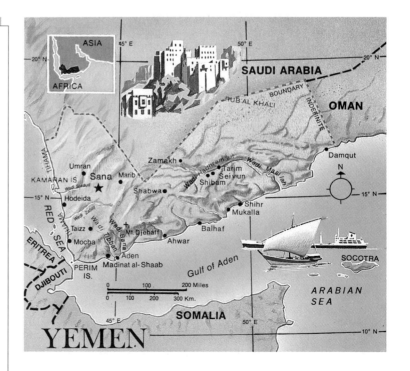

YEMEN

Aden is Yemen's leading port and the country's most important economic center.

The southern part of these western mountains reaches down into what was formerly South Yemen. Farmers grow grains and dates in the moist highlands here. Cotton growing is important along the wadis Bana and Tibban, north of the port city of **Aden.** Aden, an important center of trade, used to be the capital of South Yemen. Yemenis refer to it as the "economic capital" of the new nation.

The city of **Marib** is found just east of the western highlands, as the mountains slope off into desert. Three thousand years ago, camel caravans snaked through this city on their way north to the Mediterranean Sea. They carried spices, silks, and jewels from East Asia, and the sweet-smelling resin of two Yemeni trees, frankincense and myrrh. Today, archaeologists visit Marib to dig for the secrets of past civilizations.

Small oil deposits were discovered near Marib in 1984. The export of oil and oil products provides funds for development. At home, low-cost bottled gas and kerosene are welcome substitutes for scarce firewood. Demand for firewood was so strong before the discovery of oil that some environmentalists predicted the loss of all the north's trees and shrubs by the year 2000.

A sandy coastal plain separates Yemen's southern shore from mountains that taper off toward the east. North of the mountains, the land merges into desert—the Rub'al Khali, or Empty Quarter, of Saudi Arabia. Wadis cutting through the mountains permit crops to grow. Some of the nation's best farmland is located in the center of this eastern region, on the banks of the wadi Hadhramaut, where coffee and tobacco are major crops. Away from the mountains, summer temperatures in the south regularly rise above 130°F. (55°C.).

Many people in Hodeida and cities in the western highlands work in factories, refining oil and producing leather goods, textiles, processed food, cement, and aluminum goods. Yemen's mines produce salt and small amounts of coal and copper. Fishing is a major industry, especially in the south, where there is a healthy export trade in salted and dried fish. Aden's industry is focused for the most part on the needs of the ships that stop for refueling. Its refinery creates oil products out of imported crude oil.

Joblessness is high throughout the nation. The money sent home by more than 1 million Yemenis living abroad was an important prop for Yemen's economy. But many workers were expelled from the Persian Gulf region after Yemen backed Iraq's 1990 invasion of Kuwait.

PEOPLE

All Yemenis speak Arabic. Inhabitants of the Mahra area, in the extreme east, speak several non-Arabic languages as well.

Islam was brought to Yemen in A.D. 630, only a few years after the Prophet Mohammed began preaching, and today, all but a handful of Yemenis are Muslim. About two-thirds belong to the Shafi'i sect of Islam's Sunni branch, one-third to the Zaidi sect of the Shi'a branch. Most of the Zaidis live in the western highlands, generally in small villages. There, villagers farm or keep sheep, goats, cattle, and camels. About 10 percent of the southerners are Bedouins, nomadic herders who raise a good portion of the nation's livestock.

Tribal loyalties—the sense of being united by a common ancestor—are strong in Yemen, particularly in the north. Class distinctions are important, too. Landowners (*sayyids*) and bureaucrats (*qadis*) are on the top of the Yemeni social ladder. Service or crafts people (*bani kums*), such as butchers and carpenters, are below them. At the bottom of the social scale are the *abid*, people of African ancestry who are descended from slaves. Slavery was not banned in North Yemen until 1967.

When chewed, the leaves of the khat plant produce a mild narcotic effect.

Far weaker than it once was, this class system still guides personal decisions, especially in the western highlands. For example, women will marry into a class above theirs but never into a lower one.

The status of women has been a special concern in the south, where the government of South Yemen made special efforts to give women more power over their lives. Women were the target of special literacy campaigns, and they were encouraged to work outside their homes. In the north, women in the villages work unveiled in the fields. In the cities, they are wrapped from head to toe in bright shawls, and they are heavily veiled outside their homes. The average Yemeni woman bears seven children.

Yemeni men wear tight-fitting caps embroidered with gold or silver threads. Over these they wind brightly colored turbans. A man's robe, which reaches below the knees, is worn with an embroidered leather belt. A curved dagger, or *jambiya*, is often proudly thrust in the belt.

Since the 1960s, Yemenis in the north and the south have worked hard to make medical care and schooling more widely available. In the south, an emphasis on health care raised life expectancy from 36 years in 1960 to about 50 years in 1990. The percentage of southerners able to read jumped from 15 to 32 percent between 1967 and 1988.

Northerners saw gains, too, although less spectacular ones. Life expectancy is about 44 years. About 20 percent of all males and 2 percent of all females can read.

HISTORY

Yemen was once part of several ancient kingdoms, including the Himyarite kingdom, which was conquered in A.D. 525 by Christian Ethiopians. Christian and Jewish groups were already living there at the time. Persians defeated the Ethiopians 50 years later.

In Umran and elsewhere in Yemen, much of daily life revolves around the crowded markets.

Camels, here being washed in the sea, still serve as a means of desert transportation.

Turkey controlled the north for long periods from the 16th to the 20th centuries. A line of imams (spiritual rulers) took over upon independence in 1918. Army units ended dynastic rule in 1962 and proclaimed North Yemen a republic.

History took a different course in the south. The British West India Company occupied Aden, a small fishing port, in 1839. As a British colony, Aden became a trading center after the Suez Canal opened in 1869. Britain eventually brought the region's many sultanates, sheikhdoms, and emirates under its influence. In 1965, it persuaded 16 of these tiny states, including Aden, to form the Federation of South Arabia.

The British government withdrew its presence in 1967, and a Marxist group, the National Liberation Front (NLF), took charge of these 16 states and four others. Taking the Soviet Union as its model, the NLF tried to transform South Yemen into the Arab world's only socialist state. But massive East Bloc aid failed to lift South Yemen out of poverty. In 1988, both Yemens agreed to move toward a merger that finally occurred on May 22, 1990. Ali Abdullah Saleh, the former president of North Yemen, then became head of a five-member interim presidential council.

Because of its pro-Iraqi stance during the 1991 Gulf War, Yemen lost much foreign aid and remittances from overseas workers, although this shortfall was partially offset by rising oil revenues. In the Arabian Peninsula's first democratic elections, a single-house parliament was elected in 1993 under a new constitution. It elected a new presidential council that chose Saleh as its leader. In 1994, South Yemen attempted unsuccessfully to secede from the four-year-old union. The civil war ended when North Yemeni troops captured Aden on July 7. Subsequently, Yemen and Saudi Arabia settled a long-standing border dispute, and fighting between Yemen and Eritrea broke out over disputed islands in the Red Sea.

Reviewed by RICHARD W. BULLIET, Middle East Institute, Columbia University

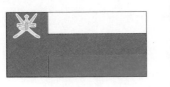

OMAN

In Muscat, the capital of Oman, the modern buildings are offset by two ancient forts the Portuguese built to guard the entrance to the harbor.

In 1970, the Sultanate of Oman's population—then numbering about 725,000—had only three schools and 12 hospital beds at their disposal. Twenty years later, the native population had grown by half, but the number of schools had multiplied to nearly 700. Oman had its own university, and the nation's hospitals and clinics had 2,800 beds.

The two factors that propelled Oman into the modern world were oil, first produced for sale in 1968, and the British-educated sultan, who wrested power from his father in 1970. While strengthening the nation's work force through schooling, the government has taken steps to broaden the nation's economic base to prepare for the day—perhaps as early as 2010—when Oman will have no more oil to sell.

THE LAND

Oman is divided into two parts: a main section, running along the Arabian Sea and the Gulf of Oman; and a small finger of land, the tip of the Musandam Peninsula, which it shares with the United Arab Emirates. It is this second part, overlooking the Strait of Hormuz, that gives Oman its strategic importance. About 17 percent of the world's oil passes through this strait on its way from the Persian Gulf to the Arabian Sea. Oman also controls several islands, including Masira, off its east coast.

The land itself is diverse. A narrow coastal plain rises sharply to form a mountainous interior, the highest point of which is nearly 10,000 ft. (3,048 m.) in the Jabal Akhdar (Green Mountain) region of the northeast. The mountainous interior slopes to a plateau fringed by desert.

Oman has one of the hottest climates in the world—temperatures of 130° F. (54° C.) are not unusual. An annual rainfall of 3 to 6 in. (8 to 15 cm.) provides some water for the springs and wells that irrigate the nation's sparse farmland, on which about 60 percent of all Omanis rely for their livelihood.

THE PEOPLE

Oman's people are largely of Arab descent. Small numbers of non-Arabs—mostly Baluchi, Zanzibari, and Indian—live in the coastal cities of Muscat (Masqat), the capital, and Matrah, the chief port. Foreigners

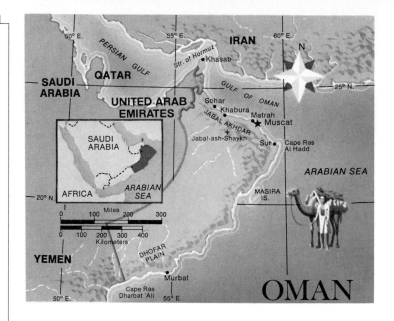

make up one-quarter of the population and half of the nonagricultural workforce. About three-quarters of all Omani citizens are Muslims of the Ibadhi sect. The rest are either Sunni or Shi'ite Muslims, with a handful of Hindus.

Until oil was discovered in the 1960s, most Omanis farmed, herded camels and goats, or caught fish along Oman's 1,000-mi. (1,690-km.) coastline. More than half the population still practices subsistence farming, and nomads still travel from oasis to oasis with their livestock herds. Dates and limes—Oman's main agricultural exports—are grown along with grain on the Batina, the fertile coastal plain northeast of the capital. Coconut palms, wheat, and bananas are grown in the southern province of Dhofar. Most Omani farmers still use traditional farming methods—one reason Oman must now import much of its food.

HISTORY AND GOVERNMENT

In 1650, the sultan of Muscat and Oman (as Oman was called before 1970) expelled the Portuguese, who had controlled the area for more than 100 years. During the 1800s, the British gained influence in Muscat and Oman through treaties that opened up trade, but the sultanate maintained its independence.

Oman has been ruled by the al-Sa'id dynasty since 1749. It has no legislature, constitution, or legal political parties. The current monarch, Sultan Qaboos bin Sa'id, rules with the aid of ministers he appoints. After ousting his father in 1970, he abolished slavery, ended many hated restrictions, squelched an armed rebellion in Dhofar, and used oil revenues to build new schools, roads, and hospitals. Regional unrest has required Oman to spend about a quarter of its resources on maintaining a small armed force. During the 1991 Gulf War, Oman let troops from nations opposed to Iraq use Omani military installations. A new, strictly advisory, Consultative Council convened in 1992.

Reviewed by RICHARD W. BULLIET, Middle East Institute, Columbia University

UNITED ARAB EMIRATES

The marketplace thrives in Abu Dhabi, the capital of the United Arab Emirates, a federation of seven tiny oil states.

About the size of the state of Maine, the United Arab Emirates (UAE) is a federation of seven small states. They are Abu Dhabi, Dubai, Sharja, Ajman, Umm al Qaiwain, Ras al Khaima, and Fujaira. In just two decades, revenues from oil and natural gas have transformed these desert states into a modern nation with one of the world's highest living standards.

THE LAND

Except for Fujaira, all the emirates lie along the Persian Gulf's southern shore, between the Qatar Peninsula in the west and the Musandam Peninsula in the east. Fujaira's coast faces the Gulf of Oman, giving the UAE a strategic location along the approaches to the Strait of Hormuz.

Salt marshes line most of the Persian Gulf coasts, giving way farther inland to barren desert. The highest point is in the eastern region, where in Fujaira the land rises to the Hajar Mountains. Here, irrigated valleys support crop growth. Elsewhere, farming is restricted mainly to the Buraimi Oasis, to an island off Abu Dhabi, and to some costly experiments with desert cultivation. Ras al Khaima, the UAE's breadbasket, contains a great fertile plain, where favorable water and climate make dairy farming possible. The UAE's farmers, who make up only 5 percent of the work force, grow dates, alfalfa, vegetables, fruits, and tobacco. Most food must be imported.

THE PEOPLE

Emirians, who make up only about 19 percent of the UAE's population, are Arabs. Guest workers from other Arab lands make up 23 percent of the population, and about 50 percent are guest workers from India. Other guest workers include Westerners and East Asians. Islam is the religion of more than nine out of 10 of these people. The rest are Hindus or Christians. About 85 percent of them work in industry or commerce.

The UAE has used much of its oil wealth to improve its citizens' standard of living. The government devotes 10 percent of its budget to education, with a specific emphasis on education for women, who are

FACTS AND FIGURES

OFFICIAL NAME: United Arab Emirates.

NATIONALITY: Emirian(s).

CAPITAL: Abu Dhabi (Abu Zabi).

LOCATION: Arabian Peninsula's eastern coast. **Boundaries**—Oman, Saudi Arabia, Qatar, Persian Gulf.

AREA: 32,276 sq. mi. (83,600 sq. km.).

PHYSICAL FEATURES: Highest point—Jabil Hafit (3,824 ft.; 1,166 m.). **Lowest point**—sea level.

POPULATION: 1,900,000 (1996; annual growth 1.9%).

MAJOR LANGUAGES: Arabic (official), Persian, English.

MAJOR RELIGIONS: Sunni Islam, Shi'ite Islam.

GOVERNMENT: Federation, with some powers delegated to central government, others reserved to the seven member sheikhdoms. **Head of state**—president. **Head of government**—prime minister. **Legislature**—unicameral Federal National Council.

CHIEF CITIES: Dubai, Abu Dhabi (Abu Zabi), Ajman.

ECONOMY: Chief minerals—crude oil, natural gas. **Chief agricultural products**—dates and other fruits, alfalfa, vegetables, tobacco, fish. **Industries and products**—petroleum, fishing, petrochemicals, construction materials, boatbuilding, handicrafts, pearling. **Chief exports**—crude oil, natural gas, reexports, dates, dried fish. **Chief imports**—food, consumer goods, machinery.

MONETARY UNIT: 1 Emirian dirham = 100 fils.

NATIONAL HOLIDAY: December 2 (National Day).

encouraged to enter the workforce. Schooling is free, and even adults are taking advantage of primary education, boosting the nation's literacy rate to around 73 percent. All housing is government-financed, as is all medical care. Since its founding in 1971, the UAE has cut the rate of infant deaths in half. Life expectancy—70 for males, 74 for females—is among the highest in the Arab world.

HISTORY AND GOVERNMENT

Two hundred years ago, piracy was a main form of revenue, and pirate ships—some of which preyed on British shipping—often hid in coves along the coasts of the Persian and Oman gulfs. To end the piracy, the British signed a series of truces with the ruling sheikhs during the 1820s. The agreements gave Britain control of the foreign affairs of the sheikhdoms, which became known as the Trucial States. The truces ended in 1971, when Great Britain withdrew from the region. Seven states declared their independence that year, and six of them united as a single country. A seventh, Ras al Khaima, joined the federation in 1972.

The UAE has taken steps to diversify its economy away from total reliance on oil and natural gas, although these commodities still account for two-thirds of the goods and services the nation produces. Industry and finance have grown. The UAE's major industries include aluminum, steel, chemicals, petroleum products, building materials, plastics, textiles, apparel, and foodstuffs. Dubai, once a pearl-diving center, has become the focus of a thriving reexport trade, buying goods and shipping them out again for a profit.

The Supreme Council of Rulers, in which the head of each sheikhdom is represented, elects one of its members as president. Members of the unicameral legislature are appointed. Abu Dhabi is the capital city.

Reviewed by RICHARD W. BULLIET, Middle East Institute, Columbia University

BAHRAIN

In the hot, arid climate of Bahrain, farmers must rely on irrigation in order to grow crops.

The first Arab state on the Persian Gulf to benefit from the discovery of oil, Bahrain may be the first to see its oil run out. For that reason, the small island nation—less than four times the size of Washington, D.C.—spent the 1970s and 1980s seeking alternative sources of income. Though oil remains key to its economic health, Bahrain has become a regional banking center and a competitive producer of aluminum, natural gas, and iron and steel. It is also an active builder and repairer of ships.

THE LAND

The State of Bahrain encompasses one large and 35 small islands in the Persian Gulf, about 17 mi. (28 km.) from the Qatar Peninsula and 15 mi. (24 km.) from Saudi Arabia's eastern coast. Running north to south, it is 30 mi. (48 km.) long and 10 mi. (16 km.) across at its widest point. The nation takes its name from the largest island, Bahrain.

Most of Bahrain Island is flat, sandy desert, rising in the center to an escarpment that reaches 445 ft. (135 m.) in height. A fertile strip 3 mi. (5 km.) wide on the main island's northern coast sustains date, fig, almond, and pomegranate trees. Bahrain's capital city, **Manama,** is also located in the north. There, Bahrain Island is connected by a causeway to Muharraq, the second-largest island, which houses an international airport and the town of Muharraq (Al Muharraq). A causeway links Muharraq Island to the island of Jazirat al Azl, a major dry-dock and ship-repair center. A third causeway, completed in 1986, links Bahrain with Saudi Arabia.

Rainfall averages less than 4 in. (10 cm.) a year. Fresh water is scarce, although there are some underground springs. The government has built large desalination plants to meet industrial and household needs. The climate is hot and humid. Temperatures regularly reach 106° F. (41° C.). Most food is imported. Bahrain's farmers, who make up 4 percent of the work force, raise poultry and grow some vegetables and fruits.

THE PEOPLE

Bahraini citizens, who made up about 63 percent of the population in 1990, fall mainly into three groups. The Baharna are descendants of Bahrain's original inhabitants. Forebears of the Hassawis emigrated from

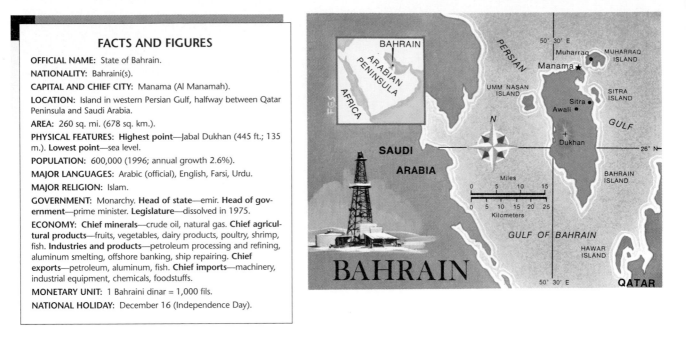

Saudi Arabia's Eastern Province. The Ajamis are descended from people who emigrated from Iran during the past 100 years or so. Non-Bahrainis are mostly guest workers from the Arabian Peninsula, Iran, and South and East Asia. Arabic is the official language, although English is widely spoken. Most people in Bahrain are Muslims.

Nearly half of all workers are engaged in manufacturing, oil and natural-gas production, and trade. More than half provide services in such areas as government and banking.

With oil production expected to cease shortly after the year 2000, Bahrainis are working to develop other industries. The fact that Bahrain boasts the Arab world's highest literacy rate helps. More than half the engineering students at the national university are women, as are three-fourths of those preparing for business and management careers.

HISTORY AND GOVERNMENT

Bahrain flourished as a trading center as early as 2000 B.C. Portugal dominated the island state for a brief period during the 1500s, after which Iran took control until its Safavid dynasty fell during the 1700s. In 1783, Arabs from Qatar conquered Bahrain. They were led by ancestors of the al-Khalifa family that rules Bahrain today. During the 1800s, Bahrain gave Britain control of its foreign affairs in exchange for military protection. The arrangement ended in 1971, when Bahrain won full independence.

Bahrain is a hereditary monarchy ruled by an emir. The emir ended a two-year experiment with parliamentary government in 1975 by dissolving the popularly elected National Assembly, but an appointed advisory council was established in 1992. The emir is head of state, and the government is run by a council of ministers that he appoints.

The government has staked future economic growth on banking and manufacturing, which require a stable political climate to thrive. That stability suffered a blow when Iraq invaded Kuwait in 1990. After the 1991 Gulf War, Shi'ite opposition groups pressed for political reforms. There is a major U.S. military base in Bahrain.

Reviewed by RICHARD W. BULLIET, Middle East Institute, Columbia University

QATAR

In little more than 50 years, oil has transformed tiny Qatar from a sleepy desert emirate into a prosperous welfare state.

On the face of it, the State of Qatar should not exist. This peninsular nation, the size of Connecticut and Rhode Island combined, is mostly desert, flat, and barren. Temperatures during the summer months regularly rise to a blistering 120° F. (48° C.), and dust storms and sandstorms are commonplace and blinding. The growing season is so short—it lasts only from January to March—that Qataris must import most of their food. The need for fresh water requires Qataris to maintain costly facilities that take the salt out of seawater.

Qataris have endured despite these hardships. Their ancestors eked out a living by herding, fishing, and pearling. By contrast, present-day Qataris are the beneficiaries of a powerful oil-driven economy. In four decades, revenues from Qatari oil and natural gas have lifted their nation out of poverty and transformed it into a modern welfare state.

THE LAND

Qatar (pronounced KAH-tar) is situated on the Persian Gulf coast of the Arabian Peninsula. It is bordered by Saudi Arabia and Abu Dhabi, the largest of the United Arab Emirates. The port city of Doha, on the east coast, is the capital and major commercial center. More than 70 percent of the population lives there. Most of the rest live in the industrial town of Umm Said, the oil-field region of Dukhan, and the east coast towns of Waqra (Al Wakrah) and al-Khor.

THE PEOPLE

Fewer than one-fourth of all Qataris are native to the country. The rest are foreign workers with temporary-resident status. They immigrated here from other nations to work in the oil and gas industries and the businesses that those industries spawned. Of the total population, about 45 percent are Arabs. Pakistanis make up 15 percent, Indians 21 percent, and Iranians about 6 percent. Egyptians and Bangladeshis are also heavily represented among the foreign workers. Arabic is the official language, although English is widely used, reflecting Qatar's long association with Great Britain. About 95 percent of the population is Muslim, and Islamic

FACTS AND FIGURES

OFFICIAL NAME: State of Qatar.

NATIONALITY: Qatari(s).

CAPITAL AND CHIEF CITY: Doha (Ad Dawhah).

LOCATION: Arabian Peninsula's eastern coast. **Boundaries**—Saudi Arabia, United Arab Emirates, Persian Gulf.

AREA: 4,427 sq. mi. (11,437 sq. km.).

PHYSICAL FEATURES: Highest point—Dukhan Heights (321 ft.; 98 m.). **Lowest point**—sea level.

POPULATION: 700,000 (1996; annual growth 1.6%).

MAJOR LANGUAGES: Arabic (official), English.

MAJOR RELIGION: Islam.

GOVERNMENT: Traditional emirate. **Head of state and government**—emir. **Legislature**—unicameral Advisory Council.

ECONOMY: Chief minerals—crude oil, natural gas. **Chief agricultural products**—fruits, vegetables, fish. **Industries and products**—oil production, fertilizers, petrochemicals, steel. **Chief exports**—petroleum products, steel. **Chief imports**—foodstuffs, beverages, chemicals, machinery and equipment.

MONETARY UNIT: 1 Qatari riyal = 100 dirhams.

NATIONAL HOLIDAY: September 3 (Independence Day).

law is the basis of the nation's legal system. Education is free at all levels but is not compulsory.

The workforce is largely dependent on the oil sector of the economy. But Qatar's oil wealth has been put to use creating new industries, including the manufacture of fertilizer, steel, and cement, and in strengthening older ones, such as commercial fishing. More than half of the labor force is employed in services or works for the government. About 70 percent of the inhabitants are not citizens of Qatar.

HISTORY AND GOVERNMENT

Inhabited for many centuries, Qatar was dominated by the sheikhdom of Bahrain, Qatar's neighbor to the west, until 1868, when the British negotiated an end to the Bahraini claim. Ottoman Turks occupied the peninsula from 1872 until, in 1916, Qatar became a British protectorate. The British recognized a sheikh in the al-Thani family as ruler. The oil that would eventually transform Qatar was discovered in 1935 and first exported in 1949. Qatar already had become a prosperous nation when Britain announced it would withdraw in 1971. Qatar first was set to join the Gulf states that became part of the United Arab Emirates. But it eventually decided to declare its independence and go its own way.

Although Qatar's oil may be depleted by 2015, its natural-gas reserves should last far longer. The nation has embarked on a program of training Qatari citizens to take over key posts in industry.

The head of state is the emir, who must be a member of the al-Thani family. His power is checked by the custom of asking the advice of others, including religious leaders, and of ruling by consensus. An advisory council, appointed by the emir, is designed to help him do this. Qatar provided assistance to the anti-Iraq alliance in the 1991 Gulf War and signed a defense pact with the United States in 1992. In 1995, the emir was deposed by his son and heir apparent in a palace coup.

Reviewed by RICHARD W. BULLIET, Middle East Institute, Columbia University

The affluent life-style of Kuwaiti citizens (left) came to an abrupt end in August 1990, when Iraq invaded the country, causing much destruction (above) and touching off the 1991 Gulf War.

KUWAIT

On August 2, 1990, Iraqi troops swept over Kuwait's northern border, and Iraq's president proclaimed the oil-rich sheikhdom a province of Iraq. Kuwait's government, headed by the same family that had ruled the land since 1752, fled into exile. A quirk of geology had placed one-tenth of the world's oil reserves under Kuwait's sands. But the oil wealth provided no security against invasion.

World reaction was swift. The United Nations demanded that Iraq's troops leave Kuwait. When diplomatic pressures and economic sanctions failed to force an Iraqi withdrawal, a multinational force led by the United States expelled the Iraqis from Kuwait. The ground phase of the Gulf War lasted only 100 hours, ending at midnight on February 27, 1991, and the emir returned to Kuwait on March 14. Limited oil exports resumed in July, but it would take several years for the economy to be restored to its preinvasion level.

LAND

Kuwait is about the size of New Jersey. It occupies an area in the northeastern part of the Arabian Peninsula, at the head of the Persian Gulf, which Arabs call the Arabian Gulf. The country is bordered on the north and west by Iraq, and on the south and southwest by Saudi Arabia.

Most of the land is flat, sandy desert, occasionally relieved by small hills. There are no rivers or lakes, and rainfall is limited. A small oasis exists at Al-Jahrah at the western edge of Kuwait Bay, and a few coastal villages draw fresh water from wells, but desalinization plants are the main source of water. **Kuwait City,** the capital, is the nation's main port and commercial center.

PEOPLE

Although most of Kuwait's population is Arab, Kuwaiti citizens made up only 39 percent of the total before the Iraqi invasion. About 39 percent of the population were citizens of neighboring Arab states. Nine percent of the guest workers and their families had come from India and Pakistan, and four percent were from Iran. During the Iraqi occupation, hundreds of thousands of guest workers, many of whom lost all they owned, fled the country. Nearly half of all Kuwaitis remained in exile in mid-1995, when the population stood at 1.8 million—well below the preinvasion figure—about 800,000 of whom were Kuwaitis. Nearly 400,000 Palestinians were expelled because of Palestinian support for the Iraqi invasion. Despite a severe labor shortage, the government was determined that Kuwaitis would never again be a minority in their own country.

Most Kuwaiti citizens are thought to have descended from the Anaiza people, who migrated to the Kuwait coastline from the desert interior during the 1700s. The ancestors of perhaps a quarter of all Kuwaiti citizens were Iranians who settled in Kuwait before 1920. Seven out of 10 Kuwaitis are Sunni Muslims; nearly all the rest are Shi'ite Muslims. Kuwait's ambitious educational program has created a highly literate population. Kuwaitis long benefited from a wide variety of social services, including retirement income, marriage bonuses, housing loans, free medical care and schooling, and guaranteed employment.

ECONOMY

Before 1946, most Kuwaiti workers were engaged in fishing, pearling, and boatbuilding. The construction of schools, roads, hospitals, and government buildings began in 1949. Oil revenues were used to provide social services, to reduce the dependence on imported food, and to develop industry and infrastructure. The government also invested in overseas real estate and foreign corporations to keep money flowing into Kuwait long after its oil reserves have run out.

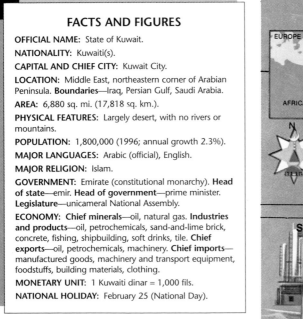

FACTS AND FIGURES

OFFICIAL NAME: State of Kuwait.

NATIONALITY: Kuwaiti(s).

CAPITAL AND CHIEF CITY: Kuwait City.

LOCATION: Middle East, northeastern corner of Arabian Peninsula. **Boundaries**—Iraq, Persian Gulf, Saudi Arabia.

AREA: 6,880 sq. mi. (17,818 sq. km.).

PHYSICAL FEATURES: Largely desert, with no rivers or mountains.

POPULATION: 1,800,000 (1996; annual growth 2.3%).

MAJOR LANGUAGES: Arabic (official), English.

MAJOR RELIGION: Islam.

GOVERNMENT: Emirate (constitutional monarchy). **Head of state**—emir. **Head of government**—prime minister. **Legislature**—unicameral National Assembly.

ECONOMY: Chief minerals—oil, natural gas. **Industries and products**—oil, petrochemicals, sand-and-lime brick, concrete, fishing, shipbuilding, soft drinks, tile. **Chief exports**—oil, petrochemicals, machinery. **Chief imports**—manufactured goods, machinery and transport equipment, foodstuffs, building materials, clothing.

MONETARY UNIT: 1 Kuwaiti dinar = 1,000 fils.

NATIONAL HOLIDAY: February 25 (National Day).

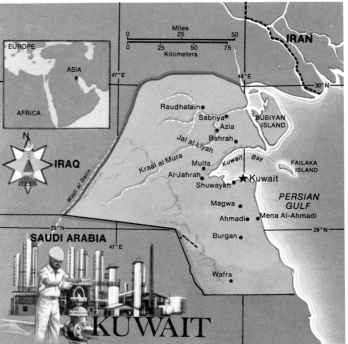

Oil and natural gas remain the mainstays of the postwar economy, although less than two percent of the labor force is needed to produce them. The costs of reconstructing the oil industry infrastructure were estimated at $8 billion to $10 billion, apart from extinguishing the hundreds of oil-well fires set by the fleeing Iraqis and cleaning up the oil lakes created by sabotaged wells that did not catch fire. The country, as expected, returned to its preinvasion production level of 1.5 million barrels of oil per day by the end of 1992. Many of the factories destroyed and looted during the occupation have yet to be repaired. To stimulate private investment in the economy, the government has paid off household debts, raised government salaries, and compensated for war damages. This spending reduced Kuwait's foreign assets significantly.

HISTORY

Kuwait, which means "little fort" in Arabic, developed from a small coastal town of the same name that was settled around 1740. In 1752, the Kuwaitis selected their first emir, Sabah I.

Kuwait's position at the head of the Gulf made it an important port. But its prosperity was constantly threatened by invasion from the interior of the Arabian Peninsula and by a Turkish attempt to rule it. The Kuwaitis sought the protection of the British, and, in 1899, the British agreed to protect Kuwait and to take charge of its foreign affairs. In 1961, by mutual agreement, the British withdrew formal protection, and Kuwait became completely independent.

That same year, Iraq claimed Kuwait's territory as its own. A show of British military might persuaded Iraq to back off. However, Iraq's refusal to accept Kuwait's northern border—after agreeing to do so upon its own independence in 1932—caused a good deal of friction between the two nations during the 1970s. At the heart of the argument was the Rumailia oil field. Most of the field lies inside Iraq, but it runs beneath Kuwait's northern border into Kuwait. One of Iraq's contentions when it invaded and annexed Kuwait in 1990 was that Kuwait had been stealing Iraqi oil from Rumailia. After Iraq was driven out of Kuwait in the 1991 Gulf War, the United Nations reinstated the 1923 border drawn by the British. Kuwait also signed a 10-year military alliance with the United States, which ordered troops and equipment to Kuwait on October 8, 1994, as Iraqi forces again massed along the Kuwaiti border in what was thought to be an effort to force the lifting of U.N. sanctions against Iraq. The Iraqi troops quickly withdrew from the border area.

GOVERNMENT

The Iraqi invasion interrupted a style of government—rule by a monarch called an emir—that had changed little for 238 years. Emirs were chosen by the Sabah family from among their members. A 1962 constitution set up a single-house, 50-seat National Assembly, which the emir dissolved in 1986. In June 1990, elections were held for a new 75-seat assembly, 25 of whose members were appointed by the emir. A prime minister appointed by the emir serves as head of government. From February 27 to June 26, 1991, the emir placed Kuwait under martial law. Multiparty legislative elections were held in 1992 and 1996. Pro-government candidates won a majority of seats in 1996.

Reviewed by RICHARD W. BULLIET, Middle East Institute, Columbia University

The Monument of Saddam's Qadissiya, a 150-foot-high tiled dome split in half, commemorates the Arab defeat of Persia in A.D. 637, and the thousands of Iraqis killed in the war with Iran.

IRAQ

Iraq was the site of several great civilizations that flourished thousands of years ago in Mesopotamia, on the rich plain between the Tigris and Euphrates rivers. Today, Iraq is once more a major force in the Middle East, yet it gets its strength not from the fertility of the plain, but from oil beneath and to the north of it. With at least 10 percent of the world's reserves—much of them in the mountainous north—Iraq has more oil than any nation other than Saudi Arabia. Revenues from these reserves, first discovered in 1927, support the Arab world's largest standing army. They have also helped Iraq fund some impressive development projects in education, social welfare, agriculture, and industry. Still, much poverty exists, and the nation cannot produce all the food it needs in spite of the abundance of fertile, well-watered soil.

THE LAND

Iraq occupies the eastern portion of the Fertile Crescent, the area that is sometimes referred to as Mesopotamia—the Greek word for "Lands Between the Rivers." Mesopotamia is the legendary site of the biblical Garden of Eden. Today, Iraq is bordered by Kuwait, Iran, Turkey, Syria, Jordan, and Saudi Arabia. The Tigris and Euphrates rivers, which originate in Turkey, have greatly influenced Iraqi life for thousands of years. (See sidebar, page 50.)

Iraq lies between the plateau of northern Arabia and the mountain ridges of southwest Iran and Turkey. The bulk of Iraq's land forms a lowland passageway between Syria and the Persian Gulf. Iraq's topography falls into three distinct zones: the northern mountains; the central plains; and the desert west, southwest, and south.

Kurdistan, the mountainous part in the north, has peaks that reach 9,840 ft. (3,000 m.). The central area lying between the Tigris and Euphrates and centered on the capital city of Baghdad is the most cultivated and irrigated area. Below Baghdad, the floodplains widen, and the river channels become braided. They form large marshy areas along the Shatt al-Arab, the name given to the channel that the rivers form after they join together about 100 mi. (160 km.) northwest of the Persian Gulf. The Shatt al-Arab is Iraq's only passageway to the sea. The desert regions are mostly uninhabited wastelands.

Temperatures range, on average, from 120° F. (48° C.) in July and August to below freezing in January. Annual rainfall averages 4 to 7 in. (10 to 18 cm.) and occurs mostly from December through April.

THE PEOPLE

As in many developing nations, Iraq's population became largely urbanized during the last half of the 20th century. Today, nearly 75 percent of Iraq's people live in urban areas, half of them in the nation's four largest cities: Baghdad, Basra, Mosul, and Kirkuk.

About 70 to 75 percent of Iraq's people speak Arabic and identify themselves as Arabs. They reside mostly in the central and southern regions and in the northern city of Mosul.

About 15 to 20 percent of the nation's people are Kurds, living mostly in the north and in Baghdad. Iraq's approximately 3 million Kurds are Muslims but not Arabs. Originally from Persia (Iran), they are an Indo-Aryan people, with kinship ties to about 17 million Kurds who live as minorities outside Iraq in Iran, Turkey, Azerbaijan, and Syria.

Fiercely independent, Kurds have long wanted their own nation. In hopes of winning greater autonomy, many Kurds sided with the Iranians during the Iran-Iraq war (1980–88). After the war, Iraqi troops used chemical weapons against them and destroyed many Kurdish villages. With Iraq's defeat in the 1991 Gulf War, the Kurds again rose up against the government. Their revolt was brutally suppressed. Hundreds of thousands of Kurds fled from their homes, and many of them died in the mountains.

Religion. Iraq is also split along religious lines. Although more than 95 percent of the people are Muslims, they are divided into two major groups: the Sunnis and the Shi'ites. The Shi'ites, who live mostly in the south, make up about 55 percent of the population. The Sunnis, who make up 40 percent, have controlled the government since a 1958 coup toppled Iraq's monarchy. Most Kurds are Sunni Muslims, but their language and customs are different from those of their Arab neighbors.

The division of the Muslim community began after the death of the prophet Muhammad in A.D. 632. After the prophet's death, the Muslims differed over who should be recognized as Muhammad's legitimate successors. The Sunnis succeeded over the centuries in having their candi-

Baghdad, the Iraqi capital, sustained much damage during the 1991 Persian Gulf War.

dates selected as caliphs, or living representatives of Muhammad's prophethood. Since the Shi'ites seldom achieved political power, their religious-belief system became a political protest movement as well. Iranian Muslims are almost all Shi'ites.

Christians constitute about 5 percent of the population. A Turkish-speaking group, the Turkomans, account for 2 or 3 percent of the population. The Turkomans, who are Sunni Muslims, live near the northern oil fields around Kirkuk and Arbil.

A substantial portion of southerners—perhaps as much as 2 percent of the entire Iraqi population—speak Persian, the language of Iran. Large numbers of this Shi'ite group were expelled from Iraq during the Iran-Iraq war (1980–88); others fled when an uprising against the government of Saddam Hussein after the end of the 1991 Persian Gulf War failed. Many Shi'ite religious shrines are located in the Iraqi cities of Karbala, An Najaf, and Kazimiyah.

WAY OF LIFE

Iraq's political history has traditionally been divided between town and tribe. In 1900, about 75 percent of all Iraqis were tribal, but most were not nomadic. Today, nomads, or Bedouin, constitute less than 2 percent of the population. Most of the rural and tribal people live in small villages where life centers around the mosque.

Housing. Village houses are flat-roofed, rectangular, and made of dried mud and brick. There are usually bright rugs on the floor, especially in the north. In the south, the floors are more likely to be covered with reed mats. Bedding is stored away during the daytime, and clothes

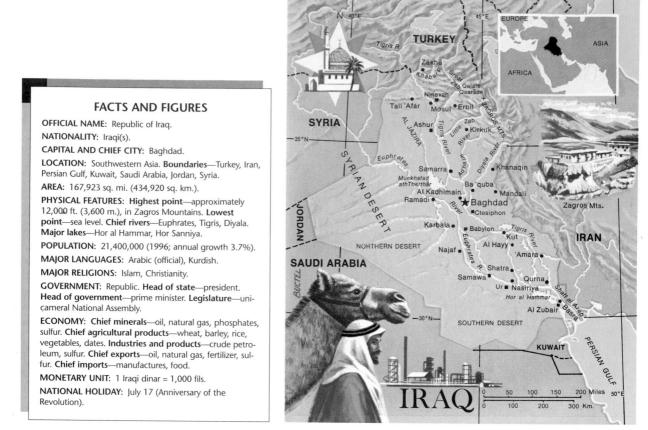

FACTS AND FIGURES

OFFICIAL NAME: Republic of Iraq.

NATIONALITY: Iraqi(s).

CAPITAL AND CHIEF CITY: Baghdad.

LOCATION: Southwestern Asia. **Boundaries**—Turkey, Iran, Persian Gulf, Kuwait, Saudi Arabia, Jordan, Syria.

AREA: 167,923 sq. mi. (434,920 sq. km.).

PHYSICAL FEATURES: Highest point—approximately 12,000 ft. (3,600 m.), in Zagros Mountains. **Lowest point**—sea level. **Chief rivers**—Euphrates, Tigris, Diyala. **Major lakes**—Hor al Hammar, Hor Sanniya.

POPULATION: 21,400,000 (1996; annual growth 3.7%).

MAJOR LANGUAGES: Arabic (official), Kurdish.

MAJOR RELIGIONS: Islam, Christianity.

GOVERNMENT: Republic. **Head of state**—president. **Head of government**—prime minister. **Legislature**—unicameral National Assembly.

ECONOMY: Chief minerals—oil, natural gas, phosphates, sulfur. **Chief agricultural products**—wheat, barley, rice, vegetables, dates. **Industries and products**—crude petroleum, sulfur. **Chief exports**—oil, natural gas, fertilizer, sulfur. **Chief imports**—manufactures, food.

MONETARY UNIT: 1 Iraqi dinar = 1,000 fils.

NATIONAL HOLIDAY: July 17 (Anniversary of the Revolution).

are kept in closets or chests. During hot summer nights, when temperatures remain above 100° F. (38° C.), many families sleep on the flat roofs of their homes.

Some nomadic Arabs still live in tents covered with goat hair, although today, most tents are made of canvas. In the southern marshes, houses (the large ones are called *mudhifs*) are made of reeds. The reeds are tied in tight bundles and bent to form a sloping roof and walls. In the larger towns and cities, most houses are built of concrete.

Diet. Dates—a source of sugar, protein, and fat—are a staple of the Iraqi diet, especially among the poor. Usually they are eaten with bread. Iraqis also eat large amounts of plain yogurt, rice, beans, green vegetables, and fresh fruit. The favorite beverage in Iraq is tea.

Social and Cultural Change

Today, nearly three-quarters of all Iraqis live in towns and cities. Almost a quarter of the nation's people live in Baghdad and its environs.

Nearly 90 percent of all Iraqis can read and write. Education is compulsory from age six to grade six. Virtually 100 percent of all children attended primary school in 1978, but only 88 percent did so in 1988. Nearly 40 percent attend secondary school. In 1992, more than 46,000 students were enrolled in higher education.

Women. Since 1968, Iraq has been governed by the Arab Socialist Renaissance Party, known as the Baath Party. The Baath Party emphasizes secularization—a decrease in the clergy's power over government and personal affairs—and increased opportunities for women. Women have made great strides in education. In 1920, few girls finished elementary school. By 1990, females accounted for about half the students in elementary school and more than 40 percent of students in intermediate and high schools. About 35 percent of university students were female. Women have made inroads in the workplace, too. Their participation increased dramatically during the 1980s, when they filled in for men who were drafted into the military. But women are still by no means equal to men in terms of pay, and they hold few high administrative posts.

Although the damage to Iraq's infrastructure during the 1991 Gulf War was not as great as originally thought, the war badly disrupted social services. Allied bombing destroyed electrical, water, and sewage systems, and there were shortages of food and medicines.

ECONOMY

The event that changed Iraq's fortunes in modern times was the discovery of oil in 1927. Iraq nationalized, or bought out, foreign oil companies in 1972, becoming one of the first Arab countries to control its oil industry completely. Oil revenues have paid for nearly all of Iraq's development programs.

Oil production slowed during the early years of the war with Iran. By 1990 Iraq had almost completely rebuilt its battered oil industry, on which it relied for about 95 percent of its export revenues. After Iraq invaded Kuwait in August 1990, an international boycott on Iraqi oil exports was imposed, and the country's refineries and other oil installations were damaged by Allied bombing during the 1991 Gulf War.

Iraqis eat a great deal of fresh fish caught in the Tigris River.

The spiral minaret of the Great Mosque at Samarra, now in ruins, was built in the 9th century.

About 30 percent of the population is involved in farming. Though Iraq exports some fruits, such as dates, it must import huge amounts of grain, meat, and dairy products. Almost all business except heavy industry and defense production is in private hands, but many factories were damaged by Allied bombing during the Gulf War. Iraq's highly urbanized and industrialized economy was slow to recover. The country still had huge foreign debts incurred during the Iran-Iraq War, and the accord that ended the Gulf War earmarked much of its future oil income to pay reparations to Kuwait. All citizens received small food rations, but by the mid-1990s, 60 percent of the labor force was unemployed and those factories still operating suffered shortages due to the economic blockade imposed in 1990. In May 1996, Iraq received permission from the United Nations to export limited quantities of oil to buy food and medicine.

HISTORY
Many of ancient Iraq's contributions to history and culture occurred during the time of the Sumerians (4000–2500 B.C.). The Sumerians devel-

oped writing, using pictographs that evolved into a standardized script known as cuneiform. They also developed the use of the wheel, techniques of metalworking, and monumental temple architecture. The Sumerians also created the first accurate calendars and the cycles of 60 minutes and 12 hours that we use today to tell time.

Iraq was one of the first areas where an empire was established. This happened during the reign of the Akkadians (2400–1900 B.C.). The empire of the Akkadians was followed by the empires of the Babylonians (2000–1600 B.C.) and the Assyrians (953–613 B.C.). The Assyrian Empire fell in the 7th century B.C. to the Babylonians, who rose to power for a second time under a strong leader, Nebuchadnezzar. During this second period of Babylonian power, the Hanging Gardens, one of the wonders of the ancient world, were built.

The Persians captured Iraq in 539–38 B.C. Iraq then became a province of the Achaemenid Empire until it was conquered by Alexander the Great in 334–27 B.C. Various empires, including that of the Romans, battled over the area until the Persian Sassanid Empire conquered Iraq in the 3rd century A.D.

The Rise of Islam.   Arabs and Muslims regained Iraq in 637. Iraq then became a base for the Arab-Muslim conquest of Iran and Central Asia.

Only scattered remains recall the ancient cities that once flourished in what is now Iraq.

During the Abbasid Caliphate from 750 to 1258, Iraq and its capital city, Baghdad, were the center of the "Golden Age" of Islam and of the Arabs. Iraq suffered a terrible blow in 1258, when it was conquered and plundered by Hulagu, a Mongol khan, or general. Hulagu and another Mongol conqueror, Tamerlane, who sacked Baghdad in 1401, are two of the most infamous names in Iraq's history. From 1514 to 1918, Iraq was under the domination of the Ottoman Empire; much of its modern culture is derived from this period.

Modern History

At the end of World War I, the League of Nations made Iraq a mandate of Britain. Although Iraq became independent in 1932, it remained under Britain's wing until 1958, when a revolution overthrew the British-backed monarchy. From 1958 to 1968, military leaders ruled Iraq. In 1968, the Baath Party came to power. Baathists emphasized Arab unity, socialism, and secularism. The beginnings of Baathist rule coincided with large increases in oil revenues.

Saddam Hussein became Iraq's president and chairman of the ruling military junta in 1979. A year later he invaded Iran in an effort to gain full control of the Shatt al-Arab waterway (Iraq's only outlet to the sea, which it shared with Iran) and to topple Iran's revolutionary regime. The war dragged on for eight years, until a cease-fire was signed in 1988. The war also nearly bankrupted Iraq, which in 1990 found itself unable to raise oil prices high enough to pay off its mounting international debts. In August 1990, when the Gulf states refused to force up the price of oil by pumping less, Hussein invaded and annexed Kuwait. The international reaction to Hussein's invasion was swift. The United Nations imposed an international embargo on Iraq, and troops from the United States and other nations landed in Saudi Arabia to block further aggressive moves. In a strange turn of events, Iraq normalized relations with Iran, but Iran remained neutral in the conflict that followed.

On January 16, 1991, when Hussein failed to withdraw from Kuwait by the U.N.-imposed deadline, a multinational force led by the U.S. launched the Persian Gulf War. Iraq was swiftly driven from Kuwait and agreed on February 27–28 to accept the allied peace terms. Subsequent efforts by Iraq's Kurds and Shiites to topple Hussein failed. The Kurds elected their own assembly in May 1992. In August, as Hussein's forces again attacked Shiite rebels in southern Iraq, the U.S., Britain, and France barred Iraqi planes from flying over the region. In October 1994, Iraqi troops massed along the Kuwaiti border in an apparent effort to force the lifting of the U.N. sanctions on Iraq. U.S. troops and military vessels were sent to the area in 1994 and 1996 to counter Iraqi threats.

GOVERNMENT

After the 1968 revolution, power in Iraq rested with the Revolutionary Command Council (RCC) and the president, who is head of state and commander in chief of the armed forces. An elected National Assembly was created in 1980, and opposition parties gained limited rights in 1991, but Hussein remained in control. In 1995, voters overwhelmingly approved his continuation in office for seven more years and the creation of a senate-like legislative body, half of whose members would be elected.

ROBERT W. OLSON, University of Kentucky

Teheran, Iran's capital and largest city, sits at the foot of the dramatic Elburz Mountains.

IRAN

Iran, known for centuries as Persia, is situated at one of the main crossroads that link Europe and the Middle East with Central Asia. The name Iran means "land of the Aryans"—a reference to the country's original settlers, Persians of Aryan stock who united the country and founded a great empire more than 2,500 years ago.

At its height, in the 6th and 5th centuries B.C., the Iranian (or Persian) Empire ruled nearly half of the ancient civilized world. Ancient Persia greatly influenced European and Asian political organization, science, art, and religion. But after many wars and invasions—by the Greeks, Arabs, Turks, and Mongols—the Iranian Empire collapsed, and the country entered a long period of decline.

The discovery of oil in 1908 gave Iran the means to add an industrial base to its largely agrarian economy. After a series of social, economic, and administrative reforms were instituted in 1961, development moved ahead with almost dizzying speed. Many of the changes brought Western influences to Iran, offending conservative Muslims, who in 1979 helped depose the autocratic shah, or king, who had urged modernization.

THE LAND

Iran has a long coastline along the Persian Gulf, and shares land borders with Azerbaijan, Armenia, Turkmenistan, Iraq, Turkey, Afghanistan, and Pakistan. The Iranian Plateau dominates the majority of this large country.

Somewhat triangular in shape, the plateau is fringed by mountains. The Elburz Range extends east and west—from Turkey to Afghanistan—along Iran's northern frontier. Iran's highest mountain peak, Mount Demavand (18,600 ft.; 5,670 m.), is located in this range. The Zagros Range, Iran's other principal mountain chain, runs southeast along the western border with Turkey and Iraq. It continues southeast along the edge of the plateau and parallel with the Persian Gulf as far as that waterway's southern end in the Strait of Hormuz. Together, the Elburz and Zagros mountains separate the arid interior plateau region, which varies in height from 1,000 to 6,000 ft. (300 to 1,800 m.), from the narrow coastal plains that border the Caspian Sea and the Persian Gulf.

Iran's principal river, the Karun, is located in the western part of the country. It is navigable for about 150 mi. (240 km.) above its mouth at the port city of Khurramshahr. There are several smaller rivers in the north and southwest. In the interior, seasonal streams flow down from the mountains in the spring, when the snow melts. The water that they carry generally evaporates quickly or is lost in the hot sands of the country's two huge deserts, the Dasht-i-Kavir (Great Salt Desert) and Dasht-i-Lut (Great Sand Desert). These two deserts cover one-third of Iran. A few small lakes dot the country, of which Lake Urmia in the north is the largest. In places, Iran's land suffers from deforestation, overgrazing, and the consequent creep of desert soil.

Climate. In the central plateau region, the climate is dry, and the seasons are clearly defined. Throughout most of the year, the days are clear and sunny. Winters can be quite cold, and summers very warm. Along the Caspian coast, the climate is generally warm and humid. In the southern coastal plains, summers are extremely hot, and the humidity is uncomfortably high. Except in the Caspian region, which is well-watered and fertile, the rainfall in Iran is scant. Heavy snows blanket the mountaintops in winter.

Natural Resources. Petroleum is Iran's most important mineral resource. The country's oil reserves are the third largest in the world. Iran's natural-gas deposits, the world's second largest, are found along the shores of the southern Persian Gulf near Bushire. There are large deposits of copper in the northwest, and smaller deposits of coal, iron, lead, zinc, chromite, sulfur, and antimony.

THE PEOPLE

Iran's population represents a considerable mixture of peoples. The majority of these are descendants of the Medes, Persians, and Parthians, the most important of the Aryan peoples who settled in ancient Iran. There are also descendants of other ancient peoples, including the Scythians, Bactrians, and Turks. The dominant ethnic groups are the Farsi-speaking Persians, who make up about 63 percent of the total population, and the Turkic-speaking Azerbaijani in the northwest, accounting for about 18 percent of the population. In addition, there are small minorities of Armenians in the northwest; Arabs along the Persian Gulf;

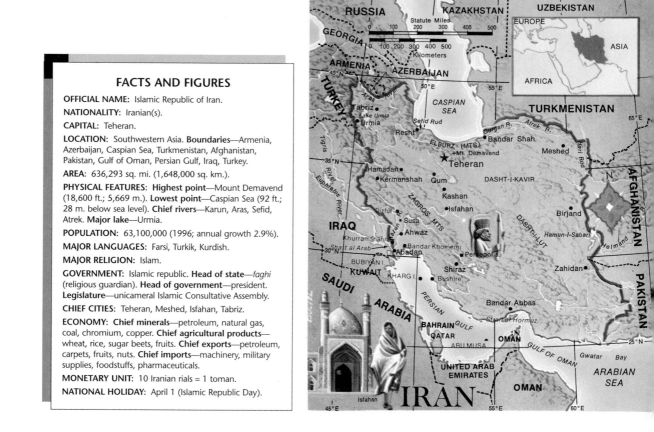

FACTS AND FIGURES

OFFICIAL NAME: Islamic Republic of Iran.

NATIONALITY: Iranian(s).

CAPITAL: Teheran.

LOCATION: Southwestern Asia. **Boundaries**—Armenia, Azerbaijan, Caspian Sea, Turkmenistan, Afghanistan, Pakistan, Gulf of Oman, Persian Gulf, Iraq, Turkey.

AREA: 636,293 sq. mi. (1,648,000 sq. km.).

PHYSICAL FEATURES: Highest point—Mount Demavend (18,600 ft.; 5,669 m.). **Lowest point**—Caspian Sea (92 ft.; 28 m. below sea level). **Chief rivers**—Karun, Aras, Sefid, Atrek. **Major lake**—Urmia.

POPULATION: 63,100,000 (1996; annual growth 2.9%).

MAJOR LANGUAGES: Farsi, Turkik, Kurdish.

MAJOR RELIGION: Islam.

GOVERNMENT: Islamic republic. **Head of state**—*faghi* (religious guardian). **Head of government**—president. **Legislature**—unicameral Islamic Consultative Assembly.

CHIEF CITIES: Teheran, Meshed, Isfahan, Tabriz.

ECONOMY: Chief minerals—petroleum, natural gas, coal, chromium, copper. **Chief agricultural products**—wheat, rice, sugar beets, fruits. **Chief exports**—petroleum, carpets, fruits, nuts. **Chief imports**—machinery, military supplies, foodstuffs, pharmaceuticals.

MONETARY UNIT: 10 Iranian rials = 1 toman.

NATIONAL HOLIDAY: April 1 (Islamic Republic Day).

seminomadic Kurds, Lur, and Bakhtiari in the Zagros Mountains; and nomadic Baluchi along the arid eastern border with Pakistan.

Language. Most Iranians speak Farsi (Persian), an Indo-European language that has changed very little over the centuries. Farsi is Iran's official language and is taught in all schools. It has been greatly influenced by Arabic, and it is written in Arabic script, from right to left. In northwestern Iran, a Turkish dialect is spoken. Certain segments of Iranian society, including the Kurds, Lur, Gilaki, and Mazanderani, speak different Farsi dialects.

Religion. Nearly all Iranians are Muslims. The official state religion under the 1979 constitution is Islam of the Shi'ite sect, the branch of Islam to which 95 percent of all Iranians belong. About 4 percent of the nation—mostly Arabs, Kurds, and other minorities—are members of Islam's Sunni branch. Many of the more than 20,000 mosques in the country are ancient buildings of rare beauty.

Small numbers of Christians and Zoroastrians also practice their faiths. The 30,000 Zoroastrians are followers of the religion that was founded in Iran and that was dominant there until the Arab conquest during the 600s. Zoroastrians believe that there are two competing spiritual forces in the universe. One force is said to represent truth and light; the other, darkness and lies.

Way of Life. Today, nearly 60 percent of all Iranians live in cities. Before World War I, more than 20 percent of the people were

The curriculum in Iranian schools emphasizes religion and the country's Islamic traditions.

nomads who wandered about the desert in search of pastureland for their horses, sheep, and donkeys. But by the 1970s, most of the nomadic people had given up their traditional way of life. Many of them now work in the oil industry, or have taken jobs in the cities.

The Iranian family is a very close-knit unit. At its center is the father or another older male, who is known as the master *(aga)*. He is absolute ruler in his home and commands total respect and obedience.

Large families are the rule in Iran, and male children are particularly desired so that the family line can be continued. Where the old traditions are still followed, it is usual for sons to remain in the family home even after they are married.

Mutton, chicken, rice, and cheese are the most common Iranian foods. The national drink is tea, which is grown on the hilly slopes around the Caspian Sea. A great delicacy is caviar, made from the eggs of the sturgeon.

As in most Muslim societies, women in Iran generally enjoy fewer rights and freedoms than do men. During modernization drives in the 1950s and 1960s, women were granted the right to vote, the Muslim practice that allowed men to have more than one wife (polygyny) at a time was outlawed, and laws were passed to protect women from being divorced and abandoned at will by their husbands. Educational opportunities for women were improved at all levels. At the same time, many women abandoned traditional Muslim roles. They gave up the custom of wearing a veil over their faces in public and began working outside their homes.

Islamic fundamentalists opposed these changes. They declared the new life-styles inconsistent with Islamic teachings. When these conservative Muslims came to power in 1979, they restored a husband's right to divorce his wife at will. They also decreed that all children below the university level be taught in either all-boy or all-girl schools. Women retained their right to vote. But the government outlawed "Western" practices such as drinking alcoholic beverages, dancing and singing in public places, and mixed swimming at beaches and pools. Western clothing styles are considered "immodest," especially for women. The government encourages traditional garb—cotton shirts and baggy trousers for men, the *chador* for women. The *chador* is a long cloth used as a head covering, wraparound, and sometimes as a veil.

Yet women remain very much a part of Iranian society. At Teheran's medical college, 30 percent of the students are women, as are 20 percent of the faculty. Ten percent of the nation's electrical-engineering students are women.

Leisure Time. Iranians celebrate various Islamic religious holidays, including the birthday of the prophet Muhammad, and Ramadan, the Muslim month of fasting. Other events include Islamic Republic Day and the New Year. The biggest festival time is the New Year, which in Iran falls on the first day of spring. The New Year is celebrated for 13 days and includes family gatherings, gift giving, and country outings. Iranians are very fond of sports and games. Since ancient times, the people of Iran have been skilled hunters, polo players, and wrestlers. Iranians also enjoy playing chess, which originated in Iran and India.

Cities. Teheran (also spelled Tehran) is the capital of Iran. With about 10 million residents, it is by a wide margin the nation's largest city. It is situated at the foot of the Elburz Mountains in the northern part of the country. A caravan town before 1910, Teheran has since developed into a modern industrial and commercial city; many of its newer areas have a distinctly European layout.

Tabriz, situated near Lake Urmia in the northwest, is another of Iran's most important cities. Tabriz is noted for the production of Persian rugs of high quality and has a number of other industries. Other major urban centers include the former capital city of Isfahan, in central Iran, and Meshed, the capital of Khorasan province in the northeast.

Art and Literature. Iranian literature, which has achieved worldwide recognition, reached its peak from the 900s to the 1500s. Many significant works of history, philosophy, mathematics, medicine, astronomy, and poetry were written during this period—despite the fact that it was a time of wars, invasions, and internal conflict.

Among the most distinguished of the classical writers were Firdausi (A.D. 940?–?1020), the author of the *Book of Kings,* an epic poem of 60,000 couplets, and the poets Rumi (1207–73), Saadi (1184?–1291), and Hafiz (1324?–?88). The most famous Iranian poet was Omar Khayyám (?–1123), whose poem *The Rubáiyát* has been widely read in the Western world. Omar Khayyám was also a respected mathematician and astronomer. Most of the classical Iranian writers wrote in Farsi, employing

The huge Abadan refinery processes hundreds of thousands of barrels of oil each day.

only a small number of Arabic words. However, since Arabic was the scientific language of the time, the most eminent Persian physicians and philosophers wrote in Arabic.

Ancient Persian architects pioneered in the development of the vault and dome and other architectural styles. The builders of that time solved the problem of building a round dome over a square base. Today, only the ruins of the beautiful ancient Persian capitals of Persepolis and Susa remain, but the influence of Persian architecture can be seen in mosques and other buildings throughout the Middle East.

Perhaps the best-known artistic creations of Iran—because they are eagerly sought after in the Western countries—are the famous hand-woven Persian rugs and carpets. Carpet weaving is a skill in which Iranians have excelled since ancient times, and it continues to be an important and profitable craft.

ECONOMY

Iran's oil-based economy, which grew rapidly during the 1960s and 1970s, lost its forward motion during the 1980s. Iran had long relied on revenues from the sale of oil abroad to modernize its military, pay for land-reform programs, and to build such things as roads and telephone lines to encourage communication and industrial growth. But oil revenues tumbled during the war with Iraq, and were further reduced by a slump in oil prices that began in 1985. By 1989, oil income amounted to about $10 billion, half its level in 1984.

Another shock to the economy was the decision in 1979 to nationalize banks and major industries. The government takeover led to a good deal of mismanagement by inexperienced officials. Thus, in 1990, Iranians were experiencing shortages in essential food and consumer goods, soaring prices, and high unemployment. All the while, the population was growing at a rate that would double its size in 20 years.

Farming.   Agriculture, which involves about 40 percent of Iran's workers, also suffered during the 1980s. Shortages of equipment and materials, from fertilizer to water pumps, depressed farm output. So did a requirement enacted after the Islamic revolution that farmers sell crops to the government at fixed prices.

Because of the dry climate in much of Iran, no more than 12 percent of the land is currently cultivated. Irrigated farms provide most of the country's food, but there is also some rain-fed agriculture in the populous northwest. Most farms are small. Wheat is the chief crop, and rice, barley, and other grains are also grown. Sugar beets, used primarily for making sugar, are grown, with the residue from the sugar-making process supporting a modern livestock industry. Cotton, tea, fruits, nuts, and vegetables are other cash crops. Sheep and goats are raised by largely self-sufficient desert nomads. Fishing is of minor importance, but some caviar is produced in the Caspian Sea.

Industry.   About 33 percent of the labor force works in mining, manufacturing, and commerce. Oil is the chief mineral product and also Iran's leading export, bringing in 90 percent of the foreign currency the country needs to pay for imports. At the end of the war with Iraq, in 1988, oil production was only about half what it had been in 1980. The oil industry has spawned a large petrochemical industry, also damaged by the war, which produces fertilizers, plastics, and artificial fibers. Metals, machine tools, and carpets are other manufactures. The government is a major employer, with more than half a million men in uniform.

Iran's agricultural production is insufficient to meet the country's demand for food.

In ancient days, Persepolis, now in ruins, was the ceremonial capital of the Persian Empire.

HISTORY

Iran was settled some 3,500 to 4,000 years ago by Aryan people who migrated from the region around the Aral Sea, in what is now Kazakhstan and Uzbekistan. During the first 1,000 years of Iranian history, several kingdoms rose and fell. In the 6th century B.C., King Cyrus the Great, of the Persian Achaemenid dynasty, defeated the rival Medes in northern Iran and united the Iranian people. Under Cyrus's rule, Persian armies conquered all of the present Middle East and Central Asia as far as what is now Pakistan. The empire founded by Cyrus flourished for more than two centuries until it was overthrown in the 4th century B.C. by Alexander the Great. Alexander and his successors established a new dynasty and extended Greek culture throughout the area.

Greek rule lasted until the 2nd century B.C., when the Parthians (a people related to the Iranians) gained control. After 350 years of rule, the Parthians were defeated by the Sassanians, who established another Persian dynasty and turned back Roman invasions. The Sassanian period (A.D. 224–641) saw a revival of Persian culture and nationalism.

Coming of Islam. During the 600s, Arab warriors swept across the Iranian Plateau and toppled the Sassanid dynasty. The Arab conquerors introduced the Arabic script and Islamic religion, which replaced Zoroastrianism as the principal faith of the Iranians.

Arab domination continued for several centuries, until the Islamic empire began to fall apart. The Arabs were followed by other foreign invaders. From about A.D. 1040 to 1500, Iran witnessed successive waves of intruders. Following a mainly peaceful movement into the area by Seljuk Turks, the Mongols under Genghis Khan and the Tatars under Tamerlane (Timur the Lame) overran the country. Iran's cities were plundered, and the countryside was left desolate.

The Safavid dynasty (1499–1722) restored a measure of Persia's former greatness. Shah Abbas I (the Great) (ruled 1587–1629), the most outstanding of the Safavid rulers, restored the cities, built new roads, and stabilized the government. Isfahan, the capital, was made into one of the world's most beautiful cities. Shah Abbas established the Shi'ite sect of the Islamic faith as the state religion and used religious zeal as a unifying force.

The Peacock Throne. The Safavid dynasty crumbled after an invasion by the Afghans in 1722. For a brief period under Nadir Shah (ruled 1736–47), Iran again became a military power. Persian armies conquered Afghanistan and reached as far as Delhi, in India. Among the treasures brought back after these conquests was the famed jewel-studded Peacock Throne. It is now preserved in a museum in Teheran, which became Iran's capital in 1788. In the 1790s, the Qajar dynasty emerged to rule Iran until after World War I.

In the 1800s, Russia, Britain, and other Western powers became involved in Iranian affairs. After two wars (1801–13 and 1825–28), Russia gained control of all Iranian land north of the Aras River. In the early 1900s, Britain acquired commercial rights to the major Iranian oil fields.

Pahlavi Dynasty. To defend their threatened independence, the Iranian people began a movement for internal reform. The Constitution of 1906 provided for representative government, and modernization efforts increased after World War I. In 1921, Reza Khan seized control of the government and eventually became prime minister. In 1925, changing his name to Pahlavi, Reza Khan was crowned shah. During World War II, he sided with Germany. When the Allies conquered Iran in 1941, he was forced to abdicate in favor of his son, Mohammad Reza Pahlavi.

A nationalist leader, Prime Minister Mohammed Mossadegh, tried to nationalize the oil industry in 1951. With the help of British and American oil interests, the Shah deposed Mossadegh in 1953. A consortium (association) of eight foreign oil companies was then granted oil-drilling rights in Iran. Using the increasing oil revenues, the Shah promoted modernization of Iran. He encouraged new technologies, built up a modern military, and widened educational and other rights for women. He also began redistributing the lands of the wealthy, often absentee, landowners among the poor.

The economy prospered under the Shah, but conservative Shi'ite religious leaders opposed the "Western" ways and new freedoms as contradictory to the traditional teachings of Islam. Rising world oil prices helped the Shah to accelerate his modernization program in the 1970s. When opposition from religious leaders grew, he made Iran a single-party state, with no opposition parties, and began to rule more autocratically. All opposition was suppressed through SAVAK, his hated secret police.

Islamic Revolution. The unpopularity of the Shah reached a crisis level in January 1979, and he fled the country. Religious leader Ayatollah Ruholla Khomeini, exiled in 1964 for opposition to the Shah, returned in February 1979, and transformed Iran into an Islamic republic in April. Iranian students demanded the return of the Shah, who was receiving medical treatment in the United States. They seized the United States embassy in Teheran on November 7, 1979, and held Americans there hostage for 444 days. The Shah died in July 1980, nearly six months before the hostages were released in January 1981.

The funeral of Iranian leader Ayatollah Khomeini in 1989 drew millions of distraught mourners.

Neighboring Iraq took advantage of the chaos and invaded Iran in September 1980. Among other things, it hoped to gain control of the Shatt al-Arab waterway that serves as a border between the two nations. Iran stopped the invasion and went on the offensive, but the war eventually settled into stalemate. About 1 million lives were lost. In 1988 a cease-fire was finally signed. Later, after its 1990 invasion of Kuwait was thwarted by multinational armed forces, Iraq agreed to return to Iran all prisoners and territory taken during the Iran-Iraq War. The countries later restored diplomatic ties. Iran remained neutral in the 1991 Gulf War.

GOVERNMENT

The 1979 constitution imposed Islamic law on every aspect of Iranian life and granted great powers to a supreme religious leader, or *faghi*. Among other powers, the *faghi* commands the armed forces, screens candidates for president, and appoints to the highest court judges who are experts in Muslim law.

The constitution also set up a one-house legislature, the Majlis. The 270 members of the Majlis, the bulk of them Muslim clergymen, are elected for four years. Until 1989, the elected president and a prime minister approved by the Majlis ran the government. In 1989, the post of prime minister was abolished, strengthening the president's role. Hojatolislam Hashemi Rafsanjani, the speaker of the Majlis, was elected to a four-year term as president in July 1989. His predecessor, Ali Khamenei, took Ayatollah Khomeini's place as the nation's supreme religious leader. Rafsanjani moved to liberalize the economy and end Iran's diplomatic isolation. He was reelected in 1993, but his support was eroded by opposition from radical clerics and public discontent with the economy.

MEHDI VAKIL, Former Ambassador of Iran to the United Nations

In much of South Asia, the marketplace is the focal point for both economic and social activity.

SOUTH ASIA

At the core of South Asia are six nations renowned for their diverse cultures and varied terrain: India, Pakistan, Bangladesh, Nepal, Bhutan, and Sri Lanka. And though situated on South Asia's fringes, two other nations are usually considered part of the region. They are the Maldives, a string of coral islands southwest of Sri Lanka, and Afghanistan, whose borders reach no farther west than Pakistan's.

All these nations are independent, and, to some degree, all are isolated from the rest of the Asian landmass by mountains, ocean, or both. Because of this isolation, geographers often refer to the core of South Asia as the Indian subcontinent. Protected from all but the most determined invaders for thousands of years, the subcontinent has been an incubator for a number of unique cultures and religions that continue to fascinate and instruct the world.

THE LAND

South Asia borders Iran on the west, Turkmenistan, Uzbekistan, Tajikistan, and China on the north, and Myanmar (formerly Burma) on the east. Most of India and parts of Bangladesh and Pakistan sit on a massive peninsula that juts south into the Indian Ocean. Two of this ocean's fingers, the Arabian Sea and the Bay of Bengal, hug the peninsula's western and eastern shores.

The island nation of Sri Lanka, just south of India, is an extension of the continental landmass. The more than 1,000 islands of the Maldives lie several hundred miles southwest of the peninsula.

South Asia's physical landscape is incredibly diverse. Its more than 1,545,000 sq. mi. (4,000,000 sq. km.) of land encompass tall mountains, desert wastelands, heavily populated flood plains, and enormous, densely packed cities. Geographers divide the subcontinent into three basic divisions: the Deccan Plateau, the Northern Mountain Rim, and the Indo-Gangetic Plain.

Deccan Plateau. This region slopes eastward from the Aravalli Range in northwest India and covers most of central and south India. Averaging 1,968 ft. (600 m.) in height, the plateau consists of several mountain ranges. The Vindhya and Satpura ranges are the traditional dividing lines between north and south India. The Western Ghats and the Eastern Ghats parallel the peninsula's shoreline. A narrow coastal plain separates the Western and Eastern Ghats from the coast on the southwest and the east, where river deltas and elaborate irrigation schemes are vital to rice production. In the northeast, rich volcanic soils nourish an impressive cotton crop.

The Thar Desert, also known as the Great Indian Desert, lies to the west of the Aravalli Range. It extends south into the Rann of Kutch and the Kathiawar Peninsula. The southern portion of the border between India and Pakistan meanders through this arid terrain.

Northern Mountain Rim. The center of this rim is dominated by the Himalayas, a great wall of mountains in the north. Ninety-five Himalayan peaks reach over 24,600 ft. (7,500 m.). These magnificent mountains extend about 1,488 mi. (2,400 km.) from the Pamir Range in the northwest to the boundary between China and the Indian state of Assam in the east.

The Himalayas are not a single continuous range. They are composed of three parallel ranges, with the highest mountains generally

Local mountaineers called Sherpas help lead mountain-climbing expeditions in the Himalayas.

SOUTH ASIA'S "HOUSE OF SNOW"

Majestic and awe-inspiring, the Himalaya Mountains form a natural wall, 100 to 150 mi. (160 to 240 km.) in width, between China in the north and India in the south. Located within the Himalayas are the Kingdom of Nepal and the much smaller Kingdom of Bhutan. At their highest level, the mountains rise like giant, snowcapped spires, often to well over 20,000 ft. (6,000 m.). Mount Everest, the world's highest mountain, soars nearly 5.5 mi. (8.8 km.) into the sky at the Nepal-China border. The name "Himalaya" means "the house of snow," and comes from the Sanskrit words *hima* ("snow") and *alaya* ("abode").

The Himalayan People. Most of the mountain people are ethnically related to the Chinese, Mongolian, and Indian peoples. They look upon the mountains with reverence, believing that gods, spirits, and strange beings live among the tall peaks.

found in the north. In the northernmost range, Great Himalayas, most of the peaks are snowcapped year round. The southernmost of the Himalayas is the Siwalik Range, a series of foothills that serve as the northern boundary of the Indus and Ganges plains.

The Himalayan kingdoms of Nepal and Bhutan are sandwiched between India and Xizang (Tibet). The world's highest point, Mount Everest, rises along the border of Nepal and Xizang in the Karakoram Range, which is near but not part of the Himalayas.

The Himalayas are the source of South Asia's greatest rivers. The Indus and Brahmaputra rivers originate in Xizang. The Ganges River also begins high in the Himalayas, inside India.

The western portion of the subcontinent's northern rim includes several mountain ranges in Pakistan and Afghanistan. Two of them, the Sulaiman and Kirthar ranges, form the western border of the Indus Plain. The Toba Kakar Range is located farther west, along Pakistan's border with Afghanistan.

The eastern section of the northern rim encompasses the Assam-Burma ranges, hill systems that stretch along India's border with Myanmar (Burma). Far lower than the Himalayas, these hills are nonetheless extremely difficult to cross, even along passes between them.

Indo-Gangetic Plain. This plain falls between the Northern Mountain Rim and the Deccan Plateau. It sweeps in an arc from the Arabian Sea to the Bay of Bengal and actually consists of two plains. One is centered around the Indus River and its tributaries in Pakistan. The other, in north-

---

They support themselves mainly as farmers and herders. On terraced slopes, they grow rice, corn, wheat, and barley at altitudes of up to 8,000 ft. (2,400 m.). They graze their sheep, goats, yaks, and other livestock on grassy slopes. Hunting, timber cutting, and tourism also provide income.

The Mountains. The Himalayas were thrust out of the earth some 60 million years ago. The parallel folds that were created are now the three ranges of the Himalayas. The first of these are the Outer Himalayas. Heavily forested in some areas, this relatively low chain of mountains, with elevations up to 4,000 ft. (1,200 m.), rims the northern Indian plains. Beyond the Outer Himalayas are the Middle Himalayas, which rise to heights of over 15,000 ft. (4,600 m.). The last range is the Great Himalayas, whose peaks start at about 18,000 ft. (5,500 m.) and reach a maximum elevation at Mount Everest, which looms above the clouds at 29,028 ft. (8,848 m.).

A fourth chain, the Karakoram range, is often associated with the Himalayas. It lies just north of the western fringe of the Great Himalayas.

Rivers. Several major rivers run through the Himalayas, including the Indus, which marks the ranges' western limit. The Tsangpo runs eastward through Xizang (Tibet) until it becomes the Brahmaputra at the eastern edge of the mountains. The Ganges, India's most sacred river, also begins in the Himalayas.

Animal and Plant Life. Dense jungles and swamps cover the valley floors of the Outer Himalayas, and various plants and trees are found up to about 12,000 ft. (3,700 m.). Tigers and leopards prowl about the forests, as do monkeys and elephants. The most useful animal in the Himalayas is the yak, a shaggy-haired, oxlike creature. Yaks are used as beasts of burden or are ridden like horses. Yak meat and milk are consumed by the Himalayan people, and the animal's hide and hair are used to make clothing and tentlike shelters.

Reviewed by P. P. KARAN, University of Kentucky; author, *The Himalayan Kingdoms*

east India and Bangladesh, has been formed over the millennia by the Ganges and its tributaries and by the powerful Brahmaputra. These intensively cultivated plains are among the most densely populated places in the world.

Climate. Almost all of South Asia experiences a monsoon climate, marked by relatively dry winters and rainy summers. During the summer, winds coming from the southwest carry moisture-laden air over the subcontinent. These winds miss the Thar Desert, western Pakistan, and Afghanistan, leaving South Asia's northwest relatively dry.

In the winter, cold air blows down from the northeast, dropping snow on the Himalayas, and rain on the peninsula's southeastern coast and on northern Sri Lanka. The subcontinent's northwest gets much of its rainfall from December through April. The Maldives have a tropical climate, with frequent, abundant rainfall.

THE PEOPLE

About 1,267,000,000 people—roughly one out of every five people in the world—lived in South Asia in 1996. Despite the population's enor-

"MOTHER GANGES"

The Ganges is India's principal river and one of the longest in the world. But to millions of Indian Hindus, the Ganges is far more. It is *Ganga Mai* ("mother Ganges"), a sacred river whose waters are believed capable of cleansing the soul of all sins and healing the body of all ills. Each year, tens of thousands of the Hindu faithful make pilgrimages in order to bathe in the Ganges.

Many Hindu temples line the banks of the Ganges. Flights of stairs *(ghats)* provide access to the holy waters and a place to sit and pray. Hindu funeral services are held on the *ghats*. The dead are cremated and their ashes scattered over the river.

The Ganges begins in the Himalayas, some 10,000 ft. (3,000 m.) above sea level. Fed by melting snows and glaciers, it winds its way through deep mountain gorges until it enters the Ganges Plain at Hardwar. Then the river runs in a generally southeasterly arc across northern India and Bangladesh, finally emptying into the Bay of Bengal. During its nearly 1,600-mi. (2,575-km.) course, it flows past Allahabad, Banaras, and Kanpur. In Bangladesh, it joins with the Brahmaputra to form a vast, swampy delta. The major tributaries of the

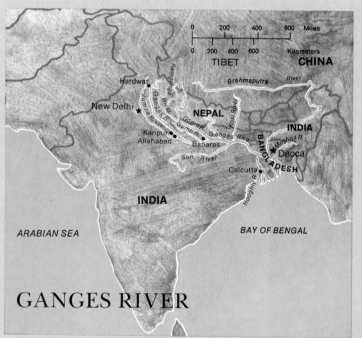

GANGES RIVER

Ganges are the Jumna, Son, Ramganga, Gogra, Gumti, and Kosi rivers.

Together with its branches, the Ganges waters an area that covers about one-quarter of all India and a large part of Bangladesh. Millions of farmers use these waters to irrigate their fields of rice and wheat.

Reviewed by B. G. GOKHALE, Director, Asian Studies Program, Wake Forest University

mous size, most South Asians share similar physical traits: dark skin, black hair, and prominent brown eyes.

Regional differences do exist, however. People in the northwest are relatively light-skinned, while those in the northeast often have noticeable Mongoloid features—high cheekbones and round faces. People in southern India and Sri Lanka tend to be darker-skinned and more slightly built than people from the north. Yet, compared with religious and regional ties, physical differences have little impact on the way South Asians think about themselves and each other.

Religion. The region is home to large groups of Hindus, Muslims, Christians, Buddhists, Sikhs, Jains, and Parsis. Religions often determine South Asians' names, what they eat and wear, their conception of the proper role of women, how they spend their leisure time, and many other behaviors. In the case of predominantly Hindu India and Muslim Pakistan and Bangladesh, religion has even decided South Asians' nationalities.

Hinduism is the predominant religion in Nepal and India, where it has been important for at least 3,500 years. Hindus worship many gods and are tolerant of different forms of worship both within and outside their religion. Hindu culture is responsible for India's caste system, with its hereditary classes of priests, warriors, merchants, and peasants. At the bottom of this social ladder are the "untouchables," landless laborers and their families. Finding ways to reduce the discrimination that results from these distinctions is a problem that has troubled India's secular governments since independence in 1947.

Islam has the second-most followers in South Asia, after Hinduism. It is the main religion in Bangladesh, Pakistan, Maldives, and Afghanistan; and in India, 11 percent of the population is Muslim. During the 700s, Islam made inroads into what is today Pakistan. But it was not until the Muslim occupation of Delhi in 1206 that Islam was promoted throughout the region, often by force. It was particularly popular among lower-caste Hindus, who were attracted to the religion by its message of equality.

Buddhism nearly eclipsed Hinduism about 1,500 to 2,000 years ago because of its optimistic outlook and rejection of castes. During the 1200s, Muslim sheiks suppressed all religions except Islam. Buddhism nearly died out in India, as did a less popular indigenous religion, Jainism. The less than one percent of the Indians who are Buddhists live in the north, near Xizang, Bhutan, and Myanmar, which have large Buddhist populations. Buddhism also flourishes in Sri Lanka.

The Buddhism of Xizang and Bhutan contains an admixture of animism, the traditional belief in the world of the spirits. This form of the religion is called Lamaism, or Tibetan Buddhism. Buddhism in Nepal has been enriched with Hindu beliefs and practices.

Sikhism is unique to India, and its adherents live mostly in the state of Punjab, where the religion was established in 1499. A blend of Hinduism and Islam, it attracted many converts from Hinduism with its vision of a casteless society and a world in which humans can control their fates.

For similar reasons, many low-caste Hindus converted to Christianity during the period that Europeans dominated South Asia. Today, about 2 percent of all Indians and 8 percent of all Sri Lankans are Christians.

Regionalism.   More than 75 percent of all South Asians live in the countryside, as their ancestors have for generations. Many share a language, such as Nepalese or Bengali, that is specific to their nation, region, state, or province. Indeed, South Asians speak at least 20 major languages and more than 1,000 dialects. Variations in climate and soil dictate what crops will grow in a given place and thus what the people who live there prefer to eat and even how well they live.

Factors such as these often add up to produce a distinctive regional identity. Compared with northerners, for example, people who live in peninsular India tend to eat spicier food, wear looser clothes, and grant women more equality.

Religious and regional strife are common in South Asia. During the 1980s and early 1990s, Sri Lanka suffered a bloody conflict between its Muslim minority, which has roots in southern India, and the Buddhist majority. In Afghanistan, attempts to secularize the government during this same period provoked devout Muslim villagers to take up arms against the government.

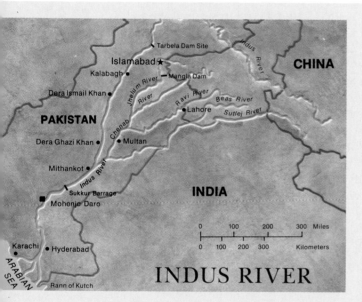

THE INDUS: "KING OF RIVERS"

The Indus is one of the great rivers of Asia. From its starting point amid the jagged mountain peaks of Xizang (Tibet), it flows across Kashmir and down the length of Pakistan into the Arabian Sea. The people of ancient India knew it as "the king of rivers." Its name comes from the Sanskrit word *sindhu*, meaning "ocean" or "great water." Between 2500 and 1500 B.C., a highly advanced culture thrived along the river's lower reaches. It was also in the Indus Plains that the Vedas, Hinduism's most sacred texts, were composed.

The Indus begins its more than 1,900-mi. (3,000-km.) course in the Trans-Himalayas of southwestern Xizang. The river churns its way in a northwesterly direction through high-walled gorges and spectacular mountain valleys. Then it veers sharply to the southwest, breaking through the Hindu Kush Mountains at Tarbela. The Indus enters the Punjab Plain near the city of Kalabagh. Below this point, the river flows parallel to a flat plain that is watered by the Indus and its tributaries. Near the town of Mithankot, the Indus is joined by its main tributaries: the Jhelum, Chenab, Ravi, Beas, and Sutlej rivers. South of the city of Hyderabad, the river divides into several branches, which empty into the Arabian Sea.

During the rainy season, the Indus is dangerously unpredictable, and its swollen waters sometimes overflow its banks for many miles. Except for flood periods, however, irrigation schemes generally make the river too shallow for large vessels. The fertile Indus Valley produces wheat, corn, rice, and a variety of fruits and vegetables.

Reviewed by B. G. GOKHALE, Director, Asian Studies Program, Wake Forest University

Population Pressures.   Throughout South Asia, soaring population growth continually threatens to wipe out hard-won economic gains. Ironically, these gains contributed to population pressures by enabling nations to improve health care. Soon South Asians were living longer. Fewer infants died, increasing the pool of young married people who had children of their own, boosting the birthrate. Health care in India, Pakistan, Maldives, and Sri Lanka has improved the most since the 1940s. Two of these nations, India and Sri Lanka, are also working to lower the birthrate. They have done it, in part, by removing barriers to education and employment for women.

Nonetheless, experts believe that the region's population will reach at least 1.5 billion before it stops growing. Already-struggling governments will have to find ways to provide schooling, health care, and other services for millions more people each year. They will also have to find ways to create many millions of new jobs each year. The result of such pressures can readily be seen in Karachi, Bombay, Calcutta, and other South Asian cities, which are overflowing with people who are both jobless and homeless.

HISTORY

The first people to occupy South Asia were probably related to some of the tribal peoples who live in Southeast Asia today. Only a few of these aboriginal peoples survive, living in the hills and plateaus where their ancestors were driven millennia ago by more powerful peoples.

South Asia's recorded history falls into five general time periods: 3000 to 1500 B.C. (Indus Valley Civilization), 1500 B.C. to A.D. 1206 (Aryan or Hindu Period), 1206 to 1757 (Muslim Rule), 1757 to 1947 (British Colonial Rule), and 1947 to the present (Independence). The articles on the separate nations, especially Pakistan and India, discuss these periods in some detail. What follows is a brief overview.

Indus Valley Civilization.   Between 3000 and 1700–1500 B.C., a dark-skinned, short-statured people called Dravidians established a civilization in the Indus River Valley, in what is now Pakistan. Their empire extended west to Kabul, now the capital of Afghanistan, and as far east as Delhi, the capital of modern India. The empire's two capitals, Mohenjo-Daro and Harappa, sprang up in the center of this prosperous agricultural region. Dravidians traded by sea with the Mesopotamians of Southwest Asia and lived in relative comfort in a number of large towns.

Hindu Aryan Period.   Light-skinned and tall, the Aryans came from Central Asia. A nomadic, stock-raising people, they had little use for towns. From 1700 to 1500 B.C. they drove the Dravidians to the south and east, along the Ganges Plain. The Aryans introduced Hinduism to the region. They enslaved many Dravidians, placing them at the bottom of their caste system, where their descendants remain today.

The Macedonian warrior Alexander the Great conquered Afghanistan in 328 B.C. and then moved into India, occupying the Punjab for two years. Adopting some of the organizational ideas from the invaders, Aryans set up a nation-state in 322 B.C. and founded the Maurya Dynasty. One Mauryan king, Asoka (274–237 B.C.), brought almost all of India under his control. Asoka became a Buddhist and sent missionaries to spread the religion. After Asoka's death, the power of the state diminished and, for nearly 600 years, control of the subcontinent was fragmented.

KASHMIR

KASHMIR

Kashmir's natural beauty masks a troubled land. In 1948, 1965, and again in 1971, Indian and Pakistani troops clashed over what had been a quasi-independent "native state," ruled by a Hindu prince. Today soldiers from both sides stare at one another across the cease-fire line that separates Pakistani-controlled Azad ("free") Kashmir from India's state of Jammu and Kashmir. Inside Jammu and Kashmir, Muslims sometimes clash with Indian troops.

Religion is at the root of Kashmir's woes. In 1947, its Hindu prince chose to make Kashmir part of India. Yet the bulk of his subjects were Muslims, and many of them had hoped to join the new Muslim state of Pakistan.

Many of Kashmir's Muslims still identify strongly with Pakistan today. But sizable Hindu and Buddhist minorities want all of Kashmir to be a part of India.

Land. Kashmir nestles in the Himalaya and Karakoram Mountains in the northeast corner of the Indian subcontinent. Its total area is approximately 86,000 sq. mi.

North India was not reunited until the Gupta Dynasty (ca. A.D. 320–550), a "golden age" during which the arts and sciences flourished. The Gupta kings were Hindus, but Buddhism was widely practiced. After their dynasty fell, central rule disintegrated, and South Asia was split into small kingdoms that were constantly at war with each other.

Muslim Rule. Arab Muslims conquered Sind, today a Pakistani province, in 711. Muslim Turks and Afghans swept into the region and established the Sultanate of Delhi in 1206. In 1526, Babur, an Islamic king from Afghanistan, led a force into India and defeated the sultans. He established Agra as the Indian capital. Babur also established what would become known as the Mogul Empire.

Expanding their rule to the south, the Moguls eventually overextended themselves. Their high taxation of Hindus sparked revolts that severely weakened the empire. After Britain began to occupy the region in 1757, the British kept the Moguls on as puppet rulers for 100 years. In 550 years of rule, Moslems created a legacy of learning, art, and increased trade with the outside world.

British Rule. Europeans had visited and traded with the subcontinent ever since 1498, when Vasco da Gama, a Portuguese explorer, touched India's shores. In 1757, British troops defeated a Bengali king and gradually established control over the entire subcontinent. About

(223,000 sq. km.), including the Indian- and Pakistani-controlled sections and a portion that Pakistan ceded to China in 1963 over India's protests.

The tallest of Kashmir's peaks, second only to Mount Everest, is Mount Godwin Austen, or K2, which rises to 28,250 ft. (8,611 m.) in the Karakoram Range. Several of Pakistan's major rivers—the Chenab, the Jhelum, and the Ravi—begin in the mountains of Kashmir. The Indus River begins in Xizang (Tibet) and flows through Kashmir.

The Vale of Kashmir, the region's most famous scenic wonder, lies in a broad, deep-set Himalayan valley in the southwestern part of the territory. **Srinagar,** Kashmir's largest city, is located in the Vale. The city's artisans produce jewelry, leather goods, silverware, wood carvings, woolen rugs, shawls, and the world-famous cashmere sweaters.

People. People in the Vale, mainly Muslims, are known as Kashmiris. South of the Vale, in the area around the city of Jammu, Hindu people called Dogra are dominant. The major language of the region is Kashmiri.

Farming, sericulture (the raising of silkworms), and lumbering are the main occupations. The richest farmland is in the Vale, where farmers grow rice, wheat, corn, and various fruits and vegetables. In the mountain regions of Gilgit and Ladakh to the north and east, herders raise sheep, goats, ponies, and yaks.

History. For many centuries, Hindu princes ruled many parts of Kashmir. Muslims conquered the southern parts of the region during the 14th century A.D. and spread their faith throughout the area. In 1846, the British colonial rulers confirmed the maharaja Gulab Singh, a Dogra, and his male heirs as the rulers of Kashmir. In 1947, one of these heirs opted to make Kashmir part of India.

The first war between India and Pakistan ended on January 1, 1949, after the United Nations arranged a cease-fire. India was left in control of about two-thirds of Kashmir, including the Vale. Pakistan got to rule the northwestern section of the region, and China later occupied part of the northeast.

Reviewed by P. P. KARAN, University of Kentucky; author, *The Himalayan Kingdoms*

one-third of the area was left in the control of 562 "native states," tiny kingdoms that relied on the British for defense, postal service, railroads, and other needs.

Britain granted independence to Afghanistan in 1919, and to British India in 1947, after partitioning it into two nations: the predominantly Hindu nation of India and the Muslim state of Pakistan. Britain later gave independence to Sri Lanka (1948) and the Maldives (1965). India gave Bhutan its independence in 1949. Nepal had been on its own since 1768.

Since 1947. The problems these nations inherited upon independence—underdeveloped economies, burgeoning populations, ethnic and regional rivalries—continue to dominate their governments' agendas during the 1990s. In some cases, these problems proved insoluble. East Pakistan, feeling shortchanged by the central government in West Pakistan, proclaimed its independence as Bangladesh in 1971. India and Pakistan fought three wars over the former native state of Kashmir, whose ownership remains in dispute.

Despite these setbacks, the region has made enormous social and economic progress since 1947, as the articles on the individual nations point out. For every unsolved problem, South Asians have solved hundreds, perhaps thousands. And they have done it with little loss to the many cultures that make South Asia unlike any other region on Earth.

Traditional shops and bazaars line many streets in Kabul, the capital of Afghanistan.

AFGHANISTAN

A landlocked country at the crossroads of central Asia, Afghanistan has been fought over for thousands of years by a dizzying list of combatants. Alexander the Great conquered most of the country in 328 B.C. In following centuries, Scythians, White Huns, and Turks invaded the land, and, in A.D. 642, Arab armies introduced Islam. The Persian rulers who came next were displaced by Turkic Ghaznavid sultans, who in turn gave way to the Mongols under Genghis Khan. Afghans fought two fierce wars with the British during the 1800s and a third in 1919.

Today, Afghanistan is emerging from still another war, a lengthy civil conflict that for a decade pitted Soviet and Afghan government troops against U.S.-armed *mujahidin,* or "freedom fighters." A third of the nation's citizens crossed into Pakistan and Iran to flee the turmoil. Through it all, the ethnically mixed Afghans, speaking more than 70 languages and dialects, remained fiercely independent, proud of their many heritages and of the nation for which their ancestors shed their blood.

THE LAND

On the map, Afghanistan looks like a tortoise with an outstretched neck. The neck of the tortoise is the most highly elevated part of the country, the Wakhan Panhandle. In this northeastern corner, the ranges of the Hindu Kush climb to the Pamir, a great knot of mountains where Afghanistan, Tajikistan, and China meet. The Hindu Kush slopes southwest into the main body of Afghanistan, forming a broad network of highlands. North of the highlands, forming part of the border with Turkmenistan, Uzbekistan, and Tajikistan, flows the Amu Darya (formerly called the Oxus), one of Asia's chief rivers. The eastern part of Afghanistan is a region of swift-flowing rivers, green and fertile valleys, and highlands. Deserts mark the south and southwest.

Afghanistan is an arid country whose agricultural life depends to a large extent on the amount of snow stored on the mountain slopes from one year to the next. Intricate irrigation systems channel water to most parts of the country. Afghanistan has a continental climate, marked by severe winters, hot summers, and extreme shifts in daily temperature.

THE PEOPLE

Though all of Afghanistan's citizens are called Afghans, its population is made up of a variety of peoples, including Pashtoon, Tajiks, Hazara, Uzbeks, and Turkomans. The Pashtoon (38 percent of all Afghans) and the Tajiks (25 percent) are the major ethnic groups. The Pashtoon speak Pashto, a language related to Farsi. The Tajiks and Hazara (19 percent of the nation) speak Dari, the Afghan form of Farsi. The Hazara are believed to be descendants of the 13th-century Mongol invaders who were led by Genghis Khan. The Uzbeks and Turkomans are of Turkish origin. Pashto is the tongue of about one-third of the population. Dari, spoken by about half of all Afghans, is commonly used in trade.

Islam, the Afghans' common religion, is the nation's main unifying force, pervading all aspects of life, despite government attempts to secularize Afghan society during the 1980s. At various times in the past, the

FACTS AND FIGURES

OFFICIAL NAME: Islamic State of Afghanistan.

NATIONALITY: Afghan(s).

CAPITAL: Kabul.

LOCATION: Southern central Asia. **Boundaries**—Turkmenistan, Uzbekistan, Tajikistan, China, Kashmir, Pakistan, Iran.

AREA: 250,000 sq. mi. (647,500 sq. km.).

PHYSICAL FEATURES: Highest point—peaks rising to more than 20,000 ft. (6,100 m.) in the Hindu Kush. **Lowest point**—Kham-i-ab, 500 ft. (152 m.). **Chief rivers**—Helmand, Amu Darya, Kabul, Hari, Arghandab, Murgab, Farah.

POPULATION: 21,500,000 (1996; annual growth 2.8%).

MAJOR LANGUAGES: Pashtu, Afghan Persian (Dari), Uzbek, Turkmen.

MAJOR RELIGIONS: Sunni Islam, Shi'ite Islam.

GOVERNMENT: Republic. **Head of state**—president. **Head of government**—prime minister. **Legislature**—unicameral Parliament.

CHIEF CITIES: Kabul, Kandahar, Herat.

ECONOMY: Chief minerals—natural gas, oil, coal, copper, talc, barites, sulfur, lead, zinc, iron, salt, gems. **Chief agricultural products**—wheat, fruits, nuts, karakul pelts, wool, mutton. **Industries and products**—textiles, soap, furniture, shoes, fertilizers, cement, carpets. **Chief exports**—fruits and nuts, natural gas, carpets. **Chief imports**—foodstuffs, petroleum products.

MONETARY UNIT: 1 afghani = 100 puls.

NATIONAL HOLIDAY: April 28 (Victory of the Muslim Nation).

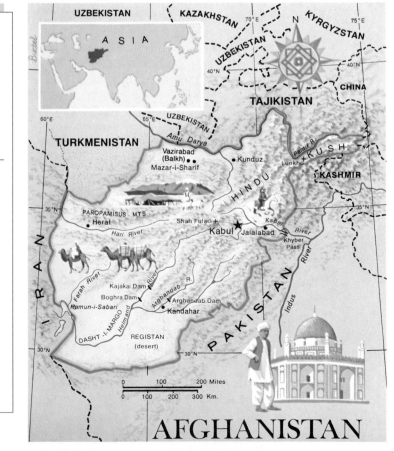

AFGHANISTAN

The twisting Khybur Pass (left), which links Afghanistan with Pakistan, has long been a favorite invasion route into Afghanistan. Once inside Afghanistan, however, foreign armies had to deal with rugged mountains and barren deserts (above), conditions with which the Afghans have long been familiar.

country was a stronghold of the Zoroastrian and Buddhist religions. Legend has it that Zoroaster, the founder of Zoroastrianism, was born in Balkh, probably during the 7th century B.C. Islam reached the country during the 7th century A.D., but it was not until 1895 that the last holdouts against Islam, the Kafirs, were forcibly converted.

The rugged nature of the land has produced a hardy, courageous people strongly identified with sedentary farming and town life. Since its geographic location has made Afghanistan a crossroads for invading armies, the Afghans have also developed excellent fighting qualities. Although they may sometimes appear arrogant and fierce to outsiders, they are friendly and hospitable to strangers and have a keen sense of humor.

Its high ranges and isolated valleys have made Afghanistan a land of many villages and small towns. Although in recent years the cities have expanded greatly, most Afghans still follow age-old customs.

Their Way of Life

A typical house in an Afghan village is square or rectangular and made of mud or mud brick. It is divided into three or four rooms furnished with rugs, pillows, and mattresses. The flat roof is made of poles reinforced with a thick layer of mud, often mixed with straw and chalk. Four walls 9 or 10 ft. (about 3 m.) high are built above the roof, which serves as a sitting room and sleeping porch in hot weather and as a place to dry fruits. More prosperous owners may erect towers on the four corners of their houses, or at least a single tower on one corner. Houses that have such towers are called *qalas*. A *qala* may house one or several family units.

Immediately inside the single large gate, there is a room called the *hujra*, for housing guests and travelers. The *hujra* is also the center of social activities for the *qala*, especially on long winter nights, when families entertain themselves with storytelling and group singing. Here, too, *sohbat* is held—a potluck meal to which everyone contributes. Round loaves of unleavened bread are a staple of the diet, which also includes goat, mutton, beef, chicken, yogurt, rice, and fruit. Most Afghans cook over wood or charcoal fires.

Everyday life centers around the fields, gardens, and vineyards on which the people depend for a living. Men find evening fellowship in the *hujra,* especially in winter. When the weather turns warm, they turn to sports and dancing. Horse racing, *ghosai,* and *buz-kashi* are popular. *Ghosai* is a vigorous wrestling game in which a player tries to reach a goal while nine teammates run interference. Each player hops on one foot and with one hand holds the other foot behind his back. *Buz-kashi* is played by two teams on horseback.

Afghans are gradually adopting Western dress in the cities, but in the villages, people still wear traditional clothing. In general, an Afghan man wears a knee-length shirt, which may be embroidered, over full trousers. In the summer he wears a cotton shawl around his shoulders, and in the winter his coat is a long woolen or quilted *chapan*. The most popular headgear is a turban wound around an embroidered cap, or a karakul (lambskin) cap without the turban.

Afghan women generally wear long-sleeved, ankle-length dresses over full trousers with embroidered ankle bands. A large cloth, or *chawdar,* is draped over the hair. In the cities before 1959, women always

City life revolves around the marketplace, where Afghans buy everything from fruits to fur.

appeared in public in a *chaderi,* a long, sacklike garment that covers the wearer from head to toe. In 1959, however, the government authorized women to appear in public unveiled if they wished.

The brutal war that followed a Communist takeover in 1978 accelerated the change in women's lives. Women became more active in the labor force, in part because of a shortage of male workers. Women are most visible in government posts and in education and medicine, two fields that they came to dominate during the 1980s. In 1990, about 60 percent of the students at Kabul University were women, compared with 10 percent in 1978. Only about 10 percent of the population can read and write, a major obstacle to modernization.

ECONOMY

Afghanistan is one of the world's poorest countries. Its wealth is in the form of mineral deposits, forests, and agricultural products. The minerals include iron ore, natural gas, copper, coal, chromium, oil, lapis lazuli, and small amounts of gold, silver, and rubies. Natural gas is Afghanistan's most important export.

Much of the country's forest wealth has been cut for timber, but there are many valuable nut trees, producing pistachios, pine nuts, walnuts, and almonds. Medicinal plants yield such products as asafetida and castor oil for local use and export.

Although only 15 percent of the land will support crops, farming and the raising of livestock are the nation's most important economic activities. Almost 70 percent of the people are farmers and shepherds. Practically all kinds of grains thrive in Afghanistan. Wheat is the major crop. Melons, apricots, figs, and apples flourish. The vineyards of Herat, Kapisa, and Kandahar yield more than 30 varieties of grapes. Oranges, corn, rice, opium poppies, and cotton also are cultivated.

Most farmers today lead settled lives, but the herders of sheep, camels, and goats still move from place to place in search of pasture. Called Kochis, these nomads may number as many as 1.5 million, or about 9 percent of the population. Karakul sheep are raised for the skins of the young lambs. These skins, prized as fur, are a leading export.

Industry, employing about 10 percent of the work force, is in its infancy in Afghanistan. Afghans produce textiles, soap, furniture, shoes, fertilizer, and cement for domestic use. The famous Afghan rugs and carpets are all made by people working at home.

HISTORY AND GOVERNMENT

In its earliest history, Afghanistan was the home of nomadic tribes. Through the centuries they were overcome by a succession of conquerors—Alexander the Great in the 4th century B.C., Genghis Khan in the 1200s, Tamerlane (Timur) in the 1300s, Baber in the 1500s, and Nadir Shah of Persia in the 1700s.

In 1747, the Pashtoon unified the tribes into an independent nation. During the 1800s, however, the nation was caught between Great Britain and Russia, as these two powers struggled for control of central Asia. In 1879, Britain defeated Afghanistan and took control of its foreign policy. Its boundaries with Russia and British India were agreed on later. During World War I, Afghanistan remained neutral. It regained control of its foreign affairs as a result of the third Anglo-Afghan War in 1919.

From their mountain bases, Afghan *mujahidin*, or holy warriors, fought a long guerrilla war against Soviet forces in Afghanistan. The Soviets finally withdrew the last of their forces in 1989. In 1992 the rebels occupied Kabul and forced President Najibullah, who had had Soviet support, from office. After Najibullah's ouster, Afghanistan became an Islamic republic. Its various rebel groups, however, disagreed on the shape of the new government and began to fight among themselves. Beginning in 1995, a new force called Taliban grew in influence.

During World War II, the country was again neutral. Trouble developed in 1947 between Afghanistan and Pakistan when an area inhabited by Pashtoon was claimed as part of Pakistan. The Afghans felt the area should be independent. The issue remains a source of disagreement.

In 1956, the Afghan government began a program to improve social and economic conditions. Transportation and health care were improved, and schools were built. Dams, reservoirs, and canals were built to provide water for irrigation and hydroelectricity. In 1964 a constitution proposed by King Mohammed Zahir Shah was approved. Afghanistan became a constitutional monarchy. But political dissatisfaction and poor economic conditions led to the military's overthrow of the monarchy in 1973. General Mohammed Daoud Khan, leader of the coup, proclaimed Afghanistan a republic and himself president and prime minister.

Recent Events. Another military coup, in 1978, resulted in the death of Daoud and hundreds of his followers. The military installed a leftist civilian regime, whose Marxist-style reforms ran counter to many Afghans' deep-seated traditions and beliefs. A nationwide rebellion nearly overwhelmed the Afghan army, triggering increased Soviet military assistance. By mid-1979, rebel forces controlled most of the countryside. Two coups—the second taking place two days after a Soviet invasion in late December 1979—left Babrak Karmal in charge. In 1986, Karmal was replaced by Mohammed Najibullah. The last Soviet troops left Afghanistan in 1989, and the *mujahidin* occupied Kabul in April 1992. A constituent assembly elected Burhanuddin Rabbani as president in December and chose a legislature from among its members. Rabbani's chief rival, Gulbuddin Hekmatyar, became prime minister under a March 1993 peace accord, but civil war continued. By 1996, much of the country was controlled by Taliban, which claimed to be an army of religious students seeking to end the disastrous fighting among various rebel groups.

ABDUR-RAHMAN PAZHWAK, Former Representative of Afghanistan to the United Nations

Mosques are the focus of much activity in Pakistan, a primarily Muslim country.

 PAKISTAN

Although Pakistan did not exist as a nation until 1947, within it are areas whose history dates back half a million years to the days when humans first learned to make crude stone tools. Pakistan's land is studded with the remains of ancient cultures and the monuments of past civilizations. Perhaps the most famous of these civilizations is that of the Indus Valley, which flourished between 2500 and 1500 B.C., and whose remains were found at Mohenjo-Daro and Harappa.

Pakistan's present culture bears the bold imprint of its past. Four-thousand-year-old toy carts dug out of the ruins of Mohenjo-Daro could be copies of the bullock carts still plying Sind province's dusty roads. Many pots used today by the village folk around Harappa, an ancient site in Punjab province, are direct descendants of those used 4,000 years ago. Pakistani Muslims still respond to daily calls to prayer, just as their ancestors did many centuries ago, and their way of life is profoundly influenced by Islamic law.

Amid these ancient places and traditions are the cities where 30 percent of all Pakistanis live. Their streets are crowded with automobiles and with men and women rushing to and from work in offices and in factories. The "noise of democracy"—the give-and-take of public debate—has brought the mass media to life since the end of authoritarian rule in the late 1980s. Despite widespread poverty and illiteracy and one of the world's fastest-growing populations, Pakistan is in rapid transition, trying to adapt its traditional culture to the demands of modern economic development.

THE LAND

Pakistan stretches 1,000 mi. (1,600 km.) from the Arabian Sea in the south to the great Himalayan Mountains in the north. It is bounded by the Arabian Sea in the south, Iran in the west, Afghanistan in the northwest, China in the north, and India in the east and southeast. Part of the northern boundary covers the disputed territory of Jammu and Kashmir, which both India and Pakistan claim. Pakistan calls the self-governing section it has long occupied Azad ("free") Kashmir.

Pakistan's four provinces are the Punjab, Sind, the North-West Frontier, and Baluchistan. The North-West Frontier contains several Tribal Areas, which Pathan (or Pashtun) tribes largely govern themselves.

Geographically, Pakistan can be divided into three main regions. First is the region of the northern highlands, the site of some of the

Small villages dot the rugged landscape near Pakistan's border with Afghanistan.

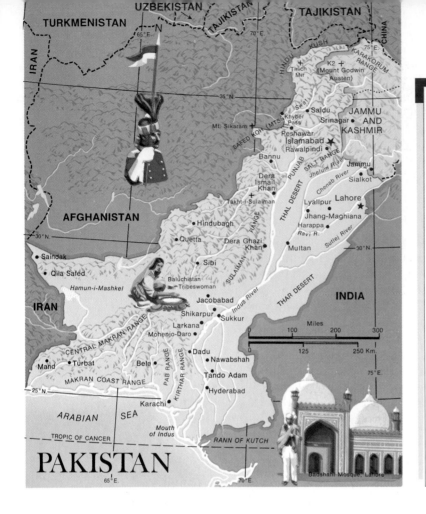

world's tallest mountains. K-2, the world's highest peak after Mt. Everest, is located in the remote Himalayan region of Baltistan. The north's rugged and well-forested mountains abound in wildlife—everything from the majestic Marco Polo sheep to the endangered snow leopard.

To the west of the Indus River is the second main region, made up of the Baluchistan Plateau. High mountain ridges rise from the plateau and reach a maximum height of 11,290 ft. (3,441 m.) at Takht-i-Sulaiman. The Baluchistan Plateau is mostly arid and barren, although some valleys have water and are cultivated. This region is home to the world's largest juniper forest.

Pakistan's third major region is the Indus River plain on the river's eastern side. The plain is fertile near the reaches of the Indus River and its tributaries. It becomes drier as it approaches the Thar Desert in the southeast. A second desert, the Thal, lies just west of the Indus River, bordering the fertile plains of Punjab. Wildlife such as bears, wildcats, and hyenas live in the plains area.

The most important river in Pakistan is the Indus, which rises in Tibet and, after flowing through mountains and ravines, enters the plains of Pakistan. (See sidebar on the Indus, page 170.) The Indus, together with its tributaries, is the mainstay of Pakistan's agriculture, which depends upon an extensive network of irrigation canals. Because of limited rainfall, mountain snow is an important source of water for the rivers that feed the canals. (See sidebar on irrigation, facing page.)

Climate

Pakistan's climate is dominated by the Asiatic monsoon. The hottest season stretches from mid-April to mid-July. Dry winds that often carry sand fan the Indus Valley in the south, where the temperatures are highest. Rain falls steadily from mid-July to mid-September. Summer rains and winter snow cool the mountains and foothills of the north and west, where subfreezing winter temperatures are common. Temperatures on the eastern plains also vary widely from season to season, ranging from 114° F. (46° C.) in June to 40° F. (4° C.) in January.

THE PEOPLE

Seven out of 10 Pakistanis live in the lowlands that abut the Indus River and its tributaries, where abundant water helps farming and industry flourish. More than half of all Pakistani workers make their living farming and fishing. About 13 percent work in mining and manufacturing.

Punjabis are the majority ethnic group, at 60 to 70 percent of the population, and they dominate the government and military. Sindhi are the second-largest ethnic group. Pathans are the next-largest group, and they share linguistic and cultural ties with Afghanistan. Next come the Baluchi of Baluchistan, and the Muhajirs, Urdu-speaking Indian refugees and their descendants.

Islam is the religion of 97 percent of the population. Most Muslims follow Islam's Sunni branch. Their lives are organized around the village mullahs and the learned *ulema,* specialists in Islamic law who pass judgment on matters of faith and law.

GROWING CROPS WITHOUT RAIN

Pakistan is one of the few countries in the world with too little rainfall to grow its crops. For thousands of years, however, the region has been a center of agricultural activity. It owes its agricultural success to increasingly elaborate irrigation schemes that draw water from the Indus River and its tributaries.

Pakistan's most fertile fields are found in the plains along the Indus River in the province of Punjab, which means "the five waters." Here the Indus and its main tributaries—the Jhelum, Chenab, Ravi, Beas, and Sutlej—form the backbone of the world's largest irrigation system.

The system was extensively developed under British rule. But it was not until 1967, two decades after independence, that the system's first major water-storage basin was formed behind the Mangla Dam. Used for flood control, the dam also powers an enormous hydroelectric power station.

The Tarbela Dam at Tarbela, at the point where the Indus breaks through the mountains of the Hindu Kush, is another essential link in the Punjabi irrigation system. The world's largest earthwork dam, it was completed in the 1970s. The dam does double duty, controlling floods and making sufficient water available at critical times when the Punjab's principal crops need it most.

Water from the Indus and its tributaries is a continuing source of friction between Pakistan and India. The 1960 Indus Water Treaty awarded India control of the main eastern tributaries, the Ravi, Beas, and Sutlej. Pakistan won control of the Indus and its western tributaries, the Jhelum and Chenab. But disputes over rights to the water still simmer, as the two nations' growing populations and thirsty industries continue to increase their demands for water.

Although more than half the population engages in some sort of farming, only 20 percent of Pakistan's land area is under cultivation. Farmers depend on oxen (above) as the principal beasts of burden. Pakistani farmers produce large amounts of grain (left) both for export and for domestic consumption.

About 20 percent of all Pakistanis belong to the Shi'ite branch of Islam. Authority under Shi'ite Islam is like a pyramid, with religious leaders called grand ayatollahs at the top. Sunnis and Shi'ites are often at odds, sometimes violently.

About 3 percent of all Pakistanis are Christians, Hindus, or adherents of lesser-known religions, such as Ahmadism. Ahmadis call themselves Muslim, but Pakistani law regards them as heretics—people whose beliefs depart from accepted doctrine. Ahmadis have suffered much abuse for their beliefs.

Way of Life

Pakistani Homes. Living conditions in Pakistan range from inadequate to opulent. Wealthy landowners, industrialists, and others may live in large, comfortable villas with all modern conveniences, including swimming pools and Jacuzzis. Middle-income families often live in apartments in the cities of Pakistan, while some have saved enough money to build houses. In the villages, the more typical houses are built of well-kneaded mud or unbaked bricks and usually have flat roofs. Many villages receive no electric service, and villagers must draw their water from wells rather than from pipes brought into the home.

   Food.   Wheat bread is Pakistan's staple food. *Chapati,* flat wheat bread baked in a *tandoor,* or brick oven, are eaten at practically every meal. The breads are supplemented with meat and vegetables. Pakistanis drink tea in great quantities. They often serve it with milk and sugar. On special occasions, they will flavor it with cardamom or other spices. *Dahi,* the Pakistani form of yogurt, is also popular. For meat, *kabobs*—broiled,

Housing conditions in Pakistan have generally improved over the last several years. In rural areas, many people reside in small, closely spaced houses (right). In the capital city of Islamabad, modern developments have sprung up to house the growing middle class (below).

The main shopping district in Rawalpindi and other Pakistani cities is the bazaar.

baked, or fried meat, either cut into cubes and pieces or minced—are popular. Pakistanis also eat *gormas* and *salans,* which are sautés or stews made of meats, vegetables, and sometimes eggs and fish. Pakistanis avoid pork, which is forbidden under Muslim religious law.

Dress. The *shawar kameez* is the common form of dress for both men and women. The outfit consists of baggy, pajamalike pants *(shawar)* and a long tunic *(kameez).*

In keeping with tenets of Islamic modesty, women wear a *dupatta,* a long scarf that is draped across the bosom and hangs behind the back on two sides. Women often cover the head with the *dupatta.*

Some women are required to live in *purdah* ("curtain"), where they remain in seclusion with other females. When they go out, these women cover their faces with a veil, or with the tentlike *burka,* which covers the entire body and allows vision through a net screen.

Men often wear some form of headdress particular to their locale. In the cities, a considerable number of men wear European clothes.

Festivals. Pakistani festivals are mostly religious in nature. The greatest occasion is the Id al Fitr, "the festival of the breaking of the fast." It follows Ramadan, the Muslim month of fasting. Early in the morning during this holiday, the family will have a light breakfast of a thin spaghetti, vermicelli, and sweet milk, pistachios, raisins, and dates. The mosques then fill with worshipers, all wearing their most festive clothing. This is followed by visits to friends and relatives, and all visitors are offered sweets. The other *id,* or festival, is the Id al Adha, ''the feast of sacrifice.'' The Id al Adha commemorates Abraham's willingness to sacrifice his son at God's command.

Pakistanis also celebrate national holidays, such as Pakistan Day, a commemoration of March 23, 1956, when Pakistan proclaimed itself an Islamic republic. Streams of colored lights adorn buildings on Pakistan Day, and people light fireworks and shoot guns into the air.

Language. Urdu, spoken as a first language by about 9 percent of the population, is Pakistan's official language. About 64 percent speak Punjabi, 12 percent Sindhi, and 24 percent a variety of other languages, including Pashto, Baluchi, and Brahui. All but Brahui (which is Dravidian) belong to the large Indo-European language family. English is officially recognized as an associate language.

Pakistan's Cities

The youngest and most modern of Pakistan's cities is **Islamabad,** the capital. Many official buildings and houses for employees of the central government have been constructed there. Islamabad is the location of the renowned Faisal Masjid (Faisal Mosque), the world's largest mosque, which is scenically set into the foothills. Islamabad lies just a few miles from the old city of **Rawalpindi,** which served as Pakistan's interim capital while Islamabad was being built.

Pakistan's largest city is **Karachi,** which dates to the early 1700s, when a fort was built there to protect the sea trade that was attracted by the

A flat wheat bread called *chapati* is eaten at practically every meal.

excellent harbor. The harbor makes Karachi practically the only outlet to the sea for Pakistan and for neighboring Afghanistan. Since 1947, the city's population has increased enormously.

Karachi has grown into a large industrial center, producing textiles and a great variety of consumer goods. The city served as Pakistan's capital from 1947 to 1959.

One of the oldest cities in Pakistan is **Multan,** in Punjab province. It dates back to 320 B.C., and was in existence when Alexander the Great invaded the region. The city has an unbroken history, and at one time it was famous as a center of learning and culture.

Faisalabad, in the Punjab, was once called **Lyallpur.** A modern industrial city and an important railroad junction, it is the home of the Pakistan University of Agriculture.

Lahore is the provincial capital of Punjab and an industrial and trade center. It is the seat of the University of Punjab, one of Pakistan's oldest universities, and it is noted for its considerable educational and cultural activities. Lahore has several mosques of historical importance, the best-known of which is the Badshahi Masjid, or Imperial Mosque, built by the Mogul emperor Aurangzeb in 1674.

Peshawar, in the North-West Frontier province, dates back many centuries to ancient Buddhist and Hindu times. It has long held strategic importance as a gateway to the subcontinent. During the 1980s, about 3 million Afghans, fleeing a war in their country, found refuge in Peshawar and elsewhere in the province.

Quetta, the provincial capital of Baluchistan, is a fertile oasis set among the province's arid mountains. In 1935, an earthquake demol-

Muslims in the Punjabi region still process sugarcane the old-fashioned way.

The carpet-weaving industry in Pakistan has emerged as an important source of exports.

ished the city, destroying many buildings of historical interest. Development of the nearby Sui gas fields has lured new industries to the region.

THE ECONOMY

Pakistan's economy is dependent on agriculture, which employs more than half the nation's workers and accounts for about 70 percent of its exports. Cotton is the most important crop, creating raw materials for export and for the nation's thriving cotton textile industry.

Wheat is the main food crop, although Pakistani farmers grow and export some highly prized varieties of rice. Other food grains include barley, maize (corn), and millet. Tobacco, sugarcane, and oilseed also are grown on a large scale. Pakistan produces and exports many varieties of fruit and vegetables. Poultry farming has made rapid strides, and fisheries are being developed scientifically. Pakistan's coast and freshwater lakes and rivers are rich sources of fish and other seafood.

People who live on Lake Manchhar in the Sind Desert rely on fish as their principal source of food.

In 1947, when the subcontinent was divided, only about 5 percent of the large-scale industries were located in the areas that became Pakistan. Since then, industry has developed rapidly. The main industries are the production of cotton textiles and carpet weaving, in which Pakistan has built up a sizable export trade. Other industries produce paper and paperboard, cement, leather products, chemicals and pharmaceuticals, fertilizers, sugar, cigarettes, and preserved food. Mineral resources, many of them being developed in Baluchistan, include natural gas, coal, salt, gypsum, chromite, iron, limestone, brine, and clay. Some petroleum is also produced.

MOHENJO-DARO

The Indus Valley civilization is one of the great mysteries of Pakistan's past. Flourishing from around 3000 to 1700 B.C., its empire stretched as far north as Kabul, in present-day Afghanistan, and as far east as Delhi, in modern India. But its economic center was the rich farmland along the banks of the Indus River and its tributaries. There, in hundreds of towns and cities, its people lived in relative comfort. Historians believe that a violent invasion by Aryans from the north triggered the civ-ilization's decline, opening the way for centuries of migrations by peoples from many parts of Asia.

Archaeologists have excavated six of the civilization's cities. The most famous, which lay buried for thousands of years until 1921, is Mohenjo-Daro, in upper Sind.

Mohenjo-Daro was amazingly well planned. About 3 mi. (4.8 km.) in circumference, it was built on a grid design, with wide avenues and a raised citadel on its western boundary. Its buildings were made of baked brick and featured stair-

Most Pakistani women still adhere to the strict dress code common to Muslim societies.

HISTORY

Ancient Times. The Indus Valley, along with some adjoining areas in what is now Pakistan, is one of the oldest cradles of civilization, comparable to those of ancient Egypt, Mesopotamia, and China. (See sidebar beginning on facing page.) In about 1700 B.C., great masses of Aryan peoples migrated from the north. The Aryans brought with them a new language, Sanskrit, the ancestor of the Indo-European languages of modern Pakistan and India. They also brought with them their own customs and religious traditions. Mixed with some of the earlier Dravidian culture, these traditions were to develop into Hinduism.

ways, bathrooms, and underground drainage. Among the public buildings were a municipal bath for ritual purposes and a central granary where the wheat, barley, and sesame collected as tax payments were stored. The city had colleges for priests, a palace, and an assembly hall. The well-to-do residents lived in large, two-story homes, with windows that opened into a central courtyard.

Archaeologists have unearthed a variety of objects, including weights and measures, games, jewelry embellished with precious stones, statues, toys, sophisticated pottery, and kitchen utensils made of lead and silver. Some of these objects suggest trade links with a number of distant cultures, including Mesopotamia, an ancient civilization that sprang up between the Tigris and Euphrates rivers in what is today Iraq.

Other ancient cities include Mohenjo-Daro's twin city Harappa, between Multan and Lahore, and Taxila, located in the north near Rawalpindi. A university built at Taxila around 275 B.C. became a center of Buddhist thought, drawing pilgrims and scholars from all over Asia.

WOMEN IN A CHANGING WORLD

The closer Amina came to graduating from a teacher-training college in Lahore, the unhappier she got. What saddened the 18-year-old was the prospect of returning to her village, where her parents had chosen a boy for her to marry. "How can I serve my country as a teacher," she asked her dormitory adviser, "when I must have a baby right away and am expected to stay at home?"

Amina's dilemma is not unusual in Pakistan. Female journalists, physicians, and teachers are fairly common. But, in gen-

Although only prime minister for 20 months, Benazir Bhutto broke new ground for Muslim women.

During the 6th century B.C., Pakistan came under the rule of the Persian Achaemenid dynasty. This was followed by Alexander the Great's invasion of the region in 327 B.C. The first empire to weld together almost all of the subcontinent was the Mauryan, which flourished from the 4th to the 2nd century B.C. Its greatest ruler, Asoka, who reigned during the 3rd century B.C., became a convert to Buddhism.

After the breakup of the Mauryan empire, Pakistan saw a succession of rulers establish themselves in different parts of the area. Among them were the Kushan, a people from central Asia; the Sassanians, a dynasty that ruled the Persian empire; then the Huns, a people who came from more easterly parts of Asia.

The Coming of Islam. During the 700s, Arabs conquered Sind in southern Pakistan. The northern part of Pakistan came under Muslim sway in the early 900s. Since then, Islam has exercised great influence upon the lives and culture of the area's people. Many of the long list of conquerors and rulers were Muslims from central Asia.

The last Asian empire of the subcontinent was that of the Moguls, a Muslim dynasty related to earlier Turkic invaders. The Moguls flourished from the 1500s to the 1700s, when control of the subcontinent passed into the hands of Great Britain.

The Struggle for Independence. Continuous pressure upon the British to grant more freedom forced them to agree to share power with provincial legislatures in 1919 and with a largely elected national legislature in 1935. Both plans fell short of the expectations of the subcontinent's political leaders, and the British decided to quit the subcontinent at the end of World War II.

As the transfer of power neared, the divisions among the region's many ethnic and religious groups surfaced. Muslims demanded a sepa-

eral, Pakistani women marry early and bear six or seven children each. Their lives, like those of women in most developing nations, are marked by poverty, drudgery, ignorance, poor health, and inequality.

For the hardships Pakistani women face, many blame the difficulty most girls have in obtaining an education. Only about a quarter of all Pakistanis can read and write. Of these, less than a third are women.

The health of Pakistani women is often poor because of malnutrition and inadequate health care, which can prove lethal during childbearing years. For every 1,000 babies born in Pakistan, about six women die from complications brought on by pregnancy or childbirth. As a consequence, Pakistan has the world's lowest women-to-men ratio—91 females to every 100 males.

Some of Pakistan's laws reinforce the prevailing attitude that women are less important than men. The nation's legal code, Islamicized under the government of Mohammed Zia ul-Haq (1977–88), mandates tougher sentences for women than for men. It also permits courts in some instances to consider a woman's evidence as less reliable than a man's.

In 1989, Benazir Bhutto's new government—the first in any Muslim nation to be headed by a woman—committed itself to improving the lives of Pakistani women. It created a ministry to deal with women's affairs. And it promised to repeal discriminatory laws, promote female literacy, and support the right of women to work outside their homes. Progress on women's issues was threatened when Pakistan's president cut short Bhutto's rule in August 1990, but she returned to power in 1993.

rate sovereign state in the areas where Muslims were in an absolute majority. Great Britain agreed, and in 1947 it partitioned British India along religious lines. Muslim-dominated areas—East Bengal, renamed East Pakistan; and the four provinces of West Pakistan—were joined to become independent Pakistan, while Hindu-dominated areas formed modern India. Both India and Pakistan claimed one Muslim-dominated region, Kashmir, and went to war over it. (See the sidebar on Kashmir, page 172.)

Independent Pakistan.   Pakistan started out in 1947 as a parliamentary democracy as part of the British Commonwealth of Nations. The British appointed Mohammed Ali Jinnah, who had spearheaded Pakistan's cause as head of the Moslem League, as the first governor-general, a largely ceremonial post. Liaquat Ali Khan became the first prime minister. By 1951, both of these able leaders were dead.

In 1956, the nation quit the Commonwealth to become a republic. General Mohammed Ayub Khan established military rule in 1958 and ran the government as president until 1969, when pro-democracy rioting forced him to resign. The army's commander in chief, General Agha Mohammed Yahya Khan, imposed martial law, suspended the constitution, and assumed the presidency.

Political activity legally resumed in 1970. Elections for the National Assembly were won by members of East Pakistan's Awami League, which wanted the east to have greater freedom to run its own affairs. Yahya Khan refused to recognize the results of the election.

In 1971, East Pakistan sought to secede from Pakistan, and civil war broke out. Troops sent from West Pakistan to subdue the unrest were defeated when India entered the war on the side of East Pakistan, which gained independence as the new nation of Bangladesh. Yahya Khan's government fell, and Zulfikar Ali Bhutto, whose Pakistan People's Party had come out on top in West Pakistan in the 1970 election, succeeded Yahya Khan as president.

A new constitution was adopted in 1973, and Bhutto became prime minister. Bhutto nationalized banking and industry, and unsuccessfully sought many other changes. After disputed elections in 1977, the army, under General Mohammed Zia ul-Haq, seized power. Bhutto was tried and convicted of complicity in the attempted murder of a political opponent. He was hanged in 1979.

Zia, who had assumed the presidency in 1978, suspended the 1973 constitution and governed under martial law. He introduced several reforms based on Islamic law.

In 1985, he permitted nonparty elections for the two-house legislature and appointed Mohammed Khan Junejo, a civilian, as prime minister. After the legislature passed measures to strengthen the presidency, Zia ended martial law and restored the 1973 constitution. Benazir Bhutto, daughter of Zulfikar Ali Bhutto, returned from exile as head of a revived Pakistan People's Party in 1986. In August 1988, Zia was killed when his plane exploded on takeoff. Multiparty elections for the National Assembly took place in November. The Pakistan People's Party won more seats than any other party, and Benazir Bhutto became prime minister.

Bhutto launched a massive social-welfare program, but her rule was generally viewed as ineffective. In 1990, President Ghulam Ishaq Khan dissolved the Assembly, ending Bhutto's government. Elections in October were won by the army-backed Islamic Democratic Alliance, headed by Nawaz Sharif. Khan dismissed Sharif in April 1993, but the dismissal was overturned by the supreme court. The subsequent power struggle between the two men paralyzed the government, and both resigned in July. After new elections in which no party won a majority, Bhutto returned as prime minister in October 1993. She cracked down on her political opponents and moved to improve relations with the United States, which had become strained due to Pakistan's nuclear-weapons program.

GOVERNMENT

Under the 1973 constitution, amended in 1985, Pakistan's president serves as chief of state. Since 1990, the president is to be elected indirectly by members of the Senate, the National Assembly, and the provincial assemblies. The prime minister, who serves as head of government, is to be nominated by the president and elected in special session by the National Assembly. A Pakistani interpretation of religious law bars women from the post of president.

The two-house legislature consists of the National Assembly and the Senate. The National Assembly has 237 elected seats—207 for Muslims, 10 for non-Muslims, and 20 seats for women. Members are elected directly by universal adult suffrage and serve five-year terms unless the president dissolves the Assembly earlier.

Eighty-four of the Senate's 87 members are elected indirectly by provincial assemblies and tribal councils. Three more are elected from the federal area of Islamabad. Half the senators are chosen every three years to serve six-year terms. The president lacks the authority to dissolve the Senate.

I. H. QUERESHI, Vice-Chancellor, University of Karachi; author, *The Pakistani Way of Life*

The Taj Mahal in Agra is a white marble mausoleum built by a Mogul emperor for his favorite wife.

INDIA

   With nearly one-sixth of the world's population, India is a vast, complicated nation, rich in history and culture, and blessed with an enormously varied landscape. Shaped like a giant pear, with its tapering end dipping into the Indian Ocean, India has been a bridge across which ideas and values have spread and a long procession of invaders have marched. It gave Buddhism to Asia, while to the West it gave its system of "Arabic" numerals. Its own traditions go back 5,000 years, and any list of its contributions to the civilizations of the world would be long and impressive.

   Everywhere in India, the contrast between old and new is striking. Monuments raised by all-powerful Mogul emperors cast their shadows on gardens cared for by government employees of the world's largest democracy. A woman may recite a 3,000-year-old prayer before starting her workday at a nuclear-power plant. An ox-drawn cart and an elephant may vie for traffic space alongside a Maruti, a zippy, Indian-built compact automobile.

   Equally sharp is the contrast between promise and reality. During the 1980s, India's economy grew at a healthy clip. Growth slowed in the 1990s, however, and the nation remains saddled with extreme unemployment and underemployment; it also has one of the world's lowest

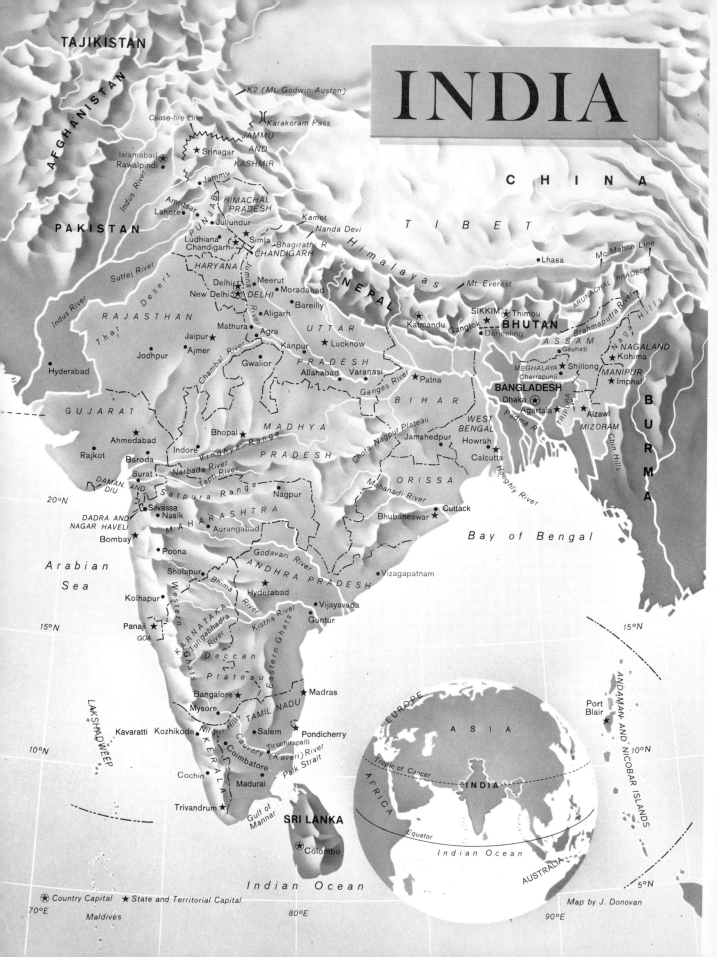

India's three major river systems originate in the snowcapped mountains of the north.

per-capita incomes—about $290 a year. India's farmers now produce enough food for the nation's huge population. But vastly uneven distribution of the benefits of development has left about half the country's 950 million people without enough money to meet their basic needs.

Such facts, however, tell only a part of India's story. Behind the figures are the Indian people. Industrious, patient, and hopeful, their lives have been profoundly shaped by the Asian subcontinent's climate, geography, and history.

THE LAND

India is the world's seventh-largest nation in terms of land area. Its topography has been shaped by three major mountain systems, two great plains, six rivers, and the rain-bearing winds called the monsoons. In the north, standing like a giant wall, are the Himalayas, one of the world's great mountain ranges, stretching for some 1,500 mi. (2,400 km.). Of the

FACTS AND FIGURES

OFFICIAL NAME: Republic of India.

NATIONALITY: Indian(s).

CAPITAL: New Delhi.

LOCATION: Southern Asia. **Boundaries**—China, Nepal, Bhutan, Myanmar, Bangladesh, Indian Ocean, Arabian Sea, Pakistan.

AREA: 1,269,340 sq. mi. (3,287,590 sq. km.).

PHYSICAL FEATURES: Highest point—Mount Godwin Austen (K2) in Kashmir (28,250 ft.; 8,611 m.). **Lowest point**—sea level. **Chief rivers**—Indus, Ganges, Brahmaputra, Jumna (Jamuna).

POPULATION: 949,600,000 (1996; annual growth 1.9%).

MAJOR LANGUAGES: Hindi (national); English (associate); Bengali, Telugu, Marathi, Tamil, Urdu, Gujarati, Malayam, Kannada, Oriya, Punjabi, Assamese, Kashmiri, Sindhi, Sanskrit (all official).

MAJOR RELIGIONS: Hinduism, Islam.

GOVERNMENT: Federal Republic. **Head of state**—president. **Head of government**—prime minister. **Legislature**—bicameral Parliament.

CHIEF CITIES: Bombay, Delhi, New Delhi, Calcutta, Madras, Bangalore, Hyderabad, Ahmadabad, Kanpur, Nagpur, Lucknow, Pune (Poona).

ECONOMY: Chief minerals—coal, iron ore, manganese, mica, bauxite, chromite, natural gas. **Chief agricultural products**—rice, other cereals, pulses, oilseed, cotton, jute, sugarcane, tobacco, tea, coffee. **Industries and products**—textiles, food processing, steel, machinery, transportation equipment, cement, jute products. **Chief exports**—clothing, cut diamonds, engineering goods, chemicals, textiles, tea. **Chief imports**—petroleum, gems, fertilizer, chemicals, machinery.

MONETARY UNIT: 1 Indian rupee = 100 paise.

NATIONAL HOLIDAY: January 26 (Anniversary of the Proclamation of the Republic).

146 Himalayan peaks, 40 rise above 25,000 ft. (7,600 m.). The Himalayan landscape ranges all the way from the lush, tropical jungles of the mountain foothills to the snowy and windswept plateau bordering Tibet, now politically part of China. In the folds of the Himalayas rise three of the great rivers of northern India: the Indus (now largely in Pakistan), the Ganges, and the Brahmaputra.

Almost in the center of the Indian subcontinent lie the Vindhya Mountains, creating, in effect, two Indias. For centuries, these mountains were a barrier to communications between north and south, and the two parts of the country were practically cut off from each other. To this day, the people of northern and southern India are markedly different.

The south Indian peninsula is bounded by two mountain systems on its eastern and western flanks—the Eastern Ghats and the Western Ghats. The two systems meet in the Nilgiri Hills. In the extreme northeast are the Lushai, Naga, and Chin hills, which form the frontier between India, Myanmar (formerly Burma), and China. These hills are the home of a number of tribal peoples. Because of the dense and often impenetrable jungle, they were isolated for a long period of time from the rest of India.

The rivers of India are held in great reverence and affection by the Hindus, the major religious group in India. The holiest of Indian rivers is the Ganges. Its plains, called the Gangetic Plains, support a large population, which depends on the river for water to grow crops and for transportation. The Gangetic Plains are especially holy to Hindus.

The three great rivers of the south are the Godavari, the Kistna (Krishna), and the Cauvery (Kaveri), which rise in the west and flow

The barren Thar Desert is one of the most sparsely populated areas of India.

The waters of the Ganges River, revered by Hindus, support an enormous rural population.

eastward to the Bay of Bengal. Their fertile plains and deltas are densely populated. Unlike the great northern rivers, which are fed by both the Himalayan snows and the monsoon rains, the rivers of the south are fed largely by the monsoon. Therefore, the volume of water in the southern rivers varies widely from season to season. Except during the summer monsoon, the south generally has little rainfall, and through the ages it has been necessary to irrigate the land to feed the people.

Upon India's great plains—the Gangetic Plains of the north and the plains of the three southern rivers—rose the great kingdoms and empires of Indian history. Today, 50 percent of the people of India live there. These lands have been farmed continuously for centuries, fertilized by the nutrients carried by the rivers.

The monsoon is as much a part of India as are the mountains, the plains, and the rivers. During the hot, dry season, from March to June, soil and vegetation become parched. The monsoon rains usually last from June through September. For most regions the summer rains are practically the only source of water. The areas of heaviest precipitation are the Western Ghats and the northeastern part of the country. Cherrapunji, in Assam State, is one of the wettest spots on earth, with an annual rainfall of some 450 in. (1,100 cm.).

THE PEOPLE

The people of India show great ethnic and cultural diversity. They speak 16 major languages and more than 1,000 dialects. The two major language groups are the northern (which includes Hindi, Gujarati, Bengali, Marathi, Oriya, Assamese, Sindhi, Punjabi, and Urdu) and the southern (which includes Tamil, Telugu, Kannada or Kanarese, and Malayalam). Hindustani, a mix of Hindi and Urdu, is spoken widely in

the north. All are official languages, although Hindi, spoken by about 30 percent of all Indians, is the national language. English, spoken by about 2 percent of the populace, is an "associate" language and the one used most in business and government communication.

In addition to language, the people of northern and southern India differ markedly in a number of ways, including their choice of food and

INDIA'S ANIMAL LIFE

India contains a kaleidoscopic array of animals, both domestic and wild. The foothills of the Himalayas teem with big game. Assam, the northeastern state, has rhinoceroses and elephants. Bengal tigers roam the delta region of the Ganges, along the border with Bangladesh. Leopards, wild boars, deer, and a great profusion of birds fill many of the forest areas. India has hundreds of varieties of reptiles, including the king cobra and pythons huge enough to swallow a small goat or calf.

Of the birds, peacocks and parrots are the most colorful, while the chief song-

Rural poverty (far left) remains a pressing problem in India. Rivers and canals (above) still serve as the main means of transport. In other regions, prolonged dry seasons make water a valuable commodity (right).

dress. In the south, rice is the staple food, while in the north it is wheat. The southerner is a coffee drinker; the northerner prefers tea. The southerner likes hot food, liberally seasoned with peppers and red-pepper powder. The northerner uses a lot of shortening in cooking. Meat is eaten more frequently in the north than in the south, where the people tend to be orthodox Hindus and therefore vegetarians.

birds are the cuckoo and the mynah. Hawks are often trained to track game birds. The mountain eagle, said to be the vehicle of the Hindu god Vishnu, is considered sacred.

In the timber areas, the elephant is both a royal animal and a beast of burden. In the past, many maharajas, or native princes, kept elephants for ceremonial parades and processions. In the deserts of Rajasthan State, the camel is the major form of transportation.

In villages the work animal is the bullock, which pulls the plows and the carts. The bullock cart is the chief form of transportation in much of rural India, where

roads become mud tracks during the rainy season.

India may have nearly one-quarter of the world's cattle. Hindus will not eat beef, because the cow is a sacred animal. It is associated with the god Krishna, who is called the Divine Cowherd.

Cattle put great pressure on India's limited resources. Some states, such as Rajasthan and Karnataka, can meet only 50 to 80 percent of their cattle's fodder needs, leaving hundreds of thousands of cattle near starvation. To feed such cattle, during the 1980s some states set up fodder-relief camps, much like famine-relief camps for humans.

Village Life

India is primarily a land of villages. More than 500,000 villages dot the countryside, and about 80 percent of India's population lives in them. Typically, these villages have fewer than 1,000 people, who live in a cluster of houses surrounded by farms and grazing areas. The villages are usually connected with the outside world by a mud path, which becomes practically impassable during the rainy season. Most of the houses are built of mud, plastered with cow dung, and thatched with the leaves of the palm and other trees.

Every village has a few wells that supply drinking water and, if there is no river nearby, water to wash clothes and pots and pans. Domestic work, such as cooking and cleaning, is performed primarily by women. Socializing at village wells keeps people informed of the activities of their neighbors and the government.

Food generally consists of fresh, unleavened bread; rice; curry; a vegetable; and red-pepper powder or green pepper for seasoning. On special days, there may be some meat (lamb or chicken) or fish. On holidays, sweetened milk or rice and other sweets are served. The two big meals are the noon lunch and the evening dinner. Breakfasts usually consist of wheat cakes or unleavened bread with tea or coffee.

CITY LIFE

In spite of the fact that India is largely a country of villages, about 20 percent of the people live in 200 towns or cities, which have always played a vital role in the nation's history. As early as 2000 B.C., India had

Cows, sacred to Hindus, are allowed to roam unmolested through city streets.

Udaipur in western India is an important commercial and administrative center.

two large urban centers, Mohenjo-Daro and Harappa, each with an estimated population of over 40,000. Today, India's major cities—Calcutta, Bombay, Delhi, Madras, Hyderabad, Ahmadabad, Kanpur, and Bangalore —each have 2 million or more residents. Calcutta, with 10 million, Bombay, with 9 million, and Madras, with 5 million, are among the largest cities in the world. Delhi, with 7.5 million, is one of the fastest-growing cities in modern history.

Crowding is the general characteristic of all Indian cities, especially since 1947, because of migration from rural areas and the influx of refugees from Pakistan. The development of city services has seldom kept pace with the increase in population. As a result, most cities are surrounded by large slum areas. In all the major cities, a considerable number of people are homeless, and most of the time they are forced to live on the sidewalks. Some families build makeshift houses of tin, bamboo, and burlap. During the dry season, thousands of men, women, and children sleep on the sidewalks. Calcutta is the worst in this respect, closely followed by Bombay and Madras. It is in these cities that the contrast between vast riches and grinding poverty is most glaring. Slums exist within the shadows of palatial homes, and the poor and the homeless wander through streets that swarm with luxurious automobiles.

The Lure of the Cities

India's cities attract people because of the promise of jobs for the thousands of rural unemployed. Here many villagers are transformed into industrial workers. Bombay, Madras, and Calcutta are important ports, have vast industrial complexes, and act as communications and transportation centers for their vast surrounding regions. Since most of India's urban hubs are either state or district capitals, they also function as centers of political life. Trade unions are well-organized and are often associated with political parties. The urban labor force, as a consequence, has become highly politicized, adding to the zest of city life.

The cities serve as pacesetters of India's cultural life. Bombay, Madras, and Calcutta have Western-style hotels and restaurants, nightclubs, art shows, and literary circles, and they are centers of India's large movie industry. (See sidebar, below.) Trade and commerce are brisk. The cities' shopping areas are crowded with people buying a large variety of goods made in India as well as products imported from the West.

INDIA'S DREAM FACTORIES

India has a unique movie industry, perhaps the biggest in the world. Studios in Bombay, Calcutta, Madras, and elsewhere produce nearly 1,000 films a year. The language may vary—Bombay produces films in Hindi, Hyderabad in Telugu, and Madras in Tamil. But three things rarely change: the story line, the format, and the emphasis on fantasy. "You could see a thousand Indian films and learn nothing about India," a prominent director, Bharat Rugachara, once complained.

India's moviegoers apparently consider the break from reality to be an advantage. They buy 5 billion tickets a year, despite the distractions of television and video rentals. Moviegoing is a family affair, so the popular Indian film has something for everyone. It features plenty of singing and dancing, and its plot lets the hero get his girl and good triumph over evil. On the way to that happy ending, the action is frantic, packed with fights, car chases, and sudden changes of scene.

This simple formula has built huge followings for film stars. The most popular are in such demand that they often make several films at once. One former superstar, Amitabh Bachchan, recalls dying on three movie sets on the same day. Like more than a few stars, Bachchan parlayed his fame into a successful political career.

India has produced its share of serious films, too. Directors such as Raj Kapoor, Shyam Benegal, Mrinal Sen, and India's most respected director, Satyajit Ray, have produced many probing films. Ray, once an advertising man in Calcutta, won a top prize at the Cannes Film Festival in 1956 with his first film, *Pather Panchali*. The more than 30 films that followed brought Ray fame in India and abroad. But for the average Indian moviegoer, Ray's portrayal of the world as a harsh, unforgiving place is all too familiar. They prefer the fantasy.

Vibrant markets are characteristic of many Indian cities. In Hyderabad (above), shoppers choose among colorful items at a market by the city gate. In arid Rajasthan (right), camel fairs are a favorite attraction.

The social, political, and cultural importance of the cities cannot be overstated. They are symbols of prosperity and progress for millions of rural people. The most advanced people functioning in literature and the arts are to be found in the cities, which have also played a leading part in the revival of the old Indian arts. The museums are packed with examples of ancient and modern Indian culture. The universities often become centers of intellectual movements, which gradually spread in ever-wider circles.

Calcutta

Calcutta, the center of a large and spreading metropolitan area, is the capital of West Bengal State. Calcutta began as an English trading post in 1690. It grew in importance because of its location on a branch of the Ganges, the Hooghly River, which empties into the Bay of Bengal. In 1773, Calcutta became the capital of British India. Although the seat of government was moved to Delhi in 1912, Calcutta remains a major port and industrial city, producing paper, iron and steel, leather goods, and jute. It is also a center of Indian cultural and intellectual life. The University of Calcutta is India's largest university, and the National Library contains more than 8 million books.

Calcutta itself provides a study in contrasts. Wide thoroughfares lined with modern, spacious buildings lie around the corner from narrow, cluttered side streets. Calcutta's main avenue, Chowringhee, is a hub of activity and entertainment, with many movie theaters and shops. Underground, an ultramodern subway system whisks people rapidly around the city.

The Maidan, a huge park in the center of Calcutta, offers areas for sports, picnicking, and just relaxing. In the Maidan is the Victoria Memorial, housing artifacts that highlight Indian life and history and the British colonial era. Other popular attractions are Calcutta's zoo, the Indian Museum—one of Asia's best museums—and botanical gardens that contain a banyan tree large enough to provide shade for more than 200 people.

Bombay

Bombay, the capital of Maharashtra State, is the center of Greater Bombay. Like Calcutta, it is a modern, cosmopolitan city, with many of Calcutta's problems. Originally a fishing village, it was acquired in the 1500s by the Portuguese, who ceded it to the British in 1661. The development of railway lines and a textile industry in the 1860s began Bombay's major period of growth. Today, it is India's major port on the west coast.

The port of Bombay, which opens into the Arabian Sea, lies on the eastern end of Bombay Island, on which the city itself is built. A huge stone arch, the Gateway to India, stands at the entrance to the harbor and is Bombay's best-known landmark.

One of Bombay's most striking sights is Marine Drive, a multilane highway. It is especially spectacular when its blazing lights are viewed at night from the crest of Malabar Hill, the city's most fashionable residential district. Other attractions include the Prince of Wales and the Victoria and Albert museums, the zoo, and the extensive gardens surrounding the Towers of Silence.

The section of the city known as The Fort is Bombay's cultural and commercial center. Its wide boulevards and large buildings give it the

Calcutta, once the capital of British India, remains one of the country's leading ports.

Cosmopolitan Bombay contains a unique mixture of skyscrapers and old colonial-style buildings.

look of a European city. Here are located most of the city's business establishments, banks, theaters, the University of Bombay, state government buildings, and the Victoria Terminus railway station. To the north is the city's industrial area, with facilities for processing the great quantities of raw cotton brought in from the surrounding countryside.

Madras

Madras, the capital of Tamil Nadu, is the principal city of southern India. More spacious than other large Indian cities, it is an important seaport as well as a major transportation center. The city has given its name to the colorful Madras cloth produced in local factories and exported to countries throughout the world. Besides textiles, the city's industries include iron foundries, bicycle factories, and engineering works. Madras was founded in 1639, when the East India Company acquired the area surrounding the present city from a local raja, or prince. The British built a trading post, named Fort Saint George, around which a thriving commercial settlement gradually developed.

By the early 1800s, Madras had become one of the administrative capitals of British India. Because of its location on the Bay of Bengal, the British developed Madras as a major port and began construction of an artificial harbor. The city currently extends for nearly 10 mi. (17 km.) along the coast of the bay. Its magnificent beaches and the Marina, a splendid shore drive that extends for 4 mi. (6.4 km.), are major attractions. The Marina begins in the south at Saint Thomé Cathedral, where the remains of the apostle Thomas are said to be buried. It continues past Madras University, state government buildings, and Fort Saint

George until it reaches its northern end at the city's harbor. Madras is also noted for its beautiful Hindu temples, its Horticultural Gardens, and its Indian art collection in the National Art Gallery and State Government Museum.

Delhi

A city with ancient roots, Delhi today is divided into two sharply contrasting sections. New Delhi, the capital of India since 1931, was built in the 20th century, while Old Delhi dates back to the 700s. As Shahjahanbad, it became one of the principal cities of the Mogul Empire (1526–1857). The two parts of Delhi form the largest city of northwestern India. Delhi is a bustling industrial and commercial center. The city stands on the west bank of the Jumna River, a tributary of the Ganges, and Hindus regard the place where these two rivers meet as a holy site.

Old Delhi is a mixture of beautiful landmarks and overcrowded slums. New factories have sprung up among the maze of narrow, winding streets, but the old city is still dominated by ancient buildings such as the 17th-century Red Fort. Not far from the Red Fort is the great mosque Jama Masjid, which rises 201 ft. (61 m.). The main thoroughfare of Old Delhi is Chandni Chauk (or Chowk)—the "Street of Silver." Today, as in ancient times, silversmiths still practice their craft along this street, but it is now filled with shops of all types. Between Old Delhi and New Delhi lies Raj Ghat, a revered shrine. Here, Mahatma Gandhi, who led the fight for Indian independence, was cremated on January 31, 1948.

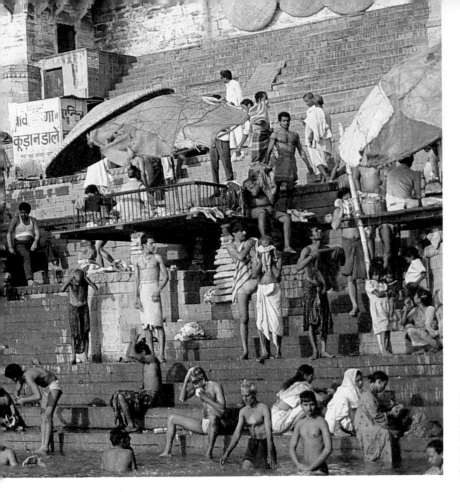

At many points along the Ganges, flights of steps called *ghats* lead down to the river's edge, enabling Hindu pilgrims to bathe in the sacred waters. Such bathing serves as a purification ritual.

In contrast to the old section, New Delhi is a modern, planned city with wide boulevards, spacious public parks, and large government buildings. A long, tree-lined avenue called the Raj Path leads to the home of the president of India. The avenue is used for parades and official processions. The presidential residence, the Rashtrapati Bhavan, and the Parliament House are popular tourist attractions. New Delhi's main shopping center is Connaught Place, a circular street surrounding a park. The University of Delhi, the Central Agricultural Research Institute, National Art Gallery, National Museum, other museums, and theaters are among Delhi's many cultural institutions.

In addition to its commercial and governmental activities, Delhi is important also as the center of northwestern India's transportation and communications network. Industries include the manufacture of cotton and wool cloth, food processing, iron foundries, printing plants, and flour and sugar mills.

RELIGIOUS LIFE

One of the most important elements in Indian life is religion. About 83 percent of the population are Hindus, and about 11 percent are Muslims. Christians account for about 2.5 percent and are evenly divided between Catholics and Protestants. There are small communities of Buddhists, Jains, Sikhs, and Jews. The Parsis, followers of the ancient Persian prophet Zoroaster, number about 100,000, of whom half live in the city of Bombay.

Hindu priests, or Brahmans (above), make up the highest group in the strict caste system.

India also has a large tribal population, estimated at about 40 million, whose religion is primarily animism. The tribal peoples believe in the existence of powerful spirits or gods, and that all natural objects have souls. Many of these tribal peoples have converted to Christianity, especially in the northeastern areas. Others are gradually being absorbed into the structure of Hindu religious beliefs and practices.

Hinduism. Hinduism has no single founder. Its ideas, beliefs, cults, and practices grew over a period of 4,000 years and were shaped by many religious and cultural movements. Hinduism embraces a spectrum of beliefs, ranging from those that border on spirit worship to those that accept the notion of a single, personal God.

THE HINDU CASTE SYSTEM

Hindu society is divided into a number of castes, or classes, into which people are born. One belongs to a caste throughout one's life unless expelled for violations of its rules. Membership in a caste traditionally means attachment to a specific profession or occupation. Marriage is within the caste and is generally arranged by the parents. Caste membership also determines social relationships, especially the sharing of food in common.

The castes are arranged in a hierarchy, with the Brahman (priest) castes at the top and the Sudras (farmers, artisans, and laborers) at the bottom of the social ladder. There are hundreds of castes among Hindus all over India. They may generally be grouped under four broad categories: the Brahmans, Kshatriyas (warriors), Vaisyas (merchants and bankers), and Sudras. Indians call these broad categories *varnas* (literally, "colors"), and each *varna* is sub-

Hindu marriages, always within the same caste, are frequently arranged by the parents.

Hinduism's roots go back to at least 1500 B.C., when the composition of the Vedas, Hinduism's sacred books, began. This early form of the religion included the belief in many gods. Each god was a personification of a natural phenomenon—thunder, lightning, rain, the sun, and the moon, for example. Early Hindus worshiped these gods through a cult of sacrifices. The early beliefs were replaced, during the period 700–600 B.C., by the philosophical theories that laid down some of the fundamental principles of Hinduism.

Essentially, there are four principles. First, the Hindus believe in God (or gods who are considered manifestations of a single God or universal spirit) as the creator and sustainer of this world. Second, they believe in

divided into a large number of castes and subcastes. Some estimates place the number of caste divisions at more than 3,000, each with varying numbers of members.

On the edge of the caste society live the untouchables. These people are regarded as members of the lowest social groups, and their physical contact is considered to be ritually polluting. The origins of untouchability go back to the 2nd century B.C., when religious concepts developed among the Brahmans required the avoidance of certain materials as unfit in Hindu ritual. People in occupations involving these materials were considered to be untouchable for ritual purposes. Although untouchables are regarded as Hindus, they are not served by the Brahman priests, and their religious rites are markedly different from those of the caste Hindus. They are often relegated to sanitation work.

Both caste and untouchability were officially abolished by the Indian Constitution of 1950. Despite their improved status, however, untouchables are still discriminated against in rural India.

a soul that is eternal and indestructible and that merges into God at salvation. Third, they believe that people have a moral responsibility for their actions.

Fourth, like Buddhists and Jains, they believe in rebirth, or reincarnation. Hindus hold that people must go through a series of births, deaths, and rebirths to atone for their sins before they may work their way to salvation. The nature and form of the next life are determined largely by one's actions in an earlier life.

Hinduism is a very tolerant religion, and Hindus generally do not try to convert people of other faiths. The caste system, though it arose independently as a social institution, soon became a part of Hinduism. (See sidebar, "The Hindu Caste System," page 210.)

Islam. Unlike the Hindus, Muslims believe in one God who is formless and must not be represented in any image. Their places of worship are the mosques. The mosque contains a place with a niche that points in the direction of Mecca (Makkah) in Saudi Arabia, the holy city of Islam. The mosque also has an assembly hall where congregational prayers are offered every Friday at noon. The Muslims are also expected to take part in specific practices. (See "The Five Pillars of Islam," page 126 in this volume.)

Both Hinduism and Islam have been great forces in the cultural history of India. They have been sources of spiritual strength and social cohesion for their followers. But in some ways their practices have tended to obstruct social and economic modernization. The caste system and its institution of untouchability have divided Hindu society into

Muslims in the courtyard of a New Delhi mosque wash their hands before entering the building.

Most monks in Hindu monasteries are disqualified from performing priestly duties.

hundreds of small, self-contained, and exclusive groups. This has made economic and social cooperation on a large scale difficult. The Hindu idea of the sacred cow has led to an excessive cattle population.

Untouchability has been the most objectionable feature of Hindu society. It condemns millions of Indians to a permanent social inferiority and economic degradation from which there is little escape. Similarly, the generally inferior position of women in Muslim society has crippled their social and cultural development. This is especially true in the custom of veiling *(purdah)*. Orthodox Hindus and Muslims have resisted attempts at rapid social change through legislation or social action, thus impeding economic progress.

FROM ANCIENT TIMES TO INDEPENDENCE

Several prehistoric towns and cities discovered by archaeologists reveal the existence of a well-established civilization as far back as 2500 B.C. The most important sites—now both part of Pakistan—are Mohenjo-Daro, in Sind, and Harappa, in the Punjab. This earliest Indian civilization existed during the time of the Egyptian pharaohs and was equally rich in its material life and sophistication. The cities were built according to well-laid plans and were busy commercial centers.

Around 1500 B.C., the Indo-Aryans migrated into India, probably from central Asia. The Indo-Aryans differed from the original inhabitants in their lighter skin color, language, social organization, and technology. Over the course of centuries, they conquered various parts of northern India. The Indo-Aryans developed the religious beliefs that were to

The Qutb Minar in Delhi serves as both a minaret and an emperor's tomb.

evolve into Hinduism. They also laid the foundations for social institutions like the caste system, cleared the land for agriculture, and developed the Sanskrit language.

During the 6th century B.C., two great religious movements—Buddhism and Jainism—arose in India. In the middle of the 6th century B.C., the Persians invaded the northwestern part of the country. They were followed by the Greeks under Alexander the Great in the 4th century B.C.

The first great Indian empire—the Maurya Empire—appeared about 324 B.C. Its greatest ruler was King Asoka, who reigned from about 274 to 232 B.C. Asoka became a Buddhist and devoted his life to the spread of Buddhism in India and Ceylon. He had cave temples excavated for Buddhist monks, and built *stupas,* semicircular mounds of brick that enshrine relics of the Buddha.

The golden or classical age of ancient India lasted from about A.D. 320 to 500. This was the period of the Gupta Empire, when literature, the arts, science, and material prosperity reached peaks of greatness. During this period, too, Hinduism became firmly established as the religion of the masses of the people.

The Ellora temples feature intricate pillars, chapels, and elephants cut from the hillside.

During the five centuries after the downfall of the Guptas, numerous small kingdoms fought against one another, and India was invaded by the Arabs and Turks. In 1206, the Turks established a kingdom in Delhi, and Muslim rulers controlled large parts of northern India. In 1526, the Moguls, who came from central Asia, began to build a great empire, with capitals in Agra and Delhi. The Mogul Empire flourished until the beginning of the 18th century.

European Invasions

The Portuguese navigator Vasco da Gama reached India in 1498 by sailing around the Cape of Good Hope. Portugese traders soon seized ports along the western coast. During the 1600s, the English East India Company set up trading stations in India. Indian peasants were exploited in the growing textile industry. The British also ordered certain traditional practices stopped, including female infanticide and *sati* (suttee), the immolation of widows along with their dead husbands.

The English were followed by the French. When the two nations were at war in Europe in the 1700s, their trading companies waged their

MONUMENTS TO THE PAST

Many people who know little about India have heard of the Taj Mahal, the marble tomb a Mogul ruler ordered built for his wife. But the Taj Mahal is only one of countless monuments that enhance the natural beauty of the Indian landscape. Almost every dynasty in Indian history left great structures behind. Their kings delighted in building great temples and palaces to reflect both their religious faith and their power. What is more, each region developed its own particular style of art, and their treasures adorn the country.

The great cave temples in the south are splendid examples of Indian artistry. Two of the finest are near Aurangabad, 230 mi. (370 km.) east of Bombay. The Ajanta cave temples there were made from a dug-out mountain to form a series of Buddhist shrines and monasteries. Between the 1st century B.C. and A.D. 600, artists crowded the cave walls with scenes of men and women, gods and angels, birds and beasts. Another group of cave temples, built at Ellora between 600 and 800 A.D., is chiefly Hindu. Ellora's most famous temple, Kailasa, was carved out of a single great rock, and its walls are adorned with larger-than-life statues of the Hindu gods.

In the north, the chief monuments are located in the cities of Agra and Delhi and in the states of Rajasthan and Bihar. The splendid Taj Mahal, world-famous for its beauty, is built of marble. It was constructed as a tomb for Mumtaz Mahal, wife of the 17th-century Mogul emperor Shah Jahan. The building took 20,000 laborers 22 years to complete.

Delhi has many renowned structures from different historical periods. Among them are the Qutb Minar, a minaret (tower used for calling Muslims to prayer) some 238 ft. (73 m.) high, and the tomb of Humayun, a 16th-century Mogul emperor.

own wars in India. From about 1800–57, the East India Company fought in many wars against Nepal, Afghanistan, and Burma (present-day Myanmar) to enlarge the British Empire.

By the second half of the 1700s, the British emerged as the chief power in India. In the middle of the next century, their troops crushed the Indians' last armed revolt against British rule, the Sepoy Mutiny of 1857–59. The following year, responsibility for the administration of India was transferred from the East India Company to the British Parliament. From 1858 until 1947, when India achieved its independence, the country was ruled by a British governor-general, who also acted as viceroy in Great Britain's relations with the hundreds of separate Indian states.

Indian nationalism grew in response to British rule. The Indian National Congress, which was organized in 1885, became a militant organization after 1905, gaining its strength from mass action. In 1920, Mahatma Gandhi assumed leadership of the organization. During the 1920s and 1930s, he led several nonviolent campaigns against the British. The British responded with a series of concessions that enlarged membership of the Indian legislatures and increased their powers. In 1935, Britain granted the provinces self-rule. After World War II, Britain began the withdrawal of its power from India.

Alongside the nationalism of the Indian National Congress there also arose a Muslim nationalistic movement led by Mohammed Ali Jinnah. Jinnah demanded the establishment of a separate sovereign state made up of areas with a Muslim majority. The British granted this demand in 1947. On August 14–15, 1947, the two independent nations of India and Pakistan were established, and a historic epoch of Indian history came to an end.

THE MODERNIZATION OF INDIA

The modernization of India, begun during the British period of Indian history, accelerated after independence was attained in 1947. Rapidly expanding cities quickly became centers of social, economic, and political change for India's predominantly rural population. Modern ideas and opportunities began to spread from the cities into the rural areas of India that were dominated by traditional life-styles. At the same time, modern communications built by the British, and the creation of a modern civil service and national judiciary, began to unite the different regions in a manner never before possible.

India's Leaders

India suffered a tragic blow with the assassination in 1948 of Mahatma Gandhi, who had done so much to win Indian independence. Jawaharlal Nehru, the first prime minister of independent India, tried to find solutions to the many problems facing the new nation.

Indira Gandhi dominated Indian politics for 20 years until her assassination in 1984.

When Nehru died in 1964, he was succeeded as prime minister by Lal Bahadur Shastri, who died in office in 1966. Shastri's successor was Indira Gandhi, Nehru's daughter. During her long tenure as prime minister, Indira Gandhi pushed for the rapid modernization of India and sought to establish India as the leader of the world's nonaligned nations.

Indira Gandhi's tenure was marked by accomplishment and controversy. Defeated in elections in 1977, when she was replaced as prime minister by Morarji Desai, she returned to power in 1980. In 1984 she was killed by Sikh extremists. She was succeeded by her son Rajiv Gandhi, who continued her economic-liberalization plans. The gap between the rich and the poor was feared to be widening, however, and political and caste-interest clashes made headlines. In 1989, Gandhi's Congress Party lost its legislative majority, and Vishwanath Pratap Singh of the National Front became prime minister. He resigned in November 1990.

During the 1991 election campaign, Rajiv Gandhi was assassinated. New Congress Party leader P. V. Narasimha Rao became prime minister in June. Rao ended many state controls over the economy, but the benefits of his reforms fell unevenly, and his party was viewed by many as corrupt. In 1996 elections, the Congress Party won only 25 percent of the legislative seats. Atal Behari Vajpayee, leader of the Hindu nationalist Bharatiya Janata Party, became prime minister in May. Two weeks later, however, Vajpayee's government, facing a no-confidence vote, resigned. A new coalition, led by H. D. Deve Gowda, took office in June.

The Golden Temple at Amritsar is the holiest shrine of the Sikhs, followers of a religion that combines elements of Hinduism and Islam. Some militant Sikhs are agitating for an independent homeland.

Indians celebrate Republic Day—January 26th—with parades and other festivities.

Problems of Modernization

India has had to solve or deal with many political, governmental, and economic problems since gaining independence in 1947. Many of these problems derive from religious and regional differences.

Religion. Religion played a key role when British India was partitioned in 1947 to create a predominantly Hindu India and a mainly Muslim Pakistan (now Pakistan and Bangladesh). As a result of this partition, millions of Hindus migrated into India from what had become Pakistan. Large numbers of Muslims from India also migrated into Pakistan. Many people died in violent Hindu-Muslim clashes that resulted from partition.

In addition, the Sikhs (members of a smaller religious group founded 500 years ago) saw their homeland in the Punjab divided between the two new countries. They, too, settled in India after losing a violent holy war against Muslims in Pakistan. The arrival in India of these millions of homeless Hindu and Sikh refugees placed heavy burdens on the Indian economy. Partition also created an economic imbalance, locating the major food-growing areas in Pakistan and the main industrial areas in India.

Religious conflict still occurs today. Sikh militants in Punjab state have demanded the creation of a Sikh nation, and the late 1992 destruction of a mosque at Ayodhya in northern India by Hindu militants sparked the worst Hindu-Muslim violence since 1947.

National Unity and Regional Fragmentation. Under Nehru, India's first need was to devise a constitution that would unify the country, create a workable political process, and tie the regions to the central government by giving them a sense of national responsibility. Until 1947, the British had ruled most of India indirectly through more than 500 local princes. The British had allowed the princes to keep nominal control of their lands, known as "native states," in return for support of British policies. After independence, India's leaders persuaded the princes to accept pensions for their lands in the interest of creating a unified country. The native states were then merged into existing states or made into new states. Although this new approach encountered resistance, it also brought to India a sense of national identity.

Government.   The Indian Constitution was adopted in 1950. It drew its inspiration from the United States Constitution and from British constitutional ideas and practices. It guarantees basic rights of equality and prohibits unequal treatment due to race, religion, or caste. The constitution decreed India to be a union of states (to date, 25 in number) and federally administered territories, of which there are now seven. Each state has a legislature, its own court system, and a governor who is appointed by India's president. The union, or federal, government is presided over by a president and a vice president, who are chosen by an electoral college made up of members of the union and state legislatures.

The real executive power of the central government is vested in a cabinet, the Council of Ministers, led by the prime minister. The union legislature has two chambers, the Lok Sabha (House of the People) and the Rajya Sabha (Council of States). The members of the Lok Sabha are elected by the people every five years. The Rajya Sabha is elected by the members of the state legislatures. The union judiciary has a supreme court headed by a chief justice. Every citizen at least 21 years of age is eligible to vote.

India's constitution has been amended many times. The political map has also changed. New states have been created and state borders adjusted in response to demands for greater local autonomy by India's many language and tribal groups. One major change, in 1966, was the division of Punjab into two separate states: a smaller Punjab, inhabited by predominantly Punjabi-speaking Sikhs; and the new state of Haryana,

Computer scientists design software using terminals and other hardware manufactured in India.

Many Christian groups run elementary and secondary schools for Indian students.

inhabited mostly by Hindi-speaking Hindus. India also took over small French colonies on the subcontinent (Karikal, Mahé, Danam, and Pondicherry) in 1959 and the Portuguese colonies of Goa, Diu, and Daman in 1961. It annexed Sikkim, a former protectorate, in 1975.

Social Change. At independence, people in the native states, the untouchables, and the tribal peoples suffered from isolation and backwardness. Special efforts had to be made to bring them into the mainstream of Indian life. These efforts included educational concessions, reservation of seats in the legislatures, and government jobs.

Equally pressing was the problem of social development. The Hindu social structure was out-of-date in many respects, and the new Hindu Codes of 1954–56 sought to change it. The new codes profoundly affected Hindu marriage customs and the organization of the Hindu family. Through the registration of marriages, marriage was made a civil rather than a religious act. Women were made eligible for inheritance rights, and divorce was permitted to Hindus. Other laws distributed power to the agencies of local and village government.

Education and Literacy. Only about 47 percent of all adult men and 33 percent of adult women can read and write. Improving literacy levels has been a major goal of the government since independence. Hundreds of thousands of new schools have been built, and approximately 85 percent of all children between the ages of 6 and 11 now attend primary schools. In the early years, they learn to read and write in their native language. Later, if they stay in school, they learn some English and Hindi.

SCHOOLING TO REACH INDIA'S POOREST

India has pressed forward economically in recent years. In an attempt to extend the reach of India's economic advances into the nation's poorest villages, promising rural children are now given the opportunity to attend boarding schools away from their villages. About 261 Navodaya Vidyalaya, or "new-look schools," have opened since the mid-1980s, under a program created by former Prime Minister Rajiv Gandhi. About 20,000 pupils enter this new educational system each year.

Children must take an aptitude test to gain entrance into these special schools. Once admitted, they receive significantly more than book learning. They are also provided a nutritionally balanced diet; free school uniforms and equipment; and close, almost parental, guidance from their teachers.

India's government plans to build a "new-look school" in each of its 448 rural districts. All but a few states have donated land for the school campuses, and most Indians support the schools. However, some object to the decision to teach students only in Hindi and English—a move that has been criticized as divorcing some students from their cultural roots. The schools' supporters defend the decision on the grounds that it gives the students the tools to break out of the isolation of village life.

A typical day at a new-look school begins with assembly programs that include news reports and speeches by students. Children learn how to make the school's chalk, candles, and other items before hitting the books.

At night, teachers and students continue to share. Said one 12-year-old attending a school in Chainsa, southeast of New Delhi: "The teachers are like relatives. When the light goes in the evening, we all sit on the ground and talk. We get guidance on what to do in life."

In many rural villages, everyday instruction is conducted in outdoor classrooms.

To help solve the overpopulation problem, the government encourages smaller families.

Fewer than one in three children in India gets a high school education. Higher education is well-developed, but there are too few jobs in India for the growing numbers of college graduates. There are now almost 5,000 schools of higher learning. Older people, who were never able to go to school as children, now enter adult-education programs in increasing numbers.

The introduction of television, radio, new roads, and government services are having a dual effect in the development of modern India. These innovations are gradually reducing the isolation long felt in many rural areas, and they are also accelerating the modernization process itself.

The Population Problem. Modern India has experienced a steady rise in population. This rapid increase is the result of better preventive medicine, public-health and hygiene measures, and a significant drop in infant mortality. Population growth is down to about 2.1 percent (compared to 3.2 percent in Pakistan). Today, the government encourages families to have fewer children, and has begun one of the most ambitious programs of population control in history. Radio and television advertising promotes family-planning programs. Generous payments are made to married couples agreeing to have no more than two children.

India's famous brightly colored fabrics are dried in the sun to help set the dyes.

Still, the average couple has three to four children. Some 65,000 babies are born each day. The result is that each year, India must build 130,000 new schools, train 330,000 new teachers, and create 3 million new jobs. It is a daunting prospect.

ECONOMY

Measured by the value of a year's output of goods and services, India has an enormous economy, ranking among the world's 12 largest economic powers. However, both in terms of output per person and income per person, India ranks among the world's least productive and poorest nations. Income is low because India's great wealth has to be shared among a large and rapidly growing population. Individual output is low because most work is still done in traditional ways, and because the nation's government-owned industries are often inefficiently run. India and Australia each produce about the same amount of coal, for example. But Australia's coal mines employ 30,000 people, while India's employ 700,000.

A major economic and social goal of India's government is to relieve the nation's widespread poverty by raising per-capita income. In recent years, efforts to slow population growth and accelerate economic growth have shown some success. Since independence, the nation's economic policies have encouraged the creation of a number of relatively sophisticated industries and a large pool of skilled labor.

Still, hundreds of millions of people living in rural areas are not part of the cash economy. They grow their own food, and trade any surplus for clothing and other necessities. At the other end of the economic spectrum are the 80 million to 100 million people, mostly in the cities, whose exceptional earnings permit them to buy the consumer goods that India's factories produce. Because consumers fuel economic growth, a major goal of India's government during the 1990s is to find ways to bring more Indians into the cash economy.

Agriculture and Food Supply

About 70 percent of India's population is engaged in agricultural activity. After several famines occurred during the 1960s, India and the rest of the world became alarmed that perhaps India's population was expanding faster than the country's capacity to increase the food supply. Large quantities of food had to be imported to feed the many people who were hungry.

The government then began a long-range program, known as the "green revolution," to increase the country's food supply. Indian agronomists developed strains of rice and wheat seeds that could double or even triple grain output. The government began to teach farmers throughout India how to grow the high-yielding hybrid seeds, which require more careful irrigation, pest control, and fertilization than do

Much of India's farmland is irrigated, often by methods used for centuries.

traditional types of seed. Production of chemical fertilizers was increased to help make the green revolution successful. Irrigation facilities were also expanded.

As a result of the green revolution, India's production of food, especially grain, began to increase more rapidly than the population during the late 1960s and early 1970s. Surpluses were stored to prevent famines, and India soon became an exporter of grains instead of an importer. The Punjab, known as the granary of India, and the Gangetic Plains are the most productive grain-growing regions. Other leading food crops are oilseeds, used to produce oils for cooking, and the peas, beans, lentils, and other protein-rich crops that make up much of the Indian diet.

India's farmers also produce many valuable cash crops. The most important are sugar, which is a major export, and jute and cotton, which are raw materials for the important textile industries. During the 1990s, the government is investing heavily in agriculture, to enable India's farmers to produce more food and earn more money.

Industrialization

Industrialization was begun by the British and continues to play a major role in the modernization of India. It is aided by rich resources of iron ore, manganese, bauxite, coal, and zinc. Also aiding industrial development are the large labor force willing to work for low wages and India's large numbers of skilled scientists and technicians. Many of the major industries—steel, machine tools, electric and transport machinery, and chemicals—are dominated by government-owned enterprises.

In some remote areas, such jobs as street cleaning are still done by human labor.

Most Indians travel between villages on open-air—and frequently overcrowded—buses.

The leading industries are textiles and steel. Other manufactures include processed food, machinery, transportation equipment, cement, and jute products. In the late 1980s, for the first time in its history, India produced more cement and synthetic textiles than it could use. It produces seven times as much steel today as it did in 1950.

India has also developed atomic energy and is capable of producing nuclear weapons. So far, however, India's government has insisted that it will produce nuclear power only for peaceful purposes. In 1989, its aerospace industry produced a surface-to-surface ballistic missile capable of carrying a 1-ton warhead up to 1,500 mi. (2,414 km.), reaching all areas of South Asia and deep into China.

India's thousands of privately owned companies are heavily regulated. During the 1980s and 1990s, the government lifted many regulations in hopes of spurring industrial growth. The move led to the biggest private-sector industrial boom in the nation's history. Hundreds of new companies started up, producing consumer goods such as televisions, computers, motor scooters, and clothing. Existing private companies expanded, and exports surged.

By the late 1990s, however, India's industrial output was only half as large as that of nations such as China and Brazil. Nonetheless, the government is putting its faith in private businesses, which it is counting on to create most of the tens of millions of new jobs that India's growing numbers of educated young people will need.

Though there are some small oil deposits in the northwest off the coast of Bombay and in the northeastern state of Assam, India must import most of the petroleum it needs. The nation's bill for imported oil is expected to rise dramatically during the 1990s, requiring India to sell more of its own goods abroad to cover energy costs.

INTERNATIONAL RELATIONS

In its relations with other nations, India has generally followed a policy of nonalignment, siding with no major power bloc. India's main difficulties have been in relations with Pakistan and China. India has gone to war with Pakistan three times—in 1947, 1965, and 1971. The first two wars involved conflicting claims over Jammu and Kashmir. The 1971 war grew out of the civil war between East and West Pakistan. Border incidents and the flight of millions of East Pakistani refugees into India led to the Indian Army's march into East Pakistan. The result was a swift victory for India and the establishment of the independent nation of Bangladesh in what had been East Pakistan. With Pakistan dismembered, India emerged as the leading power in South Asia.

Relations with the People's Republic of China turned hostile when the Chinese attacked Indian frontier areas in 1962. Since then, relations between the two countries have been uneasy. Prime Minister Rajiv Gandhi's visit to China in 1988 was a sign of warmer relations between the two countries.

New buildings are urgently needed to keep pace with urban population growth.

Huge nuclear-power plants have helped to meet India's growing energy demands.

In 1971, India and the Soviet Union signed a 20-year treaty of cooperation. A trade agreement in 1981 made the Soviet Union India's principal trading partner. With the collapse of European Communism in 1990 and the breakup of the Soviet Union in 1991, however, India began to reexamine its policies toward Western nations.

INDIA'S FUTURE

India has made enormous headway against most of the problems that confronted it upon independence in 1947. It slowed population growth. It built an industrial base that few nations can equal, achieved self-sufficiency in food production, and created a huge educated middle class. Its universities produce more engineers and scientists than any nation other than the United States and Russia. Just as important, it has proved that it knows how to make democracy work. All its leaders since independence have been freely elected.

Yet much remains to be done. India must find a way to extend its economic gains to the 40 percent of all Indians who have yet to be touched by them. The economy must continue to expand while population growth slows even more. Clearly, India is in a race with itself—one that its past successes and its values, rooted in thousands of years of history, suggest that it can win.

B. G. GOKHALE, Director, Asian Studies Program, Wake Forest University
Author, *The Making of the Indian Nation*

Fertile valleys lie nestled between towering mountains in the scenic interior of Nepal.

 # NEPAL

Nepal, South Asia's oldest nation, is landlocked between China and India on the southern slopes of the Himalayas. The Nepalese have lived on farms and in scattered villages for centuries, isolated from each other and, until midpoint in the 20th century, from non-Nepalese as well.

That isolation ended in 1951. Since then, the Nepalese have struggled to adapt the ideas and technologies of more industrial nations to their needs. Nepal has been profoundly changed as a result.

The richly textured Nepalese culture has remained relatively unchanged, however. Actually a blend of cultures—Nepalese speak 12 different languages and 36 dialects—Nepal's traditions reflect a way of looking at life that is both reverent and joyful. The Nepalese are proud of their art and architecture, and their distinctive blend of Buddhism and Hinduism is found nowhere else.

Scenic beauty is one of the kingdom's major natural resources—eight of the world's 10 highest mountains are within its borders—and tourism has become an important source of foreign currency. Yet Nepal remains one of the world's poorest nations, with a population that is growing faster than the ability of the nation's farmers to feed it.

THE LAND

Rectangular in shape, Nepal is 497 mi. (800 km.) long and from 56 mi. (90 km.) to 137 mi. (220 km.) wide. The southern part of the country, known as the Terai, features broad plains and excellent farmland. Nepal also has swamp and jungle regions that are habitats for elephants, tigers, rhinoceroses, and other wild beasts. Central Nepal, the "hill country," is mountainous and crisscrossed by many rivers and fertile valleys. In the north are the Great Himalayas, a sparsely inhabited region of towering mountains. Located along the border between Nepal and the Chinese region of Tibet is Mount Everest, the world's highest mountain at 29,028 ft. (8,848 m.).

Nepal's climate varies according to altitude. Summers are hot in the Terai and in the hill country, cool in the higher mountain regions. Winters are mild in the south and punishingly cold in the higher mountains. During the June–September monsoon season, rainfall is considerable, amounting to 30 to 60 in. (75 to 150 cm.).

THE PEOPLE

Nepal's population is a mixture of related and unrelated ethnic, religious, and tribal groups. These fall into three main divisions. First are the Newar, a people who trace their ancestry back to Nepal's earliest known history. A second group consists of Hindus who came from India during and after the 1200s. Nepali, Nepal's official language, is an Indian tongue brought in by early Hindu immigrants. Third are the tribes that originated mainly in Tibet and Mongolia. They include the Tamang, Kiranti, Magar, Gurung, and Sherpa.

The Newar live throughout the extensive Katmandu Valley in central Nepal. Most are farmers, tradesmen, and government employees. The tribal groups that came from the north long ago are primarily Buddhists.

The Gurungs, known outside of Nepal as Gurkhas, live west of Katmandu, Nepal's capital. The Gurkhas are famous as the tough mercenary soldiers who have served in both the British and Indian armies for almost

FACTS AND FIGURES

OFFICIAL NAME: Kingdom of Nepal.

NATIONALITY: Nepalese.

CAPITAL: Katmandu (Kathmandu).

LOCATION: Southern central Asia. **Boundaries**—China, India.

AREA: 56,827 sq. mi. (147,181 sq. km.).

PHYSICAL FEATURES: Highest point—Mount Everest (29,028 ft.; 8,848 m.). **Lowest point**—150 ft. (46 m.). **Chief rivers**—Kosi, Gandak, Karnali.

POPULATION: 23,200,000 (1996; annual growth 2.6%).

MAJOR LANGUAGE: Nepali (official).

MAJOR RELIGIONS: Hinduism, Buddhism.

GOVERNMENT: Constitutional monarchy. **Head of state**—king. **Head of government**—prime minister. **Legislature**—bicameral Parliament.

CHIEF CITIES: Katmandu, Biratnagar, Lalitpur.

ECONOMY: Chief minerals—mica, coal, copper, graphite. **Chief agricultural products**—rice, maize, wheat, oilseeds, jute, sugarcane, livestock. **Industries and products**—textiles, glassware, ceramics, timber, chemical products, paper, cement, metalware, craftwork. **Chief exports**—food and live animals, beverages and tobacco, mineral fuels, chemicals, basic manufactures. **Chief imports**—cotton and silk, manufactured goods, minerals and fuels, iron and steel, chemicals, machinery.

MONETARY UNIT: 1 Nepalese rupee = 100 paisa.

NATIONAL HOLIDAY: December 28 (Birthday of His Majesty, the King).

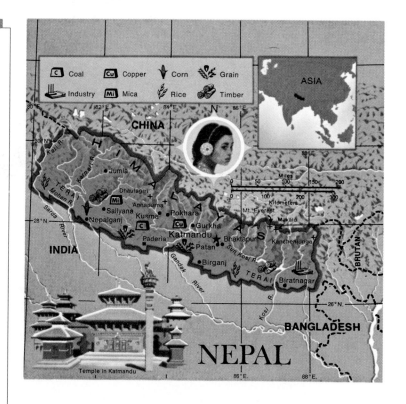

Temple in Katmandu

NEPAL

two centuries. Equally well-known are the Sherpas, a sturdy mountaineering people whose villages are situated high in the Himalayas. The Sherpas raise cattle and yaks, and some serve as porters and guides for mountain climbers.

Religion. About 88 percent of all Nepalese are adherents of Hinduism, the state religion. Buddhism is the religion of about 7 percent, and there are small groups of Muslims and Christians. A unique part of Nepalese culture is the way Hinduism and Buddhism mingle with each other. Many temples house both Hindu and Buddhist shrines, while religious ceremonies and festivals are shared by all.

Way of Life. The typical Nepalese village is made up of two-story houses of stone or mud brick, which are clustered together on hillsides above the flat valleys or above irrigated, terraced fields. In most areas, rice is the staple food. Occasionally, mixed dishes of vegetables and fish or chicken are served. Tea is the most popular drink, and among the Sherpas, it is taken with salt and butter.

Clothing is varied and generally colorful. Blouses and long skirts are worn by the women, while men wear knee-length robes and tight pants.

For the Nepalese, who are primarily farmers, family life provides its own entertainment and excitement. Weddings feature elaborate celebrations. At harvesttime, men and women perform the traditional rice dance. In October, when the herds are brought down from the highest valleys for the winter, each male Gurung brings to a clan feast the head of a ram he has killed.

Cities. Within the Katmandu Valley are the country's three principal cities—Katmandu (Kathmandu), Patan, and Bhaktapur (Bhadgaon). They are close enough to each other to be considered one metropolitan area. **Katmandu,** Nepal's capital and economic heart, is a city of nearly 450,000. Its lively streets are flanked by numerous Hindu and Buddhist temples and statues, showing the elaborate woodwork and metalwork for which Nepalese craftsmen are famous. **Patan,** "the city with a thousand gold roofs," and **Bhaktapur,** with its restored Royal Square, are two other architectural jewels.

ECONOMY

More than 90 percent of the Nepalese are engaged in agriculture or forestry. Rice, wheat, jute, millet, maize, and sugarcane are major crops. Sheep and goats graze on the lower hillsides; at the highest altitudes, cattle, yaks, and a crossbreed called the dzo, or *dzopkyo,* are raised.

Jute and sugar processing are important industries, as is tourism. Nepalese factories produce cigarettes, garments, soap, lumber, paper, chemicals, and cement, among other things.

Nepal's economy has come a long way since 1951, when the nation had virtually no schools, electricity, industry, roads, or civil service. Aid from China, India, the United States, and others has helped Nepal lay a foundation for economic growth. A highway network continues to grow, and those villages not connected to Katmandu by road are linked by radio. Most village children now have access to at least a primary school, and about one in every five young persons attends secondary school. The national university has dozens of campuses for students interested in higher education. Still, only 30 percent of all Nepalese can read and write, and skilled labor of any kind is scarce.

Elaborate woodwork and metalwork decorate many buildings in Katmandu, the capital of Nepal.

HISTORY AND GOVERNMENT

From about A.D. 300 until the mid-1700s, written accounts tell of a succession of Hindu dynasties and rulers controlling various parts of what is now Nepal. In 1769, Prithwi Narayan Shah, the ruler of the Gurungs, became Nepal's first king. The current monarch is his descendant.

Nepalese expansion southward into India resulted in conflict with the British and the Anglo-Nepali War of 1814–15. Under the peace treaty of 1815, Nepal gave up some of its territory and agreed to allow a British resident officer to be stationed in Katmandu. In 1846, a member of the Rana family forced the king to appoint him prime minister and to grant him absolute power. Thereafter, the premiership was held by the Ranas, who became the actual rulers of Nepal.

Eventually, Nepalese became dissatisfied with the isolationist policies of the Rana family. King Tribhuwan, a descendant of Prithwi Narayan Shah, escaped to India in 1950. Shortly afterward, a revolt in Katmandu broke the power of the Ranas. King Tribhuwan returned to Nepal in 1951 and proclaimed a constitutional monarchy.

Under Tribhuwan's son Mahendra, Nepal's first elected government took office in 1959. But the king soon dismissed the elected prime minister, and a new constitution in 1962 banned political parties and granted the king executive powers. King Mahendra died in 1972 and was succeeded on the throne by his son, the U.S.-educated Birendra. Amendments to the constitution in 1980 permitted direct elections to the Rashtriya Panchayat, or National Assembly (held in 1981 and 1986).

In 1990, pro-democracy protests forced King Birendra to decree a multiparty system and legalize political parties. A new constitution adopted in November made Nepal a constitutional monarchy with a two-house legislature; multiparty elections were held in 1991. After the 1994 elections, the Communist Party of Nepal formed a minority government. The centrist Nepal Congress Party regained the premiership in 1995.

DONALD N. WILBER, Editor, *The Nations of Asia*

BHUTAN

The king of Bhutan rules from a hillside palace in the capital city of Thimphu. The women in the foreground wear traditional Bhutanese costumes.

Bhutan's landscape suggests not just one nation but several. It contains forested, snowcapped mountain ranges; broad, grassy valleys; and steamy jungles that teem with exotic wildlife—all packed into a space roughly the size of Switzerland.

Statistically, Bhutan is one of the world's poorest nations. Yet its warm, hospitable people—nearly all of them farmers—never go hungry. In fact, they produce so much food they have plenty left over to sell to hungrier nations, such as neighboring India.

Bhutan's monarchy is eager to provide all Bhutanese with the benefits of the developed world—education, health care, improved housing. Yet at the same time, it is careful to isolate the Bhutanese from any threat to their traditional ways, and to maintain the landscape's natural beauty.

THE LAND

Bhutan occupies a key position between India's northern plains and Tibet, now a region of China, because it controls several mountain passes in the Himalayas. Barely 100 mi. (161 km.) wide and 200 mi. (322 km.) long, it has three main geographic areas.

Northern Bhutan lies within the Great Himalayas, where the mountains reach a height of more than 24,000 ft. (7,300 m.). The 300-mi. (483-km.) boundary with Tibet stretches along snowcapped peaks, some of which have never been scaled.

The Middle Himalayan region of central Bhutan contains several fertile valleys. These valleys are the most densely populated in the country, and they range in elevation from 5,000 to 9,000 ft. (1,524 to 2,743 m.).

Along the southern border of Bhutan lies the Duars plain, which extends into India. This is a hot, humid, and rainy area. It is inhabited by deer, tigers, elephants, and other exotic wildlife, including golden langurs, which rank among the world's rarest primates.

Bhutan's climate varies with altitude. The valleys in central Bhutan are temperate, while those in the south are subtropical. Violent thunderstorms and rain are common. Annual rainfall averages 40 in. (100 cm.) in the central valleys and 197 in. (500 cm.) in the south. Violent storms that rumble down from the Himalayas prompted the Bhutanese to call their country Druk Yul, "Land of the Thunder Dragon."

What impresses most outsiders about the Bhutanese is how conscious they are of the need to protect their environment. The nation is comparatively free of problems such as deforestation, soil erosion, and threats to wildlife that plague other nations. Some decades ago, the Bhutanese set up 10 protected areas that cover 20 percent of the land. In 1986, the government rejected a much-needed dam because it would have flooded a section of one of these areas, the Royal Manas National Park. Environmental education is taught in every school.

THE PEOPLE

Because of the harsh physical conditions in the northern mountains and in the southern Duars, most of the people live in the valleys of central Bhutan. About 50 percent of the Bhutanese are Bhotia, a people of Tibetan origin, whose forebears came to Bhutan during the 700s, bringing their culture and Buddhist religion with them. About 35 percent of the population consists of Nepali immigrants, who moved to Bhutan during the late 1800s and early 1900s to farm the southern foothills. Several smaller tribal groups account for the remaining 15 percent.

Most Bhutanese practice the state religion, Mahayana Buddhism, a reformed version of Tibetan (Lamaist) Buddhism. About 25 percent of all Bhutanese are Hindus.

Bhutan's official language is Dzongkha, which is related to classical Tibetan. Nepali is spoken in southern Bhutan, and Bhutanese speak at least 11 other languages. English, the language of instruction in the schools and colleges, is widely spoken. Unfortunately, Bhutan's schools are as widely scattered as its villages, and only 26 percent of the school-aged children attend them. Only one in five adults can read and write.

A typical Bhutanese house is a two-story building constructed of stone or mud brick. The family occupies the upper floor, while the lower is used as a barn. Beds are made of straw and yak-wool blankets.

FACTS AND FIGURES

OFFICIAL NAME: Kingdom of Bhutan.

NATIONALITY: Bhutanese.

CAPITAL: Thimphu (Thimbu).

LOCATION: Southern central Asia.

AREA: 18,147 sq. mi. (47,000 sq. km.).

PHYSICAL FEATURES: Highest point—Kula Kangri (24,783 ft.; 7,554 m.). **Lowest point**—150 ft. (46 m.).

POPULATION: 800,000 (1996; annual growth 2.3%).

MAJOR LANGUAGE: Dzongkha (official).

MAJOR RELIGION: Buddhism.

GOVERNMENT: Monarchy. **Head of state and government**—king. **Legislature**—National Assembly (Tshogdu).

ECONOMY: Industries and products—textiles, timber, metalware. **Chief exports**—cardamon, gypsum, timber. **Chief imports**—petroleum, grain, machinery.

MONETARY UNIT: 1 ngultrum = 100 chetrum.

NATIONAL HOLIDAY: December 17 (National Day).

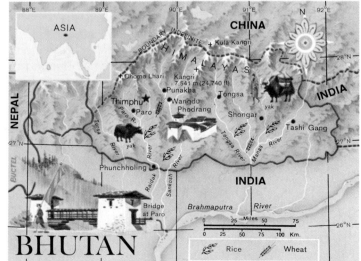

BHUTAN

In an effort to preserve traditional ways, the wearing of Bhutanese national dress is compulsory at all times. Men and boys wear the *boku,* a knee-length, white-cuffed kimono. Women and girls wear the *kira,* an ankle-length, embroidered wrap; and the *tyogo,* a small jacket.

There are few towns. **Thimphu**, also spelled Thimbu, the capital, has a population of 20,000. It is dominated by the Tashichodzong, a prime example of the Bhutanese monastery-fortresses, or *dzongs,* that function as administrative and religious centers in the nation's 18 districts. Thimphu's *dzong,* built in 1641, houses the government's offices and serves as the headquarters of the Drupka monks, members of Bhutan's dominant Buddhist sect.

Thimphu is also the site of the memorial *chorten,* or shrine, to Jigme Dorji Wangchuk, the third king, who died in 1972. When Dorji Wangchuk ascended to the throne in 1952, his kingdom had no roads, no postal system, and no air links to the outside world. During his reign, Bhutan was opened to the world.

Women command a good deal of respect in Bhutan. Family property passes to them, and they usually have sole authority over decisions that involve children.

ECONOMY

Ninety-five percent of Bhutanese workers are farmers and herders, and farming is the country's chief economic activity. A variety of crops are grown, depending on elevation and climate. Rice and buckwheat are grown up to an elevation of 5,000 ft. (1,500 m.). At higher elevations, farmers alternate crops of barley and rice, while wheat is grown up to an altitude of 9,000 ft. (2,700 m.).

Only one in 100 Bhutanese works in industry or commerce—such activities as mining, making and selling handicrafts, manufacturing cement, processing food, or turning logs into timber. Bhutanese are particularly noted for embroidered wool and silk fabrics, bronze and silver ornaments, beautifully fashioned swords and daggers, and handsomely carved woodwork. Examples of the fine wood carving may be seen in the ornate roofs and windows that adorn the old buildings in the country's many *dzongs.* Coal, dolomite, and limestone are the only minerals mined in Bhutan.

HISTORY AND GOVERNMENT

Bhutan became a separate political state some 300 years ago, when a Tibetan lama (priest) named Ngawang Namgyal proclaimed himself king. Subsequently, Bhutan was ruled by two leaders, a *je khemko,* or head abbot, for spiritual matters, and a *druk desi* for political and administrative affairs. In 1907, aided by the British, the *penlop* (governor) of Tongsa in eastern Bhutan established a hereditary line of kings.

The present king, Jigme Singye Wangchuk, came to the throne in 1972. He is assisted by an advisory council of civil servants and Buddhist leaders. The legislature is the 148-member Tsongdu, or National Assembly. Every three years, the people elect 105 members of the Tsongdu, with every family having one vote. Buddhist monastic orders appoint 10 members, and the king appoints 33. Bhutan is guided in its foreign affairs by India.

P. P. KARAN, University of Kentucky; author, *The Himalayan Kingdoms*

Colorfully decorated rickshaws crowd the streets of Dhaka, the capital of Bangladesh.

BANGLADESH

Bangladesh's flag depicts a fiery red sun setting over a sea of green rice fields, symbolizing the scenic beauty of this South Asian country. While Bangladesh is indeed beautiful, it is also one of the poorest and most densely populated countries in the world. Rivers supply it with the fertile soil that is its greatest resource. Yet they also bring the floods that are one of Bangladesh's greatest problems and the source of much of its people's misery.

Political instability has hindered Bangladesh's ability to deal with flooding and other problems. Since it declared its independence from Pakistan in 1971, this fledgling democracy has been beset by political assassinations, coups, election violence, and punishing boycotts. Despite these challenges, Bangladeshis are committed to a system of government that is acceptable both at home and in the international community, on which it relies for billions of dollars in aid each year.

THE LAND

Bangladesh—the name means "Bengal Nation"—lies astride the Bay of Bengal, where its jagged coastline runs for 357 mi. (575 km.). The Bay of Bengal, an arm of the Indian Ocean, is the only natural feature to dictate the shape of the 55,598 sq.-mi. (143,998 sq.-km.) country's irregular border. Political considerations and an attempt to keep communities intact guided Great Britain's hand in drawing that border when it carved two new nations—India and Pakistan—out of British India in 1947. As a

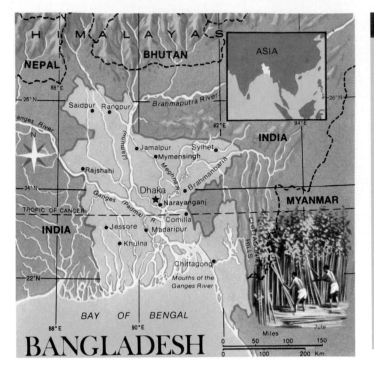

BANGLADESH

FACTS AND FIGURES

OFFICIAL NAME: People's Republic of Bangladesh.

NATIONALITY: Bangladeshi(s).

CAPITAL: Dhaka.

LOCATION: Southern Asia. **Boundaries**—India, Myanmar, Bay of Bengal.

AREA: 55,598 sq. mi. (144,000 sq. km.).

PHYSICAL FEATURES: Highest point—Mount Keokradong (4,034 ft.; 1,230 m.). **Lowest point**—sea level. **Chief rivers**—Ganges, Brahmaputra, Meghna.

POPULATION: 119,800,000 (1996; annual growth 2.0%).

MAJOR LANGUAGES: Bengali (official), English.

MAJOR RELIGIONS: Islam, Hinduism.

GOVERNMENT: Republic. **Head of state**—president. **Head of government**—prime minister. **Legislature**—unicameral National Parliament.

CHIEF CITIES: Dhaka, Chittagong, Khulna.

ECONOMY: Chief minerals—natural gas, uranium. **Chief agricultural products**—jute, tea, rice. **Industries and products**—jute manufacturing, food processing, cotton textiles. **Chief exports**—garments, raw and manufactured jute, leather, tea, fish. **Chief imports**—foodstuffs, fuels, raw cotton, fertilizer.

MONETARY UNIT: 1 taka = 100 paise.

NATIONAL HOLIDAY: March 26 (Independence Day).

result, Bangladesh, which the British called East Pakistan, is almost entirely surrounded by its giant neighbor, India. It shares a border with Myanmar, formerly Burma, on the southeast.

Four-fifths of Bangladesh occupies the large Bengal Delta, which is formed by three of the world's most powerful rivers—the Ganges, the Brahmaputra, and the Meghna. The delta is largely a flat floodplain that is crisscrossed by innumerable rivers and streams. When these waterways overflow during flood season, they deposit fertile soil along their banks. Bangladeshis use this soil to cultivate a variety of crops, including rice, the nation's chief agricultural product and food staple.

While most of Bangladesh lies less than 50 ft. (15 m.) above sea level, hilly areas exist in the far northeast and southeast corners of the country. The country's highest point, Mount Keokradong, is 4,034 ft. (1,230 m.) high. It rises from the hills of Chittagong, a district to the east of the Bay of Bengal. These hills are covered with tropical forests and teak, a valuable hardwood. **Chittagong**, Bangladesh's chief seaport, lies at the mouth of the Karnaphuli River, which runs through this district.

Bamboo grows throughout most of Bangladesh, as do mango, palm, and tamarind trees. Bengal tigers live in the Sundarbans, a swampy region in southwest Bangladesh.

CLIMATE

Bangladesh has a semitropical monsoon climate with two principal seasons—a hot, wet summer and a cooler, drier winter. The average temperature in April, usually the warmest month, is 82° F. (28° C.). In January, usually the coldest month, the temperature is 64° F. (18° C.).

Bangladesh receives an enormous amount of rainfall. The rainy season lasts from mid-March to October. Monsoons—shifts in the direction of the prevailing winds—set in around mid-May. During the monsoon season, winds from the Bay of Bengal bring rain practically every day.

Bangladesh's frequently violent weather includes monsoons, floods, and tropical cyclones.

The average annual rainfall is 100 in. (250 cm.) in the east, 65 in. (165 cm.) in the west, and as much as 250 in. (635 cm.) in the far northeast.

Monsoon rains often cause rivers to overflow and flood the surrounding countryside. In August and September of 1988, Bangladesh experienced the worst monsoon floods in its history. At one point, 75 percent of the country was underwater. More than 2,000 people died, and about 25 million others were left homeless as a result of the flooding.

Tropical cyclones often strike Bangladesh at the end of monsoon season. These fierce storms may be accompanied by huge tidal waves, or storm surges, that do their most damage to low-lying nations such as Bangladesh. In 1970, a cyclone and tidal wave that struck Bangladesh, then called East Pakistan, killed some 300,000 people, drowned millions of livestock, and destroyed most of the nation's fishing fleet. A 1985 cyclone killed an estimated 10,000 people.

THE PEOPLE

Bangladesh is one of the world's most densely populated nations, with an average of more than 2,000 persons per sq. mi. (806 persons per sq. km.). More than 80 percent of all Bangladeshis live in rural areas, chiefly in small villages, and try to make a living by farming. Their homes are one- or two-room bamboo houses with thatched roofs. There is little or no electricity or running water. The Sundarbans and the Chittagong Hill district are the least densely populated areas of Bangladesh.

About 20 percent of all Bangladeshis live in small, cramped wooden houses in Bangladesh's cities and towns. Though primarily a rural country, Bangladesh has more than a dozen cities with populations over 100,000. The largest of these is **Dhaka** (formerly Dacca), the capital. Continuously inhabited since the 400s, Dhaka now has 3.5 million people living in its metropolitan area. **Chittagong,** in the southeast, is the nation's second-largest city and chief port.

Bengalis. Most Bangladeshis are descendants of people who migrated to the area thousands of years ago from lands now occupied by Myanmar, Tibet, and northern India. Ninety-eight percent of the Bangladeshis are Bengalis—short, dark-skinned people, like their neighbors in the Indian state of West Bengal. The country's several minority groups include the Chakmas, the Marmas, the Mros, and the Tipperas, who live mainly in the Chittagong Hill district.

Unlike their mainly Hindu neighbors in West Bengal, most Bangladeshis are Muslims. In 1988, a constitutional amendment made Islam the state religion of Bangladesh, but stated that other religions could be practiced freely. About 16 percent of all Bangladeshis are Hindu, and about 1 percent are Buddhist and Christian.

Most people speak Bangla (also called Bengali), the official language. English is widely used in government, commerce, and higher education.

Hill People.　There has been a long and bloody conflict in the Chittagong Hill district between local tribespeople and the ethnic Bengalis who have been settling there in increasing numbers. The tribespeople, most of whom follow Buddhism, feel they must protect their culture and religion from the "flatlanders," as they call the Bengalis. The government is trying to ease tensions in the district by giving the people in the hills more freedom to run their own affairs. However, tribespeople insist that all nontribal people be removed from their district—a demand that will be hard for the land-starved Bengalis to meet.

Women.　Islam dominates social, political, and religious life in Bangladesh, and it heavily influences the lives of all Bangladeshis. The Muslim custom of *purdah*, which means "curtain," requires women to keep out of public view. Muslim women cover their heads with veils around strangers, avoid social contact with men they are not related to, and take part in few activities outside their homes. Muslim men do much of the shopping for their families, and generally they have more freedom than their wives do. Hindu women have greater social freedom than Muslim women, although their legal rights are limited.

Two-thirds of all Bangladeshi women get married between the ages of 15 and 19, and during their lifetimes they each bear five or six children. While about 39 percent of all men can read and write, only 18 percent of all women can read. On average, Bangladeshi women live for 49 years—two years less than men do.

Education.　In a country that has no law that requires children to go to school, only about half of all children attend primary school. In 1986, 60 percent of all school-aged children—69 percent of the boys and 50 percent of the girls—attended primary school. Only about one in five Bangladeshis attends secondary school.

Food.　Rice and fish are the most popular foods, and tea the most popular drink. Because of widespread poverty, however, many Bangladeshis do not have enough food to eat, and water is often the only drink available. Food shortages and unsanitary living conditions cause widespread disease. Malaria, which is spread by mosquitoes that thrive in Bangladesh's swampy regions, kills thousands of people each year.

Bengali Arts.　Despite their many hardships, Bangladeshis find time for art and literature. The country's warm evening air is often filled with the songs of Rabindranath Tagore, a Bengali poet from India who became prominent in Bengali literature during the late 1800s. Plays based on religious stories are popular forms of entertainment, too.

Clothing.　Bengali women traditionally wear the *sari*, a straight piece of cloth draped around the body as a long dress, with a short blouse underneath. Muslim men usually wear the *lungi,* a tight, shirtlike garment. Hindu men wear the *dhoti,* a piece of cloth wrapped around the waist and between the legs, and they often go shirtless in Bangladesh's hot climate.

THE ECONOMY

With an average annual per-capita income of $150, Bangladesh is one of the world's poorest nations. The economy is underdeveloped and depends almost entirely on agriculture. About 80 percent of the people are farmers. Most Bangladeshis farm with simple tools on farms whose average size is less than 3.5 acres (1.4 hectares).

The chief agricultural products are rice and jute, a fiber used to make twine, sacks, and burlap. Rice, the nation's basic food, grows in almost all parts of the nation. Fertile soil and a usually ample water supply allow three crops a year to be harvested in many areas of the country. Bangladesh is the world's leading producer of jute.

Industry.   Though Bangladesh has few factories, its industries produce goods that can be sold abroad, enabling Bangladesh to earn valuable foreign currency. Jute mills turn jute fiber into string, burlap sacking, and carpet backing. Jute processing is the nation's chief industry and source of its leading exports.

The manufacture of garments for export is a growing industry. Other industries include food processing and the manufacture of paper, leather goods, cement, and fertilizer. Besides jute, important export crops are wheat, tea, and tobacco. Bangladesh also exports fish, leather, and timber. Another major source of foreign exchange is the remittances from

Bangladesh's abundant rainfall and warm temperatures allow three rice crops per year.

Some Bangladeshis supplement their income by making such traditional products as pottery.

Bangladeshis who work abroad, mainly as guest workers in Arab nations of the Middle East. Still another source is the more than $1 billion a year that other nations have granted Bangladesh since it became independent in 1971.

Bangladesh needs foreign exchange to pay for needed imports, which include building materials, chemicals, coal, electric appliances, machinery, petroleum, textiles, transportation equipment, and food-stuffs. Even with imports and increased food production, Bangladesh's food supply is not increasing as fast as its population. Though its growth has slowed in recent decades, the population is expected to reach 144 million by the year 2000.

Drawbacks to Investment.   The government's attempt to encourage industrial growth in order to offset the country's dependence on agriculture and agricultural products has been disappointing. Foreign investors, especially, are wary of Bangladesh's unstable political climate, its lack of natural resources (natural gas is one of the few mineral resources), the low education level of potential employees, and the nation's underdeveloped transportation system.

The unusual need for bridges makes it both difficult and expensive to build roads and railways. Rivers still provide the country's largest single transportation network. Passenger and cargo ships, along with canoes and small wooden boats, all travel on Bangladesh's approximately 4,500 mi. (7,240 km.) of navigable waterways.

Flood Control.   The floods that deposit fertile soil on Bangladesh's farmland are vitally important to the nation's economy. Yet there is no way to control the sort of severe flooding that in 1987 and 1988 caused extensive economic damage. This flooding has become an international concern. A number of countries have begun to examine ways to assist Bangladesh in managing these annual disasters. Suggested solutions range from building dams to dredging riverbeds to enable water to course through them without overflowing.

HISTORY AND GOVERNMENT

The early history of Bengal, the region occupied by Bangladesh and the Indian state of West Bengal, is obscure. It is generally believed that about 1000 B.C., the Bang tribe, a Dravidian people, was pushed out of the upper Ganges Valley by advancing Indo-Aryans. The new territory occupied by the Bang later came to be known as Bengal. During the 3rd century B.C., the Maurya empire extended its domain over the area, and Buddhism spread under the rule of the emperor Asoka. Later, Bengal came under the control of the Hindu Gupta empire.

During the 800s, the Pala dynasty came to power. The three centuries of rule by the Pala kings is regarded as the classical period of Bengali history. The arts flowered, and a distinct Bengali culture took shape.

During the six centuries from the 1200s through the 1700s, Bengal was under Muslim rule. In this period, Islam spread rapidly in Bengal, especially in the eastern region that would become Bangladesh. Islam has played a crucial role in the region ever since. Nonetheless, rural Bengali Muslims who are descended from Hindus continue to practice ancient Hindu rites. And most Muslims and Hindus participate in each other's religious festivals.

During the 1700s, Bengal came under the control of the British, who ruled it as part of their Indian empire until 1947. In that year, Great Britain ended its rule in the Indian subcontinent. India received its independence, and at the insistence of the Muslim League, the separate nation of Pakistan was formed out of those parts of the subcontinent where the Muslims were a majority. East Bengal, which lay within the Bengal enclave of India, became the eastern wing—East Pakistan—of the new country. It was separated from the larger, western part of Pakistan by 1,000 mi. (1,600 km.) of Indian territory.

Early Years. Most of the officials sent from West Pakistan to govern East Pakistan could not speak Bangla, and they tended to treat Bengalis with contempt. Many East Pakistanis felt they had traded one colonial ruler—Great Britain—for another. To hold the two distant parts of the country together, the Pakistani government, headquartered in West Pakistan, relied on Islam. It was a mistake. The government set out to eliminate Hindu influences from the Bengali language and culture, outraging East Pakistanis. Bengali university students in Dhaka rioted in 1952 to block a proposal to make Urdu, the main language of West Pakistan, the only official language of all of Pakistan. (Today, Bangladeshis commemorate the students who died in those riots every February 21, on Martyrs' Day.)

Civil War and Independence. In legislative elections held in 1970, a majority of seats were won by the East Pakistani Awami League, which was led by Sheikh Mujibur Rahman (Mujib), whose goals included greater autonomy for the eastern region. When, by postponing the opening of the legislature in 1971, the national government prevented the successful candidates from taking their seats, riots and other disorders broke out in East Pakistan. West Pakistani troops suppressed the riots harshly, and Sheikh Mujib was arrested. In the turmoil, some 10 million Bengalis fled into India.

Border incidents between Pakistan and India eventually led to a short but full-scale war, in which the West Pakistani forces were defeated. East Pakistan won its independence as Bangladesh, with Mujib

The architecture in some districts of Dhaka resembles that of many Western cities.

becoming its first prime minister in 1972. He later became president.

Recent Events.   A war-ravaged Bangladesh was faced with enormous economic and social problems. Political disputes added to the country's disarray. In 1975, President Mujib was killed during a coup led by military officers. A series of martial-law governments followed, until, in 1977, General Ziaur Rahman (Zia) assumed the presidency. He was elected president in 1978, but was assassinated in an attempted coup in 1981.

In 1982, General Hossain Mohammed Ershad, the army chief of staff, took control of the government as president, chief martial-law administrator, and head of the Council of Ministers. After many postponements, Ershad allowed elections for Parliament in 1986. Of the two major opposition groups, only the Awami League agreed to participate in this election. The Bangladesh Nationalist Party (BNP) declined. The progovernment Jatiya (People's) Party, set up by Ershad's backers for the transition to civilian rule, won a bare majority of seats. In August, Ershad retired from the military; and in October, he was elected president. Ershad ended martial law on November 10, 1986, the day Parliament passed an amendment to the constitution that held military leaders legally blameless for any action they took while running Bangladesh. The Jatiya Party won a large majority in a second parliamentary election in 1988. Renewed protests forced Ershad's resignation in December 1990.

Parliamentary elections held in February 1991 were won by the Bangladesh National Party; its leader, Begum Khalida Zia, became Bangladesh's first woman prime minister. A new constitution adopted later that year returned Bangladesh to a parliamentary form of government in which the president's powers were largely ceremonial. After the opposition boycotted the February 1996 elections, Zia stepped down. New elections in June were won by the Awami League, led by Mujib's daughter, Sheikh Hasina Wazed, who became prime minister.

P. P. KARAN, Chairman, Department of Geography, University of Kentucky

Colombo, the capital of Sri Lanka, has one of the largest artificial harbors in the world.

SRI LANKA

Sri Lanka, formerly known as Ceylon, is a pear-shaped island 22 mi. (35 km.) from the southeast tip of India. Sri Lanka has long been known for the beauty of its rivers and waterfalls, white beaches and thick forests, and all that the land yields—tea, rubber, coconuts, spices, and gemstones. More recently, it has become known as a land of great civil unrest. The different ethnic groups that enrich the country with cultural, linguistic, and religious diversity have found themselves in often deadly conflict.

THE LAND

Sri Lanka lies in the Indian Ocean, separated from India by Palk Strait. The island is 270 mi. (430 km.) long, 140 mi. (230 km.) across at its widest point, and has an area of 25,332 sq. mi. (65,610 sq. km.). The south-central region of the country is mountainous. It is surrounded by rolling plains on the east, south, and west. Plains also cover most of the northern half of the country. The land rises dramatically from lowland rice fields plowed by water buffalo, through coconut and rubber plantations and highlands planted with tea, to grass-covered mountains 7,000 ft. (2,100 m.) high. Many rivers flow down the mountains to the ocean.

Climate. Sri Lanka's climate is tropical. While the average lowland temperature is 80° F. (27° C.), the average temperature in the mountains is 60° F. (16° C.). Average rainfall varies from 50 in. (127 cm.) a year in the northeast to 200 in. (508 cm.) a year in the southwest.

Sri Lanka's two rainy seasons help account for this difference in rainfall. Each is caused by a different monsoon—a shift in the direction

FACTS AND FIGURES

OFFICIAL NAME: Democratic Socialist Republic of Sri Lanka.

NATIONALITY: Sri Lankan(s).

CAPITAL: Colombo.

LOCATION: Island in the Indian Ocean off the southeastern coast of India.

AREA: 25,332 sq. mi. (65,610 sq. km.).

PHYSICAL FEATURES: Highest point—Pidurutalagala (8,291 ft.; 2,527 m.). **Lowest point**—sea level. **Chief river**—Mahaweli Ganga.

POPULATION: 18,400,000 (1996; annual growth 1.5%).

MAJOR LANGUAGES: Sinhalese (official), Tamil (national), English.

MAJOR RELIGIONS: Buddhism, Hinduism, Christianity, Islam.

GOVERNMENT: Republic. **Head of state and government**—president (a prime minister is appointed by the president). **Legislature**—Parliament.

CHIEF CITIES: Colombo, Dehiwala-Mount Lavinia, Moratuwa, Jaffna.

ECONOMY: Chief minerals—graphite, gemstones, ilmenite, monazite, quartz sand, limestone. **Chief agricultural products**—rice, coconuts, cassava, sugarcane, tea, rubber. **Industries and products**—cement, gemstones, ilmenite, petroleum refining. **Chief exports**—garments, tea, gems, petroleum and rubber products. **Chief imports**—textiles, machinery, transportation equipment, petroleum.

MONETARY UNIT: 1 Sri Lanka rupee = 100 cents.

NATIONAL HOLIDAY: February 4 (Independence Day).

SRI LANKA

of the prevailing winds. The southwest, which is mostly covered by tropical rain forest, experiences the stronger rainy season in summer and fall. In late fall and winter, the northeast experiences a weaker rainy season. Sri Lankans store rainwater in huge human-made lakes and tanks and use it to irrigate crops during the dry seasons.

Natural Resources. Sri Lanka has many natural resources, including its beautiful gemstones. Sapphires, rubies, moonstones, topazes, and cat's-eyes are found in the southwest. Large deposits of graphite, the leading mineral export, are also found there.

Another natural treasure is the country's variety of wildlife and fauna. More than 3,000 species of ferns and flowering plants grow there. Some common plants are orchids, poinsettias, and fruit trees. Nearly 400 different types of birds, including peacocks and flamingos, live in the forests and jungles. Sri Lanka is home to more than 100 kinds of mammals, among them leopards, buffalo, deer, bears, and monkeys. Trained elephants help in construction work and in clearing forest land. Wild elephants are now strictly protected by law to save them from extinction. There are also crocodiles, lizards, and snakes. The government has set aside land for national parks and bird sanctuaries to protect the island's wildlife.

THE PEOPLE

Sri Lanka's two largest ethnic groups—and those most often in conflict—are the Sinhalese and the Tamils. The Sinhalese make up more than 70 percent of the population. The majority of these people live in the southern and western regions of the country and speak Sinhalese. Most Sinhalese are Theravada Buddhists. As an ethnic and linguistic group, they are found nowhere else in the world.

Sri Lanka is also home to more than 2 million Tamils, who make up about 20 percent of the population. The Tamils live mainly in the north and east, speak Tamil, and are mostly Hindus. About half are Sri Lankan Tamils, descendants of people who came to Sri Lanka from the south Indian state of Tamil Nadu in ancient times. About half are Indian Tamils, whose ancestors the British brought from India to work on coffee and tea plantations, starting in the late 1800s. Sri Lanka's strong caste system keeps these two groups at odds. Sri Lankan Tamils regard Indian Tamils as being of the lowest caste.

The population also includes Moors, descendants of early Arab traders; Burghers, descendants of European colonists; and Veddas. Veddas are thought to be descendants of the island's original inhabitants.

Four out of five Sri Lankans live in rural areas and farm as their ancestors did before them. Most rural people—and many other Sri Lankans—live in extended families.

Most houses in rural areas have mud walls and thatched roofs. They often have a small veranda and are fenced. Village houses are square or rectangular, with walls of dried mud or clay blocks, floors of beaten earth or concrete, and roofs of coconut thatch or tile.

A Hindu temple in Colombo (left) and a Buddhist dagoba, or shrine (right), at Anuradhapura reflect Sri Lanka's religious diversity. Sri Lanka also has small groups of Christians and Muslims.

Tea, Sri Lanka's leading export, is grown on huge plantations in the country's highlands.

While urban Sri Lankan men often wear Western-style clothes, traditional clothing is more common. For men, this consists of a *sarong* (a long piece of cloth, usually white, which is wrapped around the body and secured at the waist) worn with a loose shirt or jacket. Sri Lankan women wear a *redde,* which is similar to a sarong, with a blouse or jacket, or a *sari* (a straight piece of cloth draped around the body as a long dress).

Rice is Sri Lanka's staple food. Orthodox Hindus and most Buddhists are vegetarians. They often serve rice with curries made of vegetables cooked in coconut milk and spices. Tea is the favorite drink.

Boys and girls are required to go to school from the ages of 6 to 16. They are taught in the language they speak at home: Sinhalese or Tamil. English is also taught. Nearly 90 percent of all Sri Lankans can read and write—an impressive figure, especially when compared with India's 36 percent literacy rate.

Artistic expression has been important to the people of Sri Lanka throughout their history. Most ancient art has religious themes. The ancient Sinhalese capital Anuradhapura is filled with *dagobas* (domed Buddhist shrines) and statues of Buddha that are important to Buddhists everywhere. Dance is an important art form. Each August, in the lovely hill city of Kandy, scores of whirling dancers in lavish costumes take part in a *perahera* (procession), a Buddhist festival to honor a tooth of Buddha.

Sri Lankans have handed down artisans' skills for generations. Handicrafts include carved wooden masks used in ritual dances and folk plays, brasswork, handloomed cotton, tortoiseshell ware, pottery, and handmade lace.

ECONOMY

About half of all Sri Lankans make their living by farming. These farmers work either on large tea, rubber, or coconut plantations; or on small farms, where they raise a variety of crops, including rice, fruits, vegetables, tobacco, and cinnamon. World prices for the plantation crops, Sri Lanka's traditional exports, have fluctuated a great deal since the 1950s, with a general downward trend. Sri Lanka is trying to reach self-sufficiency in rice production, a staple that it must still import.

More than one-third of Sri Lanka's workers provide services, in such areas as trade, government, communications, and transportation. Sri Lanka's manufacturing industry employs one-tenth of the Sri Lankan work force. The garment industry is employing increasing numbers of Sri Lankans and bringing in increasing amounts of much-needed foreign dollars.

Tourism, another source of foreign exchange, plummeted during the intense ethnic strife that began in 1983. Sri Lankans are hopeful that their beautiful beaches, sophisticated hotels, and friendly people will lure tourists back to what could become one of the Indian Ocean's premier resorts.

Sri Lanka has often had to turn to the international community for aid. In the 1980s, after ethnic violence brought the economy to a near halt, the international community pledged hundreds of millions of dollars to help Sri Lanka rebuild.

The island's commercial center and main port is the capital, **Colombo.** The docks of this port city are fragrant with tea and spices waiting to be shipped abroad.

HISTORY

The *Mahavansa,* the 6th-century epic of Sri Lanka, tells of a group of men from northern India who sailed to Sri Lanka in the 6th century B.C. They conquered the island's earliest inhabitants and set up the Sinhalese kingdom in the northern part of the island. They built complex irrigation systems to support agriculture in the face of persistent droughts. Buddhism was introduced to Sri Lanka around the 3rd century B.C., and the Sinhalese adopted this religion. Buddhism and an advanced irrigation system became the pillars of the Sinhalese kingdom, which lasted more than 1,000 years.

Rice, the staple food of Sri Lanka, is grown in terraced fields throughout the country.

As early as A.D. 500, the Tamils came from southern India to Sri Lanka to set up their own kingdom. The next 1,000 years of Sri Lankan history centered on struggles between Sinhalese kings and Tamil kings. Tamils eventually gained control of the northern half of the island, and the Sinhalese moved to the southern part of the island.

Sri Lanka's location on the ocean route between East Africa and South Asia made it a natural stopping place for traders and seafarers. Early Greeks and 8th-century Arabs knew the island, and Marco Polo visited it in 1293.

In 1505, the Portuguese became the first Europeans to occupy parts of Sri Lanka. They came in search of cinnamon and other spices. The Dutch drove out the Portuguese in 1658. At the end of the 1700s, the Dutch were challenged by the British, who in 1815 became the first Europeans to control the entire island. Sri Lanka remained under the British until 1948, when it became independent. Ceylon, the name under which the island was long known, was dropped in 1972, and the ancient Sinhalese name Sri Lanka, which means "Resplendent Land," was adopted.

Since Independence.   Sri Lanka has gone through many political crises since 1948. The worst has been the ongoing civil conflict between the Sinhalese and the Tamils. The newly independent, Sinhalese-dominated government angered the Tamils when it refused to accept Estate Tamils, descendants of the Tamils brought from India, as Sri Lankan citizens. Then, in 1956, the government made Sinhalese Sri Lanka's official language. Eventually, the law was changed to make Sinhalese and Tamil both official languages. But the Tamils began to demand guarantees that their language and culture would be protected.

The conflict escalated into guerrilla warfare in the early 1980s. Tamil separatists, who demanded an independent Tamil state, launched a terrorist campaign against the government, and some Sinhalese retaliated with attacks against Tamils. India stepped in to help end the conflict in 1987 but became embroiled in the guerrilla war when the Liberation Tigers of Tamil Eelam refused to give up the fight. India's presence also triggered an outbreak of violence in southern Sri Lanka by the People's Liberation Front (JVP), an extremist Sinhalese group, which was finally suppressed by the government in the fall of 1989. India withdrew the last of its troops in March 1990 after Sri Lanka agreed to give the Tamils greater economic and political power, but the bloody conflict between the Tamil separatists and government forces soon resumed.

On May 1, 1993, President Ranasinghe Premadasa was assassinated by a Tamil terrorist bomber. He was succeeded by Dingiri Banda Wijetunge. Chandrika Kumaratunga, the daughter of former prime ministers Solomon W. R. D. and Sirimavo Bandaranaike, who had become prime minister in August 1994, was elected president in November 1994. She named her mother prime minister and began peace talks with the Tamil rebels, but the violence continued.

Government.   After independence in 1948, Sri Lanka remained linked to the British Crown until 1972, when it became a republic. It had a parliamentary system of government headed by a prime minister until 1978. That year, a new constitution placed full executive power in the hands of a directly elected president. The president and members of the one-chamber Parliament are elected for six-year terms.

Reviewed by H. S. AMERASINGHE, Permanent Mission of Sri Lanka to the United Nations

Maldivian fishermen ply the waters in small, handsomely carved boats called *dhonis*.

MALDIVES

If a Maldivian wants to rent his own island, he can choose from hundreds in the Republic of Maldives. This archipelago, or chain of islands, is made up of over 1,200 coral islands, grouped into 19 atolls. Only about 200 are inhabited. Maldives is strategically placed along major sea lanes in the Indian Ocean.

The Maldivian atolls have long been praised for their beauty. In fact, the term *atoll*, meaning a coral island or group of islands enclosing a lagoon, comes from a Maldivian word—*atolu*.

The Land. The Maldive Islands lie several hundred miles southwest of Sri Lanka. None of the islands is larger than 5 sq. mi. (13 sq. km.), and the entire archipelago is only 115 sq. mi. (298 sq. km.) in area. The islands are low, rising no higher than 8 ft. (2.5 m.) above sea level.

The tropical climate is affected by monsoons, shifting winds that bring considerable rainfall. The weather is generally warm and humid. Coconut palms and breadfruit trees grow in abundance. The waters abound with fish, and there are magnificent tortoises.

Transportation to and from the various islands is by boat. The bicycle is an important form of transportation on land, and there are few automobiles.

The People. The origins of the Maldivian people are obscure. Their language, Divehi, is related to Sinhalese, a language spoken in Sri Lanka. For this reason, some scholars believe that the Maldivians are descendants of the Sinhalese of Sri Lanka, with a mixture of Arab peoples. Originally, the Maldivians were Buddhists, but they have practiced Islam since the 1100s.

More than 200,000 people live in Maldives, some 30,000 in the capital, **Male,** located on Male Island. The Maldivians are skilled sailors. Fishing employs 80 percent of the work force and supplies about 57 percent of the nation's exports. Dried fish (known as Maldive fish) and frozen tuna are exported to Sri Lanka and elsewhere. Locally made garments account for about 39 percent of the nation's exports.

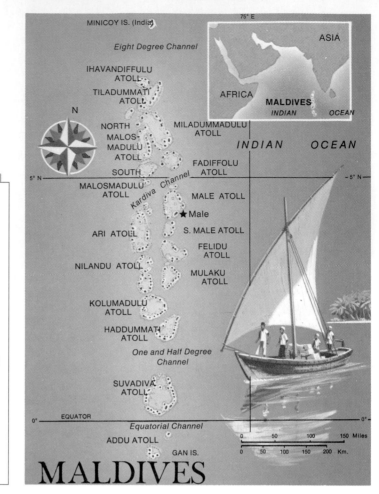

MALDIVES

The cultivation of coconuts and products derived from coconuts—copra (dried coconut meat) and coir (coconut fiber)—is another key industry. There are also some handicraft industries, such as mat making and the crafting of elegant tortoiseshell jewelry and art objects. During the 1980s and 1990s, tourism was one of the fastest-growing areas of the economy. Tourism and export revenues help Maldivians pay for the food, consumer goods, and petroleum they import. Rice, much of which must be imported, remains the staple food of the people.

History and Government. According to legend, an ancient prince of Ceylon, who with his bride was forced to anchor in a Maldivian lagoon because his ship was becalmed, became the country's first sultan. The Didi family, whose members governed Maldives as sultans for nearly eight centuries, is said to be descended from this prince.

Contact with early Arab traders led to the acceptance of Islam. Later the island came under the domination of the Portuguese and then the Dutch. In 1887, the islands became a British protectorate. Maldives attained complete independence on July 26, 1965.

In 1968, Maldives became a republic headed by an elected president under a new constitution. Maumoon Abdul Gayoom succeeded Ibraham Nasir as president in 1978. He survived a 1988 coup attempt with the aid of Indian troops, the last of which left the country in November 1989.

Reviewed by EMBASSY OF THE REPUBLIC OF MALDIVES, Washington, DC

The exotic foods of Southeast Asia have gained popularity worldwide.

SOUTHEAST ASIA

Southeast Asia is one of the world's great melting pots. Its diverse peoples moved into the region in search of a better life and greater security. This great population movement began about 4,000 years ago. Today, Southeast Asia includes the independent nations of Indonesia, the Philippines, Brunei, Malaysia, Singapore, Vietnam, Laos, Cambodia, Thailand, and Myanmar (formerly Burma). The newest of these is Brunei, which gained its full independence in 1984. The former colony of Portuguese East Timor is now part of Indonesia.

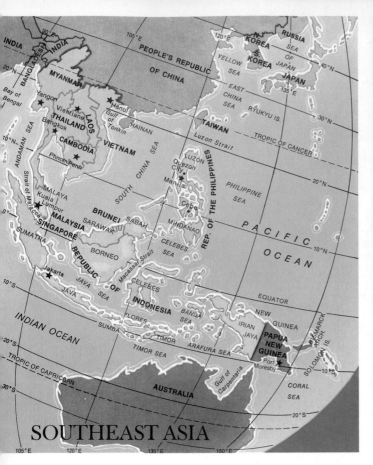

Today, most Southeast Asians reserve traditional clothing for special holidays (above).

The original inhabitants of Southeast Asia were a small, dark-skinned people, some of whose descendants still live in the highland regions of the Philippines, Indonesia, and Malaysia. Around 2500 B.C., the first major wave of migrating peoples entered the area. They were the Malays, or Indonesians, and it is their descendants who form the great majority of the populations of the Philippines and Indonesia today. The Malays formerly lived in what is now southern China, but pressure from the Chinese population in the north forced other peoples southward. These peoples in turn pressed upon the Malays, who moved through the mountain passes into mainland Southeast Asia, down the Malay Peninsula, and out into the Indonesian and Philippine islands. Skilled sailors, the Malays expanded eastward through these islands.

Other peoples followed, principally the Cambodians, the Vietnamese, the Myanmar (Burmese), and the Thai. They also moved south out of China, but settled in mainland Southeast Asia. The Thai were the last of the major peoples to settle in the area, establishing their first important kingdom during the 1200s.

These various peoples brought with them their own customs, cultures, and living patterns, but they were to be strongly influenced by still other peoples. Traders from India brought Indian ideas to Southeast Asia, especially the Hindu and Buddhist religions. Myanmar, Thailand, Laos, and Cambodia are today Buddhist countries as a result. Later, Muslim traders brought Islam to Malaysia and Indonesia, which are now predominantly Muslim. The culture and religion of Vietnam were influenced by China.

This process of infusion of both people and ideas has continued into modern times. The European powers began their colonization of the region (except for Thailand, which was never colonized) during the 1500s, bringing with them Western ideas, including Christianity. The Philippines, colonized by Spain, became largely Roman Catholic in religion. During the late 1700s and early 1800s, large numbers of Chinese and Indians came to Southeast Asia to take advantage of the economic opportunities during the height of the European colonial period. During World War II (1939 to 1945), the region was conquered by Japan. The years that followed World War II saw the appearance of the nation-states of modern Southeast Asia.

THE LAND

The nations and territories of Southeast Asia together cover an area of about 1,738,000 sq. mi. (4,500,000 sq. km.) and are inhabited by about 496 million (1996) people. Including the waters within it, Southeast Asia covers a portion of the globe as big as Europe from Ireland to Turkey. The largest country of Southeast Asia is Indonesia, which is the world's fourth most populous nation. In land area, Singapore is the region's smallest country. Its 3 million (1996) people live on only 239 sq. mi. (618 sq. km.) of land.

China is Southeast Asia's neighbor to the north. To the east, west, and south the region is flanked by seas, principally the Pacific and Indian oceans. Myanmar, the westernmost of the Southeast Asian lands, borders India and Bangladesh. Southeast Asia thus is located very strategically—east of India and south of China. These are the world's two most heavily populated countries. They are also lands with serious economic problems—problems that might be partly solved by access to the natural resources of the Southeast Asian countries.

The warm, humid climate of Southeast Asia is ideal for growing rice, tea, and many other crops.

Physically, Southeast Asia is a much-divided land. Its mountain chains, which run in a north–south direction, historically have separated some of its peoples, such as the Myanmar, Thai, and Vietnamese. Indonesia and the Philippines are also divided into literally thousands of islands, but contact was often easier among the islands than between coastal and interior regions. Southeast Asia's many divisions also made it easy to conquer the region piece by piece. This is what the European powers did from the 1500s through the 1800s, and what Japan did in 1941–42, during World War II.

The Climate. The climate in Southeast Asia is generally warm and often wet. The seasons in most countries are alternately dry and rainy, although in Indonesia there is considerable rainfall throughout the year. Myanmar and the Philippines in particular have especially deadly monsoons—violent rainstorms—with hurricanelike winds and much flooding and loss of life. The temperature rarely falls below 68° F. (20° C.) in most of Southeast Asia, except in the highlands, while the hot and dry season often brings temperatures of 90° F. (32° C.).

The Economy. Compared with both China and India, Southeast Asia is well endowed with resources and not densely populated (except for a few areas, such as the chief Indonesian island of Java), and it has a higher standard of living. Yet this standard of living is low compared with those of the United States or Europe.

Despite the great gains many of Southeast Asia's nations have made in manufacturing, the region's chief products are agricultural or mineral ones. Thailand is the world's leading exporter of rice; Cambodia, Myanmar, and Vietnam, in normal times, have also had substantial rice surpluses. The Philippines has become self-sufficient in its production of this vital grain, and Indonesia is expected to do so soon.

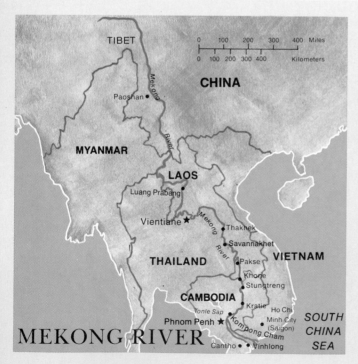

MEKONG RIVER

THE MEKONG

The Mekong, Asia's fifth-longest river, is known by many names. In the highlands of Xizang (Tibet), it is called Za Qu. In China, it is known as Lancang Jiang; in Vietnam, as Tien Giang. Mekong, its most common name, comes from the Thai expression *mae* (meaning "river") and Khong (the Thai name for the Mekong). By whatever name, this great river has played an important role in the lives of Southeast Asia's people since earliest times. Millions of Thai, Lao, Cambodians, and Vietnamese depend on water from the Mekong to grow the rice that sustains them. In addition, the river serves as an important avenue of trade and communication.

The Mekong starts in the Tanglha Range, a barren mountain wasteland in the south of China's South Qinghai province,

The juncture of a river and a canal is frequently the ideal site for an impromptu floating market.

near the Xizang border. Flowing swiftly in a southeasterly direction, the Mekong first passes through wild mountain country and steep canyons. Then, as it enters the Indochina Peninsula, the river moves at a slower pace through a region of lush green jungle and low, wooded hills. During one stretch, the Mekong forms the natural border between Laos to the east and Myanmar and Thailand to the west. Then it flows across Cambodia and the lower portion of Vietnam into the South China Sea.

The Mekong passes by the most important cities in Laos, including Vientiane, the river's main port, and Luang Prabang. It also flows by Phnom Penh, Cambodia's chief city. The Mekong Delta, south of Ho Chi Minh City (Saigon), Vietnam's largest city, has long been noted as one of the world's leading rice-producing areas. It is heavily populated. During the rainy monsoon season between June and October, the river becomes high and turbulent, and flooding is common. The Mekong's principal flood reservoir is the Tonlé Sap (Great Lake) in Cambodia's major rice-farming region.

Because of sandbars and dangerous rapids, most of the river cannot be navigated by large vessels. However, ships with a draft of up to 15 ft. (4 m.) can sail up the river to a point some 350 mi. (560 km.) from the South China Sea. The Mekong is navigable for short distances north of the Cambodian border. In southern Laos, the river drops 72 ft. (22 m.) over a series of rapids called the Khone Falls. This is the site of a hydroelectric plant, part of a larger U.N. plan to develop the lower Mekong basin.

Reviewed by RICHARD BUTWELL, California State University, Dominguez Hills; Author, *Southeast Asia, A Political Introduction*

In the more remote areas of Southeast Asia, many people adhere to traditional beliefs and customs.

Malaysia is the world's leading exporter of rubber, tin, palm oil, and tropical timber. Indonesia, Brunei, and Myanmar have substantial petroleum deposits, but coal is found only in northern Vietnam. Vietnam, Malaysia, and the Philippines also have some iron.

During the 1980s and 1990s, several of the region's nations achieved impressive spurts of industrial growth. Singapore became Southeast Asia's top manufacturing site and, in effect, the region's banker, through an expansion of its financial-services industry. Malaysia's and Indonesia's industrial sectors grew considerably. In the 1990s, Thailand's factories were producing about one-quarter of the nation's goods and services. The laggards in the industrial area during the 1980s and 1990s were those nations like Vietnam, Cambodia, and Myanmar whose economies were hobbled by excessive government controls, war, or both.

THE PEOPLE

Racially, almost all of Southeast Asia's peoples are of Mongoloid stock. Most have darker skin than the Han, China's dominant ethnic group. The area's major foreign minorities are the Chinese and Indians. Europeans have been relatively few in number, even during the colonial period.

Indonesia and the Philippines are probably the two least-complex countries ethnically. More than 90 percent of their inhabitants are of the broad Malay or Indonesian group. Singapore—often referred to as a "third China"—also is a fairly homogeneous country. Three out of four of its inhabitants are of Chinese descent. Cambodia's countryside is populated largely by Khmer, but the country has had large Chinese and Vietnamese minorities as well.

The other countries have serious ethnic problems. Myanmar has four major minority groups: the Karen, Kachin, Chin, and Shan. Members of these groups have taken up arms against the central government, which has been dominated by the majority Myanmar (Burman) people since independence in 1948. In Malaysia, half the population is non-Malay. The number of Malaysian Chinese, in fact, almost equals the number of Malays. Thailand has important, largely unassimilated Malay, Miao, Vietnamese, and Lao minorities. In Laos, the Lao, the strongest ethnic group, inhabit only the lowland area near the Mekong River. In Vietnam, differences between the majority Vietnamese and the minority Montagnards (mountain people) cause friction. In addition, the influx since 1975 of hundreds of thousands of Indochinese refugees has further strained the delicate ethnic balance in many Southeast Asian nations.

Part of the blame lies with the artificial borders drawn by the former colonial powers. Malays live in Thailand and Singapore as well as in Malaysia; and Vietnamese live in Cambodia, Laos, and Thailand as well as in Vietnam. Myanmar's Shan minority is more closely related to the majority Thai of Thailand than to the ruling Myanmar people of Myanmar. Thus, there are sometimes stronger links between peoples divided by frontiers than among those living within the borders of a particular country.

Language. Southeast Asia's diverse peoples speak a variety of tongues. The main ones of the insular, or Malay, countries—Indonesia, the Philippines, and Malaysia—are closely related, being of common

Something of the French colonial atmosphere persists in Ho Chi Minh City, the former Saigon.

Jakarta (left), the capital and largest city of Indonesia, has expanded rapidly in recent years, thanks in part to the country's large oil reserves (right).

Malay origin. The governments of Malaysia and Indonesia are working to create a single national language for the two nations, known as Bahasa Indonesia in Indonesia and Bahasa Malaysia in Malaysia. In the Philippines, no one Malay dialect is predominant. English is more widely spoken than any single regional language. Of the mainland Southeast Asian languages, only Thai and Lao are closely related.

Customs and Beliefs. There are important differences in the ways the various Southeast Asian peoples look at life. Most people in Myanmar, Thailand, Laos, Cambodia, and Vietnam are Buddhists. Yet Vietnamese Buddhism is at least as different from the Buddhism of the other four countries as Roman Catholicism is from Protestantism. Nine out of 10 people in Indonesia are Muslims. The same percentage are Christians in the Philippines, but there are many Muslims in the southern Philippines. Thailand, too, has a Muslim minority of Malays in the south. Almost all the Malays of Malaysia are Muslims, but due to the large number of Chinese, less than half the total population is Muslim.

The Chinese follow a variety of religious beliefs—Confucianism, Buddhism, Taoism, Christianity, ancestor worship, spirit worship, or often some combination of these beliefs. These Chinese do not believe that a person must serve only one spiritual master. There are Christians in all of the Southeast Asian countries, though their numbers vary greatly. Only the Philippines has a Christian majority, the result of its conquest and conversion by Catholic Spain. About 10 percent of the people of Vietnam were Roman Catholic before the Communist victory in 1975. Living mostly in the south, they had political and economic importance out of all proportion to their numbers. Many fled Vietnam during a government campaign against Catholics during the 1970s.

Throughout the entire region, however, most people, especially the rural peasants (who account for about 70 percent of the region's population), also believe in spirits, regardless of their formal faith. Thai and Laotian Buddhists, for example, honor the Buddha, but they also believe in *phi* (as the spirits are called). Such spirits inhabit all objects—rivers, trees, rocks, plants, and the like. They are believed, among other things, to be able to cause pain at night by pulling toes, and to end the life of a loved one if not properly appeased with offerings of flowers and food.

Buddhists in the mainland Southeast Asian countries also believe in reincarnation—the process of being born over and over again. A man who is born again as a dog, for example, is thought to have lived a bad life in his previous existence; a dog reborn as a man, on the other hand, lived a good life. Such Buddhists do good deeds to acquire "merit" in order to be born as a higher being in their next incarnation.

There have always been at least two major ways of life in all the countries of Southeast Asia. Formerly a few people lived in and about the courts of the various kings, but perhaps over 95 percent lived in the countryside. Today, although most people still live in rural areas, increasing numbers of them have moved to one or another of the several large cities that serve as the capitals and commercial centers.

The Major Cities. The largest of Southeast Asia's cities is **Jakarta,** capital of Indonesia. Other important cities are **Bangkok,** the capital of

Manila, the capital of the Philippines, serves as one of the leading financial centers of Southeast Asia.

Thailand; **Ho Chi Minh City** (Saigon), Vietnam's largest city, and **Hanoi,** the Vietnamese capital; the city-state of **Singapore;** the Philippines' largest city and capital, **Manila;** Myanmar's capital, **Yangon (Rangoon);** Cambodia's capital of **Phnom Penh;** Malaysia's rapidly growing capital city of **Kuala Lumpur;** and the Laotian capital, **Vientiane.** In all of the big cities of Southeast Asia, many young people, attracted by the excitement of city life, arrived before enough jobs were created for them. As a result, there is a relatively high level of unemployment.

Life in the Countryside. From the mid-1970s until the late 1980s, farm families in Vietnam, Cambodia, and Laos were forced to work on large state-owned farms. These cooperatives proved to be impractical. Today the average farm family throughout Southeast Asia grows most of its own food on land it owns or rents. Increasingly, families have been producing enough of a surplus to be able to supply city dwellers with vital foodstuffs. The families use the money they earn to purchase such things as bicycles (an important means of transportation) and sewing machines. Many so-called smallholders also produce rubber and other export crops, while still other rural people work on big rubber and other plantations. Rice is the major export of mainland Southeast Asia, and most of the farmers here are engaged in the backbreaking labor of seeding, carefully transplanting, and harvesting the grain.

Most villages in Southeast Asia today have a school for children to attend, at least until they are old enough to go to high school. The high schools are usually located in a centrally situated town, to which the students walk or bicycle.

The tiny sultanate of Brunei is by far the wealthiest country in Southeast Asia.

In Thailand (left) and elsewhere in mainland Southeast Asia, most people are Buddhists. Many young men live in Buddhist monasteries for a year or more.

In many parts of Southeast Asia, people still live in houses (usually thatched) built on stilts. This is especially true in those areas where heavy rains result in flooding. Building a house on stilts provides protection from wild animals as well as from burglars. It also provides a built-in place to shelter the family work animal, usually a water buffalo.

Food and Dress.   Rice is the staple food in almost all parts of Southeast Asia, and it is frequently eaten with a very pungent sauce. Fish is the primary protein food. Meat is fairly scarce and comparatively costly. Buddhists are not supposed to eat the flesh of fish, fowl, or any other animal, but many do so. Muslims do not eat pork. Many of the favorite dishes of the Chinese in Southeast Asia, on the other hand, include pork as one of the prime ingredients. Vegetables and fruits are both plentiful, especially fruits, but vegetables form a surprisingly small part of the average Southeast Asian's regular diet.

Most people in the countryside throughout Southeast Asia—men as well as women—have traditionally worn shirtlike garments of one kind or another. In Myanmar they are called *lungis;* in Indonesia, *sarongs* (for men) and *kains* (for women). Traditional clothing is sometimes worn even in the major cities, particularly in Myanmar's capital of Yangon, where almost everybody still wears the colorful, attractive *lungis*. Most city dwellers, however, today wear Western-style clothing.

Life in even the rural regions is changing today, although not as rapidly as in the cities. Most rural towns have radios, often located in some public place. Television is increasingly accessible, particularly in the cities, as are VCRs and videos.

Traditional art forms are also changing, though slowly, under the impact of the outside world. The *wayang,* or shadow-puppet play, has historically been Indonesia's chief type of dramatic entertainment. The *pwe,* or folk opera, is the traditional Myanmar popular art form. Both the *wayang* and the *pwe,* while still generally popular, are rapidly losing ground today to movies, produced either locally or in the United States, India, or Japan.

HISTORY

European colonial rule began in Southeast Asia with the arrival of the Portuguese, who seized Malacca on the west coast of the Malay Peninsula in 1511. The Philippines was a Spanish colony for more than three centuries, from the second half of the 1500s until the United States ousted Spain in 1898. The Dutch colonial conquest of Indonesia began during the 1600s, but was not really completed until the early 1800s. Myanmar (formerly Burma), Malaysia (formerly Malaya), and Singapore became British colonies during the 1800s. France took over Cambodia, Vietnam, and Laos—together known as French Indochina—during the same period.

The Europeans contributed much to the development of modern Southeast Asia, though not always intentionally. In 1830, there were probably only 10 million people in all of Southeast Asia. The colonial powers ended local wars, which had been taking a high toll of the population, and they introduced improved health and sanitation measures, which also increased the population. The first universities in Southeast Asia were in the Philippines—Santo Tomás in Manila and San Carlos in Cebu—and were established by the Spanish. Other universities and schools were built, and roads, railroads, and some industries were developed. New crops, such as rubber, were introduced; and old crops, such as rice, were made commercially profitable.

Southeast Asia, however, was still governed by Europeans in the interests of Europeans. Self-government was only grudgingly introduced, except in the Philippines after the Americans had taken over from the Spanish. The Western presence, however, foreign as it was, stimulated group consciousness, or nationalism, among the subject peoples. And during the 1900s, increasing demands were heard for an end to colonial rule altogether. During World War II, Japan conquered all of Southeast Asia in six months, and the region suffered greatly under enemy occupation. After the war, there was an intensification of nationalist feeling and of the struggle for independence, when the European powers tried to regain control. One by one, however, the various colonies gained their independence, and the Southeast Asian nations we know today took shape.

RICHARD BUTWELL, *California State University, Dominguez Hills*
Author, *Southeast Asia, A Political Introduction*

Even in Yangon, Myanmar's capital, men and women still wear the traditional *lungi*, a skirt-like garment.

MYANMAR

The people of Myanmar, formerly Burma, call their country the Golden Land. The name may come from the Myanmar custom of decorating Buddhist pagodas with gold leaf, which makes them glitter in the sunlight. The term may also refer to the golden glow of Myanmar's bountiful rice crop just before harvesttime, for Myanmar grows enough rice to export large quantities of the grain. Or it may refer to the fact that the sun shines throughout many months of the year. Whatever the reason, it is an appropriate name. For Myanmar—which itself means "swift and strong"—is a country that is well endowed with fertile land, great forests rich in valuable wood, and important mineral resources.

Since its independence in 1948, however, Myanmar has been unable to translate these blessings into economic strength. One reason is chronic warfare between the central government and insurgent groups that want more autonomy for ethnic minorities. Another reason is eccentric and erratic leadership, especially during the three decades that General Ne Win dominated the nation's government either directly or indirectly. As a result, Myanmar entered the 1990s as one of the world's poorest and least-developed nations. Politically, it faced the challenge of satisfying the average Myanmar's long-suppressed desire for a greater voice in the nation's affairs.

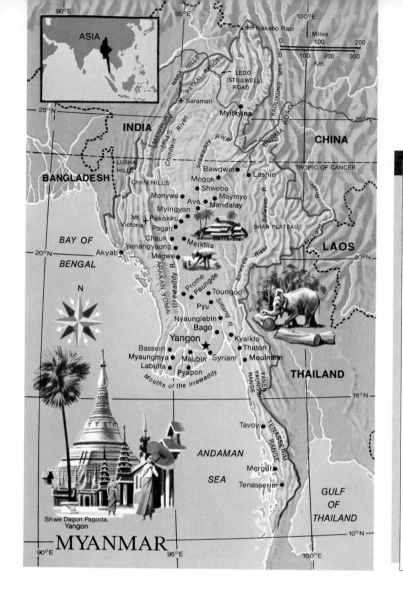

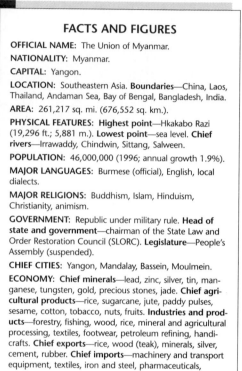

MYANMAR

FACTS AND FIGURES

OFFICIAL NAME: The Union of Myanmar.

NATIONALITY: Myanmar.

CAPITAL: Yangon.

LOCATION: Southeastern Asia. **Boundaries**—China, Laos, Thailand, Andaman Sea, Bay of Bengal, Bangladesh, India.

AREA: 261,217 sq. mi. (676,552 sq. km.).

PHYSICAL FEATURES: Highest point—Hkakabo Razi (19,296 ft.; 5,881 m.). **Lowest point**—sea level. **Chief rivers**—Irrawaddy, Chindwin, Sittang, Salween.

POPULATION: 46,000,000 (1996; annual growth 1.9%).

MAJOR LANGUAGES: Burmese (official), English, local dialects.

MAJOR RELIGIONS: Buddhism, Islam, Hinduism, Christianity, animism.

GOVERNMENT: Republic under military rule. **Head of state and government**—chairman of the State Law and Order Restoration Council (SLORC). **Legislature**—People's Assembly (suspended).

CHIEF CITIES: Yangon, Mandalay, Bassein, Moulmein.

ECONOMY: Chief minerals—lead, zinc, silver, tin, manganese, tungsten, gold, precious stones, jade. **Chief agricultural products**—rice, sugarcane, jute, paddy pulses, sesame, cotton, tobacco, nuts, fruits. **Industries and products**—forestry, fishing, wood, rice, mineral and agricultural processing, textiles, footwear, petroleum refining, handicrafts. **Chief exports**—rice, wood (teak), minerals, silver, cement, rubber. **Chief imports**—machinery and transport equipment, textiles, iron and steel, pharmaceuticals, peanut oil, paper.

MONETARY UNIT: 1 kyat = 100 pyas.

NATIONAL HOLIDAY: January 4 (Independence Day).

THE LAND

Almost as big as Texas, Myanmar is the largest nation in mainland Southeast Asia. On a map, it resembles a diamond-shaped kite complete with its tail. The country's long coastline fronts on the Bay of Bengal and the Andaman Sea, which form part of the Indian Ocean. Myanmar's neighbors include India and Bangladesh to the west, and China, Thailand, and Laos to the north and east. Snow-covered Himalayan mountain peaks in the far north, rising to over 15,000 ft. (4,600 m.), mark Myanmar's borders with India and China.

Mountain ranges extend along the western and eastern sides of the country like the two arms of an inverted V. In the west, the Arakan mountain chain, extending in a series of ridges known as the Naga, Chin, and Lushai hills, forms the border with India. This area is thinly populated and has little land suitable for agriculture. To the west of the Arakan Mountains, along the Bay of Bengal, is a narrow strip of land watered by rivers and streams that flow down from the mountains. This area contains rich farmland.

The Shan Plateau (also called the Shan Highlands), the eastern arm of the inverted V, extends southward into the Tenasserim mountain range. These highlands and mountains serve as a dividing line between Myanmar and Thailand. Myanmar's great central basin lies between the Shan Plateau and the Arakan Mountains. This lowland area is drained by the important north-south river systems of Myanmar—the Irrawaddy and its tributaries, including the Chindwin, the Sittang, and the lower reaches of the Salween. This vast delta is the center of Myanmar's major economic activity—rice production.

Located close to the equator, Myanmar has a tropical monsoon climate. Annual rainfall varies from about 200 in. (500 cm.) near the coast to a mere 30 in. (77 cm.) in the central "dry zone." Annual temperatures in southern Myanmar average about 80° F. (27° C.) and are slightly cooler in the northern lowlands. During the March–May hot season, temperatures in central Myanmar often rise above 100° F. (38° C.).

Economy. Agriculture, including forestry, is central to Myanmar's economy, employing about 65 percent of the country's workers. In addition to rice, Myanmar's rich soil produces grains, cotton, sugarcane, tobacco, peanuts, sesame, and pulses (peas, beans, lentils). Forests blanket nearly three-fifths of the land. The production of wood, particularly teak, is a major industry. Teakwood became Myanmar's major export in 1985.

Mineral resources are plentiful. The Myanmar mine lead, zinc, tungsten, copper, gold and silver, tin, precious stones, and jade, and they produce a considerable amount of petroleum, coal, and natural gas. Other than fishing, mining, and lumbering, industry is limited in Myanmar. Factories produce cement, textiles, fertilizers, tile, jute, pharmaceuticals, and steel, and there are a number of plants for processing foodstuffs, wood, and minerals. Myanmar's craftsmen are noted for their excellent wood and ivory carvings, silk weaving, and handmade jewelry.

The lumber industry uses elephants to help move around heavy beams of teak, Myanmar's chief export.

A Buddhist priest painstakingly restores a statue in Yangon's Shwe Dagon Pagoda, one of the world's largest Buddhist shrines. Most of the people of Myanmar are devout Theravada Buddhists.

Since 1948, the nation's economy has been based on socialist ideas and the retention of traditional Buddhist values—something Ne Win called "The Burmese Way to Socialism." During the 1960s, the government took control of all important industries. Though farming was not nationalized, distribution of farm products was. During the late 1980s and early 1990s, the government took several halting steps to permit free enterprise in areas such as trade.

THE PEOPLE

The population of Myanmar, which includes a good number of Chinese residents, is primarily Mongoloid in origin. More than 1 million Indian and Bangladeshi immigrants also live there.

The great majority of the people speak Myanmar (or Burmese), the language of the Myanmar (Burman) people—the ethnic group that makes up about 68 percent of the population. Other languages are spoken by members of the other main ethnic groups, including the Shan, Karen, Rakhine, Mon, Chin, Kachin, and Kayah peoples.

English is commonly spoken as a second language and is taught from the elementary schools upward. Roughly 5 percent of Myanmar's people speak Chinese or Indian languages such as Hindi, Tamil, or Urdu. The Myanmar alphabet is based on scripts taken from Indian languages, particularly Pali, which is used in writing Myanmar Buddhist texts.

About 85 percent of the people practice Theravada Buddhism, an early form of the religion that is prevalent in mainland Southeast Asia. Animism—the traditional belief in good and evil spirits—is also practiced, as are Christianity, Islam, and Hinduism.

Early Migrations. It is unclear who Myanmar's original inhabitants were. Migrations into Myanmar from Central Asia began at least 2,000 years ago. First came the people of Mon-Khmer stock, who settled in the delta and Tenasserim areas and spread Buddhism and other elements of their culture throughout Myanmar. Early in the first centuries A.D., the Tibeto-Myanmar peoples began arriving in the area. These more recent arrivals included the Pyu, Myanmar, Chin, and, much later, the Kachin.

The third major group of immigrants was the Shan-Thai, who at one time dominated a South China kingdom called Nanchao. The main branch of Shan-Thai people are those who populated Thailand, Laos, and the Shan state of Burma. They were driven from their kingdom in China during the Mongol conquests during the 1100s and 1200s. Myanmar also has smaller groups of hill peoples, generally related to the Mon-Khmer, the Tibeto-Myanmar, and the Shan-Thai.

The various Myanmar ethnic groups can be distinguished mainly by their dress and speech. Myanmar men and women wear a *lungi,* or skirt, while a Shan male wears wide, cuffless trousers. There are also variations in shoes and head coverings, methods of tying knots, jewelry styles, and the colors and designs of textiles used by the different groups. A Myanmar-speaking person from Tavoy or Mergui in the south, for example, has an accent quite different from someone living in Mandalay, in the central part of the country.

Way of Life. In their daily lives, most Myanmar cling to traditional values and customs. In both the rural areas and the cities, Myanmar prefer to wear traditional garments rather than Western-style clothing. Modern household appliances, radios, and movie theaters are now found in the cities, but most Myanmar live without access to them. Automobiles, trucks, bicycles, and motorbikes are found on all the roads, but the average rural Myanmar either walks or travels by oxcart. Although some farmers work their fields with modern tractors, most rely on plows drawn by water buffalo and oxen. Elephants are often used to carry heavy loads, particularly in the lumber industry.

About three out of every four of Myanmar's people live in small farming villages, mainly in the river valleys and delta floodplains of lower Myanmar. A typical Myanmar family lives in a bamboo house elevated on stilts. Usually the family eats and relaxes on a long porch outside. Most men and women wear short jackets, skirts, and open sandals. Often the men wear colored headbands made of cloth.

Besides the cultivation of crops, life in the rural areas centers around the family, which includes uncles, aunts, and cousins. Children are taught to show "respect," which in Myanmar is an important ritual involving correct manners and bearing and the use of proper forms of address. For example, one addresses an elderly person or one who has a high status as *U,* a title of respect meaning "mister" or "uncle" (as in the case of U Thant, former secretary-general of the United Nations). An important occasion in the life of every Buddhist male child is the Shinbyu ceremony, which marks a boy's readiness to become a morally responsible Buddhist. After the ceremony, the boy enters the local monastery for a short stay.

In general, women have equal status with men in Myanmar. They operate nearly all of the bazaar stalls and shops in local markets. Yet women in high government posts are rarities, although women have ruled Myanmar and are now active in politics and the professions.

Education. Education is highly prized in Myanmar. One of the traditional duties of the monks is to study the Buddhist scriptures. Another duty is teaching children, and, before independence in 1948, most elementary education was provided by Buddhist monastery schools. Since independence, the Myanmar government has extended public education throughout the land. Although only four years are compulsory, about two-thirds of Myanmar's people are literate. Although schools and universities were closed after protests in 1988, generally low-cost college and professional education is available to anyone who qualifies through exams.

Cities.   One in four Myanmar live in about 50 cities, only a few of which are major urban areas. **Yangon (Rangoon),** the nation's capital, is the largest city, with a population of more than 3 million. Located on the Yangon River, it is the country's main port, a key industrial and commercial center, and the hub of Myanmar's transportation and communications network.

Myanmar's second-largest city is **Mandalay** (pop. 500,000), which is situated on the Irrawaddy River. Mandalay is an active port and trading center, with several busy markets. The old city, the center of Myanmar's traditional culture, contains many ancient buildings and pagodas.

HISTORY AND GOVERNMENT

Myanmar's history as a unified nation began during the 11th century A.D., when King Anawratha founded the first Myanmar dynasty at Pagan, a city on the Irrawaddy River. Anawratha ruled from 1044 to 1077. During the next two centuries, the Myanmar conquered most of the other peoples in the area and absorbed their cultures, which included Theravada Buddhism. Pagan became a magnificent city architecturally and a cultural center comparable to Athens during the Golden Age of Greece. Libraries

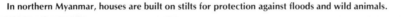

In northern Myanmar, houses are built on stilts for protection against floods and wild animals.

Pedicabs compete with buses and trucks for transportation on many streets in Yangon.

and seminaries were established, beautiful Buddhist temples were built, and Myanmar developed into a firmly rooted Buddhist society, which it remains today.

At the end of the 1200s, Mongol armies led by Kublai Khan invaded Myanmar. The Myanmar kingdom was split into warring factions, and the Pagan dynasty collapsed. The nation's decline was only temporary, however. By the late 1400s, a new Myanmar dynasty known as Toungoo—named for one of its capitals—had come to power. Under King Bayinnaung, who ruled from 1551 to 1581, the Myanmar once again unified and even extended their kingdom. The dynasty was brought down after an uprising of the Mon in 1740.

The Konbaung dynasty, the third and last, was founded by King Alaungpaya (ruled 1752–60), who defeated the Mon and reestablished royal authority over all of Burma, as Myanmar was then called. During the 1760s, the new dynasty defeated the Siamese (Thai) and repelled Chinese invasions. From 1782 to 1820, the nation's political and military power was at its height. The Burmese pushed westward to Assam and Manipur. But westward expansion brought the nation into conflict with the British in India, and three Anglo-Burmese wars were fought during the 19th century. After the last of these, in 1885, the British conquered what remained of the Kingdom of Burma and annexed it as a province of India. Later, in 1937, Burma was made a separate colony within the British Empire.

During World War II, Japanese forces invaded and occupied the nation, and much of it was devastated. After the Japanese were driven out in 1945, Burmese nationalists, led by Aung San, continued their efforts to win independence for their country. The nationalists were successful, although Aung San and six cabinet members were assassinated in 1947. On January 4, 1948, Great Britain granted Burma full independence. A new constitution, adopted four months earlier, provided for a British-style parliamentary democracy, under which the nation began to develop into a democratic socialist state.

Ne Win's Rise to Power.   During its early years, the new Republic of the Union of Burma came under attack by various rebel groups, including Communists and guerrillas who pressed minority and regional demands for independence. Amid a political crisis in 1958, the army chief, General Ne Win, stepped in and ran a caretaker government until 1960, when elective government returned. Two years later, he seized power in a coup and set up a single-party state.

Ne Win's government put all important industries in the government's hands. Most of the nation's commercial and technical people, Indians and Chinese, were driven out. In 1974, a new constitution was adopted, and Ne Win—no longer in the army—assumed the presidency. Although the single-party government was constitutionally elected, it was a dictatorship.

Incompetence and corruption stifled economic growth, and some experts believe that the black market—supplied by goods smuggled from neighboring nations—grew to become larger than the regular economy. Eventually, many of the nation's key exports, including rice, teakwood, and rubber, would be smuggled out of the country, as would half the world's illegal supply of opium. The nation became isolated from the foreign investment that its economy desperately needed.

Recent Developments.   In 1981, Ne Win left the presidency but held onto his power by remaining head of the Burmese Socialist Program Party, the sole legal party. Under new leaders, the nation tried to broaden its contacts with foreign nations. In 1987, in an attempt to cripple the black market, the government made the highest-denomination banknotes worthless. This act precipitated widespread riots during the spring and summer of 1988. Soldiers and police gunned down protesters, killing thousands. In July 1988, Ne Win took responsibility for the riots and resigned his post as party head.

A nationwide revolt followed his appointment of a protégé as chairman of the party and president of the country. After another government was unable to halt the pro-democracy protests, the army took over in September 1988 and declared martial law. General Saw Maung, head of the junta that called itself the State Law and Order Restoration Council (SLORC), promised multiparty elections. In June 1989 SLORC substituted native spellings for the country's name and for those of many cities. Burma became Myanmar; Rangoon became Yangon.

SLORC also jailed or placed under house arrest opposition leader Aung San Suu Kyi, the daughter of independence leader Aung San. Nonetheless, in May 1990 her National League for Democracy won a sweeping victory in the nation's first free elections since 1962. SLORC refused to turn over power to the new government and intensified its crackdown on the opposition. In 1992, Saw Maung resigned as head of SLORC. His successor, General Than Shwe, lifted martial law and signed peace accords with most ethnic rebel groups. Aung San Suu Kyi, the 1991 Nobel Peace Prize winner, was released from house arrest on July 10, 1995, but SLORC remained firmly in control.

FRANK N. TRAGER, New York University; author, *Burma from Kingdom to Republic*

The Buddhist spires that once dominated Bangkok's skyline are now dwarfed by modern buildings.

 # THAILAND

Thailand, whose name means "Land of the Free People," is the only Southeast Asian country that has never been a colony of a European power. Visitors to Thailand who expect to find a nation frozen in the past are always startled by what they find. Thailand, which has borrowed freely from the West without losing its special Asian identity, is a dynamic society. Its location at the heart of Southeast Asia has enabled it to become a regional hub of international activity. The nation's ability to adapt new ideas and technologies to suit its needs is a source of pride for the Thais. And so are Thailand's exquisite beauty and rich culture, a culture built on more than 5,000 years of tradition.

THE LAND

On a map, Thailand looks like a blooming flower, with its stem reaching down into the Malay Peninsula. Strategically located, the nation is about the same size and shape as Central America. It shares borders with Myanmar (Burma) in the north and west, Laos in the north and east, Cambodia (Kampuchea) in the southeast, and Malaysia in the extreme south. A short stretch of the Salween River separates Thailand from Myanmar, while the Mekong River serves as a dividing line between eastern Thailand and Laos.

The nation's five main geographic regions, distinct in terms of their natural resources, are the north, the northeast, the central plain, the south, and the eastern shore. In the north, thick teak forests cover the

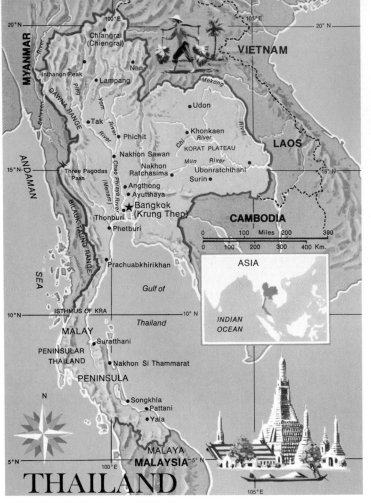

region's vast mountain ranges and steep river valleys. The country's highest point, Inthanon Peak, is located here, reaching 8,452 ft. (2,576 m.) above sea level. The most densely populated region is the agriculturally rich central plain. The Chao Phraya, Thailand's most important river, dominates the central plain. Four tributaries of the Chao Phraya River— the Ping, Wang, Yom, and Nan—flow from this region. All but one of Thailand's former capitals have been located on the banks of this river.

One-third of the country lies on the northeastern Khorat Plateau, which rises 1,000 ft. (304 m.). Seasonal droughts and poor water-holding capacity make this the country's poorest section.

Fisheries and aquaculture lend new economic progress to the narrow coastal plains along the eastern shore of the Gulf of Thailand. Rolling hills and mountains extend from the plains, but provide adequate land for upland crops.

Humid tropical forests cover much of southern Thailand. Rubber plantations and coconut cultivation dominate this portion of the Malay Peninsula.

Climate. Thailand's climate, which is tropical and subtropical, is determined largely by the shifting winds of the monsoons. During the cool season, from November to February, a dry monsoon brings refreshing winds from China. The wet monsoon, coming off the Indian Ocean in the south, carries heavy rainfall from May to October. A hot season stretches from February to May. Regional variations in temperature occur. The north is generally the coolest portion of the country. Rainfall averages about 60 in. (150 cm.) annually, with the heaviest rainfall occurring in the south and southeast.

THE PEOPLE

Thailand's population is relatively homogeneous. Approximately 85 percent of the people belong to one of four ethnic groups known collectively as the Core Thai. These four ethnic groups share traditional values and culture and speak a dialect of one of the languages of the large Tai family of languages. The Central Thai, living near Bangkok, make up about 36 percent of the population and are politically and economically dominant. The Thai-Lao, or Northeastern Thai, are the second-largest of the Core Thai groups. They are closely related to, and far more numerous than, the people living in neighboring Laos. The Thai-Lao make up about 32 percent of Thailand's total population, and they inhabit much of the impoverished northeastern plateau region. Northern Thai, making up 8 percent, include several smaller groups of Core Thai.

Historically, Thailand's government has encouraged assimilation of minority peoples and collected little information about them. Chinese, variously estimated at between 6 percent and 14 percent of Thailand's population, are the largest minority. Many have taken Thai names or married into Thai families, making an accurate count of their numbers impossible. Less numerous minorities, many of them living within Thailand's borders as a result of past border wars, include the Ngio (or Shan), Phutai, and Saek, who speak Tai dialects. Also, there are the Khmer, many of them from war-torn Cambodia; Malays, in the peninsula; and the isolated Karen, Meo (or Hmong), and other minorities of the north and northwest, known collectively as the "hill peoples."

Religion.   About 95 percent of the people are Buddhists. Roughly 4 percent are Muslims (mainly Malays of the south), while other religious groups constitute the remainder. Every morning, Buddhist monks carrying small bowls and wearing saffron robes venture out among the people to receive food. On holy days and during festivals, food is brought to them in their temple-monasteries, or *wats*. Hundreds of these *wats* dot the countryside. Every boy is expected to put on a monk's robe and serve in a *wat* for three months. The most elaborate is Wat Phra Keo (Temple of the Emerald Buddha), situated within the Grand Palace in Bangkok.

Language and Education.   Thai is the national language, and the official dialect that is used in Bangkok. While the phonetic language is related to Chinese, King Ramkhamhaeng, an early leader, based the written alphabet on the Cambodian script. English is generally taught as a second language, and many Thai speak it fluently. Six years of education is compulsory for all children. Upon completion of secondary school, a student can attend one of the country's 23 universities. An estimated 89 percent of adult Thai are considered literate.

Way of Life.   Thailand is still largely a nation of small villages, most of which are located along the coast or near the rivers. Rivers and *klongs* (canals) play an important role in Thai daily life, although many *klongs* in Bangkok have been filled up in order to widen traffic-congested streets. Many people still live in floating houses moored to the riverbanks. They earn their living by selling various products from their floating stores.

Traditional-style houses in the villages are made of wood or bamboo. The roofs are generally made of thatch or sometimes corrugated iron. When located near the water, the houses are usually built on stilts as a protection against floods. Buddhism influenced traditional Thai arts, with the temples ranking among the best examples of Thai architecture. New public buildings, as well as private homes, successfully preserve the grace of traditional architectural design while using modern construction materials and techniques.

Boiled or steamed rice is the principal food. It is eaten together with fish, pork, chicken, meat, and vegetables, which are often fried and heavily spiced. At home, as well as in restaurants, the Thai delight in eating a wide variety of traditional Thai and Chinese dishes. Fish sauce and hot peppers are indispensable ingredients in Thai cooking. Fruits such as mango, mangosteen, rambutan (a Malayan fruit related to the litchi nut), and pineapple are found in abundance.

Boats, buses, cars, taxis, three-wheeled motorbikes, and other vehicles are used as means of transportation by the Thai. The different regions of Thailand are served by a network of road, rail, water, and air transport. Communications, especially radio and television broadcasting, and paved all-weather roads are dramatically changing the traditional life-styles of Thailand's rural areas.

Water buffalo provide the main source of power for about 30 percent of all small farms in Southeast Asia. Farmers choose this ancient energy source because it remains more efficient than a tractor, which consumes gasoline instead of grass and provides no natural fertilizer. Following a tour of the farm regions in the 1970s, Bhumibol Adulyadej, Thailand's king, concluded that the lack of water buffalo contributed to rural poverty. The Royal Buffalo and Cattle Bank, which he established, has since loaned 7,000 animals to farmers.

Thailand grows enough rice to meet its own needs and still have tons left over to export.

The thriving textile industry, centered in Bangkok, is the fastest-growing sector of the economy.

Among the sports popular in Thailand are traditional Thai boxing (in which the hands, feet, elbows, and knees may be used), *takraw* (wicker ball), kite flying, and cockfighting. Western sports such as rugby, soccer, and basketball have also gained favor with the Thai.

Among Thai festivals, perhaps the most colorful is the Surin Roundup, which takes place every October at Surin, in the eastern part of the country. Thousands of people come to watch elephant races and the parade of the "war elephants," a re-creation of the pageantry of ancient times, when elephants were used in battle.

ECONOMY

Historically, Thailand has been a farming country, and most Thai workers are farmers. In recent years, however, the relative importance of agriculture has declined somewhat, as the industrial sector has grown. Agricultural products now account for about 16 percent of the annual output of goods and services; industry accounts for about 24 percent.

About 59 percent of the working population is involved in some form of agricultural activity. Most cultivate rice on tiny plots that average just 7 acres. The Thai's high productivity of rice, cassava, maize, sugar, and manioc (the source of tapioca) makes Thailand one of the world's leading agricultural exporters. Thailand is the world's largest exporter of tapioca.

The total natural-resource sector contributes greatly to Thailand's export economy. Thailand is the world's second-largest exporter of rubber, which is grown in the Malay Peninsula. It is the world's fifth-largest producer of tin. The vast northern forests provide teak and other wood products. Increased activity along the eastern shore of the Gulf of Siam has made Thailand a leading exporter of canned tuna.

Riverboats plying the Chao Phraya River connect Bangkok with important cities downstream.

Government policies during the 1980s converted this traditionally agricultural nation into an industrial one. Mining and manufacturing goods now account for approximately 60 percent of the nation's exports. The government encouraged foreign investment by reducing corporate and private taxes and providing special industrial incentives. Japanese companies recognized the opportunity, and the factories they created in Thailand helped transform the nation into a newly industrialized country (NIC). Thailand now competes comfortably with the affluent "four dragons" of industry: Hong Kong, Korea, Taiwan, and Singapore. Industrial exports include textiles, toys, processed food (largely canned pineapple), integrated circuits, and artificial flowers.

The entire nation has yet to benefit from Thailand's industrial wealth. Individuals in Bangkok earn about eight times more than their counterparts in rural areas. To help alleviate poverty in the countryside, the government began encouraging tourism "up-country," in the nation's most isolated regions. Tourism has long been Thailand's top foreign-exchange earner, but few tourists ever got far outside Bangkok.

Cities. Thailand is divided into 73 administrative areas, within which are more than 49,000 towns and villages. The most important of the urban areas are the two cities of **Bangkok** (Krung Thep) and **Thonburi,** which are separated only by the Chao Phraya River. These two ancient cities, together with other nearby communities, make up the **Bangkok Metropolis,** Thailand's preeminent urban area. Designed to attract tourism, this cosmopolitan complex boasts 17 luxury hotels, the world's largest restaurant, and three of the world's biggest nightclubs. **Chiang Mai,** the regional center for the north, is Thailand's second-largest city. Bangkok is also Thailand's chief port.

HISTORY

Archaeological evidence indicates that people in what is now northeastern Thailand, in the village of Non Nok Tha, cultivated the world's first rice 5,000 years ago. Recent studies also point to early bronze metallurgy in nearby communities. These two factors provided the impetus for social and political organizations. Thus, these early technological innovations most likely were transmitted to China, not from China, as was long believed.

In 1238, Thai chieftains overthrew the Khmer at Sukothai, establishing the Thai Kingdom. They named it Sukhamhaeng, "Dawn of Happiness." In 1350, a new centralized kingdom emerged at Ayutthaya. Its first ruler, Rama Thibodi, established the official religion of Buddhism and compiled a legal code based on Hindu sources and Thai tradition. During this period of the Ayutthaya Kingdom (1350–1767), Thailand expanded its frontiers and became the dominant nation of mainland Southeast Asia. It also established contact with European trading powers such as Holland, Portugal, and Great Britain.

In the late 1700s, Burma (now Myanmar) overwhelmed the kingdom. However, Rama I, founder of the present ruling dynasty, routed them, changed the country's name to Siam, and established Bangkok as the nation's capital. Successive rulers became preoccupied with European

Most Thais are devout Buddhists. The Temple of the Emerald Buddha (below) is Bangkok's oldest.

colonialism. That Thailand was never a colony is a source of great pride, and it can be attributed to the efforts of two kings who ruled during the mid-1800s. King Mongkut, or Rama IV (popularized in the Rodgers and Hammerstein musical *The King and I*), and Chulalongkorn, or Rama V, are most responsible for introducing extensive reforms. Slavery was abolished, outmoded royal customs were ended, and the power of the aristocracy was limited. For the most part, however, only the top level of Thai society was changed. Life for most Thais remained the same.

Thailand's 19th-century rulers modernized the government, the army, education, and transportation to meet the threat of the European powers then carving out colonial empires in Southeast Asia. And it invited Western advisers to assist in the modernization efforts. Thailand lost much of its former territory, however, and had to agree to a series of treaties that limited its control of foreign trade, taxes, customs collections, and jurisdiction over foreigners.

Until 1939, Thailand was known as the Kingdom of Siam (the word means "Free"). At that time, Thailand's rulers allied themselves with Japan and changed the country's name to Thailand. They sought to enlarge the country's borders to include the much greater area inhabited by the Thai-speaking people. They did manage to annex a number of border areas in Laos, Myanmar (Burma), Cambodia, and Malaya during the early years of World War II. But when Japan's power waned, Thailand made peace with Britain.

After the war, the Thai government attempted to deal with the political difficulties associated with modernizing the country. These and other pressures enhanced the importance of the military in Thailand's political life, putting military officers in a position to stage several military coups, the most recent in February 1991. During periods of military rule, Thailand's constitution has usually been suspended and the legislature dissolved. But the king, though largely powerless, has remained as head of state and has served as a unifying element.

GOVERNMENT

In 1932, a revolution transformed the Thai monarchy of King Prajadhipok from an absolute to a constitutional monarchy. In 1980, females became eligible to reign as monarch for the first time. The 1991 constitution, the fifteenth since the 1932 coup, makes the king head of state, a largely ceremonial post. The king appoints an advisory Privy Council.

True executive power lies in the hands of the prime minister, who heads the government. There is a two-house National Assembly. Members of the House of Representatives are popularly elected; members of the Senate are appointed by the military. Following the installation of a pro-military prime minister after elections in March 1992, there were widespread protests. The army's brutal suppression of the demonstrations was widely condemned, the prime minister was forced to step down, and the constitution was amended to specify that the prime minister must be an elected member of parliament. Chuan Leekpai, who became prime minister after September 1992 elections, was succeeded by Banharn Silpa-archa in July 1995. After elections in November 1996, General Chaovalit Yongchaiyut became head of another coalition civilian government.

PRACHOOM CHOMCHAI, Chulalongkorn University, Bangkok

Until 1975, Laos was a kingdom whose ruler lived in the Royal Palace (above) in Luang Prabang.

LAOS

A small nation, about 600 mi. (965 km.) long and in some places barely 50 mi. (80 km.) wide, Laos is a land of dense jungle, rugged mountains, fertile floodplains, and overpowering beauty. Streams cascade down the mountains, feeding the region's most important river, the Mekong, and flooding the rice paddies that supply the bulk of the nation's food.

Laos was a power in the region from 1353 to 1707, when it ruled over parts of present-day China, Cambodia, Myanmar (Burma), Thailand, and Vietnam. It became a French colony in 1893; won its independence in 1953; and remained a kingdom until 1975, when a Communist government abolished the monarchy. Laos's ruling Communist party—the Lao People's Revolutionary Party—permits Laotians to run privately owned businesses alongside state-run enterprises.

THE LAND

Laos is situated in the rugged mountainous interior of the Indochina peninsula, an extension of the vast Asian landmass to the north. The eastern part of Laos, bordering on Vietnam, lies along the high ridges of the Annamese Cordillera. The rugged plateaus and mountains in the north and east range in height from 500 to 4,000 ft. (150 to 1,200 m.). In places, limestone under the plateaus is eroded into karsts—areas honeycombed with fantastic fissures, caves, and underground channels.

Climate. The country's climate is generally warm. Temperatures range from about 82° F. (28° C.) in summer to between 60° and 70° F. (15° and 26° C.) from November through February. March and April are usu-

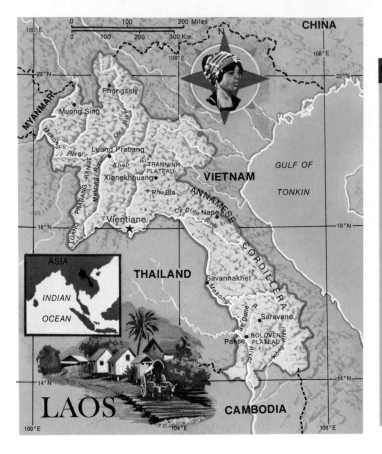

FACTS AND FIGURES

OFFICIAL NAME: Lao People's Democratic Republic.

NATIONALITY: Lao or Laotian(s).

CAPITAL: Vientiane.

LOCATION: Southeastern Asia. **Boundaries**—China, Vietnam, Cambodia, Thailand, Myanmar.

AREA: 91,429 sq. mi. (236,800 sq. km.).

PHYSICAL FEATURES: Highest point—Phu Bia (9,250 ft.; 2,820 m.). **Lowest point**—594 ft. (181 m.). **Chief river**—Mekong.

POPULATION: 5,000,000 (1996; annual growth 2.9%).

MAJOR LANGUAGES: Lao (official), French, English.

MAJOR RELIGIONS: Buddhism, animism.

GOVERNMENT: Communist republic. **Head of state**—president. **Head of government**—prime minister. **Legislature**—National Assembly.

CHIEF CITIES: Vientiane, Savannakhet, Luang Prabang.

ECONOMY: Chief minerals—Tin, gypsum, and rock salt are mined. Unexploited minerals include iron, copper, gold, lead, sulfur, coal. **Chief agricultural products**—rice, corn, tobacco, coffee, cotton, citrus fruits. **Industries and products**—tin mining, teak, bamboo, silk weaving, pottery, leathercraft, silverwork. **Chief exports**—electricity, wood products, coffee, tin. **Chief imports**—food, petroleum, motor vehicles, tractors, bicycles, machinery, electrical equipment, cotton, steel, other metals.

MONETARY UNIT: 1 new kip = 100 at.

NATIONAL HOLIDAY: December 2 (National Day).

---

ally dry, hot months. From May to October, southwest monsoon winds deposit about 10 in. (25 cm.) of rain each month. During the dry season, from November to April, rainfall averages less than 1 in. (2.5 cm.).

Resources. Laos's natural resources, largely untapped, include teak, tin, lead, silver, and gold. The churning Mekong River serves as this landlocked nation's major transportation route and as its western border with Thailand. Water transport has long been the chief means of moving people and goods within Laos. Today, most land transport occurs on foot, although bicycles, Japanese motorbikes, and several thousand trucks and cars frequent the unpaved highways. Laos has no internal railroad. Railroad tracks link the capital, Vientiane, with Bangkok, Thailand. An improved highway runs east from Savannakhet to the Vietnamese border and continues through Vietnam to the seaport of Da Nang.

Cities. Laos has only a few cities of importance, the chief ones being **Vientiane** and **Luang Prabang**, both on the Mekong River. Vientiane is the largest city and major commercial center, and it has been the nation's capital since 1560. The country's main airport is located here. Luang Prabang is about 130 mi. (210 km.) northwest of Vientiane. The former royal capital, it is primarily a market town, where farm goods, fish, and lumber are sold.

THE PEOPLE

Laos embraces 68 different ethnic groups, each with a distinct culture. Most of their languages fall into two language families, the Sino-Tibetan of China and the Mon-Khmer of Southern Asia.

Lowlanders. The Sino-Tibetans include the Lao, who make up about half of all Laotians. Laotians refer to them as Loo Lun-Lao (Laotians of the valleys), because they prefer to live within the broad floodplains of the Mekong Valley, surrounded by irrigated rice fields and lush tropical vegetation. Their outlook on life is expressed in the Lao saying, "Everyone must live simply." Lao is the nation's official language.

Lao villages are small, normally containing 300 to 500 people. Houses are usually constructed of bamboo and are raised 6 to 8 ft. (1.8 to 2.4 m.) above the ground on wooden piles. The space beneath the houses is used to store tools and to secure livestock at night. An elevated granary stands a short distance from each family's living quarters.

Settlements are often quite isolated during the height of the monsoon rains in July and August, when the only vehicles that can move in rural areas are oxcarts. Farmers use this period for rest, since it follows the arduous plowing and transplanting of rice seedlings in May and June. The dry season, which comes after the November harvest, is a time for traveling and for visiting friends and relatives. By March, Laotians look forward to another rice-growing season.

Hill Tribes. The Kha and other Lao-Theung (Laotians of the mountainsides) live at middle elevations and make up about 25 percent of the population. They speak a language that belongs to the Mon-Khmer language family. The Kha, descendants of the Indochina peninsula's original inhabitants, were once thought of as savages or slaves.

The Loo-Soung (Laotians of the mountaintops) live at the highest elevations and account for about 13 percent of the population. They include such tribes as the Hmong (formerly Meo) and the Tai.

These mountain dwellers live in small, scattered hamlets. They practice swidden, or slash-and-burn agriculture, on the steep slopes near their homes. This primitive form of agriculture consists of cutting down vegetation, burning it, and using the ashes for fertilizer.

Among the Loo-Soung are the Hmong tribes. The United States recruited and trained many of these highlanders to fight the Pathet Lao, the Communist guerrilla army, during the Vietnam War. After the Pathet Lao's victory in 1975, many Hmong fled to Thailand and eventually to the U.S. One in 10 Laotians, including some of the nation's most highly educated citizens, fled abroad after the Communists took over.

Life in the hills is rigorous, and the tribesmen have few possessions. Families work long hours to clear and burn the brush and then to plant and harvest dry (or hill) rice, the staple crop. Occasionally they journey to lowland towns to trade. Although the upland peoples make up about 40 percent of the population, they remain isolated from the lowlanders, who took advantage of them and even enslaved them in the past.

Religion and Education. The Laotians are Buddhists, although many people still believe in local spirits, or *phi*. Village life centers around the local temple, with its guesthouse, monastery, and monastery school. Although officially opposed to religion, the Communist government recognizes Buddhism's importance in Laotian life and has left it alone.

The French established public schools, and education was made compulsory in 1951. But most villagers still received their education from Buddhist monks. Since 1975, many new schools have been built, and the literacy rate has climbed past 41 percent. There is a university in Vientiane, and many students attend universities in the Soviet Union.

During the dry season, villagers flock to the city markets to buy fresh vegetables.

THE ECONOMY

When Communists took power in 1975, they tried resettling many of the country's farmers on large cooperative farms. However, Laotian families, used to raising their own food on small plots, resisted these huge state-owned farms. In 1988, the government began dismantling the cooperatives and distributing the land to individual families. The government also allowed private ownership and encouraged profit-making enterprises.

Less than 6 percent of Laos is under cultivation. Rice accounts for 90 percent of the tilled acreage. Expanded irrigation now allows two annual crops, although drought continues to plague the countryside.

Laos has little industry. Laotian factories employ a total of 5,000 workers, and the nation's chief manufacturing export is toothpicks. Tin, timber, and coffee are also exported. But they pale in importance next to Laos's sale of electricity to Thailand. Electricity accounts for 90 percent of Laos's earnings in foreign currency, which it uses to help pay for needed imports—largely food, fuel oil, consumer goods, and machinery.

HISTORY

Originally, the Lao, the Thai, and other speakers of Sino-Tibetan languages were inhabitants of southern China. There they developed a characteristic way of life centered around the growing of wet rice in valley bottoms. Sometime during the first centuries A.D., these peoples began moving south and west. Eventually they reached as far west as Myanmar (Burma) and as far south as Thailand's great Menam (Chao Phraya) floodplain. Organized along semifeudal lines, with a military and governing elite, the newcomers conquered, absorbed, or enslaved the local peoples.

In A.D. 1353, Fa Ngoun, the first historic Lao ruler, united several princely states into Lan Chang (Lan Xang), the kingdom of "one million elephants." By the early 1700s, feuding among rival states led to the kingdom's being split into three sections: the kingdoms of Luang Prabang, Vientiane, and Chanpasak. During the 1800s, most of Laos was taken over by Siam (now Thailand). Siamese control continued until 1893, when the French, seeking to expand their colonial power in Indochina, ousted the Siamese from the Lao states.

Laos became a protectorate within what was to become French Indochina, a union of Laos, Cambodia, and Vietnam. The French governed the Lao states indirectly through the king of Luang Prabang.

Laos was granted virtual independence as a self-governing state within the French Union in 1949. Complete independence came in 1953. But as a result of fighting between royal government troops and Communist Pathet Lao rebels, Laos remained divided.

In 1960, army officers led an uprising against the government, and their forces occupied a strategic area of the country. During 1961–62, several nations met in Geneva, Switzerland, to try to resolve Laos's problems. As a result, Laos's neutrality and independence were guaranteed. In Laos, neutralists, conservatives, and Communists formed a coalition government, with Prince Souvanna Phouma as prime minister.

During the Vietnam War, Laos tried to remain neutral. But the North Vietnamese moved troops and supplies to South Vietnam along a trail that ran through eastern Laos, and the U.S. bombed the trail. In 1975, following Communist victories in Vietnam and Cambodia, the Communist Pathet Lao took control of Laos, and many Laotians fled to Thailand.

After 1975, Laos depended heavily on assistance from Vietnam and the former Soviet Union. Although most of the 50,000 Vietnamese troops stationed in Laos during the 1980s have been withdrawn and the Laotian government has actively sought aid from Thailand and other Western nations, ties between Vietnam and Laos remain strong.

The republic's first constitution, drawn up by a Supreme People's Council elected in 1989, was approved in 1991. It provides for a strong president elected for a five-year term by the National Assembly.

FRANK M. LeBAR, Coeditor, *Laos, Its People, Its Society, Its Culture*

The magnificent ruins of Angkor date from the 1100s, when Cambodians worshipped their kings.

CAMBODIA

Cambodia is a troubled land with a glorious past. In recent years, it has struggled to retain its identity through periods of invasion, misrule, and civil war. These conflicts have severely tested the resilient Khmer culture, which was forged over a period of 2,000 years by influences from much of the continent and even from Europe. Cambodia's golden age occurred eight centuries ago, when the Khmer Kingdom of Angkor ruled an empire that dominated much of Southeast Asia. At home, Khmer artisans built monuments whose ruins still dazzle the world. Much later, Cambodia became a French-protected state—in effect, a colony—for nearly a century before gaining full independence in 1955.

Cambodia (known as Kampuchea from 1975 to 1990) was a monarchy at independence and then a republic. It was later ruled by two Communist regimes, the first of which (1975–1979) was responsible for the deaths of an estimated 1.5 million to 3 million Cambodians. In 1993, after multiparty elections, Cambodia became a constitutional monarchy.

THE LAND

Cambodia, along with Thailand and Myanmar (formerly Burma) to its west, is the historic rice bowl of mainland Southeast Asia. Still, about 75 percent of the country, which is about the size of the state of Missouri, is forested. The 16 percent of its total land area that will support crop growth is very fertile. Cambodia's soil can be among the most productive for growing rice in all of Asia. However, a decline in all agricultural production resulted from Cambodia's involvement in the Indochina War, the reign of terror of the late 1970s, and the civil war that followed.

The Mekong River, which flows from Laos through east-central Cambodia into Vietnam, is the source of water for the traditional rice-producing central portion of the country, where most of the population lives. One of the Mekong's tributaries, the Tonle Sap River, exhibits unusual seasonal behavior. During the dry season, the Tonle Sap flows southeast, joining the Mekong at Phnom Penh. However, flooding and melting snow from Tibet during the May-to-October monsoon season cause it to change direction, flowing back into the lake from which it gets its name. The largest body of water within Cambodia, Tonle Sap—which means "Great Lake"—expands to about eight times its dry-season size.

Rainfall is variable. The coast receives nearly 200 in. (510 cm.) a year, while Phnom Penh gets less than 60 in. (150 cm.). Temperatures range from about 70° to 95° F. (21° to 35° C.). The monsoon season is hot and humid, yet temperatures are highest during the dry season.

THE PEOPLE

About 90 percent of Cambodia's population are Khmer, which is what ethnic Cambodians have historically called themselves. About 5 percent are Vietnamese, the Khmer's traditional enemies, and about 1 percent are ethnic Chinese.

FACTS AND FIGURES

OFFICIAL NAME: Cambodia.

NATIONALITY: Cambodian(s).

CAPITAL: Phnom Penh.

LOCATION: Southeastern Asia. **Boundaries**—Thailand, Laos, Vietnam, Gulf of Thailand.

AREA: 69,898 sq. mi. (181,035 sq. km.).

PHYSICAL FEATURES: Highest point—Mount Aural (5,948 ft.; 1,813 m.). **Lowest point**—sea level.

POPULATION: 10,900,000 (1996; annual growth 2.9%).

MAJOR LANGUAGES: Khmer (official), French.

MAJOR RELIGION: Theravada Buddhism.

GOVERNMENT: Constitutional monarchy. **Head of state**—king. **Head of government**—prime minister. **Legislature**—National Assembly.

CHIEF CITIES: Phnom Penh, Battambang, Kompong Cham, Pursat.

ECONOMY: Chief minerals—iron ore, coal, copper, phosphates, gold, zircons. **Chief agricultural products**—rice, rubber, corn, poultry, livestock. **Industries and products**—rice milling, fishing and fish processing, wood and wood products, sugar refining, handicrafts. **Chief exports**—natural rubber, wood, soybeans, sesame. **Chief imports**—food (including food aid), machinery, pharmaceuticals, textiles, electrical equipment, chemicals, consumer goods.

MONETARY UNIT: 1 new riel = 100 sen.

NATIONAL HOLIDAY: November 9 (Independence Day).

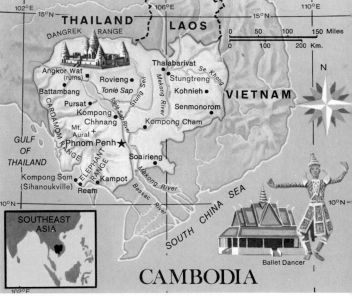

Ballet Dancer

CAMBODIA

Food is plentiful only after the crops cultivated during the rainy season are harvested.

Khmer fall into three groups: the Khmer Loeu (upper Khmer), or hill tribes; the Khmer Kandal (center Khmer) of the rice lands; and the Khmer Krom (lower Khmer), whose numbers reach into Vietnam's Mekong Delta. All Khmer speak the Khmer language, which has its own alphabet. Many educated Khmer also speak French.

About 80 percent of the people live in the rural areas. Most reside in villages, or *kampongs*, of approximately 100 to 400 people. They generally build their houses on stilts of bamboo and thatch and keep small gardens and a few fruit trees nearby. Farmers cultivate rice paddies only during the rainy and flood seasons.

Theravada Buddhism is the traditional religious faith of 95 percent of the people. Before 1975, a central feature of every village was a *wat*, or religious compound, consisting of a temple, a guesthouse, and dormitories for monks. Buddhism lost its legal protection under the 1976 constitution, and the Khmer Rouge (Communist) regime closed down temples and even destroyed some. The temples were reopened after 1979, but a 1985 law barred men less than 50 years old from becoming monks. The schools in temple compounds, where monks used to teach, are operated by the government and offer secular education. Nevertheless, most Cambodians still pursue the Buddhist goal of nirvana (escape from perpetual physical reincarnation), and they believe in traditional animistic spirits that inhabit objects and both plague and protect humankind.

Only 48 percent of the population is literate, a situation that the government vows to change through increased emphasis on education. In 1975, the Khmer Rouge closed down the nation's schools and killed every teacher they could find. A severe shortage of both teachers and textbooks persisted into the 1990s. In the countryside, older monks serve as teachers, because no other teachers exist. Otherwise, life in the rural areas—despite chronic food shortages—has largely returned to the way it was before 1970.

The Khmer Rouge attempted to eradicate the traditional Khmer culture. It destroyed almost all of the nation's books, Buddhas, pagodas, traditional costumes, and musical instruments, making it nearly impossible for scholars to piece together an accurate picture of Cambodia's cultural traditions. One of the few documents not destroyed was a handwritten catalog listing 1,170 traditional Khmer music pieces. Working

Cambodia's schools, now finally reopened, suffer from a severe lack of teachers.

largely from memory, the nation's seven surviving music teachers had managed to set down 500 of them by 1990.

Artists, dancers, and musicians were among those tortured and murdered. Only 10 female and seven male dancers from Cambodia's Royal Ballet survived the terror—a tragedy for Cambodian dance, which master dancers pass along by word of mouth and example.

THE ECONOMY

Cambodia's economy was prosperous, if largely agricultural, in the years before the early 1970s, when the war in Vietnam spilled over the border and engulfed the country. Rice and rubber were grown for export, the former by small landholders, and the latter on plantations. A modest industrial sector included rice mills, wood processing, fish products, sugar refining, textiles, paper, and jute mills. War and political upheaval during the 1970s caused severe food shortages and a famine that was alleviated by international relief efforts.

During the 1980s, flooding, drought, and civil war continued to slow recovery, although there were major gains in fishing and in rubber plantings. The government reduced its control of the economy. By 1990, about 70 percent of the economic resources were in private hands. The experiment in massive collective farming was abandoned in favor of a return to the sort of mutual-aid teams that are traditional to Cambodia.

Cambodia's most prominent natural resource, Asia's last giant stand of hardwoods, covers 70 percent of the land. Timber production doubled during the late 1980s. However, uncontrolled lumbering and minimal replanting have caused erosion, increased flooding, and the destruction of many spawning areas for fish.

HISTORY

The people of Cambodia rightly take great pride in their history. The earliest Khmer kingdom, founded in the 1st century A.D., was Funan, a Chinese name probably derived from the Khmer word *phnom*, or "mountain." An Indian Brahman who immigrated from the northwest is thought to have ruled the kingdom during the 2nd century and introduced Hindu customs and the Indian legal code. The kingdom was taken over by Khmer during the late 500s, and Khmer god-kings ruled from their capital in Angkor from the 800s to the 1200s. At its height, the Khmer Empire covered most of present-day Vietnam, Laos, and Thailand, extending from the Vietnamese coast to the Thai-Myanmar border.

The first Khmer god-king is thought to have been Kambu Svayambhuva, from whom the name of Cambodia, or Kampuchea, is said to be derived. (*Kambuja-desa* means "land of the lineage of Kambu.") It was during the reign of Suryavarman II (1113–50) that construction was started on the magnificent temple complex of Angkor Wat, one of the true wonders of the world. Planned as a monument to the monarch's divinity, it may be the world's largest religious structure. Walls nearly half a mile (0.8 km.) long portray the Hindu concept of the universe. A central tower represents Mount Meru, home of the gods; the outer walls symbolize the mountains enclosing the world; and a vast moat, surrounding the complex, stands for the ocean beyond. When Hinduism gave way to Buddhism as the nation's major religion, the temples were altered to reflect the change.

The violent Khmer Rouge regime in the 1970s imposed a reign of terror upon the Cambodian people.

The ancient Cambodian state was impressive in other respects, too. Agriculture was its great strength. More than 12 million acres (4.8 million hectares) of wet rice land were irrigated by a vast network of canals, producing two or three crops a year. Building and maintaining Angkor Wat and such an extensive complex of waterways, however, proved to be too great a burden. Cambodians turned to Buddhism and gave up their worship of the god-kings. Angkor, abandoned, was no longer the heart of Khmer civilization by the 1400s, when the capital was moved south to Phnom Penh. Attacked by its neighbors to the east and west, the Vietnamese and the Thai, Cambodia eventually was reduced in size to its present-day dimensions.

In 1863, King Ang Duong surprised the Vietnamese and the Thai by inviting the French to establish a protectorate over his country. The French agreed, but the move cost Cambodia its independence, as it became little more than France's colony. Along with Vietnam and Laos, two other lands France ruled, Cambodia became part of French Indo-china.

The Modern Era. Japan ruled Cambodia during World War II, when it conquered all of Southeast Asia. With Japanese encouragement, the Cambodians declared their independence in March 1945. When France managed to reestablish its presence in Indochina, King Norodom Sihanouk, who had taken the throne in 1941, campaigned for independence. France granted Cambodia independence within the French Union on November 9, 1953.

In order to enter politics, Sihanouk gave up the throne to his father in 1955. His party won the parliamentary elections that year, and he became prime minister. As his first act, he pulled Cambodia out of the French Union, a move that gave Cambodia full independence. Sihanouk became head of state in 1960, holding that post until his premier, Lon

Nol, ousted him in 1970, and parliament declared the nation a republic. At the time, Communist rebels known as the Khmer Rouge ("Red Khmer") controlled much of the country. The Khmer Rouge took power in 1975 and renamed the nation Democratic Kampuchea.

The Khmer Rouge leader, Pol Pot (the nom de guerre of Saloth Sar), wanted to build a Communist society almost overnight. To do so, the Khmer Rouge turned the nation into a huge labor camp, emptying the cities and relocating their residents to the countryside, where they worked alongside peasants on collective farms.

The newly organized villages contained three classes: a small group of Khmer Rouge officials at the top; "base people," the original inhabitants; and "new people," those resettled from the cities. Past membership in a group that the Khmer Rouge considered opposed to Communism often brought a death sentence. Estimates of the dead—from murder, malnutrition, and overwork—range from 1.5 million to 3 million. The Pol Pot regime has been described as "autogenocidal" for its attempt to obliterate an entire segment of its own people.

The Vietnamese invaded Cambodia on Christmas Day, 1978, and installed Khmer Rouge defector Heng Samrin as head of a new people's republic. Under a 1981 constitution, the government was run by a Council of Ministers chaired by Hun Sen. The Kampuchean People's Revolutionary Party (KPRP) was the sole legal party until 1991, when it accepted multipartyism and was renamed the Cambodian People's Party (CPP).

Following the 1979 overthrow of the Khmer Rouge, the government faced resistance from three major groups—what was left of Pol Pot's Khmer Rouge, supported by China, and two non-Communist groups headed by Prince Norodom Sihanouk and former premier Son Sann, who were supported by the United States and the non-Communist nations of Southeast Asia. The non-Communists formed an uneasy alliance with the militarily stronger Khmer Rouge, and their government-in-exile held Cambodia's seat in the United Nations until 1990. In 1989, Vietnam withdrew almost all of its troops from Cambodia, and in June 1991 the four factions declared a cease-fire. On October 23, they signed a comprehensive peace accord. Sihanouk was named head of a 12-member interim coalition government (the Supreme National Council) and later was reinstated as head of state. Hun Sen remained head of the government, and much of the CPP bureaucracy remained in place. U.N. peacekeeping forces oversaw the cease-fire and organized and supervised democratic elections held in May 1993. The royalist party (Funcinpec) won 58 of 120 seats in a constituent assembly; the CPP won 51 seats. Sihanouk returned to the throne on September 24, 1993. The Khmer Rouge continued its armed insurrection until 1996, when many of its supporters defected and made peace with the government.

GOVERNMENT

The four parties elected to seats in the assembly in May 1993 shared power until the assembly wrote a new constitution making Cambodia a constitutional monarchy, with a king as head of state and commander of the armed forces. The heads of the two most powerful parties became "first" and "second" premiers, and the constituent assembly became a National Assembly with the power to pass laws by a two-thirds vote.

RICHARD BUTWELL, Author, *Southeast Asia, A Political Introduction*

Vendors from the countryside bicycle into Hanoi, Vietnam's capital, to sell flowers and other goods.

VIETNAM

Conquest has played a significant role in the lives of the people of Vietnam for more than 2,000 years. Alternately they have conquered other peoples and have themselves been conquered by foreigners. The peoples conquered by the Vietnamese, without exception, have declined in number, vitality, and importance following the conquest. The Vietnamese, however, survived 1,000 years of Chinese colonial rule, both French and Japanese imperialism during the 1800s and 1900s and, more recently, a war that involved the United States.

Vietnam emerged from the last of these conflicts stronger than ever before in its history, at least militarily. Indeed, not long after the war, it became an invader itself again, occupying adjacent Cambodia.

Yet this incessant warfare left Vietnam—one of Southeast Asia's richest lands in terms of natural resources—in an almost preindustrial stage of development. Unable to serve even the nation's food needs with a state-controlled economy, Vietnam's Communist leaders made an about-face in 1987. They permitted ordinary citizens to sell crops and manufactured goods and provide services for a profit.

THE LAND

Geography is an important factor in any country's development. A major reason for China's past influence on Vietnam is the fact that the Vietnamese share their northern border with China. Cambodia and Laos are the country's neighbors to the west, while the waters of the South China Sea and the Gulf of Thailand wash Vietnam's shores to the east and south. Located in the extreme southeast corner of the great Asian landmass, Vietnam is a coastal country with about 2,150 mi. (3,450 km.) of shoreline. Because of the geographical exposure that results from this

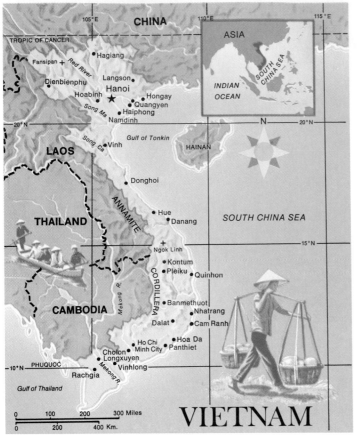

coastline, France entered Vietnam during the 1800s, hoping to use it as a base for invading adjacent China from the south.

During the period of rule by France that ended in 1954, Vietnam was part of a colonial political framework called French Indochina. The name "Indochina," a geo-cultural term, reflected the reality of its location between India and China, two great Asian countries that influenced both the culture and the politics of the lands that lay between them. The entire mainland Southeast Asia, which is peninsular in shape, is also known geographically as the Indochinese Peninsula.

The Vietnamese often describe the geography of their country in cultural terms—its appearance resembling a peasant carrying two rice baskets on opposite ends of a pole. The northern basket is dominated by the Red River Delta, while the Mekong Delta forms the southern basket. In fact, these are the two main rice-growing regions of Vietnam. But the country has three other regions as well: the Northern Highlands, the Annamite Cordillera range, and the central Coastal Lowlands.

The Northern Highlands border Laos and China. Forests and jungles cover much of this thinly populated region. Vietnam's highest peak, Fan Si Pan, rises 10,312 ft. (3,143 m.) in these highlands.

The Red River Delta is situated between the Northern Highlands and the Gulf of Tonkin. The north's chief agricultural region, this delta provides irrigation with the aid of canals and dikes to control flooding. The forest-covered chain of mountains, the Annamite Cordillera range, extends from the Northern Highlands to within 50 mi. (80 km.) of Ho Chi Minh City (formerly Saigon).

Rice production and fishing are the chief means of livelihood in the Coastal Lowlands that cover east-central Vietnam. However, the Mekong Delta is the south's main agricultural region. Over half of the south's population lives in this area.

Climate.   Like the rest of Southeast Asia, Vietnam is affected by the monsoons that create two basic seasons, wet and dry. The dry season extends from November to April, while rains begin in April and can last into October. Rainfall during this season may be as heavy as 72 in. (183 cm.) in both Hanoi, the capital city, and Ho Chi Minh City. The temperature in the south tends to be more moderate and consistent throughout the year, averaging in the low 80s F. (28° C.), while the mean temperature in the north is in the upper 80s F. (30° C.). Both the north and south can experience daytime temperatures above 100° F. (38° C.) during the wet season.

THE PEOPLE

Ethnic Vietnamese constitute 85 to 90 percent of the population. Chinese, accounting for about 3 percent of the population, make up the nation's largest single minority group. They are a majority in the southern city of Cholon. Ethnic Cambodians, or Khmer, and Cham are two smaller groups. Their ancestors inhabited south and central Vietnam before the Vietnamese migrated there. More numerous collectively than any of these groups are the *Montagnards,* the hill people of northern and central Vietnam. These Muong, Miao, and Tai are less materially advanced than the majority Vietnamese.

In the early 1990s, Vietnam's population was growing at the alarming rate of 2.5 percent a year—something that a government-set limit of two children per family failed to reduce. The regulation had little effect except in the cities, where a slash in rice rations—the punishment for exceeding the two-child limit—was most easily enforced.

Religion.   The most widespread religion is Buddhism of the *Mahayana* (Greater Vehicle) school that came to the country by way of China. Another form of Buddhism is the Hinduized *Hinayana* Buddhism of neighboring Cambodia, Laos, Thailand, and Myanmar (Burma). About 80 percent of all Vietnamese are either practicing Buddhists or nominal followers. Roman Catholicism was widespread in South Vietnam before the Communists' 1975 victory, which caused many Christians to flee to other lands. Confucianism, Taoism, and indigenous sects that combine elements of the major religions are also found. Many of the country's inhabitants, primarily the minorities of the highlands, practice animism, or spirit worship.

Though not encouraged by the Communist government, religion has remained important in Vietnam, especially to older people. In an effort to channel this religious energy toward "building socialism," the government set up a wholly new Buddhist organization in 1980. Buddhist training schools were reopened, allowing for an increase in monks. During the late 1980s, the National Assembly passed a law that restored vast amounts of land to the monasteries, allowing monks to support themselves by growing their own food.

Way of Life.   About 20 percent of the Vietnamese live in the cities. The majority of these reside in two- or three-room apartments. Street vendors fill the main thoroughfares, and cafés—a remnant of the many

The Vietnamese government allows only limited religious freedom. Cao Dai (left), a sect founded after World War I, claims over one million followers. The faith incorporates elements of several world religions.

years of French rule—dot the central business areas. Urban dress often shows the lingering influence of the West.

The majority of Vietnamese people live in small, rural villages. The village has been the traditional focus of Vietnamese society. A *dinh*, or temple compound, occupies the center of most villages. Most homes are constructed of wood or bamboo with roofs of palm leaves or straw, although sheets of metal and plastic are sometimes used in the north, where the climate is cool. Rural women tend to wear the traditional costume, the *ao dai*, a full-length tunic, slit to the waist and worn over loose-fitting white or black trousers. Men and women wear conical hats for protection.

Language. The Vietnamese language is composed of single-syllable words that do not change. The same word, however, can have different meanings, which are expressed through different levels of pitch. Although Vietnamese has been enriched with many Chinese literary, philosophical, and technical terms, it is basically unrelated to the Chinese language. Chinese ideographs, or characters, were originally used in written Vietnamese. But they came into disuse after Portuguese and French missionaries in the 1600s invented *quoc-ngu,* a system of using Roman letters.

Because of Vietnam's ethnic mixture, many other languages are spoken in the country, although Vietnamese, the official language, is spoken by nine out of 10 people. French, the language of colonial French Indochina, is still fairly widely spoken among the older elite. The American political and military presence in the south from 1954 to 1975 left many southerners fluent in English. The Chinese in Vietnam speak various dialects, while languages such as Mon-Khmer and Malayo-Polynesian predominate in the relatively localized areas where minorities speaking these tongues are found. Vietnam's literacy rate is high, with about 94 percent of the population able to read and write.

Chief Cities. Vietnam's largest city, once the capital of the southern part of the country, is **Ho Chi Minh City,** named after the Vietnamese Communist leader who died in 1969. Formerly called Saigon, it is the south's major port and the center of the nation's finance and industry. The metropolitan area of Ho Chi Minh City includes **Cholon,** where many of the south's factories are located. Many Vietnamese of Chinese ancestry live in Cholon, which has a more traditionally Vietnamese appearance than Ho Chi Minh City. Westernized under French control after the mid-1800s, Ho Chi Minh City is far more cosmopolitan than Cholon. It has many European-style buildings and wide boulevards. Its population increased considerably during the Vietnam War (1959–75), when people from the countryside sought refuge in the city.

Danang, the second-largest city in southern Vietnam, has port facilities that make it important to that part of the country. During the war, it was the site of a large air force base and other military installations. Next in size among southern cities is **Hue,** situated about 50 mi. (80 km.) from the 17th parallel, which once divided the northern and southern parts of Vietnam. Hue was the old imperial capital of Vietnam and the center of learning and traditional Vietnamese culture. In 1968, fighting destroyed much of the city.

Hanoi, the former capital of the northern part of the country, and the capital after the two parts were united, is Vietnam's second-largest city. It is situated in the Red River Delta. Under Communists, it was rapidly industrialized until the mid-1960s, when wartime bombing forced the evacuation of many of its industries, as well as much of its population. **Haiphong,** an industrial city that also serves as Hanoi's port, was a major supply depot during the war years.

Once the Vietnam War ended in 1975, new buildings began to spring up in Hanoi.

Many fishermen depend on the rich waters of the South China Sea for their livelihood.

ECONOMY

Vietnam's economy is mainly agricultural, with farming, fishing, and forestry employing about two-thirds of the work force. Rice is the main crop—heavily exported since 1989—although maize, sorghum, cassava, and sweet potatoes are also grown in large amounts, as is rubber. Fish and rice are the staples of the Vietnamese diet.

Vietnam's considerable mineral resources, the bulk of them in the north, include phosphates, coal, manganese, bauxite, chromate, and offshore oil deposits. Though coal and other minerals are exported, they remain underdeveloped. Vietnam's industries include food processing, textiles, machine building, mining, cement, chemical fertilizer, glass, tires, oil, and fishing.

Despite these assets, Vietnam is one of the world's poorest countries. Its poverty is in large measure the result of the many years of resistance and warfare between 1940 and 1975. The anticolonial war with France (1946–54) prevented economic reconstruction after the exploitative occupation of the Japanese during World War II. American bombing knocked out a large portion of the manufacturing facilities of the north during the Vietnam War (1959–75), while Communist guerrillas, members of the Vietcong, disrupted rice-growing in the south.

Vietnam's invasion of neighboring Cambodia in late 1978, less than three years after the war's end, put a terrible burden on Vietnam's treasury for the next 10 years. Little money was left for development purposes, and the nation gained nothing by expanding the state-controlled economic system to the south.

In 1987, the nation's leaders decided to weaken the state's grip on the economy and permit privately owned, profit-making enterprises. It instituted a program of *doi moi,* or renovation. Farmers were allowed to lease land on long-term contracts that could be handed down to their children. The government ended subsidies that kept rice prices artificially low, dismantled farm collectives, and permitted private businesses and family farming.

Other reforms followed. Farmers were permitted to sell on the open market, for a profit, any goods they had not pledged to the state. By 1990, this reform had boosted the average farm family's income by as much as 300 percent. More important, it had resulted in increased output, catapulting Vietnam in 1989 from being a rice importer to becoming the world's third-largest rice exporter.

The reforms took hold less quickly in the north than in the south, which had previous experience with free enterprise. Yet signs of free-market activity were clearly evident in the north by 1990. Independent businesses such as sidewalk cafés, restaurants, video shops, and open-air markets began to crop up all over the city of Hanoi.

Doi moi had less immediate success in the industrial area. In part, this was because Vietnamese consumers had little money to spend for manufactured goods. A bicycle, for example, cost the average state worker about one month's salary in 1990. So, instead of buying an entire bicycle, the average Vietnamese was apt to purchase one piece-by-piece —a seat one year, handlebars the next, and so on.

Despite its gains, the new economic policy created a good deal of resentment, especially among people who failed to benefit from it immediately. This included the unemployed, who made up perhaps 20 percent of all urban workers in 1990, and the majority of workers whose sole source of income was their low state salaries. By 1990, about 30 percent of the income Vietnamese workers earned came from private sources, including family-owned farms and businesses.

Throughout the 1970s and 1980s, Vietnam relied heavily on foreign aid from the Soviet Union and other nations. But with its own economic problems, the Soviet Union made it clear it was eager to cut back its aid.

After years of near famine, Vietnam has suddenly become the world's third-largest exporter of rice.

The ancient royal capital of Hue was the scene of heavy fighting during the Vietnam War.

A key revenue source put in jeopardy by changes in Eastern Europe was the earnings of Vietnamese living abroad. In 1990, some 200,000 Vietnamese "guest workers" living in the Soviet Union and in Eastern European countries regularly sent money to families back home. But with a shift in Eastern Europe from state-controlled to free-enterprise economies, and the breakup of the Soviet Union, many of the Vietnamese workers were no longer needed or could no longer be supported.

Aid from the former Soviet Union ended in 1991. To fill the gap in revenues, Vietnam sought to improve its relations with China and to attract economic aid and investment from non-Communist countries. In an effort to reduce its budget deficit, the government also halted subsidies to state enterprises in 1991. Military expenditures were also reduced when Vietnam withdrew its forces from Cambodia. Among the most attractive fields for Western investment was exploration for offshore oil and natural gas. The U.S. trade embargo that had been imposed on North Vietnam in 1964 and extended to the entire country after the Communist victory in 1975 was finally lifted in 1994. The following year, Vietnam was the first Communist nation to be admitted to the Association of Southeast Asian Nations (ASEAN).

GOVERNMENT

With the adoption of a new constitution in April 1992, economic reform was followed by limited political reform. The new constitution formalized the free-market economic reforms that had been implemented since the 1980s. The former collective presidency (Council of State) was replaced by a single president elected from within the legislature, the National Assembly, which was given greater powers. Members of the National Assembly are elected by universal adult suffrage for a five-year term. The Council of Ministers was also abolished, replaced by a cabinet headed by a prime minister whose powers were also enhanced. The Vietnamese Communist Party remained the only legal political party and was to continue to guide policy, but it was no longer to be involved in the day-to-day running of the government. More than 80 percent of the legislators elected under the new constitution in July 1992 were new, although 90 percent were members of the Vietnamese Communist Party.

HISTORY

The original inhabitants of the central and eastern portions of mainland Southeast Asia were primarily the Malay peoples, who now constitute the majority populations of Malaysia, Indonesia, and the Philippines. About the 4th century B.C., these and other peoples were pushed south and southwest as the Vietnamese, whose earliest known home was near modern Canton in China, moved into the Red River Delta region of northern Vietnam.

Chinese pressures forced the Vietnamese to move southward. When the Chinese attempted to rule the Vietnamese indirectly, through puppet governments, the Vietnamese rebelled. The Chinese reacted by taking over Vietnam and incorporating it into their empire, ruling it from 111 B.C. to A.D. 939. In 939, the Vietnamese were able to throw off Chinese rule only to experience it again in the early 1400s. In 1427, led by Le Loi, a national hero, Vietnam again resumed its independence from imperial Chinese rule.

Much as they disliked the Chinese, the Vietnamese were influenced by this long contact. The Vietnamese borrowed so heavily from Chinese religion, philosophy, language, arts, dress, food, and political organization that many foreigners referred to the subsequently independent land as "Little China." Yet in much of its long history, Vietnam has defined itself as China's enemy, a fact memorialized in folk song and legend.

The tomb of Ho Chi Minh in Hanoi has become a shrine to the Communist revolutionary leader.

The Vietnamese played the role of aggressor toward peoples to the south of them. They defeated the kingdom of Champa in central Vietnam, and the subjugated Cham became an underprivileged ethnic minority in a larger Vietnamese state. Similarly, the Khmer of Cambodia, whose once-great empire extended from Myanmar to the Southeast Asian coast, were overcome by the Vietnamese and forced to withdraw into a state of a much smaller size. As the borders of the Khmer empire shrank, an impoverished Cambodian minority was left stranded in the Mekong Delta region.

France invaded Vietnam in 1858, consolidating its control there by 1883. France was to remain Vietnam's ruler until 1954, although the Japanese were actually in control as the occupying power from 1940 to 1945.

The Vietminh, headed by Ho Chi Minh, a Communist and nationalist, led the resistance against Japan and, later, against the restoration of French rule after World War II. In 1954, Vietminh forces defeated the French at Dien Bien Phu in the Red River Delta. The Vietnamese reached a settlement with the French that divided Vietnam at the 17th parallel into the separate—and, by agreement, temporary—states of North and South Vietnam. The Communist north and non-Communist south agreed to schedule elections that would be followed by reunification. But in 1956, South Vietnam's leaders refused to take part in the elections.

The Vietnam War.   North Vietnam's rulers felt cheated of certain victory in the elections. Civil war between the north and south began in earnest in 1959, and before long each side had the support of different world powers. The United States entered the conflict on the side of South Vietnam, committing 500,000 troops a year at the war's height. Armed by the Soviet Union and able to sustain immense casualties, the north pursued victory relentlessly. The U.S. pulled out its troops in stages between 1969 and 1973, when all parties—including the Vietcong, an antigovernment guerrilla army in South Vietnam—signed a cease-fire. Without U.S. troop support, South Vietnamese troops were overrun by North Vietnamese forces in 1975. On July 2, 1976, the victors declared Vietnam unified and named it the Socialist Republic of Vietnam.

The Postwar Era.   Vietnam emerged from the war with the world's fourth-largest army and the most experienced military machine in Southeast Asia. With their own foreign enemy gone, the Vietnamese almost immediately moved against the neighboring Cambodians, whose easternmost territory Vietnam had absorbed more than a century earlier. In 1979, the Vietnamese entered Phnom Penh, Cambodia's capital, and drove out its Communist rulers. They were replaced with a puppet government that was willing to serve Vietnam's interests. This move angered the Chinese, who supported the ousted regime, as did Vietnam's alliance with the Soviet Union. In 1979, Chinese troops temporarily crossed into Vietnam. After Vietnam withdrew from Cambodia in 1989, it stationed most of its troops near the Chinese border as a precautionary measure.

Vietnam normalized relations with China after the signing of a U.N.–supervised Cambodian peace accord in October 1991. Full U.S. diplomatic relations were restored in 1995, when Vietnam was also admitted to ASEAN and adopted its first civil code. Many hoped that the ending of Vietnam's isolation, coupled with economic liberalization at home, would help to solve the nation's social and economic problems.

RICHARD BUTWELL, *California State University, Dominguez Hills*

Kuala Lumpur, the capital of Malaysia, has emerged as one of the leading cities of Southeast Asia.

MALAYSIA

Founded in 1963, the Federation of Malaysia, in Southeast Asia, is one of the world's youngest countries. Its people—a mixture of many races, nationalities, and cultures—have forged a national state out of territories that were part of the British Empire. Malaysia consists of 11 states on the Malay Peninsula and two former British colonies on the island of Borneo. Until 1965, it also included the island country of Singapore. The territories that make up Malaysia have been important in history because of their natural resources and their favorable location.

THE LAND

Malaysia is divided into two parts, separated by roughly 400 mi. (640 km.) of the South China Sea. Western Malaysia occupies the southern half of the Malay Peninsula. The eastern and larger part of Malaysia is composed of the two states of Sarawak and Sabah on the northern quarter of the big island of Borneo. A long, forested mountain range runs much of the length of the Malay Peninsula. To the east and to the west of these heights are low-lying plains that reach to the sea. A large part of these lowlands is covered by swamps and thick forests and is unsuitable for cultivation. The western lowlands of the peninsula are the most heavily populated areas. Here are located the principal cultivated lands and the main mining centers. Few people live along the peninsula's eastern coast, which is a generally undeveloped region of dense jungle and swampland. The peninsula's major rivers are the Pahang and the Perak.

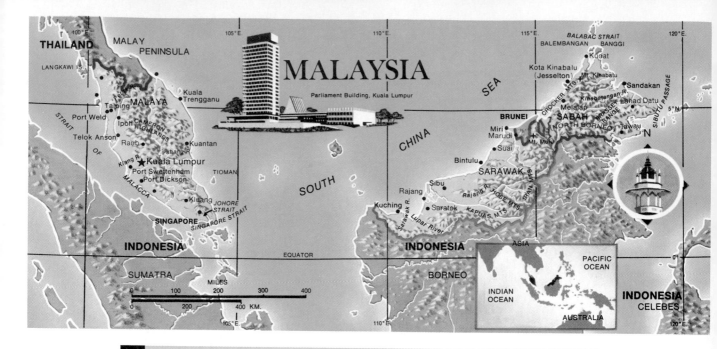

MALAYSIA

Parliament Building, Kuala Lumpur

East Malaysia, formerly North Borneo, consists of Sarawak and Sabah, which share the island of Borneo with Brunei and Kalimantan, an Indonesian territory. East Malaysia is largely a land of coastal swamps, rain forests, and rugged mountain ranges. Only about 18 percent of the country's people live in this region. The Crocker Range, Malaysia's tallest mountain range, extends from Sabah into Sarawak.

Climate. Malaysia has an equatorial climate with generally high temperatures. Rainfall is heavy, particularly during the late-autumn and early-winter months, and the annual average is more than 100 in. (240 cm.). Although days are often hot and humid, nights are cool because of the sea breezes. In the mountains, temperatures are cooler, and there is considerably less humidity.

Natural Resources. Malaysia is the world's largest producer of tin, palm oil, rubber, and tropical timber. Malaysia also exports copper, and there are substantial oil and natural-gas reserves in the South China Sea. Beginning in the 1970s, the production of petroleum grew dramatically, and it now accounts for about 13 percent of Malaysia's foreign earnings. Malaysia also has extensive deposits of iron ore and bauxite.

THE PEOPLE

Malaysia's inhabitants include people of various racial and ethnic backgrounds. The native Malays make up about 49 percent of the population and live largely in rural areas. They are closely related to the Filipino and Indonesian peoples.

Malaysians of Chinese extraction are mostly urban. They make up about 31 percent of the population. About 9 percent of the population is Indian, their ancestors coming from India, Pakistan, Sri Lanka, and Bangladesh. Several aboriginal tribal groups, living mostly in Sarawak and Sabah, make up 11 percent of the population. The nation's ethnic diversity has sometimes created problems, and the government must take care that no group feels excluded in development. Nonetheless, economic policy aims to improve the status of the *bumiputras* ("sons of the soil," or Malays).

Language and Education.   The official language of the country is Bahasa Malaysia (Malay). Indonesia and Malaysia are cooperating to standardize the spelling of their almost-identical languages. English is widely spoken in business and government. Chinese and Tamil are also commonly spoken. Tribal dialects exist, too, in Sarawak and Sabah in East Malaysia.

Children receive nine years of free, compulsory education in schools that must teach Malay and English. There are many teacher-training and technical colleges and several universities, the largest of which is the University of Malaya in Kuala Lumpur.

Religion.   By constitutional definition, all Malays are followers of Islam, which was introduced into the region by Arab and Indian traders. People of Indian ancestry are mainly Hindus. Those of Chinese background are mostly Buddhists, although some are Taoist or Christian.

Malaysia leads the world in tin production. The metal is easily accessible by strip-mining methods.

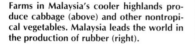

Farms in Malaysia's cooler highlands produce cabbage (above) and other nontropical vegetables. Malaysia leads the world in the production of rubber (right).

Some tribal peoples practice the animist faiths of their ancestors, and there is a scattering of converts to Christianity.

Way of Life. Modern buildings are found in all of the cities and larger towns, but in the villages, people ordinarily live in traditional Malay homes. Erected on small posts a few feet above the ground, these dwellings offer protection against floods and wild animals. The walls of matting and the thatched roofs can be constructed quickly and inexpensively; houses are cool and comfortable in the warm climate.

Many styles of dress are worn. In the cities and towns, men often wear a loose shirt, trousers, and sandals. In the countryside, the sarong —a wraparound skirt reaching from the waist to the knees and sometimes lower—is usually worn. Many men also wear a brimless black velvet cap called a *songkok*. City women frequently wear Western-style clothes. Still, the most popular costume for women in cities and villages is the gaily colored sarong and blouse. Indian women favor saris and blouses, while Chinese women wear the pajamalike *sam-foo* or the *cheongsam*, a close-fitting dress with a slit skirt.

Malaysian food includes dishes made with rice, vegetables, fish, chicken, and meat. Many dishes are heavily spiced with curry sauces. Fruits, such as bananas, durians (a large, prickly fruit), and mangosteens (a reddish brown fruit that combines the taste of peach and pineapple), are abundant. Since the majority of the people are Muslims, many Malaysians do not drink alcoholic beverages. Tea and coffee are the favorite drinks. People of Indian and Chinese ancestry eat foods that are adapted from the native cooking of their homelands.

Malaysians are fond of outdoor sports, particularly soccer, rugby, swimming, tennis, and cricket. There are large amusement parks in the principal cities. Among the different forms of entertainment are Chinese and Malay operas, puppet shows, the classical Malay dramatic play called the Menora, and traditional dancing known as *joget*. Celebrations take place on the main holidays. These include the Islamic holy day Hari Raya Puasa, the Chinese New Year, the Hindu Festival of Lights, and Freedom Day (August 31), the national holiday.

Cities. Malaysia's capital, **Kuala Lumpur,** is the largest of the country's cities. It is situated on the Klang River in the heart of a tin- and rubber-producing region. The city is a blend of old Moorish-style architecture and modern structures such as the imposing Parliament House complex, the National Museum, and the University of Malaya.

Sabah's capital, **Kota Kinabalu,** is a major port and important trading center. Sarawak's leading city and capital is **Kuching,** located on the Sarawak River. Livestock trading, fishing, and timber exporting are its main industries. Malaysia's major ports include Port Swettenham, Telok Anson, Port Weld, and Pinang (George Town).

The Economy. About 34 percent of all Malaysians earn their living from agriculture. Most farms are small and are worked by the farmer and his family, who consume much of what they raise. The most important crops raised on these smaller farms are rice, coconuts, fruits, and vegetables. Malaysia grows much rice, but must import more to feed its people. Rubber, oil palms, and coconut trees, the chief cash crops, are grown mainly on large plantations. The processing of agricultural products and timber milling remain important, but mineral-related industries are expanding rapidly, employing about 11 percent of the work force. About 15 percent of Malaysia's workers manufacture components for electrical and electronic equipment, or work in the textile or plastics industries, or in the entirely Malaysian automobile industry.

Malaysians work at various handicrafts, including basketry, silverware, handweaving of shawls and sarongs, and the making of batik cloth. The batik process involves coating fabric with wax, cutting designs out of the wax, and then dyeing the unwaxed parts of the fabric.

In the swampy terrain of East Malaysia, many people still travel to market on river ferries.

GOVERNMENT

Malaysia is a constitutional monarchy. The *yang di-pertuan agong*—meaning "king" or "supreme head of state"—is elected for a term of five years. He is chosen from among the rulers of the nine original Malay states and elected by them. The king appoints the prime minister and cabinet from among the members of Parliament but has little real power. A majority of Senate members are appointed by the king; the remainder are elected by the legislatures of Malaysia's 13 states and two territories. All members of the House of Representatives are popularly elected. Mahathir Mohammed, who heads the dominant party in the ruling National Front coalition, has been prime minister since 1981.

HISTORY

The first groups of Malay people moved into the Malay Peninsula about 2000 B.C. For many centuries, these people lived scattered along the coast in small villages. From A.D. 8 to the end of the 1200s, the ancient Indonesian Buddhist kingdom of Srivijaya dominated much of the peninsula. Later, for a shorter period, the Hindu kingdom of Madjapahit on Java gained control. The founding of the port of Malacca in the early 1400s aided the spread of Islam. The city grew into one of the principal trading centers in Southeast Asia, attracting Arab merchants who converted the inhabitants to the Muslim faith.

In 1511, the Portuguese captured Malacca, beginning more than four centuries of European colonial rule in this region. Malacca was taken by the Dutch in 1641, and, in 1786, the British occupied the offshore island of Penang. British influence in the area expanded rapidly during the 1800s, and eventually all of the Malay states came under British control. By the early 1900s, the British were also firmly entrenched in Sarawak and North Borneo (now Sabah).

Under British rule, rubber plantations were established, mining was expanded, and railroads were built. In 1941–42, during World War II, Japan overran Southeast Asia, including Britain's colonies. In 1945, however, the British regained control. Three years later, they organized the nine Malay states into the Federation of Malaya, which became independent in 1957. At that time, Malacca (now Melaka) and Penang (now Pinang) became states in the federation. From 1948 to 1960, the federation was rocked by a Communist uprising that was finally put down with British military assistance.

In 1961, Malaya's premier, Tengku (Prince) Abdul Rahman (later Malaysia's first prime minister), suggested organizing a Malaysian state by adding Singapore, Sarawak, Sabah, and Brunei to the Federation of Malaya. After two years of negotiations, the Federation of Malaysia was established on September 16, 1963. Brunei, a British-protected state in North Borneo and later an independent nation, decided not to join; and Singapore left the federation in 1965.

Despite serious racial disturbances involving the Malay and Chinese communities, Malaysia has flourished as one of the most promising of the Southeast Asian nations. Its living standard is the fourth-highest in Asia. Malaysia is a founding member of the Association of Southeast Asian Nations (ASEAN), which seeks to advance cooperation among the countries of the area.

RICHARD BUTWELL, California State University, Dominguez Hills

The island city-state of Singapore thrives as the financial center of Southeast Asia.

SINGAPORE

In the early 1800s, Singapore was an unimportant little Southeast Asian island covered by jungle and swampland. But in 1819, a farsighted Englishman named Sir Stamford Raffles, acting on behalf of the British East India Company, leased Singapore from a Malay prince and set up a trading station. By the century's end, the trading post had grown into a thriving port city, and the island was a key outpost of the British Empire. British rule ended in 1963, when Singapore joined the Federation of Malaysia. Two years later, it left the federation to pursue an independent course. Today, the diamond-shaped city-state is Southeast Asia's financial center, and its people enjoy one of Asia's highest standards of living.

Singapore is like many nations in its need to forge a national identity among groups with strong ethnic and religious loyalties. It is also like many well-run business enterprises, especially in its government's detail-oriented style of management. This unusual mix of qualities has made Singapore's society one of the world's most intriguing, and its economy a model for the developing world.

THE LAND

Singapore consists of one large island and 55 islets. It is located just off the southern shore of the Malay Peninsula, separated from the mainland by the narrow Johore Strait. The island is connected to the mainland by a causeway. South of the island is the Singapore Strait, which separates Singapore from several islands belonging to Indonesia. West to east, Singapore Island is 26 mi. (42 km.) wide. North to south, it spans 14 mi. (23 km.). Most of the people live in the city of Singapore at the southern end of the island. The rest live in scattered villages. The central portion of Singapore is hilly, but the coastal areas are flat. The island's climate is hot, humid, and rainy.

THE PEOPLE

About 76 percent of Singapore's 3 million people are ethnic Chinese, descended mainly from immigrants who settled in Singapore during the past 150 years. Most of them speak Mandarin or other Chinese dialects. Malay-speaking descendants of the original Malay inhabitants now amount to 15 percent of the population. About 6 percent of all Singaporeans are of Indian background, and their principal language is Tamil. The language of instruction at all levels of schooling is English. Most children attend schools that emphasize the language they speak at home as a second language.

Most of Singapore's Chinese, retaining traditional beliefs, adhere to a mixture of Confucianism, Daoism (Taoism), and Buddhism. Nearly all the Malays are Muslims, while the Indian population is mainly Hindu. Christians may be found among all of the ethnic groups.

Compulsory national service for all males over 18 has helped create a sense of common identity among all citizens, and the importance of mutual respect for all ethnic groups is a constant theme of government. Malay, Chinese, and Indian Singaporeans prefer to socialize and marry within their own groups, however, and some friction exists between them.

Way of Life. Singapore combines both Eastern and Western ways in its pattern of living. The country is virtually 100 percent urban and has no separately defined cities. Tall office buildings and modern apartment houses line the broad avenues, side by side with buildings in the Victorian style popular a century ago during colonial times. But along the side streets, the atmosphere becomes more traditionally Asian. Here are found stalls and small shops run by Chinese, Indians, and Malays. Although many people wear Western clothing, it is not unusual to see Indian women in saris and others in traditional Chinese and Malay dress, reflecting the cultural diversity in this international crossroads.

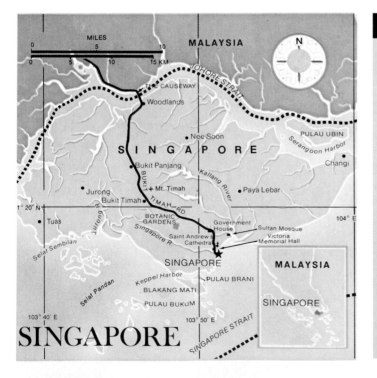

SINGAPORE

FACTS AND FIGURES

OFFICIAL NAME: Republic of Singapore.

NATIONALITY: Singaporean(s).

CAPITAL AND CHIEF CITY: Singapore.

LOCATION: Southeastern Asia. **Boundaries**—Malaysia, Singapore Strait, Indonesia.

AREA: 239 sq. mi. (618 sq. km.).

PHYSICAL FEATURES: Highest point—Mount Timah (581 ft.; 177 m.). **Lowest point**—sea level.

POPULATION: 3,000,000 (1996; annual growth 1.1%).

MAJOR LANGUAGES: Chinese, Malay, Tamil, English (all official).

MAJOR RELIGIONS: Buddhism, Islam, Christianity, Hinduism, Sikhism, Daoism, Confucianism.

GOVERNMENT: Republic. **Head of state**—president. **Head of government**—prime minister. **Legislature**—unicameral Parliament.

ECONOMY: Chief agricultural products—rubber, copra, fruits and vegetables, fish, pork, poultry. **Industries and products**—petroleum refining, electronics, oil-drilling equipment, rubber products, processed food, ship repairs, financial services. **Chief exports**—computer equipment, rubber, manufactured goods. **Chief imports**—aircraft, petroleum, chemicals.

MONETARY UNIT: 1 Singapore dollar = 100 cents.

NATIONAL HOLIDAY: August 9 (National Day).

The streets of Singapore, although crowded with people wearing Western-style clothing, still manage to maintain a traditional Asian atmosphere.

Old-style wooden junks, sampans, and fishing vessels crowd the waterfront, in sharp contrast to the modern ocean liners and cargo vessels that visit Singapore's bustling harbor. Both European and Asian culture are represented in the city's libraries and museums. The city of Singapore also has a splendid botanical garden, an outstanding symphony orchestra, and printing facilities that produce excellent books and periodicals for publishers around the world.

Education. About nine of every 10 Singaporeans can read and write. Education is free, and children must attend school for six years. Two-thirds of primary-school students go on to secondary schools. Standards are high. About 10 percent continue their educations at such places as the National University of Singapore, Singapore Polytechnic, and the engineering-oriented Nanyang Technological Institute.

ECONOMY

From the days of Sir Stamford Raffles to the present, trade has been the lifeblood of Singapore, which is a major transshipment port. Goods from other Southeast Asian lands flow through Singapore on their way to Japan, Europe, and the United States. From Singapore's crowded docks and wharves sail ships carrying rubber, copra (dried coconut meat), timber, spices, and other products of the region. Other ships carry electronic goods, processed petroleum, and similar industrial products that reflect Singapore's status as Southeast Asia's premier manufacturing site. Storage and handling facilities for ships and cargo are among the most modern in the world.

Since independence, the government has emphasized manufacturing products for export. It cleared marshy land on the island's west coast, built hundreds of factories, and invited manufacturers from other nations to lease them. Hundreds of manufacturers accepted, taking advantage of Singapore's inexpensive, industrious, and well-educated labor force.

During the 1980s, oil refining became the largest industry in terms of the value of its product. Following closely in size were the electronics industry; transportation equipment and marine services, including ship-building and repair; textiles; electrical machinery; and the processing of canned and frozen food.

The nation imports food and raw materials from neighboring lands. It also imports heavy industrial equipment and various manufactured goods. Singapore is the banker for much of the region, and a popular tourist site.

Singaporeans devote their limited farmland to the intensive cultivation of poultry, orchids, garden vegetables, and fruits. Rice, a main dietary staple, is imported, as are other foodstuffs.

During the 1980s, construction helped fuel economic growth. The government instituted an ambitious program of public works that provides modern housing for most Singaporeans, up-to-date ports, and a rapid-transit system that will eventually be 41.5 mi. (66.8 km.) long.

During the 1990s, Singapore is positioning itself to become one of the world's most innovative economies. To achieve that goal, it is taking steps to nurture and attract research and development, technology, and automation.

HISTORY

A center of trade during the 1200s and 1300s, Singapore lost its role during the early 1400s, when the port of Malacca was founded in what is now Malaysia. By the time Sir Stamford Raffles arrived in 1819, the island was virtually uninhabited. The trading post Raffles founded grew steadily. In 1826, it was merged with Malacca and Penang to become the British Straits Settlements, which became a crown colony in 1867.

In 1869, the Suez Canal was opened, enabling countries in Europe and Asia to trade more easily with one another. Because of its location at the crossroads of Southeast Asia, Singapore once again began to flourish. It became even more important during the early 1900s, when the British constructed large naval and air bases on the island. Despite its elaborate defenses, however, in 1942, the island fell to the Japanese, who occupied it until World War II ended in 1945.

Britain granted Singapore internal self-government in 1959. In 1963, Singapore joined the Federation of Malaya and the former British colonies of Sarawak and Sabah on Borneo to form the new state of Malaysia. Singapore left the federation in 1965 to become an independent country.

GOVERNMENT

Members of Singapore's single-house Parliament are elected by universal and compulsory suffrage for a five-year term. The leader of the party holding a majority of seats in Parliament heads the government as prime minister. When self-rule began in 1959, a Singapore-born Chinese named Lee Kuan Yew took charge of the island's government. As head of the People's Action Party (PAP), he became the country's first prime minister in 1965. In 1990, after overseeing Singapore's rise to prosperity, Lee passed PAP's leadership to Goh Chok Tong, although he remained in the cabinet. In 1991, the constitution was revised to convert the formerly ceremonial post of president into a popularly elected executive position with increased power. The nation's first direct presidential elections, won by Ong Teng Cheong, took place in 1993.

RICHARD BUTWELL, *California State University, Dominguez Hills*

Jakarta, the Indonesian capital, has grown into a sprawling metropolis of 9 million people.

INDONESIA

Rich in natural resources, the Republic of Indonesia is the largest nation in Southeast Asia and the fifth most populous nation in the world. Situated between the Pacific and Indian oceans, it spans a distance greater than that between the east and west coasts of the United States. A lush island nation with a rich cultural past, it is engaged in a mammoth effort to modernize its economy.

Indonesia was once famous for its spices, and it was in order to find a shorter route to these "Spice Islands" that Christopher Columbus and Ferdinand Magellan set sail on their voyages of discovery. Beginning in the early 1600s, the Dutch gradually assumed control over the area, developing it into a colony called the Netherlands East Indies. In 1949, the colony won formal independence as the Republic of Indonesia. It gained Dutch-held Western New Guinea, now Irian Jaya, in 1963. In 1976, East Timor, a former Portuguese colony, also became part of Indonesia.

THE LAND

Indonesia is an archipelago consisting of more than 13,500 islands and tiny islets. More than 6,000 of these islands are inhabited. The islands stretch like a bridge of stepping-stones between the Asian mainland and the continent of Australia. Mountains rise steeply and often to great heights on many of the islands. The highest of these mountains, located on Irian Jaya (the Indonesian part of New Guinea), are permanently capped with snow. Many of Indonesia's mountains are active or inactive volcanoes. Probably the most famous Indonesian volcano is Krakatau (Krakatoa) on an island in the Sunda Strait. In 1883, Krakatau erupted in one of history's worst instances of volcanic activity.

The rugged mountains on the island of Java have many active and inactive volcanoes.

Climate. Because Indonesia is on or near the equator, its climate is tropical. Temperatures are usually high, but vary according to height above sea level. Most of the major cities—where 25 percent of all Indonesians now live—are located along the coasts or on the lowland plains. Here the weather is generally very warm and humid. Seasonal winds known as monsoons buffet the islands, resulting in two main seasons, a wet and a dry. Throughout most of Indonesia, the rainfall is enough to make the land green and rich all year round. But on some of the smaller islands of the southeast, the dry season is long and severe. There the land is suitable mainly for grazing cattle and growing crops that require little moisture.

The Greater Sunda Islands. The five major islands of Indonesia are Java; Sumatra; Kalimantan, the Indonesian portion of Borneo; Sulawesi, formerly Celebes; and Irian Jaya, the Indonesian part of New Guinea. The first four form the Greater Sunda Islands, with an area of about 493,000 sq. mi. (1,277,000 sq. km.).

For nearly all of Indonesia's history, **Java** has been the most important of these islands. Today, two-thirds of Indonesia's people, about 124 million, live on this densely populated island, which is about as large as New York State. Fortunately, Java's soils are very fertile, particularly along the northern coastal plain, due in part to the ash from the island's numerous volcanoes. Farming is the primary means of support for most people on Java, although the bulk of Indonesia's manufacturing industry is found there, too. Java is also a source of oil and natural gas. Jakarta, Indonesia's capital, is located on Java.

Sumatra is Indonesia's second most important island. A long chain of mountains, the Bukit Barisan, extends along Sumatra's southwestern coast. The interior of the island is densely forested, and the eastern coastal region is covered by swampland. Sumatra has a great many large plantations, which produce rubber, tea, coffee, tobacco, and palm oil. Sumatra is Indonesia's principal producer of petroleum and natural gas. Tin, mined on offshore islands, and bauxite are other resources.

Borneo is the third-largest island in the world, and most of it is Indonesian territory, called Kalimantan. The remaining portion of the island consists of Sarawak and Sabah (parts of Malaysia) and the oil-rich nation of Brunei. Much of Kalimantan is mountainous terrain and nearly impenetrable jungle. Most of the population lives along the coast. Rice and rubber are the principal agricultural products. Mineral resources include natural gas, oil, nickel, copper, bauxite, tin, diamonds, gold, and silver. Forestry is a major economic activity.

Sulawesi (Celebes), the last of the Greater Sunda Islands, consists of four mountainous peninsulas. Because the rugged terrain divides island-ers in one section from those in another, the population of more than 10 million consists mostly of small groups of people with different lan-guages, customs, and religious beliefs. The island's chief products are rice, maize (corn), dried coconut meat (copra), coffee, and various wood products, including rattan (palm). Ujung Pandang, formerly called Ma-cassar (Makassar), is the island's principal city. It was once an important colonial spice center. Although spices are no longer the island's most important commodity for export, the city is still the chief trading center for eastern Indonesia.

The Lesser Sunda Islands. Across the Banda and Flores seas from Sulawesi are the Lesser Sunda Islands, totaling about 28,000 sq. mi. (73,000 sq. km.). Of this group, the most interesting is **Bali.** An island of rare beauty, Bali is noted for its ancient Hindu culture. Like Java, Bali is densely populated, and its people are mostly farmers who work tiny, irrigated rice fields. Less densely populated and mostly too dry for wet rice are the islands of Flores, Sumba, Lombok, and Timor.

The Moluccas (Maluku). Hundreds of islands make up this group, known historically as the Spice Islands and located between Sulawesi and Irian Jaya. The principal islands are Ceram, Buru, Ambon (Amboina), Ternate, Halmahera, and Tidore. From these islands came the rich spices —cloves, nutmeg, and mace—that led to the colonization of Indonesia by the European sea powers. Copra, coconuts, spices, sago, coconut oil, and timber are the islands' most important products.

Irian Jaya. The easternmost area of Indonesia is Irian Jaya, the In-donesian part of New Guinea. (The other, or eastern, portion of New Guinea is the major part of Papua New Guinea.) Covered by dense for-ests, Irian Jaya has a population of more than 2 million Irianese, most of whom live at a modest level of technology. In the interior are the Jaya-wiyaya Mountains (Snow Mountains), whose highest peak, Puncak Jaya (Mount Carstensz), is 16,400 ft. (4,999 m.) high. Most of the people on Irian Jaya live along the coast. In fact, much of the interior of the island has only recently been explored. The Indonesian government plans to develop Irian Jaya by resettling Javanese families there.

Animals and Plants. The animals and plants of Indonesia are divided roughly into two groups by an imaginary line called the Wallace Line, after the naturalist who established it. The line runs north-south between Kalimantan and Sulawesi. West of the line, the plants and animals are

FACTS AND FIGURES

OFFICIAL NAME: Republic of Indonesia.

NATIONALITY: Indonesian(s).

CAPITAL: Jakarta.

LOCATION: Southeastern Asia. **Boundaries**—Malaysia, Brunei, Papua New Guinea, Indian Ocean.

AREA: 751,236 sq. mi. (1,904,570 sq. km.).

PHYSICAL FEATURES: Highest point—Puncak Jaya (Mount Carstensz) (16,400 ft.; 4,999 m.). **Lowest point**—sea level. **Chief rivers**—Barito, Asahan, Kampar, Rokan, Hari, Musi, Solo.

POPULATION: 201,400,000 (1996; annual growth 1.6%).

MAJOR LANGUAGES: Indonesian (Bahasa Indonesia, official), English, Dutch, Javanese.

MAJOR RELIGIONS: Islam, Christianity, Hinduism.

GOVERNMENT: Republic. **Head of state and government**—president. **Legislature**—DPR (House of Representatives).

CHIEF CITIES: Jakarta, Surabaya, Bandung, Medan, Semarang, Palembang, Ujung Pandang, Padang, Malang, Surakarta, Yogyakarta.

ECONOMY: Chief minerals—oil, tin, natural gas, nickel, bauxite, copper. **Chief agricultural products**—timber, rice, cassava, peanuts, rubber, cocoa, coffee, copra. **Industries and products**—petroleum, textiles, mining, cement, fertilizers, timber. **Chief exports**—manufactures, petroleum, natural gas, timber, rubber, coffee, tin, animal and vegetable oils, tea, copper. **Chief imports**—machinery and transportation equipment, chemicals, mineral fuels, crude materials.

MONETARY UNIT: 1 rupiah = 100 sen (sen no longer used).

NATIONAL HOLIDAY: August 17 (Independence Day).

much like those of Southeast Asia. There are dense tropical rain forests, vast numbers of palm and banana trees, and a great many varieties of wildflowers. Among the animals in this region are the orangutan, the tiger, the wild buffalo, and—very rarely now—the elephant and the rhinoceros. Another animal found here is the mouse deer *(kantjil),* a tiny creature whose legendary cleverness at outwitting larger enemies has made it the hero of Indonesian folktales.

East of the Wallace Line, animal life is much more like that of Australia. Some of the more unusual creatures include the kangaroo and the brilliantly feathered bird of paradise. The reason for the sharp difference in natural life is probably the fact that the western islands of Indonesia, which lie in shallow waters, were once a part of mainland Asia. But the eastern islands, which are surrounded by deep seas, were always separated from the continent, and therefore did not develop the same type of wildlife.

Natural Resources.   Indonesia has large deposits of several valuable minerals, including petroleum, natural gas, copper, nickel, sulfur, manganese, tin, iron, bauxite, and coal. Forests are another natural resource, and supply large amounts of teakwood, ebony, and sandalwood. Quinine, used in the treatment of malaria, is manufactured from the bark of the cinchona tree. Bamboo and rattan are used to make wicker chairs and other furniture. Since it is surrounded by the sea, Indonesia has an abundance of different kinds of fish, which form an important part of the Indonesian family's daily diet.

THE PEOPLE

There are 300 distinct, if related, ethnic groups in Indonesia. From island to island—and even within each island—different languages are spoken, and different customs are observed. Most Indonesians are of Malay ethnic stock. They are usually slight in build and have brown skin and straight black hair. But in the easternmost islands of Indonesia, the people are bigger, darker in skin coloring, and curly-haired. These are the Irianese, the dominant people of Irian Jaya, whose language and culture are quite different from those of the majority of Indonesians.

On a technological level, the Irianese lag behind most other Indonesians. The government is trying various policies to narrow the gap

Indonesia has scores of ethnic groups. Each group has developed its own distinctive customs.

between the Irianese and the majority population. Many Irianese regard themselves as different from other Indonesians, however, and the task is not easy.

The Javanese and the Sundanese, Indonesia's largest ethnic groups, live on the island of Java. They make up nearly 60 percent of Indonesia's population. Their way of life shows traces of the old culture of the Indonesian kingdoms of past centuries, which were influenced by Indian religious (Hindu, Buddhist) and cultural ideas. The Sundanese are now orthodox Muslims, but many Javanese mixed Islam with their earlier Hindu and spirit-worshiping religions. As a result, there is a sharp difference in Javanese society between strict Muslims, known as *santri,* and those who practice less orthodox Islam, who are known as *abangan.*

The ancient shrine to Buddha at Borobudur reflects the Buddhist heritage of many Indonesians.

Youngsters enjoy the camping trips and other activities offered by Pramuka youth groups.

The Batak and Minangkabau peoples of Sumatra are the most important of Indonesia's minor ethnic groups. Both are considered to be among the most enterprising people of Indonesia. The Batak and Minangkabau have provided modern Indonesia with many of its leaders.

Dayaks predominate in the interior of Kalimantan, while a mix of other ethnic groups have settled in coastal areas of the island. On Sulawesi, the Buginese and Makassarese, well-known traders and seafarers with their own traditions, predominate. Amboinese predominate in the Moluccas. Some of the country's more than 4 million Chinese residents have been permitted to become Indonesian citizens, but the Chinese are resented in many parts of Indonesia because of the wealth they accumulated in business during colonial times.

Language.   About 250 languages and dialects are spoken in Indonesia. The official language is Bahasa Indonesia, understood throughout the land. Of the many dialects, Javanese is the most widely spoken.

Religion.   Islam is the major religion of Indonesia, having been introduced to the area some 500 years ago. Indonesia has the largest Muslim population of any country in the world, with nearly nine out of 10 Indonesians adhering to that faith. About one-fourth of the Muslims consider themselves devout and identify with the orthodox Islam practiced by Arabs and Iranians in the Middle East. The remaining Muslims mix older Hindu-Buddhist beliefs with those of Islam.

Many devout Muslim men wear a black velvet cap called a *pit ji.* Orthodox Muslim women sometimes wear a white scarf over their heads, especially on Friday, the Muslim Sabbath. But Muslim women in Indonesia do not veil their faces, as is often the custom in the Middle East, and they enjoy a relatively high social position. Women make up about 10 percent of the members of the Indonesian parliament and more than 30 percent of the justices of the supreme court.

People on Bali are among the 2 percent of all Indonesians who are Hindu. In interior regions of other islands, particularly where the mountainous terrain and forests cause isolation, many other peoples cling to spirit and ancestor worship and other older forms of religion. About 9

An instrument called a *tjanying* is used to make a traditional *batik* design.

percent of all Indonesians are Christian—two-thirds of them Protestant, one-third Roman Catholic.

Traditional Art Forms. Indonesians are famous for their high-quality handicrafts. Batik, a way of dyeing cloth, is especially important. Wood-carvers also produce beautiful items. Many traditional Indonesian homes have hand-carved wooden figures at the entrance, and complex designs carved into pillars, roofs, porch ceilings, and walls. Intricate stone carvings adorn the facades of many historic Hindu and Buddhist temples found on the island of Bali, in central Java, and elsewhere.

An important part of Indonesian culture is the *wayang (wajang),* or shadow play, which dates from the time of the Indonesian Hindu kingdoms. These plays are acted out by leather puppets, which cast shadows on a lighted screen. The puppet performers are accompanied by a narrator and an orchestra, or *gamelan,* that consists of musicians playing traditional Indonesian instruments.

ECONOMY

Indonesia's main economic goal is providing jobs for all who want them. To this end, the nation has made great gains since independence. Yet the goal remains elusive, because several million people enter the job market each year. Competition for jobs has kept most Indonesians' personal incomes low. Many workers are unemployed, underemployed, or willing to work for low wages—about half the pay, in fact, that workers in Malaysia and Thailand demand.

Ironically, these low wages have helped Indonesia attract foreign investment from places like Japan, Taiwan, South Korea, the United States, Germany, and Australia. Hundreds of foreign companies have set up factories in Indonesia, providing jobs in such areas as shoe-

More than half the Indonesian population is involved with some form of agriculture.

making, toy making, textiles, electronics, paper manufacturing, and petrochemicals. These new private enterprises are helping Indonesia create
jobs and lessen its dependence on the petroleum industry for export
revenues.

Farming.   About 56 percent of all Indonesian workers are involved
in agriculture. Rice, the basic food for Indonesians, is the chief crop.
Most Indonesians eat rice with various spices and sometimes pieces of
fish, chicken, or meat. Maize (corn) and cassava (a plant whose roots
provide a starchy food) are the main crops in areas too dry for growing
rice. Maize and cassava are also grown as second crops during the dry

In a village on Komodo Island, stilts help protect the houses from flooding at high tide.

season on Java, Bali, and other islands where rice is the preferred wet-season crop. Other Indonesians work on small holdings or large plantations that produce tree crops such as rubber, coconuts, and palm oil.

Farm output has been boosted in recent years by high-yielding hybrid seeds and educational programs that teach farmers how to make better use of fertilizers, pesticides, and irrigation. Not long ago, Indonesia was the world's major importer of rice. In the 1990s, the nation's farmers are able to supply almost all the nation's rice. To keep people in rural areas from pouring into the cities in search of work, the government has tried to equip landless individuals with nonfarm job skills. Handicraft cooperatives provide training and marketing help. And the government has ambitious plans to resettle more than 500,000 landless families from crowded Bali and Java on the less crowded Outer Islands, where farmland is relatively plentiful.

Forestry and Fishing. Teak is grown on plantations in Java, while natural forests support a forestry industry in Kalimantan, Sumatra, and other islands. The government now demands that loggers build plywood and other wood-processing industries to help Indonesia industrialize.

Petroleum, drilled onshore and offshore, is one of Indonesia's most valuable exports.

The aviation industry and most other manufacturing businesses are concentrated on the island of Java.

Fish is the main source of animal protein in the Indonesian diet, but commercial fishing is relatively undeveloped. This is because Indonesian fishermen lack the modern trawlers and freezing facilities used by Japanese and other foreign fishing fleets. Most of Indonesia's fish are caught in the sea, but increasing amounts are produced in freshwater ponds.

Mining. Indonesia seeks to develop its rich mineral resources by limiting exports of unprocessed minerals and encouraging miners to build smelting and other processing plants. Oil and natural gas are the principal minerals produced. In the early 1980s, petroleum-based products—largely crude and refined oil—accounted for about 75 percent of the nation's exports. By 1990, that figure had dropped to about 40 percent, as the price of oil dropped, and Indonesia began to emphasize other products, including liquefied natural gas, or LNG. Today, Indonesia is the world's largest exporter of LNG, primarily to Japan, Taiwan, and South Korea. During the 1990s, the coal industry has seen fast growth. Indonesia's low-sulfur coal is in great demand in Western Europe.

Oil and natural-gas exports provide about half the government's income from taxes and about half the foreign currency it needs to buy the equipment for continued development. Unless new petroleum reserves are discovered, however, Indonesia may end up importing more oil than it exports during the 21st century.

Indonesia is also a leading producer of tin, which is smelted on Bangka Island. Nickel is produced on Sulawesi, where there is a large smelter, and on islands off the northwest coast of Irian Jaya. Bauxite is mined and processed into alumina on and around Bintan Island, and the alumina smelted into aluminum at Asahan in northern Sumatra.

Manufacturing. Most manufacturing, except for wood- and mineral-processing industries, is concentrated on Java, and it is here that the industrialization of Indonesia's economy is most evident. The drop in oil prices during the 1980s persuaded Indonesia to find ways to encourage more manufacturing. It is doing so, in part, by welcoming foreign companies that wish to take advantage of Indonesia's low wages and abundant raw materials. It has also been selling some of the state-owned industries to private buyers, as a way of making these enterprises more efficient.

During the early decades of independence, the government invested heavily in the development of basic industries, such as steel, fertilizers, chemicals, cement, and petrochemicals. These industries supply the materials needed to support other industries. For example, the small automobile industry needs steel, rubber, tires, aluminum, and other basic products. In turn, the automobile industry creates a market for spark plugs, light bulbs, upholstery, and other parts. The growing textile and clothing industry uses synthetic fibers produced by the petrochemical industry and puts large numbers of Indonesians to work sewing clothing for export.

CITIES

Jakarta, which is situated in northwestern Java, is the capital of Indonesia. With a population of about 9 million, it is by far the nation's largest city. It is also the country's leading seaport and its most important center of trade and communications. Six-lane highways cut through the city, and they are lined with modern buildings and crowded with cars and bicycles. **Surabaya,** with a population of 3.5 million, is second only to Jakarta as a port and manufacturing city, and it is the center of Indonesia's manufacturing industries. **Bandung,** the most modern Indonesian city, has a population of 1.1 million. A popular resort town, it is the home of the country's leading technical institute. Another important Javanese city is **Yogyakarta,** one of the old royal capitals and a center of fine arts and traditional Indonesian culture.

Western-style resorts have drawn large numbers of American and European tourists to Indonesia.

Jakarta has evolved into one of Asia's busiest centers of commerce and communication.

Sumatra's principal city is **Medan,** home to 1.7 million people. Its busy port at **Belawan** handles most of the island's exports. **Palembang,** on the Musi River, has about 650,000 residents, and it is an important outlet for petroleum and rubber products. Its industries include shipyards and ironworks. Other leading Indonesian cities are **Banjarmasin** on Borneo, with a population of about 325,000; **Ujung Pandang** (formerly Macassar), the largest city on Sulawesi, with nearly 500,000 people; and **Ambon** in the Moluccas, with about 90,000 residents.

HISTORY AND GOVERNMENT

In 1891, Dutch scientists working on Java discovered human bones hundreds of thousands of years old. These were the remains of the famous Java Man, who many scientists believe was one of the earliest human beings. Yet today's Indonesians are descended from Malay people who began immigrating to the islands only 4,000 to 5,000 years ago.

Even in ancient times, the Indonesian islands were important in international trade, for the islands lay along the sea route that connected China, India, Persia, and the Roman Empire. Ships from many lands docked at Indonesian ports to take on cargoes of spices, resins, and precious woods, which were the principal items of this trade. The Indonesians themselves were skilled seafarers and merchants, and their trading ships traveled as far as the shores of India and China. Although the Indonesian islands were never under a single government before the period of Dutch colonial rule, they were tied to each other by a long history of contact and trade.

India's Influence. The many traders who visited the islands introduced foreign ideas and customs to the Indonesians. Indian culture, including the belief in royal power, became the most important influence by the early centuries A.D. The classical Indian idea of an all-powerful king appealed to ambitious Indonesian rulers, who until then had been little more than tribal chiefs. Both the Hindu and Buddhist faiths of India were adopted by the Indonesian ruling class. Indian ideas also filtered down to the rest of the people. Hinduism mixed with, or sometimes replaced, traditional animistic beliefs.

Several Hindu and Buddhist Indonesian kingdoms came to power on the larger islands. The two greatest of these kingdoms were Sriwijaya (from the 600s through the 1200s) in southern Sumatra, and Majapahit (from the 1200s to the 1500s) in eastern Java. Both kingdoms were trading powers, and they controlled much of the commerce of the islands.

The Coming of Islam.   During the 1200s, the famous traveler Marco Polo became the first known European to visit the Indies. Shortly after Marco Polo's visit, the powerful Mongol emperor of China, Kublai Khan, attempted to conquer Java, but his army was defeated. Between the 1100s and the 1400s, the religion of Islam was brought to Indonesia by traders from India and the Malay Peninsula. Islam gained a foothold in the coastal cities, whose princes were trying to break away from the powerful Hindu kingdoms on Sumatra and Java. Eventually, Islam spread to nearly all of the Indonesian islands and became the area's major religion.

The year 1511 marked the beginning of European involvement in Indonesia. The Portuguese captured Malacca, which gave them control of the narrow strait between the Malay Peninsula and Sumatra. The Portuguese were followed by the Spanish, Dutch, and British. During the 1500s, the great European sea powers competed for control of the Indies, particularly the Spice Islands (the Moluccas).

Dutch Rule.   Early in the 1600s, the Dutch East India Company set up trading posts in the Spice Islands and on Java. The Dutch established their main base at the present-day city of Jakarta. Gradually, the Dutch extended their influence to the rest of the islands. By the end of the 1600s, Holland was the major European power in what became known as the Dutch, or Netherlands, East Indies.

Dutch rule spread slowly through the islands. On the larger islands, particularly Sumatra and Java, many large plantations were developed by the Dutch and other non-Indonesians. On some of the islands, such as Java, the Dutch ruled directly. But in the outlying islands, the Dutch merely backed the local ruler or tribal chief, and the people there had little contact with European social, political, and economic ideas. As a result, Indonesia did not develop as a unified nation, but rather as a group of islands with varied customs and life-styles. These regional differences made it difficult to unify the nation after independence.

The Dutch governed with a firm hand while exploiting Indonesia's natural riches. Resentment against Dutch rule led to the rise of an Indonesian independence movement, which began in 1908 with the founding of the Budi Utomo ("noble endeavor"), an association of Javanese intellectuals. Other nationalist groups were formed during the next two decades, including the Indonesian Nationalist Party (PNI) in 1927. The PNI was led by Sukarno (many Indonesian people have only one name), who later became the first president of the Republic of Indonesia.

To pacify the nationalist groups, the Dutch established a Volksraad ("people's council") in 1918 to give Indonesians some voice in their own government. But nationalist feeling continued, and an unsuccessful Communist-led rebellion took place in 1926–27. Many of the leaders of the independence movement, including Sukarno, were later jailed or sent into exile.

During World War II, the Japanese occupied Indonesia (1942–45). In order to win support in their war against the Allies, the Japanese released the imprisoned leaders and encouraged the nationalist movement. Toward the end of the war, the Japanese allowed nationalist leaders Sukarno and Mohammed Hatta to establish an Indonesian-run government.

Independence. On August 17, 1945, a few days after Japan's surrender to the Allies, the nationalist leaders declared independence for Indonesia. However, the Dutch did not recognize this new government, and four years of fighting and lengthy negotiations followed. Finally, in December of 1949, the Dutch recognized the independence of what was first called the United States of Indonesia. In 1950, it was renamed the Republic of Indonesia.

The 1945 constitution, providing for a strong presidential form of government, was retained. Sukarno became the new country's first president. In 1950, a new constitution provided for a parliamentary form of government, with a president, vice president, premier, cabinet, and one-house legislature.

The parliamentary system proved to be unworkable in Indonesia, where some 30 political parties vied for power. President Sukarno responded in 1959 by reinstating the 1945 constitution by decree. In so doing, he gained almost unlimited authority as head of government and head of state. He called his concept of government "guided democracy," with himself as "President for Life."

In addition, he created a People's Consultative Assembly and gave it the power to choose presidents and propose broad national policy. The Consultative Assembly consists of the 500 members of the House of Representatives (parliament) and an equal number of representatives from various national groups and organizations, including the military, labor and religious groups, and the professions. It meets only once in its five-year term.

The House, which convenes once a year, is made up of 400 elected and 100 appointed members. Under the concept of *dwi fungsi,* or "dual function," many of the appointed members of the House are military officers, who serve in government posts at all levels.

President Sukarno directed the government in an increasingly dictatorial manner, ignoring some severe economic and social problems. He quarreled with neighboring lands, opposing the creation of the new state of Malaysia in 1963. He worked closely with major Communist nations, particularly China, and favored the Indonesian Communist Party at home. In 1965, Indonesian Communists attempted to strengthen their hand by kidnapping and killing six senior army generals. Led by General Suharto, the military struck back and wiped out the plotters. Right-wing death squads went on a rampage, killing perhaps 100,000 or more people suspected of Communist sympathies. The violence was especially savage in Java and Bali.

The Suharto Era. Suharto succeeded Sukarno as president. Unlike his predecessor, President Suharto placed major emphasis on economic development. Both foreign aid and private investment were welcomed, and the country's standard of living, which had been declining, improved significantly during the 1970s and 1980s. A major expansion of colleges and universities took place as the government sought to develop educated personnel to help modernize the country.

Pope John Paul II visited Indonesia's comparatively small Christian community in 1989.

Under Suharto, regular elections have been held at five-year intervals since 1972, and these have generally been free of irregularities and corruption. However, a de facto government political party, Golkar—a federation of labor, farmer, youth, women's, and other groups—has been sufficiently favored by the Suharto regime as to ensure its electoral victories in both the House and the People's Consultative Assembly. Golkar won about 67 percent of the vote in the 1992 elections, and Suharto won a sixth term as president in 1993.

In pursuit of national unity, the government has effectively required previously divisive ethnic, religious, and regional political parties to come together in only two opposition groups, the Muslim-oriented United Development Party and the Indonesian Democracy Party (IDP). Military personnel cannot vote. The first serious challenge to Suharto's rule occurred in 1996, when street protests erupted over a government attempt to replace Sukarno's daughter, Megawati Sukarnoputri, as leader of the Indonesian Democratic Party.

Internationally, Indonesia under Suharto has played a leadership role in improving regional relations. Jakarta is the headquarters of the Association of Southeast Asian Nations (ASEAN), an organization that seeks to strengthen economic, political, and social ties among the nations of Brunei, Indonesia, Malaysia, the Philippines, Singapore, and Thailand. Indonesia has also worked to establish close political and economic relations with the United States, Japan, and Western Europe, which it sees as the main source of development assistance, investment, and markets for Indonesian goods.

RUTH McVEY, School of Oriental and African Studies, University of London
Editor, *Indonesia, Its People, Its Society, Its Culture*
Reviewed by RICHARD BUTWELL, California State University, Dominguez Hills

BRUNEI

Brunei, one of the wealthiest nations in the world, is headed by a sultan, who rules the tiny country from a magnificent palace in the capital city of Bandar Seri Begawan.

About the size of the state of Delaware, the oil-rich nation of Brunei gained its independence from Great Britain in 1984 after 96 years as a British protectorate. Brunei is located on the lush green northwest coast of the huge island of Borneo, which it shares with parts of Malaysia and Indonesia. Sir Muda Hassanal Bolkiah, a sultan, is the nation's political and religious leader. He is the 29th hereditary sultan to rule the country in a line that dates back 500 years. Over one-quarter of all Bruneians live in Bandar Seri Begawan, the capital and largest city.

THE LAND

Brunei is divided into two parts. The parts are separated and surrounded on all land borders by the Malaysian state of Sarawak. The western section consists mostly of low and swampy coastal plains. The eastern section is hilly and rises to over 6,000 ft. (1,800 m.) in the southeast. The country has a hot and humid equatorial climate with considerable rainfall. Dense rain forests cover 75 percent of the land.

THE PEOPLE

About 65 percent of all Bruneians are ethnic Malays. About 25 percent are Chinese, and the rest are largely Dayaks and members of other groups native to Borneo. Malay and English are official languages, but many also speak Chinese. Islam is Brunei's official religion.

The government uses income from its oil resources and worldwide investments to provide free education and free medical care, and to subsidize food and housing costs. It has built new houses for about one-third of the Bruneians who lived in "water towns" of wooden houses built on stilts above water. Made of wood, the new homes are simple one-room rectangular structures with porches. The sultan, thought to be

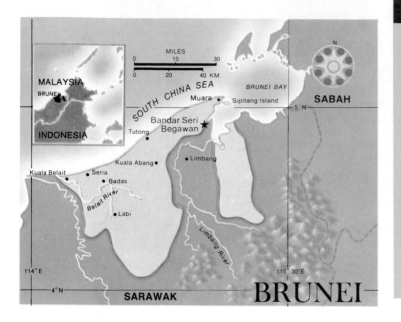

the world's wealthiest man, lives in a 1,788-room palace that also contains government offices. He moves easily among his subjects. The nation's income, per person, is one of the highest in the world.

THE ECONOMY

Oil and liquefied natural gas (LNG) are Brunei's main exports and sources of income. Much of the oil is produced near the town of Seria by foreign companies working under contract with the government of Brunei. More than 40 percent of the labor force is engaged in producing oil and natural gas and in construction. Most of the rest provide services, especially in government work, or are involved in trade. Farming and fishing employ nearly 4 percent of the workforce. Crops, grown in cleared areas of the coastal plains, include rice, sago, pepper, coconut, and fruit. About 80 percent of the country's food is imported. As part of a long-term plan to encourage industrial growth, the government has upgraded its deepwater port at Muara, created the world's largest gas-liquefaction plant at Lumut, built an international airport at Bandar Seri Begawan, and founded the Royal Brunei Airlines.

HISTORY

Once a powerful Muslim sultanate, by the early 1500s, Brunei controlled all of northwestern Borneo—the form of the word *Brunei* that Europeans gave to the entire island. After 1600, Brunei began to decline, and by the late 1800s, it included only its present area. By terms of a treaty signed in 1888, Brunei came under Great Britain's protection. In 1959, Brunei regained control of its internal affairs; Great Britain remained responsible for defense and foreign relations. At that time, both Malaysia and Indonesia threatened to annex the oil-rich sultanate. Both countries eventually established friendly relations with Brunei. The sultan accepted full independence for his country on January 1, 1984.

Reviewed by RICHARD BUTWELL, California State University, Dominguez Hills
Author of *Southeast Asia, A Political Introduction*

Manila, capital of the Philippines, is also the country's largest city, chief port, and cultural center.

PHILIPPINES

The Philippines, the first Western colony in Asia to regain its independence, began its resumed freedom on July 4, 1946, as a democracy. A Spanish colony for more than three centuries and a United States possession for 48 years, the islands were given increasing self-government under U.S. rule. Seven presidential elections were held during the first quarter century of independence, and the Philippines gained widespread respect as Southeast Asia's first and oldest continuously functioning democracy.

Philippine democracy collapsed in 1971, however, when President Ferdinand Marcos, refusing to limit his time in office to two terms, declared martial law. Another 15 years passed before a peaceful popular uprising in 1986 toppled his government and gave Philippine democracy a second chance.

THE LAND

The Philippines is an island country that stretches about 1,100 mi. (1,770 km.) north to south along Asia's southeastern rim. Its physical division into 7,107 islands and islets kept their inhabitants isolated from one another before Spanish conquerors unified the islands under one rule. During the 1980s, this same insular separation prevented a Communist insurrection from spreading more rapidly and helped the army to contain it. The nation's total coastland is 13,997 mi. (22,540 km.), more than twice that of the U.S. The ocean depths off the eastern Philippines are among the greatest in the Pacific, reaching 34,000 ft. (10,400 m.).

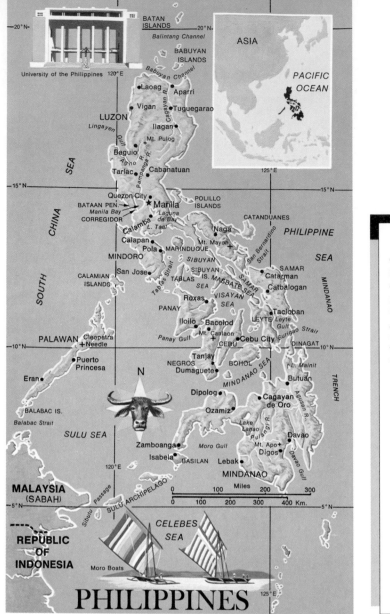

University of the Philippines

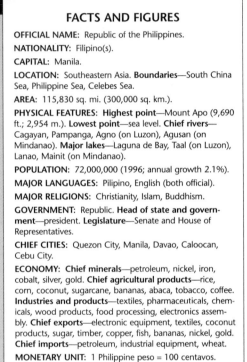

PHILIPPINES

FACTS AND FIGURES

OFFICIAL NAME: Republic of the Philippines.

NATIONALITY: Filipino(s).

CAPITAL: Manila.

LOCATION: Southeastern Asia. **Boundaries**—South China Sea, Philippine Sea, Celebes Sea.

AREA: 115,830 sq. mi. (300,000 sq. km.).

PHYSICAL FEATURES: Highest point—Mount Apo (9,690 ft.; 2,954 m.). **Lowest point**—sea level. **Chief rivers**—Cagayan, Pampanga, Agno (on Luzon), Agusan (on Mindanao). **Major lakes**—Laguna de Bay, Taal (on Luzon), Lanao, Mainit (on Mindanao).

POPULATION: 72,000,000 (1996; annual growth 2.1%).

MAJOR LANGUAGES: Pilipino, English (both official).

MAJOR RELIGIONS: Christianity, Islam, Buddhism.

GOVERNMENT: Republic. **Head of state and government**—president. **Legislature**—Senate and House of Representatives.

CHIEF CITIES: Quezon City, Manila, Davao, Caloocan, Cebu City.

ECONOMY: Chief minerals—petroleum, nickel, iron, cobalt, silver, gold. **Chief agricultural products**—rice, corn, coconut, sugarcane, bananas, abaca, tobacco, coffee. **Industries and products**—textiles, pharmaceuticals, chemicals, wood products, food processing, electronics assembly. **Chief exports**—electronic equipment, textiles, coconut products, sugar, timber, copper, fish, bananas, nickel, gold. **Chief imports**—petroleum, industrial equipment, wheat.

MONETARY UNIT: 1 Philippine peso = 100 centavos.

NATIONAL HOLIDAY: June 12 (Independence Day)

Located in the western Pacific Ocean about 500 mi. (800 km.) southeast of China, the Philippines is northeast of Borneo and directly south of Taiwan. The country has a land area approximately the size of Italy's. The two largest islands, accounting for two-thirds of this territory, are heavily populated Luzon in the north and Mindanao in the south. The smaller islands that lie between these two main islands are known collectively as the Visayas. Ten other islands make up most of the remaining land area of the country. Only 154 of the Philippine islands have land areas over 5.5 sq. mi. (14 sq. km.).

A large part of the country is mountainous, part of a belt of volcanoes circling the Pacific. Mount Apo on Mindanao is the highest. Earthquake tremors are frequent, and major earthquakes occur every decade or so. In 1976, an earthquake centered on Mindanao killed 8,000 people. A less-powerful quake hit Luzon in July 1990, killing more than 1,000.

Less than one-third of the land will support crops. Forests cover more than half the nation's land surface, and on many islands they are being cut down to provide farmland for the Philippines' growing population. Deforestation is one of the nation's major environmental problems, in large part because it causes scarce topsoil to wash away.

Climate.   The climate of the Philippines is tropical. Rainfall averages more than 80 in. (200 cm.) annually, but varies considerably from region to region. Most parts of the Philippines experience wet and dry seasons. Typhoons often cause flooding and much loss of life and property as well as widespread power failures. Temperatures average from 75° to 85° F. (24° to 30° C.). April and May are the hottest months, while the cool season extends from November to February.

Natural Resources.   The Philippines is fairly rich in natural resources. Nonetheless, they have not been exploited to advance the country's overall economic development. Profits from them have been used more to enrich individuals than to fuel the nation's growth as investments. Few areas in the world have as wide a range of mineral resources or have deposits as extensive. Copper, gold, lead, nickel, iron, silver, zinc, chromite, cobalt, and manganese are the leading mineral deposits. Fish are plentiful in the area's waters.

THE PEOPLE

Filipinos have a strong sense of collective identity despite the fact that 116 languages and dialects are spoken on the islands. One reason is that 92 percent of all Filipinos are Christian, most of them Roman Catholic. The Philippines is the only Christian country in East Asia, a result of Spanish colonial Catholicization. Five percent of the population, largely on Mindanao, is Islamic.

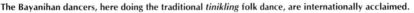

The Bayanihan dancers, here doing the traditional *tinikling* folk dance, are internationally acclaimed.

334

The University of Santo Tomas, founded in 1611, is the oldest university in the Philippines.

The fact that a majority of Filipinos also speak English, in addition to their local dialects, contributes to this sense of oneness. English is one of two official languages, and its widespread use makes the Philippines the third-largest English-speaking land in the world, after the U.S. and Britain. The country also produces English-language literature that is of high quality. Pilipino, a language based on the Tagalog dialect of Luzon, is the other official language. Growing numbers of Filipinos speak Pilipino. Radio, television, movies, and comic books have significantly contributed to its expanding use. Since 1988, all official government communications have been written in Pilipino. Pilipino is expected to replace English as the language of instruction at the university level during the 1990s.

The Philippine population, already the world's 17th largest, is expected to double between 1990 and 2015. Such rapid growth will surely add to the nation's unemployment problems. It will also cause further environmental damage, through increased slash-and-burn farming and uncontrolled logging.

The ancestors of today's Filipinos, the Negritos, are thought to have walked to the islands from Borneo and Sumatra, crossing land bridges that existed some 30,000 years ago. Later, people of Malay ethnic stock, closely related to the Indonesians and the majority Malays of Malaysia, came from the south, first on foot and then by boat. About 95 percent of today's Philippine population is Malay. The next-largest group, the Chinese, accounts for 1.5 percent.

Filipinos intermarried freely with the formerly ruling Spanish and the immigrant Chinese, although they did not do so to the same extent with the Americans, who were not in the Philippines for the same long period. Also, resident Americans were usually not single. The result is that a high percentage of Filipinos in the top social and economic groups are of mixed ethnic background. Almost all Filipinos have Spanish names, another legacy of the colonial era.

Partly as a result of such factors, three different Philippine societies have emerged. One includes the Westernized, predominantly English-speaking, fair-skinned, and affluent Filipinos who constitute the ruling, business, and professional class. It is concentrated in metropolitan Manila and the major provincial capitals. The second society, embracing about half the population, includes the farm families that live in rural *barrios* (villages), who are very likely to be poor, speak a local dialect, and have darker skin and be less adequately clothed than members of the first group. The third group is the urban poor, who have migrated from *barrios* to the cities and are largely underemployed. They often live in crowded squatter settlements. In 1990, more than 40 percent of all Filipinos were either unemployed or underemployed.

Education. Most Filipinos, wherever they live, are literate—a high 88 percent. The figure is higher in the cities than in the more-depressed rural areas. The quality of education is generally good through the college level. The success of the education system is reflected by the ease with which Philippine-educated doctors and nurses qualify for employment in the U.S., and Filipino engineers in Europe and the Middle East. Large numbers of Filipinos historically have pursued graduate studies in the U.S. The state-operated University of the Philippines, modeled after the U.S. land-grant college system, produces well-trained graduates, as do many of the private institutions, especially the church-related schools. But many graduates also have trouble finding jobs that take advantage of this education, and are forced to accept employment much below their skill levels.

Way of Life. The Filipino life-style is a blend of the different cultures that have influenced the islands in historic times, but, almost invariably, Filipinos have added their own unique touch to what they have borrowed from others. Christianity came with Spanish rule, but Filipinos also established two denominations of their own: the *Aglipayan,* or Philippine Independent, Church (formed in 1902) and *Iglesia ni Kristo,* "Church of Christ" (founded in 1914). Philippine newspapers are clearly modeled after those in the once-ruling U.S., but the bombastic style of their columnists is characteristically Filipino. Even the daily speech of the urban Filipino intermixes Pilipino, English, and a little Spanish.

Western-style dress is widespread in the Philippines, but all Filipinos who can afford to do so dress up for festivals in fiesta dress—also a mix of the Spanish and indigenous. The *balintawak* dress, with its butterfly shoulders, is the formal costume for women. On special occasions, men wear a shirt called the *barong tagalog,* made of pineapple fiber. They wear it outside the pants—a practice that began in the 1800s as a nationalist symbol of opposition to continued Spanish rule. The Spaniard

In some rural Philippine villages, people live in stilted houses with thatched roofs.

tucked his shirt in, so the Filipino refused to, proclaiming his rejection of Spanish ways.

Cities. About 41 percent of all Filipinos live in cities or large towns. **Cebu City,** on the east coast of Cebu island, is the oldest city in the Philippines. It was founded in 1565. **Davao,** on Mindanao, is the major metropolis of the south. **Bacolod,** on Negros, is a major sugar center, and **Iloilo,** on Panay, is an important port. **Quezon City** was the nation's capital from 1948 to 1976. **Zamboanga,** on Mindanao, is a rapidly developing industrial city.

The Philippines' capital and largest city is **Manila,** which is also one of the great cities of Asia. A bustling metropolis of about 8 million people, it is the islands' chief port and the commercial and cultural center. In 1975, Manila and many nearby communities, including Quezon City, were joined into a greater Manila, known as **Metro Manila.** Manila was once ruled by the Muslim warrior Rajah Soliman. In 1571, the Spaniard Miguel López de Legazpe captured it and rebuilt it as a Christian city.

ECONOMY

The Philippines is a largely agricultural country that appeared to be making a successful transition to a more industrialized nation in the 1950s, 1960s, and 1970s. But excessive government spending and borrowing and declining world prices for Filipino raw materials (agricultural and mineral) combined to depress the economy severely during the 1980s.

In 1990, after a few years of steady economic growth, the economy was battered once again by an earthquake on Luzon and soaring oil prices. The oil-price hike, caused by an international embargo on Iraqi oil, was especially harmful. The Philippines imports more than 95 percent of its fuel supplies and had relied heavily on oil imports from Iraq.

Most Filipinos are farmers. Only 15 percent of them own the land they till. The rest are tenants who must pay much of their earnings to landlords. Yields from wet-rice cultivation have increased dramatically as a result of hybrid seeds and improved farming methods. Rice is grown primarily on the northern island of Luzon, while corn dominates the diet of the Filipino in the central and southern parts of the country. Once rice importers, Filipinos now meet their own food needs.

Copra (dried coconut meat), sugar, and abaca (Manila hemp) are other major agricultural products, and these are exported abroad. One in four Filipinos makes a living in some aspect of the coconut industry. Fish, when available, is the Filipino's main source of protein, but the fishing industry is underdeveloped. Forestry and wood products are also important elements in the economy.

Copper is the main mineral mined and processed in the country. Textiles, machinery and transport equipment, processed foods, chemicals, wood processing, and electronics assembly are among the chief manufactured goods. One in 10 Filipinos works in manufacturing of some kind, which accounts for 33 percent of the nation's annual output of goods and services. The extensive Philippine coastline tempts smugglers, who cheat the government out of badly needed taxes. Cigarettes and liquor are the main illegal imports.

Part of the problem of the Philippine economy in the first half of the 1980s was the draining off of resources by President Ferdinand Marcos, who fled the country in 1986. The successor government of President Corazon Aquino moved to improve the economy, but was faced with a multibillion-dollar foreign debt, among other problems. Her major economic goal was to encourage private industry and rural development. She also promised to break up the huge farms and distribute land to 4 million landless peasant families—a reform that the Philippines badly

Rice fields thrive in the rich soil beneath Mount Mayon, one of many active volcanoes in the Philippines.

needs. But the Philippine Congress, whose membership is dominated by landlords, blocked her program, leaving 80 percent of the country's farmland in the hands of 20 percent of all landowners. The same 20 percent receives half of the nation's income—the most inequitable distribution in all of Southeast Asia.

GOVERNMENT

The Philippines resumed its independence in 1946 with democratic governing institutions modeled after those of the United States: a president, Senate, and House of Representatives. The Philippine two-party system between 1946 and 1971 also resembled American political parties, except for the fact that there were absolutely no differences between the parties, and politicians frequently left one party to join the other. The Supreme Court was also patterned on the U.S. model.

A parliamentary government was adopted in 1973, after President Ferdinand Marcos proclaimed martial law. But it was considerably modified by the time martial rule ended in 1981. When the Marcos regime fell in 1986, the government consisted of a president and a one-house legislature. It also relied very heavily on the army to maintain itself in power.

The failure of Filipino democracy after 1972 primarily reflected the fact that the country attempted to operate democratic political institutions in a nonegalitarian social setting. Only the wealthy could afford to run for political office, particularly on the national level. Campaign costs were high, and millions of votes were openly bought during each presidential election. The Filipino press was largely free before Marcos, and it became free again only after his fall from power. In rural areas, continued opportunity to work on a plantation or to till tenant land was often dependent on support of a patron's favored candidates. Filipino politics were also violent, with many deaths during elections, but force and intimidation were also used in support of the local power figure.

There has always been nominal opposition to the party in power in the Philippines, and, between 1946 and 1969, relatively peaceful rotation of occupants of the presidency and of seats in the Senate and House of Representatives occurred. The real opposition to the wealthy ruling elite, however, came from the Communists—represented by the *Hukbalahaps (Huks)* in the late 1940s and early 1950s. This first Communist assault on Filipino participatory government was unsuccessful, largely because of reform and amnesty policies. From the late 1970s, a new and better-organized Communist guerrilla threat developed. The "New People's Army," the military wing of the Philippine Communist Party, reached its peak strength during the last years of the Marcos era.

The Filipino people showed their preference for honest and democratic rule after the 1986 presidential election, when they demonstrated against vote fraud by the Marcos government. The election's ultimate winner, Corazon Aquino, soon appointed a commission to write a new constitution. The new document, approved in 1987, essentially reestablished the U.S.-style system that Marcos had scrapped. Aquino's successor, Fidel Ramos, made efforts to dismantle state and private monopolies and encourage foreign investment, leading to a spurt of economic growth. He also began negotiations with the Communists and with the Moro National Liberation Front, a Muslim secessionist group in the south; in 1995 he signed a peace accord with three rebel military groups.

Corazon Aquino swept to power in the 1986 "People's Revolution," replacing Ferdinand Marcos.

HISTORY

The Philippines' history as a nation began in the 1500s with the conquest of the archipelago by Spain. The country's name, indeed, honors Philip II of Spain. Before Spanish rule, the majority Malay peoples of the islands had never been united under a single government. They lived under literally hundreds of local chieftains. They were not even able to communicate with one another because they did not speak a common language. The islands probably would not have been brought together in their present political configuration except for the unifying fact of Spanish colonial rule.

The Filipinos' first ancestors may have come to the islands as early as 30,000 years ago, continuing to do so down to the time of the Spanish intrusion. It was only in the 1300s and 1400s, however, that the people of the Philippines were drawn into the main currents of Southeast Asian life. In the 1300s, parts of what was to become the modern Philippines were ruled as an outlying portion of the Sumatra-based Madjapahit empire. Islam, sweeping across neighboring Indonesia during the 1400s, established a strong foothold on the southern island of Mindanao.

Ferdinand Magellan claimed the islands for Spain in 1521, but was killed by a warrior resisting the intruders. If it had not been for the arrival of the zealously Christian Spaniards at this time, the Philippine islands, like Indonesia, might have been completely converted to the Muslim faith. The Muslims were never completely integrated into national life under either Spain or the U.S.

More than 200 revolts against Spanish rule occurred between 1565, when Spain established a permanent presence in the islands, and 1898, when Spain ceded the archipelago to the U.S., its foe in the Spanish-

American War. Philippine nationalism really began to coalesce after the execution of three priests in 1872. The Filipinos had almost ousted the Spanish from the islands by the time the Americans took over in 1898. The two most revered Filipino patriotic heroes are the nationalist writer José Rizal, martyred in 1896, and Andres Bonifacio, founder of the organization that launched the final push for independence from Spain.

The American Years. Filipinos celebrate June 12 as independence day rather than July 4, the anniversary of the end of U.S. rule. It was on June 12 that Philippine nationalists declared their freedom in 1898, setting the stage for the proclamation of the first Philippine republic a year later. In 1902, however, Filipino nationalists surrendered to the Americans. A war with Spain that started in the Caribbean had spread to the western Pacific and made the anticolonial Americans colonial rulers in Asia.

The U.S. progressively introduced the Philippines to internal self-government, beginning with a two-house legislature in 1916. The internally self-ruling Philippine Commonwealth was created in 1934 and independence pledged in a decade. The United States was not able to grant independence in 1944 as promised, however, because Japan occupied the islands between late 1941 and 1945, during World War II. Filipinos and Americans fought valiantly, if unsuccessfully, to defend the islands, and the U.S. was welcomed back to the Philippines with enthusiasm in 1945. General Douglas MacArthur, who promised, "I shall return," when he was forced to quit the islands when they were invaded by Japan, led the liberation of the Philippines.

Modern Events. Economic dislocation caused by the Japanese occupation, widespread corruption, and a Communist revolt posed problems for a democratic Philippines from the start of its resumed independence. The insurgency was contained, however, and renewed Communist rebellion did not become serious until the late 1970s, after President Ferdinand Marcos declared martial law and a feeling of oppression had spread among the peasant masses. Marcos banned political parties, and the once-vital Philippine democracy ceased to beam as a beacon in the world of newly independent states. Partly because of worsening economic conditions and army brutality under the Marcos regime, the Communist insurgency spread until, by the mid-1980s, it had become a major problem. A Muslim secessionist insurrection in the south also threatened the government. The Marcos regime detained political opponents—Communist, Muslim, and democratic. Marcos seized the properties of personal foes and turned them over to his cronies. Marcos and his friends became wealthy during this period.

The assassination of opposition leader Benigno Aquino in 1983 and vote fraud during the 1986 presidential election marked Marcos' downfall. His opponent in that election, Aquino's widow, Corazon, subsequently became the seventh president of an independent Philippines. Candidates endorsed by her swept the congressional elections held in 1987. Aquino, who survived several attempted coups, was succeeded as president by former defense minister Fidel Ramos after elections in 1992. In 1991, the United States abandoned Clark Air Force Base, and, in late 1992, it relinquished control of the sprawling Subic Naval Base. The outcome of the May 1995 elections strengthened Ramos' ability to enact further social and economic reforms during the remainder of his term.

RICHARD BUTWELL, California State University, Dominguez Hills

CENTRAL AND NORTH ASIA

Siberia occupies the vast northern expanse of Asia. Many residents of the frigid uplands of Eastern Siberia make their living herding reindeer.

Central and North Asia are two of the continent's most diverse and fascinating regions. At least 40 different ethnic groups reside there—26 in North Asia alone.

North Asia begins where European Russia ends, at the eastern edge of the Ural Mountains, and it extends to the Pacific Ocean. Central Asia stretches east from the Caspian Sea all the way to the Great Wall of China. Politically, much of Central Asia and virtually all of North Asia were part of the Soviet Union until December 1991, when the Communist empire ceased to exist as one state. Five former Central Asian Soviet republics—Kazakhstan, Uzbekistan, Turkmenistan, Tajikistan, and Kyrgyzstan—gained independent status, but they all remained part of the Soviet Union's successor, the Commonwealth of Independent States. Another Central Asian country is Mongolia, and a huge chunk of the region belongs to China.

Although most people think of all of North Asia as Siberia, geographers divide it into three parts: Western Siberia, Eastern Siberia, and the Far East. The region's northern edge borders the Arctic Ocean. To the south, it shares boundaries with Kazakhstan, Mongolia, and China's Heilongjiang Province.

The article on China in this volume discusses China's portion of Central Asia: the regions of Xizang, Xinjiang, and Nei Monggol. The article on Russia, in Volume 4 of LANDS AND PEOPLES, has a long section on the Russian region of North Asia. Articles on the five new independent republics and on Mongolia follow this introduction.

NORTH ASIA

North Asia—Western Siberia, Eastern Siberia, and the Far East— accounts for about one-third of the Asian landmass. Its vegetation, from north to south, includes a sort of boggy, treeless plain called tundra;

taiga, a sometimes swampy area forested primarily with cone-bearing trees; and forested and nonforested steppe, or dry grasslands.

Western Siberia.   With 80 percent of North Asia's population, Western Siberia is a vast lowland plain that extends east from the Urals to the Yenisey River. North Asia's most productive farms and factories are located here. Natural resources include coal, iron ore, petroleum, natural gas, and timber. The area's farmers grow grains such as wheat, rye, and oats and run a dairy industry. Industrial centers include Novosibirsk, Omsk, Novokuznetsk, Barnaul, and Kemerovo.

Eastern Siberia.   This broad plateau lies between the Yenisey River on the west and the Lena River on the east. Its climate is rigorous, with

Many former Soviet citizens are now free to rediscover their Islamic roots after years of religious suppression.

ISLAM IN THE FORMER SOVIET UNION

Since the 7th century, Central Asia has been the easternmost outpost of Islam, and many of its cities, primarily Samarkand and Bukhara, later flourished as great centers of Muslim learning.

When the Soviets took over in the 1920s, most Islamic schools (known as *madrassas*) were closed and the number of mosques was sharply reduced. Although the Communist authorities were somewhat more tolerant of Islam than of Christianity, the ensuing modernization process (which transformed nomadic herdsmen into factory workers) and lack of religious instruction resulted in a widespread decline in the number of believers. The political upheaval of recent years has led to a religious revival and to the establishment of many Islamic parties and organizations.

Like the majority of Muslims worldwide, most of the approximately 50 million Muslims who now live in the former Soviet republics belong to the Sunni branch of Islam. The other branch, Shiite Islam, is the state religion of Iran and is closely linked with Islamic fundamentalism.

The major Islamic countries—Egypt, Saudi Arabia, Turkey, and Iran—have been closely following the developments in Central Asia and trying to gain influence there. Most of them have concentrated on forging closer economic links and on helping the former Soviet citizens to rediscover their religious roots by supporting religious instruction. Saudi Arabia donated 1 million copies of the Koran, Egypt has been sending its Islamic teachers to the region, and Central Asian Muslim scholars and educators are being invited to study in Cairo and in Turkey.

Despite their new openness toward religion, Kazakhstan, Kyrgyzstan, Turkmenistan, and Uzbekistan continue to be predominantly secular states, with Islam playing only a minor role in public affairs. Tajikistan, on the other hand, has been the scene of a bloody confrontation between Communist and Islamic forces, the latter supported by fundamentalist guerrillas from Afghanistan.

subfreezing temperatures 180 days a year. The bulk of the land consists of tundra and taiga, where the native people raise reindeer, hunt, and fish. In the far south, where some steppe exists, farmers produce wheat, oats, and other grains. The major industries are focused on the mining of gold, diamonds, bauxite, nickel, and other minerals. Eastern Siberia's main cities are Krasnoyarsk, Irkutsk, Chita, Ulan-Ude, and Angarsk.

The Far East. Mountains cover three-fourths of the Russian Far East, many of whose rivers drain into the Pacific Ocean. Two strategically important parts of the region are the Russian island of Sakhalin and the 56 Kuril Islands, which the Soviet Union seized at the end of World War II and annexed in 1947. Japan wants the four southernmost islands back, but as of 1996 the issue remained unresolved. The Kurils and the Kamchatka Peninsula contain more than 70 active volcanoes.

The frozen steppes of China's Inner Mongolia Autonomous Region support large numbers of wool-producing sheep.

The Far East's climates range from Arctic to monsoonal. The Amur and Maritime areas, on the mainland west of Sakhalin Island, are the most heavily populated. The major cities are Khabarovsk, Komsomolsk-na-Amure, and Vladivostok. The winters are severe, and the summers cool.

Gold, lead, tin, zinc, and other minerals are mined here. Wheat, oats, rye, rice, soybeans, and other crops are grown to meet local needs. The fishing industry is important, accounting for one-third of Russia's catch. Industries include canning, ore smelting, paper manufacturing, and timber production.

CENTRAL ASIA

Land. Much of Central Asia is either mountainous or desert. In the west, two large deserts occupy large parts of Turkmenistan and Uzbekistan: the Kara-Kum (Black Sand) and the Kyzyl-Kum (Red Sand). Most people in these two republics live in fertile valleys or in oases in the foothills of such mountain ranges as Kopet Dagh, on the border with Iran, and Tien Shan, one of the major Central Asian mountain systems.

The northern part of Kazakhstan features steppeland, where Kazakh nomads once wandered with their herds. South of the steppe, the formerly arid regions are now intensively irrigated and devoted to the cultivation of cotton and fruit.

Tajikistan and Kyrgyzstan are mostly mountainous, with permanently snowcapped peaks in the Tien Shan and Pamir ranges. Most of Mongolia is a flat upland, whose average height is nearly 1 mi. (1.6 km.) above sea level.

Living conditions in Siberia are somewhat less harsh now that most villages have electricity.

Climate. Owing to its location, most of Central Asia receives very little rain. Temperature range is enormous, from the record low of −81° F. (−63° C.) in the highlands of Tajikistan, to the 158° F. (70° C.) reputedly recorded in the Kazakhstan steppe.

People. The present borders of the five new Central Asian states were drawn in 1936, at the height of the Stalinist Soviet Union. Allegedly "nationality based," they are, in fact, rather artificial. The main Central Asian ethnic groups—Uzbeks, Kazakhs, Turkmen, Kyrgyz, and Tajiks—live in most of the republics. The first four are Turkic-speaking peoples, whose languages are mutually understandable. Tajiks are an Iranian people who resemble Europeans in appearance. Mongolians are the classic representatives of the Mongoloid racial group.

The former Soviet Central Asia also has large numbers of Russians and Ukrainians, many of whom have settled there since the 19th century. In Kazakhstan, Russians and Ukrainians represent more than 40 percent of the population.

Most of Central Asia's non-Europeans are Sunni Muslims (see "Islam in the Former Soviet Union," page 342). In Mongolia, the predominant religion before the Communist period was Tibetan Buddhism (known as Lamaism), but decades of atheist propaganda suppressed most religions.

The largest Central Asian city is the capital of Uzbekistan, Tashkent. With 2.1 million people, it is a cosmopolitan metropolis, and its airport serves as a refueling stop for flights from Moscow to Southeast Asia.

Economy. Traditionally, Central Asia was home to nomad herdsmen, and livestock breeding remains one of the mainstays of the economy. During the 20th century, however, Soviet Central Asia has undergone profound changes. Massive irrigation works transformed large expanses of land into cotton plantations. Rapid industrialization, mainly based on the extensive mineral wealth of the region, has turned many Central Asian cities into pollution-ridden centers containing mammoth factories.

HISTORY

North Asia was at one time exclusively the home of numerous nomadic tribes. In the Far East and on the shores of the Arctic Ocean, these peoples lived by hunting seals, whales, and walrus. Inland, other bands spent their days fishing, hunting, and herding reindeer. In the south, on the grasslands and in the mountains, nomads raised sheep, horses, and other livestock.

Central Asia was for centuries a busy crossroads between China, Southwest Asia, and Europe. The famous Silk Road, known since the 3rd century B.C., served as the main communication artery. The Sogdians, who were Iranian, were its first known inhabitants. Buddhism and Christianity found their way to Central Asia before Arab Muslims conquered it during the 7th and 8th centuries, implanting Islam. So many Turkic peoples migrated to the region from the east that it came to be known as Turkestan.

During the early 1200s, Mongol tribes in the east united under Genghis Khan. His armies conquered northern China and Siberia and swept west, taking Turkestan, Afghanistan, and the Caucasus. After his death, one of his sons ruled Turkestan. Another laid claim to China, eastern Siberia, and the Far East. A third ruled Russia and held a claim to western Siberia until the Mongol Empire fell apart in the late 1300s.

European Russians began settling among the fur-trading Siberian peoples during the late 1500s and early 1600s. By the 1800s, Russia had begun exiling convicts there. The Trans-Siberian Railway hastened settlement after work on it began in 1891, as peasants migrated to Siberia in search of land. Most of the Russian population in Siberia today is concentrated in the narrow belt along the railroad.

Russians have also made inroads into Central Asia, absorbing most of Turkestan into their empire by the mid-1800s, and dividing it into five republics during the 1920s. In 1990, there were more than 8 million ethnic Russians in the region. Despite the nationalist fervor of most of the new governments after the demise of the Soviet Union in December 1991, only about 335,000 Russians chose to return to their mother country. It is more than likely that the multiple economic, social, and cultural links between Central Asia and Russia will persist for many years.

The newly independent republics of Central Asia—Kazakhstan, Uzbekistan, Turkmenistan, Kyrgyzstan, and Tajikistan—were the founding members of the Commonwealth of Independent States (CIS), a loose alliance replacing the defunct Soviet Union. From December 1991 on, they tried to forge new identities while maintaining close links with Russia. All the republics pledged to introduce democratic practices and free-market economies, but the results have not been impressive. With the exception of Kyrgyzstan, the governments continue to be authoritarian, and economic reforms are proceeding slowly.

Mongolia, another Central Asian country, became the second Communist nation in the world in 1924. In 1990, the first free elections took place, but the Communists won. In 1996, however, Mongolia elected its first non-Communist government.

Mountainous areas of Kazakhstan receive substantial snowfall during the winter.

 # KAZAKHSTAN

Kazakhstan, the second largest of the former Soviet republics, was a proving ground for several grandiose Soviet projects. It was also one of the four Soviet republics with stockpiles of nuclear weapons.

In the 1950s there was a massive campaign to transform the "virgin lands" of Central Asia into productive agricultural lands. The results were expansive cotton and wheat farms that turned Kazakhstan into the biggest producer of cotton in the former Soviet Union. About the same time, the Baykonur space center was built near Syr Darya; most Soviet spaceflights were launched from there. By the 1980s, industrialization had turned several Kazakh locations into huge, polluted cities.

Since becoming independent in December 1991, Kazakhstan has tried to assert its new identity, but it remains linked to Russia in countless ways. Although the government of Nursultan Nazarbayev is authoritarian, the society is somewhat more open than during the Communist era. Nuclear disarmament had been completed by May 1995.

THE LAND

With an area twice the size of Alaska, landlocked Kazakhstan is a vast expanse of mostly flat or gently undulating land in the center of Asia. Its borders touch Russia on the west and north, China on the east, Kyrgyzstan and Uzbekistan on the south, and Turkmenistan and the Caspian Sea on the southwest. Large irrigation projects have changed the face of the steppes in the north and the desert and semidesert in the south. The only mountainous areas occur in the northeast (the Altai range) and in the southeast, on the border with China and Kyrgyzstan.

The climate of Kazakhstan is marked by huge seasonal differences in temperature. Winters are extremely cold, particularly in the north, and very long, lasting from October through April. Temperatures have been known to drop as low as −49° F. (−45° C.). Summers are short, hot, and dry, with a July average temperature in the south of 84° F. (29° C.). There are also wide swings of temperature between day and night, sometimes as much as 55° F. (31° C.).

The Shriveling Aral Sea. Kazakhstan's streams and rivers drain into a large system centered on the Caspian and Aral Seas and Lakes Balkhash and Tengiz. The Aral Sea has become a victim of an ill-conceived irrigation scheme that diverts water from the Amu Darya and Syr Darya rivers. The sea has lost about 70 percent of its water and is too salty and polluted to support fish. Lakeside fishing villages have become ghost towns that now lie several miles inland.

THE PEOPLE

The nomadic Kazakhs have always shared the area of present-day Kazakhstan with other groups, including the Kyrgyz (Turkic-speaking ethnic cousins of Kazakhs), Uzbeks, Kara-Kalpak, and Turkmen. In the late 19th century, about 400,000 Russian settlers arrived, followed by other immigrants. During World War II, German and other ethnic groups from the European part of Russia were forcibly resettled in Kazakhstan.

FACTS AND FIGURES

OFFICIAL NAME: Republic of Kazakhstan.

NATIONALITY: Kazakh(s).

CAPITAL: Almaty.

LOCATION: Central Asia, south of Siberia. **Boundaries—** Russia, China, Kyrgyzstan, Uzbekistan, Turkmenistan.

AREA: 1,049,200 sq. mi. (2,717,428 sq. km.).

PHYSICAL FEATURES: Highest point—Khan Tengri Peak (22,949 ft.; 6,997 m.). **Lowest point—**Karagyie Depression (433 ft.; 132 m. below sea level). **Chief rivers—**Irtysh, Ishim, Tobol, Syr Darya. **Major lakes—** Balkash, Tengiz, Zaysan, Alakol.

POPULATION: 16,500,000 (1996; annual growth 0.9%).

MAJOR LANGUAGES: Kazakh (official), Russian.

MAJOR RELIGIONS: Islam, Christianity.

GOVERNMENT: Republic. **Head of state—**president. **Head of government—**prime minister. **Legislature—** Parliament.

CHIEF CITIES: Almaty, Semipalatinsk, Petropavlovsk, Uralsk.

ECONOMY: Chief minerals—coal, iron, bauxite, copper, lead, zinc, silver, gold, oil, gas. **Chief agricultural products—**wheat, vegetables, fruit. **Industries and products—**cast iron, steel, rolled metal, cement. **Chief exports—**mineral resources, agricultural products. **Chief imports—**machinery, consumer goods.

MONETARY UNIT: Tenge.

NATIONAL HOLIDAY: December 16 (Independence Day).

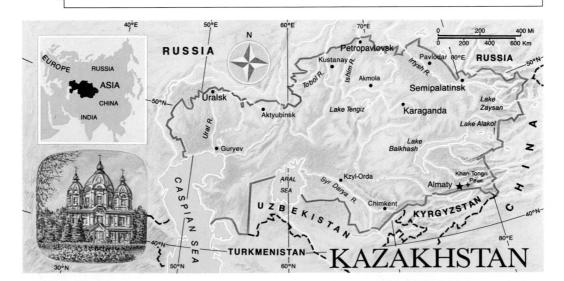

Kazakh "cowboys" (above) round up cattle in a manner not unlike that of their nomadic ancestors. Much Kazakh social life revolves around the bazaar (right), where people buy food and other goods.

Kazakhs account for only 42 percent of the population of Kazakhstan, and Russians for 37 percent. About 1 million Kazakhs live in China and Mongolia, and more than 1 million live in Russia and Uzbekistan. Kazakhs are Sunni Muslims, but most are secular.

Way of Life.   During the 1930s nomadic Kazakhs were forced by the Soviet regime to become collective farmers. Many resisted this pressure and fled to China, but by the 1990s there was very little left of the traditional Kazakh ways. Some women still occasionally wear the national costume—a long dress with a stand-up collar—but most Kazakhs, particularly the younger generation, prefer contemporary clothing.

Almaty.   Previously known as Alma-Ata ("father of apples"), the city was founded in 1854 on the site of a Silk Road oasis called Almatu ("apple tree"). It is the present capital of Kazakhstan, but the government has designated a more northerly city, Akmola, to become the new capital of the country in 1998.

Education.   The languages of instruction are Russian and Kazakh, but there are also schools for other ethnic groups. Several institutes of higher learning are located in Almaty and other regional centers.

ECONOMY

Historically, Kazakhstan was a sparsely populated land with very few permanent settlements. Nomadic groups moved freely across great distances. During the Soviet era, the region and its people underwent a profound change. First the nomads were made into farmers, then the "virgin lands" campaign of the 1950s created enormous cotton and wheat farms, and in the next decade industrialization began.

About 90 different minerals have been discovered in the republic, including copper, lead, zinc, silver, tungsten, tin, and cobalt.

The republic is now dotted with steelworks, copper and zinc plants, lead smelters, and cement and textile factories. Although many of these mammoth complexes are just several decades old, they often resemble old 19th-century industrial mills in England. Soviet economic bosses paid little attention to worker safety; employees in these factories have been inhaling lead fumes and carcinogenic agents for years.

Post-Communist Developments. Compared to those of its Central Asian neighbors, Kazakhstan's government seemed more determined to implement economic reforms, and even invited foreign experts to provide advice about a transition to a free-market system. By the mid-1990s, however, little actual progress had been made. Foreign entrepreneurs complained of too much red tape and constant government interference.

In May 1992, Kazakhstan's president secured a $10 million investment by Chevron, a U.S. company, for the development of the Tenghis oil field near the Caspian Sea. By 1996, however, little actual money had arrived in the country.

A new currency, called the *tenge,* was introduced in the fall of 1993. Despite continuing dependence on Russia, Kazakhstan now has more trading partners, with China being the largest.

HISTORY

The word "Kazakh" appears in historical records from the 11th century, with a general meaning of "riders of the steppe." During the 16th century, Kazakhs created a nomadic state headed by a "khan" (and therefore known as a "khanate"). This empire then split into three "hordes," each of which was ruled by a tribal chieftain called a "sultan."

In the following century, Kazakhs were repeatedly ravaged by raids from the Mongol Oyrat Empire, and in the 1700s they came under the influence of the Russians. Between 1822 and 1848, all three Kazakh hordes were disbanded. The Russians erroneously referred to Kazakhs as Kyrgyz (while the Kyrgyz were called Kara-Kyrgyz).

A small Kazakh nationalist movement developed in the early 20th century, and, in the turmoil of the civil war after the Bolsheviks seized power in 1917, the nationalists set up an independent government. It did not last for long, however, and from 1920 onward, Kazakhstan fell again under the rule of Moscow. First an autonomous republic, Kazakhstan became a union republic in 1936.

Independent Kazakhstan. Kazakhstani President Nursultan Nazarbayev has been praised for his pragmatism and his ability to handle interethnic tensions. He has had to be ever mindful of the more than 6 million Russians living in the north of the country. Because of this significant minority, the government has decided to move the capital to the northern city of Akmola, which is closer to industrial centers.

Government. The first post-Communist parliament, which replaced the old Supreme Soviet, was elected in March 1994, but was dissolved a year later because of alleged improprieties in the elections. New parliamentary elections took place in December 1995. A rewritten constitution was approved in a referendum in August 1995. The decisive political power remains in the hands of the president.

IRINA RYBACEK / Reviewed by EDWARD W. WALKER, Ph.D., Columbia University

Tashkent, the capital of Uzbekistan, has taken on a very modern look in recent years.

UZBEKISTAN

Of the five new central Asian republics that arose out of the disintegration of the Soviet Union, Uzbekistan has the most colorful, distinguished history. The ancient Silk Road that connected Europe with China passed through the southern part of Uzbekistan's territory, and the capital of the sophisticated 14th-century empire of Timur (or Tamerlane) was at present-day Samarkand. The names of the other two major Uzbek cities, Tashkent and Bukhara, evoke exotic images of Mongol warriors and of caravans carrying spices, silks, and beautiful rugs.

THE LAND
Located in the heart of Asia between the rivers Syr Darya and Amu Darya, Uzbekistan is bordered by Kazakhstan to the west and north, Kyrgyzstan and Tajikistan to the east, and Afghanistan and Turkmenistan to the south. The border with Kazakhstan runs through the Aral Sea. Because of the large irrigation system that uses the waters of both Amu and Syr Darya, the surface of the sea has shrunk by more than one-third, making the water too salty and too toxic to sustain life.

The center of Uzbekistan is taken up by the sparsely populated Kyzyl Kum (Red Sands) desert. The most densely populated part of the republic is its easternmost protrusion. There, between the Tien Shan mountain range and the foothills of the Pamir-Alai range, lies Tashkent and the fertile Fergana valley, the industrial heart of the republic.

Uzbekistan has an arid, hot climate, with summer temperatures often climbing above 105° F. (40° C.). The city of Termez, in the south, was reportedly the hottest place in the former Soviet Union.

THE PEOPLE

Uzbeks are the largest Turkic-speaking group after the Turks themselves; apart from their own republic, they also live in Kyrgyzstan, Tajikistan, Turkmenistan, and Afghanistan. Uzbeks are Sunni Muslims.

In Uzbekistan, the ethnic Uzbeks account for more than 70 percent of the population. Russians represent about 8 percent, and other nationalities include Ukrainians, Koreans, Armenians, Kazakhs, Tajiks, and Kara-Kalpak. The Kara-Kalpak live in an autonomous region.

Tashkent. This city, the capital of Uzbekistan, traces its beginnings to the 2nd century B.C. In the Middle Ages, it was a busy trade center. Devastated in a 1966 earthquake, it was rebuilt into a modern, cosmopolitan city of 2.1 million people; only a few historic sites remain.

Samarkand. Known to the ancient Greeks as Marakanda, Samarkand was first mentioned in writing in 329 B.C., when Alexander the Great conquered it. In A.D. 1370 it became the capital of Timur's empire and the cultural center of Asia; for many decades, Samarkand was known as "the precious pearl of the world." The old center of the city dazzles with its beautiful Bibi Khanym Mosque and three *madrassas* (Muslim schools) at the Registan Square. The present population is about 370,000.

Bukhara. This 1,000-year-old city is the most Asian of Uzbekistan, much less glamorous than Samarkand and much more traditional than Tashkent. From the 16th until the late 19th century, Bukhara was a center of religious learning; it had about 100 *madrassas*. Its streets are still lined with old bazaars and mosques. Bukhara, a famous type of Oriental rug with geometrical designs and reddish colors, is named after the city.

Way of Life. Uzbekistan was thrust into the 20th century during the Soviet period, but many old customs and traditions survive. On holidays people still dress in national costumes, with characteristic bright colors and embroideries; many houses are decorated with colored rugs and folk art; and traditional festivals, which usually include some horseback-riding events, are still celebrated.

FACTS AND FIGURES

OFFICIAL NAME: Republic of Uzbekistan.

NATIONALITY: Uzbek(s).

CAPITAL: Tashkent.

LOCATION: Central Asia. **Boundaries**—Kazakhstan, Kyrgyzstan, Tajikistan, Afghanistan, Turkmenistan.

AREA: 172,700 sq. mi. (447,293 sq. km.).

PHYSICAL FEATURES: Highest point—Twenty-Second Congress of the CPSU Peak (15,233 ft.; 4,645 m.). **Lowest point**—Munbulak Depression in Kyzyl Kum (40 ft.; 12 m. below sea level). **Chief rivers**—Amu Darya, Syr Darya.

POPULATION: 23,200,000 (1996; annual growth 2.3%).

MAJOR LANGUAGES: Uzbek, Russian.

MAJOR RELIGION: Islam.

GOVERNMENT: Republic. **Head of state**—president. **Head of government**—prime minister. **Legislature**—unicameral Supreme Soviet.

CHIEF CITIES: Tashkent, Samarkand, Namangan.

ECONOMY: Chief minerals—natural gas, oil, coal, gold, marble. **Chief agricultural product**—cotton. **Industries and products**—chemicals, fertilizers, textile manufactures, fur farming. **Chief exports**—cotton, gold, heavy machinery. **Chief imports**—light manufactures, foodstuffs.

MONETARY UNIT: 1 sum = 1,000 sum-coupons.

NATIONAL HOLIDAY: September 1 (Independence Day).

Cultural Heritage. Uzbekistan has a long cultural tradition. After being conquered by the Arabs, the region was for centuries an important Islamic center. A famous 11th-century encyclopedist, al-Biruni, was probably born in the present Kara-Kalpak region. In the 15th century, an observatory was built at Samarkand by Prince Ulugh-Beg, a distinguished Islamic mathematician. Uzbek literature began to flourish in the 1920s. Tragically, its two major authors, Abdalrauf Fitrat and Abdullah Qadiri, were killed in the Stalinist purges.

ECONOMY

Under Soviet rule, Uzbekistan became the third-largest cotton producer in the world. Another important product is the silkworm, cultivated since the 4th century A.D. Fergana Valley is also a fruit-growing region.

For centuries, Uzbeks have raised Karakul sheep, an animal native to the region. The black curly fur of the Karakul lamb is world famous.

The disintegration of the Soviet economic sphere in the late 1980s led to many hardships, and they are far from over. In March 1994, the government introduced a package of economic reforms aimed at privatization, protection of private ownership, and stimulation of individual entrepreneurship. Foreign observers, however, have pointed to widespread corruption.

HISTORY

The area of present-day Uzbekistan was known in ancient times as Transoxania, or the land beyond the River Oxus (the classical name for Amu Darya). Arabs entered the region in the late 7th century A.D.; by 750, they had it under their control.

The term Uzbek is derived from a monarch named Özbeg (ruled A.D. 1313 to 1341), the greatest ruler of the Kipchak khanate. He is best-known for converting the tribes of central Asia to Islam. In the late 15th and 16th centuries, Uzbeks were united under the leadership of Muhammad Shaybani. He seized all of Transoxania and extended his rule to modern Afghanistan; his dynasty ruled these lands until 1598.

Russians began to penetrate the region as traders in the 16th century, and by the 19th century they had become politically dominant. The emirate of Bukhara was the last part of the region to fall when, in 1868, it became a protectorate of Russia, a status it retained until 1917. The Uzbek Soviet Socialist Republic was formed in 1924.

Independence. In September 1991, the Uzbek Communist Party renamed itself the Popular Democratic Party. Its leader, former party boss Islam A. Karimov, was elected president in 1991 in the nation's first popular contested election. In a March 1995 referendum, he had his mandate extended until 2000. Just as in Soviet times, over 99 percent of the voters approved. Karimov maintains that Central Asia is not ready for democracy yet and that political and economic changes must be gradual. Yet he seems to move in the opposite direction. By 1996, foreign observers agreed that Uzbekistan was the most repressive Central Asian republic. At the same time, the country aspires to a predominant position in the region.

Government. Opposition parties are banned and their leaders exiled. President Karimov exercises almost unlimited power.

IRINA RYBACEK / Reviewed by EDWARD W. WALKER, Ph.D., Columbia University

KYRGYZSTAN

In some areas, Kyrgyzstan's Tien Shan mountain range towers to heights of 4 miles or more.

A small, landlocked Central Asian country, Kyrgyzstan was until December 1991 one of the 15 constituent republics of the Soviet Union, and in reference books was referred to as Kirghizia. In the mid-1900s, Kyrgyzstan was generally considered more democratic than its four neighbors.

From about the 3rd century B.C. until the 15th century A.D., the area adjoined the important Silk Road, a trade route between Europe and China. Russians arrived in the mid-1800s.

THE LAND

Kyrgyzstan lies in the western part of the Tien Shan range; half of its area is at elevations of 20,000 ft. (6,100 m.) or higher. The scenery is quite spectacular, with snowcapped peaks and high alpine plateaus. The 37-mi. (60-km.)-long Inylchek Glacier is one of the largest in the world. The country borders Kazakhstan to the north, China to the southeast, Tajikistan to the south, and Uzbekistan to the west.

The Fergana Valley in the southwest and the lowlands along the Chu and Talas rivers are the most densely inhabited parts of Kyrgyzstan. The capital of the republic, Bishkek (until 1991 called Frunze), is located on the Chu River. It stands on the site of an old Silk Road settlement, which became a Russian garrison in the late 19th century. The main river of Kyrgyzstan, the powerful Naryn (upper Syr Darya), is dammed by five huge power stations.

The blue, salty Issyk Kul Lake, in a basin about 5,250 ft. (1,600 m.) above sea level, is locally believed to harbor a monster trout; in any case, the lake is certainly full of fish and a favorite with anglers. Because of the many hot springs rising from its floor, the lake retains a pleasant temperature for most of the year. The lake and the surrounding mountains are dotted with campsites and several resorts.

The climate is characterized by great differences in temperature: the highest temperature ever recorded was 109° F. (43° C.), and the lowest was −65° F. (−54° C.). Summers in the valleys are very hot and dry; the winters turn bitterly cold.

THE PEOPLE

The Kyrgyz, who represent about 52 percent of the population of Kyrgyzstan, are Turko-Mongolian people whose original homeland was probably in southern Siberia. From there they migrated southward to the Tien Shan range sometime during the 12th century, and later became known as accomplished livestock breeders and herdsmen. Their language belongs to the Turkish family, and is so similar to other Turkic languages that a Kyrgyz speaker can readily understand a Turk, an Azerbaijani, an Uzbek, or a Kazakh.

Until the modern era, the Kyrgyz were nomads. During the Soviet period, however, they were forced to abandon their old ways. The ancient traditions still survive in various horseback games that people play on Sundays. One of them, called *keshkumai,* in which a man chases a woman on horseback and tries to kiss her, apparently reflects the ancient ritual of the taking of the bride. Some men still wear traditional white felt caps or fur-trimmed hats and felt boots with leather overshoes, but more elaborate costumes are worn only during special ceremonies.

Religious Kyrgyz are generally Sunni Muslims. After decades of official Soviet atheism, many people are now beginning to rediscover their religious roots.

Education and Cultural Life.   Under Soviet rule, education was made compulsory, and illiteracy was largely eradicated. Although the Russian

---

FACTS AND FIGURES

OFFICIAL NAME: Republic of Kyrgyzstan.

NATIONALITY: Kyrgyz.

CAPITAL: Bishkek.

LOCATION: Central Asia. **Boundaries**—China, Tajikistan, Uzbekistan, Kazakhstan.

AREA: 76,600 sq. mi. (198,394 sq. km.).

PHYSICAL FEATURES: Highest point—Victory Peak (24,400 ft.; 7,440 m.). **Lowest point**—Fergana Valley (1,600 ft.; 488 m.). **Chief rivers**—Naryn, Chu. **Major lake**—Issyk Kul.

POPULATION: 4,600,000 (1996; annual growth 1.6%).

MAJOR LANGUAGES: Kyrgyz (official), Russian.

MAJOR RELIGION: Islam.

GOVERNMENT: Republic. **Head of state**—president. **Head of government**—prime minister. **Legislature**—bicameral Assembly of Legislatures.

CHIEF CITIES: Bishkek, Osh, Dzhalal-Abad.

ECONOMY: Chief minerals—oil, gas, uranium, mercury, antimony. **Chief agricultural products**—cotton, sugar beets, tobacco. **Industries and products**—coal mining, food processing, textiles. **Chief exports**—wool, mercury, antimony, cotton. **Chief imports**—machinery, fuel, foodstuffs.

MONETARY UNIT: 1 som = 100 tiyin.

NATIONAL HOLIDAYS: December 2 (National Day) and August 31 (Independence Day).

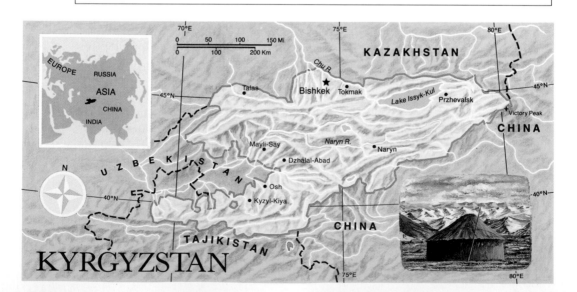

language has not been very popular, it has served as a useful common tongue. Most broadcasting and newspapers use both Russian and Kyrgyz.

A rich oral tradition of epic and lyric poetry has found its expression in the long poem called *Manas*, "the Iliad of the steppes," which was first written down in the mid-1800s. Reflecting old myths and legends, the poem celebrates the heroic feats of Manas and his son and grandson, all of whom defended their homeland against enemies. The best-known modern writer is Chingiz Aitmatov, whose critically acclaimed *Tales of the Mountains and Steppes* has been translated into English.

ECONOMY

Sheep raising is Kyrgyzstan's main economic activity in the mountains, while cattle raising and cultivation of cotton, sugar beets, and tobacco predominates in the lowlands. The Chu Valley is known for its many orchards and vineyards.

Minerals—which include coal, mercury, antimony, and uranium—are found around the Fergana Valley. During the Soviet era, the republic developed some food-processing plants and other light industry. Cotton spinning and manufacturing of leather and sheepskin coats are particularly important industries.

Kyrgyzstan is one of the poorer Central Asian republics and recent years have brought much hardship: the old Moscow-directed economy has collapsed and a new system has not yet replaced it. Privatization and other reforms have not been very successful, and by the mid-1990s, unemployment had reached about 20 percent.

HISTORY

Kyrgyzstan has been crisscrossed by nomads since prehistoric times. In the early 19th century, the area belonged to the Kokand khanate. Then, during the 1860s and 1870s, the region was colonized by Russians. Until 1926 the Kyrgyz people were called "Kara-Kyrgyz" by Russians, while the word "Kirghiz" was applied to the Kazakhs.

During the civil war following the Bolshevik Revolution, the area witnessed a number of anti-Bolshevik uprisings, but by the mid-1920s, the new Soviet state had asserted its power. The present boundaries were drawn in 1936, with complete disregard for ethnic lines of settlement. That same year, the Kirghiz Soviet Socialist Republic was set up.

New Beginnings.   Since late 1991, Kyrgyz leaders have been among the strongest supporters of the Commonwealth of Independent States, a loose alliance that replaced the defunct Soviet Union. The forging of a new national identity has been complicated by ethnic tensions between the Kyrgyz and the Russians (more than one-fifth of the population), and also between the Kyrgyz and the Uzbeks.

President Askar Akayev, former head of the Kyrgyz Academy of Sciences, is credited with supporting democracy. Several new political parties were founded in 1995.

Government.   The nation's first post-Communist constitution was adopted in 1993. Unlike his Central Asian counterparts, President Akayev was reelected in December 1995—winning 72 percent of the vote—in a contest that Western observers generally considered free and fair. A 1996 referendum gave the president the right to dissolve the legislature at will.

IRINA RYBACEK / Reviewed by EDWARD W. WALKER, Ph.D., Columbia University

Turkmen traditionally wear a *tilpek,* the sheepskin hat modeled by the street vendor above.

TURKMENISTAN

This newly independent Central Asian country, also known as Turkmenia, was, from 1936 until December 1991, one of the 15 member republics of the Soviet Union. The disbanded Communist empire was immediately replaced by the Commonwealth of Independent States, consisting of 10 former Soviet republics; Turkmenistan, together with its four Central Asian neighbors, joined this loose alliance.

THE LAND

Situated in southwest Central Asia, Turkmenistan is a Spain-sized country bordered by the Caspian Sea to the west, Kazakhstan and Uzbekistan to the north, and Afghanistan and Iran to the south. Most of its area is taken up by the Kara Kum (Black Sand), one of the world's largest deserts. The outskirts of the Kara Kum are ringed by oasis settlements.

Along the border with Iran rise the only mountains to be found in the country, the Kopet-Dag range. Its highest peak rises to 9,652 ft. (2,942 m.). The range is geologically unstable and subject to earthquakes.

The major river is the Amu Darya, which forms the boundary with Uzbekistan in the north. Smaller rivers include the Tedzhen and the Murgab in the southeast and the Atrek in the southwest. The Kara Kum Canal is the world's largest irrigation project. It has transformed Turkmenistan's landscape, making possible the establishment of cotton plantations on the once arid lands.

Although Turkmenistan lies at the same latitude as Italy, its climate is quite different. Turkmenistan has a climate marked by great extremes in temperature. In summer the temperature is usually above 95° F. (35° C.), while in winter it drops as low as −29° F. (−34° C.). What very little rain occurs, usually falls in the spring.

THE PEOPLE

The majority of the people are Turkmen, or Turkomans, descendants of warrior desert tribes that have inhabited the region for centuries. These ancestors arrived in Central Asia around A.D. 600. After the Arab invasions in the 7th century, they accepted Islam. Of mixed Caucasian and Mongoloid stock, they are closely related to Turks.

Russians comprise the largest minority in Turkmenistan (about 10 percent); there are also Uzbeks, Kazakhs, Ukrainians, Armenians, and Azerbaijani. Most Turkmen live in rural settlements and villages, while the immigrants have settled in cities. Half of the population is urban.

Ashkhabad. The capital and major city, Ashkhabad experiences some of the hottest weather in the former Soviet Union. Founded in 1881 as a Russian garrison, the city was almost completely devastated by a one-minute earthquake in June 1948, which killed about 110,000 people.

Way of Life. As nomads and horsemen warriors, Turkmen are known for their strong tribal loyalties. Many of the republic's inhabitants continue to live in traditional ways, with some women still covering their faces in public. A woman's outfit typically includes narrow trousers worn under ankle-length dresses in bright colors; men traditionally wear a long coat or tunic over a white shirt.

Education and Cultural Life. Historically, the educational center of the area was at Bukhara (now in Uzbekistan). In the early 1900s, Muslim reformists established schools in Kerki and Chardzhou. During the Soviet period, primary and secondary schools were founded in most large towns, and several institutes of higher learning came into existence.

ECONOMY

Although historically a herding region, Turkmenistan was industrialized during the Soviet era, with cotton production and mineral extraction as the leading economic activities.

FACTS AND FIGURES

OFFICIAL NAME: Turkmenistan.

NATIONALITY: Turkmen.

CAPITAL: Ashkhabad.

LOCATION: Central Asia. **Boundaries**—Kazakhstan, Uzbekistan, Afghanistan, Iran, Caspian Sea.

AREA: 188,500 sq. mi. (488,215 sq. km.).

PHYSICAL FEATURES: Highest point—Mount Rize (9,652 ft.; 2,942 m.), near Ashkhabad, on the border with Iran. **Lowest point**—Akchakaya (266 ft.; 81 m. below sea level). **Chief rivers**—Amu Darya, Tedzhen, Murgab, Atrek.

POPULATION: 4,600,000 (1996; annual growth 2.4%).

MAJOR LANGUAGES: Turkmen, Russian.

MAJOR RELIGION: Islam.

GOVERNMENT: Republic. **Head of state**—president. **Head of government**—prime minister. **Legislature**—bicameral Parliament.

CHIEF CITIES: Ashkhabad, Mary (Merv), Tedzhen.

ECONOMY: Chief minerals—oil, gas, uranium, iodine, bromine, sodium sulfate. **Chief agricultural product**—cotton. **Industries and products**—oil extraction, carpet making, food processing, engineering and metal processing. **Chief exports**—natural gas, cotton, oil, carpets, butter, wine, fish. **Chief imports**—light manufactures, transportation equipment, grain.

MONETARY UNIT: Manat.

NATIONAL HOLIDAY: October 27 (Independence Day).

The Kara Kum Canal, which was started in the 1950s and is projected to reach Krasnovodsk on the Caspian Sea, irrigates large expanses that have been turned into cotton plantations. For decades, Turkmenistan produced over 10 percent of all the Soviet Union's cotton. The raising of Karakul sheep, which produce beautiful wool, is another important agricultural activity. Turkmenistan's production of silkworm cocoons was the largest such operation in the former Soviet Union.

After World War II, Turkmenistan became one of the Soviet Union's largest producers of natural gas. Oil-extraction activities developed near the Caspian Sea, and uranium deposits are mined.

The most famous traditional industry is carpet and rug making; "Bukhara" rugs have been exported to at least 50 countries. Other light industries, particularly food processing, and some heavy industries have developed since the 1950s.

During the Soviet era, Moscow provided steady subsidies, thus offsetting the disadvantages of an economy relying primarily on a single product, namely cotton. With this support now gone, the economic situation has deteriorated badly. Turkmenistan's problems have been exacerbated by the failure of other former Soviet republics, primarily Ukraine, to pay for shipments of gas.

Yet there is some hope for better days to come, thanks primarily to Turkmenistan's large deposits of oil and gas. The republic's leaders are even talking about Turkmenistan as "the future Kuwait." More cautious observers point out, however, that political instability and ethnic tensions will probably delay this bright future.

HISTORY

The word "Turkmen" was mentioned in Chinese sources as early as the 8th century A.D. For centuries the Turkmen social system was tribal, with individual tribes being either independent or part of adjoining states. In the 14th century, the region of present-day Turkmenistan was part of Timur's empire, and for most of the 19th century, it nominally belonged to the emirate of Bukhara.

When the Russians came to the area in the 1870s, the fierce Turkmen warriors put up stubborn resistance. They were finally defeated by Russian troops in 1881, when 20,000 Turkmen were massacred.

During the civil war that followed the Bolshevik Revolution in 1917, a small British force came from Iran to help the anti-Bolshevik Social Revolutionaries, but to no avail. Ashkhabad was captured in July 1919, and soon thereafter the whole region came under Soviet rule. The Turkmen Soviet Socialist Republic was established in 1924.

Independence. Relying for seven decades on Moscow, the country was not prepared for independence. Former Communists—renamed the Democratic Party of Turkmenistan—still hold power, but in the mid-1990s, there seemed to be some internal tensions. Antigovernment demonstrations took place in 1995 as a result of disastrous economic conditions.

Government. Turkmenistan is a republic headed by a president. In the 1992 elections, Saparmurad Niyazov was the only candidate and won 99.5 percent of the vote. In a January 1994 referendum, he had his term extended by five years (until 2002).

IRINA RYBACEK / Reviewed by EDWARD W. WALKER, Ph.D., Columbia University

Tajikistan's Varzab River is fed by runoff from glaciers found on the towering Tien Shan mountains.

 # TAJIKISTAN

Tajikistan is a remote mountainous country in the heart of the Asian continent. For most of the 20th century, it was one of the 15 constituent republics of the Soviet Union. A civil and religious war in 1992 resulted in thousands of deaths (estimates vary from 20,000 to 100,000) and the displacement of about 600,000 people. In the mid-1990s, the country was in turmoil, with shortages of everything, including bread.

THE LAND

More than half of the republic's area lies at elevations above 10,000 ft. (3,049 m.). Two major mountain systems, the Pamirs and Tien Shan, dominate the eastern and central part of the country, with the highest peak of the former Soviet Union, Mount Communism, rising to 24,590 ft. (7,497 m.). Two lowland areas contain most of the population: the western part of the Fergana Valley, forming a northernmost promontory of Tajikistan, and the valleys south of the capital, **Dushanbe.**

The higher peaks are covered with snow year-round; there are also many glaciers, including one of the world's largest, the 50-mi. (80-km.)-long Fenchenko Glacier. The inaccessible wilderness supports rich animal life that includes deer, bear, wildcat, and an occasional Asian tiger.

THE PEOPLE

The Tajiks, who constitute 65 percent of the population, trace their origins back to 3000 B.C. They speak an Indo-European language of the Iranian branch, which is similar to the Farsi dialect of Afghanistan.

Physically, Tajiks often resemble Europeans; some have blond or red hair and blue eyes. Centuries-long intermingling, however, has erased any clear-cut ethnic distinctions.

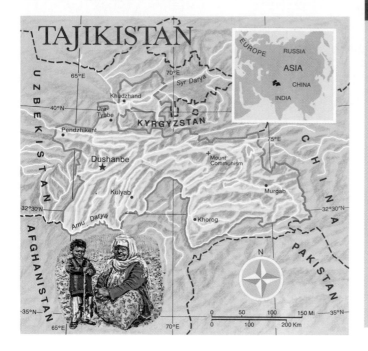

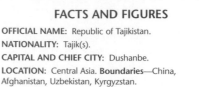

Uzbeks comprise the largest minority in the country (almost 24 percent), followed by Russians, Tatars, Germans, Kyrgyz, and Ukrainians. The country has the highest birthrate in Central Asia; about one-third of its population are children under age 9.

Way of Life. Despite many inroads of modern lifestyles, a great many inhabitants of this republic still live in a very traditional way. The typical settlement is a rural *qishlaq,* consisting of small, flat-roofed family houses built along a river. The national costume includes an embroidered skullcap known as a *tubeteyka.*

Religion. Of all the Central Asian republics, Tajikistan has the largest proportion of Muslims, about 85 percent of the population. Most belong to the Sunni branch, but some remote communities in easternmost Tajikistan, in the Gorno-Badakshan Autonomous Region, are Shi'ite Muslim. Even before the country became independent, Communist forces combated Islamic opposition, which was supported by Afghan fundamentalist *mujahidin.* In 1992, a full-scale war erupted. The heaviest fighting subsided in early 1993, but individual incidents have continued ever since, and the country remains unstable.

ECONOMY

Since prehistoric times, the inhabitants of this area had to use irrigation to produce crops. Cotton, fruits, and mulberry trees for silkworms have been cultivated for centuries; dried apricots, almonds, and grapes are important export items. New irrigation projects built in recent years have led to the expansion of wheat, barley, and rice cultivation.

Tajikistan has many minerals, particularly in the north. Coal and some precious and nonferrous metals are extracted, but much of the mineral wealth has not yet been tapped. There are also rich deposits of uranium, which caused some international worries when the country became independent. In early 1992, however, the Tajik president assured the United States that Tajikistan would not sell its uranium to any country to use in nuclear weapons. Industry includes textile production, food processing, and production of agricultural equipment and fertilizers.

Tajikistan was among the poorest of the Soviet republics, and the civil war of recent years has only made matters worse. About 35,000 houses were destroyed in the fighting and there are shortages of basic goods, building materials, water, gas, and medicines. The government depends heavily on Russian economic assistance.

HISTORY

Settled for several millennia, the region of present-day Tajikistan was among the conquests of Alexander the Great in 328 B.C. Successive conquerors include Persians, Arabs, Mongols, Turks, and Russians.

In the 1860s and 1870s, present-day Tajikistan became incorporated into the Russian Empire. In the early 1920s, the area was the scene of an anti-Communist revolt. In 1924 a Tajik Autonomous Region was created as part of Uzbekistan. Tajikistan attained the status of a full Soviet republic in 1929 and, from then until 1991, was firmly controlled by Moscow.

The End of the Soviet Era. In August 1991, Tajikistan's Communist president, Kakhar M. Makhkamov, backed the leaders of the coup in Moscow. When the hard-line coup failed, Makhkamov resigned. His successor outlawed the Communist Party and declared Tajikistan's independence. The Communists, however, quickly struck back. In October 1991 a former Communist Party boss, Rakhman Nabiyev, was elected president by a slim majority. This comeback was violently opposed by pro-Islamic forces, which deposed Nabiyev in September 1992. Two months later, the ruling Islamic faction was in turn ousted, and Emomali Rakhmonov, a Communist backed by Moscow, took over. He was elected president in November 1994, but observers claimed that the election was fraudulent.

Tajikistan has continued to be one of the major trouble spots of the former Soviet Union. In the mid-1990s, the government tried to introduce some minor economic reforms, including the issuance of a new currency —the Tajik ruble—but these efforts have not brought relief. As long as the religious and civil war continues, there is little hope for economic recovery.

The religious conflict has been exacerbated by rivalries between various clans whose members continue to fight with each other. There have been a number of political murders as well. The Commonwealth of Independent States (CIS) maintains a force of about 25,000 troops (mainly Russian) on the Tajik-Afghan border, but because it is such a remote region, few journalists go there. Only occasionally does a report appear about a new bloody clash.

GOVERNMENT

The pro-Russian government has outlawed all political parties and organizations except the Communist Party, and a tight police regime has been in force since late 1992. Talks between representatives of the Tajik government and the Tajik opposition in exile, begun in the spring of 1994, have brought no peaceful settlement. A new constitution was approved in a referendum in November 1994.

IRINA RYBACEK / Reviewed by EDWARD W. WALKER, Ph.D., Columbia University

Government buildings in Ulan Bator, Mongolia's capital, stand in the shadow of rolling hills.

MONGOLIA

Mongolia is a sparsely populated nation with more than twice the land area of Texas but only one-eighth that state's population. It shares the vast Mongolian Plateau with portions of China and Russia.

The plateau is the traditional home of the Mongol people. During the 13th century A.D., the various Mongol tribes, united under Genghis Khan, swept down from the plateau to carve out a great empire that eventually stretched from China to eastern Europe.

But the empire of the Mongols did not last. Only one-third of the 6 million Mongol people live in Mongolia today. Of the rest, 3.5 million live under Chinese rule and 500,000 live in Russia. Once called Outer Mongolia, this mountainous landlocked nation has now discarded Soviet domination and is headed forward on its own.

THE LAND

The Mongolian Plateau is made up of three general regions. The northwest is a massive mountain complex etched with river basins and featuring permanently snow-covered peaks rising to more than 14,300 ft. (4,300 m.). The central region consists of the Gobi, a great desert, and rolling, grass-covered plains dotted with oases. The southeast contains many mountain chains plus an extensive zone of lowlands. Mongolia covers a little less than half the plateau. It is bordered by Chinese territory to the south and east and Russian territory to the north.

On average, the nation sits about 1 mi. (1.609 km.) above sea level, with one peak reaching nearly three times that height. The continental climate is marked by limited rainfall and extremes in temperature. In Ulan Bator, the capital, January's temperatures average –17° F. (–27° C.). In July, at the height of the short summer, the average is 64° F. (18° C.).

Vegetation, Animal Life, and Mineral Resources. With the exception of the Gobi, most of Mongolia is prairie and grassland. This provides the Mongols, whose economy is based on stockbreeding, with excellent pastures. Mountains are generally treeless, except in the northwest.

Mongolia has more livestock per person—about 10 animals for each inhabitant—than any other country. The most important farm animals are camels, horses, cattle, yaks, sheep, and goats. Despite this abundance, Mongolia's city dwellers—about half the population—often suffered meat shortages, in part because Mongolia used to ship most of its meat to the Soviet Union.

Outside the cities, two-humped camels and compact horses provide the most common forms of transportation. Inside the cities, rubber-tired, horse-drawn carts are as plentiful as automobiles, trucks, and buses.

Wild animals are abundant and include valuable fur-bearing species, such as sable, ermine, marten, and fox. Minerals found in Mongolia include coal, iron, oil, copper, lead, silver, tungsten, and gold.

THE PEOPLE

The Mongols belong to one of the major racial divisions, the Mongoloid, of which they are the classic type. They make up about 90 percent of the nation's population, and are divided into numerous tribes with different dialects, customs, and dress. The major tribal group is the Khalkhas in the east, who number more than 1.5 million—about 78 percent of the population. Non-Khalkha Mongols—Durbets and others in the north, Darigangas in the east—number about 260,000.

Non-Mongol groups, including the Turkic-speaking Khotons, Kazakhs, and Tuvinians, account for six percent. The Khotons are farmers, while the Kazakhs and Tuvinians are stockbreeders like the Mongols. Another group is the Tungus, nomadic hunters who originated in Siberia. Small groups such as the Oirats in the west and the Buryats are emigrants from the former Soviet Union.

The Mongol Way of Life. Traditionally, all Mongols were nomads, who traveled with their livestock herds from season to season, seeking pasture. Their circular, felt tents, called yurts, were well-suited to the nomadic life. Their herds provided most of the family's food—meat, butter, cheese, and *airag,* or fermented mare's milk.

In recent years, remote Mongolia has greatly increased its contact with the outside world. Mongolian youth have taken a particular liking to Western rock music. With the end of one-party Communist rule in 1990, there was also a resurgence of interest in Mongol traditions, history, and culture.

MONGOLIA

After Mongolia became the world's second Communist nation in 1924, Mongolia's nomads were encouraged to settle down in fixed homes to work as farmers or to raise livestock on state-owned collectives. Others—just over half of all Mongolians—now live in Ulan Bator or other urban or semiurban centers. In 1990, the government formally renounced socialism and declared its intention to transform the country's economy into a free-market system. Many state enterprises were privatized, but pastureland remains under state ownership.

Urbanization has spawned a popular culture that includes such Western staples as rock music and blue jeans. The political reforms of the early 1990s were accompanied by a revival of traditional Mongolian culture, including the reintroduction of the traditional Mongolian script in the schools.

Wrestling, archery, and horse racing are the most popular sports. The Mongols have always been renowned for their horsemanship, and in rural areas riding is still a necessary skill.

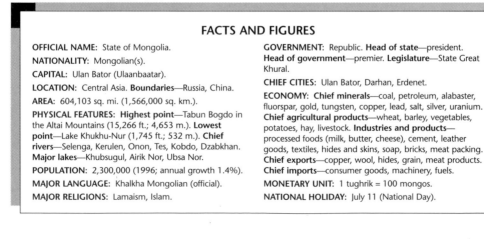

FACTS AND FIGURES

OFFICIAL NAME: State of Mongolia.

NATIONALITY: Mongolian(s).

CAPITAL: Ulan Bator (Ulaanbaatar).

LOCATION: Central Asia. **Boundaries**—Russia, China.

AREA: 604,103 sq. mi. (1,566,000 sq. km.).

PHYSICAL FEATURES: Highest point—Tabun Bogdo in the Altai Mountains (15,266 ft.; 4,653 m.). **Lowest point**—Lake Khukhu-Nur (1,745 ft.; 532 m.). **Chief rivers**—Selenga, Kerulen, Onon, Tes, Kobdo, Dzabkhan. **Major lakes**—Khubsugul, Airik Nor, Ubsa Nor.

POPULATION: 2,300,000 (1996; annual growth 1.4%).

MAJOR LANGUAGE: Khalkha Mongolian (official).

MAJOR RELIGIONS: Lamaism, Islam.

GOVERNMENT: Republic. **Head of state**—president. **Head of government**—premier. **Legislature**—State Great Khural.

CHIEF CITIES: Ulan Bator, Darhan, Erdenet.

ECONOMY: Chief minerals—coal, petroleum, alabaster, fluorspar, gold, tungsten, copper, lead, salt, silver, uranium. **Chief agricultural products**—wheat, barley, vegetables, potatoes, hay, livestock. **Industries and products**—processed foods (milk, butter, cheese), cement, leather goods, textiles, hides and skins, soap, bricks, meat packing. **Chief exports**—copper, wool, hides, grain, meat products. **Chief imports**—consumer goods, machinery, fuels.

MONETARY UNIT: 1 tughrik = 100 mongos.

NATIONAL HOLIDAY: July 11 (National Day).

Religion and Language. For years, Mongolia's Communist government suppressed religion, but its influence never died out completely. Shamanism, an ancient animistic faith, was at one time Outer Mongolia's main religion. It is still practiced in remote rural areas. Islam, practiced in the western provinces, is the religion of two of the Turkic peoples, the Kazakhs and the Khotons.

Lamaism, the Tibetan form of Buddhism, was introduced into Mongolia in the 1500s and became the state religion. For more than 300 years, the Jebtsun Damba Khutukhtu ("Living Buddha") was the Mongols' spiritual and secular ruler. The last Living Buddha died in 1924, the year Mongolia became a Communist state. At the time, Mongolia had about 800 monasteries and 100,000 Buddhist monks. By 1990, only one monastery remained open, and there were about 110 monks; however, a freer political climate has led to a religious revival and the reopening of many monasteries.

Of the various Mongolian dialects, the most important is the one spoken by the Khalkhas. It is Mongolia's official language. Originally, Khalkha Mongolian was written in a script that resembles Arabic. At Soviet urging, Mongolia adopted the Russian (Cyrillic) alphabet. But the old script reappeared as a nationalistic spirit spread across the nation in 1990.

Economy. Livestock remains the foundation of the Mongolian economy. It is also the basis of much of the country's industry. About 90 percent of Mongolia's exports consist of live animals and animal products, such as meat, butter, wool and hair, hides, and furs. Agricultural products, besides livestock, are mainly wheat, millet, oats, barley, hay fodder, potatoes, and vegetables. Coal mining is the most important mineral industry.

In the early 1990s, Mongolia began to transform its economy into a mix of state-owned and privately owned enterprises. The chief problem

The free, nationwide elections in Mongolia have reduced the domination of the Communist Party.

of the economic transformation is the heritage of dependency. By 1994, Japan and the United States had replaced the Soviet-bloc countries as the major foreign-aid donors. Despite some $300 million of aid already delivered and about $400 million more promised, the results have been discouraging: prices and unemployment have risen, and there are shortages of everything, particularly energy. Meat, bread, flour, and other staples are rationed.

Cities. **Ulan Bator**, the capital and largest city of Mongolia, has a population of nearly 700,000. It is the economic center of the country and the seat of government. With Soviet aid, Ulan Bator developed into a modern city with broad avenues, a university, museums, hotels, housing developments, and an airport. Other Mongolian cities include **Choibalsan**, **Uliassutai**, **Tsetserlik**, and **Sukhe Bator**.

HISTORY AND GOVERNMENT

Many kingdoms and peoples rose and declined on the Mongolian Plateau. But it was not until Genghis Khan united the various warring tribes in the early 1200s that the Mongols created their great empire. After his death in 1227, portions of the empire were administered by his sons and grandsons, under the leadership of one son elected as khan, or ruler, of all the Mongols. By 1260, the empire had been divided into several khanates, and its unity had been destroyed.

The chief khanate, comprising China and Mongolia, was ruled from Beijing by Kublai Khan, a grandson of Genghis Khan. It was known as the Yüan dynasty in China and lasted until 1368. After the Manchus conquered China in 1644, they gradually extended their power to Mongolia. By the mid-1700s, they had overrun the entire Mongolian Plateau.

The Chinese revolution of 1911 gave the Outer Mongolians a brief chance to assert their independence under Russian protection. In 1919, the nation became a Chinese province once more. Soviet troops with some Mongolian units marched into Urga (now Ulan Bator, or "Red Hero") in 1921. In 1924, Outer Mongolia declared itself the Mongolian People's Republic. Technically still part of China, it was in fact a self-governing satellite of the Soviet Union.

The efforts of post-Communist Mongolian leaders to turn the country into an independent sovereign nation have been hampered by the "feed-me" mentality created by a 70-year dependence on Moscow in political and economic matters. To emphasize their unique Mongol history, the present rulers are reclaiming the medieval hero Genghis Khan.

Government. In 1990, the Communists' constitutionally sanctioned monopoly on power was ended and opposition parties were permitted to field candidates for the Khural, or national assembly. The new Khural, in which the Communists retained a majority, set to work on a constitution. Adopted in January 1992, the new constitution renounced socialism, proclaimed Mongolia a parliamentary republic headed by a popularly elected president, and committed the country to neutrality in international affairs.

In June 1996, the democratic opposition won a sensational landslide victory and received 50 seats in the Khural, against 25 seats won by Communists. The election marked the definitive fall of Communism in Mongolia.

TAO CHENG, Trenton State College

One-quarter of the world's people live in East Asia, many in huge cities like China's Shanghai.

EAST ASIA

Signs of change—and of a kind of tug-of-war between traditional and modern ways—appear everywhere:

• A teenage girl in Nagasaki, Japan, dreams of a career in medical research. Yet each week she pauses in her studies to attend a class in the ancient Japanese art of ceremonial tea making.

• A family with roots in Hong Kong for generations wonders if it should quit that British colony before 1997, when China is scheduled to take administrative control.

• In Beijing, China, a street sweeper brandishes a broom made of bundled sticks while standing beneath a huge billboard that promotes Japanese-made electronic appliances.

• In Taiwan, the 18-year-old son of a rice farmer takes a job in a factory that builds high-tech computer components.

Since World War II ended in 1945, East Asians like these have experienced the most dizzying sort of political, economic, and social change. During that time, East Asia served as a mammoth testing ground for competing ideas on economic development. China and North Korea experimented with socialist approaches to development. Japan, South Korea, Taiwan, Hong Kong, and Macau put their faith in government-assisted free enterprise. The results, so far incomplete, directly affect more than 1.4 billion people, and through them, the rest of the world.

East Asians make up 25 percent of the world's people. Yet they inhabit less than 7 percent of the world's land, only a small fraction of which sustains crops. As the region's nations and territories move into the future, the harsh reality of scarce resources and bulging populations informs every major decision their governments make.

THE LAND

East Asia covers a huge area. East to west, it extends 3,800 mi. (6,080 km.) from Japan's eastern edge to China's western border with Tajikistan, Kyrgyzstan, and Kazakhstan. North to south, it stretches about 2,700 mi. (4,320 km.) from China's northernmost point in Manchuria to its southern island of Hainan.

Geographically, the region is immensely varied. Much of western and northwestern China is desert and semidesert, for example, and 14 percent of China's land is forest and woodland. River valleys and coastal plains provide fertile farmland for this basically agricultural region.

Yet the dominating feature of East Asia's landscape is its height. More than two-thirds of China consists of high plateaus, mountains, and upland hills. The Korean Peninsula is a largely mountainous plateau that juts southeast from China. South Korea's highest peak rises, not on the peninsula, but on Cheju, a volcanic island off the southern coast. A spectacular mountain range covers two-thirds of the island of Taiwan. Northeast of Taiwan, Japan's major islands are dominated almost completely by steep mountains, hills, and volcanoes. Insular Hong Kong sits on a rugged granite ridge. Of all of East Asia's separate political entities, only tiny Macau, the Portuguese colony 17 mi. (27 km.) west of Hong Kong, is uniformly low and flat. East Asia's rugged topography has meant that most people in the region live where their ancestors did, along the fertile and often painstakingly irrigated coastal plains.

Islands—East Asia has nearly 7,000 of them—are another characteristic of the region. More than 400 islands lie off China's 9,000-mi. (14,481-km.) coast, including the islands of Hong Kong, Macau, and Taiwan. About 3,000 more are scattered off the western and eastern shores of the

YANGTZE RIVER (CHANG jIANG)

To the Chinese, it is known as Chang Jiang ("long river"), and it is the wellspring of much of China's history and life. To the rest of the world, it is better known as the Yangtze—the longest river in Asia and the third-longest in the world. Originating high in Qinghai Province in the Tibetan Highlands, the Yangtze alternately rages and flows 3,430 mi. (5,520 km.) through eight provinces, past some of the world's most breathtaking scenery, to its mouth in the East China Sea. Together with its tributaries, the Yalong (Yalung), Min, Jialing, and Han rivers, the Yangtze carries millions of tons of freight a year, and its delta provides the Chinese with their chief rice-growing region. Along its banks lie some of China's major cities—Chongqing, Wuhan, and Nanjing—whose commercial importance is due largely to this mighty river. And the area drained by the river is one of the most densely populated in China.

From its source, the Yangtze rushes first east and then south through Qinghai

YANGTZE RIVER

Korean Peninsula. Most Japanese live on the four largest of the nation's 3,000 islands and islets. All told, East Asia has 31,831 mi. (51,340 km.) of shoreline.

The sea plays a vital role in East Asians' lives. It is a major source of food, and it provides the lanes over which ships carry goods to and from the rest of the world. Container ports in Japan, South Korea, Taiwan, and Hong Kong are among the largest in the world.

Centuries ago, the sea played another role, enabling many distinctive cultures to form and flourish in isolation. Japan's remoteness kept its people free from the domination of others for thousands of years. On the continent, mountains and vast deserts served as barriers to all but the most intrepid travelers and warriors. Ways of life as unique and fascinating as those of Xizang (Tibet) and neighboring Xinjiang (Sinkiang) were the result.

The Climate

East Asia's climate varies with its geography. In China alone, geographers have noted seven distinct climate zones. Winters are extremely cold in the northeast, where winds blow down from Siberia. The winds come off the Pacific Ocean during the summer, bringing warm and humid air.

Summers are also warm and humid in central China, which is sometimes subjected to tropical typhoons and cyclones. Winter temperatures rarely drop below freezing there.

South China—including Taiwan, Hong Kong, and Macau—experiences a tropical-monsoon climate, with short, mild winters and hot, humid summers. Typhoons bring heavy rains off the South China Sea.

and Yunnan provinces. Turning sharply eastward again, it flows snakelike across Yunnan and into the fertile Red Basin of Sichuan (Szechwan) province. At the city of Batang, some 600 mi. (960 km.) from its source, the river begins a series of spectacular falls that lower its level from 16,000 ft. (4,800 m.) above sea level to 630 ft. (190 m.) by the time it reaches Chongqing. Called by various names in its upper course, the Yangtze proper begins at Yibin (Ipin), south of Chongqing, where it merges with the Min River. Here the river first becomes navigable for small boats. About 250 mi. (400 km.) from Chongqing lies the gateway to the magnificent triple gorges of the Yangtze. Their names—Bellows Gorge, Witches' Gorge, and the Gorge of the Western Grave—evoke both their beauty and the terror with which they are regarded by sailors who must navigate the tortuous twists and turns.

At Jichang, the gorges end, and the river takes a more leisurely course on its journey to the sea. Beyond Jichang, the Yangtze is choked with junks, sampans, and other small rivercraft, which form virtual floating cities. At this point, the river also becomes navigable for oceangoing ships. Here the lower course of the Yangtze begins.

The triple city of Wuhan, one of China's greatest industrial centers, lies on the Yangtze's lower course, at its junction with the Han River. At Wuhan is the Yangtze Bridge, which links north and south China. This double-deck steel bridge, built in 1957, is considered by many Chinese to be one of their great modern engineering feats. Past Wuhan, the river courses northwest until, near Shanghai, it finally empties into the East China Sea.

Reviewed by C. T. HU, Columbia University
Coauthor, *China: Its People, Its Society, Its Culture*

YELLOW RIVER (HUANG HE)

The Yellow River (in Chinese, Huang He) has been called China's Sorrow. For this great river, which was the cradle of China's civilization, has often threatened to ruin that civilization by floods. The unpredictable waters of the vast river have destroyed millions of lives and acres of farmland. For the people who live along the river's banks, life is a constant gamble. For this reason, few cities have grown up on the river's banks—Lanzhou (Lanchow), Kaifeng, Zhengzhou (Chengchow), and Jinan (Tsinan), are the most important. And although the river is the second-longest in China (after the Yangtze), its waters defy navigation in all but a few places.

From its source in the Tibetan Highlands of Qinghai (Tsinghai) province, the

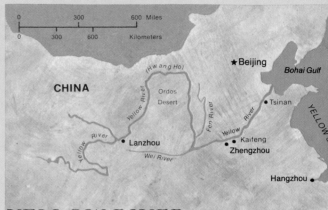

YELLOW RIVER

Yellow River begins its 2,900-mi. (4,700-km.) journey eastward across North China to its mouth in the Gulf of Chihli (or Bo Hai), an arm of the Yellow Sea. The course of the river has changed many times in its history.

Southwest China, a largely mountainous zone bordering Vietnam, Laos, and Myanmar, experiences mild winters and, in the mountains, cool, rainy summers. In the west, Xizang's high plateau, surrounded by mountains, experiences severe winters and mild summers. Xinjiang has an arid desert climate, cold in the winter and oven-hot during the summer.

Summers in the mountain ranges and semidesert lowlands of northern Xinjiang and Nei Monggol (Inner Mongolia) are warm, with July temperatures topping off around 82° F. (28° C.). Winter winds whip down from Siberia, making this climate zone as bitterly cold as those in the northeast.

North China's climate has a direct effect on the climates of the Korean Peninsula and Japan. Winters on the Korean Peninsula are intensely cold, due to the monsoon winds that bring frigid, dry air from Siberia and North China. The same winds cross the Sea of Japan, picking up moisture and depositing it as heavy snow on the west coasts of northern Honshu and Hokkaido, Japan's northernmost island. But because it is surrounded by the sea, Japan never experiences winter temperatures as cold as those on the continent, and its climate, in fact, bears resemblance to that of the eastern United States.

Summer months on the Korean Peninsula are hot, and most years during the summer or early fall, a typhoon swoops off the South China Sea, bringing hurricane-force winds and torrential rain.

Japan is often subjected to the same typhoons. In addition, its oceanic climate often makes the summer air so moist that it gives the heat an oppressive feel.

At one time, it flowed into the East China Sea.

One of the few places where the Yellow River is navigable for small vessels is the Mu Us (Ordos) loop in Nei Monggol (Inner Mongolia). This stretch of the river encircles the Mu Us Shamo (Ordos Desert). Beyond the Mu Us loop, the river is joined by its main tributaries, the Wei and Fen rivers. From here the river passes through a series of gorges that form the entryway to the great plain of North China. This fertile plain of the Yellow River covers parts of five provinces and merges with the Yangtze River plain to the south. Here, where the Yangtze and Yellow River valleys converge, was the center of the early imperial dynasties of China. In this area, too, the yellow-colored deposits of silt (tiny particles of rock) that give the river its color and name begin to accumulate. The flooding of the river is caused mainly by the continual buildup of silt, which elevates the water level above the surrounding plain. Although dikes have been built, they are often unable to hold back the floodwaters.

Because of the floods, the vast agricultural potential of the Yellow River delta has never been realized. The Chinese embanked and deepened the river for the first time about 220 B.C., and efforts to check its raging waters have continued since that time. The Grand Canal, constructed in ancient times to connect the Yellow and Yangtze rivers, now extends from Beijing to Hangzhou (Hangchow), a distance of some 1,200 mi. (1,900 km.), but much of it is choked with silt. The canal is now being rebuilt as part of a long-term plan to control the Yellow River to make it work for, not against, the people of China.

Reviewed by C. T. HU, Columbia University
Coauthor, *China: Its People, Its Society, Its Culture*

THE PEOPLE

Digging near China's capital of Beijing in 1927, archaeologists discovered "Peking Man," the fossil remains of an extinct species of human known as *homo erectus*. Members of this species stood erect when they moved, and they learned to use tools and fire and to hunt game. Fossil remains suggest that they lived in several parts of the world roughly 300,000 to 1 million years ago.

Today's humans belong to the species of *homo sapiens* (thinking man), and, in East Asia, the dominant racial group is Mongoloid. The characteristics of this group include straight black hair, medium stature, and dark, almond-shaped eyes.

Ethnic Variety. The three main cultural areas—China, Japan, and the Korean Peninsula—each have relatively homogeneous populations. About 94 percent of all Chinese are Han Chinese, the nation's dominant group. The remainder belong to 55 different ethnic groups. Among the largest are the Zhuang (Chuang), Uighur, Hui, Yi, Tibetan, and Miao.

Koreans are also a distinct ethnic group. A small Chinese minority lives in South Korea.

Japan's population is virtually all Japanese. Among the non-Japanese are several thousand Ainu, an indigenous group in northern Japan, and a sizable Korean community.

Languages. East Asians speak many different languages. Chinese has a number of variations, including Putonghua (Mandarin), Yue (Cantonese), Wu (Shanghainese), and Minnan (Hokkien-Taiwanese). Putonghua, the dialect of Beijing, is the official language of China and Taiwan. More people speak it than any other language in the world.

China's Tibetan, Mongolian, Zhuang, Uighur, and other minorities speak their own languages. Yue and English are the official languages of Hong Kong. Portuguese is Macau's official language, although most business is conducted in Yue.

In origin, Japanese and Korean appear to be unrelated not just to Chinese but to each other. Japanese and Korean do have similar grammatical structures, however, leading some scholars to suggest a kinship between the two. Others see a faint link to the Altaic family of languages, which includes Mongolian and Turkish. These links are unproven. Japanese and Koreans both originally took their forms of writing from Chinese ideographs (picture writing), adapting them to their own needs.

Shared Influences. China's civilization has had a deep impact on the Korean and Japanese civilizations. The Koreans borrowed their form of rural housing and settlement patterns from the Chinese. Koreans also took from the Chinese—and passed on to the Japanese—a good portion of their vocabulary and their knowledge of stock breeding, musical instruments, and certain Buddhist beliefs. Ideas and skills that the Japanese later borrowed directly from China helped them create an advanced society in Japan. The values taught by the Chinese philosopher Confucius (551–479 B.C.) and his disciples still shape the thoughts and actions of today's Japanese and Koreans, especially those in South Korea. The Communist governments of North Korea and China weakened their citizens' ties to Confucianism, which encourages family loyalty, in an effort to shift individual loyalty to the state.

Way of Life. East Asians live in cultures that are blends of the ancient and the new. The technology at the disposal of ordinary citizens varies according to the local level of economic development. Farmers in China, the two Koreas, and Taiwan often plow their fields with water buffalo, while those in Japan generally use modern farm machinery. People in Beijing and Shanghai often bicycle to work, while those in Hong Kong have the option of riding aboard gleaming subways. Many Japanese commuters take high-speed "bullet trains" to and from their jobs.

Living conditions vary, too. In Nei Monggol (Inner Mongolia), most people live settled lives. But some still follow herds of livestock and inhabit portable houses called yurts. In Hong Kong, millions are housed in towering apartment complexes. Thousands of families live on small boats in Hong Kong's harbor. In Japan, where urban living space is scarce, the average family lives in a two-room apartment, with everyone sleeping in the same room.

China's large and growing population also experiences cramped conditions, especially in the cities, where several families in one apartment building may share a single toilet and kitchen. In the countryside, most peasants make do without electricity in small houses with wood-fueled stoves.

Religion. Throughout East Asia, the worship of spirits (animism) and of ancestors was once widespread. But the Communist governments of China and North Korea have largely eradicated the practice in their countries. Reverence for ancestors remains strong elsewhere in East Asia, however, especially in Japan, where it is incorporated into Japan's native religion, Shinto.

Most of the world's religions have adherents throughout East Asia, even in China, which lifted its opposition to religious observance during

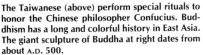

The Taiwanese (above) perform special rituals to honor the Chinese philosopher Confucius. Buddhism has a long and colorful history in East Asia. The giant sculpture of Buddha at right dates from about A.D. 500.

the 1980s. Religion is unlikely ever again to become a major force in China, however. Still, among minority groups—the Tibetan Buddhists, for example, or the Uighur Muslims—religion remains important. Among other Chinese, Taoism and Buddhism are still vital to millions. The nation also contains more than 20 million Muslims and 10 million Christians.

Buddhism is the most important religion in South Korea, Taiwan, Hong Kong, and Macau. But other religions are strong there, too. About 10 percent of all Taiwanese and 28 percent of all South Koreans identify themselves as Christians. And although, strictly speaking, Confucianism is not a religion, South Koreans uphold its tenets with almost religious devotion.

HISTORY

Its size and varied topography make East Asia a source of many histories, not just one. Yet the histories of China, Korea, and Japan share many common themes.

The Formation of Nations

One of the world's earliest civilizations developed in China's fertile river valleys. China's early people were quick to learn the arts of growing wheat, making silk, working with bronze and then iron. Knowledge of these skills spread throughout East Asia as the Chinese civilization grew more powerful.

In 1990, Koreans held a march in favor of reunifying their country, divided since the end of World War II.

Between 600 B.C. and A.D. 900, the Chinese developed and expanded their empire. Under government supervision, canals were dug to irrigate more fields and to allow easier transportation of crops and goods. To tighten communication links and extend their rule throughout the land, succeeding dynasties built an elaborate network of roads.

Advances in civilization spread from China into the Korean Peninsula and from there to the Japanese islands. Between A.D. 200 and 400, a structured society took shape in Japan. Later, Japanese copied much that they liked about the Chinese way of life, including their imperial form of government. Some Japanese nobles even modeled their palaces and clothing after those of the Chinese.

Influences from the West

Contacts with the West grew after the Portuguese and Spanish reached China during the 1500s and the Dutch and English arrived during the early 1600s. Suspicious of the newcomers, the Chinese opened only the port of Guangzhou (Canton) to foreigners. Chinese opposition to imports from the West led to the Opium War with Great Britain (1839–1842). This war and another one with Britain and France (1858–60) resulted in more Chinese ports being open to trade, and to China's cession of Hong Kong to the British.

In 1853, the United States forced Japan to open its ports to Westerners. Japan lost no opportunity to learn from the West, and soon it had adopted such Western concepts as shipping ports, public education, and central banking, and such technologies as the telegraph, the steam engine, and gas lamps. Soon, Japan had become a major force in the region. It gained control of Korea and Taiwan in 1895. Japan won a war against Russia in 1905, becoming the first Asian nation to defeat a foreign power. In 1910, Japan annexed Korea.

China's central government disintegrated during the years after its last war against foreign influence, the Boxer Rebellion (1900). The nation became a republic in 1912, but was unable to achieve true unification until 1926. Soon afterward, a civil war began between the ruling Nationalist Party and the Communist Party. In 1937, both sides accepted an uneasy truce in order to confront the Japanese, who invaded that year. The conflict became global after the United States entered World War II against Japan in 1941.

After World War II

At the war's end in 1945, U.S. forces occupied southern Korea and Japan, and Soviet troops occupied northern Korea. Portuguese and British colonial administrators returned to Macau and Hong Kong, which the Japanese had occupied throughout the war. The Chinese government, in the hands of the Nationalist Party, regained Taiwan.

In 1949, Communist forces took over China and renamed it the People's Republic of China. The Nationalists fled to Taiwan, where they set up the Republic of China's government-in-exile. Now China had two governments, each claiming to be the rightful leader of all China.

In 1948, Korea also got two governments: the Democratic People's Republic of Korea in the north and the Republic of Korea in the south. In 1950, hoping to reunite the nation under Communist rule, soldiers from the north attacked the south. Three years of fierce warfare ended with a truce. All East Asian nations and territories then turned to the task of developing their economies from the ground up.

By the 1990s, China and North Korea had made great advances in industrializing their economies. But nowhere were the gains described almost universally as "miraculous" as in South Korea, Hong Kong, Taiwan, and Japan.

The Economic Transformation

When the wars stopped—1945, for Japan, Macau, and Hong Kong; 1949, for China and Taiwan; 1953, for North and South Korea—the immediate task was to pick up the pieces. Picking up the pieces meant building, or rebuilding and extending, the roads, railways, ports, and government structures without which no modern economy can function.

To achieve their economic and social goals, the Chinese and the North Koreans copied the Soviet economic and political model. In part, that meant Communist Party control of the government, and tight government control and ownership of all land and economic enterprises. All farms were collectivized, or brought together in large units and worked, not by individual farmers, but by brigades of them. Industries were nationalized, and government planners went to work setting prices for all goods. All workers became government employees.

Japan, Taiwan, South Korea, Hong Kong, and Macau took a different path. Their governments created conditions that allowed privately owned enterprises to flourish. In Japan, Taiwan, and South Korea, land was redistributed to small farmers, who were encouraged to use modern farming methods. Their governments—and those of Hong Kong and Macau as well—invested heavily in public-works projects, creating employment and essential facilities like ports and railroads. In some cases the governments built and ran industries to produce materials such as steel that are basic to all manufacturing. Finally, they encouraged the development of businesses that manufacture products for sale abroad.

This export orientation was crucial. Exports were the only way these resource-poor nations could earn money to import the food, fuel, and raw materials that they needed to survive.

This free-enterprise recipe was extraordinarily successful. It enabled Japan, with a population half that of the United States, to become the world's third-largest economy in terms of the value of the goods and services it produces each year. In 1990, Japan's income, divided among its citizens, became the highest of any nation's. Its exports sell so well abroad that Japan earns many billions of dollars more than it can possibly spend on imports. By the year 2000, it has been estimated that Japan, with 2 percent of the world's population, will be producing 15 percent of the world's products.

Though far smaller than Japan's economy, South Korea's export-oriented economy expanded during the 1970s and 1980s with astonishing speed. Since 1988, South Korea has ranked among the world's top 10 trading nations.

Taiwan's economy grew about 4,000 percent during the 1970s and 1980s—four times faster than the world economy as a whole. Hong Kong, another robust free-market economy, exports about 90 percent of its manufactured goods.

The two socialist nations, North Korea and China, also made great economic progress. In both nations, people today are better off in terms of housing, health care, and education than their forebears were at mid-century. In an attempt to achieve more rapid modernization, China adopted some of the elements of a free-market economy during the late 1970s, 1980s, and early 1990s. Among other moves, it permitted individual farmers and entrepreneurs to make a profit from their work. By contrast, North Korea remains adamantly opposed to such moves.

Although China's national income, divided among its citizens, had increased to about $2,500 a year by the mid-1990s, it remains one of Asia's poorest nations, burdened by its enormous population. North Korea's per-capita income during this same period was only about $900 per year. These figures compare with about $10,000 in Macau, more than $11,000 in South Korea, $12,000 in Taiwan, and nearly $25,000 in Hong Kong. An economic slowdown caused Japan's per-capita income to decline from more than $25,000 in 1990 to about $20,000 in 1994.

THE FUTURE

In a region where change has been so rapid and in many ways unexpected, one can only wonder about the future. How powerful will East Asian economies become, and how will their leaders use that power? Will China and North Korea move closer to a free-market economy? How much political give-and-take will the traditionally authoritarian governments of South Korea and Taiwan be willing to accept? How will the prosperity of Hong Kong and Macau be affected when China resumes control late in the 1990s? As the overall economy of East Asia begins to rival that of Western nations, how will the world react? Amid these questions and scores of others, the only certainty for East Asia over the next century is more change—change that builds on the extraordinary dynamism of the 1990s.

The 1,500-mile-long Great Wall of China is the longest such fortification ever built.

CHINA

Students of China, the world's oldest continuous civilization, tend to divide their studies into two parts. The first part deals with traditional China—the civilization from ancient times to the coming of the West in the mid-1800s. The second area of study deals with modern China, emphasizing the many changes that have taken place since the 1800s.

China in the traditional period has often been described as changeless. By contrast, modern China has undergone sweeping changes in virtually all its institutions—political, economic, and social. In 1949, a Communist revolution sought to achieve an egalitarian society quickly by extreme, radical measures. A "second revolution" began in the 1980s, emphasizing economic modernization and reforms to achieve a higher standard of living for China's masses.

Many people find all these changes bewildering. Yet it is necessary to understand them, for what happens to more than 1 billion Chinese—one-fifth of the human race—also affects the entire world.

THE LAND

In land area, China is the third-largest country in the world, surpassed only by Russia and Canada. It lies almost entirely within the temperate zone, north of the Tropic of Cancer, and it has a wide variety of geographical features. Within China's borders are tall mountains, great rivers, fertile plains, and forbidding deserts. In size as well as latitude and climate, China and the United States are generally comparable. Beijing (Peking), China's capital, is only one degree farther north than Washington, D.C., the U.S. capital.

Most of China is covered with mountains, hills, and plateaus. Only about 12 percent of the land consists of plains.

China's Regions. China's mountains and great rivers both extend from west to east, dividing the country into three distinct regions. The first, in the west, embraces the lofty highlands of Xizang (Tibet). The second, to the north of Xizang, is the Xinjiang–Nei Monggol (Sinkiang–Inner Mongolia) region. Large parts of these two regions consist of mountains, deserts (including the great Gobi in Nei Monggol), or high plateaus that are suitable only for pasture. Although these two regions comprise about half of China's land area, they contain only about 5 percent of its people.

The third major region is Eastern China, where 95 percent of the population is concentrated. In contrast to the west and northwest, where one can travel for days without seeing a single person, the fertile plains of Eastern China are crowded with millions of people engaged in farming. Eastern China also contains the nation's most important industrial centers.

Eastern China is itself composed of three subregions: the Northeast (Manchuria), the North, and the South. These subregions are divided by mountain ranges and differ significantly in vegetation and climate. China's three major rivers—the Huang He (Yellow River), the Xijiang (Si Kiang), and the Chang Jiang (Yangtze), China's longest river—flow through the farmlands of the North and South and serve as important inland navigation routes.

FACTS AND FIGURES

OFFICIAL NAME: People's Republic of China.

NATIONALITY: Chinese.

CAPITAL: Beijing.

LOCATION: Eastern Asia. **Boundaries**—Mongolia, Russia, Kazakhstan, Kyrgyzstan, Tajikistan, North Korea, Yellow Sea, East China Sea, Hong Kong, Macau, South China Sea, Gulf of Tonkin, Vietnam, Laos, Myanmar, India, Bhutan, Nepal, Pakistan, Afghanistan.

AREA: 3,705,390 sq. mi. (9,596,961 sq. km.).

PHYSICAL FEATURES: Highest point—Mount Everest on China-Nepal border (29,028 ft.; 8,851 m.). **Lowest point**—Turfan Depression (below sea level). **Chief rivers**—Chang Jiang (Yangtze), Huang He (Yellow), Si (West), Amur. **Major lakes**—Tungting, Poyang, Tai, Hongze.

POPULATION: 1,217,600,000 (1996; annual growth 1.1%).

MAJOR LANGUAGES: Chinese in various dialects, notably Mandarin (official), Shanghai, Hakka, Hokkien, Cantonese.

MAJOR RELIGIONS: Mixture of Confucian, Daoist, and Buddhist beliefs and practices; Islam; Christianity.

GOVERNMENT: Communist republic. **Head of state**—president. **Head of government**—premier. Effective power is exercised by the leaders of the Chinese Communist Party. **Legislature**—unicameral National People's Congress.

CHIEF CITIES: Shanghai, Beijing, Tianjin, Shenyang, Wuhan, Guangzhou, Harbin, Chongqing, Nanjing, Xián, Lüda (Dairen), Chengdu, Changchun, Taiyuan.

ECONOMY: Chief minerals—petroleum, natural gas, coal, lignite, iron, bauxite, tin, tungsten, lead, copper, antimony, uranium. **Chief agricultural products**—rice, wheat, maize, sorghum, cotton, oilseeds, sugarcane, tea, tobacco, rubber. **Industries and products**—livestock raising (hogs, sheep, cattle), fishing, iron and steel, textiles, agricultural machinery and implements, chemical fertilizers, vehicles, household goods. **Chief exports**—textiles, garments, electronic equipment, petroleum and petroleum products, foodstuffs, crude materials, manufactured goods. **Chief imports**—machinery and vehicles, chemicals, manufactured goods, steel, yarn, fertilizers.

MONETARY UNIT: 1 yuan = 100 fen.

NATIONAL HOLIDAY: October 1 (National Day).

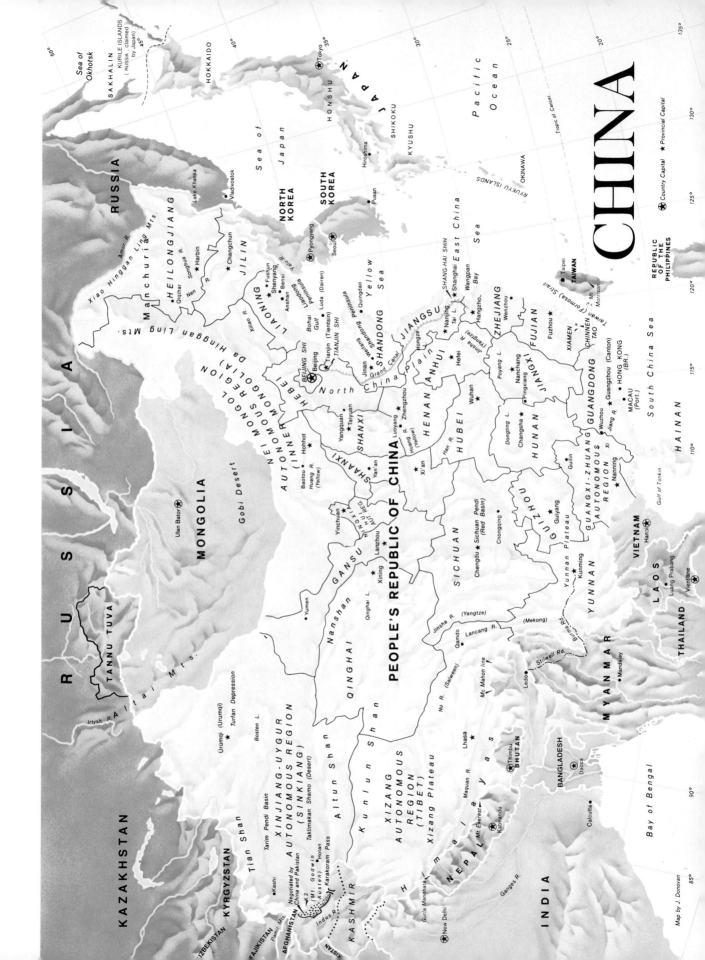

CHINA

⊕ Country Capital   ★ Provincial Capital

REPUBLIC OF THE PHILIPPINES

Tropic of Cancer

Pacific Ocean

Sea of Okhotsk

SAKHALIN

KURILE ISLANDS (RUSSIA, claimed by Japan)

HOKKAIDO

RUSSIA

Amur R.

Xiao Hinggan Ling Mts.

Lake Khanka

Vladivostok

Manchuria Mts.

HEILONGJIANG

Qiqihar

Harbin

Songhua R.

Nen R.

Changchun

JILIN

Xiliao R.

Da Hinggan Ling Mts.

LIAONING

Fushun

Shenyang

Benxi

Anshan

Liaodong Peninsula

Luda (Dairen)

Bohai Gulf

JAPAN

HONSHU

Tokyo

Hiroshima

KYUSHU

SHIKOKU

Sea of Japan

NORTH KOREA

Pyongyang

SOUTH KOREA

Seoul

Pusan

Yalu R.

NEI MONGGOL AUTONOMOUS REGION (INNER MONGOLIA)

Hohhot

Baotou

Huang R. (Yellow)

MONGOLIA

Ulan Bator

Gobi Desert

Yumen

TANNU TUVA

Altai Mts.

Irtysh R.

KAZAKHSTAN

KYRGYZSTAN

Tian Shan

Ürümqi (Urumqi)

Bosten L.

Turfan Depression

Tarim Pendi Basin

Kashi

XINJIANG-UYGUR AUTONOMOUS REGION (SINKIANG)

Taklimakan Shamo (Desert)

Holan

K. Godwin (Mt. Austen)

Karakoram Pass

Negotiated by China and Pakistan

Pamir Mts.

AFGHANISTAN

KASHMIR

Indus R.

PAKISTAN

UZBEKISTAN

TAJIKISTAN

Guria Mandhata

New Delhi

INDIA

Ganges R.

Calcutta

Bay of Bengal

BANGLADESH

Dacca

NEPAL

Mt. Everest

Kathmandu

Thimbu

BHUTAN

H i m a l a y a s

Lhasa

Maquan R.

XIZANG AUTONOMOUS REGION (TIBET)

Xizang Plateau

Kunlun Shan

Altun Shan

QINGHAI

Qinghai L.

Xining

Nanshan

GANSU

Lanzhou

Yinchuan

NINGXIA HUI AUT. REG.

SHAANXI

Yan'an

Xi'an

Taiyuan

SHANXI

Yangquan

HEBEI

BEIJING SHI

Beijing

Tianjin (Tientsin)

TIANJIN SHI

North China Plain

Grand Canal

Huang R. (Yellow)

Jinan

SHANDONG

Zhengzhou

Luoyang

HENAN

JIANGSU

Nanjing

Tai L.

Hongze

SHANG-HAI SHIH

Shanghai

Wuhan

Hefei

ANHUI

Han R.

Changsha

HUBEI

Yangtze R.

Hangzhou

Wangpan Bay

ZHEJIANG

Wenzhou

East China Sea

Yellow Sea

Weihai

Shandong Peninsula

Qingdao

Jinsha R. (Yangtze)

Chengdu

SICHUAN

Sichuan Pendi (Red Basin)

Chongqing

Qamdo

Lancang R.

Nu R. (Salween)

Mekong

Mc Mahon line

Stilwell Rd.

Ledo

Burma Rd.

MYANMAR

Mandalay

THAILAND

LAOS

Luang Prabang

Vientiane

VIETNAM

Hanoi

YUNNAN

Kunming

Yunnan Plateau

GUIZHOU

Guiyang

Guizhou Plateau

GUANGXI-ZHUANG AUTONOMOUS REGION

Nanning

HUNAN

Dongting L.

Pingxiang

Nanchang

Poyang L.

JIANGXI

FUJIAN

Fuzhou

Wenzhou

ZHEJIANG

Gulf of Tonkin

HAINAN

Xi Jiang R.

Wuzhou

Guilin

Gulin

GUANGDONG

Guangzhou (Canton)

HONG KONG (BR.)

MACAU (Port.)

South China Sea

XIAMEN

CHINNEN TAO

Taiwan (Formosa) Strait

Taipei

TAIWAN

Mt. Morrison

RYUKYU ISLANDS

OKINAWA

PEOPLE'S REPUBLIC OF CHINA

Map by J. Donovan

The shape of China's coastline is determined to a great extent by its hill systems. North of Hangzhou (Hangchow) Bay, with the exception of the Liaodong (Liaotung) and Shandong (Shantung) peninsulas, the coast has low, sandy beaches. South of Hangzhou Bay, the coast is generally rocky.

Internally, China is divided into 23 provinces, three municipalities (Beijing, Shanghai, and Tianjin [Tientsin]), and five autonomous regions. Smaller administrative units control local affairs. China considers Taiwan its 23rd province. The Nationalist government in Taipei, Taiwan's capital, also regards Taiwan as a Chinese province, and claims to be the nation's sole legitimate government. In the late 1990s, Great Britain and Portugal will turn the colonies of Hong Kong and Macau (Macao), on the Chinese coast, over to China. (Separate articles on TAIWAN, HONG KONG, and MACAU appear in this volume.)

Climate. China's vast size accounts for numerous variations in its climate. In the winter, cold, dry air flows down from the plateaus of the northwest, making China colder than any other part of the world at the same latitude. In the summer, warm, wet air flows inland from the South China Sea, and most of the country is hot and humid. Heavy rains at that time cause frequent floods. In August and September, typhoons strike the southeast coast, causing great destruction.

Temperatures in China vary from region to region. Winter temperatures in northern Manchuria may fall to −17° F. (−27° C.). By contrast, the

XINJIANG: CHINA'S "NEW DOMINION"

The Xinjiang-Uygur Autonomous Region comes as a surprise to travelers who are familiar only with the people and terrain of Eastern China. Larger than most European nations and mostly desert, Xinjiang accounts for 17 percent of China's land and little more than 1 percent of its people.

The region's nearly 15 million people occupy a network of oases on the lower slopes and valleys of the Tien Shan and Pamir mountain systems. China's lowest point, 505 ft. (154 m.) below sea level, is found here, at the center of the Turfan Depression. This basin covers about a third of Xinjiang (pronounced *shin-chyahng*). Many people who live on its ingeniously irrigated oases descend into underground shelters to escape the peak hours of summer heat.

The People. Xinjiang is the home of some 7 million Uygurs, a dark-skinned people who speak a language related to Turkish. Like the Kazakhs and the Kirghiz, two smaller Turkic groups who live in Xinjiang, the Uygurs are practicing Muslims. They trace their history back to the Uygur kingdom that flourished in Xinjiang from the 900s to the 1100s, and before that to a nomadic people that in the 500s established an empire from Mongolia to the Black Sea. Small numbers of Mongols, Uzbeks, Hui, and members of other "national minorities" also live in Xinjiang. And so do millions of Han-Chinese, China's dominant ethnic group, many having been moved there from Eastern China after 1949.

Xinjiang's people earn their living primarily as farmers and herders of yaks, camels, horses, sheep, and cattle. In recent years, however, the development of mineral resources, especially oil, has increased the size of the industrial labor force.

Village Life. The Uygurs, members of the Sunni branch of Islam, have built numerous places of worship throughout their settlements. Although several hundred thousand live in Xinjiang's capital, Ürümqi,

temperature in the tropical south at the same time may reach a balmy 68° F. (20° C.).

Far more rain falls on south China than on north China. Rain is heaviest in the southeast, ranging from 60 to 80 in. (152 to 203 cm.) annually. It steadily decreases toward the north and northwest to less than 10 in. (25 cm.). In north China, rainfall occurs almost exclusively during the summer months. In the south, there is some rain every month, although most falls during the summer.

The growing season for crops varies with the regions. In the far northeast, it is less than 140 days. Along the tropical south China coast, crops can be grown all year long.

Animal and Plant Life.   China has a wealth of animal life. Among the larger mammals are different species of deer and bear, the giant panda, kiang (wild ass), wild boar, tigers, leopards, wolves, and monkeys. Valuable fur-bearing animals like sable, marten, mink, and fox are found in the north and northeast. Rodents and various kinds of birds abound. Snakes, alligators, and tortoises are also found. Since the 1970s, the government has set up more than 60 nature preserves.

Freshwater fish, which form an important part of the Chinese diet, include perch, shad, sturgeon, bass, and pike. Hogs, sheep, and goats are the most important domestic animals raised for food. The chief work animals are donkeys, oxen, camels, occasionally horses, and, in the south, water buffalo.

most Uygurs are village people, and their lives are centered on village affairs.

During most days of the year, they dress like other Chinese, except for the men's embroidered skullcaps, whose pattern varies according to region. On feast days and holy days, they wear traditional clothes. Women are especially striking in tight-waisted dresses, jangling jewelry, gaily embroidered vests, and colorful caps and veils.

The Silk Road. In traditional China, Xinjiang was a bridge between East and West. Trade caravans that were headed for the Middle East or India along the "Silk Road" halted at the region's oases for water, food, and other supplies. These routes brought two major religions to Xinjiang—Buddhism, from India, and much later Islam, from the Middle East. Between A.D. 200 and 900, thousands of caves were dug out of cliffs and decorated to Buddha's glory. Islam, first brought to Xinjiang by Muslim traders in the late 600s, gradually supplanted Buddhism as the region's major religion.

New Dominion. From time to time, powerful Chinese imperial dynasties imposed their rule on the region. In the 1700s, the Qing (Manchu) dynasty seized the region and later named it Xinjiang, which means "New Dominion." The Communist government renamed it the Xinjiang-Uygur Autonomous Region in 1955, implying more independence than actually exists.

Xinjiang is militarily important to China, because it is sandwiched between Mongolia, Kazakhstan, Kyrgyzstan, and Tajikistan on the north, and Pakistan, India, and Xizang (Tibet) on the south. For this reason, China has often moved quickly to suppress minority demands for more rights. In 1985, Uygur students staged demonstrations in Beijing, Shanghai, and Ürümqi. They called for an end to nuclear testing in the region, the relaxation of family-planning regulations, and increased rights for minorities. In 1990, Chinese troops put down an uprising south of the ancient trading center of Kashgar, near the Soviet border.

China's vast territory includes many different types of terrain. The deserts and semi-arid grasslands of Inner Mongolia (top) lend themselves to raising horses and other livestock. Terraced fields (above) bring even steep hillsides under cultivation in south China. The exotic karst scenery of cone-shaped mountains in Guangxi (left) has long inspired Chinese painters.

Forests were cleared in China's main agricultural areas centuries ago. Today, only about 12 percent of the land is covered with forests, mainly in Manchuria and the thinly populated parts of the northwest and southwest. Trees used mainly for timber are the evergreens, oak, elm, and birch. There is a wide range of fruit trees, shrubs, and flowering plants.

China's major food grains are wheat, which is grown in the north, and rice, which is grown in the south. Other food grains include millet, barley, and sorghum, grown mainly in the north, and corn. Vegetables are the main supplement to grains in the Chinese diet. China also produces soybeans, tea, cotton, jute, bamboo, and tobacco.

Mineral Resources. China is well endowed with most of the important ores, fuels, and other minerals used by industry. It is one of the world's leading producers of coal, its most important mineral. There are smaller deposits of iron ore, much of it in Manchuria. China is the world's largest producer of antimony and tungsten.

Though coal provides about two-thirds of the energy China uses, the development of large onshore and offshore oil and natural-gas reserves plays an expanding role in China's economy. China sells crude oil to other nations and is the world's tenth-largest producer of natural gas.

THE PEOPLE

About nine of every 10 Chinese live on only 15 percent of China's land—for the most part, the 11 percent of the land that supports crop growth. The most heavily populated and most intensely cultivated regions are in the eastern part of China: Manchuria, the North China Plain, the middle and lower Chang Jiang River valleys, and the southeast. The eastern coastal province of Jiangsu (Kiangsu), for example, has over 1,000 people per sq. mi. (2.59 sq. km.). Population density decreases sharply toward the northwestern and western borders of China. Nei Monggol has fewer than 30 persons per sq. mi. (2.59 sq. km.), and Xizang, the most sparsely populated region, fewer than three.

Confronting Urbanization

While nearly eight out of every 10 Chinese live in the countryside, more than 200 million live in cities. Some 20 cities have populations of over 1 million. China's seven largest cities and their surrounding areas contain close to 50 million people—an average of 7 million per city. Shanghai, China's largest city, has nearly 13 million people in its metropolitan area.

China's cities would be much larger if the government had not taken steps in the 1950s to check the flow of people from the countryside. Living standards in China's cities are two or three times higher than those in rural villages, in large part because the state has built most industries in urban areas. The wide social and economic gap between country and city has caused some resentment in the villages. But villagers cannot just pick up and move to the cities. Except in extraordinary circumstances, such a move has been against the law since 1958.

The law was prompted by the flood of rural people into the cities after 1949, as jobs opened up in expanding city industries. Government officials became alarmed. Providing housing, water, electricity, and sewage systems for the new migrants was costly, and officials feared that the newcomers would create squatter settlements if they couldn't find housing. Over the years, the government has actually resettled millions of city dwellers in the countryside to relieve crowding.

The legal barriers to migration are maintained partly by a rationing system. In the cities, ration coupons are needed to buy grain, oil, and other food staples. But the coupons are good only in their own localities. In addition, city police make unannounced inspections, usually at night, to look for people who do not have legal permission to live in a city.

A comparatively small proportion of China's enormous population lives in the cities. Still, simply through natural increase (the Chinese population doubled between 1950 and 1990), urban areas (above) are rapidly becoming overcrowded. The government is trying to control the explosive growth rate by campaigning for smaller families. Official policy calls for couples to limit themselves to one child (right).

Slowing Population Growth

China has also had great success in slowing down overall population growth. Between 1950 and 1990, China's population doubled in size, from 563 million to more than 1.1 billion. Such growth poses a serious problem. For although China can feed its newborns, population growth of that magnitude, if permitted to continue, would prevent the nation from achieving a high standard of living. China remains one of the world's poorest nations, despite enormous gains in industry and agriculture since 1950.

To control rapid population growth, the government launched a massive campaign in the mid-1970s to encourage young people to marry late and have few children. In the 1980s, the government called for a target family size of three, and introduced incentives to limit the number of children to one or, in special circumstances, two. These measures helped slow population growth dramatically. Nonetheless, China continues to have about 18 million new mouths to feed each year—a heavy drain on its resources.

Ethnic Diversity

The vast majority of the people of China—about 94 percent—are known as Han-Chinese. Han was the name of the first long-lasting imperial dynasty (206 B.C.–A.D. 220). All the Han use a common written form of Chinese and share the same cultural characteristics. They occupy the most productive agricultural areas of China.

China also has many different minority peoples, ranging numerically from a few thousand each to almost 8 million. The larger nationalities have been organized by the Communist government into so-called autonomous (self-governing) regions. At present, there are five such regions, designated for the Zhuang (Chuang), the Uighurs, the Hui (Chinese Muslims), the Tibetans, and the Mongols.

The Zhuang.   With a population of more than 8 million, the Zhuang are the largest minority group in China. They are concentrated mainly in south central China, in the Guangxi (Kwangsi) Autonomous Region. Others live in Yunnan and Guangdong (Kwangtung) provinces. The Zhuang are a settled agricultural people, like the Han. They have had long and extensive contacts with the Han and are culturally more assimilated with the Han-Chinese than the other ethnic groups. However, their spoken language and some of their customs are somewhat different.

The Uygurs.   The Uygurs, numbering about 7 million, live in the Xinjiang-Uygur Autonomous Region. They speak a language related to Turkish, and practice the religion of Islam. They are primarily farmers. (See sidebar, page 380.)

The Hui.   These are descendants of Chinese who adopted Islam. There are more than 4 million Hui, and they are indistinguishable from the Han. Most live in northwest China, where the Ningxia (Ningsia) Hui Autonomous Region was created in 1958. Other Hui communities are found in Gansu (Kansu), Xinjiang, Qinghai (Tsinghai), Hebei (Hopei), and Yunnan provinces.

The Tibetans.   Historically, the most nationalistic of the minority areas has been Xizang (Tibet). There are about 5 million Tibetans, but only about 1.4 million of them live in Xizang, where about 500,000 Han Chinese also live. Most of the rest live under Chinese rule elsewhere in China. A majority of those in Xizang are farmers, although several thousand are nomadic herders, roaming about the region's northern plateau with flocks of yaks, sheep, horses, and camels. Tibetans are followers of the Lamaist version of Buddhism. Priest-kings called Dalai Lamas ruled Xizang for centuries under China's protection. From 1911 to 1950, it was an independent nation. (See sidebar, page 386).

The Mongols.   The Mongols, who number about 3 million, live in the Nei Monggol Autonomous Region (Inner Mongolia), in the Northeast, and in Northwest China. The typical Mongol is either a nomad, who

LAMAISM: XIZANG'S "STATE RELIGION"

Visitors to Xizang (Tibet) are usually fascinated by its ancient culture, and most of all with the intensity of its Buddhist religion. The Tibetan form of Buddhism is known as *Lamaism*. The Tibetan word *lama* means "superior one." Xizang's lamas are monks who act as religious teachers and spiritual guides.

In Xizang (pronounced *sit-sang*), Lamaism is an integral part of daily life. Paths throughout this former kingdom are lined with small shrines, and in thousands of places, prayer flags flutter in the wind. On the streets, ordinary people regularly spin cylinders, called prayer wheels, that contain written prayers. Long lines of pilgrims at every major religious site indicate that the oppression during the early decades of Communist rule did little to weaken Lamaism's power. Tibetans may be the most religious people in the world.

Origins of Lamaism. Buddhism was established in Xizang after A.D. 700 by a monk from India, where the religion originated. Named Padmasambhava ("born of the lotus"), he founded Xizang's first monastery and order of monks. The religion spread rapidly, mingling with rituals from Xizang's traditional religion, Bon, which involved a belief in spirits and magic.

travels with herds of sheep, goats, cattle, and horses, or, where soil conditions permit, he is a settled farmer. The settled Mongols outnumber the nomads. The Mongols are also followers of Lamaism.

Pressures on Minorities. Under Communism, China redoubled its efforts to achieve greater national unity, in part by finding ways to integrate the many ethnically and culturally different minorities into the national fold. The government adopted severe measures against all social and political groups that were identified with the interests of the national minorities. After putting down a Tibetan revolt in 1959, for example, the government began a systematic attempt to suppress Tibetan culture.

Taking another tack, the government ordered many thousands of young men and women in China to settle in the border regions, where most of the minorities live. The goal was not just to dampen regional nationalism with the influx of Han-Chinese, but also to ease the tensions caused by the large concentrations of young people in China proper.

The branch of Buddhism that is the basis of Lamaism is *Mahayana*. It resembles Christianity in significant ways, for it, too, is concerned with the afterlife and the salvation of the individual. Mahayana Buddhism teaches that the souls of good people go to a paradise where they enjoy eternal bliss, but usually only after living through several incarnations, or lives, with the actions in one life having moral consequences in the next. The wicked are consigned to numerous hells.

Ritual. The worship of Lamaism consists chiefly in the recitation of prayers and sacred texts, and in the chanting of hymns accompanied by the music of horns, trumpets, and drums. Lamas, who at one time added up to 20 percent of Xizang's population, are summoned to worship three times a day by the tolling of a bell. They are seated in rows according to their rank. Religious rites include the use of rosaries, prayer wheels, prayer flags, holy relics, talismans, and mystical incantations.

On holidays, the temples, shrines, and altars of the lamas are decorated with symbolic figures. Worshipers bring offerings of milk, butter, tea, and flour.

Dalai Lamas. During the late 1200s, Kublai Khan, the Mongol conqueror who became emperor of China, made Lamaism the state religion of his empire. He also appointed a high-ranking lama as priest-king of Western Xizang. Three hundred years later, Altan Khan, a Mongolian chieftain, gave Xizang's priest-king the title of Dalai Lama and bestowed it posthumously on the priest-king's two dead predecessors. *Dalai* is the Mongolian word for "ocean," marking the Dalai Lama as someone whose superiority and wisdom are "ocean-wide." Xizang's Buddhists believe that Dalai Lamas are reincarnations of the first of the line. A Dalai Lama is succeeded, after his death, by a toddler that a committee decides is the reincarnation of the first Dalai Lama.

The 14th Dalai Lama fled Xizang with more than 100,000 of his followers in 1959, after a failed uprising against Chinese rule. Between 1960 and 1980, the number of lamas actively practicing their vocation inside Xizang is thought to have dropped from 110,000 to several thousand. The people nonetheless remained devout. Most monasteries were closed or destroyed before the Beijing government became more tolerant of religious observance. The Dalai Lama, still a sort of god to millions of Tibetans, lives in India, some 1,300 mi. (2,092 km.) from Xizang's capital city of Lhasa. In 1989, he was awarded the Nobel Peace Prize for his nonviolent struggle to regain autonomy for his homeland. His goal is a self-governing Xizang, with China in charge of defense and foreign affairs—something the Chinese say they will never permit.

Following the death of Mao Zedong (Mao Tse-tung) in 1976, the government softened its policy toward the autonomous regions. The nation's minorities are now allowed to observe their traditional customs and religions and to speak their own languages. Religious freedom has been largely restored. Most of the Tibetan monasteries and temples destroyed during the Cultural Revolution are being rebuilt.

Values and Religion

Traditionally, the Chinese believed that the world was peopled not only by human beings but also by supernatural forces that accounted for happenings that were obviously not man-made. They worshiped gods of all sorts—harvest gods, river gods, town gods, kitchen gods, gods of disease, gods of war, and many others. But the Chinese did not recognize one awesome, supreme divinity in the same manner as Jews, Christians, and Muslims do.

The government has grown more tolerant of religion. Devout Buddhists still perform traditional ceremonies.

Their relationship with the spiritual forces, the gods, and the ancestors was ritualized. They paid homage to the spirits, offered sacrifices, and sometimes engaged in fasts and meditations. However, the main purpose was to achieve harmony between people and the "other world," largely by appeasing the gods and spirits.

Ancestor Worship. The oldest and most widespread of religious practices in traditional China was ancestor worship. At one time, most homes had a small altar with wooden tablets inscribed with the names, titles, and birth and death dates of the deceased members of the family. Offerings of food and wine were made to the ancestors, who, it was believed, watched over their descendants as guardians and benefactors.

Confucianism. China's traditional values derived from the teachings of Confucius (K'ung Fu-tzu), who lived from 551 to 479 B.C. Confucianism was not a religion with deities and a priesthood, but rather, a moral and social philosophy. It was taught in academies, and examinations for government jobs tested candidates' knowledge of a group of books that spelled out Confucian ideas.

Confucianism stressed the need for a harmonious social order based on strict ethical rules and respect for human dignity. According to Confucians, human nature is at its best in love between parents and children. For this reason, traditional Chinese placed great emphasis on the teaching of respect between parents and children. People who are respectful to their parents, Confucius taught, can be expected to be faithful to their

A stone statue of Kuan Yin (left), the goddess of mercy, dates from the 6th century A.D.

A statue of Buddha (right), dating from the T'ang dynasty (A.D. 618–906), is bronze covered with gold.

friends and loyal to their ruler. Confucians believed that the ideal, unified state required men of education and superior wisdom to lead it.

Taoism. Originally a philosophical system that developed in the 6th century B.C., Taoism emphasized harmony between man and nature and advocated passive behavior. Over the centuries, it became a religion, with gods, temples, and a priesthood. Taoism was very influential in China, but its importance faded as Buddhism's grew and the government gave official support to Confucianism, which used ancestor worship as a form of religious expression.

Buddhism. Coming to China from India around the beginning of the Christian era, Buddhism became China's predominant religion. The Buddhism that flourished in China was the Mahayana variety, which taught that everyone could attain salvation through faith and sincerity. Buddhism offered an outlet for those concerned with the "other world."

Islam. Although Islam existed in China as early as the 700s, its spread was slow. Today, an estimated 25 million Muslims are scattered throughout the country. They tend to isolate themselves from non-Muslim Chinese, and to try to preserve their customs and religious rituals. Islam is based on the belief in one God, named Allah, whose prophet was Muhammad.

Christianity. Not until the arrival of Jesuit missionaries in the 1500s did Christianity begin to win important converts in China. Many Jesuits —members of the Society of Jesus, a Roman Catholic religious order—

became favorites at the imperial court and were given official posts. The modern phase of Christian missionary work began at the time of China's defeat by European powers in the mid-1800s. Christianity teaches that hope is found in God's love, perfectly expressed in Jesus Christ and offered freely to all. More than 11 million Chinese share these beliefs.

The Government and Religion.   Until the death of Mao Zedong in 1976, organized religion was scorned by the Communist government, which considered all forms of religion to be superstition. Christians were persecuted most severely, because of their former ties with foreign missionaries. Christian churches were closed and never reopened. Taoist and Buddhist organizations were stripped of their priesthoods and their main source of income, their lands. Their temples were turned into warehouses or meeting places. During the frenzy of the Cultural Revolution in the 1960s, Red Guards wrecked temples, religious statues, and home ancestral tablets. Only Islam was permitted to exist as an organized religion, in large part because China wished to maintain good relations with the governments of Muslim countries.

In 1978, the government revised its policy toward religion and became more tolerant. Much of traditional ritual survives or has been revived, especially in the countryside. With its energy dissipated, however, it is unlikely that religion in China will ever again become a major force among the majority of people.

The Changing Family

In traditional China, the family was the cornerstone of the society. Keeping the family together from generation to generation was considered the most important task of its members. Allegiance to one's family, including distant cousins, was considered more binding than allegiance to the state.

Family size and structure in traditional China varied according to social position. Well-to-do rural landlords and government officials had the largest families, and poor peasants had the smallest. As a rule, three generations—grandparents, their children, and grandchildren—lived under the same roof as an extended family.

In modern times, however, particularly under the Communist regime, this traditional pattern of the family has drastically changed. For one thing, state-sanctioned organizations compete with the family for members' loyalty. Among such groups are the Young Pioneers, for children; the Communist Youth League, for teenagers; and, for adults, work units and the 47-million-member Communist Party. For another thing, the family is no longer solely responsible for its members' economic security. The state, acting through work units such as the factory, workshop, or cooperative, provides support and benefits when the family cannot. Three-generation families can still be found in the cities as well as rural villages. Yet the extended-family pattern has largely given way under Communism to the nuclear pattern—parents and children living in one house, the grandparents in another.

Nonetheless, the family is still vitally important in China, especially in the countryside. Peasant families are required by law to support their aged or disabled members. Also, since 1979, the family has been the most important unit of production, as it was before 1949. In 1979, families were allowed to rent land from the state, and their incomes were linked

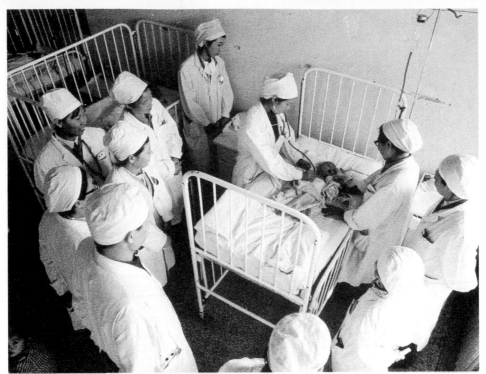

Since 1949, better medical care and public health have nearly doubled the life expectancy at birth.

to their output. This shift signaled the decline of the government's 30-year effort to attach families to larger units—mutual-aid teams of up to a dozen families, collectives of 20 to 30 households, and combinations of collectives called communes.

In 1987, a typical farm family had five or six members, which was about the same size as a moderately well-off peasant family in traditional China. Most urban families are smaller.

Both the state and society expect children, especially sons, to look after their elderly parents. Often, however, grandparents are the ideal solution to the child-care and housework problems of younger couples.

Marriage

The belief in the perpetuation of life through the family explains in part the importance that the Chinese attached to marriage in traditional China. Marriages were arranged by parents and elders, and children were expected to comply with their wishes. In 1950, the Marriage Law guaranteed everyone the freedom to choose his or her marriage partner. However, many children, especially in the countryside, still rely on parents to make matches for them. In rural China, there are relatively few opportunities to meet potential mates, and little privacy for courtship. As a result, parental introductions and professional matchmakers continue to play a major role in arranging marriages. In most cases, each of the young people has the right to veto a proposed marriage.

Urban families play a limited role in marriage arrangements. This reflects the diminished role of city families in providing long-term security and benefits for their members. City dwellers are as likely to find mates within their work units or other organizations as they are from introductions by parents and relatives.

Modern China has experienced dramatic changes on the retail level. Most Chinese have discarded their drab "Mao" outfits for more stylish Western fashions (above). Economic reforms have made food (left) and many consumer goods readily available, though often at high prices.

Urban weddings are usually smaller and more subdued than those in the countryside. More guests will be work-unit friends of the bride and groom than distant kin or associates of the parents. The wedding ceremony focuses on the bride and groom as a couple rather than as members of families. For a city couple, a brief honeymoon trip takes the place of the three-day celebration in which the entire village takes part in the countryside.

Women

In traditional Chinese society, women were expected to be subordinate to fathers, husbands, and adult sons. A young woman had little to say in the decision about her marriage partner. When married, she had to leave her family's home and village to live in a family and community of strangers, where she would be subservient to her mother-in-law. Far fewer women than men were educated.

Today, the position of women has changed greatly. The Marriage Law of 1950 gave women full legal equality with men. Women with sufficient reason can sue their husbands for divorce, and many have done so. Women now attend universities, serve in the People's Liberation Army, and join the Communist Party.

The greatest change in women's status has been their movement into the paid labor force. Almost all urban women and the majority of rural women work outside their homes. Both in cities and in the countryside, nurseries have been set up for the care of small children. Usually these nurseries employ elderly women, so that the younger ones may work or go to school.

In many respects, however, women remain disadvantaged. Generally the jobs they hold in industry are lower-paying and less desirable than those of men. In the countryside, male workers are also better rewarded than female workers, and most skilled jobs are held by men. In addition, Chinese women, like working women everywhere, suffer the double burden of full-time work outside the home and most of the chores in the home as well.

Educational opportunities for young women remain more limited than those for men. There are fewer female students than male students in both rural and urban secondary schools and universities.

The Chinese government encourages all of its citizens to engage in some sort of daily exercise.

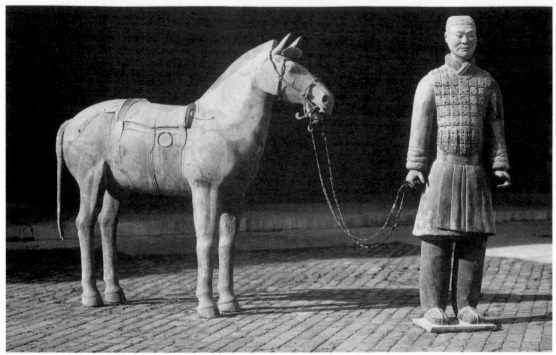

The soldier and horse above are part of an "army" of 7,000 life-size sculptures found buried near the tomb of Ch'in Shih-huang-ti, the first Chinese emperor.

CHINA'S PAST

During China's long history, a number of patterns were established. One of them was the continuous expansion of the Chinese people from their original home in the North China Plain. In time, the country's vast territory, large population, and cultural achievements made it the dominant civilization in East Asia. Neighbors like Korea, Annam (now part of Vietnam), Burma (now called Myanmar), and others paid tribute to the Chinese emperors.

Because of its geographical isolation, China had relatively little contact with other centers of civilization until modern times. As a result, the Chinese gradually came to consider themselves as the center of the civilized world. They considered all other people barbarians who could be civilized only by exposure to Chinese culture.

Chinese Dynasties. China became a unified empire in the 3rd century B.C., after which there was a long succession of imperial dynasties, or ruling families. Some of them were long-lasting, notably the Han (206 B.C.–A.D. 220), the T'ang (A.D. 618–907), the Ming (1368–1644); and the last imperial dynasty, the Qing, or Manchu (1644–1912). In between were a number of short-lived dynasties, some lasting less than 20 years.

Most of the dynasties were founded and ruled by the Han-Chinese. Occasionally, however, people on China's northern borders defeated Chinese armies and established themselves as rulers of the Chinese empire. The best known are the Yuan, founded by the Mongol leader Kublai Khan in 1260, and the Qing, founded by the Manchus from Manchuria.

Chinese dynasties rose and fell in a cyclical pattern. A new dynasty usually came to power after a period of disunity and civil war. Once established, it enjoyed a period of stability and economic prosperity. This period was followed by a period of disintegration and collapse, paving the way for a new dynasty.

Unifying Factors.   The relatively changeless character of traditional China was largely due to Confucianism, a moral philosophy that dominated Chinese life for more than 2,000 years. The teachings of Confucius stressed the need for a harmonious social order based on strict ethical principles. Education in Confucianism was the chief method by which people became government officials. Their knowledge of four key Confucian texts was tested in competitive civil service examinations that were held at regular intervals. Only a small portion of the candidates passed.

In theory, old China had four classes: scholars, farmers, craftsmen, and merchants, in that order. Farmers were held in high esteem because they produced the nation's food. Merchants were held in contempt because they produced nothing themselves, but merely bought and sold. In reality, however, there were just two classes: the ruling class of Confucian scholars, and everyone else.

Yet people could move up in the social order. It was not uncommon for a farmer's son to receive a classical Confucian education and become a government official. Women were not allowed to compete in the examinations, although some of them, especially those from upper-class families, were educated at home.

The Chinese written language, as well as the broad acceptance of Confucianism, served as a strong unifying factor in the nation's past. The Chinese spoke many different dialects, and still do. Even today, residents of Beijing may not understand the speech of a person from Shanghai. But they can read each other's newspapers without difficulty, because the Chinese written language has been the same since the 3rd century B.C. (See sidebar, page 402.)

Another major force contributing to Chinese unity was the centralized state. The imperial government had a great deal of control over all parts of the country, and even illiterate peasants assumed that rule by an emperor and an administrative bureaucracy was the norm.

CHINA IN MODERN TIMES

The modern era of China's history began not so much because of great changes within China itself but because of the coming of the West. In the early 1800s, China was still very much an isolated empire in East Asia that clung to its age-old civilization. The collision between the dynamic West and tradition-bound China has been likened to an irresistible force meeting an immovable object.

The first clash, often called the Opium War of 1839, occurred when Great Britain used force to open China to trade. China's defeat resulted in the signing of the first of a series of "unequal treaties." Each time China was defeated by one or more Western powers, it lost some of its territories and some of its rights as an independent state. In addition, the Western powers and Japan claimed "spheres of influence" in all parts of China. By the end of the 1800s, the once-great empire of China was virtually reduced to the status of a colony.

Creation of the Republic

Foreign aggression and devastating internal rebellions combined to sap the strength of the decaying Manchu dynasty. At the same time, new ideas of democracy, nationalism, and individualism, brought to China by the Western powers, attracted increasingly large numbers of Chinese

金世界无产者同被压迫人民、被压迫民族联合起来，反对

Wall posters seen almost everywhere in China extol the virtues of the Chinese Communist system.

intellectuals. Some advocated reforms; others worked for a revolution. While the reformers met with little success, the revolutionaries under Dr. Sun Yat-sen (1866–1925) overthrew the Manchu dynasty and established a republic in 1912.

With no real military power to support him, Sun Yat-sen was soon forced to give up his position as provisional president of the republic in favor of Yuan Shikai, the former commander of the imperial army. Yuan undermined the new parliamentary system of government and sought to restore the monarchy with himself as emperor. He died of natural causes in 1916 amid widespread rebellions. A period dominated by "warlords" began as military leaders in various parts of the country fought each other for control of the central government in Beijing.

Meanwhile, the revolutionaries under Sun Yat-sen organized the Guomindang (Kuomintang), or Nationalist Party, and developed a base in South China. After Sun's death in 1925, leadership of the Guomindang gradually was assumed by Jiang Jieshi (also spelled Chiang Kai-shek). In 1926, Jiang led his army on a northern expedition against the warlords. He defeated most of them and finally established a new national government, the Republic of China, in Nanjing (Nanking).

China under Jiang suffered from internal dissension and threats from abroad. Within China, the Communist Party, founded in 1921, challenged the authority of the Guomindang government and staged armed rebellions. The threat from abroad was a militaristic Japan bent on expanding its empire by conquest in China. In 1931, the Japanese took the first step, occupying the northern province of Manchuria.

Communist Defeat and Victory.   During the early 1930s, Jiang's armies succeeded in ousting the Communists from their bases in South China and drove them to the remote northwest. The Communist retreat became famous as the "Long March." Under Jiang's leadership, the Nationalist government pushed forward with modernization plans and made impressive gains.

Fearing a unified and strong China, the Japanese attacked again in July 1937, beginning eight long years of a war of resistance. Threatened by a common enemy, the Nationalists and the Communists formed a cautious alliance.

When World War II ended, the Communist forces had grown in numbers and strength, while the Nationalist government was beset with problems. Prices soared, the morale of the Guomindang army sank, and the government lost popular support because of inefficiency and corruption. Despite efforts of the United States to bring peace between the two parties, civil war raged all over China.

In the end, Jiang and his government were forced to retreat to the island of Taiwan (Formosa). On October 1, 1949, the Communists under Mao Zedong proclaimed the founding of the People's Republic of China in the ancient city of Beijing.

The People's Republic

The Communists took control of a nation that was exhausted by two generations of conflict. They quickly set up political and economic structures that mimicked those of the Soviet Union: Communist Party control of the nation's government, and tight government control and ownership of all economic enterprises, from farming to industry.

During most of the 1950s, China's economy made great gains. Life began to improve for millions of people who only a few years before had been facing starvation.

But the political turmoil did not end with the Communist takeover. In some ways, it was a natural outgrowth of Communist ideology. In other ways, it was the result of disputes among Communist Party leaders over the goals of the revolution.

Ideology.   The idea of class struggle, or conflict, is an integral part of Communist thought. Even before the Communists came to power, Mao Zedong had portrayed China's people as members of several social classes. The workers and peasants—the "proletariat"—were to be the masters of the new society. They were to be supported by the army, officially called the People's Liberation Army, which was to be drawn from the ranks of the workers and peasants.

The landlords in the countryside and the capitalists in big cities were considered enemies of the proletariat. If they did not reform under the new order, they would be eliminated.

As it happened, the land-reform movements in the early 1950s did away with the landlords—millions were killed. At the same time, private property was confiscated or put under state control. The middle classes —the "bourgeoisie"—were screened according to their attitude toward the new regime. All were required to go through "thought reform," a type of intensive indoctrination, designed to make intellectuals and others accept the Maoist doctrine of socialism. In China of the 1950s, anyone with a high school education was considered an intellectual.

A typical midday meal for farm workers often includes rice, fresh fruit, and salted eggs.

Another source of turmoil was infighting among Party leaders. Since the beginning, the political history of the People's Republic has been marked by an ongoing power struggle between two main factions. In the early years, a radical faction, led by Mao, the Party chairman, was uncompromising in its emphasis on a classless society and a permanent revolution. Its goal was the complete elimination of social and economic inequalities in China.

In the early 1960s, after the failure of Mao's Great Leap Forward—a scheme to revitalize the economy quickly—a more moderate faction emerged. It was led by Liu Shaoqi (Liu Shao-chi), the state president, and his protégé, Deng Xiaoping (Teng Hsiao-ping), the general secretary of the Communist Party. This group thought that economic development was more important than ideology. It sought to raise living standards in China by modernizing the economy and offering profit and bonus incentives to increase production.

Cultural Revolution. Mao believed that material incentives were corrupting the masses and dragging the country back toward capitalism. In the spring of 1966, he launched a massive political attack on Liu, Deng, and other moderates. Millions of youths, organized as Red Guards, assaulted Party and state organizations, rooting out leaders who would not bend to the will of the radical faction. The movement, which became known as the Great Proletarian Cultural Revolution, produced so much violence and disorder that in time, Mao became alarmed and joined with the army to stop it.

The conflict between radical and moderate leaders continued behind the scenes, however, and in 1975, it erupted again. Mao's wife, Jiang Qing (Chiang Ching), and three associates of the Cultural Revolution, who were later dubbed the "Gang of Four," launched a media campaign against Deng. In the aftermath, Deng was stripped of all his official positions.

After Mao. The death of Mao in September 1976 touched off another scramble for power. Within one month, the Gang of Four was arrested and imprisoned amid public jubilation. In August 1977, the Communist Party leadership restored Deng to all his previous posts, symbolizing the growing consolidation of control by moderate Party officials opposed to the radicalism of the previous two decades.

In 1976, the leadership adopted economic-modernization policies aimed at increasing production and personal income. Some production for profit was permitted to both farmers and business enterprises, and foreign investment in China was approved. The result of these and other reform policies was to stimulate China's economic growth considerably.

The leadership also moved to meet the demands for greater freedom in almost all fields. Artists, writers, and journalists were encouraged to adopt more critical attitudes toward the government, although open attacks on the Party's authority were not permitted.

In December 1982, the National People's Congress adopted a new state constitution, the fourth since 1949. It provided a legal framework for reforms in China's social and economic institutions.

Efforts to change the political structure, however, were less successful. In the spring of 1989, students who wanted a more democratic government took over Tiananmen Square in Beijing, and their protest spread to 80 other cities throughout China. After some indecision, the government ordered the army to suppress the demonstrations. Soldiers killed

The Young Pioneers, inspired by Mao Zedong, played an active role in the Cultural Revolution.

In recent years, the housing for much of China's rural population has improved dramatically.

about 1,000 people in Beijing. Afterward as many as 10,000 people were arrested, although many of them were later released. As China celebrated the 45th anniversary of the Communist revolution in 1994, Deng's economic reforms continued, but political dissent still was not permitted.

CHINESE SOCIETY UNDER COMMUNISM

Life in the Countryside

A peasant's life is dictated as much by the seasons as by the state, which, for the first 30 years of Communist control, experimented with various ways of organizing rural society. In 1979, farm families were permitted to lease land from the state and keep earnings from the sale of surplus crops. This changed their lives, doubling their incomes in very short order, and many were able to purchase "luxuries"—better clothing, more efficient farm equipment, and sturdier homes. Many were able to move from their two- or three-room cottages, made of mud bricks and thatch, into new cottages of clay bricks, tiled roofs, and glass windows. (Windows are usually made of sealed paper stretched over a frame.)

Kerosene lamps provide light after dark, and a kerosene stove provides heat. On cold nights, ducts pipe heat from the stove through the beds, which are made of clay or brick. The rest of the furniture usually amounts to no more than a wooden table and six or seven wooden chairs, for family members at mealtime. Meals generally consist of vegetables and rice in the south, or vegetables and wheat or millet in the north. Poultry or pork is sometimes added.

The rhythm of farming differs, according to the region. North of the Chang Jiang (Yangtze) River, where land can be relatively dry, irrigation is a concern, and families spend a lot of time carrying or directing water to their fields. Winter wheat is planted in the fall and harvested during the summer, when soybeans and corn are planted. April and May, crops such as cotton and millet are planted. Plowing, planting, nurturing, and harvesting go on all year round, except in the winter, when families fix up their homes and farms.

Rice growing is the focus of most farm families' lives south of the Chang Jiang. Fields are plowed and fertilized in the early spring, flooded, and then planted with seedlings. Family members then weed the paddies constantly, letting the water run off as the rice plants mature. After harvesting and threshing, the fields are prepared once more, either for a second or third rice crop or for another cereal.

Life in the Cities

Urban families look to their work units—whether in a factory, newspaper, or government office—for the housing, old-age security, and other benefits that in the countryside are still the responsibility of the family. But while sickness benefits and pensions are relatively easy to obtain, housing is not.

Typically, a family of five has no more than two rooms, and shares a kitchen and toilet with several other families. Electric lighting, where it exists, is as often as not a bare 40-watt light bulb. Some city apartments have running water, though many families in crowded urban centers like Shanghai make do with street-level water taps and public toilets. In Shanghai, China's largest city, one in five residents had inadequate housing or none at all in 1990, according to government records. In the central city, nearly 1 million people had living space of less than 6 by 6 ft. (1.82 by 1.82 m.).

Guangzhou (Canton) is the leading city and chief port of south China.

Living space is cramped in China's cities because their populations more than doubled during a period when the government built very little new housing. More apartments were constructed between 1985 and 1990 than during the previous 30 years, yet space remains critically short. Young married couples, who enjoy priority in housing allocations, sometimes have to wait five years to be assigned a room of their own.

Once a couple is assigned a room or an apartment, it is likely to be in poor shape. Rents, which amount to only 2 to 10 percent of the average wage, fail to cover even the cost of repairs. The government of Shanghai announced plans to double rents in 1990, and it hoped to persuade workers to save money to buy their own homes.

For most city dwellers, that will be hard to do. Although they work six days a week, their wages are low. After basic expenses, they have only about 15 percent of their pay left over for clothing or to be saved for items such as sewing machines, televisions, and bicycles.

Despite these awesome housing problems, city dwellers are better off than their country cousins in many ways. They work less hard, for one thing. In order to spread the work around, factories hire more people than they need. Still, they must be at their places of work six days a week, get no vacation, and have only seven public holidays off each year.

HOW PEKING BECAME BEIJING

The world's oldest continuously used language, Chinese is spoken and written today by more people than any other language. Chinese writing goes back more than 3,500 years, to a time when major events were recorded on bone and shells.

Chinese is written with ideographs, or "characters," that represent word meanings rather than sounds. As a rule, a single character stands for each word. While written Chinese is uniform throughout the country, spoken Chinese varies from region to region. Yet the spoken dialect of one region is often incomprehensible to the people of another.

The Chinese written language now contains over 40,000 characters. A well-educated person might recognize 25,000 words, although no more than 5,000 are in common use. The difficulty of mastering written Chinese has contributed to China's high rate of illiteracy. In 1990, about 250 million Chinese were either totally or partly illiterate.

Language Reforms. To help more people learn to read and write, the government developed a three-part program of language reform. In 1956, the government adopted as the common spoken language of China a Beijing dialect known as *puthongua*. *Puthongua* was in use throughout China by 1977, although hundreds of regional dialects continued to be spoken.

A second language reform was the adoption of a simplified method of writing that reduced the number of strokes needed to form characters. Characters became easier to learn and write.

A third language reform was the creation of a new writing system that uses a Romanized alphabet. Known as *pinyin*, it was encouraged mainly to help spread *puthongua* in regions where other dialects are spoken. So far, however, its use has not become widespread. Most Chinese prefer to write with their traditional characters. However, *pinyin* has replaced more familiar spellings in China's English-language publications. The U.S. government has adopted *pinyin* spellings for all names of people and places in China. And that's how Mao Tse-tung became Mao Zedong and Peking became Beijing.

Many buildings in Shanghai, China's chief port and industrial center, show a strong European influence.

Urban workers rise early, often before first light. Women cook breakfasts of tea, vegetables, and a cereal such as rice gruel in communal kitchens or, if they are lucky, on a one-burner stove of their own. Before work, some workers exercise in a park before taking a bus or bicycling to the factory or workshop in which they are likely to remain for life.

Shanghai is an important city, and not just because of its huge, 12.8-million population. A port on the east coast of China, Shanghai underwent rapid development after the country was opened to trade with the West in the 1800s. It rose to become the main center of commerce, foreign trade, banking, industry, and shipping, as well as education and publishing.

Beijing, China's capital and second-largest city, has a population of about 8 million people. Lying in the North China Plain, it has existed since ancient times. Except for brief periods, it has been the capital for centuries. Today, Beijing is China's center of higher learning and culture as well as the seat of government.

Education

Since the Communist revolution in 1949, education in China has wavered between two goals: fostering social equality and furthering the nation's economic development. During the Great Leap Forward (1958–61) and the Cultural Revolution (1966–76), education sought to narrow the social gap between urban and rural populations, between workers and peasants, and to "rectify" the tendency of educated people to look down on manual labor.

Chinese kindergartens are run by groups ranging from the armed forces to neighborhood committees.

Economic development became education's main goal after Mao Zedong's death in 1976. Under Deng Xiaoping's leadership, schools stressed vocational and technical skills needed to help China modernize and to produce "more able people." In 1985, all children were required to attend school for nine years, a reform that was implemented in about 75 percent of China by 1995. School attendance was higher in major cities and developed coastal areas and lower in rural areas and small towns.

Primary Schools. By 1991, 100 percent of all Chinese children of primary-school age went to school, compared with only 20 percent in 1949, when the Communists took control of the country. During that same period, the proportion of the population unable to read and write dropped from 80 percent to 22 percent.

These achievements were dimmed somewhat by the fact that not all primary-school students graduated, and that those who did so often performed poorly. The success rate was lowest in rural areas, where many parents preferred that their children work to increase the family's income.

Education for many children begins at age 3, when they enter kindergarten. Children usually enter primary school at the age of 6 or 7 and attend classes six days a week. Most primary schools have a five-year course of study, except in such cities as Beijing and Shanghai, which have six-year primary schools. The school year consists of two semesters with a long vacation in July and August.

The gap between rural and urban education is a wide one. Urban schools generally prepare students for further education and high-level jobs, while rural schools prepare students for manual labor in lower-skilled jobs.

Urban school courses consist of Chinese, mathematics, physical education, music, drawing, nature, history, and geography. A foreign language, usually English, is added to the curriculum in about the third grade. Rural schools may offer only Chinese and mathematics, along with Communist moral training and ideology, which urban schools are also required to teach. Communist morality stresses love of the motherland, the Communist Party, and the people.

Starting in the fourth grade, students are usually required to labor two weeks each semester on farms or in workshops to relate classroom studies to actual experience. Most schools have after-hour activities at least one day a week that involve students in recreation and community service that stress Party values.

Secondary Education. Chinese secondary schools are called middle schools and are divided into junior and senior levels. Junior middle schools offer a three-year course of study that students begin at age 12. The great majority of students, particularly in rural areas, go no further than junior middle school. Senior middle schools offer a two- or three-year course that students begin at age 15. In 1992, about 50 million students attended either regular or technical middle schools. Since vocational education was reemphasized during the late 1970s, the proportion of students in vocational middle schools increased, and four weeks of each year are set aside for physical labor and technical training. In rural areas, some students use this time to work in agriculture, and some secondary schools run their own factories.

Higher Education. In 1993, more than 3 million students pursued education beyond middle school in universities, colleges, and teacher-training and vocational institutes.

China's institutions of higher learning were virtually shut down during the early years of the Cultural Revolution, when tens of thousands of students joined militant Red Guard units in support of Mao Zedong's radical policies. The end result was a critical shortage of trained people to meet China's needs. The restoration of the higher-education system began in 1976, when entrance exams—not simply good political credentials—were once again required for admission to universities. A major effort was also begun to improve the quality of higher education, with emphasis on scientific research and training. After the pro-democracy student demonstrations of 1989, students were required to undergo a year of political education before being allowed to attend college. A lack of funds and qualified teachers, however, has meant that China is unable to offer higher education to all students who want it.

To help meet the demand for higher education and develop a trained workforce, China has created numerous alternatives to conventional schools. Besides "workers' colleges" in factories and elsewhere, the government sponsors correspondence schools and "TV universities." A typical TV-university student spends up to six hours a day for three years watching some of China's best teachers hold forth on videotape. Students who pass final exams are entitled to the same pay as graduates of conventional universities.

Arts and Leisure

China's arts are as old as painting on silk, which has been traced back to the 3rd century B.C., and as modern as the television screen. In the 20th century, practically all of the country's arts have undergone great changes as a result of revolutionary political upheavals.

Theater. Traditionally, Chinese theater has served as both a medium of popular entertainment and as an arena for political debate. One of the most popular kinds is the Beijing Opera, which has flourished for about 200 years. It is not opera in the Western sense, but an intricate, highly stylized form of theater that combines spoken dialogue, song, dance, pantomime, and acrobatics. A strong rhythmic accompaniment to the acting is provided by small drums, stringed instruments, flutes, clackers, gongs, and cymbals. Body movements may express such actions as riding a horse or rowing a boat. No sets and few props are used. The traditional repertoire of Beijing Opera includes more than 1,000 works, most based on historical novels about political and military struggles.

Literature. Traditional literature in China dates from the Eastern Zhou (Chou) dynasty (770–256 B.C.) and includes the five central texts of Confucian thought as well as the *Shijing (Shih Ching)*, an anthology of poetry. Fiction, however, was rarely regarded as literature by China's elite class of scholars and rulers.

During the Republican period, two of China's foremost writers, Lu Xun (Lu Hsun) and Ba Jin (Pa Chin), challenged that attitude by making literature serve political ends. In 1918, Lu wrote a short story titled "Diary of a Madman." It was a complete break with the past, using vernacular prose rather than the traditional literary writing style. The story is a study of perception: only a "madman" can see the exploitation of China's peasant masses. The madman is horrified as he recalls the practice of families selling their daughters into marriage, concubinage, and prostitution. In the 1930s, Ba Jin depicted the struggle of modern youth against the age-old Confucian family system. One of his novels, *Family,* deplored the practice of arranged marriages that deprived young people of the right to make their own choices.

After 1949, all art was subordinated to the goals of the Communist revolution. Literature had to expose the ills of capitalist society and trum-

Ancient scroll art shows the elegance of life at the Chinese imperial court.

A folk-dance troupe recreates a historical scene at the Beijing opera house.

pet the growing strength of socialism. But some writers produced works that, between the lines, could be taken as criticism of Mao and the Communist Party. The Cultural Revolution caused a sharp decline of all creative activity, and writers became active again only after the death of Mao and the arrest of his wife, Jiang Qing. In novels, short stories, and articles, writers condemned the political leadership that gave rise to the extreme disorder of the Cultural Revolution. Some blamed the political system itself.

Libraries. In 1949, China had only 55 public libraries, most of them concentrated in major coastal cities. Though the Communist government strove to develop library services throughout the country, libraries remained scarce or inadequate. By the early 1980s, the government saw the lack of libraries as a major obstacle to modernization and made a strong effort to increase library services. In addition to public libraries at the county level and higher, cultural centers offer limited library services to people in small cities and towns. The national library in Beijing, housed in a new building that opened in 1987, is one of the world's largest libraries.

Newspapers. The *People's Daily* and the *Liberation Army Daily*, official organs of the Communist Party and the army, are among China's most influential daily newspapers. The *Workers' Daily* covers major domestic and overseas news as well as labor matters. Local morning and evening newspapers are extremely popular and usually sell out soon after they arrive at the newsstands.

Movies. With the establishment of the People's Republic, filmmaking was brought under the control of the Ministry of Culture. All films were expected to support the new government and its policies.

China's film industry continued to develop after 1949, and produced more than 600 feature films over the next 17 years. Severely restricted

Gymnasts strike a pose as spectators hold cards aloft that depict the Himalayas.

during the Cultural Revolution, the movie industry again flourished as a medium of popular entertainment after 1976. Domestic films played to large audiences, and tickets for foreign-film festivals sold quickly. But during the 1980s, the government condemned thriller and martial-arts films as socially unacceptable. In 1986, it transferred control of the film industry to the new Ministry of Audio, Cinema, and Television to bring it under "stricter control and management."

Radio and Television.   During the 1980s, radio and television broadcasting expanded rapidly in China. By 1990, there was one radio receiver for every 5.4 persons. Television, which was first seen in Beijing in 1958, reached two-thirds of the population in 1990. Radio broadcasts are often relayed over a vast loudspeaker system, and most TV viewing takes place in community centers.

During the late 1980s, TV and radio programming's emphasis on political lectures and statistical information gave way to more popular entertainment. Radio shows now include soap operas based on popular novels, as well as a variety of Chinese and foreign music. Education makes up about 25 percent of TV programming, and news makes up 15 percent. The rest is made up of movies, drama, music, dancing, children's programs, and sports.

Sports.   Almost everyone in China engages in some kind of daily athletic activity ranging from calisthenics to table tennis. Athletic activity is associated with military preparedness, and the theme of "defending the motherland" is prevalent in sports articles.

The Chinese place heavy emphasis on team sports, rather than those that feature individual skills. Competition is conducted on a "friendly" basis, and combative sports like Western-style boxing, which is considered brutal, have been outlawed.

THE ECONOMY

When the Communist Party came to power in 1949, its chief goal was to repair damage to the economy caused by World War II and the civil war between Nationalist and Communist forces. It brought inflation under control and transferred ownership of most industry to the state. In agriculture, it took land from landlords and prosperous farmers and parceled it out to the 60 to 70 percent of farm families who owned little or no land.

By 1952, Communist leaders could turn to their long-range goals. These included industrializing the economy, improving living standards, narrowing income differences, and producing modern military equipment.

State Planning. In 1953, China adopted the Soviet model of central economic planning. Under the First Five-Year Plan (1953–57), the government concentrated its efforts on the rapid buildup of heavy industry. All modern industries became either state-owned or were converted into joint public-private enterprises under state control.

Agriculture also underwent extensive changes. The government encouraged farmers to organize large collective units. By 1957, about 93 percent of all farm families had joined collectives, where their incomes were based solely on the amount of labor they contributed. Each family was allowed to keep a small private plot on which to grow vegetables and raise livestock for its own use.

Industry boomed during the First Five-Year Plan, but agriculture lagged, persuading Mao Zedong to scrap the Second Five-Year Plan. In its place, he called for heroic efforts to achieve a "great leap" in agricultural and industrial production. This "Great Leap Forward" lasted from 1958 to 1961.

People's Communes. In agriculture, the plan called for the formation of people's communes. These were created by combining from 20 to 30 collectives of about 22,000 members each. Communes were supposed to increase efficiency by moving farm families into dormitories, feeding them in communal mess halls, and moving whole teams of laborers from one task to another. In industry, revolutionary zeal was supposed to motivate the work force to increase output.

China's fledgling automobile industry helps meet the needs of government agencies and the military; demand for private cars remains small.

In Shenzen (left) and other "special economic zones," joint ventures with foreign firms have led to skyscraper construction and other large-scale projects.

The Great Leap Forward proved to be a disaster. After the first year, agricultural production fell sharply. Widespread famine occurred, and perhaps 14 million people died of starvation. To prevent even more deaths, the government had to import huge amounts of grain.

For a time, industrial production did "leap," but soon the excessive strain on workers and equipment began to tell. Production plummeted by 38 percent in 1961, and the entire country was plunged into a depression. Faced with economic collapse, the government decided to give top priority to restoring agricultural output. The development of light industry was given second consideration, and heavy industry third.

Cultural Revolution. Following a brief period of recovery and growth, political upheaval once again shattered the economy. The Cultural Revolution, especially from 1966–68, reduced production in factories and mines, and farm production stagnated.

In 1975, Premier Zhou Enlai (Chou En-Lai) outlined a new set of goals designed to make China a "front-rank" economic power by the year 2000. The plan called for a program of modernization to accelerate production in agriculture, industry, science and technology, and national defense. The plan became known as the "Four Modernizations."

Free-Market Incentives. After Mao Zedong's death in 1976, Deng Xiaoping's reform government set out to accomplish the goals of the Four Modernizations. It aimed to increase production by offering incentives, or rewards, for higher output.

The program begun by the reform leaders in 1980 was a mix of a planned, socialist economy with some features of a free-market economy. In agriculture, individual farm families were allowed to lease land from the state in exchange for the right to sell any surplus crops for profit. Agricultural production was also stimulated by establishing farmers' markets in urban areas as well as in the countryside, where families could sell their surplus. In addition, farm families were allowed to produce, for profit, any goods and services that were in short supply.

By late 1984, almost all farm families were working leased plots of land, and the commune system had practically vanished. The new policies quickly achieved results. By 1985, farm output almost doubled.

In industry, market forces were also put into play. Managers of state-owned businesses were given greater decision-making power, and they were allowed to reward productive workers with bonuses. Individuals were allowed to set up their own businesses. Independent cobblers, tailors, tinkers, and vendors once again became common sights in the cities. By the mid-1980s, these reforms had produced substantial results. Industrial production was about 25 times that of 1952.

In trade, the reform program made China more open to the outside world. Chinese business enterprises were allowed to negotiate directly with foreign firms, and foreign investment in China was legalized. These changes benefited the nation's economy and brought it into the mainstream of international trade.

The new hybrid economy generally raised standards of living, although growth in large and inefficient state-run enterprises lagged

Small, family-owned businesses are helping meet consumer demand for many household items.

behind that of the private sector, and millions of surplus rural workers were unemployed or underemployed. By the mid-1990s, China's standard of living was still well below those of advanced industrial nations. But nearly everyone in China had adequate food and clothing, consumer goods increased in both quantity and quality, and the government had begun to alleviate the scarcity of urban housing.

Inflationary Pressures. Although the reform program achieved many successes, it also created some serious problems. Whenever the government relaxed its controls over prices, inflation threatened the country. As people rushed to buy consumer goods, the cost of living began to soar. In 1994, prices rose more than 25 percent. Tensions were also created by the widening income gap between people who were ''getting rich'' and those who were not, and by rising crime and corruption.

In the 1990s, as conservatives and reformers struggled to control China's future, government policies shifted back and forth from efforts to bring the economy under state control and slow the rate of growth to encouragement of free-market reforms and foreign investment.

Agriculture

China has the world's largest agricultural economy, and one of the most varied. In 1992, nearly 59 percent of all workers were engaged in farming, fishing, or forestry. Except for hauling, mechanization has lagged in agriculture, and most of the labor is done by hand.

China leads the world in the production of rice, which makes up almost half of the country's total grain output. The nation ranks third in the world as a producer of wheat. Wheat is the staple food in north China

China is the world's leading producer of rice, the country's chief crop and staple food.

China is striving to become one of the world's leading industrial nations by the year 2000. Textiles (left) and steel (right) are among China's principal manufactured products.

and is eaten in the form of steamed bread and noodles. Corn is grown in most parts of the country, but most Chinese consider it less desirable than rice or wheat. Much of the crop is used for animal food.

China is by far the largest producer of cotton in the world. Since the 1980s, it has become a major exporter of the crop. Tea and silk have traditionally been important commercial crops, and the market for them continues to be substantial at home and abroad. Agricultural exports earn foreign revenue that China needs to buy industrial equipment from other countries.

Industry

China has made great progress in developing industry since 1949. In 1990, one in four workers was employed in industry and commerce, and almost one in 20 was employed in mining and construction. The nation's industries remain unable to meet the country's needs, however, in large part because much of China's technology and distribution networks are outmoded. China can manufacture nuclear weapons and launch space satellites, and it is one of the world's largest producers of oil and coal. Yet factories often have to shut down for long periods because of severe energy shortages. The coal fields are located far from the industrial centers, and the nation's underdeveloped transportation system makes it difficult to get the coal to where it is most needed.

China's tourist trade suffered a severe blow in the wake of the Tiananmen Square crackdown.

Besides coal and oil, major industries in China include iron and steel, machinery, armaments, and textiles. China has had remarkable success in expanding consumer industries. The annual production of television sets increased from about 500,000 in 1978 to nearly 14 million in 1992. Dramatic gains were also made in the production of washing machines and refrigerators.

China's foreign trade, which by 1990 accounted for about 2 percent of the world's trade, grew rapidly during the 1980s. Its leading trade partners in the mid-1990s are Japan, Hong Kong, and the United States.

GOVERNMENT

In theory, the People's Republic of China, a socialist state, is governed by workers and peasants who are guided by the ideas of the German philosopher Karl Marx, the Soviet revolutionary leader V. Lenin, and Mao Zedong. In reality, political power is shared by the Communist Party, the government (or state), and the army. The Party controls the army and dictates policy to the government, which executes it.

State Constitution. The formal structure of the government is outlined in the 1982 state constitution, which replaced three previous ones. Reflecting Deng Xiaoping's determination to lay a lasting foundation for modernization and a stable society, it provides a legal basis for broad changes in China's social and economic institutions. It moved the country another step away from its Maoist past and from the strict precepts of Marxist-Leninist doctrine.

The constitution plays down class struggle and gives top priority to economic development. To that end, it seeks the cooperation of large groups outside the Communist Party that can make important contributions toward modernization. Accordingly, Article 1 of the constitution describes China as a "people's democratic dictatorship." This means that the system is based on a broad alliance of the working classes led by the Communist Party.

Citizens' Rights.   Probably because of the excesses committed during the Cultural Revolution, the 1982 constitution details the "fundamental rights and duties" of citizens. The right to vote and run for office, for example, begins at age 18. Religious freedom is guaranteed, as well as the "freedom not to believe in any religion." The constitution further proclaims that "citizens of the People's Republic enjoy freedom of speech, of the press, of assembly, of association, of procession, and of demonstration."

These rights were guaranteed in the earlier 1978 constitution, as were four important rights that the 1982 constitution leaves out. Rights omitted from the 1982 charter include the right to speak out freely, to air views fully, to hold great debates, to display posters with innovative ideas, and to strike. Party leaders considered these rights too risky for an era of rapid modernization.

The 1982 constitution does, however, provide a legal framework for freer economic policies. For example, it gives members of the rural collectives the right "to farm private plots, engage in household sideline production, and raise privately owned livestock." The 1982 constitution also permits and encourages extensive foreign participation in China's economy.

In 1989, troops violently crushed a student-led movement for democracy in Beijing's Tiananmen Square.

The Legislature.   The constitution calls the National People's Congress (NPC) "the highest organ of state power." The NPC's approximately 3,000 members are elected by provincial congresses to serve five-year terms. The NPC meets annually for about two weeks to approve or reject new policies, laws, the budget, and changes among high government officials. During the intervals between yearly meetings, its functions are carried out by a Standing Committee of about 150 members.

Although the NPC has played a greater role in recent years, it does not determine the political course of the country. This remains the function of the Communist Party. Basically, the NPC plays a consultative role and serves as a symbol of the Communist regime's popular base.

The Executive.   The primary instrument of executive power is the State Council, a body similar to a cabinet in other countries. Members include China's premier, five vice premiers, and the heads of ministries and other government agencies. Theoretically responsible to the NPC, the State Council actually takes its orders from the Communist Party Secretariat. Senior members of the State Council are also influential members of the Party.

The Communist Party.   With 54 million members, the Chinese Communist Party dominates virtually every area of society. In all important government, economic, and cultural institutions, its role is authoritative and unquestioned. However, China is too large and socially diverse to be ruled by decree from Beijing. Party leaders rule instead by building a consensus for new policies among Party members, influential non-Party people, and the population at large.

In theory, the highest source of authority within the Chinese Communist Party is the National Party Congress (not to be confused with the National People's Congress). The Party Congress, which is supposed to meet at least once every five years, in reality does little more than approve the decisions of the top Party leadership. The approximately 1,500 delegates do serve a useful function, however, by communicating the Party's new policies to local governments and organizations and helping to ensure that they are carried out.

The Party Congress elects a Central Committee, in which political power is formally vested. However, the Central Committee's large size—189 full members and 130 alternate members—makes it necessary to delegate authority to its smaller, elite bodies. The three highest-ranking power groups within the Party are, in order of importance:

(1) The Politburo (Political Bureau) Standing Committee, the innermost circle of power, whose seven members hold the most important Party and government posts;

(2) The Politburo, consisting of about 20 full members and two alternate members;

(3) The Secretariat, the principal administrative apparatus of the Communist Party. It consists of the Party's general secretary and five secretaries, and is, in reality, the Party's inner cabinet.

Members of the Communist Party comprise just over 4 percent of China's total population. To qualify as Party members, applicants must be at least 18 years old and go through a one-year probationary period. During the 1980s and 1990s, approval was based more on education and skills than on total commitment to Party principles.

C. T. HU, Columbia University; coauthor, *China: Its People, Its Society, Its Culture*

HONG KONG

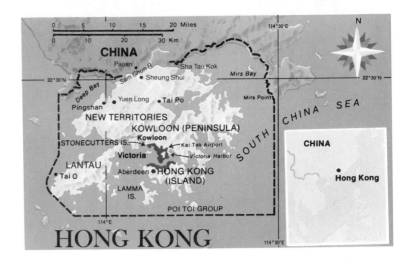

HONG KONG

In 1841, Britain's foreign secretary flew into a rage when he learned that his superintendent of trade in China had acquired Hong Kong Island. "A barren rock with hardly a house upon it!" he fumed.

Today, that "rock" is anything but barren. One of the most densely populated spots on earth, it is the center of Great Britain's Dependent Territory, or colony, of Hong Kong. Hong Kong is an amazingly efficient moneymaking machine, thanks to free trade, low taxes, hardworking residents, and excellent communications.

Soon, Hong Kong—"fragrant harbor" in English—will change hands again. On July 1, 1997, the entire colony will become a Special Administrative Region of the People's Republic of China. Besides the main island, Hong Kong includes 235 nearby islands and a small piece of China's mainland, Kowloon Peninsula. China has promised to let Hong Kong keep its free-market economy and local government for 50 years.

Hong Kong's skyline includes the dramatic 70-story Bank of China, Asia's tallest building.

Hong Kong is the most important center for manufacturing and commerce in Southeast Asia.

THE LAND

Hong Kong owes its existence as a trading center to the fact that its chief natural resource, its deep harbor, is located at the mouth of the Pearl (Zhu) River estuary on China's southeastern coast. During the 1700s, British trading ships sailed up the Pearl River to Canton (Guangzhou), just 90 mi. (145 km.) from Hong Kong.

The British acquired Hong Kong Island (30 sq. mi., or 78 sq. km.) in 1841, and Kowloon Peninsula (5 sq. mi., or 13 sq. km.) in 1860. It leased the New Territories (376.6 sq. mi., or 975 sq. km.) for 99 years in 1898. The New Territories include 235 islands and the mainland north from Kowloon Peninsula to the Chinese border.

The entire colony is hilly and rugged, with mountain slopes close to the coast. The hills are covered with scrub and trees, planted to stop erosion. About 12 percent of Hong Kong is woodland, 9 percent fishponds and farmland, and 16 percent is reclaimed land.

Hong Kong Harbor teems with vessels of all descriptions, ranging from sampans and junks to ocean liners and supertankers. The single runway of Hong Kong's Kai Tak Airport, which handles millions of passengers a year, extends into the harbor from Kowloon Peninsula. The peninsula and the narrow coastal strip of Hong Kong Island that faces it across the harbor are the colony's busiest and most crowded parts. About two-thirds of Hong Kong's people live in these two areas, which are linked by a cross-harbor tunnel and a sleek subway.

Tsimshatsui, the southern end of Kowloon Peninsula, has luxurious hotels and shopping plazas. The waterfront of Hong Kong Island is dominated by high-rise office towers, apartment buildings, hotels, and freeways. Behind them are the narrow alleys, steep streets, and tenements of the island's older sections.

New land is continually being reclaimed from the harbor. Parks and new towns in the New Territories, built on landfill, are linked to the urban areas by a railroad, new highways, and ferries. New roads have been constructed to provide access to China. A two-runway airport on Chek Lap Kok, a small piece of land off Lantau Island, is scheduled for completion in 1997. In 2006, a new container port will open on landfill along Hong Kong Island's western coast. Hong Kong is already the world's most active container port.

Though Hong Kong is just south of the Tropic of Cancer, at about the same latitude as Hawaii and Calcutta, its climate is not tropical. During the winter, gusts of cold air come from Siberia. Hot, wet monsoons (tropical winds) blow up from the south in the summer. The average annual rainfall is 87.6 in. (222.5 cm.).

THE PEOPLE

About 98 percent of Hong Kong's people are ethnic Chinese. The remaining 2 percent is made up of Filipino, British, Indian, American, and other ethnic groups. Hong Kong's only true natives are the Hakka, farmers in the New Territories, and the Tanka, a nomadic boat people that have fished the local waters for centuries.

English and Cantonese, the Chinese dialect of Canton, are official languages. Mandarin, the Beijing dialect that 70 percent of all Chinese speak, is taught in Hong Kong's schools.

Hong Kong's educational system is patterned after the British model. By 1995, officials expect that one in four of all young people of college age will be attending a postsecondary school—either one of three universities or a technical institute.

Hong Kong celebrates the British queen's birthday, Easter, Christmas, and traditional Chinese festivals. The Chinese New Year, falling anywhere from January 21 to February 28, is a three- to five-day celebration with firecrackers and feasting. People exchange presents, and children receive "lucky money" in red envelopes.

Many men and women wear Western clothing. However, the Chinese *cheongsam*, a fitted dress with a slit skirt, is popular with women. Movies are a favorite form of entertainment, as are Hong Kong's rich performing arts, ranging from Western operas to Chinese folk dances.

Half the people of Hong Kong live in public housing. In the 1990s, the government is building about 40,000 apartments a year. Still, around 400,000 people live in squatters' shacks. Officials have devised a massive environmental-protection plan to tackle the problems of waste disposal and noise, air, and water pollution.

THE ECONOMY

Hong Kong is a free port. Import duties are charged on only a few items. Goods from the People's Republic of China and other nations are sent there, unloaded, and reexported to other countries. Hong Kong is valuable to China, providing a port through which it can trade with South Korea, Taiwan, and other countries with which it has no diplomatic relations. China also owns hotels, department stores, and even factories in

State-of-the-art factories in Hong Kong produce large quantities of precision electronics parts.

Hong Kong. Hong Kong accounts for about 35 percent of the foreign currency China needs to pay for imports—an incentive for China to "let Hong Kong be Hong Kong" after 1997.

Although trade is important, manufacturing is the mainstay of Hong Kong's economy. Almost 70 percent of the colony's workforce is employed in the plastics, toy, watch, textile, clothing, and electronics industries. Hong Kong is the world's largest manufacturer of toys.

Only 1 percent of the workforce is engaged in farming and fishing. Half of Hong Kong's food and water is imported from China.

HISTORY

Canton was opened to foreign trade in 1685. British traders exported tea and silk from there, and began selling opium to the Chinese in 1773. When China tried to stop the opium shipments, the British retaliated with a military campaign that in 1841 pressured the Chinese into giving up Hong Kong Island. After another show of force, China granted Britain Kowloon Peninsula in 1860. In 1898, Britain leased the New Territories from China for 99 years.

Hong Kong is administered by a governor who is appointed by the British monarch. The governor heads the Executive Council, which directs the territory's affairs, and the Legislative Council, which enacts laws and oversees government spending.

Britain's lease on the New Territories runs out on June 30, 1997. In 1984, Britain agreed to return all of Hong Kong to China at the end of that day. Hailing the idea of "one country, two systems," China promised to permit Hong Kong a good deal of freedom, especially in financial matters, until 2047.

China and Hong Kong approved a constitution for Hong Kong in 1990 called the Basic Law. The document offers few guarantees of individual freedom, worrying Hong Kong residents. Until 1985, Hong Kong's Legislative Council consisted of civil servants and members appointed by the governor, largely in deference to China's wishes. By 1995, however, all of its members were directly or indirectly elected. The extension of British democracy was bitterly denounced by China, which said it would disband the legislature and other elected institutions in 1997.

Reviewed by DAVID CHUENYAN LAI, University of Victoria (Canada)

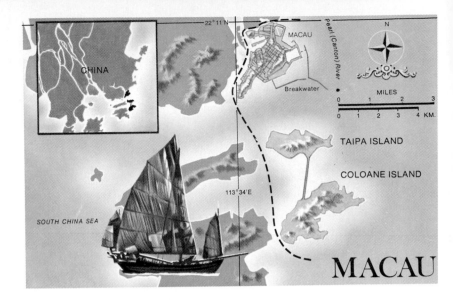

MACAU

The oldest surviving European settlement in Asia, Macau—a Portuguese-run territory of China—was used by Portuguese traders as early as the 1550s. That's almost three centuries before the British acquired Hong Kong Island, which sits 40 mi. (64 km.) northeast of Macau on the far side of the Pearl (Zhu) River estuary. This 6-sq.-mi. (16-sq.-km.) enclave consists of two islands and a peninsula on the South China Sea. Called the "Latin Orient" for its mix of Portuguese and Chinese cultures, and the "Las Vegas of the East" for its emphasis on tourism and gambling, Macau retains a centuries-old sense of adventure and intrigue. Its harbor is too shallow for today's heavy ships, so the few that still call there must lie offshore. Casino gambling is its major industry, but it also produces and exports textiles and fireworks through Hong Kong.

LAND AND PEOPLE

Macau—from the Cantonese A-Ma-Gau, (City of God)—is located in the Pearl (Zhu) River estuary and comprises the city of Macau and the islands of Taipa and Coloane. Originally, most of the inhabitants were Portuguese traders and missionaries. Today, Chinese make up 95 percent of the population, and Macanese—Macau-born Portuguese and Eurasians—make up 3 percent. Another 1 percent is made up of guest workers from other nations, especially Thailand. Many Chinese citizens cross the border each day to work in Macau.

The mixture of Portuguese and Chinese cultures is striking. Roman Catholic churches stand next to Chinese temples. Streets with Portuguese names are lined with the shops of Chinese merchants.

About 98 percent of Macau's people live on the crowded peninsula. Taipa and Coloane, linked to each other and to the mainland by a bridge and a causeway, are rural in flavor. Once a haven for pirates, they contain beautiful beaches and homes, hotels, and farms. Macau buys almost all its food and water from China.

HISTORY

During the 1500s, Macau was an important trading center between Japan and Europe. For centuries the Portuguese paid a yearly rental to China. The Chinese agreed to recognize Portugal's right of "perpetual

The Macau cityscape has a unique combination of Portuguese, Chinese, and modern architecture.

FACTS AND FIGURES

OFFICIAL NAME: Macau (also spelled Macao).

NATIONALITY: Macanese.

CAPITAL AND CHIEF CITY: Macau.

LOCATION: Southern coast of China at the mouth of the Pearl (Zhu) River, 40 mi. (64 km.) west of Hong Kong.

AREA: 6 sq. mi. (16 sq. km.).

PHYSICAL FEATURES: Macau is a narrow, hilly peninsula, linked by bridge to the island of Taipa, which is linked by causeway to the island of Coloane.

POPULATION: 400,000 (1996; annual growth 1.2%).

MAJOR LANGUAGE: Portuguese.

MAJOR RELIGIONS: Buddhism, Roman Catholicism.

GOVERNMENT: Chinese territory under Portuguese administration. **Head of state**—president of Portugal. **Head of government**—governor. **Legislature**—unicameral Legislative Assembly.

ECONOMY: Chief agricultural products—rice, vegetables. **Industries and products**—tourism/gambling, fishing, textiles, fireworks. **Chief exports**—textiles, clothing, toys. **Chief imports**—raw materials, consumer goods, foodstuffs.

MONETARY UNIT: 1 pataca = 100 avos.

NATIONAL HOLIDAY: June 10 (Day of Portugal).

occupation'' in 1887. Portugal changed Macau's status from overseas province to territory in 1974. In 1987, Portugal agreed to return Macau to China on December 20, 1999. Like Hong Kong, Macau—as a Special Administrative Region of China—is to be allowed a 50-year period of free enterprise and local independence. China will be responsible for defense and foreign policy.

GOVERNMENT

The territory of Macau is administered by a governor appointed by the Portuguese government, a cabinet of five secretaries, and a legislative assembly. The cabinet secretaries are selected by the governor. Of the 23 members of the legislative assembly, seven are appointed by the governor, eight are elected by direct vote, and the remaining eight are elected by professional and workers' groups. Macau sends one elected representative to the Portuguese parliament.

Reviewed by PAUL VARLEY, Department of East Asian Languages and Culture,
Columbia University

A bustling street in Taipei, the capital of Taiwan, typifies the vibrancy of the island country.

TAIWAN

Taiwan, the mountainous island off the coast of China, was for centuries a haven for fishermen, a few foreign seafarers, and rebels. The island was still a relatively undeveloped agricultural area when 2 million Chinese Nationalists arrived in 1949, fleeing their longtime foes, the Communists, who had taken over the mainland.

Today, Taiwan—officially known as the Republic of China—is one of Asia's most advanced industrial centers. Its flourishing economy, based on high technology and exporting, is a model of development. Taiwan ranks with South Korea, Singapore, and Hong Kong as one of the "Four Tigers" challenging Japan's place as the major supplier of Asian products to foreign countries.

Taiwan's development is more than economic. Recently, its institutions have been undergoing a gradual democratization, lending weight to the axiom that one result of economic freedom is political freedom.

THE LAND

The Republic of China consists of the island of Taiwan, the islands of Quemoy and Matsu, and the 11 islands of the Pescadores chain, which lie between Taiwan and the mainland. The island of Taiwan lies 100 mi. (160 km.) off the southeast coast of mainland China across the Taiwan Strait. By far the largest of the islands making up the Republic of China, Taiwan is about 240 mi. (386 km.) long and 85 mi. (137 km.) wide.

The thickly forested Chungyang mountain range bisects Taiwan from north to south. East of the range, the mountains fall in sharp peaks and gorges to the ocean. This spectacular coastline inspired Portuguese explorers to name the island Formosa, meaning "beautiful." West of the range, the mountains gradually give way to a broad, fertile, and well-cultivated plain, where most of the people live.

The median temperature in this subtropical climate is about 75° F. (23° C.). June to September is the wettest and hottest period. Monsoon winds bring heavy rains to the south during the summer and to the north during the winter. In addition, the islands are regularly lashed by violent typhoons that sweep up from the South China Sea early in autumn. Located in an earthquake zone, Taiwan periodically experiences tremors.

Taiwan has small deposits of coal, natural gas, limestone, marble, dolomite, and asbestos. But scarce energy resources have made industry heavily reliant on foreign oil. Since 1977, the government has put three nuclear-power plants into operation. These and a fourth plant now supply most of the island's electricity.

THE PEOPLE

About three-quarters of all Taiwanese live in cities or towns. One out of five people—more than 4 million in all—are concentrated in Kaohsiung, the important southern port, and Taipei, Taiwan's capital city. Increasingly, life in Taipei resembles city life anywhere in the world. Jets crisscross above Chiang Kai-shek International Airport. Modern skyscrapers line busy streets choked with traffic. Cultural offerings include everything from opera to rock music. To a lesser degree, other Taiwan cities engaged in international trade have also become more cosmopolitan. Kaohsiung is one such city. So are Keelung, the northern port and shipbuilding center, and Taichung, an industrial city in central Taiwan.

The native Taiwanese, who make up 84 percent of the population, are descended from the Chinese who migrated to Taiwan in the 1700s and 1800s. About 14 percent of the population consists of Chinese (and their offspring) who fled to Taiwan in 1949. It is this group of Nationalist Chinese, so called because of their ties to the Nationalist Party, who led Taiwan's government from 1949 until very recently.

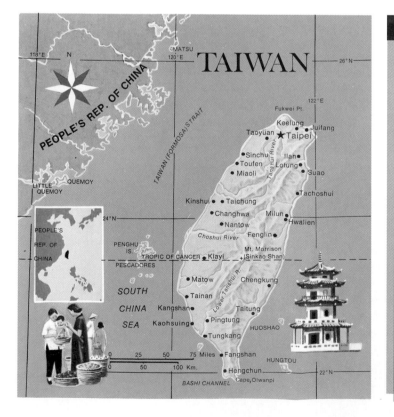

FACTS AND FIGURES

OFFICIAL NAME: Republic of China.

NATIONALITY: Chinese.

CAPITAL: Taipei.

LOCATION: Island nation in the western Pacific Ocean, about 100 mi. (160 km.) off the coast of mainland China.

AREA: 13,892 sq. mi. (35,980 sq. km.).

PHYSICAL FEATURES: Highest point—Sinkao Shan (Mount Morrison) (13,113 ft.; 3,997 m.). **Lowest point**—sea level. **Chief rivers**—Tanshui, Choshui.

POPULATION: 21,400,000 (1996; annual growth 1.0%).

MAJOR LANGUAGES: Mandarin Chinese (official), Taiwanese, Hakka Chinese.

MAJOR RELIGIONS: Buddhism, Confucianism, Daoism, Christianity.

GOVERNMENT: Republic. **Head of state**—president. **Head of government**—premier. **Legislature**—unicameral National Assembly and unicameral Legislative Yuan.

CHIEF CITIES: Taipei, Kaohsiung, Taichung, Tainan.

ECONOMY: Chief minerals—coal, natural gas, limestone, marble, asbestos. **Chief agricultural products**—rice, sweet potatoes, sugarcane, fruits. **Industries and products**—electronics, textiles, clothing, chemicals, food processing, plywood, sugar milling. **Chief exports**—electrical machinery, textiles, footwear, foodstuffs, wood products. **Chief imports**—machinery and equipment, chemicals, petroleum, metals, foodstuffs.

MONETARY UNIT: 1 new Taiwan dollar = 100 cents.

NATIONAL HOLIDAY: October 10 (National Day).

Many Taiwanese adhere to Confucianism. The birthday of Confucius is observed with much ritual.

About 250,000 aborigines, or native Taiwanese, live in the island's eastern and central mountains. Of Malayo-Polynesian descent, they dominated the island until the Chinese began settling in great numbers in Taiwan during the 1100s.

Mandarin Chinese is the official language, but Taiwanese and Hakka dialects are also spoken. Many Taiwanese older than 50 also speak Japanese, the result of half a century of Japanese rule.

More than 95 percent of the people practice Buddhism, Taoism, or Confucianism, or a mixture of these religions. About 5 percent practice Christianity, and there is a small Muslim population as well.

Confucian values, which stress the promotion of human welfare through education, have fostered an enthusiasm for learning. Free education for children from age 6 to age 15 was introduced in 1968, boosting the literacy rate to 94 percent. Seven out of 10 graduates of junior high school continue their education in three-year senior high and vocational schools. The largest of the island's 105 public and private universities is Taipei's National Taiwan University, a public institution.

Ancient Chinese traditions continue to determine the values and way of life for the great majority. The most popular festival is the celebration of the Lunar New Year. Business activity virtually stops for a week before and after as families gather to observe ageless rituals and enjoy parades and fireworks. Another big day in Taiwan is Double Ten (the 10th day of the 10th month). Also called National Day, it marks the anniversary of the October 10, 1911, uprising that gave birth to the Republic of China.

THE ECONOMY

Taiwan has one of the world's most dynamic economies, growing 9 percent a year since 1960. This growth is astounding, considering that in 1945, when Japan returned Taiwan to China after World War II, the island had one industry, the milling of sugarcane. For 50 years, Taiwan's agricultural economy had been geared to producing food and raw materials for Japan.

An important feature of the economic planning that the Nationalists introduced in 1953 was a program of land reform. Only a quarter of Taiwan's land can be used for growing crops. Nonetheless, farmers there produce more rice than Taiwan can consume, thanks to advances in biotechnology, cultivation methods, and mechanization. Only 17.5 percent of Taiwan's workers are farmers. Taiwan exports rice, but it must import large amounts of corn, soybeans, wheat, barley, and sorghum.

Government policies, combined with aid from the United States, helped set the stage for Taiwan's economic miracle. In 1966, the Taiwanese opened their first "export processing zone" (EPZ). The government offered incentives, such as five-year tax holidays and a ban on strikes, for foreign companies to build factories within these EPZs. The EPZs became magnets for foreign investment.

Taiwan's early success on the world market was based on high, labor-intensive production. By the late 1970s, however, labor costs were rising, and Taiwan was facing serious competition in such industries as textiles, plastics, and consumer electronics. The competition came from countries less developed than Taiwan, and from developed nations that had cut manufacturing costs with robots and other new technologies. In response, the Taiwan government lent a hand to industries able to benefit from high technology. Among other things, it opened an industrial park for high-technology companies in Hainchu, south of Taipei. By 1988, more than 100 companies had been lured to the park with such incentives as tax breaks, low-interest loans, and investment money provided by the government.

Despite Taiwan's emphasis on high technology, many traditional crafts are still cultivated.

Taiwan's terraced paddies have helped make the island self-sufficient in rice, the staple food.

The government also works hard to improve the economic environment. In 1990, it completed 14 key public-works projects, including two north-south highways, new harbor facilities, several flood-control projects, and an upgrading of its telecommunications system.

Taiwan suffers from the sort of environmental problems that accompany swift industrial growth everywhere. Heavy polluters, such as petrochemical and plastics manufacturers, are important to its industrial base. Taipei's air quality is roughly three times worse than that of Los Angeles. Taiwan's intensely farmed landscape contains vast quantities of pesticides and fertilizers. The crush of people—Taiwan has the world's second-highest population density—only adds to the problem.

Fortunately, Taiwan's economic success will permit it to pay for expensive pollution-control and cleanup measures. In 1987, the government set up the Environmental Protection Agency (EPA), which has announced new programs to combat pollution and boost recycling.

HISTORY

For a thousand years, Taiwan was a remote outpost of the Chinese empire. Its geographic isolation made it a refuge for pirates and hardy settlers from many other parts of Asia. Although a few Chinese from Fujian province across the Taiwan Strait began arriving in the 600s, the first sizable colony of Chinese was the rebel kingdom established by Cheng Ch'eng-kung (Koxinga) in 1661 in defiance of the Manchus. His army, mostly from Fujian, held out for two decades before the Manchus regained control of the island in 1683.

After 200 years of Manchu (Qing dynasty) rule, Taiwan was ceded to Japan following China's defeat in the Sino-Japanese War of 1894–95. The Japanese reorganized the land-tenure system, developed a sugar-export industry, and built roads and railways. Beginning with the second Sino-Japanese War in 1931, however, Chinese nationalism fueled a growing political resistance. Japan's defeat in World War II brought the return of

Taiwan to China in 1945. In 1949, when Communist forces took over the mainland, the Nationalist government of the Republic of China assumed control of the island. Since then, both the Nationalists and the Communists, each of which considers itself China's legitimate government, have considered Taiwan a province of China.

The admission of the People's Republic of China to the United Nations in 1971 ended the Nationalist government's official status as the United Nations representative of China. Eight years later, in 1979, the United States recognized the People's Republic of China as the sole legitimate government of China. It did so with the understanding that reunification of the province of Taiwan with the mainland was to be accomplished without the use of force.

Chiang Kai-shek, the first president, served until his death in 1975. He was succeeded by his son Chiang Ching-kuo, who served as premier from 1975 to 1978, and as president from 1978 until his death in 1988. In 1987, he ended four decades of martial law, and he gradually reformed the political system to grant more power to the Taiwanese majority. His successor, Lee Teng-hui, was Taiwan's first native-born president. The first multiparty elections for seats in the Legislative Yuan were held in 1989. In 1991, in the first general elections for the National Assembly since 1948, political power shifted to a new generation. Less than 22 percent of those persons winning seats were born on the mainland. In 1992, for the first time, the entire Legislative Yuan was born on Taiwan. A law making the discussion of Taiwanese independence or the advocacy of Communism a criminal offense was repealed in 1992. Taiwanese investment on and trade with the mainland have increased dramatically despite restrictions on direct commercial ties. Relations deteriorated in the mid-1990s, particularly after Lee Teng-hui visited the United States in 1995. Angered by Lee's pursuit of an independent image for Taiwan, China conducted missile tests and war games off the Taiwanese coast immediately preceding Taiwan's first direct presidential elections in 1996.

GOVERNMENT

For more than 40 years, the Kuomintang ruled through a presidential structure established by a 1946 constitution. According to this constitution, the National Assembly elected the president for a term of six years. It also presided over five administrative councils, or *yuans:* executive, legislative, judicial, examination, and control. Members were theoretically elected to three of these bodies: the Control Yuan, which investigated wrongdoings; the National Assembly, which elected the president; and the Legislative Yuan, which passed laws. Because the government claims to represent all of mainland China, no general elections were held on Taiwan between 1948 (when the last general elections were held in mainland China) and 1991, when the aging legislators representing mainland China were forced to retire. Between 1949 and 1990, despite special elections that were held to fill some seats in the yuans with native Taiwanese, membership in the National Assembly shrank from 3,045 to 692 as its elderly members died. The National Assembly elected in 1991 revised the Taiwanese constitution to provide for direct elections of the president and vice president. Lee Teng-hui won Taiwan's first direct presidential elections, which were held in March 1996.

RICHARD A. WILLIAMS, Central Connecticut State University

Skyscrapers line the streets of Pyongyang, the capital and largest city of North Korea.

NORTH KOREA

Kim Il Sung, who led North Korea from its creation in 1948 until his death in 1994, was viewed by his people as almost a god and was referred to as the "Great Leader." He created a tightly organized, disciplined society with a government and economy largely modeled after Europe's former Communist states. North Korea, however, departed from the European model by stressing a goal of its own: *chuche*, or national self-sufficiency.

Since 1990, South Korea has been urging North Korea to unite with it to form one nation. Just before his death, Kim Il Sung had agreed to an unprecedented meeting with his South Korean counterpart, and several bilateral talks have since taken place. By 1996, however, the talks had brought no results.

Kim Il Sung's successor, his son Kim Jong Il (known as the "Dear Leader"), has continued in his father's footsteps. The task is a difficult one, because the country is beset by problems. In 1993 and 1994, for example, North Korea was in the forefront of international attention because it was believed that the government was developing nuclear weapons. A year later, severe flooding led to widespread food shortages. Meanwhile, a number of defections of high-level officials took place. The stability of North Korea thus seems rather shaky.

THE LAND

North Korea—officially the Democratic People's Republic of Korea —occupies 55 percent of a mountainous peninsula that juts out of northeastern China. The nation is roughly the same size as Pennsylvania.

North Korea is bordered on the west by the Yellow Sea and on the east by the Sea of Japan. Its major rivers, the Yalu and the Tumen, mark

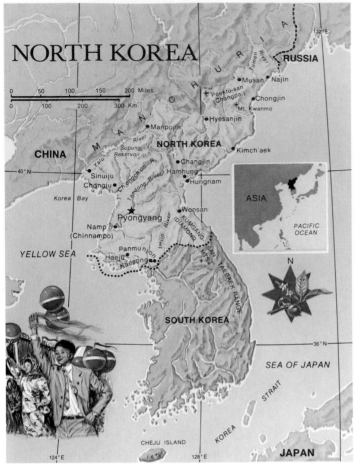

NORTH KOREA

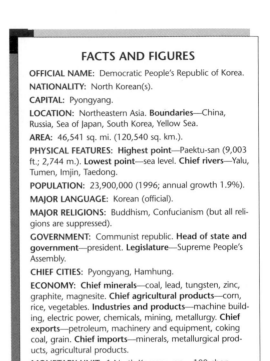

the nation's long northern border with China. Both rivers begin on the steep slopes of Mount Paektu, North Korea's highest peak, and are important sources of hydroelectric power. To the south, a jagged cease-fire line, established after the Korean War (1950–53), cuts northeast from the Han estuary across the 38th parallel. This line runs through the center of a 1.24-mi.-wide (2-km.-wide) "no-man's-land" and forms North Korea's border with South Korea.

North Korea is better endowed with forests and minerals than is South Korea. Four-fifths of the land consists of mountains or uplands. The central section is an almost continuous mass of forested mountains, the source of most of North Korea's valuable minerals and timber. The Taebaek Range, which extends into South Korea, runs parallel to the east coast. The Diamond Mountains, noted for their forest-covered ridges, waterfalls, and splendid views, are part of this range.

Farmland is largely confined to the Yalu and Tumen river valleys, the narrow coastal plain on the east, and the wider plain on the west. The eastern coast has some good harbors and access to some of the world's best fishing grounds. North Korea's capital city, Pyongyang, is situated on the large Northwestern Plain, which contains rolling hills and flatland and most of the nation's farms and factories.

The nation's climate is temperate. Winters are long, dry, and more severe than those in South Korea. Most rain falls during the short, hot summers.

THE PEOPLE

About half of all North Koreans live on the northwestern plain. About a fourth live in the mountainous central region, and another fourth live in the heavily cultivated eastern coastal lowlands.

About two-thirds of all North Koreans live in cities and large towns. **Pyongyang,** the nation's capital and largest city, is an important industrial and commercial center. Other leading North Korean cities are **Hamhung,** an industrial city on the east coast; **Hungnam,** the port for Hamhung; and the ports of **Wonsan** and **Chongjin**.

Koreans are descended from various Tungusic peoples (related to the Mongolian people), who migrated into the Korean Peninsula from Central Asia several thousand years before the birth of Christ. According to Korean folklore, the Tungus were joined (around 1100 B.C.) by a group of Chinese led by a legendary figure named Kija. Chinese culture had a strong impact on the early Koreans.

North Korea is a highly regimented society, yet to one foreign observer in early 1994, it seemed a "well-oiled dictatorship where everybody knows the rules and plays by them." Since 1953, the North Korean government has managed to weaken traditional ties to Confucianism, a system of beliefs that emphasizes strong family ties. Instead, North Koreans have been taught to revere their leaders. A state newspaper said in early 1996 that Kim Jong Il was "an outstanding great master of witty remarks as well as the greatest man ever known in history." The self-proclaimed "Dear Leader" was also said to compose operas that are better "than all the operas mankind has ever created."

The government approves all marriages and determines where in the country people may live. To increase the population, the government has encouraged large families. With a shortage of both skilled and unskilled labor, women are required to work at full-time jobs.

North Koreans eat mostly rice, corn, winter root vegetables, and a national dish called kimch'i (a spicy pickled cabbage with garlic). Meat is eaten just once or twice a week.

Language. The people of North and South Korea speak the same language, Korean. The Pyongyang regional dialect is considered the "official Korean language" in North Korea.

Religion. Religion is suppressed in North Korea, although some Buddhist temples and shrines are kept open for their historic importance. Kim's government especially persecuted Christians, many of whom fled to South Korea to build new lives. In place of religion, North Koreans are forced to pay homage to Kim Jong Il's family and to *chuche*.

Education. Education is free and compulsory for 11 years. This includes one year in kindergarten; four years in primary school, called People's School; and six years in secondary school. Younger children attend free, state-run nurseries while their parents are at work. Training after high school is available at Kim Il Sung University, at medical and technical schools, and in adult schools in factories and rural areas. About 95 percent of all North Koreans can read and write.

Traditional Arts. Kim's iron rule stifled artistic freedom, requiring all culture, art, and recreational activities to celebrate the "Great Leader." Yet Koreans on both sides of the demilitarized zone share a rich artistic and literary tradition. Much of early Korean poetry dealt with the country's natural beauty and with life in the royal court, where many poets

North Koreans celebrate their holidays with great fanfare.

were employed. Some poetry dealt with universal emotions, as in the case of the love poems of Hwang Chini (1506–44), Korea's most famous woman poet.

Magnificent Korean pottery was created during various dynastic periods. The gray-green bowls of the Koryo period (A.D. 935–1392) are highly regarded throughout the world. Korea's rich musical tradition includes both royal court music and ballet and folk songs and dances.

Koreans have also made important technical and scientific advances. Their printers used movable type before Europeans did, and their scientists built one of the world's earliest astronomical observatories. A Korean admiral used history's first ironclad warships ("turtle boats") to defeat a Japanese invasion in 1592.

ECONOMY

After the Korean War, the government took control of all land and industries. In hopes of freeing the nation from the need of relying on any outside country, North Korea developed industries around its strength—natural resources, especially iron ore, coal, and hydropower. The government maintains a tight grip on the economy, and state-owned industries produce 95 percent of all goods.

The concentration on heavy industry and a strong defense has caused chronic shortages of consumer goods. On average, North Korean earnings per person are less than one-fifth those of South Koreans.

Agriculture. After 1953, collective farms, worked cooperatively by all farmers, replaced privately owned farms. Today, there are about 3,700 collective farms in North Korea, concentrated mostly on the Northwestern Plain. About 300 families live on each farm. The government tells these communal farms how much to produce. The farms must meet these quotas, but individual farm families can raise food for themselves on the small, rent-free plots assigned to them. Rice is the major crop. The nation is largely self-sufficient in food production.

Industry. Mining and industry are also regulated. Coal, iron ore, lead, and zinc are the principal minerals. Along with imported petroleum, they are used to produce the steel, machinery, fertilizers, and chemicals needed to modernize the country's farms and industry.

An attempt to modernize North Korea's factories by borrowing money and importing Western machinery backfired during the 1970s. When North Korea's exports failed to grow as expected, the government found itself unable to pay even the interest on its loans. Eventually, during the 1980s, it stopped trying, leaving its lenders in Japan and elsewhere poorer by $4 billion. To the government's chagrin, the nation's credit record discouraged subsequent foreign investment.

HISTORY

Until going their own ways as separate nations in 1948, North and South Korea shared one of the longest continuous histories of any nation, going back some 5,000 years. The early history of Korea is shrouded in legend. It revolves around the ancient kingdom of Choson, which came into being about 2300 B.C. The Chinese established the colony of Lolang in Korea during the 2nd century B.C., but the Koreans drove them out five centuries later. By then, three small kingdoms had emerged. The kingdom of Silla eventually defeated its two rivals and united the peninsula under its own rule. The united Silla dynasty that followed (A.D. 668–935) brought in an era of great cultural and scientific achievement, as well as relative peace and prosperity. Internal troubles led to the decline of the Silla, and during the 900s the Koryo dynasty arose in its place. In 1231, Mongols invaded from China, and eventually Korea's kings accepted Mongol control.

The Mongol Empire collapsed in the late 1300s. A period of uncertainty followed, until a Korean general named Yi Sung-gy established the Yi dynasty (1392–1910) with Chinese help. The nation's capital was moved from Kaesong to Seoul.

But Korea still found itself threatened by China and Japan. Both countries wanted to control Korea in order to expand and to protect their own borders from attack. Following an unsuccessful Japanese invasion that lasted from 1592–98, Korea came under partial control of the Manchu from the north. For the next few centuries, Korea shut itself off from the rest of the world, becoming a hermit nation.

During the 1800s, Russia, Japan, and China competed for control of Korea. After the Russo-Japanese War (1904–5), the victorious Japanese moved into the peninsula and annexed Korea in 1910. The Japanese modernized Korea, developed industries, and built new railroads. They also held all key government and industrial posts. The Japanese were driven out in 1945, after their defeat in World War II. (See SOUTH KOREA in this volume for the story of Korea's division after World War II.)

North Korea Since 1953. North Korea, occupied by Soviet troops in 1945, developed along Communist lines. Kim Il Sung served as premier from 1948 to 1972 and as president under a revised constitution from 1972 until his death on July 8, 1994. His death, which took place during a time of tensions over North Korea's nuclear program, provoked a frenzy of mourning. Kim's oldest son appeared to assume de facto control. In October 1994, the United States and North Korea signed an accord designed to lead to the eventual dismantling of the North Korean nuclear program. In 1996, amid reports that famine threatened the country, North Korean troop movements increased tensions between the two Koreas.

Reviewed by PAUL VARLEY,
Department of East Asian Languages and Culture, Columbia University

With over 10 million people, Seoul, the South Korean capital, ranks among the world's largest cities.

SOUTH KOREA

In 1953, the future looked anything but bright for the five-year-old Republic of Korea, the southern half of a nation that had been split in two. It had been shattered by three years of all-out war. Its largely agricultural economy had ground to a halt and, for all intents and purposes, it had practically no experience with either modern industrial techniques or democratic institutions.

Thirty years later, however, South Korea was being hailed as one of the 20th century's economic marvels. It had become—along with Taiwan, Hong Kong, and Singapore—one of the Pacific Rim's "Four Tigers," able and eager to compete with Japan for an impressive share of world trade.

Its political development failed to move as fast as its economy, however. Understandably jittery, with soldiers of the south and north glaring at each other across a demilitarized zone, South Korea's leaders regularly used the need for national security to justify authoritarian measures. Yet the late 1980s brought refreshing changes on the political front, and in the 1990s, South Koreans were beginning to enjoy freedoms to match their economic gains.

THE LAND

South Korea—often referred to simply as Korea—occupies less than half of the mountainous Korean Peninsula and contains about two-thirds of its people. The peninsula extends 600 mi. (966 km.) from north to south and averages 135 mi. (217 km.) in width. South Korea's share of the peninsula, 38,023 sq. mi. (98,480 sq. km.), makes it about the size of Indiana. It is bordered by the Sea of Japan on the east, the Yellow Sea on the west, and the East China Sea on the south. Its only land boundary is formed by the Military Demarcation Line (MDL) that marks the line of separation between North and South Korea.

South Korea's principal mountain ranges are the Taebaek, which extends into South Korea from North Korea, and the Sobaek. Most people live in the western lowlands of these ranges, though some settlements exist in the east, where the mountains drop directly into the sea.

Some 3,000 islands dot the west and south coasts. The largest, Cheju, contains South Korea's highest peak, the 6,396-ft. (1,950 m.) volcanic Mount Halla. The major rivers are the Naktong, which irrigates the southeastern coastal plains; the Han, which flows through South Korea's capital city of Seoul; and the Kum, which along with the Han provides water for crops in the western lowlands.

The climate is temperate. Winters are mildest in the southwest, near the city of Kwangju, and long and cold in Seoul, South Korea's capital. Summers are short and hot. Monsoon winds bring hot, moist air from the Pacific Ocean. At least one typhoon comes off the East China Sea each summer, bringing hurricane-force winds and heavy rain. Southwest Korea falls within an earthquake zone and experiences occasional tremors. South Korea's scarce natural resources include anthracite coal, tungsten, iron ore, limestone, kaolinite, and graphite.

FACTS AND FIGURES

OFFICIAL NAME: Republic of Korea.

NATIONALITY: South Korean(s).

CAPITAL: Seoul.

LOCATION: Northeastern Asia. **Boundaries**—North Korea, Sea of Japan, Yellow Sea.

AREA: 38,023 sq. mi. (98,480 sq. km.).

PHYSICAL FEATURES: Highest point—Mount Halla (6,398 ft.; 1,950 m.). **Lowest point**—sea level. **Chief rivers**—Naktong, Han.

POPULATION: 45,300,000 (1996; annual growth 0.9%).

MAJOR LANGUAGES: Korean (official), English.

MAJOR RELIGIONS: Confucianism, Buddhism, Christianity, Chondogyo.

GOVERNMENT: Republic. **Head of state and government**—president. **Legislature**—National Assembly.

CHIEF CITIES: Seoul, Pusan, Taegu, Inchon, Kwangju.

ECONOMY: Chief minerals—coal, tungsten, graphite. **Chief agricultural products**—rice, barley, vegetables. **Industries and products**—electronics, automobiles, chemicals, shipbuilding, steel, textiles and clothing, footwear, food processing. **Chief exports**—electronic and electrical equipment, textiles and clothing, footwear, steel, automobiles, ships. **Chief imports**—machinery, oil, transportation equipment, grains.

MONETARY UNIT: 1 South Korean won = 100 chun.

NATIONAL HOLIDAY: August 15 (Independence Day).

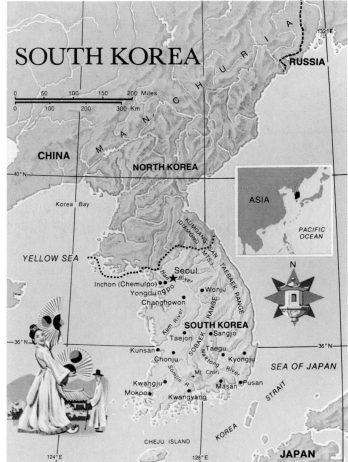
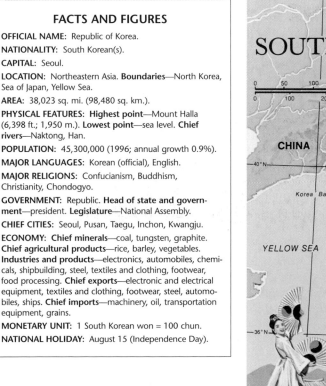

The circle dance, performed in traditional costume, is one of many folk customs still practiced.

THE PEOPLE

Industrial development in South Korea turned a population that was primarily rural in 1965 to one that was 65 percent urban in 1990. About a third of South Korea's population is concentrated in the four major cities of **Seoul**, **Taegu**, **Pusan**, and **Inchon**. **Seoul**, South Korea's capital and largest city, is located near the west coast. Its gleaming new office buildings, hotels, and apartment houses, rising next to centuries-old palaces and Buddhist temples, symbolize South Korea's rapid transformation into a modern industrial state. Another sign of industrialization is Seoul's growing pollution problem. **Pusan,** the nation's second-largest city, is a major port. Other important cities are **Taegu,** an industrial city in central South Korea; **Inchon,** the port of access to Seoul; and the southwestern industrial city of **Kwangju.**

The Korean War (1950–53) forced hundreds of thousands of northerners to flee to the south. Today, 10 percent of South Korea's people are of northern origin.

The values taught by the ancient Chinese philosopher Confucius (K'ung Fu-tzu) took root in Korea's villages centuries ago and continue to dominate South Korean thinking and behavior. Students are taught to obey teachers, children to obey their parents, the young to obey their elders, and wives to obey their husbands. South Korea's legal code, shaped by Confucianism, puts women at a disadvantage in some ways. Inheritance laws, divorce codes, and head-of-household privileges are heavily weighted in favor of men.

Like their counterparts in other Asian nations, South Korean parents much prefer having boys than girls. At one time, parents even practiced infanticide, killing newborn girls, who were looked upon more as financial obligations than assets. The ability to learn a fetus' sex led to a spate of abortions of female fetuses during the 1980s. The government outlawed such abortions when it became clear that by the year 2010, they would result in a lopsided male-female birth ratio of 126 males for every 100 females.

Language. The Seoul dialect of the Korean language prevails in South Korea. Koreans write their language in *hangul,* an easy-to-learn alphabet developed during King Sejong's reign in 1443. Literary and upper-class Koreans continued to use Chinese ideographs into modern times, however. The Korean language has also borrowed many words from Japanese and English, which is taught widely in high schools.

Religion. Most South Koreans rely on Buddhism and Confucianism for spiritual and ethical guidance. During the Choson dynasty (1392–1910), an emphasis on Confucian teachings reduced Buddhism's influence. Yet Buddhist temples are found throughout the country. Ancestor worship and shamanism—the belief in an unseen world of gods and demons—have also been part of South Korea's culture for centuries.

Christianity has increased in popularity since World War II, claiming 16 percent of the population as adherents. Today, South Korea has the largest Christian population of any Asian country outside the Philippines.

Education. More than 90 percent of South Korea's people can read and write. Technical training, which prepares students for jobs in industry, begins in the middle grades. Primary schooling is free, but parents must pay for their children's middle schools, high schools, and universities and colleges. About 90 percent of children aged 12 to 17 attend secondary school. Because the universities have room for only a tenth of the student population, competition for admission is fierce.

ECONOMY

The division of the Korean Peninsula in 1945 left South Korea with few natural resources, most of the peninsula's arable land, and a largely unskilled labor force. The influx of northern refugees and the need to maintain a strong military added additional burdens. Yet through the planned development of an export-oriented economy, South Korea became one of the industrialized world's fastest-growing economies.

Agriculture. Two of every five South Koreans live in farm households. The figure was far larger in 1965, when more than two of every three South Koreans lived on farms. These farms—mostly on the western and southern coasts—are owner-operated. Rice, barley, vegetables, and legumes are the chief crops. Despite heavy use of fertilizers and high-yielding seeds, rising demand and a series of poor harvests have made South Korea a net importer of rice since 1977. South Korea's modern trawler fleet has made it one of the world's major fishing nations.

Industry. During the early 1960s, the government lured foreign investment with a work force that regularly put in 54-hour workweeks, accepted relatively low wages, and was forbidden to strike. The modern technology South Korea gained when factories were set up on its shores enabled Koreans to develop thriving export industries of their own.

From 1962 to 1971, South Korea's exports increased at a rate of 40 percent a year. Today, the nation's major exports are textiles, clothing, electrical machinery, footwear, steel, automobiles, ships, and fish. South Korea must import all fuels and most industrial raw materials. During the 1990s, it hopes to use its well-educated labor force to expand production of computers, computer chips, robots, and other "high-tech" goods.

South Korea's economy is dominated by huge conglomerates, or *chaebol,* established after World War II. The size and connections of these family-owned businesses give them tremendous clout.

HISTORY

Until the 1945 defeat of Japan, which had ruled the peninsula for 35 years, Koreans in the north and south shared 5,000 years of culture and history. (For details of Korea's history before 1945, see the entry on NORTH KOREA.) In 1945, at the end of World War II, Soviet troops occupied the northern half of the peninsula, and United States troops occupied the southern half. When Soviet troops refused to leave, the country was divided along the 38th parallel. A U.S. military government controlled the south until August 1948, when the Republic of Korea (South Korea) was established. The Soviet Union established the Democratic People's Republic of Korea (North Korea) a month later.

On June 25, 1950, Soviet-supported North Korean troops invaded South Korea in an attempt to unify the peninsula under Communist rule. Only the arrival of military forces from the United States and other nations—under U.N. leadership—saved South Korea from defeat. The fighting ended with an armistice in July 1953, and the Military Demarcation Line was established as a border between the two warring nations. Talks held since then have failed to reach an agreement for officially ending the war or reunifying Korea.

South Korea Since 1953. Syngman Rhee, South Korea's first president, led the country from 1948 until 1960, when student protests forced him to step down. In 1961, a military coup brought Park Chung Hee to power. After two years of martial rule, Park was elected president in 1963. He was reelected in 1967, 1971, and 1978.

In 1972, South Korea's constitution was amended, increasing President Park's power at the expense of the national legislature, the National Assembly. The amendments authorized the president to issue decrees and to restrict civil liberties. In October 1979, Park was assassinated. Two months later, Chun Doo Hwan, an army general, took control. His government declared martial law in mid-May 1980, imprisoning political activists and banning all demonstrations.

In 1987, Chun picked General Roh Tae Woo as his successor. Roh, who became president following multiparty elections held later that year, pressed for political reforms, including a more democratic constitution. In 1991, North and South Korea became U.N. members. That same year, the two Koreas signed a nonaggression pact. Former opposition leader Kim Young Sam won the December 1992 presidential election.

In 1996, former presidents Chun and Roh went on trial for their roles in the 1979 coup and in a 1980 massacre of pro-democracy demonstrators in Kwangju.

Government. In 1987, the National Assembly approved a new constitution, which took effect in February 1988. The constitution calls for direct presidential and National Assembly elections. It changed the presidential term from seven years to five years, and it revoked the president's power to dissolve the National Assembly. It also guaranteed several human rights, freedom of expression, habeas corpus, and the right of workers not associated with defense industries to join unions.

South Korea's president heads the government. The single-house legislature, the National Assembly, has 299 seats, and its members are elected to four-year terms. Anyone over the age of 20 can vote.

Reviewed by PAUL VARLEY,
Department of East Asian Languages and Culture, Columbia University

Mount Fuji, called *Fuji-san* by the Japanese, is clearly visible from Tokyo, 62 miles away.

 # JAPAN

At the end of World War II, Japan lay in ruins. Two million of its people had died in the war, a third of them civilians. Air raids had devastated its cities, and at least 13 million Japanese were homeless. Industry was at a standstill, and even farm output had declined. Many Japanese wore rags and were half-starved. All were mentally and physically exhausted. For the first time in its history, Japan was a conquered nation occupied by a foreign power.

Today, there is a new Japan, throbbing with life and vitality. It has become one of the top two or three trading nations in the world. Its people are prosperous. "Bullet trains" speed between Japan's rebuilt cities at 120 mi. (193 km.) per hour, and giant bridges and tunnels join the nation's main islands.

This transformation into an economic superpower, which is often called "the Japanese miracle," is due in no small part to some admirable —and traditional—characteristics of the Japanese people. Among them are a belief in the value of hard work, skill in developing group cooperation, and high standards in education.

Prosperity has created new challenges, however. The price for Japan's success has included explosive urban growth and overcrowding, water and air pollution, and damage to many of the nation's scenic treasures. Hills have been hacked down for factory sites or homesites, while mountains have been defaced by highways to accommodate city tourists. Many famous beauty spots have been obscured by hotels, restaurants, and trinket shops. For a time, Mount Fuji, Japan's highest mountain peak, almost disappeared from sight because of smog created by factories and cars. Today, that smog is gone, thanks to some of the world's most rigorous standards for auto emissions and industrial air pollution. In other areas, Japan still struggles to balance development with environmental protection.

It is also struggling with the charge by a few of its trading partners that some of its success has come at their expense. Thus, Japan finds itself torn between pride in its accomplishments and fear that other nations will take steps to discriminate against it. For this reason, the Japanese believe that their country's main hope for success in the future lies in increased international cooperation. Japan in the 1990s is taking a much more active role in world affairs, especially in Asia, where it is a dominant force.

THE LAND

The more than 3,000 Japanese islands form a long, relatively narrow chain, lying about 100 to 500 mi. (160 to 800 km.) off the east coast of Asia. From north to south, its four main islands are Hokkaido, Honshu, Shikoku, and Kyushu. Superimposed on a map of North America, they would stretch from Montreal, Canada, almost to the Gulf of Mexico. The most densely populated part of Japan, the island of Honshu, lies on the same latitude as North Carolina. The islands are bounded on the east by the Pacific Ocean and on the west by the Sea of Japan, the Korea Strait, and the East China Sea.

In area, Japan is smaller than France, yet its population is twice France's in size, with most Japanese squeezed into lowland plains that lie mainly along the seacoasts. More than 80 percent of Japan is covered with jagged mountains that are virtually uninhabitable, and only about 12 percent of Japan's land area is suitable for cultivation. Nonetheless, Japanese farms are so productive that, along with Japan's fishing fleet, they supply more than 70 percent of the nation's food.

The largest lowland plain is the region around Japan's capital city, **Tokyo,** on Honshu's southeast coast. More than 11 million people live in the Tokyo metropolitan area, which has one of the heaviest concentrations of people in the world. Packed alongside it are **Yokohama,** with about 3 million people, and **Kawasaki** with over 1 million.

More than 12 million people live on the plain around **Osaka,** which is 340 mi. (547 km.) southwest of Tokyo. Osaka itself has over 2.5 million people, while the port city of **Kobe** and the old capital of **Kyoto** have almost 1.5 million each. The area between Tokyo and Osaka contains one-third of Japan's total population.

More than three-quarters of all Japanese live in cities, making living accommodations cramped. Outside the cities, in the suburbs, land costs are far higher than those in New York City or London's suburbs. To buy land for a house, families in suburban Tokyo must put aside much of

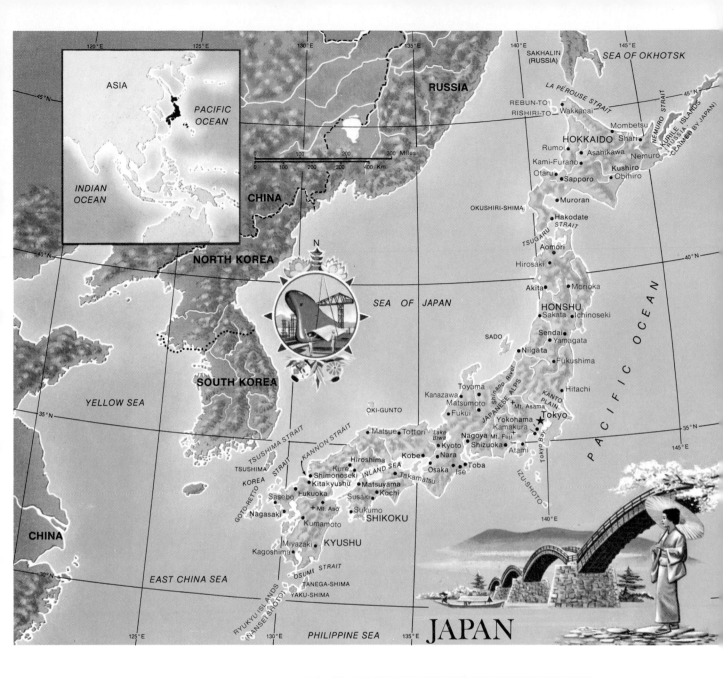

ASIA

PACIFIC OCEAN

INDIAN OCEAN

120°E 125°E 130°E 135°E 140°E 145°E

SEA OF OKHOTSK

SAKHALIN (RUSSIA)

RUSSIA

LA PÉROUSE STRAIT

45°N

REBUN-TO
RISHIRI-TO •Wakkanai Mombetsu

HOKKAIDO Shari

KURILE ISLANDS (RUSSIA) CLAIMED BY JAPAN

NEMURO STRAIT

Rumoi •Asahikawa Nemuro
Kami-Furano Kushiro
Otaru •Sapporo •Obihiro

NORTH KOREA

40°N

OKUSHIRI-SHIMA •Muroran
Hakodate
STRAIT
TSUGARU
•Aomori
Hirosaki

N

SEA OF JAPAN

•Akita •Morioka

HONSHU
•Sakata Ichinoseki
Sendai• •Yamagata
SADO Niigata• •Fukushima

40°N

PACIFIC OCEAN

SOUTH KOREA

35°N

YELLOW SEA

OKI-GUNTO

Toyama •Hitachi
Kanazawa• Shinano River KANTO PLAIN
•Matsue •Tottori Matsumoto JAPANESE ALPS +Mt. Asama
Lake •Fukui Yokohama •Tokyo ★
Biwa Kamakura
Kyoto• Nagoya Mt. Fuji Shizuoka
Kobe •Nara TOKYO BAY •Atami

TSUSHIMA STRAIT KANNON STRAIT
Hiroshima Osaka •Ise •Toba
KOREA STRAIT Kure• INLAND SEA
TSUSHIMA Shimonoseki• •Matsuyama Takamatsu
Kitakyushu• •Kochi
GOTO-RETTO Sasebo Fukuoka• •Susaki
Nagasaki• +Mt. Aso •Sukumo SHIKOKU
•Kumamoto

35°N

145°E

140°E

IZU-SHOTO

CHINA

30°N

EAST CHINA SEA

RYUKYU ISLANDS (NANSEI-SHOTO)

OSUMI STRAIT
TANEGA-SHIMA
YAKU-SHIMA

Miyazaki• KYUSHU
Kagoshima•

PHILIPPINE SEA

125°E 130°E 135°E

JAPAN

FACTS AND FIGURES

OFFICIAL NAME: Japan.

NATIONALITY: Japanese.

CAPITAL: Tokyo.

LOCATION: Eastern Asia. **Boundaries**—La Pérouse Strait, Pacific Ocean, Philippine Sea, East China Sea, Korea Strait, Sea of Japan.

AREA: 143,749 sq. mi. (372,310 sq. km.).

PHYSICAL FEATURES: Highest point—Mount Fuji (12,389 ft.; 3,776 m.). **Lowest point**—Tokyo (about 11 ft.; 3.4 m.). **Chief rivers**—Shinano, Ishikar, Tone. **Major lake**—Biwa.

POPULATION: 125,800,000 (1996; annual growth 0.2%).

MAJOR LANGUAGE: Japanese (official).

MAJOR RELIGIONS: Shinto, Buddhism, Christianity.

GOVERNMENT: Constitutional monarchy. **Head of state**—emperor. **Head of government**—prime minister. **Legislature**—Diet.

CHIEF CITIES: Tokyo, Yokohama, Osaka, Nagoya, Sapporo, Kobe, Kyoto, Fukuoka, Kawasaki.

ECONOMY: Chief minerals—coal, iron, manganese, uranium, zinc, copper, lead, gold. **Chief agricultural products**—rice, sugar, vegetables, fruits. **Industries and products**—metal and engineering industries, electrical and electronic products, chemicals, textiles. **Chief exports**—machinery, motor vehicles, electronics. **Chief imports**—petroleum and other fuels, wheat, soybeans, sugar, cotton.

MONETARY UNIT: 1 yen = 100 sen.

NATIONAL HOLIDAY: December 23 (Birthday of the Emperor).

FUJIYAMA: JAPAN'S SACRED MOUNTAIN

Mount Fuji, or Fujiyama, is Japan's highest mountain and the one closest to the hearts of the Japanese people, who call it *Fuji-san*. An almost perfect volcanic cone, this world-famous symbol of Japan has inspired countless poems and paintings since ancient times. It is on the island of Honshu, about 62 mi. (100 km.) southwest of Tokyo. Mount Fuji's snowcapped peak is clearly visible from the city.

Mount Fuji is actually the site of three volcanoes. The youngest began to form some 10,000 years ago. Its many eruptions covered the earlier volcanoes with a composite mixture of ash, cinders, rock fragments, and lava. Though it last erupted in 1707, geologists still classify it as active. Five small lakes and stands of virgin forest lie at its foot.

In size as well as in beauty, Mount Fuji is one of the world's major volcanoes. It soars to a height of 12,388 ft. (3,776 m.). Its crater measures 1,640 ft. (500 m.) in diameter. The diameter of its base, including the broad lava fields around it, is roughly 25 to 30 mi. (40 to 48 km.).

Climbing Mount Fuji began as a religious practice and has been carried on throughout the ages. Members of a sect that combines both Buddhist and Shinto beliefs consider the mountain sacred. Numerous shrines and temples dot its slopes, and a shrine shares the summit with a weather observatory.

Nowadays, many people climb Mount Fuji simply for pleasure. During the climbing season, which runs from July 1 to August 26, it is crowded with tens of thousands of people each day. Roads run more than halfway up the mountain. From there, climbers can walk to the summit in about five hours. To avoid summer crowds, some people risk avalanches to climb to the top in winter.

their earnings. When they can finally build their house, it is likely to be small and of poor quality. Renting a place to live is also very expensive. A typical apartment is often no larger than a good-sized room in an American city. Despite these drawbacks, people flock to cities like Tokyo, where life is varied and exciting, and where decisions are made that affect all of Japan and much of the rest of the world.

Climate. Japan's climate is temperate, roughly comparable to the east coast of North America. The surrounding oceans tend to make the winters and summers in Japan more moderate than those experienced on North America's east coast. They also bring more humidity and rain. Late autumn and winter are relatively dry, and most of Japan at that time enjoys long stretches of mild, sunny weather.

One exception to this rule is the west coast of Honshu, on the Sea of Japan. Winter winds from Siberia blow across the sea, which separates the Japanese islands from the Asian mainland. The winds pick up considerable moisture along the way and may dump as much as 72 in. (183 cm.) of snow on this part of Honshu.

Moderate temperatures and ample rainfall combine to make most of Japan luxuriantly green eight months a year. In other respects, however, nature has been less kind to Japan. In the late summer and early fall, parts of the country are likely to be struck by typhoons—storms with hurricane-force winds that cause great devastation. Japan also has many active volcanoes that sometimes erupt. Numerous faults run beneath the islands, and earthquakes are frequent; most of them are mild.

THE JAPANESE PEOPLE AND THEIR HISTORY

The origins of the Japanese people are obscure, but human skeletons dating from about 8000 B.C. are of a Mongoloid people closely related to the Chinese and Koreans. Historians believe that most of these early inhabitants probably came to Japan over a long period of time from northeastern Asia. There is evidence that many crossed over from the Korean peninsula, the closest point of the mainland to Japan. Yet it is possible that some early Japanese may have come from as far away as the South Pacific by a process of island-hopping.

One thing is certain: the various migrations to Japan halted by A.D. 400. From that time until the present, there has been no migration of any consequence into the Japanese islands. The Japanese people jelled more than a thousand years ago into a very homogeneous group with only one sizable ethnic minority, the Ainu. (See sidebar, page 444.)

Today, the Japanese tend to think of themselves as a racially "pure" people comprising a single great family. The largest ethnic minority in Japan now is a Korean community of about 700,000. They are the remainder of an even larger number who were brought to Japan during World War II to replace Japanese workers who had gone into the armed forces. Even today, the Japanese do not accept these Koreans as full members of their society.

Japanese myths maintain that the nation was founded in 660 B.C. by its first emperor, Jimmu, a direct descendant of the sun-goddess Amaterasu. Evidence found in tombs indicates, however, that the first emperors did not reign until sometime after A.D. 300. Japan's present emperor, Akihito, is descended from a family that seems to date from the early 500s. This is undoubtedly the longest-reigning family in the world.

Learning from China.   Under early imperial rule, the Japanese court in the province of Yamato began to borrow heavily from China's more advanced civilization. The Chinese writing system was adopted early in the 5th century. Buddhism, the principal religion of China at the time, was introduced in the year 552.

Buddhism was a great civilizing force as well as a vigorous new faith. Japanese converts to Buddhism voyaged to China to study. After many years, they returned home as skilled artists, musicians, poets, and craftsmen. The imperial court, which moved to Kyoto in 794, became a center of Buddhist learning and literary creativity. By the 900s, Japan was transformed into an advanced society whose culture was a unique blend of Chinese influences and Japan's own native traditions.

Japan's leaders also tried to create a strong central government in which the emperor would have all the power and majesty of China's emperors. By the mid-800s, however, Japan's emperors were reduced to figureheads, allowed to reign but not to rule. Real power was held by great landowning noblemen, who inherited high government posts. With few exceptions, Japan's emperors have been politically powerless ever since.

The Shoguns.   The decline in the power of the central government spurred provincial leaders to form vigilante bands of warriors for protection. Soon they were fighting each other for control of the country. In 1185, one of these leaders, Minamoto Yoritomo, defeated his rivals and set up a military government to rule Japan. He took the title of *shogun*, which means chief commander of the emperor's army.

THE AINU: JAPAN'S NATIVE PEOPLE

Before migrating groups arrived from the Asian mainland, the Ainu occupied most of the Japanese islands. Gradually, the newcomers conquered and absorbed the Ainu and became the main body of Japanese people. Today, fewer than 20,000 Ainu survive as a distinct cultural group, living mainly on the northern island of Hokkaido. Through intermarriage, they are rapidly being assimilated into the larger culture. Pure-blooded Ainu are rare.

Many anthropologists place the ancestors of the Ainu in the Caucasian, or white, race. In certain physical ways—heavy beards, wavy hair, and a light complexion—they seem more European than Asian. Their language, with several dialects, has no link to any other.

The Ainu culture's decline began after 1868, when the country embarked on rapid modernization, and accelerated after World War II. Traditionally, Ainu men engaged in hunting and fishing, while women gathered wild fruit and nuts, or dug for edible roots and bulbs with sticks. Today, they generally work as farmers and in the commercial fishing industry.

Ainu communities are still based on kinship groups, each headed by a chief. Other traditions also survive. Young women are commonly tattooed on the face and arms to indicate their readiness for marriage. Both men and women frequently wear earrings. Adult males never shave their beards.

The Ainu don traditional clothes on ceremonial occasions. Ainu religion is a form of nature worship, which holds that spirits control such forces as the wind, rain, hail, and fire. The Ainu also pay homage to the spirits of their ancestors.

Although the Ainu language has no written form, a rich Ainu folklore exists. Since the introduction of compulsory education, younger generations tend to consider Japanese more important than the Ainu language.

Yoritomo created a political system that was very similar to the feudal order that existed in Europe at the time. It was based on personal ties of loyalty and service that knights owed to their overlords. Knights were called *samurai*—those who "served." Their unwritten code of honor became known as *bushido*—"the way of the warrior." For almost 700 years, Japan was ruled by shoguns and their samurai retainers.

Japan's first contact with the West occurred in 1543, when a Portuguese ship landed off the coast of the southern island of Kyushu. Portuguese firearms made a great impression on Japan's overlords, and soon a lively trade developed with Portugal, Spain, Holland, and England. Jesuit missionaries, Roman Catholic priests who belonged to the Society of Jesus, followed in the wake of Portuguese traders. By the early 1600s, some 300,000 Japanese had been converted to Christianity.

Isolation. In 1600, Tokugawa Ieyasu became shogun and chose as his military capital the town of Edo, which would later become Tokyo. Under Ieyasu and his successors, known as the Tokugawa shoguns, Japan began a period of peace and stability that lasted 250 years. The shoguns achieved this period of relative calm by imposing strict controls that "froze" Japan's feudal order as it existed around 1600.

In time, any contact with the outside world was considered a threat to Japan's stability. The Tokugawa shoguns began to see European traders and missionaries as forerunners of military conquest. They crushed Christianity, expelled the traders, and closed Japanese ports to their ships. By 1641, only a limited number of Dutch and Chinese traders were allowed to do business in Japan. They were restricted to the port city of Nagasaki, in western Kyushu, where they were closely guarded. By such means, Japan effectively isolated itself from the rest of the world.

Japan's isolation ended on July 14, 1853, when a powerful U.S. Navy squadron entered Edo Bay (now Tokyo Bay). The squadron's commander, Commodore Matthew Perry, bore a letter from U.S. President Millard Fillmore. The letter demanded that Japan open its ports to American ships and trade.

Japanese leaders knew that resistance would be futile. The following year, Japan signed a treaty with the U.S., agreeing to open its ports to American ships. European countries soon made similar treaties with Japan. These treaties gave the West special privileges in Japan and greatly angered the Japanese people.

The Rush to Modernize. In 1863, samurai forces rose up against the government of the shogun and eventually toppled it. On January 3, 1868, they announced the "restoration" of rule by the emperor Meiji. In reality, however, the emperor remained merely a symbol of the nation.

Shoppers and strollers flock to The Ginza, Tokyo's main shopping and entertainment district.

During the period known as the Meiji Restoration, Japan underwent revolutionary changes designed to modernize it. The feudal system was abolished, and the country embarked on a program of rapid industrialization. Its leaders created a constitutional government and adopted a Western legal system. Education was made compulsory for all children, and to meet the needs of Japan's armed forces, all males were required to serve in the military.

Within a few decades, Japan was transformed into a modern nation and a world power. The Japanese government ended the "unequal treaties" that gave Western powers special privileges in Japan.

The Push for an Empire.   Japan sought to acquire an empire, fighting two wars for control of foreign territories and succeeding in both. The first, with China in 1894–95, ended with Japan acquiring the island of Formosa (Taiwan). The second war was with Russia, Japan's chief rival for domination of Korea and the Chinese province of Manchuria. In 1904–05, Japan surprised the world by winning a series of spectacular victories on land and sea against Russian forces. As a result, Japan won important rights in Manchuria and gained a free hand in Korea, which it annexed in 1910.

In World War I, Japan fought on the side of the victorious Allies against Germany. With a minimum of effort, it acquired almost all of Germany's island empire in the Pacific. At the 1919 peace conference in Versailles, France, Japan sat as an equal power with its Western allies.

During the 1920s, Japan developed a system of parliamentary government patterned after Great Britain's. But democracy was not deep-

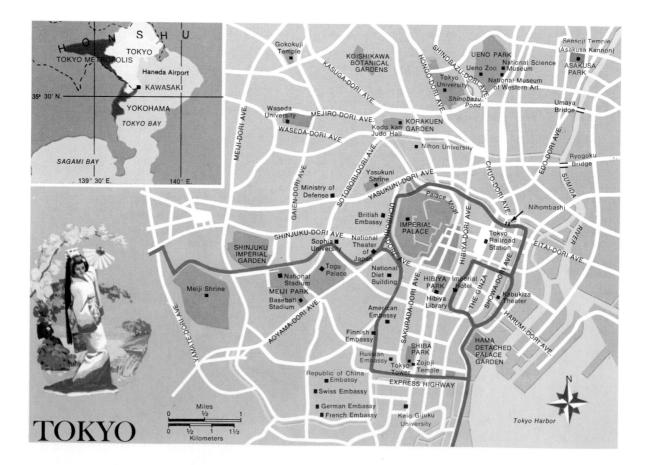

TOKYO

Tokyo, the capital of Japan, is also one of the world's largest cities. Its numerous skyscrapers (left) resemble those of any Western metropolis. But just a few blocks away, a typical side street (above), entered through a gateway called a *torii*, retains much distinctly Japanese charm.

rooted in Japan, and many people distrusted it. In the early 1930s, a worldwide business slowdown crippled Japan's trade, and hard times set in. Extreme nationalist groups believed that the solution to the problem was to expand Japan's empire by military conquest.

World War II. As the economic depression deepened, military leaders took control of the government. Japan invaded and annexed Manchuria in 1931. Japanese expansion in northern China led to a full-scale war with the Chinese in 1937.

The outbreak of World War II in Europe created new opportunities for Japan's military leaders. Following the fall of France in June 1940, Japanese troops began moving into Indochina, a French colony. This prompted the United States to stop shipping vital war materials, especially petroleum, to Japan. In retaliation, Japan attacked the U.S. naval base at Pearl Harbor, Hawaii, on December 7, 1941.

The war against the United States and its allies proved to be the greatest disaster in Japan's history. It cost Japan 2 million lives, including almost 200,000 who were killed in the atomic bombing of the cities of Hiroshima and Nagasaki. On September 2, 1945, Japan surrendered. For the first time in its proud history, Japan had been conquered—and would be occupied—by a foreign nation.

Postwar Changes. As a result of the war, Japan was stripped of all its military conquests, including Taiwan and Korea, and its armed forces were disbanded. Under U.S. General Douglas MacArthur, commander of the occupation forces, Japan was given a democratic constitution.

The cenotaph in Hiroshima's Peace Memorial Park commemorates Japan's war dead.

Perhaps its most interesting provision was the renunciation of war "forever." Economic and social reforms were also introduced.

Japan became an independent nation once again on April 28, 1952, when a peace treaty signed in 1951 in San Francisco, California, took effect. Since then, Japan has been ruled by moderate conservative governments that have maintained close cooperation with the West. Parliamentary democracy has become progressively stronger, and the nation's economy has grown tremendously. By the mid-1990s, Japan had become a world leader in every type of industrial production and appeared to be pushing ahead of most of the nations of the West.

THE POWER OF THE GROUP

A Japanese proverb maintains that "the nail that sticks up gets hammered down." The proverb sums up a characteristic of the Japanese people—intense loyalty to groups of all kinds and dislike of individualism. Put another way, the Japanese like team players, not "stars."

Japanese life has always centered on groups. Before the Meiji Restoration, the most important ones were the family, the feudal lord and his samurai retainers, and the rural village. The samurai have long since gone, and village life has declined, but family ties remain strong in Japan. Most elderly parents still live with their children, although tiny city apartments are making this arrangement increasingly difficult.

Next to family, the most important group in Japan is the company. Japanese employees establish strong ties to their organizations. They wear company pins, sing company songs, and go on company outings.

Most Japanese take part in organized group activities eagerly. There are hobby groups for everything from flower arranging and tea ceremonies—two traditional art forms—to the martial art of judo. The Japanese are enthusiastic tourists, and sight-seeing is almost always done in groups.

Why the Japanese place so much emphasis on group activities and solidarity is uncertain. Some think it is a way of coping with one of the country's oldest problems—many people living in a limited amount of space. Overcrowded conditions make cooperation and self-discipline essential if life is to be tolerable.

Harmony. The virtue most admired by the Japanese is harmony, for the success of the group depends on it. When a group has to make a decision, it is vital that all the members accept it. Decisions reached by a majority are not satisfactory—they leave too many people with the feeling that they are "losers."

The Japanese system of decision making rests on lengthy discussions in which all members express their points of view. Confrontations must be avoided, so opinions are expressed cautiously in language that is indirect and perhaps even vague. Eventually, there is a meeting of minds, and the decision will be very nearly unanimous.

The emphasis on group loyalty and harmony has done much to shape the personality of the Japanese people. On the surface, at least, they seem to be quite unemotional. They will rarely show affection in public, except toward young children. The tendency of Western people to kiss or embrace openly seems very strange to them. Japanese smile a good deal, but often to hide embarrassment or anger. They seldom raise their voices or scold. Among their friends, they are polite to a fault. A very formal people, they observe thousands of rules of etiquette.

Company picnics and other functions help nurture a strong sense of loyalty to one's employer.

The Japanese do not make class distinctions based on income, mainly because there are few extremes of wealth and poverty. Most of them, however, are very conscious of status or rank based on age, length of service in a company or government bureau, or leadership in a group. They see no reason why the aged should try to act young, or a company president should act like "one of the boys." Such behavior would seem extremely awkward to them.

Respect. The Japanese commonly show their respect by bowing. The higher a person's status, the deeper and longer are the bows that he or she will receive. In the family, aged parents receive the deepest bows, the first dip in the bathtub, and the seat of honor in the house.

The Japanese language has endless gradations of politeness that reflect status. Humble forms apply to oneself, while increasingly polite forms apply to people of higher rank. For example, a person who is admired for his wisdom is reverently addressed as *sensei,* or teacher. Among men, a very close friend may be addressed as *kun*. If his name is Tanaka, he would be addressed as Tanaka-kun. Almost everyone else, male or female, single or married, is called *san*, the equivalent of Mr., Mrs., or Miss. If a person's name is Suzuki, he or she would be called Suzuki-san. Except for children and intimate friends, people are almost never called by their first names.

WOMEN'S CHANGING ROLE

In feudal Japan, women were almost entirely subservient to men. From early childhood, a daughter was taught that she first owed obedience to her father, then to her husband, and in late life to her sons. The traditional Japanese homemaker served her husband almost slavishly. As recently as the 1920s, it was not uncommon to see her walking in the street laden down with young children and heavy bundles. Her husband walked before her, unencumbered by any burdens.

Since the end of World War II, the status of women in Japan has improved considerably. Much of it is due to the country's postwar constitution. It states: "There shall be no discrimination in political, economic, or social relations because of sex."

In recent years, more and more women have taken jobs in business and industry. Today, they comprise about 40 percent of the work force. Among them are many teachers, doctors, and small-business executives. Women executives in large companies are very rare, however, and almost as exceptional in the government ministries. The great majority of women employees hold low-status jobs and earn only about half as much as men doing the same work. About a third of all women employees are part-time workers.

Part of the problem lies in the fact that only a third of all university degrees go to women. Some parents feel that an expensive four-year college education is less important for a daughter than for a son.

But the future looks brighter for women in even the biggest Japanese companies. A 1986 law made sexual discrimination at the workplace illegal. There is a huge demand for university graduates—a demand that in the 1990s, male graduates can only begin to fill.

Married homemakers tend to have a limited social life. As a rule, Japanese men enjoy socializing with their business or work groups more than with their wives. A wife seldom goes out with her husband to din-

Statistically, Japan is a Buddhist country, with a vast majority of the population professing that religion. The Daibutsu (above), or Great Buddha, in Kamakura, attracts Buddhists and non-Buddhists alike. But Japan's native religion is Shinto, a faith marked by many elaborate ceremonies (left). Many Japanese consider themselves both Shintoist and Buddhist, celebrating joyous occasions with Shinto rites and solemn ones with Buddhist rites.

ners or parties. By and large, her social life is restricted to her children, a few close relatives, and some female friends she has known since school days.

JAPAN'S RELIGIONS

Japan's oldest native religion is Shinto, "the way of the gods." It is founded on the nature myths, legends, and rituals of the ancient Japanese. Today, there are thousands of Shinto shrines in Japan, often in places of great natural beauty. Some are still visited by eager sightseers, but these visits have little religious significance. Shinto survives today mainly in annual shrine festivals that give the Japanese an opportunity to wear traditional clothes and celebrate boisterously.

The modern Japanese tend to wear traditional costumes only on holidays and special occasions.

Buddhism was introduced to Japan from China before A.D. 555, and eventually it exerted a great influence on the country's fine arts, social institutions, and thought. It began to decline during Tokugawa times, when people became more concerned with the "here and now" and less with the hereafter. Yet most Japanese still consider themselves members of one of the major Buddhist sects, and many families keep ancestral tablets on small Buddhist altars in the home.

The Japanese see no conflict in having two religions, and most consider themselves both Shintoists and Buddhists. In fact, the two religions seem to complement each other very well. Such joyous events as birth and marriage are celebrated with Shinto rites. Funerals and communion with the dead are observed with Buddhist rites.

About 1.5 million Japanese are Christians—about 60 percent Protestant and 40 percent Roman Catholic. Christians have played a major role in education and social work and are widely admired as people of high moral principles. During the Christmas season, Japanese department stores enthusiastically display Christmas decorations and play Christmas carols.

Japanese society during Tokugawa times was dominated by Confucian thought. Confucianism in Japan was not a religion. It had no deities and no priesthood. As a philosophy, it emphasized the need for harmonious living, ethical conduct, and proper etiquette. Today, few Japanese think of themselves as Confucians, yet most of them are strongly influenced by Confucian concepts in their everyday lives.

FAMILY LIFE

Until modern times, marriages in Japan were arranged by parents. Typically, the parents of an eligible daughter would ask a relative or friend to find a suitable husband for her. The use of a go-between assured that there would be no angry confrontations between the families.

If the parents were satisfied that the proposed match was a good one, the young couple was expected to obey their wishes. It was believed, or hoped, that love would develop after the marriage.

Today, young people no longer feel obliged to marry partners chosen by their parents, yet many of them willingly accept their parents' guidance. One reason is that young Japanese tend to socialize in groups and are quite shy in one-on-one situations. As a result, they often lack confidence in their ability to choose appropriate marriage partners. A first meeting between a young man and woman is still commonly arranged by their parents. If, after a few dates, the two feel that they are personally compatible, they will become engaged. Go-betweens are still employed to investigate family backgrounds. One advantage of this system is that almost everyone who wants to get married can count on finding a mate.

Most Japanese are married in a traditional Shinto ceremony. The bride usually wears a kimono and a white headdress called a *tsuno-kakushi,* or horn-hider. Its purpose is to conceal the proverbial female horns of jealousy, and it signifies that the bride will never be jealous of her husband. The groom almost always wears Western-style clothes. Many grooms favor a cutaway, a formal coat with tails in the back.

After the ceremony, there is a reception and dinner at which many toasts are drunk. Later, individual guests approach the newlyweds, bow, and offer wishes for future harmony, fertility, and prosperity. October and November are the most popular months for getting married, for then the honeymooners can enjoy the brilliant colors of autumn.

A Woman's Domain. Japanese wives today have much more independence than their mothers and grandmothers had. The old Japanese saying, "When the husband calls, the woman jumps," rings false today. Today, the typical Japanese husband is considerate of his wife's feelings and refrains from giving her orders. More and more, in fact, the wife

A typical Japanese meal includes *tsukemono,* or pickled vegetables, and soybean-based *miso* soup.

Ikebana, the art of flower arranging, enjoys great popularity among Japanese women.

considers the household her domain and runs it with little interference from her husband. Although the husband is still the main provider, the wife controls the family finances and often puts her husband on an allowance.

The modern Japanese family centers on the mother, not the father. Fathers spend so much time at work and socializing afterward, they are rarely home when their small children are awake. The mothers are expected to hold their families together, and for the most part, they succeed.

Children. In few societies are the ties between a mother and her children as close as they are in Japan. When a Japanese mother has to go out shopping, she rarely trusts a baby-sitter to care for her infant child. Instead, she straps the child to her back and carries it with her. When the mother does household chores, she keeps her child near her or strapped to her back.

The Japanese believe that close physical contact is a natural form of affection. Typically, a Japanese child sleeps with its mother from infancy until the birth of a second child. Then the new baby sleeps with the mother, and the older child sleeps with the father. At least until they reach grade-school age, children continue to sleep with their parents. The mother and father bathe with their young children and sometimes use the occasion to have heart-to-heart talks with them.

By Western standards, Japanese children seem pampered and overprotected. The mother rarely spanks her children or even criticizes them. Yet when the time comes for her to teach them proper behavior, she has little difficulty in getting them to comply. Generally they want to please her, especially when she praises them with words like *o-riko* (nice child) and *joru* (skillful). By the time they enter grade school, Japanese children are well-behaved, polite to their teachers and other adults, and considerate toward each other. As they grow older, the children's dependence on their parents for affection and security is transferred to their school and work groups.

The House.   Japanese homes are built of very light materials and are designed to let in as much air and sunlight as possible. Walls are often made of balsa wood and paper panels that slide open or can be removed entirely. Though pleasant in the summer, they lack central heating and are cold in the winter. The only heat comes from the *kotatsu,* a small pit in the floor of one room that contains a charcoal-burning *hibachi.* A low table covers the kotatsu, and a quilt is stretched over the table and surrounding area. During the winter, the family members eat, read, talk, and watch TV around the kotatsu, their feet dangling inside it, their laps covered by the quilt.

The Japanese have found other ways to keep warm. They take long, steaming-hot baths in a deep wooden tub, and drink hot tea often. They sleep on thick, heavy comforters called *futons* that they stretch out on the floor, one next to another. Then they cover themselves with quilts and huddle close together for additional comfort. During the day, the bedding is easily folded up and stored in a closet.

A typical home is quite small and cramped, averaging less than 200 sq. ft. (18.6 sq. m.) in Tokyo. Kitchens are especially tiny and inconvenient, and Japanese homemakers are reluctant to show them to visitors.

The newer Japanese homes and city apartment buildings feature Western-style kitchens with modern refrigerators and gas ranges. Western beds, chairs, and other furniture are becoming popular with families that can afford them. Many Japanese are even giving up their traditional baths for Western-style showers.

The blocks-long Nishiki market in Kyoto draws throngs of shoppers looking for holiday foods.

Food Preparation.　Rice is still the main food in the Japanese diet, and it is very easy to prepare in an electric cooker. Vegetables such as cucumbers, radishes, eggplant, cabbage, and gourds can be bought pickled and ready to serve. Other vegetables can be cooked in oil for only a minute or two over a very hot fire. Fish, a Japanese staple, is eaten raw, sun-dried, fried, or broiled. It may also be lightly cooked in a clear soup. Desserts are plain, usually a piece of fresh fruit or a bowl of rice with hot tea poured over it.

Formerly, the Japanese homemaker had to spend much of her day shopping at various small neighborhood stores for her food, which was always fresh. Now, supermarkets are everywhere in the cities, stocked with foods from all over the world. These and modern refrigerators make it unnecessary for her to make daily shopping trips.

A typical Japanese homemaker begins her day before anyone else in the house and is the last to go to bed at night. Yet she does not feel "trapped," and she places less emphasis on an outside career than do Western women. She cherishes her role as mother and homemaker and derives great satisfaction from being the dominant figure in the family.

EDUCATION

The Japanese are probably the most education-conscious people in the world. From the time of the Meiji Restoration, government leaders have stressed the importance of education to Japan's development. Today, education is considered central to the nation's economic success.

Japanese schools, which are under considerable central control, have achieved a remarkably uniform level of excellence. The Ministry of Education regularly compares Japan's level of educational achievement with that of other nations and is not satisfied unless it ranks at or near the top. It constantly pressures the schools to raise their standards.

All children must attend six-year elementary schools and three-year junior high schools. One result is almost 100 percent literacy, an attainment rare among nations. Another is an eagerness to pursue more

Much of a Japanese mother's self-image rests on how well her children do in school.

"EDUCATION MAMAS"

Japan's ardent pursuit of education puts a good deal of pressure on mothers, who hold themselves responsible for their children's performance in school. If a mother's children do well, she will be praised by teachers, friends, and neighbors. If they do poorly, her image suffers. As a result, mothers become what the Japanese call "education mamas"—assistant teachers and hard taskmasters, ambitious

schooling. About 94 percent go on to senior high schools. About 40 percent of all high school graduates continue on to higher education. This is less than the U.S. rate of about 50 percent, but well ahead of the nations of Western Europe.

Education in Japan is more demanding than it is in the U.S., except at the university level. The school day is longer, the school week is five and a half days, and summer vacation is little more than a month. Discipline in the schools is strict, with daily homework assigned from the first grade on. All students are expected to study a foreign language, generally English, in junior high school. Math students are expected to complete calculus in senior high school. About half of all students receive outside tutoring or attend after-school academies for further drill and instruction.

Education and Careers. The great educational striving in Japan is in part due to traditions like Confucianism that emphasized the importance of learning. But modern Japanese have an even more compelling reason for pursuing education. In no other society does a successful career in business or government depend so much on an individual's educational achievement.

The best companies and the most important government ministries recruit the graduates of the top-ranking universities and virtually assure them of lifetime jobs with steady advancement. Those who graduate from other universities usually settle for lesser jobs, but they, too, can count on security and white-collar status. As a result, almost every student who is ambitious for success seeks to enter a university, where there is room for only two of every five applicants. Only one of every six candidates to a top-ranking university gets in.

In Japan the most prestigious institutions of higher learning are the national, or public, universities. Tokyo University ranks at the top of the list; after it come other former "imperial" universities such as Kyoto and Kyushu. Next come the leading private universities such as Keio and Waseda.

for their children's academic success.

Starting with the first grade, children are given homework that is often too difficult for them to do without help. Sometimes the homework is not easy for the mother, either, because many changes have taken place in teaching since she went to school. To prepare herself, she studies at home and often consults with her children's teachers. Keeping one step ahead of her children is a challenge that the Japanese mother takes seriously.

A mother's reputation as a tutor is likely to be well-known in the community. At group meetings of parents and teachers, for example, she may hear teachers praise or criticize her, in the mild Japanese manner, depending on how well her children are doing in school. On certain days, she and other mothers are required to observe their children in the classroom. Teachers evaluate each child's performance aloud, directing their comments to the mother. It will be clear to all whether or not the mother has succeeded in her role as an assistant teacher.

A typical Japanese mother pushes her children hard to do well in school, but she also pushes herself hard. At exam time, she shares their anxiety and excitement. Their success will be her greatest reward; their failure, her greatest sorrow.

Entrance to the national universities is based on merit, rather than social status or the ability to pay. As a result, these universities draw the best students from all walks of life.

Examination Hell. Students who wish to continue their education after junior high school must pass stiff entrance exams both for senior high school and university. The pressure to pass these exams, which are given in February and March each year, is so great that the Japanese call it "examination hell."

During the "examination season," almost everyone in Japan gets caught up in the excitement. Experts appear on TV talk shows to give advice to parents. Newspapers and magazines report on the records of high schools in advancing students to universities. On street corners, in shops, and at dinner, the upcoming examinations are the main topic of conversation.

Exam results are posted on school bulletin boards. Anxious parents and their children begin to gather around the schools 24 hours in advance. When the results are put up, some people fear to look. If a student has succeeded, the parents will be all smiles. If not, they will be terribly gloomy. Students who fail often enroll in special "cram" schools to try again the next year.

Apart from entrance exams, competition in Japanese schools is limited. Grades are not given much importance, and differences in ability are played down. Hardly anyone is ever "flunked out." Once students are admitted to a school, rivalry is subordinated to loyalty and friendship within the group.

Students who get into the top universities often let their studies slide for a while, perhaps in reaction to the punishing years of secondary education. They may devote themselves to sports, hobbies, or political

Japanese students must pass strenuous examinations to attend both high school and college.

Kabuki theater is considered the most versatile form of Japanese drama.

activities. Eventually, though, they settle down to prepare for the next round of exams they will take to enter the business world or government service.

ARTS AND LEISURE

Although the Japanese subordinate their individuality to the group, they still retain a strong sense of self-identity, which they express in a variety of hobbies and other pastimes. The majority of Japanese are skilled in at least one art, whether it is music, dancing, drama, or painting. There are both traditional and modern forms, and each one has a large number of devoted followers.

Traditional Arts

Poetry. Literally millions of Japanese express themselves by writing poetry. Poetry magazines and study groups are very popular, and each year there is a national poetry contest. The winning poems are read in the presence of the emperor, who contributes a poem of his own. Generally the Japanese prefer the old forms like *haiku*, which attempts to convey moods and scenes with great sensitivity in 17 syllables. Bashō, a master of haiku in Tokugawa times, wrote this example:

An ancient pond.

A frog jumps in.

The sound of water.

In the original Japanese, the poem's first line contains five syllables; the second, seven; and the third, five. To capture so much in so few words takes the kind of control and sharp insight that the Japanese admire in all their arts. Calligraphy, a way of combining art and penmanship, is a required course in schools.

Drama. Traditional drama also flourishes in Japan and has many followers. *No* theater, which originated in the 1500s, is a highly stylized form of drama that combines music, dance, and poetry. The players wear masks that may express emotion as movingly as any human face, and the story is chanted with great formality. *Kabuki* developed in the late 1600s and was popular among the urban merchant classes. It features elaborate sets, sentimental plots, and action that is often violent. *Bunraku*, which dates from the same period, uses puppets that are almost life-size. They act out their roles so convincingly that the viewer often forgets that they are not flesh-and-blood actors.

Nature. Most Japanese find fulfillment in their love of nature. Nature hikes and outings are extremely popular and provide needed respites from the pressures of society. Even at home the Japanese are reminded of nature in the tiny landscape gardens they cultivate. Generally they seek to create a miniature replica of great mountains, forests,

THE JAPANESE LANGUAGE

Spoken Japanese, which dates from prehistoric times, is not particularly difficult, but written Japanese is extremely difficult to learn. Written Japanese began about 1,300 years ago, when the Japanese began to borrow Chinese writing. At first, this was a picture language, like Egyptian hieroglyphs. The Japanese, however, used the Chinese characters, called *kanji*, to represent images and sounds in their own spoken language. These kanji are the basis

Women spend years learning the many intricacies of the Japanese tea ceremony.

and bodies of water. This is accomplished by the artful arrangement of a few rocks, bushes, and dwarf trees, and a pond or a stream. Another extension of this love of nature is flower arranging *(ikebana),* practiced by both men and women. Many department stores have exhibitions of both traditional and new forms of this art.

Tea Ceremony. The tea ceremony *(chanoyu)* is a traditional art that aims at creating a beautiful experience. It is a very formal way of serving tea that emphasizes the beauty of the pottery and the grace of the host

of the Japanese written language. Scholars know thousands of kanji, and 1,850 of them are used in everyday reading of newspapers and magazines. A student must learn nearly 900 kanji by the end of sixth grade.

In addition to kanji, there is a group of 48 characters called *hiraganas,* which are used mainly to represent the sounds of prepositions, participles, and other less important parts of speech, and also 48 *katakanas,* used mainly to represent the sounds of foreign words that have come into the Japanese language. Japanese also learn one or another system of *Romajis,* which are Japanese words represented in the Roman alphabet. (Usually in the seventh grade, students also begin to learn English.)

A few people have suggested that this difficult language be simplified, perhaps reduced to an alphabet such as Western nations use. But most Japanese would rather not change, for the whole rich literature of the centuries would then be largely lost. A number of foreign words, particularly scientific terms, have entered the Japanese language. But Japanese is rich in the ways in which it can express fine shadings of personal feeling and delicate differences in the sights, sounds, and smells of things.

or hostess in their slow and deliberate movements. The mood that the tea ceremony seeks is one of complete spiritual calm and detachment from worldly concerns. Traditionally, during the 1500s, warriors resting from battle would practice this ceremony.

Mass Culture

Leisure activities made possible by a high standard of living and advanced technology are often referred to as "mass culture." Enthusiasm for spectator sports is characteristic of modern industrial societies. So are such popular leisure pastimes as watching TV, reading, and going to the movies. No Westerners outdo the Japanese in their pursuit of mass culture.

Mass Communication. Practically every Japanese household has at least one television set, and most have color TVs. Japan has two government networks, known as NHK, supported by a tax on TV sets. One of them broadcasts educational programs, including instruction in foreign languages and mathematics. The other competes with the private networks in presenting general-interest programs such as news, drama, comedy, and quiz shows. American movies and TV shows are very popular in Japan. They are presented on home screens with dubbed-in Japanese voices.

The Japanese are exceptionally avid readers, a fact that is reflected in the huge circulations of their newspapers. Average daily newspaper circulation amounts to about one copy for every two people, a ratio that is among the highest in the world and almost twice that of the U.S. Because Japan is a small country, its major newspapers are either national or regional, rather than local.

Perhaps the most striking aspect of Japanese newspapers is their sameness. Virtually the same news appears on almost the same pages of every newspaper. The next to the last page of each, for example, is always devoted to news of crime, accidents, and human-interest stories. The papers have very few interpretive articles, and even the points of view expressed in the editorials seem similar—a reflection, perhaps, of the fact that most Japanese share a single view of the world.

Nonetheless, Japanese newspapers maintain high journalistic standards. They have large numbers of reporters who provide full coverage of both national and international news, and stories are carefully edited to make sure they are accurate.

Japanese magazines offer more variety than the newspapers, but their circulations as a rule are smaller. A few monthlies are general-interest magazines that feature serious articles. A large number of weeklies are specialty magazines covering a wide range of interests, from knitting to sports. Others tend to be sensational and deal in gossip about celebrities.

Literature. The end of World War II produced an immediate boom in the publication of Japanese books. Promised freedom of expression, writers rushed to complete manuscripts and get them into print. Japanese literature showed great vitality as it reached out to a truly mass audience. Novels reflected the demoralization of the Japanese people at the end of the war, and some were harshly critical of the army. In more recent years, a familiar theme of Japanese novelists is the desire to escape from the pressures of modern industrial society.

Film. The postwar period also developed into a golden age for Japanese moviemakers. U.S. occupation forces encouraged the film industry to provide entertainment for a people that sorely needed it. Soon the Japanese were producing movies that ranked with the best in the world, and many of them were acclaimed in Western countries. Among the most popular films in Japan and abroad were those of the director Akira Kurosawa. They include *Rashomon, To Live,* and *Seven Samurai.*

In recent years, moviemaking in Japan has declined due to the competition of television. The major studios have been reduced to turning out low-budget "junk" films, but a few independent producers keep alive the high artistic standards achieved in the golden age after World War II.

Sports. Practically every Western form of athletics is enjoyed in Japan. The most popular Western sport is baseball, which the Japanese call *basuboru.* Professional baseball teams are sponsored by business firms and have English names such as Giants, Dragons, and Whales.

The Japanese are also avid golfers. In 1990, about 18 million people played the sport on more than 1,700 golf courses. Many of these courses belonged to resorts that promoted two-day golfing weekends.

The most popular sport native to Japan is sumo wrestling, which may be 2,000 years old. Sumo wrestling is vaguely associated with Shinto rites, and the referees wear robes similar to a priest's. The contestants wear only loincloths and tie their hair up in the traditional Japanese topknot. Sumo wrestlers are immensely heavy and strong. At the peak of his career, a sumo wrestler will weigh about 310 pounds. Sumo wrestling makes a very lively television show, and champions have huge followings in the main cities.

Sumo wrestlers begin grappling only after completing an elaborate set of rituals.

Baseball has become enormously popular in Japan. Some teams have their own cheerleaders.

Amusement Areas. Mass culture thrives in many forms in modern Japan. City amusement areas have thousands of bars, cafés, and restaurants that are usually filled with people. Huge department stores that offer a wide variety of standardized goods cater to large numbers of customers. They often have a children's zoo on the roof, restaurants, a theater, and a gallery for art exhibits, which are usually of high quality.

Since the end of World War II, Japan has been flooded by Western mass culture, especially from the United States. The opening of a 204-acre Disneyland near Tokyo in 1983 was further evidence of this trend. Some Japanese fear that eventually their culture will become indistinguishable from that of the West.

Others doubt it. In premodern times, they say, Japan borrowed heavily from Chinese culture. More recently, during the Meiji era, Japan borrowed extensively from the culture of the West. Yet always the Japanese molded and adapted whatever they borrowed to suit their own tastes and purposes. By the same process, the Japanese are likely to retain their distinctive cultural identity in the future.

JAPAN'S ECONOMY

Japan's remarkable recovery from the devastation it suffered in World War II, and its rise since 1950 to become an economic giant, has been widely acclaimed as "the Japanese miracle." Today, the name "Japan" conjures up images of modern, efficient factories, computers, robots, and endless streams of automobiles pouring out of the holds of ships. Actually, the Japanese economy is amazingly robust, not just in manufacturing and trade, but in farming and fishing as well.

Agriculture

Though Japan's land is not extraordinarily fertile, and Japanese farms are quite small, Japan's farmers and fishermen are able to supply all but 30 percent of the nation's food. In most of Japan, the average farm is no larger than 2.5 acres (1 hectare). The high productivity of Japan's farm acreage is the result of a long growing season, plentiful rainfall, skillful farming techniques, and a great deal of hard work.

Since the end of World War II, Japanese farmers have made increasing use of modern technology, including machines and chemical fertilizers and insecticides. This has greatly reduced the need for farm workers. Until about 1950, almost half the population was engaged in agriculture. Today, only 8 percent of Japanese workers are engaged in farming, fishing, and forestry, many of them only part-time. Japan's fishing fleet, one of the world's largest, accounts for nearly 15 percent of the global catch.

About 40 percent of Japan's agricultural land is devoted to irrigated rice cultivation. On the rest, farmers grow dry-field crops such as grains,

The Japanese fishing industry is one of the largest and most efficient in the world.

Although some rice farmers continue to cultivate their crops by hand (left), the greater efficiency of advanced agricultural machinery (above), introduced during the 1970s, has caused Japan's rice production to become almost completely mechanized.

vegetables, fruits, and tea. Because so little of Japan's land can be cultivated, the nation's resourceful farmers often plant vegetables on terraced hillsides or on small plots in mountain valleys.

Manufacturing and Trade

While Japan's population has more than doubled since 1952, the standard of living has improved immeasurably, thanks in large part to the great expansion of manufacturing industries. Today, one-third of all Japanese workers are engaged in manufacturing, mining, and construction.

Japan has achieved its industrial growth despite its lack of the very natural resources on which its factories depend. The country has practically no domestic sources of oil, iron ore, lead, coal, copper, zinc, or other minerals. It must import all of these vital resources.

Japan depends on foreign trade to pay for the raw materials its factories require. Japanese steel, ships, machinery, computers, cars, and a host of other products are sold all over the world. The most basic fact of economic life in Japan today is its dependence on the outside world. It depends on other nations not just for raw materials, but for the money it needs to pay for them. Slightly more than half of Japan's workers are involved in trade and services.

Postwar Opportunities. Japan's spectacular industrial growth can be attributed to a number of factors. For one thing, the country already possessed a skilled and educated work force with long experience in industry. For another, the destruction of out-of-date factories during the war actually benefited Japan afterward. Japan's destroyed factories were replaced by brand-new ones that were often superior to their aging counterparts in the U.S. and Europe.

Also, the U.S. assumed the responsibility for Japan's defense, relieving it of the burden of supporting large military forces. The breakup of the *zaibatsu*—giant, family-owned business combines—encouraged competition and growth. The U.S. and its allies reduced barriers to trade between nations everywhere after the war, and worldwide commerce flourished. Freer trade provided new opportunities for Japan to sell its products abroad.

But Japan's brilliant success must also be attributed to certain distinctive characteristics of Japanese society, particularly in its system of lifetime employment. This system makes for a loyal and enthusiastic work force that takes pride in its products. Workers monitor their output so carefully that there is no need for inspectors to control the quality of manufactured goods.

Cooperation. The Japanese system fosters a spirit of cooperation, rather than competition. At the white-collar level, junior executives are recruited after graduation from the top-ranking universities. Often their scores on company examinations are less important than the fact that they attended the same school as their employers. This, it is assumed, will foster mutual loyalty and harmony in the workplace.

The new recruits become a distinct company group based on the year they were hired. Throughout their careers, they will advance together in pay and rank, although the more able will be given more important assignments. They will not be asked to serve under anyone from their own group or a younger group. To prevent this from happening, all but a few will be retired when they reach the ages of 55 to 60. Only the ablest members of the group will continue on to the top executive posts. Financial loss due to early retirement is often offset by part-time employment in a subsidiary company.

This system eliminates competition to the group by younger subordinates. A younger man doesn't try to outshine his superior in order to win his job—that would be useless. He may at times disagree with his superior, but in the end he will support him loyally. Everyone feels that he is part of a team, and a spirit of cooperation prevails from one level of management to another.

The "Salary Man." A male executive with a large company or a government ministry is known in Japan as a "salary man." The term implies that he is a successful white-collar employee who can count on a regular paycheck regardless of business conditions. Even during a recession, he will not be laid off.

His company provides a typical salary man with other benefits that enable him to live well. He receives sickness and accident benefits and a

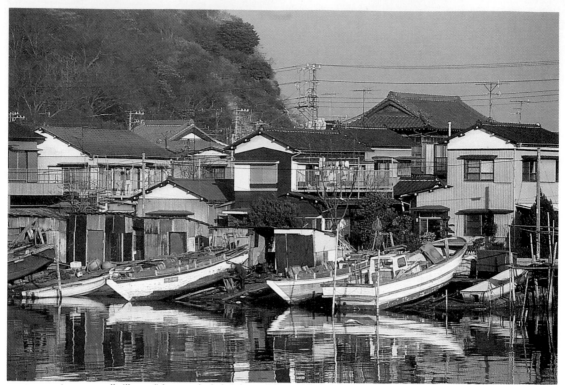

In some small villages, fishermen dock their boats right outside their homes.

retirement pension. These are important advantages in a country whose public-welfare services provide only modest assistance. Inexpensive company housing may be available to him, as well as a company inn where he may spend his vacations. He attends parties and athletic meets sponsored by his company. At least once a year, he is treated to an overnight trip to the countryside with other employees. On these trips, conflicts that have developed in the workplace are smoothed over, and the solidarity of the group is reaffirmed.

The salary man's superiors take a personal interest in his problems both at work and at home. He can call on them to help his daughter enter a school, find a job for his son, or even to counsel him about marital problems he may be having.

In return for the company's commitment to him for life, the salary man works diligently. He does not object to working overtime without extra compensation, if the need arises. As a rule, he doesn't take all the vacation time he is allowed. He would consider that selfish and disloyal to his work associates and superiors. He is proud to be a member of a large, stable organization, and even derives a sense of power from it. He is likely to regard his status as more desirable than that of either the independent businessman or professional.

Blue-collar Workers. The system of lifetime employment applies to blue-collar workers as well as executives, and has strongly influenced the organization of labor unions. Instead of separate craft unions, each large company has a union that represents all workers. This union is often affiliated with a nationwide labor federation. Because the company guarantees workers job security, union members tend to identify with the company's interests. They may bargain hard for higher wages and better working conditions, but as a rule, they do not engage in prolonged strikes. The number of workdays lost in strikes is less than a third of that in the U.S. and Great Britain. Union members also do not oppose technological advances. They know that if their old skills are no longer needed, the company will train them in new skills.

The company, on its part, wants goodwill and harmony with its permanent force of workers, and it will rarely lay off workers. As a result, the rate of unemployment in Japan in recent decades has usually been below 2 percent.

The system of lifetime employment does not apply to all workers. Those who are not covered by it include workers in small industrial plants or retail shops, and most women, who have always been looked on as temporary workers.

Japan's top businessmen today are the salaried executives who manage, but do not own, the large companies. Although their salaries are quite modest, their positions give them great power and prestige. In traditional Japan, a preoccupation with making profits from business activities was regarded as unethical and unpatriotic. To some extent, this attitude still persists today. Japanese business managers derive satisfaction not so much from quick profits, as from long-term growth that increases the company's share of its market and wins it national and international prestige.

In pursuing the goal of growth, they work closely with the Japanese government. The powerful Ministry of International Trade and Industry (MITI) sets production goals for specific industries, oversees the pur-

Japan's highly efficient steel industry exports nearly one third of its output.

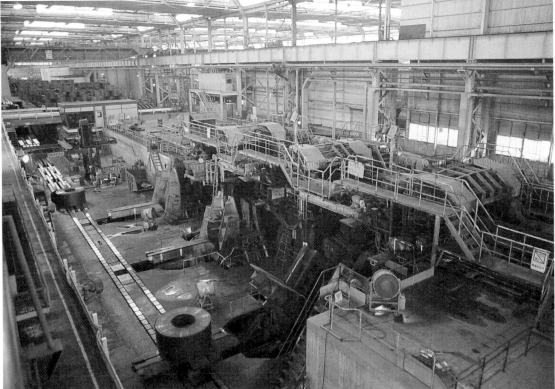

Japan exports 60 percent of the passenger cars it produces, many to the United States.

chase of foreign technology, and encourages competition between companies. Though MITI's role in providing guidance to industry has waned in recent years, there is still considerable cooperation between government and business. Business accepts direction from the government, yet there is ample opportunity for free, competitive enterprise.

Challenges. As an industrial giant, Japan faces many challenges. With few natural resources, it must depend on the outside world for the fuel and raw materials that its industries use.

The shakiness of Japan's reliance on others was brought home in 1973, when the price of oil rocketed, causing a major crisis for Japanese industry. Japan responded to the "oil shock" by developing alternative sources of energy, chiefly nuclear power.

Japan also began moving away from "smokestack industries" that rely heavily on imported raw materials and fuel. Steel and shipbuilding, for example, are in decline. High-technology industries such as computers, microelectronics, and fiber optics, which have low material and energy costs, are on the rise.

While Japan's dependence on foreign imports of raw materials and fuel has lessened, it is still huge. To pay for them, Japan exports a vast amount of manufactured products all over the world. During the late 1980s, Japanese exports increased dramatically, while imports increased only slightly. As a result, Japan spends far less on other nation's goods than it earns from its exports—a source of friction between Japan and many of its trading partners, who feel that this imbalance hurts their own industries.

Because of Western criticism, Japan has occasionally imposed limits, or quotas, on some of its exports. By 1994, the trade imbalance raised the possibility of a trade war between Japan and the United States.

Another Western complaint is that Japanese taxes make it difficult for Western companies to sell their products in Japan. Actually, Japanese import tariffs are on a par with those of most industrial nations. Some Japanese suggest that Western companies would do better in Japan if their representatives spoke Japanese.

Others sympathize with outsiders who find it hard to understand the way Japanese companies do business. Japanese companies tend to buy products and services mainly from companies with which they have had a long association. In such associations, personal friendship and trust are important, and such ties cannot be established quickly.

GOVERNMENT AND POLITICS

The constitution that U.S. occupation authorities drew up for Japan after World War II went into effect in 1947. The great majority of the Japanese people enthusiastically embraced it. They welcomed the opportunity to return to democratic rule after years of authoritarian rule by military leaders.

The Diet. The new constitution stripped the Japanese emperor of all claims to power, defining his role as merely "the symbol of the state and the unity of the people." Real power was placed in the hands of the Diet, or parliament. A bicameral legislature, the Diet consists of an upper house, the House of Councillors, and a lower house, the House of Representatives. Councillors are elected for six-year terms, with half their seats up for election every three years. Representatives are elected for four-year terms.

The House of Representatives has the last word in Japan's political system. It elects one of its members prime minister. The prime minister, in turn, selects members of the cabinet. The House of Representatives can remove the prime minister at any time with a vote of "no confidence." Instead of resigning, however, the prime minister can call for new elections for the lower house, in hopes of winning the support of a majority of the newly elected representatives.

The 1947 constitution also spells out the rights of the Japanese people. Among them are the right of all men and women 20 years of age or older to vote, the right of workers to bargain through unions, and the right of everyone to receive an equal education.

Political Parties. The ruling political party in Japan from 1955 to 1993 and again from January 1996 was the Liberal Democratic Party (LDP), which was formed in 1955 by the merger of two moderate, agrarian-based, conservative parties that joined forces to offset the rising strength of more liberal parties. The LDP is actually a coalition of factions that work together to retain power, although at times competition between those factions is fierce and the party controls the legislature by only slim margins. From July 1989 to July 1992, the LDP lost control of the upper house of the Diet—the first time since 1955 it had not controlled both houses. The LDP managed to stay in power for such a long time because of its record in achieving economic success, but there was mounting public dissatisfaction over a series of financial scandals that had contributed to the fall of six LDP governments between 1982 and 1993.

The funeral of Emperor Hirohito in 1989 marked the formal end of a reign that began in 1926.

In the July 1993 elections, the LDP lost its majority in the lower house of the Diet for the first time since 1955. It still had the largest number of seats of any party, however, and remained a powerful political force. Morihiro Hosokawa of the Japan New Party then became head of a seven-party non-LDP coalition government that pledged to end corruption and give greater political representation to urban voters. He was forced to resign in April 1994 amid charges of financial improprieties. His successor, Hata Tsutomu, resigned after only two months in office. The SDPJ, which had withdrawn from the ruling coalition in April, then joined forces with its former arch-rival, the LDP, to form a new coalition government. On July 29, 1994, Murayama Tomiichi became Japan's first Socialist prime minister since 1948. He resigned in January 1996 and was succeeded by Hashimoto Ryutaro of the LDP.

Consensus Politics.   The Japanese have molded the system of Western parliamentary democracy to suit their own needs and style. The great value that they place on harmony and consensus, for example, is reflected in the way that bills are passed in the Diet. Government leaders negotiate with the various political parties over proposed legislation long before it is presented to the Diet. The result is that almost two-thirds of the bills adopted by the Diet are generally passed unanimously. In Japan, a moderate, centrist public has created a political system that is extremely effective in converting the popular will into political action.

THOMAS SHIBATA, Tokyo Metropolitan University
CHARLES G. CLEAVER, Grinnell College
IRA PECK, author, *Japan* (Scholastic World Culture Series)

Sydney, the largest city in Australia, is also the chief distribution center for the South Pacific area.

AUSTRALIA AND NEW ZEALAND

Australia and New Zealand stand apart from all other South Pacific nations, and from each other as well. Geographically, they reach farther south than any of the region's other nations. Culturally, the overwhelming majority of people in both nations trace their ancestry to the British Isles. These two facts for a long while made Australians and New Zealanders feel very much alone, as if they were manning outposts of British civilization in a hostile environment.

By the 1980s, that attitude had largely evaporated. For one thing, both nations had become more worldly, as they absorbed growing numbers of immigrants from Asia, the Pacific islands, and Southern and Eastern Europe. For another thing, they had become more sensitive to the needs of their indigenous peoples—the Australian aborigines and the New Zealand Maori. For still another, Australians and New Zealanders realized that their future prosperity depends on close trade links, not just with the West, but with Asia.

Nonetheless, Great Britain's imprint on both nations remains indelible. English is the official language of both nations, and both belong to the loose confederation of former British colonies called the British Commonwealth. Australia and New Zealand have the same head of state—the United Kingdom's Queen Elizabeth II. Their parliamentary democracies have roots in Great Britain, as does their commitment to the rule of law. Indeed, their systems of common (unwritten) law grow directly out of England's.

Unlike Australia, New Zealand is quite mountainous and has a much-indented coastline.

And yet both of these nations are completely independent. This fact was underscored by New Zealand's 1985 decision to refuse docking rights to the nuclear-powered or nuclear-armed warships of its most powerful ally, the United States, and by the Australian government's 1993 announcement that it planned to sever Australia's ties to the British crown by the year 2001. This independent spirit is also reflected in literature and art. Maori carvings and aboriginal paintings are as unique as the kiwi bird of New Zealand and the kangaroo of Australia.

THE LAND

The two nations have distinctive landscapes. Located just south of the islands of Southeast Asia, Australia and its southern island of Tasmania are part of a single continent. In land area, it is similar in size to the continental United States. Australia sits mainly on a low plateau, much of it flat, dry, and with little vegetation.

In contrast, New Zealand is a group of largely mountainous islands situated about 1,200 mi. (1,930 km.) southwest of Australia. Compared with Australia's expanse, it is quite small in land area—approximately the size of Victoria, Australia's smallest mainland state. On the other hand, New Zealand is slightly larger than the United Kingdom, and it is as geologically complex as a continent.

Its three major islands are North Island, South Island, and Stewart Island, and all are different. Although a good portion of North Island was formed by volcanic action, three-quarters of New Zealand consists of sedimentary rocks that are more than 500 million years old.

Climate. Australia is large enough to have six different climate zones. They range from tropical in the north to the mild marine climate on Tasmania and the mainland's southeast coast, where most Australians live. But most of the continent is semiarid or arid.

New Zealand's single climate region is of the mild marine variety. New Zealanders experience only a few days a year of either subfreezing weather or of temperatures that rise above 90° F. (32° C.). Stewart Island, jutting only about 200 mi. (322 km.) farther south than Australia's Tasmania, is generally colder than the "winterless north" of the North Auckland Peninsula.

Resources. Much of the land in both countries is suitable for grazing. Together, they have more sheep than any other two nations in the world. Farm products—especially cheese, meat, and wool—account for nearly half of New Zealand's export income. Two of New Zealand's more important industries, forestry and paper production, rely on the forests that cover more than 35 percent of the nation. Both New Zealand and Australia have well-developed fishing industries that take advantage of the plentiful resources of the sea.

Besides coal, gold, and iron sands, New Zealand has few mineral resources worth exploiting. Australia, on the other hand, produces and exports more than 20 important minerals, ranging from bauxite and petroleum to platinum and industrial diamonds.

THE PEOPLE

Australia's population of 18.3 million in 1996 is roughly five times the size of New Zealand's, which numbers about 3.6 million. More than four of every five people in each country live in or near cities, where the manufacturing and service industries are concentrated.

The two nations' ethnic makeups differ in important ways. About 75 percent of all New Zealanders and more than 90 percent of all Australians have roots in Europe. Asians make up about 4 percent of Australia's population, aborigines about 1 percent. About 9 percent of all New Zealanders are at least half Maori in descent. Another 3 percent are islanders from other parts of Polynesia who have immigrated to New Zealand in search of work.

Australia and New Zealand combined have more sheep than any other two countries in the world.

Australia's generally mild climate makes outdoor sports possible practically year-round.

Native Peoples.   The aborigines and Maori have quite different histories. The aborigines first arrived in Australia about 38,000 years ago, having walked from Southeast Asia over a land bridge that no longer exists. By the time European settlers arrived in the late 1700s, there may have been as many as 300,000 aborigines, belonging to about 500 tribes and speaking many languages. Today, there are a little more than 200,000. Some live a settled, traditional life in remote areas, although most are of mixed descent and live in and around urban areas.

The Maori are unrelated to the aborigines. They are Polynesians, descended from people who sailed to New Zealand, possibly from what is now French Polynesia, around 1,000 years ago. Disease and warfare reduced their numbers from around 250,000 in the 1820s, when European settlers began arriving in force, to about 42,000 in 1896. They rebounded to about 400,000 during the 20th century. Nearly all Maori today live on North Island, their traditional homeland.

Immigration.   Both nations have relied to a great degree on immigration to increase their numbers. Australia's population has more than doubled since 1945, in large part because of a planned program of "assisted" immigration. Today, one of every five Australians is foreign-born. Many have roots in Southern Europe, Asia, and South America, adding a more cosmopolitan feel to Australia's cities.

Immigrants accounted for about 25 percent of New Zealand's population growth during the 20th century. Though most came from the British Isles, New Zealand has long welcomed other Europeans, including those from Scandinavia, Southern Europe, and Eastern Europe. In recent years, Asia and the Pacific islands have been the two largest sources of newcomers.

HISTORY
Exploration.   A Dutchman, Abel Tasman, explored parts of Australia and New Zealand in 1642, and before him, Chinese, Arab, Portuguese, and Spanish seafarers carried news of Australia back to their homelands.

Credit for the English influence on both nations must be given to Captain James Cook, the Royal Navy lieutenant who claimed both lands for the British Crown during his first voyage to the area in 1769 and 1770. Cook spent six months charting New Zealand's islands. Then he sailed west and located New Holland, as Australia was then called, and spent nearly five months exploring its uncharted east coast.

Settlement. In 1788, Britain founded a penal colony at Port Jackson (Sydney), not far from the spot where Cook had first landed 18 years earlier. Free settlers followed, and soon Port Jackson became an important whaling center. Kororareka (now Russell) on New Zealand's North Island became a stopover for whalers from the United States, Britain, and France. The British eventually set up small whaling stations on New Zealand's North and South islands. Traders supplying the whalers followed, and they exchanged goods with the Maori, who welcomed the newcomers at first but later resisted them.

Australian settlement spread from Sydney to Tasmania in 1803 and to Western Australia in 1827. By 1859, all six of Australia's modern states had been colonized. A gold rush in 1851 brought more people, trade, and wealth to the land.

During the 1830s, Australian sheep ranchers journeyed to New Zealand and bought up land from the Maori. At the same time a private group in Britain made an elaborate plan to colonize New Zealand. These facts persuaded Britain to annex the islands, making them first part of Australia's colony of New South Wales and later an entirely separate colony.

The Maori resisted, but were no match for the armed might of the settlers. Eventually they lost most of their best land. In Australia, most aboriginal lands were absorbed by large sheep stations (ranches).

Both nations' economies got a boost in the 1880s with the invention of refrigerated ships. At last Australian and New Zealand farmers had the means to export dairy goods and meat to Europe.

Independence. Australia became the independent Commonwealth of Australia on January 1, 1901. New Zealand, which had been largely self-governing since 1853, won its independence on September 26, 1907, when it was proclaimed a dominion of the British Empire.

Troops from the two nations fought gallantly in World War I as "Anzacs" (members of the Australian and New Zealand Army Corps). Nearly 8,600 died in a single battle, at the Gallipoli Peninsula in northwest Turkey. Troops from both nations fought hard in several theaters during World War II, when U.S. forces provided their main defense at home.

After the war, the two countries moved to make themselves more secure against the possibility of attack. New Zealand became a major voice for the smaller powers in the United Nations. Australia launched a campaign to lure immigrants from all over Europe, on the premise that there was security in numbers. Though the policy excluded Asians, it was gradually altered. During the late 1980s, about one-third of all newcomers to Australia were Asian.

Over the past 40 years, Australians and New Zealanders have shed their sense of isolation. They are committed to making their multicultural societies work at home. Abroad, they are eager to link their economies to those of the burgeoning nations of Asia, in order to enter the 21st century as vital members of an interdependent community of nations.

The Australian coat of arms features an emu and a kangaroo, animals found only in Australia.

AUSTRALIA

Australia—the continent and the nation—is a land of continual surprise. Of the six continents, it is the smallest, the oldest, the flattest, and, after Antarctica, the driest and most sparsely populated. It is also the only one that is occupied by a single nation. The Commonwealth of Australia was formed in 1901 after the British had maintained colonies there for 113 years.

Australia's climate, land, and wildlife show astonishing variety. The north can be jungle-hot, the south mild, and the eastern mountains ice-cold. Australia's "Red Centre" is a desert wasteland, but many of its coastal regions are fertile and densely forested. In winter (June to August "down under" in the Southern Hemisphere), the mountains of New South Wales, one of the nation's six states and two territories, are covered with snow. And from the kangaroo to the platypus, the gum tree to the spear lily, the continent nurtures animals and plants found nowhere else on earth.

Such facts of nature shaped the activities and beliefs of Australia's native, or Aboriginal, peoples for thousands of years. Australia's unique landscape began shaping the thoughts and activities of Westerners in 1788, when the first boatloads of settlers, half of them convicts, arrived from England.

Today, as Australia becomes a vast melting pot, welcoming people from 120 nations, its geography and climate remain potent forces. They determine where Australians live, what types of work they do, how they relax, and how they view themselves and their world.

THE LAND

Australia is about the size of the continental United States. North to south, from Cape York Peninsula in the state of Queensland to Southeast Cape in the island state of Tasmania, the continent is about 2,000 mi. (3,220 km.) long. West to east, from Steep Point in the state of Western Australia to Cape Byron in the state of New South Wales, it measures about 2,400 mi. (3,860 km.).

The continent's 22,000-mi. (36,735 km.) coastline is remarkably even, because it has been smoothed out by water washing against it for millions of years. There are two large indentations: the Gulf of Carpentaria on the northern coast, and the Great Australian Bight on the south.

Along the northeast coast is one of the most spectacular natural wonders of the world—an enormous underwater garden. The Great Barrier Reef, the longest coral formation in the world, runs for 1,250 mi. (2,010 km.). Some 600 little islands lie in this gigantic marine playland, and they are separated from the mainland by from 10 to 100 mi. (16 to 160 km.) of shallow water. (See sidebar, page 497.)

Millions of years of wear and tear by wind and rain have worn away the ancient mountains of Australia, making this the flattest of all the continents. There are three great natural regions: the Great Western Plateau; the Central Lowlands; and the Great Dividing Range, or Eastern Highlands.

Great Western Plateau. Geologists think that the Great Western Plateau may be 3 billion to 6 billion years old. Much of the interior of the plateau is desert—the Great Sandy Desert, the Gibson Desert, the Great Victoria Desert. The plateau also contains the so-called "gibber" plains, vast stretches covered with pebbles or consisting of barren land with some grassland and spiky bushes.

Among the many dramatic outcrops is the majestic Ayers Rock, the world's largest monolith (large rock) and a sacred site of the Loritja and Pitjanjatjara tribes, who call it Uluru. Thousands of years ago, members of these Aboriginal tribes painted scenes from their legends on the walls of the rock's caves.

Mineral wealth is found in all parts of Australia, but this dry western area is literally a treasure trove. The Hamersley Range contains important iron ore deposits. Valuable minerals such as lead, zinc, silver, copper, uranium, nickel, gold, and industrial diamonds are found in many parts of the Great Western Plateau.

Some southwestern areas of the Western Plateau receive rain relatively regularly. Farmers and ranchers have developed these areas, with the aid of irrigation projects, into croplands and livestock stations.

Central Lowlands. Stretching south from the Gulf of Carpentaria, the Central Lowlands contain some of Australia's finest pastureland. An unusual feature of this area is the Great Artesian Basin, 670,000 sq. mi. (1,735,300 sq. km.), where water is found deep underground. This basin catches water from rivers that run inland from the eastern mountains. Ranchers have sunk thousands of bores to make this artesian water avail-

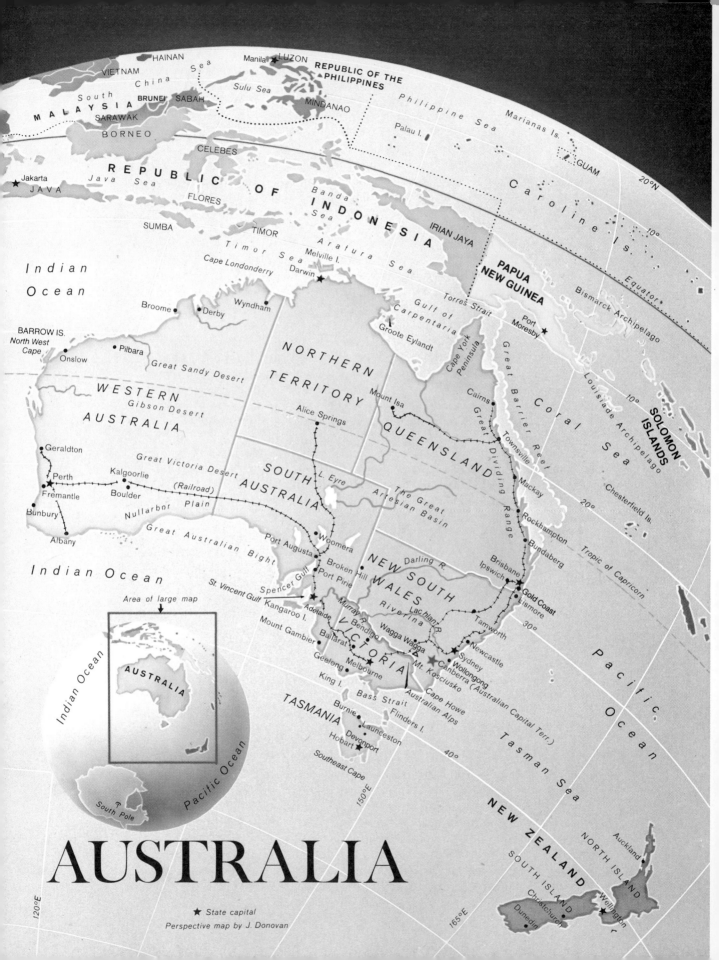

HAINAN
VIETNAM
China *Manila* ★ LUZON **REPUBLIC OF THE PHILIPPINES**
Sea
South Sulu Sea MINDANAO _Philippine Sea_ Marianas Is.
MALAYSIA BRUNEI SABAH
SARAWAK _Java_ CELEBES GUAM
BORNEO _Sea_ _Caroline Is._
20°N

Jakarta **REPUBLIC OF** 10°
★ JAVA _Java_ Sea **INDONESIA** IRIAN JAYA
FLORES Banda _Equator_
Sea
SUMBA Palau I.
TIMOR Arafura _Sea_ **PAPUA NEW GUINEA** SOLOMON ISLANDS
Timor Sea Melville I. Bismarck Archipelago
Indian Cape Londonderry Darwin ★ Torres Strait Port
Ocean Gulf of Moresby ★ Louisiade Archipelago
Carpentaria
Broome Wyndham Groote Eylandt Cape York Peninsula 10°
Derby
BARROW IS. Chesterfield Is.
North West **NORTHERN** _Coral_ 20°
Cape Onslow Pilbara Cairns _Sea_
Great Sandy Desert **TERRITORY** Townsville
WESTERN Mount Isa **QUEENSLAND** Mackay
Alice Springs Great Barrier Reef
Gibson Desert **AUSTRALIA** Rockhampton _Tropic of Capricorn_
Geraldton Great Victoria Desert L. Eyre **SOUTH** Bundaberg
Perth ★ Kalgoorlie Brisbane
Fremantle Boulder (Railroad) **AUSTRALIA** _The Great_ Ipswich ★ Gold Coast
Bunbury Nullarbor _Plain_ _Artesian Basin_ Lismore
Albany Great Australian Bight Darling R. **NEW** Tamworth 30°
Port Augusta Woomera **WALES** Lachlan R.
Indian Ocean Broken Hill Newcastle
St. Vincent Gulf Spencer Gulf Port Pirie _Riverina_ Sydney
Area of large map Kangaroo I. ★ Adelaide Murray R. Wagga Wagga Wollongong
Mount Gambier Bendigo **VICTORIA** Canberra (Australian Capital Terr.)
AUSTRALIA Ballarat Geelong Melbourne Mt. Kosciusko _Pacific_
King I. Bass Strait Cape Howe
Indian **TASMANIA** Australian Alps _Ocean_
Ocean Burnie Flinders I. _Tasman Sea_
Launceston 40°
Devonport
Hobart ★ **NEW**
South Pole _Pacific Ocean_ Southeast Cape **ZEALAND** Auckland
NORTH ISLAND
SOUTH ISLAND Wellington
Christchurch
Dunedin

AUSTRALIA

120°E 150°E 165°E

★ State capital
Perspective map by J. Donovan

able for irrigating grazing land and pastureland. The water contains too much salt and other minerals to be used for watering croplands.

Lake Eyre, in the state of South Australia in the southern part of the Central Lowlands, is a vast, dry depression. At 52 ft. (16 m.) below sea level, it is the continent's lowest point. As far as anyone can tell, it has filled only twice in history. Judging from the many dinosaur fossils found there, scientists figure that at one time, its shores held lush vegetation. Today, the lake is a giant basin of dried, salty mud.

South of the lake, the ruggedly beautiful Flinders Ranges are composed of rocks 1 billion years old. To the southeast, between the Lachlan and Murray rivers in New South Wales, is some of Australia's richest farmland and best grazing land.

Eastern Highlands.   The Great Dividing Range is a system of plateaus, hills, and low mountains that parallel the east and southeast coasts for 1,250 mi. (2,000 km.). Its climate is tropical in the north, subalpine in the south. The range includes the Blue Mountains, west of Sydney, and the Australian Alps, northeast of Melbourne. Mount Kosciusko, Australia's highest point, rises 7,310 ft. (2,228 m.) in the Snowy Mountains.

Along the coast, on the eastern and southern sides of the Dividing Range, are the great cities of Australia—Sydney, Melbourne, and Bris-

The Trans-Australian Railway runs nearly 300 miles across the Nullarbor Plain without a curve.

FACTS AND FIGURES

OFFICIAL NAME: Commonwealth of Australia.

NATIONALITY: Australian(s).

CAPITAL: Canberra.

LOCATION: Southern Hemisphere, between the Indian and Pacific oceans. **Boundaries**—Arafura Sea, Coral Sea, Pacific Ocean, Tasman Sea, Great Australian Bight, Indian Ocean, Timor Sea.

AREA: 2,967,896 sq. mi. (7,686,850 sq. km.).

PHYSICAL FEATURES: Highest point—Mount Kosciusko (7,310 ft.; 2,228 m.). **Lowest point**—Lake Eyre (52 ft.; 16 m. below sea level). **Chief rivers**—Murray, Darling, Murrumbidgee.

POPULATION: 18,300,000 (1996; annual growth 0.8%).

MAJOR LANGUAGE: English (official).

MAJOR RELIGIONS: Anglicanism, Roman Catholicism.

GOVERNMENT: Independent, self-governing federation. **Head of state**—British monarch, who is queen of Australia. **Head of government**—prime minister. **Legislature**—Parliament.

CHIEF CITIES: Sydney, Melbourne, Brisbane, Perth, Adelaide, Newcastle, Canberra, Wollongong, Hobart.

ECONOMY: Chief minerals—bauxite, coal, iron ore, copper, tin, silver, uranium, nickel, tungsten, mineral sands, lead, zinc, diamonds, natural gas, oil. **Chief agricultural products**—livestock, wheat, fruits, sugarcane. **Industries and products**—mining, industrial and transportation equipment, food processing, chemicals. **Chief exports**—wheat, barley, beef, lamb, dairy products, wool, coal, iron ore. **Chief imports**—transportation equipment, machinery, textiles, petroleum products.

MONETARY UNIT: 1 Australian dollar = 100 cents.

NATIONAL HOLIDAY: January 26 (Australia Day).

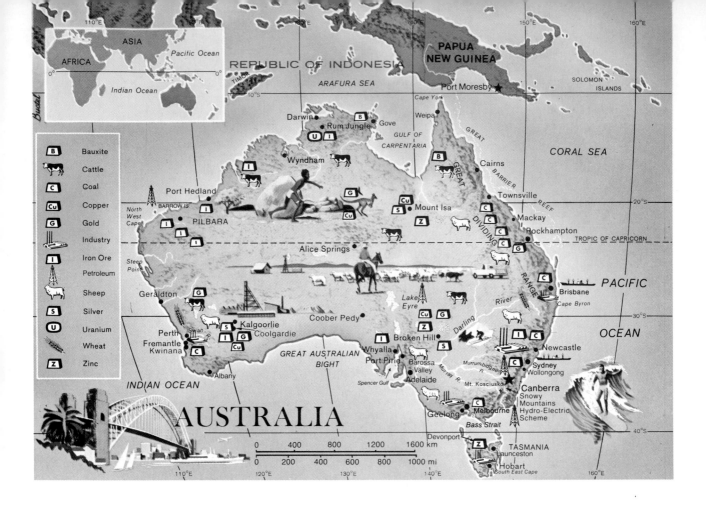

AUSTRALIA

Legend:
- B — Bauxite
- 🐄 — Cattle
- C — Coal
- Cu — Copper
- G — Gold
- ⚒ — Industry
- I — Iron Ore
- Petroleum
- 🐑 — Sheep
- S — Silver
- U — Uranium
- Wheat
- Z — Zinc

Scale: 0 400 800 1200 1600 km / 0 200 400 600 800 1000 mi

bane—as well as many other smaller towns and cities. Along the western slope is the "fertile crescent," a well-watered area where many large farms and sheep stations, or ranches, are located.

The Great Dividing Range is Australia's main watershed. Several short, swift rivers flow eastward or southward to the coast. The long inland rivers that supply water for the fertile lands flow away from the coast and, because of the flat terrain, are leisurely and slow-moving.

The 1,600-mi.-long (2,570-km.) Murray, the greatest of Australia's rivers, forms the major part of the boundary between the states of New South Wales and Victoria before it enters the state of South Australia and empties into the sea. The Murray, with its tributaries—the Darling, Murrumbidgee, and Lachlan (flowing into the Murrumbidgee)—forms the main watering system of Australia. Floodwaters in the upper reaches of these long, lazy-moving rivers may take weeks to reach distant parts of the country.

The island of Tasmania is a southern extension of the Eastern Highlands. It is separated from the mainland by the Bass Strait, where huge deposits of oil and natural gas were discovered in 1965. Shaped like a shield, Tasmania—the smallest of Australia's six states—has a mountainous interior. Plunging streams and rivers have been harnessed to generate electricity, helping Tasmanians expand mining and factory operations. A fertile island, it has many small farms, and is an important source of dairy products and wool.

Mount Olga rises majestically above Australia's vast Central Lowland region.

Climate and Rainfall

Australia's seasons may seem reversed to people who live in the Northern Hemisphere. The Australian summer—and the school summer vacation—begins in December, just in time for Christmas. Despite the warm weather, Australians celebrate Christmas in much the same way as people in other English-speaking countries do—by caroling in the streets, opening gifts, and eating turkey and plum pudding.

The northern third of the continent is semitropical, suffering extreme temperatures from October to May, when it is hot and sticky. The rest of the continent lies within the temperate zone and enjoys milder weather. This mildness is due, in part, to Australia's global position, wind patterns, and the absence of great land barriers. Thus, Australians can enjoy outdoor sports nearly all year, and the cattle that roam Australia's "stations" (ranches) do not need to be sheltered even during the winter.

Despite the inviting climate, Australia suffers from a lack of rainfall. About one-sixth of the continent—a belt along the eastern seaboard, the northern coast, and parts of the southern coast—receives more than 40 in. (102 cm.) of rain annually. Enormous interior areas have an average annual rainfall of less than 10 in. (25 cm.). The major cities of Australia have grown up in the areas where rainfall is comparatively plentiful.

Unique Plant Life

An amazingly varied and abundant plant life flourishes on this dry continent. In 1770, this abundance so impressed the men who sailed on Captain James Cook's voyage of discovery that Cook named the place where they anchored Botany Bay.

Many of Australia's 13,000 native plants are unique to the continent. Some 2,000 rare flowers bloom on the southwestern heathlands and in

The livestock industry thrives in Australia, where nearly 60 percent of the land is pasture.

the western coastal regions. After a rainfall they give the land the appearance of a brilliantly colored painting. One unusual native wildflower is the kangaroo paw, a red-and-green plant that is shaped like the hind foot of a kangaroo.

Although vegetation varies with climate, national and state parks with extraordinary flowers and trees are within an hour's drive of every capital in the country. Along the east coast, one finds the honeyflower; the lovely native fuchsia; and the spear lily, a plant that regularly grows 12 ft. high and has clusters of vivid red blooms. The Christmas bush, Christmas bells, and coachwood burst into bloom at Christmastime. Orchids grow wild, but many of the more than 600 species are also cultivated for export.

Throughout Australia, one finds the eucalyptus, or gum tree, of which more than 500 varieties grow in all kinds of climate and soil. The commonwealth's coat of arms depicts sprays of the sweet-smelling acacia, known as the wattle tree. This name comes from the fact that early settlers found acacia saplings just right for interlacing, or wattling, the framework for mud-plaster walls and roofs.

Unusual Animals and Birds

Australia's isolation for millions of years permitted animals that disappeared elsewhere to survive and develop. Nearly half of Australia's native mammals are marsupials, animals whose females carry their immature offspring in a pouch until the babies are fully developed. The most famous is the kangaroo. There are 40 types of kangaroos, ranging from the red kangaroo, which may grow taller than a person; the wallaby, often the size of a large dog; and the rat kangaroo, less than a foot (0.3 m.) long.

Australia's geographic isolation from the rest of the world allowed unusual types of animals to evolve. Over 40 species of kangaroo live in Australia. They carry their babies, or joeys, in pouches (above). The gentle koala (left) spends most of its time in eucalyptus trees, where it feeds on the leaves.

The koala is the best-loved marsupial. In its natural habitat, the koala spends its days sound asleep in eucalyptus trees. This once made the koala an easy target for hunters who prized its fur. A law protecting the koala stopped the slaughter.

The duck-billed platypus, Australia's strangest mammal, has four webbed feet and a long, ducklike snout. The platypus represents a stage in evolution between reptile and mammal. It is a mammal that lays eggs.

Birds as strange and special as the native animals abound in Australia. The emu, Australia's largest bird, cannot fly but is a fast runner. Equally distinctive is the black swan, its black plumage highlighted by a red beak. The lyrebird, a great mimic, has been known to sing more than 40 different calls in one concert.

For more than 150 years after the first British settlement in 1788, most Australians took their continent's unique plants and animals for granted. They did little to ensure their survival. Today, laws protect endangered plant and animal species. Projects that threaten the environment—a dam in Tasmania, logging operations in eastern rain forests, for example—have been shelved or reduced in size. The environment has

Tasmania's numerous bodies of water have become an important source of hydroelectric power.

become a political issue, as Australians realize the value of balancing development with conservation.

Farmers and ranchers have a pressing environmental problem—the salt poisoning of much of Australia's topsoil, to the point that it cannot sustain crop growth. Settlers who created pastureland by clearing trees and shrubs from hills unknowingly caused the problem. The government is trying to stem the loss of land with a number of programs, including the planting of 1 billion trees by the year 2000.

Natural Resources

Australia's most valuable agricultural resource is the vast grassland in the eastern and central areas where sheep graze. The export of wool continues to be a primary source of foreign currency.

All of Australia's six states have important mineral resources. The minerals are often found in the exposed rocks that crop up over much of the continent. Iron ore, lead, zinc, silver, copper, uranium, nickel, and gold are produced in Western Australia, South Australia, the Northern Territory, and parts of Queensland and western New South Wales. Mineralized rocks that once contained major deposits of gold can be found in a belt along the eastern portion of the continent, from western Victoria to northern Queensland. The gold is now largely worked out, but some huge deposits of copper, lead, zinc, and silver remain. Both areas hold smaller amounts of tin, tungsten, mica, manganese, cobalt, and other metals. Bauxite for aluminum is also an important Australian resource.

Australia is a major exporter of coal. Opals, lovely iridescent gems, are found in the sediment of the Great Artesian Basin in Queensland, in New South Wales, and in South Australia.

In the 1960s, important commercial oil fields were discovered in Queensland, west of Brisbane. Offshore fields in the area of Victoria and on Barrow Island, Western Australia, have proved of great value. Natural gas was also found there.

Australia's eucalyptus trees provide a fine supply of hardwoods and also help to fill the country's newsprint and paper needs. The supply of softwoods is being replenished by extensive planting.

Australia does lack a most important natural resource—sufficient water. Much is being done to use the available water to provide irrigation and hydroelectric power.

PEOPLE

In the 1770s, England was faced with the problem of what to do with its large convict population. For some years, considerable numbers had been transported to America, especially to the colonies of Virginia and Maryland. But America's War of Independence closed off this outlet. Soon the English jails were overflowing with men, women, and children, many of whom had committed relatively trivial offenses.

It was Sir Joseph Banks, a naturalist who accompanied Captain James Cook on his voyage of discovery in 1770, who suggested Botany Bay as an appropriate spot for a penal settlement. On May 13, 1787, Captain Arthur Phillip set sail from Portsmouth to be governor of New South Wales, a new English colony. Phillip's 11 ships carried 1,487 people, 736 of them convicts. Besides the prisoners, the ships carried government officials, Royal Navy marines and sailors, merchant seamen, a minister, and a doctor.

The convicts ranged in age from John Hudson, a chimney sweep of 9, to Dorothy Handland, a rag dealer of 82. Hudson had stolen some clothes and a handgun; Handland had told a lie in court. Both were ordered "transported" for seven years.

None of the convicts aboard the First Fleet, as the flotilla came to be known, had been charged with murder, rape, or prostitution. The most serious offenses these criminals had been convicted of were mugging, cattle theft, and highway robbery.

The most common offense was minor theft. A woman of 70 had stolen 7 pounds of cheese. A black man from the West Indies had up-rooted 12 cucumber plants. An 11-year-old boy had taken 10 yds. of ribbon. The youngest girl aboard, Elizabeth Hayward, 13, had stolen a gown and a silk bonnet.

The voyage of 15,000 mi. (24,135 km.) took eight months. The First Fleet anchored in Botany Bay on January 20, 1788. Six days later, Captain Phillip moved the fleet a few miles north to a more hospitable site, where the city of Sydney now stands. He described the site as "the finest harbour in the world." The day they arrived there, January 26, is now celebrated every year as Australia Day.

Two weeks later, on behalf of the British Crown, Phillip and his assistants took formal possession of the eastern half of the continent and the island of Tasmania. The Aborigines, natives of the country, looked on but did not protest.

Aboriginal Peoples

Like the British, the ancestors of the Aborigines who watched that ceremony had come from someplace else as many as 38,000 years before. They had walked to the continent from Asia, moving across a land bridge that disappeared 5,000 years ago.

When the First Fleet arrived, perhaps as many as 300,000 Aborigines lived in Australia, and they spoke about 300 different languages. Essentially hunter-gatherers, they had no knowledge of agriculture. The Aborigines were nomadic people who belonged to one of many large tribes. They moved about in clans of 10 to 50 people. The women and children fished and gathered edible plants and seeds. The men hunted and fought, often with the boomerang—a heavy weapon that seemed to hover in the air. The "return" boomerang, more curved than the hunting stick, is a sort of toy.

The Aborigines lived simply, although their societies were organized in complex ways. Clan elders, usually always males, enforced strict rules of conduct, including those concerning marriage and childbirth. They also passed on tribal myths—stories that linked humans to each other, to all other objects in the environment, and to the past and the future. A clan's group identity came from its totem, usually a plant or animal that acted as a symbol for the clan and was thought to protect it.

The settlers treated the Aborigines with contempt. In little more than 100 years of white settlement, the Aborigines' numbers dropped 80 percent, to about 60,000. Diseases brought by the settlers were partly to blame. Many were killed in clashes with settlers. In Tasmania, the entire Aboriginal population vanished.

Aboriginal Peoples Today. Several decades of government programs designed to protect the Aborigines have enabled their population to

Australia has many minority groups. Aborigines, the original inhabitants of Australia, are demanding an end to discrimination (left). Asian immigrants have settled in many cities (below).

The government has set up numerous schools that address the needs of Aborigine children.

grow to about 270,000, less than a third of whom are people of unmixed descent. White Australians have become more sensitive to the Aborigines' needs, thanks in part to government action and in part to pressure from Aboriginal groups, including the National Aboriginal Conference (NAC). The NAC, a group of 36 selected Aborigines, advises the national government on Aboriginal matters.

Many Aborigines maintain features of tribal life in the Northern Territory and Western Australia. But most live a settled life in and around towns and cities, especially in the southern states, where most Aborigines are of mixed descent.

The federal government provides Aborigines with special social benefits. The Aboriginal Development Commission (ADC), a federal agency, helps Aborigines set up businesses, and provides funds for housing. In 1993 the government granted Aborigines who could prove a long-standing relationship to vacant, unleased government land the right to reclaim their land through the courts.

Yet even Aborigines who choose to become part of the mainstream tend to remain on its fringes. There are exceptions. People of Aboriginal descent have become noted political figures, sports stars, actors, ballerinas, university graduates, writers, and artists. Yet compared with other Australians, the average Aborigine has more health problems, less education, and fewer job skills.

The Settlers

Between 1788 and 1868, the British transported 161,000 convicts to Australia. Only about 25,000 were women, a fact that some feel left a masculine stamp on the nation's rough frontier society.

Australians used to be ashamed of the origins of their country. That attitude is changing. Recently, descendants of the early settlers formed the Fellowship of the First Fleeters, and Australians who trace their roots to the first arrivals flocked to join.

The inexperienced pioneers showed great enterprise. Some drove sheep or cattle across the mountains to the plains beyond. Others made their way through the forests along the coast, cutting timber. And still other groups settled down to farm cleared land.

In the early days, the governors of the colonies had the right to grant land free to anyone who agreed to hire, feed, and clothe convicts. As settlements spread beyond the mountains, ownership of land was established by living, or "squatting," on it.

The settlers needed additional land for the sheep industry. The first sheep had been brought to Australia from the Cape of Good Hope in 1787. By skillful breeding, the settlers developed a hardy type of sheep that produced excellent wool. The sheep industry was perfectly suited to the dry climate of Australia's vast interior.

Transporting criminals to all but Western Australia ended in 1850. The next year, gold was discovered on the central plains of New South Wales, spurring a great wave of immigration. Newcomers came from all over the Western world, but mostly from Great Britain.

Prospectors opened up the continent by trekking inland. Adventurers and tradesmen followed. In 10 years, the population tripled. Many settlements became flourishing cities as prospectors turned to farming and other ways to make a living. To meet their needs, the settlers constructed roads and railroads, started businesses, and built schools.

New Australians

In the 19th century, Chinese-Australian conflicts in the goldfields led many colonies to prohibit settlement by most peoples of non-European stock. An unofficial "white Australia" policy developed. It gave Australia a predominantly homogeneous population and a life-style similar to that of Western Europe and North America. But Australia was often attacked for discriminating against people of non-European ancestry. All restrictions were scrapped in 1972, and today, Australia accepts immigrants from more than 120 different countries.

The move toward a more multicultural society took a giant step between 1945 and 1965, when Australia helped pay the transportation costs of more than 2 million immigrants. Most came from Great Britain. But large numbers came from countries like Italy, Yugoslavia, Greece, Germany, and the Netherlands.

After immigration laws were relaxed in the 1970s, increasing numbers of Indians, Chinese, and other Asians entered Australia to stay. Australia has also accepted hundreds of thousands of refugees from troubled lands such as Czechoslovakia, Lebanon, Vietnam, and Kampuchea. The result is that in 1990, half of all Australians had either been born in another country or had a foreign-born parent.

Fully 5 percent of the population have roots in Asia. One section of Sydney, the Cabramatta district, has the air of a miniature Indo-Chinese city. English is a first language for only 25 percent of the students at Cabramatta High School, where 25 percent of the students are practicing Buddhists.

The Sporting Life

Australians are mad about sports. They love to participate in them, watch them, argue about them, bet on them. Children fantasize about wearing Australia's green and gold—the national colors—in international competition. For young and old alike, heroes tend to be athletes.

The largest spectator sport, football, is really four different sports: rugby league, rugby union, soccer, and Australian National Rules. More than any other sport, soccer reflects the ethnic shifts in Australia's post-war population. The rosters of the professional teams are dominated by

Australians are great sports enthusiasts. Rugby is popular among men and, to a lesser extent, women (below). Australians enjoy countless types of water sports along the many miles of beaches (bottom).

New Australians, people with names like Kosmina, Katholos, Bertogna, and Senkalski. Australian Rules is especially popular in the southern states and Western Australia.

In the summer, cricket becomes the nation's passion. Every major city has a cricket arena, seating from 30,000 to 90,000 spectators. Water sports such as swimming, surfing, skin diving, and sailing are popular year-round, as might be expected in a country where 95 percent of the people live within 10 miles (16 kilometers) of the seashore.

Tennis, lawn bowling, track, cycling, and golf are all very popular, as is running. The annual Sydney-to-Bondi Fun Run regularly draws 25,000 participants. Interest in horses is great, and horse races draw large crowds, as do automobile races. In recent years, basketball has become popular, and basketball courts are springing up all over the country.

On the field, Australians are fierce competitors. Friendly and open off the field, they emit emotions on the field that show just how much they hate to lose. To increase their chances of winning in the international arena, the government set up the Australian Institute of Sport to develop state-of-the-art coaching techniques.

LIFE IN THE CITIES

The least densely populated nation in the world, Australia is also the most highly urbanized. Fully 85 percent of all Australians live in cities. The chief cities are the nation's capital, Canberra, and the state capitals, all of them ports. Nearly 40 percent of the population live in two of these capitals: Sydney, in New South Wales, and Melbourne, in Victoria. Like the other state capitals—Brisbane, Adelaide, Perth, and Hobart—these cities have grown rapidly in recent years, keeping pace with population increases and the expansion of trade and manufacturing. Canberra and Darwin, the capital of the Northern Territory, have also grown.

An afternoon of lawn bowling is a particularly popular pastime for many Australians.

In 1988, spectacular celebrations throughout the country marked Australia's 200th anniversary.

Australian cities tend to grow outward rather than upward, because Australians prefer houses and gardens to apartments. Since the work-week is from 35 to 40 hours, most workers have some time left every day for sports or gardening when they return from their jobs. Near their homes are inexpensive facilities for tennis, cricket, golf, lawn bowling, and swimming.

Australians live well. Their wages are generally lower than those in the United States, their taxes higher, and the prices they must pay for many necessities are also higher. But they do not have extremes of poverty and wealth. Health services are good and available to all under a government-sponsored insurance plan.

Industrial Growth

Most of Australia's factories are located in or near its cities. Australian manufacturing firms mainly supply the small domestic market and account for only about 15 percent of the nation's output of goods and services. The manufacturing sector employs about 16 percent of the labor force. Traditionally, manufacturing's growth was helped by import taxes that protected local businesses from foreign competition. Many of these taxes were reduced or phased out in the 1980s and 1990s.

Australia's iron and steel industry is a strong one, buttressed by its wealth of coal and iron ore. Subsidiaries of major U.S., Japanese, and British automobile companies produce cars there. In fact, Australia's economic growth depends in part on the investment of foreign businesses.

Australians enjoy traditional Christmas decorations, even though the holiday falls during their summer.

The nation's factories also produce sophisticated machinery such as diesel locomotives, power turbines, earth-moving equipment, and computer equipment. Two relatively new industries, based on discoveries of oil and natural gas, are the petroleum and petrochemical businesses. Shipbuilding, paperboard, fishing, and canning are important industries.

The nation's mineral industry is enormous. It is a world leader in the production and export of aluminum, alumina, bauxite, cobalt, copper, industrial diamonds, gold, iron ore, lead, nickel, silver, and uranium.

LIFE OUTBACK

The sparsely settled interior of Australia is known as the Outback. That is the area of many of the great cattle ranches, or stations. They have been so successful that Australia has become a major world exporter of beef and veal.

The Outback is a vast, largely flat, dry, lightly populated land. There are cattle stations that vary from a few thousand acres to one that is about 6,300 sq. mi. (16,300 sq. km.) in area. The Australian stockman, or cowboy, often uses trucks, jeeps, and planes these days instead of horses.

Sheep farmers, called graziers, take care of thousands of sheep. Some graziers lead fairly isolated lives, while others are part of holdings so large that they form little communities of their own. Sheep are run in all the states, but the larger sheep stations are found in Queensland, New South Wales, and Western Australia.

Aircraft and two-way radio do much to relieve the isolation of the Outback. The radio lets neighbors talk together even though they may be miles apart. It brings news and advice to the homestead and links farm families to medical care. The Royal Flying Doctor Service, supported by the government, carries physicians and dentists to people who live in remote areas.

Many Australians live on large wheat farms. Other farms produce dairy products, fruit, and corn. Wheat, barley, and oats are grown in all the states. Sugarcane, tobacco, and cotton grow in the warmer areas.

Smaller farms, found in areas near cities, provide fruits and vegetables as well as dairy products. Many of the market gardens, fruit farms, and vineyards are run by Australians newly arrived from similar farms in Europe. About 9 percent of Australia's land is suitable for farming. Only 6 percent of all Australian wage earners work in agriculture.

EDUCATION

The Australian colonies early introduced free, compulsory education. Today, children must attend school between the ages of 6 and 15 or 16, depending on which state they live in. The state governments operate the schools. In addition to free schools, Australia has many independent schools, mainly operated by religious denominations. More than 25 percent of all primary- and secondary-school students attend these independent schools, often at great expense to parents. More and more, Australians see a university education as a necessity, and many parents believe that a private education will give their children an edge in university admissions.

The Australians have had to improvise to meet the problems of educating children in the remote areas. In some cases, children travel almost 50 mi. (80 km.) each way to school. Farther out, schools are established wherever there are eight or nine children. But in the isolated Outback, children and their teachers speak to one another on two-way radios, supplemented with videocassettes.

Perth (below) and other big cities in Australia resemble those in the U.S. By contrast, parts of Australia are so remote that medical care must be provided by physicians and dentists working with the Royal Flying Doctor Service (right).

The arts thrive in Australia. The unusual saillike design of the Sydney Opera House has become a symbol of Australia's largest city. *Picnic at Hanging Rock* (left) and other Australian films have received rave reviews worldwide.

Beginning in 1988, Australia's 19 universities and most public colleges and institutes of technology were consolidated into a smaller number of large, federally run schools. The nation's first private university was founded in 1987. University education, once free, now costs a small annual sum, which students may pay at enrollment or after graduation.

THE ARTS

The arts in Australia—both the "high arts," like sculpture and serious literature, and the "low arts," like rock music and soap operas—have thrived down under. The first writers of literature with an "Austra-

THE UNDERWATER GARDEN

Australia's Great Barrier Reef, the world's largest coral reef, is a string of multicolored, rocklike ridges. These ridges parallel Queensland's coast for 1,250 mi. (2,000 km.). Tourists flock to the area to snorkel or scuba dive, or just to gaze in wonder through glass-bottomed boats.

This coral mass is made of the hardened secretions of billions of tiny sea animals called polyps. To protect their soft bodies, the polyps secrete calcium carbonate, which hardens into limestone. These outer skeletons attach themselves to the skeletons of dead polyps beneath them, enabling the reefs to grow.

The Great Barrier Reef has been growing for 10,000 years. At one time, its many sections were attached to the mainland. Over the years, the shoreline receded, leaving the reefs standing alone offshore.

There are some 300 species of coral polyps, and they come in many different colors. The delicate pink and purple sea fans look like flowers. More than 1,400 species of fish, some more brightly colored than the coral, swim in the water near the reefs.

One person who learned to be wary of the Great Barrier Reef was Captain James Cook. In 1770, on the voyage of discovery that took him to Botany Bay, his ship ran aground on a coral ridge. The ship limped to shore, where his crew made repairs. Today, Endeavour Reef, the coral outcropping that nearly ended Cook's voyage, bears the name of his ship.

lian voice" were late-19th-century bush poets like A. B. "Banjo" Paterson, who wrote "Waltzing Matilda," and Henry Lawson, who wrote short stories as well as verse. When Lawson died in 1922, the nation honored him with a state funeral. Marcus Clarke wrote about convict life in *For the Term of His Natural Life*. In 1901, Stella Franklin, who grew up in a squatter's family, wrote the autobiographical novel, *My Brilliant Career*.

In more recent times, Australia has produced important prose writers such as Morris West, Shirley Hazzard, Alan Moorehead, Christina Stead, Colleen McCullough, Thomas Keneally, and Patrick White, the novelist who won the 1973 Nobel Prize for Literature. Sally Walker's *My Place* is a quest for her Aboriginal roots. Three major contemporary poets are the Aborigine Kath Walker, Les A. Murray, and David Malouf.

In the performing arts, Australia has produced more than its share of notable figures. Dame Nellie Melba (1861–1931), the great soprano, was born Helen Mitchell. She took her stage name from her native city, Melbourne. Joan Sutherland was for decades one of the most celebrated sopranos in the world. Many of the nation's popular singers and musicians—including members of such rock bands as Midnight Oil, AC/DC, INXS, the Hoodoo Gurus, and Silverchair—are widely known.

Between 1834 and 1853, Port Arthur, Tasmania, served as Australia's main penal colony.

The Australia Broadcasting Commission helps fund new work by Australian composers and playwrights, and performances by Australian musicians and actors. The government also supports opera, ballet, and orchestral companies, which have performed around the world.

Australia has produced many world-class painters. Early landscape artists such as Arthur Streeton and Charles Conder painted vivid scenes of the lonely Outback, a tradition that Fred Williams continued after World War II. Sidney Nolan, perhaps Australia's best-known painter, produced a famous series on the Australian Robin Hood, Ned Kelly. Albert Namatjira, an Aborigine, used watercolors to interpret the landscapes of his tribal lands. Before his death in 1959, he spurred an interest in Aboriginal art that remains strong decades later.

Helped by the government, the Australian film industry had a remarkable revival during the 1970s and '80s. Among the films that earned worldwide respect were *Picnic at Hanging Rock*, *Gallipoli*, *The Man from Snowy River*, *The Year of Living Dangerously*, and *My Brilliant Career*.

HISTORY

Dutch Discovery. During the 2nd century, the Greek mathematician and geographer Ptolemy sketched a landmass south of Asia and a body of water we now know as the Indian Ocean. He called the land *terra australis incognita*, or "unknown southern land."

The Dutch were the first Europeans to learn about this land. In 1606, Willem Jansz, commander of the Dutch vessel *Duyfken*, landed on the eastern side of the Gulf of Carpentaria. In the years that followed, Dutch seamen and traders visited the continent's western and southwestern coast. Dutch navigators explored and named parts of the coast. Captain Tasman discovered Tasmania and explored Australia's north coast. But the Dutch decided against settlement.

English Arrival.   In 1688, the adventurer William Dampier sailed into King Sound, on the northwest coast. His later descriptions of the barren land discouraged further English explorations.

It was not until April 20, 1770, that another English ship visited the continent. The ship was the *Endeavour*, and it was captained by James Cook of the Royal Navy. Cook was on his way back to England after exploring New Zealand. After stopping to pick up plant specimens in what he would call Botany Bay, he sailed north, passing by a harbor he named Port Jackson, later to become the site of Sydney. Finally he reached the tip of the continent, which he called Cape York.

On August 22, the entire ship's company landed on a nearby island. Hoisting the British flag, Cook claimed possession of the entire eastern coast of the continent in the name of King George III of England. He called the region New South Wales.

At the end of his voyage, all of the coast had been mapped except the southern and southeastern parts. English and French navigators finished the job between 1798 and 1802, some years after the English had begun to settle New South Wales with convicts.

Exploration.   It would take another 100 years before all of Australia was explored. The first step for members of the First Fleet was to move inland in search of better farmland. Captain Phillip, the first governor of New South Wales, explored all the way to the Blue Mountains.

Australia's major cities are found in the coastal areas. The city of Gold Coast (below), a popular tourist resort, is located just a few miles south of Brisbane, the capital of Queensland.

Convict settlements were established at Hobart, on Tasmania; at Moreton Bay, which would later become Brisbane; and in Western Australia. Free settlers began to arrive in small numbers, and many convicts who became free stayed on in Australia. Other settlements were gradually established— at Perth, on the Swan River; at Adelaide; and at Melbourne.

The Blue Mountains hemmed in the settlers around Port Jackson for 25 years. The mountains lie about 50 mi. (80 km.) to the west. In 1813, a party of explorers found a way to the far side of the mountains and saw the fertile country beyond. By the end of the 1800s, the opening of Australia was practically complete.

Australia became an independent nation on January 1, 1901, 113 years to the month after the First Fleet anchored in Sydney Harbor. The six self-governing colonies—Queensland, New South Wales, Tasmania, Victoria, South Australia, and Western Australia—joined to become the Commonwealth of Australia. Australia also administers the huge, sparsely settled Northern Territory, which was granted self-government in 1978, and a number of island territories. The Australian Capital Territory includes the capital city, Canberra. This federal territory was carved out of the state of New South Wales in 1902, between Sydney and Melbourne, Australia's two major cities.

AUSTRALIA'S STATES AND TERRITORIES

STATE	AREA (Approx.)		POPULATION	CAPITAL CITY
	(Sq. Mi.)	(Sq. Km.)		
New South Wales	309,500	801,600	6,023,500	Sydney
Victoria	87,900	227,600	4,468,300	Melbourne
Queensland	666,800	1,727,200	3,155,400	Brisbane
South Australia	379,900	984,000	1,466,500	Adelaide
Western Australia	975,100	2,525,500	1,687,300	Perth
Tasmania	26,200	67,800	472,100	Hobart
Northern Territory	519,800	1,346,200	170,500	Darwin
Australian Capital Territory	900	2,330	299,400	Canberra

ELLEN TIMSON, CONVICT

In 1829, a 17-year-old freckle-faced girl from London, England, was convicted of stealing a man's watch. Her name was Ellen Timson, and her sentence was one that, these days, most judges would consider extreme. She was ordered to Australia "for the rest of her natural life."

Ellen made the four-month journey to Australia aboard the prison ship *Lucy Davidson*, which carried only women convicts.

GOVERNMENT

Although they had delayed forming an independent nation until 1901, the Australian colonies had pioneered in developing features of democratic government that have been widely accepted. Australian voters were the first to use the secret ballot. Australia was also a leader in the drive for compulsory voting and for woman suffrage.

The constitution that the Australian people enacted created a parliamentary democracy on the British model. The federal government of Australia retains control of foreign trade; defense; immigration; customs; external trade and commerce; postal, coinage, banking, and social services. It also controls the collection of income taxes and distributes grants to the states. The states control education, law enforcement, health services, and other key local functions.

Australia is a member of the British Commonwealth. Thus, Queen Elizabeth II of Great Britain is queen of Australia and is represented by a governor-general and six state governors. They have limited power, because ordinarily they act only on the advice of elected officials.

The Federal Parliament is made up of a 72-member Senate (12 members from each state, two from each territory) and a 148-member House of Representatives, whose members are allocated to the states and territories roughly on the basis of population. House members serve three years. Senators serve six years, with half elected every three years. The election system is designed to ensure minority-party representation.

The actual head of the federal government is the prime minister. He is the leader of the political party that holds a majority in the House of Representatives, and he is assisted by a cabinet. The prime minister holds office only so long as he and his party retain the confidence of a majority of the representatives.

DEPENDENCIES

Besides its two internal territories, the Northern and the Australian Capital, Australia is responsible for administering several islands and island groups that are referred to as external territories. The inhabited

Once in New South Wales, she was assigned to live and work with free settlers.

But this teenager with tattoos on her upper arms, including a heart with the words "I love," couldn't seem to stay out of trouble. She was returned more than once to the Female Factory in Parramatta, near Sydney. The Female Factory was a women's prison. Given a job as a weaver there, Ellen continued to push her luck. Once, she did time in the factory's jail for "mutinous and outrageous conduct."

Her luck changed in 1832, when she married David Bowerman, a tenant farmer and former convict who had served out his sentence. Ellen and Bowerman had four children before he died in 1839. She then married Edward Stanton, another former convict, and had seven more children with him.

They lived a rough, often dangerous frontier life on an isolated farm in Dungog. Ellen worked hard—on the farm and, records show, behind a hotel bar.

Ellen's great-great-great granddaughter, Norma Tuck, thinks she got a good deal. "Pretty well without exception," she said, "everyone who was sent out here was 100 percent better off than if they had kept on in England." Her view of Ellen? "We think she was rather a bad hat in some ways, but we rather like her."

The Parliament House in Canberra, Australia's capital, was dedicated amid much fanfare in 1988.

territories include Norfolk Island in the South Pacific Ocean; Jervis Bay Territory (formerly part of the Australian Capital territory); and the Cocos (Keeling) Islands, Christmas Island, Heard Island, and the McDonald Islands in the Indian Ocean. The uninhabited territories are the Coral Sea Islands, Ashmore Island and Cartier Island in the Timor Sea, and part of Antarctica.

The Antarctic Division of the Department of Science and Technology operates three permanent research stations on the 2,400,000 sq. mi. (6,216,000 sq. km.) that Australia claims as its Antarctic Territory. As with other such claims, Australia's is not recognized internationally. Australia signed the 1959 Antarctic Treaty outlawing military use of Antarctica.

TOWARD THE 21ST CENTURY

For two centuries, Australians cherished their ties to Great Britain and other Western nations. These associations remain important for Australia, both economically and culturally, despite the government's stated intention to make Australia a republic by the year 2001. Australia anticipates showcasing itself to the world when Sydney hosts the Summer Olympic Games in the year 2000. Australia is an active member of the South Pacific Forum, and it is clear to most Australians that their nation's future economic health depends on close links with Asia.

These links have been developing for decades. As the 1990s began, five of the seven top markets for Australian goods were Asian: Japan, South Korea, China, Hong Kong, and Taiwan. Asian companies, primarily Japanese, have invested heavily in Australian businesses. And, at current immigration levels, Australians of Asian descent are expected to swell to 7 percent of the population by the year 2025. Thus, Australia in its third century will surely reinvent itself—again.

Reviewed by BRUCE W. PRATT, Editorial Director, *The Australian Encyclopedia*

Auckland, New Zealand's largest and fastest-growing city, has fine harbors on two coasts.

NEW ZEALAND

Distance and isolation have always been the central facts about the South Pacific nation of New Zealand. It is 12,000 mi. (19,300 km.) from Europe and 1,200 mi. (1,930 km.) from Australia, its nearest neighbor. Until the 20th century, New Zealand remained one of the least-known countries in the world. Today, it is respected everywhere as a modern, flourishing nation, and it has one of the highest standards of living in the world.

THE LAND

About the size of Colorado, New Zealand includes three main islands—the North Island, the South Island, and Stewart Island—and several smaller ones, not all of them occupied. Among the smaller islands are the Chatham group, some 400 mi. (640 km.) southeast of Wellington; and the Kermadecs, about 500 mi. (800 km.) northeast of the North Island. About 1,000 mi. (1,609 km.) from top to bottom, with the sea never more than 70 mi. (113 km.) from any given point, New Zealand contains some of the world's most unusual and beautiful geographical features.

The South Island

The South Island, which New Zealanders refer to as the Mainland, is the largest of the three principal islands, and the one with the most varied landscape. It is dominated by the Southern Alps, a massive moun-

NEW ZEALAND

FACTS AND FIGURES

OFFICIAL NAME: New Zealand.

NATIONALITY: New Zealander(s).

CAPITAL: Wellington.

LOCATION: South Pacific Ocean. **Boundaries**—Pacific Ocean, Tasman Sea.

AREA: 103,737 sq. mi. (268,680 sq. km.).

PHYSICAL FEATURES: Highest point—Mount Cook (12,349 ft.; 3,764 m.). **Lowest point**—sea level. **Chief rivers**—Waikato, Clutha. **Major lakes**—Taupo, Te Anau, Manapouri.

POPULATION: 3,600,000 (1996; annual growth 0.9%).

MAJOR LANGUAGES: English, Maori (both official).

MAJOR RELIGION: Christianity.

GOVERNMENT: Constitutional monarchy within Commonwealth of Nations. **Head of state**—British monarch represented by a governor-general. **Head of government**—prime minister. **Legislature**—House of Representatives.

CHIEF CITIES: Auckland, Christchurch, Manukau, North Shore, Wellington.

ECONOMY: Chief minerals—natural gas, iron, sand, coal, timber. **Chief agricultural products**—fodder and silage crops, wool, meat, dairy products. **Industries and products**—food processing, wood and paper products, textiles, machinery, transportation equipment, banking, insurance, tourism. **Chief exports**—beef, wool, dairy products. **Chief imports**—petroleum, cars, trucks, machinery and electrical equipment, iron and steel, petroleum products.

MONETARY UNIT: 1 New Zealand dollar = 100 cents.

NATIONAL HOLIDAY: February 6 (Waitangi Day).

tain chain that runs down the island's west coast. Although only occasionally rising higher than 11,000 ft. (3,300 m.), these mountains provide magnificent Alpine scenery, with snowfields, crevasses, and glaciers that descend through rain forests almost to sea level. Soaring to 12,349 ft. (3,764 m.), snowcapped Mount Cook is New Zealand's highest mountain. The Maori, New Zealand's native people, call it Aorangi, "the cloud piercer." Mount Cook is located in one of the island's seven national parks, where visitors can enjoy mountain climbing, hunting, and hiking.

The mountains contain three vast glaciers—Tasman, Fox, and Franz Josef. Another attraction is the superb skiing. Airplanes take skiers to the heads of these glaciers for the long, smooth runs to the bottom, sometimes as much as 16 mi. (26 km.) of uninterrupted skiing. This part of the South Island also abounds in beautiful, deep glacial lakes.

The southwestern coast, below the Alps, is deeply indented by isolated fjords, similar to those in far-off Norway. Fringed by mountains rising straight out of the sea, the fjords are among New Zealand's most dazzling beauties. The Fiordland, too, has been made a national park, and some of it remains unexplored. One of its highlights is Sutherland

Falls, the fourth-highest waterfall in the world. Milford Sound, with its cone-shaped Mitre Peak, is the best-known fjord. Two of the others are Dusky Sound and Doubtful Sound.

Stretching from the foothills of the Alps to the east coast of the South Island are the vast open spaces of the region known as the Canterbury Plains. Farther south are the rolling hills and pleasant valleys of the Otago and Southland districts.

Across Foveaux Strait from the South Island is 600-sq.-mi. (1,700-sq.-km.) **Stewart Island**, known to the Maori as the Isle of the Glowing Sky. It is a peaceful spot with unspoiled beaches, forests that provide a haven for wildlife, and fewer than 600 inhabitants.

The North Island

The North Island's landscape has a special drama all its own. Cutting across the center of the island is one of the most active volcanic complexes in the world. Tongariro National Park—one of the island's three national parks—includes Mounts Tongariro, Ngauruhoe, and Ruapehu. To the west of these three active peaks is the symmetrical cone of Mount Egmont, rising over 8,000 ft. (2,400 m.) from the rich lands of the Taranaki district. Egmont, extinct for some 250 years, is often compared to Japan's Mount Fujiyama. Today, there are many fine ski trails in both the Tongariro and Egmont regions.

To the north of Mount Egmont are the Waitomo Caves, three huge limestone grottoes. Visitors marvel at the grotesque shapes of their stalactites and stalagmites, eerily lit by thousands of tiny glowworms.

Still farther north, centered around the old Maori town of Rotorua, is New Zealand's thermal region. Here, spouting geysers like Pohutu and the Prince of Wales Feathers put on spectacular performances, sending up plumes of hot water as high as 100 ft. (30 m.). There are also boiling

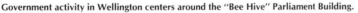

Government activity in Wellington centers around the "Bee Hive" Parliament Building.

Milford Sound is the best known of the many fjords that indent the coast of the South Island.

mud pools that plop and bubble, and fumaroles—where steam and gases rise into the air. Here, too, it is possible to catch a fish in one stream and cook it by plunging it into the next, for hot and cold springs exist practically side by side. The hot, mineral-rich springs are said to have beneficial effects for people suffering certain diseases, but they also give the area a distinct sulfurous odor that takes some getting used to.

There are several lovely lakes in the volcanic and thermal districts. Among them is New Zealand's largest, 238-sq.-mi. (616-sq.-km.) Lake Taupo, located almost in the center of the North Island.

Seaside resorts are strung out all along the east coast, from the Bay of Plenty to the Bay of Islands, and the area offers deep-sea fishing for marlin, shark, and tuna. In the North Auckland region—or the Northland, as New Zealanders call the long peninsula north of Auckland—there are protected stands of giant kauri trees. These are all that are left of the ancient kauri forests that once grew all over the North Island. One tree is over 2,000 years old.

Climate

New Zealand's climate is strongly influenced by the sea that surrounds the islands. In the Fiordland, moisture-laden winds from the sea bring abundant rainfall, sometimes reaching as high as 250 in. (635 cm.) a year. Westerly winds from the sea make New Zealand's weather highly changeable, with bright blue skies one minute and gray threatening ones

New Zealand generates nearly 10 percent of its electricity supply from geothermal springs.

the next. Temperatures are moderate, however, without great extremes of hot or cold.

Since New Zealand is below the equator, the seasons are the reverse of those in the Northern Hemisphere—a situation that occasionally causes problems for New Zealanders and foreigners alike. At the warmest time of year, New Zealanders eat a heavy Christmas dinner that faithfully follows its English original down to plum pudding with brandy sauce. Under his beard and red suit, Father Christmas perspires in the midsummer sun. Location in the Southern Hemisphere also means that temperatures tend to get increasingly colder as one moves toward the south, rather than the opposite.

Resources

The many rivers that drain its mountain ranges and lakes are New Zealand's most important natural resource. Often too short or too turbulent to be navigable for great lengths, many of them have been harnessed to provide cheap electricity for New Zealand's homes and industries. Waterpower provides almost 90 percent of the nation's electricity. Since the North Island has the larger population and the smaller hydroelectric potential, cables under Cook Strait carry power north. At a large geothermal plant at Wairakei, just south of Rotorua, underground steam drives giant turbines, generating more electricity for the North Island.

New Zealand's mineral resources include coal, most of which is mined in mountainous Westland in the South Island. Quarries in many parts of the country produce the limestone that, when crushed, is so vital to New Zealand's agriculture. The South Island's Otago region was the country's gold-rush center in the 1880s, but very little gold is mined there today. In the North Island, iron sands are used by New Zealand's developing steel industry. Natural gas, an important energy resource on the North Island, is also being converted into petroleum as part of a plan to reduce oil imports.

New Zealand's forests are another valuable natural resource. At first, both Maori and Europeans cut down and burned off trees to clear land for agriculture. Later, an active trade developed in New Zealand timber. Many of the island's forests—including those of ancient kauri trees—were destroyed.

But eventually, under government reforestation programs, new trees replaced the old. During the 20th century, scientists introduced trees native to other countries; and today, there are thriving forests of California pine, Japanese cedar, European larch, and Australian eucalyptus trees in New Zealand, side by side with the country's own rimu, matai, totara, tawa, and beech trees. Forests cover about one-quarter of New Zealand's land area, and their products—from pulp and paper to timber and furniture—are important exports.

Rare Plants and Animals

Because of its geographical isolation, New Zealand has some forms of plant and animal life not found anywhere else. These are one of the country's unique attractions for visitors. The best known is the flightless, long-beaked kiwi, New Zealand's unofficial national bird. Other native birds are the tui and the bellbird, both of which have lovely, melodious songs. There are also the kea, a large greenish parrot that preys on sheep; and the takahe, which, until 1948, was thought to be extinct.

Strangely, New Zealand has no land snakes. The tuatara lizard, New Zealand's lone reptile, is an accidental living fossil that should have been extinct 100 million years ago. Besides its two sighted eyes, the tuatara has a sightless third eye—in the middle of its forehead.

In addition to the kauri and other New Zealand trees, there is the scarlet-flowered pohutukawa, sacred to the Maori; the nikau palm; and the rata, which twines around other plants, using them for support and decorating them with its bright, fragrant blossoms.

CITIES

Wellington.   The country's capital and second-largest city, Wellington was founded in 1840 by immigrants assembled by the New Zealand Company, an association founded in 1837 to colonize New Zealand. Company officials named the settlement after the Duke of Wellington, who in 1815 had defeated the French forces of Napoleon Bonaparte at the Battle of Waterloo.

Located on the southwestern tip of the North Island, overlooking Cook Strait, Wellington is blessed with one of the world's deepest natural harbors. The port area, with its miles of docks for oceangoing ships, also has ferry and hydrofoil connections to the South Island. From the harbor, cable cars climb the steep hills on which Wellington is built.

As the seat of government since 1865, Wellington is the site of New Zealand's parliament and main government offices. A sizable proportion of Wellingtonians are government employees. Wellington's Dominion Museum has exhibits depicting New Zealand life and history. Wellington is the home of Victoria University, one of New Zealand's six universities.

Auckland. Near the northern end of the North Island is Auckland (pronounced AWK-luhnd), New Zealand's largest city. With its port and industrial center, it is also the country's fastest-growing city.

Built on an isthmus between two harbors, Waitemata and Manukau, Auckland separates two seas, the Pacific Ocean and the Tasman Sea. A soaring bridge connects the city to its north-shore suburbs. Auckland's location and excellent port facilities have made it a focal point for much of New Zealand's trade and shipping. It is also a major industrial center, with a wide variety of manufacturing plants and an iron and steel industry based on local iron sands.

In recent years, Auckland has become the city with the largest Polynesian population in the world. In addition to the Maori who live there, new arrivals from all over the South Pacific make their home in the city. Most are from former New Zealand territories—Western Samoa, the Cook Islands, Niue, and the Tokelaus—where jobs and opportunities are scarce. By and large, the newcomers stay in self-contained communities, where culture and customs are familiar.

The busy, modern metropolis offers an exciting introduction to the country as a whole. The city's War Memorial Museum has one of the best collections of Maori artifacts in the world, including the only surviving Maori war canoe. (See sidebar, page 515.) Auckland University is known for its engineering, fine arts, and architecture schools. About 3 mi. (4 km.) outside the city, visitors drive to the top of Mount Eden, one of several extinct volcanoes in the area. Only a few minutes away, miles of beaches afford excellent swimming and surfing, and of course there is always sailing.

Christchurch. Christchurch is New Zealand's third-largest city and the largest one on the South Island. In its origins and atmosphere, it is the most English of all New Zealand's cities. Set in Canterbury Plains, it was founded in 1850 by a group of settlers sponsored by the Church of England. The city's major landmark is the single spire of its Gothic-style cathedral. Named for a college in Oxford, England, Christchurch is proud of its excellent educational facilities—among them, the University of Canterbury, Lincoln College, and the boys' school Christ's College.

Through its port of Lyttelton, 7 mi. (11 km.) away, Christchurch exports the wheat, wool, meat, and other products of the plains area. Christchurch's thriving industries include fertilizers, engineering, clothing, electrical equipment, and furniture.

Dunedin. Dunedin sits on the Otago Peninsula about 200 mi. (320 km.) down the coast from Christchurch. Its name, Gaelic for Edinburgh, recalls Dunedin's founding in 1848 by the lay association of the Free Church of Scotland.

In the 1860s, Dunedin was a base for gold prospectors. Today, the city is a manufacturing center, with iron and brass foundries and woolen mills. The products of these industries are shipped from Dunedin's harbor of Port Chalmers, as are the agricultural products of the Otago area. The University of Otago, in Dunedin, is the oldest in New Zealand.

People of European extraction and the native Maori people are almost completely integrated.

PEOPLE

Measured in terms of recorded history, New Zealand is a very young country. The story of its development was written by two different peoples—the Maori and the white settlers and their descendants—both of whom played vital roles in molding the modern nation.

Two Peoples—One Nation

The Maori (pronounced MAU-ree, not may-oh-ree), a brown-skinned Polynesian people, lived in New Zealand for some hundreds of years before Europeans sighted the land in 1642. Almost 200 years more passed before Europeans began to settle New Zealand in large numbers. The Maori word for "white man" is *pakeha*, believed to have originally meant "imaginary beings resembling men." *Maori* itself means "normal," "usual," or "ordinary." In New Zealand today, the gap between the two peoples is steadily being closed.

At first, the arrival of Europeans brought the Maori more sophisticated methods of killing, as well as new diseases to which they had no resistance. As a result, during the 1800s, the Maori population declined from perhaps 250,000 to less than 40,000. But the 1900s brought a reversal of this trend. Although few full-blooded Maori now exist in New Zealand, by 1989, about 404,000 New Zealanders, about 12 percent of the population, were thought to be half Maori or more in descent. Because the Maori population is growing faster than the nation's, one expert predicts that by the year 2015, 30 percent of all New Zealanders will be half Maori in descent.

The Maori have had full citizenship rights since 1865. Today, they live, dress, and work the same as *pakeha* New Zealanders, with whom they are almost completely integrated.

Nonetheless, many problems remain. More and more Maori have left their old, close-knit communities and moved to the cities. The transition to an urban way of life creates tension, which is often compounded by lack of understanding shown by whites. Compared with other New Zealanders, the Maori have less success in school, more trouble with the law, and higher unemployment.

Both government and private agencies have been set up to deal with these problems. Attempts are also being made to preserve the Maori's rich cultural heritage and even to teach it in schools. The goal is for all New Zealand children to grow up with an appreciation of their bicultural roots. Finally, the government is wrestling with the touchy question of the Maori's right to land that they argue was taken from them. (See sidebar, page 517.)

LIFE-STYLES

Observers often conclude that many New Zealanders are "more English than the English." This may be due to the orderly flower gardens in front of most homes, to a certain manner of speech found in educated New Zealanders, and to the sentimental care with which many English institutions have been transplanted. But today, the Englishness of New Zealand is largely an illusion. Immigrants from Asia, Oceania, and European nations other than Great Britain are all mingling in the special blend that is the New Zealander.

Outdoor Life. New Zealand's population is small in relation to its land area. One result is that most New Zealanders are house owners rather than apartment dwellers. Another is that every New Zealander has easy access to open country, and that outdoor activities and sports play an important part in New Zealand life.

New Zealanders give their leisure time with great energy to cricket, tennis, golf, soccer, outdoor bowling, skiing, hiking, mountain climbing,

The ski resorts on South Island are busiest during the June-to-September winter season.

New Zealanders of English descent are sometimes said to be "more English than the English."

horse racing, swimming, sailing, and surfing. But however popular these are, none of them generates as much enthusiasm as does rugby football. Rugby is not a sport but a national cause in New Zealand. Every winter, New Zealanders focus on it fanatically.

Arts and Crafts.   Perhaps because so much energy had to be devoted to building up a young country, New Zealand has not produced many great artists. In the late 1800s, Charles Heaphy and Frances Hodgkins were among the first to capture the country's beauty on canvas; and William Pember Reeves, a poet and politician, wrote lyrically about his homeland.

During the 20th century, many New Zealanders—short-story writer Katherine Mansfield and novelist Janet Frame, to name two—felt that, for a time, at least, they had to go abroad to write. Today, more and more contemporary New Zealand artists are staying at home, drawing on the life around them for inspiration. The late Sylvia Ashton-Warner was one. She wrote novels and nonfiction based on her experiences as a teacher in Maori schools. Among the writers who provide personalized views of New Zealand life in their fiction today are Maori novelists Patricia Grace, Keri Hulme, and Witi Ihimaera; and Maurice Shadbolt, Maurice Gee, and Frank Sargeson.

New Zealanders are avid potters and ceramists. The nation has some 4,000 professional potters and another 40,000 who practice the craft as a hobby. About 4,000 more create ceramics, weaving, jewelry, and carved art objects. Maori carving, on display in major museums, is a respected indigenous art form.

ECONOMY

Endowed with mild temperatures and fertile soils, New Zealand was first settled as an agricultural country. Today, it has one of the most efficient agricultural industries in the world, and in spite of the fact that about 84 percent of its people live in urban areas, agricultural products are the country's most valuable exports.

There are some 55 million sheep in New Zealand, raised wherever the land is suitable for grazing. They have made the country the world's leading exporter of mutton and lamb and the second-largest exporter of wool. One principal sheep-raising area is still the South Island's Canterbury Plains.

Although sheep are the mainstay of New Zealand's agriculture, there are also some 6.5 million cattle. About 40 percent are dairy cattle, and New Zealand is one of the major exporters of butter, cheese, casein (a milk protein), and skim-milk powder. Most of the dairy farms are located in the North Island.

New Zealand's grain crops include wheat, barley, and oats, which are grown principally on the Canterbury Plains. A wide variety of vegetables are raised; and hay, grass, and clover are important as fodder crops for livestock.

The products of New Zealand's orchards—mainly in the Otago and Nelson areas of the South Island, and Hawke's Bay in the North Island—include apples, peaches, pears, cherries, citrus fruits, and subtropical fruits such as the tamarind and Chinese gooseberry. Fresh or canned, these are becoming more important exports. Berries are also grown, and near Auckland and Napier, in Hawke's Bay, there are vineyards that produce fine wines.

Industries

Great Britain was once New Zealand's most important trading partner. Today, New Zealand directs most of its trade to Asia—particularly Japan—and to Australia and the United States.

To develop the economy, there has been a growing emphasis on manufacturing, including the production of automobiles, furniture, re-

New Zealand has become the world's leading exporter of lamb and mutton.

frigerating equipment, clothing, light engineering, and electronics. Investment from foreign companies has led to the development of oil refining, steel manufacturing, and the use of hydroelectricity to produce aluminum from imported bauxite. About 41 percent of New Zealand's work force is involved in manufacturing and commerce, 47 percent in services and government, and 12 percent in agriculture and mining.

HISTORY

New Zealand's history began with the arrival of the Maori. Although there are many theories, the exact origins of this Polynesian people are lost in history and time. Many scholars believe the Polynesians came from somewhere on the mainland of Southeast Asia. By great feats of seamanship, the Polynesians eventually spread north to Hawaii, as far west toward South America as Easter Island, and south to New Zealand. In this way, they populated the area now referred to as Polynesia.

Since the Maori had no written language, their history was passed from one generation to the next by word of mouth. According to tradition, the Maori's ancient homeland is Hawaiki—a far-off place in central Polynesia, possibly one of the Society Islands near Tahiti. Hawaiki is considered the place to which all Maori return after death.

It has been estimated that the Maori came to New Zealand between A.D. 700 and 1100. They came in hardy vessels made of hollowed logs, and the vessels were either outriggers or double canoes. Sturdy and well equipped, they carried men, women, and children; plants and seeds; and even dogs and rats.

Early Life in New Zealand. Because the new arrivals first saw mountains shrouded with mist, they called their new home Aotearoa, "the land of the long white cloud." According to the mythology they developed, the country had been fished up from the ocean by a legendary Polynesian hero—"the man Maui, linked by his lineage with the gods." So the northern island came to be known as Te Ika a Maui ("Maui's fish"); and the southern, Te Waka a Maui ("Maui's canoe").

At first, the Maori depended for survival on hunting the moa, a large, flightless bird that has long been extinct. Gradually, they developed skills in shelter building, weaving, agriculture, fishing, and bird snaring. As life became more comfortable, carving and other decorative arts reached a high level. Using tools made of hard New Zealand greenstone (a kind of nephrite, or jade), the Maori carved the arching prows of their canoes and the gateposts of their villages and hilltop forts, or *pas*, to which they retreated during times of conflict with other tribes. They also carved intricate *tikis*, or fertility symbols, out of the greenstone itself. Every aspect of Maori life was regulated by ritual and a religion that has been described as mythology mixed with magic.

Recurrent wars were another important part of Maori life, and battles were ferocious. A proud people, the Maori believed in *utu*, or revenge, for any insult or slight.

Ritual played a significant role in war, too. Since many Maori were cannibals, the dead and captured were often eaten. Vanquished chiefs usually preferred this fate to its alternative—slavery. In spite of wars, however, by 1600, the Maori had become an agricultural people, and they had made the land their home.

THE MAORI'S MASTER BOAT BUILDERS

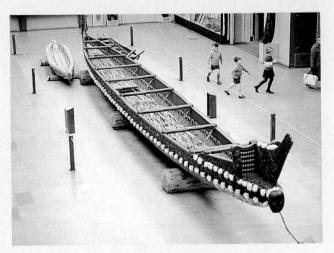

Accomplished seafarers, the Maori were also patient and expert builders of small craft for coastal fishing and use on lakes and rivers. But their great feats of boat construction involved the large war canoes, or *waka taua*, which could carry as many as 100 men on raids along the coast. These massive canoes, often 70 ft. (21 m.) long and 5 ft. (1.5 m.) wide, impressed Captain James Cook, and he studied them closely on his 1773 voyage to New Zealand. "The People show great ingenuity and good workmanship in building and framing their Boats or Canoes," he wrote.

They were seaworthy, too. "We have observed other war-canoes cross the Bay of Islands in perfect safety when it was thought imprudent to lower the ship's boats," a British ship captain remarked in 1820.

The canoes took two years to build. After selecting an appropriate tree—usually a giant kauri or totara—the Maori spent days felling it with stone tools and fire, and then stripping away its head. Left with a large log, they hollowed it out with hot coals and stone tools; hauled it to the shore; smoothed the hull inside and out; installed flooring and thwarts, or seats; and added tall, elaborately carved figureheads and stern pieces, which they often painted black.

The figureheads caught Cook's attention. "Most common," he wrote, "is an od design'd figure of a man with as ugly a face as can be conceived, a very large tongue sticking out of his mouth and large white eyes made of the Shells of sea ears."

The canoe makers used cord made of plaited flax to lash all the pieces together. They often painted the hull red with a mixture of burned ocher and shark oil. On special occasions, long streamers of feathers hung from the figureheads and stern pieces, giving these fierce war vessels a festive, even lighthearted, look.

European Contacts

Abel Tasman. In 1642 the Dutch East India Company sent two ships commanded by its best navigator, Abel Janszoon Tasman, to hunt for a southern continent. In December of that year, Tasman sighted "a large, high-lying land," and began mapping it. He called it Staaten Landt, but the Dutch later named it Nieuw Zeeland, after their own southwestern province. In a landing attempt, Tasman made contact with the Maori, who killed four of his crewmen. He sailed on, and Nieuw Zeeland was left to its belligerent inhabitants for more than a century.

Captain Cook. In 1769, New Zealand was visited by the greatest seaman and navigator of his time, the Yorkshireman Captain James Cook. He, too, was searching for the legendary southern continent. On a ship named *Endeavour*, Cook and his crew of 90 circumnavigated the islands, charting them with remarkable accuracy. Sir Joseph Banks, a naturalist on board the *Endeavour*, recorded precise information on the islands' plant and animal life. Banks also noted that "the almost certainty of being eaten as you come ashore adds not a little to the terrors of shipwreck." But after some hostile first encounters, Cook established reasonably good relations with the Maori.

Cook returned to New Zealand twice, in 1772 and 1777. There were other expeditions as well, including several led by Frenchmen.

By the end of the 1700s, as Europeans learned more about New Zealand, the country slowly began to be opened up. At first, the rich harvest of the southern seas attracted Australian, American, British, and French whalers and seal hunters. Busy whaling stations were built on the coasts of both of New Zealand's islands. Competition among them grew so fierce that at times it approached piracy, and soon several kinds of whales were almost exterminated. Trade in flax and timber also developed rapidly. The strong flax fiber, used for ropes, was bartered by the Maori for imported goods. (Guns and rum were the preferred items.) The northern ports where these activities centered became colorful, frontier-type towns.

Settlement, Expansion, and Development

In the early 1800s, the economic crises that followed the Napoleonic Wars brought poverty to working-class people in Europe. Thousands emigrated—especially from England—in search of a better life. Missionaries came from England, too, and began converting Maori to Christianity.

New Zealand Becomes an English Colony. By 1840, England had decided to annex New Zealand. In that year, a treaty was signed with the Maori chiefs at Waitangi, in the North Island. (See sidebar, page 517.) The Maori recognized Queen Victoria as their sovereign, and they received guarantees of their property rights.

In 1837, Edward Gibbon Wakefield, a specialist in what he called "the art of colonisation," had set up the New Zealand Company to organize settlement of the new colony. He hoped to create an English society in the South Seas. With assistance provided by the company, thousands of people immigrated to New Zealand. But Wakefield's plans were soon forgotten. The new settlers began to build a different society from the one he had envisioned.

All over New Zealand, a period of development began. The hilly, open country of the South Island was ideal sheep-grazing land. Sheep farmers were soon exporting wool to Australia and England as well as supplying high-quality lamb and mutton for New Zealand's tables. Grain crops—mainly wheat and barley—were also raised in the South Island. In the 1860s, gold was discovered in the south. This brought a rush of prospectors—some of whom had followed the hunt for gold around the world, from California to Australia to new Zealand—but the large finds were quickly worked out.

In the North Island, there was progress, too. The foundations of a thriving dairy industry were laid by English farmers who brought in Jersey and Guernsey cows. All kinds of vegetables were raised on farms similar to those in central England, and pear and apple orchards were planted as well. Since the North Island still depended on acquiring land from the Maori, farms and settlements tended to be small.

Self-Government. Yet on both islands, cities were being built, and in 1852, when there were some 50,000 European settlers, England granted

New Zealand self-government. Six provinces—Auckland, Wellington, New Plymouth, Nelson, Canterbury, and Otago—were set up, and a central parliament was established at Wellington. The governor, Sir George Grey, planned for the peaceful development of New Zealand, with Maori and Europeans working together.

The Maori Wars. But trouble was brewing in the North Island. As more and more settlers arrived, pressure on the Maori increased. At the same time, Maori opposition to further land sales was growing. In 1860, in spite of the Waitangi treaty, land disputes flared into open war. Conflict continued throughout the 1860s, but the settlers finally proved too strong. By 1872, the Maori wars were over.

With the return of peace, the government concentrated on attracting more settlers and on building up the economy. The country's merchant marine was enlarged, and soon New Zealand's ships were calling at ports all over Asia and the South Pacific. But the greatest strides in the country's economic development began in 1882, when an experimental refrigerator ship took a cargo of meat on the long voyage to England. The *Dunedin* was a trailblazer. Vast new markets were now open to New Zealand.

The 20th Century

With exports ensuring a strong economy, New Zealand became one of the most progressive countries in the world. Women were granted the

MAKING THE TREATY OF WAITANGI WORK

An 1840 pact designed to promote cooperation and trust between the English Crown and the Maori became a source of friction in the 1980s, and it is expected to trouble New Zealanders well into the next century. The pact is known as the Treaty of Waitangi. It was signed on February 6, 1840, by representatives of England's Queen Victoria and by 45 Maori chiefs.

New Zealanders celebrate the day every year as National Day. Yet some Maori have come to view the treaty's signing as the beginning of their culture's decline. In 1990, on the 150th anniversary of the signing, protesters tried to shout down a speech being given by the current British monarch, Queen Elizabeth II. And Maori have demanded that the government honor the treaty and return about half of the nation's land—all the government owns—to them.

The cause of the conflict is a brief, hastily drawn, and confusingly translated document. In essence, it contains an English promise to respect Maori land rights in exchange for a Maori promise to sell land only to the English Crown.

It is unclear whether the more than 400 Maori chiefs who eventually signed the treaty really understood what they were giving up. For example, they promised to yield sovereignty, or supreme authority, to England's queen. But the word *sovereignty* was translated into Maori with the word *kawanatanga*, which merely means "governorship."

In any event, the treaty never worked. After four years, the British government let the settlers buy land on their own terms directly from the Maori. Those terms rarely benefited the Maori, who in 1990 owned less than 5 percent of New Zealand's land.

The Waitangi Tribunal, a quasi-judicial body, has been given authority to settle more than 150 Maori land-rights claims. Deciding who owns about half of New Zealand's land area and even its offshore fishing grounds won't be easy. The Tribunal is expected to take 50 years just to unravel the current claims.

vote in 1893. Land was redistributed, and an income-tax bill was passed. A welfare program—including unemployment insurance, old-age pensions, workmen's compensation, and family allowance—went into effect. The world's first system for government arbitration of industrial disputes was set up. By stages, education became "free, secular, and compulsory." During this time, too, the first steps were taken to bring the Maori more fully into the life of the country. In 1907, New Zealand gained independence—dominion status within the British Empire, which later became the Commonwealth of Nations.

Two World Wars.   The outbreak of World War I marked the real beginning of the country's participation in world events. New Zealand sent food and supplies to England and other Empire countries, and an expeditionary force to fight in France and the Middle East. These troops were respected for their bravery wherever they fought. At Gallipoli, in Turkey, in 1915, they and the Australians made the name ANZAC (Australian and New Zealand Army Corps) one to be reckoned with. New Zealand suffered tragic losses in the war. Of a population of just over 1 million, nearly 17,000 were killed.

World War II saw the nation's resources even more completely mobilized. Once more, vast quantities of food were shipped to England. Once more, New Zealanders saw action in many theaters of war—in Europe, in the Pacific, and in North Africa.

GOVERNMENT

New Zealand's constitutional procedures are based on those of England. The British Crown is represented by a governor-general, and the basic lawmaking body is a one-chamber parliament, usually referred to as the House of Representatives.

Parliament consists of 97 representatives, four of whom must be Maori elected on a separate slate. Elections are held at least every three years, and every citizen of New Zealand over the age of 18 has the right to vote. Since 1993, any party receiving at least 5 percent of the vote is guaranteed a seat in the legislature, increasing the influence of small parties in national politics and leading to a succession of coalition governments.

NEW ZEALAND AND THE WORLD

For some years after 1907, when New Zealand achieved dominion status, England was still home—an assured market and a protective parent. But World War II brought an awareness that New Zealand is close to Asia, though not exactly a part of it. New Zealand recognized the People's Republic of China in 1972 and began to play a leading role in Asian and Pacific affairs. Trade with Japan and South Korea stepped up.

In 1985, New Zealand was a key participant in the negotiations that led to the Treaty of Rarotonga, which established a South Pacific Nuclear Free Zone. The U.S. declared in 1986 that New Zealand's antinuclear policy ended U.S. promises to defend New Zealand under the ANZUS (Australia, New Zealand, U.S.) Treaty, which was then 35 years old. Virtually all trade barriers between Australia and New Zealand were abolished in 1990. In 1994, high-level ties between the United States and New Zealand resumed.

JOHN MALE, Former Chief, Advisory Services
Division of Human Rights, United Nations

Oceania is made up of thousands of islands, many of them lush, balmy paradises.

OCEANIA

Oceania—a region of some 25,000 islands spread out over an ocean that covers one-third of the world's surface—is notable for several important "lasts." It was the last major area of the world that humans populated. It was the last major area that Westerners explored, the last to be colonized, and the last to shed the colonial experience for self-government. It was also the last to be examined by archaeologists—experts on the ways of peoples in the past.

During the 1990s, archaeologists are still uncovering clues that add to our understanding of the islanders' origins, of how different groups of islanders are related, and of how islanders lived before the impact of Western cultures. The ongoing discoveries make Oceania a fascinating region to study. And so do the insights Oceania provides into the fragile relationship between humans and their environment.

Oceania, a vast region in the Pacific, is not always defined the same way. Generally, experts agree that its northern border is marked by Hawaii, its eastern extreme by Easter Island, and its western edge by the islands of Palau and New Guinea. Oceania's southern limit includes New Zealand and, in the reckoning of most experts, the continent of Australia as well.

In this volume, the modern nation states of Australia and New Zealand are explored in a separate section (pages 473–518). Irian Jaya, the Indonesian province that makes up the western part of New Guinea, is discussed with Indonesia (pages 313–328). An article in Volume 5 of LANDS AND PEOPLES examines Hawaii, and another in Volume 6 covers Easter Island.

This section is concerned with the rest of Oceania: 9 territories variously associated with the United States, New Zealand, and France; 13 independent nations; a U.S. commonwealth; and a colony of the United Kingdom. These islands and island groups cover a total land area of 3,565 sq. mi. (9,233 sq. km.), about half the size of New Jersey. They are home to about 7 million people—slightly less than the population of Los Angeles and its suburbs.

Immense distances separate the islands of Oceania from one another, and even more immense distances separate Oceania from the industrially developed centers of Western Europe and North America. These distances have helped keep Oceania isolated from the mainstream of history until quite recent times. Until World War II, there were still people in Oceania who had encountered only a handful of administrators, missionaries, and settlers from the outside world.

Oceania's isolation did not end until World War II. For three years, from 1942 to 1945, hundreds of thousands of troops from Asia, Europe,

COUNTRIES AND TERRITORIES OF OCEANIA

NAME	LAND AREA[1] sq. mi./sq.km.	POPULATION (1995–96)	CAPITAL	POLITICAL STATUS
MICRONESIA				
Federated States of Micronesia	271/702	100,000	Kolonia	Indep. (1986) *
Guam	209/541	153,000	Agana	U.S. territory
Johnston Atoll	1.1/2.8	327	None	U.S. territory
Kiribati	264/684	79,000	Tarawa	Indep. (1979)
Marshall Islands	70/181	100,000	Majuro	Indep. (1986) *
Midway Islands	2/5.2	453	None	U.S. territory
Nauru	8.2/21	10,000	Yaren Dist.	Indep. (1968)
Northern Marianas	184/477	51,000	Saipan	U.S. commonwealth
Palau (Belau)	177/458	17,000	Koror	Indep. (1994) *
Wake Island	2.5/6.5	302	None	U.S. territory
				* In free association with the U.S.
MELANESIA				
Fiji	7,054/18,270	800,000	Suva	Indep. (1970)
Irian Jaya	162,918/421,981	1,700,000	Jayapura	Indonesian province (1962)
New Caledonia	7,243/18,760	185,000	Nouméa	French territory
Papua New Guinea	178,260/461,693	4,300,000	Port Moresby	Indep. (1975)
Solomon Islands	11,599/27,556	400,000	Honiara	Indep. (1978)
Vanuatu	5,699/14,760	200,000	Vila	Indep. (1980)
POLYNESIA				
American Samoa	77/199	57,000	Pago Pago	U.S. territory
Cook Islands	93/240	19,000	Avarua	Self-governing *
Easter Island[2]	64/166	2,000	Hanga Roa	Chilean island
French Polynesia	1,413/3,660	220,000	Papeete	French territory
Hawaii[3]	6,449/16,705	1,200,000	Honolulu	U.S. state
Niue	100/260	1,800	Alofi	Self-governing *
New Zealand[4]	103,737/268,680	3,600,000	Wellington	Indep. (1907)
Pitcairn Islands	18/47	73	Adamstown	Colony of U.K.
Tokelau	4/10	1,500	None	N.Z. territory
Tonga	277/718	106,000	Nuku'alofa	Indep. (1970)
Tuvalu	10/26	10,000	Funafuti	Indep. (1978)
Wallis & Futuna	106/274	15,000	Mata-Utu	French territory
Western Samoa	1,097/2,842	200,000	Apia	Indep. (1962)
				* In free association with New Zealand
Australia[4]	2,941,100/7,617,850	18,300,000	Canberra	Indep. (1901)

NOTES: [1] Land area is often smaller than total area, which is reported in the "Facts and Figures" boxes that accompany individual articles. [2] An article on Easter Island appears in Volume 6 of LANDS AND PEOPLES. [3] An article on Hawaii appears in Volume 5. [4] For convenience, a separate section of this volume considers Australia and New Zealand, which are usually considered part of Oceania.

OCEANIA

PACIFIC OCEAN

CHINA

SOUTH CHINA SEA

OKINAWA

TAIWAN

PHILIPPINE SEA

PHILIPPINES

LUZON

MINDANAO

BORNEO

CELEBES (SULAWESI)

SERAM

TIMOR

LESSER SUNDA ISLS.

JAVA

INDONESIA

IRIAN JAYA

NEW GUINEA

PAPUA NEW GUINEA

ARAFURA SEA

AUSTRALIA

TASMANIA

BONIN ISLS.

VOLCANO ISLS.

MARCUS IS.

IWO JIMA

MARIANAS ISLS.

SAIPAN

GUAM

YAP ISLS.

PALAU ISLS.

FEDERATED STATES
OF MICRONESIA

CHUUK

M I C R O N E S I A

MARSHALL ISLS.

ENIWETOK

BIKINI

KWAJALEIN

WAKE IS.

PEALE
WILKES

SAND IS.
EASTERN IS.

MIDWAY ISLS.

Tropic of Cancer

HAWAIIAN ISLS.

KAUAI
NIIHAU
OAHU MOLOKAI
LANAI MAUI
KAHOOLAWE HAWAII

JOHNSTON IS.

P O L Y N E S I A

FANNING IS.

CHRISTMAS IS.

LINE

ISLS.

EQUATOR

International Date Line

180°

OCEAN IS.

TARAWA

GILBERT ISLS.

KIRIBATI

PHOENIX ISLS.

TUVALU

CANTON
ENDERBURY

NAURU

TOKELAU

ATAFU
NUKUNONO
FAKAOFO

WESTERN SAMOA

AMERICA SAMOA

TUTUILA AUNUU

NIUE

TONGA

Tropic of Capricorn

MARQUESAS ISLS.

NUKU HIVA
HIVA OA

TUAMOTU ISLS.

SOCIETY ISLS.

BORA-BORA
RAIATEA TAHITI
HUAHINE MOOREA MEHETIA

COOK ISLS.

RURUTU
RIMATARA TUBUAI
TUBUAI ISLS. RAIVAVAE

GAMBIER ISLS.

PITCAIRN IS.

RAPA

ADMIRALTY ISLS.

MANUS

BISMARCK ARCH.

BUKA
NEW IRELAND
NEW BRITAIN BOUGAINVILLE

TROBRIAND ISLS.
SANTA ISABEL
NEW GEORGIA
MALAITA
GUADALCANAL
SAN CRISTOBAL

WOODLARK IS.
D'ENTRECASTEAUX ISLS.

CORAL SEA

CHESTERFIELD ISLS.

SOLOMON ISLS.

M E L A N E S I A

ESPIRITU SANTO
VANUATU
HUON ISLS.
EFATE

BELEP ISLS.

NEW CALEDONIA

LOYALTY ISLS.

WALPOLE ISLAND
ISLE OF PINES

WALLIS ISLS.

HOORN ISLS.

FUTUNA ISLS.

FIJI

VANUA LEVU
VITI LEVU

NEW ZEALAND

NORTH IS.

SOUTH IS.

TASMAN SEA

AUCKLAND IS.

CAMPBELL IS.

EQUATOR
0 200 400 600
0 200 400 600 900
Statute Miles

EQUATOR
0 300 600 900
0 300 600 900
Kilometers

and America fought a bloody war in Oceania. At that time, Oceania's military importance became apparent, and no great power or nation on Asia's Pacific Rim could ever ignore it again.

It also became impossible for Oceania's people to avoid the outside world. The war threw thousands of islanders into close contact with outsiders, either as co-combatants or workers on military bases. The troops from the various warring nations were among the last outsiders to meet truly isolated cultures. At the same time, the island people developed a whole range of new habits and new desires that could not be satisfied within their traditional economic and social systems.

Sometimes the clash between the islanders' way of life and the material wealth and power of the outside world produced strange results. Among the strangest were the cargo cults, forms of religious worship that grew up in parts of Oceania after World War II. In these cults, "the good" was the coming of a new age, symbolized by a cargo of such things as cars, trucks, refrigerators, furniture, and canned goods. All these things the islanders had seen on foreign air bases during the war, but had rarely been able to own. The people believed that if some local or foreign leader were properly prayed to or paid, he would reveal the secret of how to obtain the cargo. Often the normal life of a village would come to a halt while the people built an airstrip and lit fires to guide in the expected cargo-carrying airplane.

Cargo cults reflect the islanders' sense of frustration when faced with the wealth and technology of the outside world. Present administrations in Oceania are trying to speed up political, economic, and educational development to give the people many of the benefits available in the industrialized countries.

THE LANDS OF OCEANIA

Oceania is situated in one of the most unstable areas of the earth's crust. Earthquakes and volcanic eruptions have occurred and continue to occur along both edges of the Pacific Ocean, in Asia and America. The

THE LURE OF TAHITI

Few Pacific islands have the romantic allure of Tahiti, the largest of the more than 130 islands and islets of French Polynesia. Today, this lush, mountainous island is a magnet for tourists. Most of them hope for a taste of the earthly paradise that European explorers and sailors first described more than two centuries ago. And few of these newcomers are disappointed, although the Tahiti of legend—that of a simple, care- and problem-free society—may

Although Tahiti's capital city of Papeete bustles (left), the rest of the island retains an idyllic charm.

earthquakes and volcanic eruptions that take place in the vast area in between are not as well known, yet it is because of them that all of the smaller islands came into existence.

Continental Islands

The larger island groups—such as New Guinea, New Caledonia, the Bismarck Archipelago, and the Solomon Islands—are subject to volcanic activity. However, they are not volcanic in origin. They are known as continental islands because they are made up of geologically ancient rock that owes its origin to the vast folding process that established the basic landforms of the Southeast Asian area. New Guinea is situated on the northern extremity of a continental shelf that extends from the northern coast of Australia.

Natural Resources. Mineral deposits occur in meaningful quantities only on the larger continental islands, where there exists a variety of rock and soil types. Oil, gold, nickel, and copper are among the minerals that have already been discovered on these islands. Continental islands are also more likely to have better natural forests. This is true, for instance, in New Guinea, where the timber industry, although relatively young, is already important.

High Islands and Low Atolls

The remaining islands of Oceania are either high volcanic islands or low coral atolls. Both the high islands and low atolls are of volcanic origin. The atolls are literally sitting on top of sunken volcanic islands.

High islands were formed as a result of volcanic activity and, consequently, are composed almost entirely of volcanic rocks and soils. They vary in size from large islands of over 4,000 sq. mi. (10,360 sq. km.), such as Viti Levu in the Fiji group, to small ones of less than 1 sq. mi. (2.6 sq. km.). They also vary in appearance. Some resemble a volcano, such as the small island of Kao in the Tonga group, which is an almost perfect volcanic cone. Many others have a sharp and broken outline, which may

never have existed. Even Paul Gauguin, the artist whose bold, brightly colored paintings helped perpetuate the legend, found the reality of Tahiti far different from its myth. When he arrived in 1891, he was horrified by Papeete, the territorial capital. It reminded him of "the Europe I had thought to shake off," he said. "It was the Tahiti of former times that I loved."

Yet even in former times, Tahitian society—the one few visitors tried to comprehend—could be harsh. The land was divided among hereditary chiefs, called *arii*, who were thought to have *mana*, or supernatural power. Warfare was constant. Cult worship of Oro, the god of war, sometimes involved human sacrifice.

Visitors today discover an even more complex society, altered by centuries of contact with the West. Papeete and its surrounding towns form an urban hub of more than 70,000 people. Tahitians, all of whom are French citizens, are a multicultural blend of Polynesians (70 percent), Europeans (12 percent), Chinese (5 percent), and people of mixed race. Tahitians violently protested against the temporary resumption of French nuclear testing on the nearby Mururoa atoll in 1995. Their island remains one of the world's most idyllic settings, and Tahitians want to keep it that way. Nevertheless, the economic impact of the 1996 cessation of French testing was expected to be considerable.

be familiar from tourist posters of some of the islands of the Society and Samoan groups. Still others, like the main Fiji Islands, have been subjected to longer periods of erosion, which has broken up the volcanic rock and filled the valleys with the rich soil. There is also the possibility that minerals may be found, as was the case in the Fiji Islands, where gold and manganese deposits have been discovered.

The surface of low islands, or atolls, is composed entirely of coral sand. A typical atoll is never more than 20 or 30 ft. (6 or 9 m.) above sea level, and consists of a ring of long, narrow islands and a reef enclosing a lagoon. Atolls are formed as a result of the sinking of high volcanic islands and the simultaneous upward growth of the coral reefs surrounding them. A coral reef is not made of rock, but of living and dead organisms. Live coral is composed of billions of tiny creatures surrounded with lime. It is this that gives coral its solid appearance.

Natural Resources. Coral atolls have little in the way of natural resources except their incredible beauty. Their coral sand can support very few plants apart from the coconut. Minerals are nonexistent, unless one considers guano a mineral. Guano, which is used as a fertilizer for crops, is the name given to seabird droppings that have been deposited over the centuries and solidified. Guano is found extensively throughout the islands of the Pacific, including the atolls.

The more highly concentrated deposits of phosphate on Nauru and Banaba (Ocean Island) are different from ordinary guano. It is believed that these deposits are made up of the droppings of huge prehistoric birds, now extinct. The droppings may have been submerged and compressed and then pushed up above sea level again.

A major regional resource, relatively untapped by the islanders themselves, is the ocean fish. For a long time, the Pacific was a rich hunting ground for whales, although now their numbers have been sadly depleted. Today, it is a major source of bonito and tuna. Perhaps one day the sea and the minerals hidden from view on the ocean floor will provide the wealth this area now seems to lack.

THE COOK ISLANDS

Though not an independent nation, the Cook Islands has operated much like one since 1965. Its 19,000 (1990) people run their own internal affairs through a popularly elected 24-member parliament. New Zealand, about 2,300 mi. (3,700 km.) to the southwest, controls foreign affairs and defense. Islanders can opt for full independence at any time.

The islands fall into two groups: the six Northern Islands and the nine Southern Is-

Cook Islanders sun-dry split coconuts in the first step toward preparing copra, the leading coconut-product export.

Climate

Situated almost completely in the tropics, Oceania is subject to relatively high temperatures. It has more than adequate rainfall all year round.

Winds and currents in the Pacific are linked and follow a similar pattern. In general, they flow in huge circles, clockwise in the Northern Hemisphere and counterclockwise in the Southern. The area in between the two wind systems is known as the "doldrums." The doldrums is a highly unstable area, where wind conditions can vary from dead calm to the destructive fury of hurricanes and typhoons. The doldrums seem to follow the sun, reaching the Tropic of Cancer in June and the Tropic of Capricorn in December. As they move, they interfere with the steady trade winds, bringing uncertainty and, quite often, devastating destruction.

The relatively high temperatures have an important effect on agriculture. High temperatures raise the soil temperatures. Then when a large amount of rainfall is added, the soils are often partly destroyed for crop planting. As long as the soils are covered by thick rain forest and other natural vegetation, they are protected from the heavy rains, erosion, and loss of the valuable minerals that support plant life. But once the vegetation is removed and the soils are exposed to rain and intense sunlight, their valuable ingredients tend to leach out quickly.

THE PEOPLE

The peoples of the Pacific are usually divided into three groups: Micronesians, Melanesians, and Polynesians. These divisions were based on the observations of Europeans in the area. They believed that certain groups of islanders with common physical and linguistic characteristics, living in a definable geographical area, could be distinguished from other groups. In fact, only one of these groups—the Polynesians—meets these tests. Nevertheless, the terms do have a useful geographical meaning, and it is in that sense that they are used here.

lands. The Northern Islands are mostly low-lying coral atolls. Some are so near sea level that waves wash over them during hurricanes. The largest islands are in the southern group, where about 90 percent of Cook Islanders live.

Rarotonga, 27 sq. mi. (70 sq. km.) in area, is the largest of these islands, all of which were formed by volcanoes. Among its many mountain peaks is Te Manga, the highest, which rises to 2,142 ft. (653 m.). A coral reef surrounds the island, sheltering its many beaches from the surf. Approximately half of all Cook Islanders live on Rarotonga, mostly along the shoreline. About 5,000 live in Avarua, the capital of the Cook Islands.

Eighty-one percent of the islanders are full-blooded Polynesians, and another 15 percent are part Polynesian. Europeans had little effect on the islanders until the 1820s, when missionaries began to convert them to Christianity. Britain declared the islands a protectorate in 1888, and New Zealand law was established on them in 1901.

Today the Cook Islands struggles to build its economy on a blend of tourism, garment manufacture, and the export of fruit and fish. Progress has been slow, in part because of the enormous distance between the islands. They are scattered over a patch of the Pacific that is three-fourths the size of the Mediterranean Sea.

PITCAIRN ISLANDS

Britain's last colony in the Pacific consists of the islands of Pitcairn, Henderson, Duicie, and Oeno, known collectively as Pitcairn Islands. The islands—only Pitcairn is inhabited—are located about halfway between Peru and New Zealand. In 1790, Pitcairn's high cliffs and remoteness made it an ideal hideout for the British sailors who had staged a mutiny aboard the HMS *Bounty*. In 1990, 42 of the 54 people who

The tiny population (only 54 in 1990) of Pitcairn Island is almost entirely descended from the mutineers of the HMS *Bounty* and their Tahitian wives.

Micronesia ("small islands") sits north of the equator (except for Nauru, which is just south of it) and includes the islands north of New Guinea to the borders of Oceania. The people within this area have little in common with one another. Some of them speak Polynesian languages, but most use non-Polynesian languages that are unrelated.

Melanesia ("black islands") encompasses the islands south of the equator and west of Polynesia and includes New Guinea. Apart from the fact that most of the people of this area have darker skins than the people in the two other areas, the residents of Melanesia have little in common with one another.

Polynesia ("many islands") lies within the vast triangle formed by Hawaii, New Zealand, and Easter Island. The people within this area share a common basic language, social system, and religious beliefs.

Where the People Came From

The mixed character of the Pacific islanders reflects their different origins. Most experts believe that the migrations came first from Southeast Asia, perhaps 40,000 to 50,000 years ago, during the Ice Ages of the Pleistocene era. Sea levels were lower then, and New Guinea and Australia may have been linked by a land bridge.

These first inhabitants were nomads, who lived off what they could hunt or find. They moved out of Southeast Asia, across the narrow seas to New Guinea, and onto the Australian mainland. After the melting of the ice cap, peoples who had a slight knowledge of farming and of the other skills required to settle permanently moved into and through New Guinea and into the other islands of Melanesia. These people were the direct ancestors of today's Australoids—the Aborigines of Australia and the peoples of the New Guinea highlands. For the most part, today's Melanesians are Australoids, with some mixing by latecomers to the region.

Centuries later, other people with a more highly developed material culture came into Micronesia from Southeast Asia through what is now

lived on Pitcairn Island were descendants of the mutineers and their Tahitian wives.

Though only 1.75 sq. mi. (4.5 sq. km.) in area, Pitcairn is half-covered with fertile soil. That was more than enough to nurture crops for the nine British mutineers and 19 Polynesians (six men, 12 women, and a little girl) who accompanied them. But it fell short in 1856, when the population had reached 192. The islanders were resettled on Norfolk Island, 930 mi. (1,500 km.) east of Australia. Six homesick families returned to Pitcairn over the next eight years, and it is mostly their descendants who live on Pitcairn today.

Life is simple and revolves around the family and the Seventh-Day Adventist Church. Children attend primary school on the island. Older students often go to New Zealand to study, and many never return. One quarter of the population was over 65 in 1990.

Adamstown, the island's only settlement, sits on a plateau about 400 ft. (122 m.) above the landing at Bounty Bay. When a passing ship anchors offshore, islanders journey out to exchange mail and passengers, and to ferry ashore the food, fuel, machinery, and building materials they need to survive. Islanders fish and practice subsistence farming and sell handicrafts to passing ships. The island also earns money by issuing postage stamps that are prized by collectors.

called Indonesia. To these were added groups from Asia and the Philippines. Finally, descendants of these predominantly Southeast Asian peoples moved out of Micronesia into Polynesia.

According to one theory, the people we know as Polynesians gathered first in the Tonga-Samoa area in about A.D. 300. From there they moved to the surrounding islands. In time—probably about A.D. 1000—another center developed farther east in the Tahiti area. From there, Polynesians sailed to Hawaii in the north, Easter island in the east, and New Zealand in the south.

Differences and Similarities of the People

As in many societies the world over, the family—the most important social unit—became the basic political unit throughout Oceania. In Polynesia, there was great unity among family groups. This unity extended over whole islands and, in some cases, over groups of islands. This political unity was made possible by the existence of a common language and social system.

In Melanesia, on the other hand, there were literally hundreds of groups speaking completely dissimilar languages. In New Guinea today, there are said to be about 650 different languages. Often only a few hundred persons make up a language group. For centuries, contacts with other groups in Melanesia mainly took the form of warfare or some limited trading activities. Added to this was the constant struggle for survival. As a result, people lived in a state of insecurity.

Using the Land.   To a Western European or an American, there were obvious similarities among the people. One example was their attitude toward land and work. All these peoples lived completely on what they could produce or take from the land. They hunted birds, wild pigs, and other animals. They gathered fruits, building materials, and firewood. They grew crops. Land meant life. As a result, land was of prime importance in their social system and played a preeminent role in their religious practices.

Among the people of Oceania, control over the use of land was never the exclusive right of one person. The idea of exclusive individual ownership of land was unknown. Individuals shared in the use of land with other members of their group for specific purposes.

The Islanders' Ideas About Work.   Another example of attitudes that were fairly common to all islanders was their attitude toward work. Labor was not an end in itself. One worked for socially desirable ends. Houses had to be built and maintained. Gardens had to be established and cared for. Food had to be prepared; communities had to be defended; tools and weapons had to be fashioned. These activities, mainly done in a group and in some cases only seasonally, were carried out only when they were necessary.

The idea of working regular hours each day, day after day, for no purpose except to earn money, was quite strange to islanders. To them, money was important only as a means of getting the goods the Europeans had to offer—steel axes, knives, and trinkets. Once these desires were met, the islanders' interest in work depended on how important money was to their way of life. This, in turn, depended upon what Europeans could offer and the extent to which the islanders became dependent on a money economy.

OCEANIA'S DISCOVERY BY THE WEST

The Explorers.   The first contacts between Europeans and the islanders began with the coming of the European explorers. It was these explorers who did much to spread the somewhat exaggerated picture of the idyllic life led by Pacific islanders. The islands are beautiful. But what the explorers and their chroniclers often omitted from their glowing accounts were the conditions of life on the islands. Fruit was abundant, but meat was not. Little was said about rainstorms and hurricanes. Endemic malaria, other fevers, and intestinal parasites were scarcely mentioned. No hint was given that the openhearted welcome that Europeans received might be related to the axes, knives, and other useful tools they brought.

The early visitors learned little about the islanders' moral and social systems, let alone their motivations. They began to become apparent only to people who lived on a particular island for longer than a few weeks. Of those who did, many were "beachcombers"—sailors who left their ships to settle on South Pacific islands.

The Missionaries.   Most of the intruders into the Pacific who came to stay were hardy souls. The Christian missionaries represented the Protestant and Puritan churches of Western Europe and North America. These men and women were endowed with great bravery and fortitude, and they were driven by their fervor to convert the "heathen."

To the missionary, the legendary, idyllic, work-free life of the Pacific islanders, with its reputed sexual freedom, represented the very essence of heathenism. In addition to saving souls, they tried to impose a whole new moral and social order on the islanders. The missionaries wanted to build their own ideal society in the Pacific—one that placed a premium on the virtues of uprightness, obedience, thrift, and hard work. It placed little emphasis on such notions as comfort and enjoyment. Often narrow and bigoted, many missionaries condemned anything non-European or "native."

For some years, the missionaries made little or no headway. But when European traders, planters, and settlers appeared on the scene, the island leaders felt overwhelmed. Needing an ally, the islanders turned to the missionaries as the only persons willing to support their interests. In return for the missionaries' support, the island leaders announced their conversion to Christianity. Mass conversions followed, mainly in the Polynesian areas, where the authority of the chiefs meant something. In this way, Christianity—in name, at least—was established throughout Polynesia by the 1850s. True conversion to Christianity took much longer. The task was much more difficult in Melanesia, where the chiefs' power was less strong and the work of conversion had to proceed almost person by person. In fact, it still is going on today.

The Christian missionaries did a lot for the islanders. For many years, missionaries provided most of the education and health services.

On the negative side, however, the missionaries destroyed the islanders' native religious beliefs, ceremonies, music, art, and dancing. In this way, they undermined the basis of the islanders' social systems and contributed to a complete collapse of their way of life. In Hawaii and a few other places where the islanders have been able to integrate themselves into the new Western way of life, the negative effects of change have not been as serious. But where such integration has not taken place, which is the case over almost all the rest of Oceania, serious problems remain.

The Settlers.   The next decisive influence in the Pacific was the settlers. Their forerunners were the traders and whalers who came to Oceania for such products as sandalwood and oils. The traders established relations with the islanders, and in this way introduced them to many Western influences. But these brief contacts had only a limited effect on the lives of the islanders.

The settlers first came to Oceania to cultivate coconuts. They exported to Europe the soft inside of the nut in the form of copra (dried coconut meat). In Europe, copra oil was extracted for use in a variety of ways.

At first, the traders arranged to collect coconuts at ports of call in the islands. Then they began to show the islanders how to dry the pulp. Finally, as the demand grew and the inadequacies of these arrangements became clear, Europeans decided to settle on the islands and grow the coconuts themselves.

Problems of all kinds followed wherever settlement took place. Trouble arose between the islanders and the settlers because of misunderstandings over land dealings. This often led to bloodshed and left behind bad feelings on both sides.

Often settlers took the law into their own hands. On some islands, the settlers began to organize puppet governments that they controlled. They would set up one of the leading chiefs as king. This practice accounts in large part for the origins of the "kings" in places like Hawaii, Fiji, and Tahiti. The people of the islands participated only slightly in these European-run governments.

By the last quarter of the 1800s, chaotic situations had developed in a number of island centers. In Fiji, the king begged Queen Victoria of Great Britain to help him control the activities of her subjects, and, in 1874, the British government assumed responsibility for the Fiji Islands.

An equally chaotic situation developed in Samoa, leading to a decision by the U.S. and Germany to divide and annex the island group in 1899.

The Growing Influence of the World Powers. The world powers were reluctant to become involved in Oceania. However, these seafaring nations did acquire a few islands. Great Britain claimed New Zealand in 1840, and France acquired the Society Islands in 1842 and New Caledonia in 1853. Between 1874 and 1901, almost every island group in the Pacific became a protectorate or a colony of either Germany, France, the United States, or Great Britain.

In the early 1900s, Great Britain transferred responsibility for some of its Pacific possessions to its own former colonies of Australia and New Zealand. These new Pacific nations and Japan were given Germany's Pacific colonies as League of Nations mandates after Germany's defeat in World War I. After Japan's defeat in World War II, the former mandated territories were placed under the United Nations trusteeship system.

OCEANIA AFTER 1900

After these territories were acquired, great emphasis was placed on inducing people to settle their differences according to the legal codes introduced by the new administrators. This was seen as part of the Europeans' "civilizing mission" in the islands. Yet colonial administrators undermined the old systems of leadership and authority and failed to replace them with new ones with which islanders could identify.

The new systems of law and order did have a positive side—they eliminated warfare. Ending the constant fear of death at the hands of one's enemies had an effect that is hard to overestimate. With the fighting ended, for example, villages could be built in valleys near good sources of water, instead of on inconvenient but more defensible ridges.

The new administrators also brought health and educational services with them. They were assisted by the missionaries, who in many cases did more in providing these services than the governments.

In many of the islands, there had once been a single economy that provided food and shelter for the community. Now there were two economies. The old one still existed in varying degrees. The new economy was based on European-owned and -run plantations or mines. Asians participated as traders. The local people participated only as the providers of the land and sometimes as laborers.

Expanding Economies

The Europeans, in addition to growing and producing copra, began to experiment with a variety of other tropical products, such as rubber, sugar, coffee, cacao, and tea. They also began the large-scale production for export of such tropical fruits as bananas and pineapples. Until World War II, however, production in most of the islands was limited mostly to sugar and copra. The main exception was Hawaii, whose tropical products could be shipped relatively easily to U.S. markets.

Another European economic interest was minerals. Gold was found in New Guinea and was the mainstay of the economy before World War II. Gold was also important in Fiji. In New Caledonia, large deposits of nickel and chromium have been worked since the early 1900s.

These economic activities and the commercial and trading activities to which they gave rise required skills that the islanders simply did not have. At first, Europeans overcame this problem by importing laborers from nearby countries of Asia—Chinese, Indians, Filipinos, and Vietnamese. Eventually the practice became too expensive, or local governments prohibited it. So the Europeans had to turn to the local population. As an inducement to work for money, the colonial governments imposed head taxes on every able-bodied male, which had to be paid in cash.

After World War II, the pace of change in Oceania accelerated. The islanders became increasingly aware of their problems and pressed for change. One result was greater investment by administering nations in economic-development projects—roads, schools, factories, and ports.

Islanders also gained more control over their governments. Western Samoa was the first island group to win independence, in 1962. By 1990, most of the islands were either independent, or their voters had chosen a form of self-government somewhat short of independence. The Cook Islands and Niue, for example, opted to turn over their foreign affairs and defense to New Zealand, but to remain otherwise self-governing. The Federated States of Micronesia, the Marshall Islands, and Palau (Belau) accepted a form of independence that grants only defense responsibilities to the U.S. The Northern Marianas became a commonwealth of the U.S., like Puerto Rico.

OCEANIA'S FUTURE

Although these developments give hope for Oceania's future, there are still problems to solve.

Micronesia. In Micronesia, the possibilities for true economic self-sufficiency are not universally bright. Nauru is perhaps the best off, having used its phosphate earnings to create a welfare state. Kiribati, perhaps the worst off, is trying to build fishing and tourism industries to reduce its reliance on copra. In between these two poles are Guam and the former U.S. trust territories, whose links with the United States should assure a continuation of aid to supplement development efforts.

Melanesia. Violence broke out during the 1980s in both Fiji and New Caledonia for the same reason—the anger of indigenous peoples who found themselves outnumbered by immigrants or the descendants of immigrants. A 1987 military coup in Fiji removed Fijians of Indian origin from political power. But in New Caledonia, native Kanakas seeking independence were outvoted by settlers of French, Asian, or Polynesian background who wished to keep the territory French. France has promised a local referendum on independence in 1998.

In the remaining parts of Melanesia—Papua New Guinea, the Solomon Islands, and Vanuatu—developing a sense of unity and nationhood is a major challenge. Even now the people of the various parts of Melanesia still often have only limited contact with one another and think of themselves more as members of a village or family than a nation.

Polynesia. Prospects for economic self-sufficiency are strong in Polynesia. Copra is an important product here, but there are also others, such as sugar, tropical fruits, and vegetables. Tourism has also become a lucrative industry in such places as Hawaii, Samoa, and parts of French Polynesia. The fact that the population is concentrated on islands grouped close together has helped the people in Polynesia to adapt their social and political life to the demands of the modern world.

JOHN MILES, Senior Political Affairs Officer, United Nations

Micronesians can pursue many of their traditional crafts outdoors in the year-round balmy weather.

MICRONESIA

As its name suggests, Micronesia consists of small islands, some 2,000 of them, about 125 of which are inhabited. In total land area, Micronesia is roughly the size of Rhode Island. Yet its islands are scattered over an area of the Pacific Ocean between Hawaii and the Philippines that is larger than the continental United States.

Four island chains—the Marshalls, the Gilberts, the Carolines, and the Marianas—dominate the region. Johnston Atoll and the equally iso-

GUAM

Only 32 mi. (51 km.) long and 4 to 10 mi. (6.4 to 16 km.) wide, Guam is the largest island in the Mariana chain as well as the largest in Micronesia. At the very west of the Pacific Ocean, it lies 1,600 mi. (2,574 km.) east of the Philippine capital of Manila. Its 1994 population was 200,000, including some 20,000 U.S. military personnel and their dependents.

The northern two-thirds of this volcanic island is a high limestone plateau

An old fort dates back to the days when Spain colonized Guam. Guam was one of the first Pacific islands to be settled by Europeans. Spain ceded Guam to the U.S. in 1898.

lated islands of Nauru, Wake, and Midway are also in Micronesia. Politically, Micronesia is divided into 10 distinct units: five independent nations; four U.S. territories; and one U.S. commonwealth.

THE LAND

Micronesia's 2,100 islands contain 1,189 sq. mi. (3,079 sq. km.) of land and are spread over approximately 4,497,000 sq. mi. (11,649,000 sq. km.) of the Pacific Ocean. With a few exceptions, the islands lie north of the equator. The exceptions are Nauru, which sits 26 mi. (42 km.) south of the equator, and several of the Gilbert Islands (now part of Kiribati). Two Kiribatian island groups south of the equator, the Phoenix and the Line islands, are culturally part of Polynesia, not Micronesia.

Micronesia's islands are mostly high volcanic islands or low coral islands. Volcanic islands account for most of the land area. Examples include Guam and most other islands in the Mariana chain; and Kosrae, Ponape, Truk, and Palau, on the Carolines. Yap, also in the Carolines, is sedimentary rock that was lifted off Asia's continental shelf.

The remainder of Micronesia's islands are mostly sand and coral, built up over thousands of years by billions of calcium-secreting organisms called polyps. The thin soil cover and scarcity of salt-free water keeps vegetation on coral islands to a minimum. Volcanic islands generally have rich soil, rivers and streams, and lush vegetation.

Daily temperatures average 81° F. (27° C.) year-round, and humidity is generally high. Trade winds blow cooling air from the northeast from December to March. Rain is plentiful, averaging 85 to 150 in. (216 to 381 cm.) a year, depending on location.

THE PEOPLE

Micronesia's population is culturally diverse. Micronesians speak 11 main languages and several dialects.

Inhabitants of the high volcanic islands have traditionally been subsistence farmers. Their societies are complex, often involving several

with no rivers or streams. The southern third is quite different, full of waterfalls, dense jungle, and picturesque villages.

About half of the people on Guam are descended from the island's original inhabitants, the Chamorro. The Chamorro lived on Guam as long as 3,000 years ago. No pure-blooded Chamorro exist today because of intermarriage and diseases brought by Europeans. From an estimated 80,000 in 1668, the Chamorro's numbers shrank to about 1,500 in 1783.

Spain laid claim to Guam in 1565 and was forced to cede it to the United States in 1898. The U.S., which used it as a naval station, lost it to the Japanese in 1941. U.S. forces won it back in 1944, and, the next year, it became the headquarters of the U.S. Pacific fleet.

In 1950, the U.S. made Guam an "unincorporated territory of the United States," granted U.S. citizenship to Guamanians, and permitted limited self-government. Guamanians elected their first governor in 1970. In the 1990s, a bill was moving through the U.S. Congress that would shift Guam's status again to that of a self-governing commonwealth within the U.S. political system. Guamanians feel that commonwealth status will boost their chances of becoming economically self-sufficient. About half of all Guamanians work for either the territorial or the federal government.

classes of commoners, chiefs, and paramount chiefs. Inhabitants of the low coral islands, on the other hand, have generally relied on the sea for their food. Over the centuries, they developed into skillful seafarers.

Recent decades have seen an acceleration of change as young people migrate to administrative centers in search of wage-paying jobs. One by-product of this shift away from traditional customs and support systems has been an alarming increase in crime, alcoholism, and suicide.

Economies.   Except for Nauru, no island or island state in Micronesia is economically self-sufficient. Nauru supports itself from the sale of phosphate and the earnings generated by investments. Kiribati, a former British colony, relies heavily on aid from Australia and Great Britain. All the other political entities rely on a combination of U.S. aid and government jobs that are underwritten by the United States. Finding a way to enable these island economies to pay their way is an awesome challenge.

HISTORY

Humans have inhabited the Micronesian islands for at least 4,000 years. The first settlers seem to have come from the Philippines and Indonesia to the Marianas, Yap, and Palau. Centuries later, in another wave of settlement, Melanesians landed on the eastern Marshalls. Their descendants then moved west, settling Kosrae, Ponape, and Truk, and eventually sailing to the outer islands of Yap and Palau.

Ferdinand Magellan's Spanish expedition landed on Guam in 1521. Spain claimed the Marianas in 1565, and its missionaries brought Roman Catholicism to the Carolines in the early 1700s. British and American whalers made Micronesia's islands ports of call during the first half of the 1800s. Protestant missionaries began to arrive after 1870.

Western Dominance.   By 1889, Germans controlled the Marshalls, Nauru, the Carolines, and the Northern Marianas. Britain established a protectorate over the Gilberts in 1892 and annexed them in 1915. Spain ceded Guam and Wake Island to the U.S. in 1898.

Germany abandoned its Micronesian holdings at the start of World War I in 1914, and Japan quickly filled the vacuum. After taking Guam in December 1941, Japan controlled all of Micronesia. The entire region was subjected to heavy fighting and intense aerial bombing during World War II. U.S. forces finally drove the Japanese out in 1944 and 1945.

In 1947, the United Nations made Micronesia into a "strategic trust," with the United States as trustee. The six districts of the U.N. Trust Territory of the Pacific Islands were Palau (Belau), the Marshalls, Ponape (Pohnpei), Truk, Yap, and the Northern Marianas. U.S. forces began testing nuclear weapons on Bikini Atoll, in the Marshall Islands, in 1946.

Self-Government.   Nauru won independence in 1968, Kiribati (on the Gilberts) in 1979. The Northern Marianas became a U.S. commonwealth in 1978. The remaining five districts broke into three self-governing units: the Federated States of Micronesia (FSM), the Republic of the Marshall Islands, and the Republic of Palau. The FSM and the Marshall Islands signed a Compact of Free Association with the United States, which declared them independent in 1986. In December 1990, the U.N. Security Council formally terminated the trust territory status of the Northern Marianas, the FSM, and the Marshall Islands. Palau, the world's only remaining U.N. trust territory, finally voted to accept a similar compact in November 1993; it gained formal independence on October 1, 1994.

Some of the islands that make up Palau barely rise out of the sea.

PALAU

The Republic of Palau (Belau) lies in the North Pacific Ocean southeast of the Philippines, where it forms the western end of the Caroline Islands chain. Palau's more than 20 islands, eight of which are inhabited, range from mountainous, volcanic Babelthuap (Babeldoab) to tiny coral atolls barely above sea level. Babelthuap, the second-largest island in Micronesia after Guam, makes up about 80 percent of Palau's land area. About two-thirds of the people live in the capital of **Koror**, on Koror Island. A new capital is to be built on Babelthuap. The islands have a hot, humid climate.

THE PEOPLE

Palau's inhabitants are of mixed Micronesian, Polynesian, and Malayan origin. English, Japanese, and a variety of local languages—including Palauan, Sonsorolese, Angaur, and Tobi—are spoken. Most Palauans are Christians, primarily Roman Catholics. A local non-Christian religion called Modekngei (Modignai) is practiced by about one-third of the population. Education in Palau is compulsory for children between the ages of 6 and 14. More than 90 percent of Palauans can read and write.

ECONOMY

Most Palauans work for the government or are engaged in subsistence farming and fishing. Coconuts, cassava, bananas, and sweet potatoes are the chief food crops. Some copra, fish, and handicrafts made from shell, wood, and pearl are exported. In 1991 a Japanese consortium agreed to build an international airport on Babelthuap as part of an effort to increase tourism. Palau is heavily dependent on U.S. aid, which provides about 90 percent of all revenue.

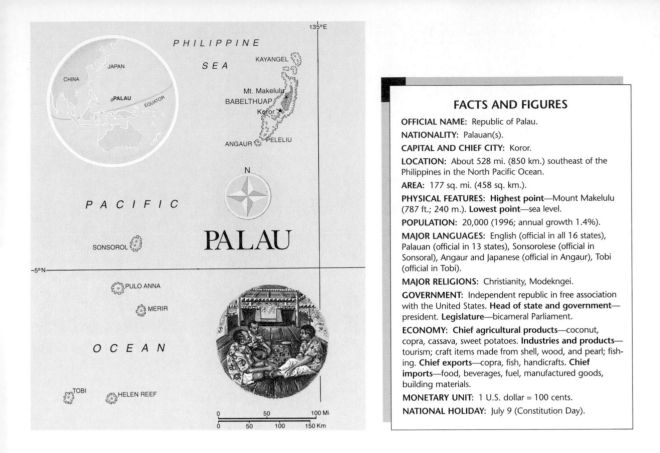

HISTORY AND GOVERNMENT

Probably settled from Indonesia about 4,500 years ago, Palau was formally annexed by Spain in 1896. The Spanish possessions in Micronesia were sold to Germany in 1899 and occupied by Japan during World War I. From 1920 until Japan's defeat in World War II, Palau was administered by Japan as part of a League of Nations mandate.

In 1947 Palau became part of the United Nations Trust Territory of the Pacific Islands, administered by the United States. When the rest of the Trust Territory was formally terminated by the U.N. Security Council in 1990, Palau remained under U.S. administration. Palau signed a Compact of Free Association with the United States under which it would become self-governing, with the United States remaining responsible for its defense. The compact was approved in seven successive referenda, but failed to gain the 75 percent majority required to override a nuclear ban in Palau's 1981 constitution.

In 1991 the United States suggested that Palau begin negotiations on independence if it could not approve the compact. In 1992 voters approved a constitutional amendment to require a simple majority for compact approval, which was obtained in 1993. The United States was permitted to use Palau for military purposes during a crisis, and was required to clean up any nuclear or toxic accidents in Palauan waters. The 1993 vote paved the way for Palau's independence, which was formally declared on September 30, 1994. Palau's government is headed by a president who is directly elected for a four-year term. There is an elected bicameral legislature made up of a Senate and a House of Delegates. Each of Palau's 16 states has its own elected governor and legislature.

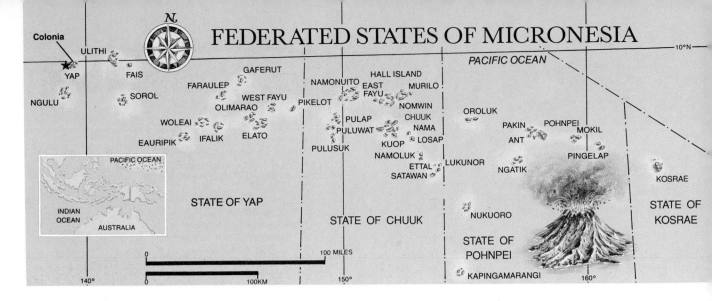

FEDERATED STATES OF MICRONESIA

Voters in four districts of the United States Trust Territory of the Pacific approved a new constitution on May 10, 1979. On that date, the four districts—Yap, Chuuk, Pohnpei, and Kosrae—were joined together as the Federated States of Micronesia (FSM). Though largely self-governing, the FSM remained part of the U.S. Trust Territory until November 3, 1986, when it achieved independence in "free association" with the U.S.

THE LAND

The FSM covers all the islands in the Caroline archipelago except for those in the extreme west, which belong to the Republic of Belau (Palau). The state of **Yap** is centered on Yap Proper, four closely grouped islands that are linked by bridges. Seventy percent of all Yapese live in Yap Proper, which is the site of the state capital, Colonia.

The state of **Chuuk** is made up of 15 island groups that contain nearly 300 islands. The 11 main islands, all volcanic, are enclosed inside the Chuuk Lagoon by a lengthy barrier reef. One of these islands, Moen, is the state capital and commercial center.

The state of **Pohnpei** consists of the volcanic island of Pohnpei and eight coral atolls. The island accounts for nearly all the state's land area. The state and federal capital, Kolonia, is on Pohnpei Island.

The state of **Kosrae** consists of the island by that name and a smaller one, Lelu, to which it is linked by a causeway. River valleys stretch from Kosrae's mountainous interior to the ocean. Lelu is the state's commercial center. The village of Tofol on Kosrae serves as the state capital.

THE PEOPLE

FSM is the most populous of the former U.S. Trust Territories. Fewer than 1 percent of the people are Polynesians. The rest are Micronesians who are often called Carolinians. Eight languages are spoken, including English, the official language. Most Yapese are Roman Catholic, while the rest of the FSM's Micronesians are Protestant.

In some areas of the Federated States of Micronesia, the people weave thatch from palm leaves to use in the construction of their homes.

Land ownership is very important. Except in Kusaie and among Polynesians, property passes from generation to generation matrilineally—through the mother. In Truk, the oldest male descendant of an island's first settlers holds a good deal of prestige.

ECONOMY

About 70 percent of the islanders rely on subsistence farming and fishing. Of those in the paid labor force, about two-thirds work for the government, whose main source of revenue is U.S. aid. The government earns some money from taxes and by licensing foreign ships to fish in the FSM's waters.

Since independence, the government has spent heavily on such essentials to economic growth as roads, bridges, sewer systems, docks, power plants, and airports. The largest private industry is construction.

The FSM relies heavily on imports. The main export is copra (dried coconut meat). Important crops include black pepper, tropical fruits and vegetables, coconuts, cassava, and sweet potatoes. Relatively new industries include seaweed farming and the processing of sun-dried fish.

HISTORY AND GOVERNMENT

The Micronesians are descended from people who began migrating from Southeast Asia about 3,000 years ago. European and American traders and missionaries began to influence life in the Carolines during the early 1800s. Between 1885 and 1945, the islands were ruled by Spain, Germany, and Japan. In 1947, at U.S. urging, the United Nations made the islands part of the U.N. Trust Territory of the Pacific Islands.

The FSM became a self-governing entity in 1979 and independent in 1986, four years after signing a Compact of Free Association with the U.S. The FSM won control of domestic and most foreign affairs, and the U.S. retained responsibility for its defense. The United Nations Security Council formally approved the arrangement in December 1990.

MARSHALL ISLANDS

War wreckage on the beaches bears grim testimony to the pivotal battles fought on the Marshall Islands during World War II.

The Republic of the Marshall Islands consists of two parallel island chains, the Ratak ("sunrise") chain in the northeast and the Ralik ("sunset") chain in the southeast. Approximately 800 mi. (1,287 km.) long, the chains lie about 150 mi. (241 km.) apart. The two chains' more than 1,150 islands and islets are grouped in 29 atolls, five low islands, and 870 reefs. Few of the islands rise more than 5 ft. (1.5 m.) above sea level. The highest point on any of the islands, 34 ft. (10 m.), is found on Likiep Atoll of the Ratak Chain. If pollution warms the earth, as many scientists fear, rising sea levels could submerge the Marshalls over the next century.

The atolls are coral rings whose beaches partly or totally enclose bodies of water called lagoons. The three islands of Delap, Uliga, and Darrit (D-U-D Municipality), on the Majuro Atoll, serve as the nation's capital. Causeways link the atoll's southern islands with a road that runs 35 mi. (56 km.) from end to end. More than one-third of all Marshallese live here. Most work in tourism or for the government.

The world's largest atoll, Kwajalein, consists of 97 islands with a total land area of of 6.5 sq. mi. (16.5 sq. km.). U.S. troops captured it from the Japanese after fierce fighting in 1944. The lagoon the atoll surrounds, 900 sq. mi. (2,304 sq. km.) in size, is the splashdown point for test missiles launched from California, 4,500 mi. (7,245 km.) away.

The Ralik chain also includes the atolls of Bikini and Eniwetok, the sites of 66 nuclear-bomb tests between 1946 and 1958. Bikini and most of Eniwetok are too radioactive for human habitation. The 350 inhabitants of Rongelap Atoll, the site of radioactive fallout from a nuclear blast on Bikini, relocated elsewhere in 1985.

THE PEOPLE

Almost entirely Micronesian, the 43,000 Marshallese inhabit 24 of the 34 atolls and islands scattered over about 772,000 sq. mi. (2,000,000 sq. km.) of the Pacific. More than 60 percent of all Marshallese live on the Majuro and Kwajalein atolls, where jobs are available in government, tourism, or in support of the U.S. missile facility.

Sizable groups also live on Arno, 35 mi. (56 km.) from Majuro, and on Ailinglapalap and Jaluit, in the Ralik Chain. The people on Jaluit grow bananas and breadfruit and export copra, seashells, and handicrafts. The 56 islands of Ailinglapalap Atoll are where the paramount chiefs of the Ralik Chain traditionally lived. Most of the other inhabited atolls and islands have between 90 and 1,000 people.

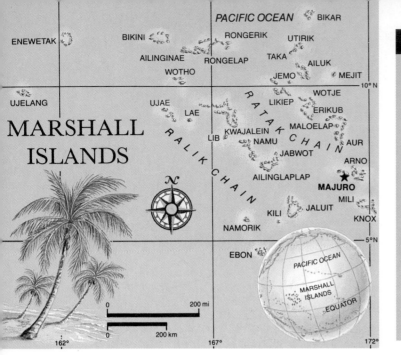

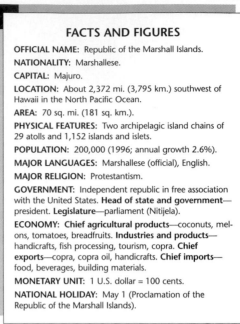

Marshallese society is organized matrilineally. Every Marshallese belongs to his or her mother's clan and has the right to use that clan's land. The head of each clan coordinates clan affairs and acts as a sort of intermediary between the commoners and chiefs, or *iroij*. The highest of these aristocrats, the paramount chiefs, are called *iroij laplap*.

ECONOMY

Agriculture and tourism are the strengths of the Marshallese economy. Farming takes place on small farms. The key crops are coconuts, tomatoes, melons, and breadfruit. A few cattle ranches produce meat. Industry is limited to handicrafts, fish processing, and copra.

The government, heavily subsidized by U.S. aid, employs three-quarters of all wage earners. U.S. aid is guaranteed until 2001 under the Compact of Free Association. In the future, deep-sea mining ships may be able to extract valuable metals from the ocean floor.

HISTORY AND GOVERNMENT

A Spanish explorer put the Marshalls on European maps in 1529, but Europeans ignored the islands for years. In 1767 and 1788 the islands were explored by British ships. One of the ships in 1788 was commanded by Captain John Marshall, after whom the islands are named.

American whalers and missionaries frequented the islands during the 1800s. The islands were a protectorate of Germany from 1885 to 1914, when Germany abandoned the islands and was replaced by Japan. U.S. forces drove out Japanese defenders in 1944 and 1945.

After the war, the Marshalls became part of the U.S.-administered U.N. Trust Territory of the Pacific Islands, along with Palau and what have become the U.S. Commonwealth of the Northern Marianas and the independent Federated States of Micronesia. The Marshall Islands became internally self-governing in 1979. A compact making them independent in "free association" with the U.S. was approved by the islanders in 1983, by the U.S. in 1986, and by the U.N. Security Council in 1990.

Nauru owes its prosperity to the rich phosphate deposits that cover 80 percent of the island.

NAURU

The tiny Republic of Nauru (pronounced na-OO-roo), situated just south of the equator, is one of the most isolated islands in the Pacific. It is also one of the world's richest nations, recently earning about $100 million a year for its approximately 5,000 native inhabitants.

Nauru owes its wealth and independence to the high-quality phosphate deposits that cover four-fifths of the island. But the phosphate, used in making fertilizer, is being worked out rapidly. It is expected that the deposits will be exhausted by the year 2000.

Though their present source of income will have disappeared, no one expects the well-educated Nauruans to go hungry. For decades, they have invested more than half their income in other businesses, including a shipping company, an airline, and real-estate and mining ventures in Australia, Hawaii, and elsewhere. If these businesses continue to produce income, Nauruans and their descendants can look forward to a future of comfort.

THE LAND

Nauru is an oval island 8.2 sq. mi. (21 sq. km.) in size, located in the west-central Pacific Ocean. It lies 33 mi. (53 km.) south of the equator and halfway between Sydney, Australia, and Honolulu, Hawaii. Along with Ocean Island in Kiribati and Makatea in French Polynesia, it is one of the Pacific's three great phosphate-rock islands. Its perimeter, some 12 mi. (19 km.) long, contains sandy beaches that rise to a fertile strip about 200 yds. (192 m.) wide. All Nauruans live on this strip, many in solar-powered, ranch-style homes.

A coral reef forms a plateau inside this fertile area, and the plateau contains the nation's wealth—the droppings of huge prehistoric birds

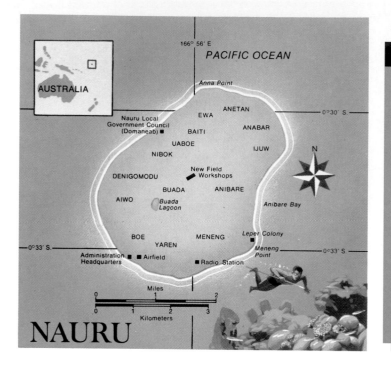

FACTS AND FIGURES

OFFICIAL NAME: Republic of Nauru.

NATIONALITY: Nauruan(s).

CAPITAL: No official capital. The seat of government is located in the Yaren District.

LOCATION: Southwestern Pacific Ocean.

AREA: 8.2 sq. mi. (21 sq. km.).

PHYSICAL FEATURES: Coral island, most of which is a plateau at 200 ft. (61 m.).

POPULATION: 10,200 (1995; annual growth 1.3%).

MAJOR LANGUAGES: Nauruan (official), English.

MAJOR RELIGIONS: Nauruan Protestant Church, Roman Catholicism.

GOVERNMENT: Republic. **Head of state and government**—president. **Legislature**—unicameral Parliament.

ECONOMY: Chief mineral—phosphate. **Chief agricultural product**—coconuts. **Industries and products**—phosphate mining, financial services, coconut products. **Chief export**—phosphate. **Chief imports**—food, fuel, building materials, machinery.

MONETARY UNIT: 1 Australian dollar = 100 cents.

NATIONAL HOLIDAY: January 31 (Independence Day).

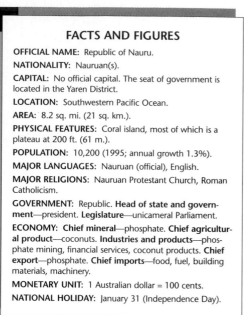

that over thousands of years turned into phosphatic rock. Nauruans call this barren area Topside. The phosphate is strip-mined, ground into fertilizer, and shipped mainly to Australia, New Zealand, and Japan.

Denuded of topsoil, most of the Topside area will not support vegetation. Coconut trees and vegetables are grown on about 500 acres (200 hectares) of the plateau. Temperatures range between 76° and 93° F. (24° to 33° C.), and rainfall is sparse except during the wet season, which runs from November to February. Nauru has no rivers or streams, and most water is imported as ballast in ships that arrive to take away the phosphate.

THE PEOPLE

The Nauruans are a mixture of Pacific peoples who evolved into a homogeneous group after centuries of intermarriage. Nothing is known of their origin or of how their ancestors came to Nauru.

Their distinct language seems to comprise elements of languages from the Gilbert, Caroline, Marshall, and Solomon islands. German missionaries translated the Bible into one of the most widely used dialects, providing the basis for a standard Nauru language. Nauruan is the nation's official language, although English—spoken with an Australian accent—is used for government and commercial purposes.

Education is free and compulsory for Nauruan children between the ages of 6 and 16 and for non-Nauruans from 6 to 15. The government sends many students to colleges and technical schools abroad, mainly in Australia. Two-thirds of the Nauruans are Protestants, the rest Roman Catholics.

Most native Nauruans work for the government or in the phosphate operations, which are largely conducted by managers from Australia and about 2,500 workers from other Pacific islands and Hong Kong. People of European and Chinese descent make up 16 percent of the population.

Government subsidies keep prices low for food and consumer goods, and the government also finances welfare benefits and social services for those who need them.

Nauruans enjoy life. Most families have automobiles, which they take on frequent drives around the perimeter road. Many go fishing in their own power boats.

HISTORY

Europeans first learned about Nauru in 1798, when it was visited by a British whaling ship captained by John Fearn. Finding the land "extremely populous" and attractive, he named it Pleasant Island. In the years that followed, Nauru received its share of European traders and beachcombers. The Europeans sold firearms and alcohol to the islanders, adding to the fierceness of tribal disputes. In the 1870s, tribal warfare reduced the population to about 1,000.

In 1888, Germany annexed the island. Missionaries arrived in 1899, introducing Western education and Christianity. But it was not until the turn of the century, when an Englishman discovered the rich phosphate deposits, that Nauru began to have economic value to Europeans. An English company acquired the phosphate mining rights, and mining operations began in 1906.

In 1920, Nauru was granted as a League of Nations mandate to Australia, Great Britain, and New Zealand. Australia administered the island for all three governments. These three countries also acquired the assets of the phosphate company. Royalties were paid to Nauruan landowners and into various trust funds to be used for public purposes or to be held for use by the Nauruans when the supply of phosphate ran out.

During World War II, Nauru was occupied by Japanese forces, and, in 1943, 1,200 Nauruans were forcibly removed to Truk in the Caroline Islands. At the end of the war, 743 survivors returned to Nauru. They arrived on January 31, 1946. (January 31, remembered in Nauru as Deliverance Day, would be the date chosen as Nauru's Independence Day in 1968.) At the end of World War II, Nauru became a United Nations Trust Territory, and Australia continued to administer it, as before, on behalf of Great Britain and New Zealand.

Gradually, Nauruans gained a larger role in their island's administration, and, in 1967, they negotiated for their independence. New Zealand, Australia, and Great Britain agreed to sell the phosphate industry to the Nauruan government, and Nauru received its independence.

THE GOVERNMENT AND FUTURE OF NAURU

Nauru has a parliamentary system of government. Its unicameral parliament has 18 members, each elected for three years. All Nauruans at least 20 years old are required by law to vote. Parliament elects the nation's president, who serves as head of state and chief minister.

The Nauruans are optimistic about their future. Their young people are well-educated, and their leaders are energetic and willing to make imaginative decisions. The fact that the island will one day be unable to support them does not seem to daunt them. Through investments in new businesses and attempts to seek ways to restore their mined-out land to fertility, they are trying many ways to guarantee their island's future.

JOHN MILES, Senior Political Affairs Officer, United Nations

Kiribati hopes to develop its many miles of unspoiled beaches into tourist resorts.

KIRIBATI

The Pacific island nation of Kiribati, formerly the British colony of the Gilbert Islands, became an independent republic in 1979. The ceremonial transfer of power took place on the principal island of Tarawa, which was the scene of savage battles during World War II. Today, Tarawa is the capital of Kiribati, which is fighting its own battle, this time for economic self-sufficiency. With that goal in sight, Kiribatians are engaged in some imaginative schemes to create steady sources of revenue from tourism, fishing, copra, and a host of smaller industries.

THE LAND

Kiribati (pronounced KIR-uh-bas) is situated in the southwestern Pacific Ocean, east of the island of New Guinea and southwest of Hawaii, around the point at which the international date line cuts the equator. Scattered across 2,000,000 sq. mi. (5,180,000 sq. km.) of ocean, the islands have a total land area of only 264 sq. mi. (683.8 sq. km.).

Kiribati's islands are atolls, coral islands that consist of reefs surrounding circular bodies of water called lagoons. Christmas Island, one of the northern Line Islands, is the largest coral island in the world, and it accounts for nearly half of Kiribati's land area.

There are three groups of islands—the Gilbert Islands, the Phoenix Islands, and eight of the 11 Line Islands. (The other three are uninhabited U.S. dependencies.) Phosphate-rich Banaba (Ocean Island), whose peo-

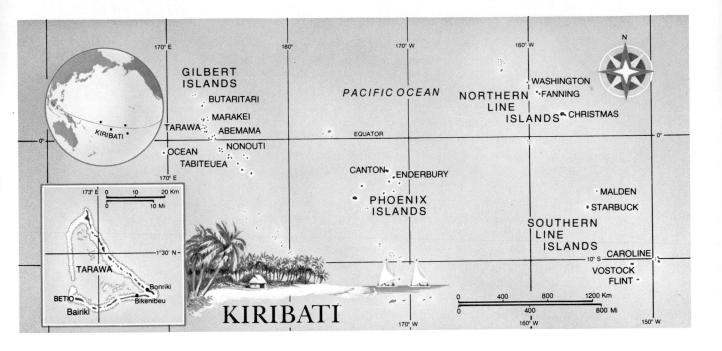

KIRIBATI

FACTS AND FIGURES

OFFICIAL NAME: Republic of Kiribati.

NATIONALITY: Kiribatian(s).

CAPITAL: Tarawa.

LOCATION: Southwestern Pacific Ocean.

AREA: 332 sq. mi. (861 sq. km.).

PHYSICAL FEATURES: Made up of 33 islands, most of which are coral reefs.

POPULATION: 79,400 (1995; annual growth 1.9%).

MAJOR LANGUAGES: English (official), Gilbertese.

MAJOR RELIGIONS: Protestantism, Roman Catholicism, Seventh-Day Adventism, Bahaism.

GOVERNMENT: Republic. **Head of state and government**—president. **Legislature**—unicameral House of Assembly.

ECONOMY: **Chief agricultural products**—coconut palms, breadfruit, bananas, papaws. **Industries and products**—fishing, shrimp raising, small local industries. **Chief export**—copra. **Chief imports**—foodstuffs, clothing, tobacco, bicycles and other consumer goods.

MONETARY UNIT: 1 Australian dollar = 100 cents.

NATIONAL HOLIDAY: July 12 (Independence Day).

ple were resettled on the island of Rabi (or Rambi) in the Fiji group after World War II, was also made part of Kiribati against the wishes of the Banabans. Banaba, one of three great phosphate-rock islands in the Pacific, was made uninhabitable by the extensive mining operations.

The climate of Kiribati is pleasant, with an average annual temperature of 80°F (27°C). Easterly trade winds blow throughout the year. Rainfall is irregular and varies widely from island to island, creating occasional droughts. Typhoons most often occur from November to March, although they can batter the islands with high hurricane-force winds at any time.

THE PEOPLE

Most of the hardy and proud seafaring people of Kiribati are of Micronesian or Polynesian descent. The 2,900 people of Banaba, however, are ethnically distinct from the other inhabitants of Kiribati. English and a local language, I-Kiribati, are spoken on the islands.

Christian religions predominate. The islanders are almost equally divided between Protestants and Roman Catholics. There are a small number of Seventh-Day Adventists, members of the Church of God, and

Baha'is. Most children between the ages of 6 and 15 attend government-run schools. There are several secondary schools, some run by missionaries, a teacher training college, a technical institute, a marine training school, and a center of the University of the South Pacific. Some students attend universities in Fiji, New Zealand, Australia, and Britain on scholarships. More than 90 percent of the people can read and write.

The Marine Training Centre is a unique school, training sailors, engineers, and officers for service on international cargo ships. Set up in 1967 with aid from the United Nations and Great Britain, it is now run by a group of German shipping companies. After nine months of instruction, the centre's graduates ship out, mostly on German ships. The money Kiribati's seafaring citizens send home is important to the nation's economy, accounting for about 12 percent of the value of its annual output of goods and services.

Agriculture is almost nonexistent, due to the poor quality of island soil. Yet coconut palms cover most of the islands, and many islanders are engaged in harvesting coconuts and preparing their meat, copra, for export. Islanders also grow breadfruit, bananas, and papayas, and they raise pigs and poultry for their own use. Locally caught fish such as kingfish, snapper, and tuna make up the main part of their diet.

The government is encouraging commercial fishing, which has great potential. Raising brine shrimp (used as fish food) is important on Christmas Island. The great deposits of phosphate rock, for which the island of Banaba was noted, were nearly exhausted when the British Phosphate Commission, which administered the mining operations, withdrew in 1979. However, the Kiribati government planned to reopen the mines during the 1990s. The Kiribati government pays some of its bills with money earned from a fund that was established with some of the profits of earlier mining operations. Kiribati relies heavily on grants and loans from other nations, particularly Australia.

To curb expensive food imports, Kiribatians have set up several small businesses, including a biscuit factory. To boost exports, they have begun a garment business. And to develop their tourist trade, they have sought the help of resort builders from Europe and elsewhere.

HISTORY AND GOVERNMENT

The islands are thought to have been settled from the Marshall Islands some 2,000 years ago. European navigators first sighted the islands in the 1500s and early 1600s. A British protectorate over the Gilbert and Ellice islands was proclaimed in 1892. In 1915, the British annexed the islands as the Gilbert and Ellice Islands Colony.

The Japanese invaded and occupied several of the islands during World War II, and were not driven out until 1945. The Ellice Islands (now Tuvalu) broke away from the Gilberts in 1975. The Gilbert Islands gained full internal self-government in 1976. They became the independent republic of Kiribati in 1979.

Kiribati has a one-house legislature, the National Assembly. It has 39 elected members and one nominated representative of the Banaban community. An elected president serves as head of the state and government. All citizens 18 years old and over have the right to vote. Elections are held every four years.

HAROLD M. ROSS, St. Norbert College

The reefs that surround many of the Melanesian islands force large ships to anchor offshore.

MELANESIA

Melanesia takes its name from the word *melanin,* the pigment responsible for the color of human hair, eyes, and skin. Because the people of this region have the most heavily pigmented skin of all Pacific islanders, Western explorers called the region Melanesia, the "dark islands."

Geographically, the region consists of the enormous island of New Guinea and the outlying islands to its east; the Solomon Islands; New Caledonia; the islands of Vanuatu; and Fiji. Politically, Melanesia is made up of four independent nations as well as a French territory and an Indonesian province. Irian Jaya, the province that occupies the western half of New Guinea, is discussed in this volume's article on Indonesia. This section will introduce you to the island's eastern portion, the independent nation of Papua New Guinea.

THE LAND

In land area, Melanesia covers 371,803 sq. mi. (963,020 sq. km.). Its hundreds of islands are spread out over 3,279,364 sq. mi. (8,494,000 sq. km.) of ocean, an area about as large as the continental United States. The region is situated in the Southwest Pacific, northeast of Australia and south of the equator.

Most of the islands are volcanic in origin. Some of the largest, including New Guinea, New Caledonia, and the Fiji island of Viti Levu, are continental islands, formed of rock that has been thrust up from beneath the ocean. Generally, these volcanic and continental islands are mountainous and heavily forested, particularly on their eastern coasts, which receive most of the rain. The western coasts often consist of woodland or grassland.

Three quarters of Papua New Guinea is dense rain forest. Like Melanesians elsewhere, most Papua New Guineans live on the rich coastal plains and the river valleys of the interior.

548

Early missionaries converted many of the native Melanesian people to Christianity.

Melanesia is rich in minerals, including manganese, bauxite, gold, copper, and nickel. High-quality oil has been discovered in Papua New Guinea. The region's climate is tropical, generally hot and humid with plentiful amounts of rain.

THE PEOPLE

Culturally, Melanesians are immensely varied. In color, they range from a rich brown to a blue-black. Living in small, isolated groups for thousands of years, they developed hundreds of different languages—

NEW CALEDONIA

New Caledonia, a French overseas territory, is a divided land. Physically, the central mountain chain on the cigar-shaped main island separates the dry west coast from the tropical and forested east coast. Economically and socially, New Caledonians live in two separate societies. One society, the Melanesian, is black, rural, and poor. The other, composed largely of French immigrants or their descendants, is white, urban, and well-off.

This unhappy split was caused by colonial policies that favored white over Melanesian interests. Resentment and distrust

New Caledonians take advantage of the balmy climate to air-dry coffee, one of the island's chief agricultural products.

more than 900 in Papua New Guinea and more than 300 in the Solomon Islands alone.

Most Melanesian societies today retain their traditional structures. New Caledonia is the exception. There, nearly a century and a half of French colonial rule altered age-old patterns.

Wealth—generally reckoned in pigs, small valuables, and crops—is important in Melanesia. Village leaders are "big men"—people who are able to acquire wealth and distribute it generously, putting others in their debt. In a few smaller islands, such as the Trobriand Islands, east of New Guinea, power is held not by "big men" but by hereditary chiefs.

The status of Melanesian women in these societies is not high. On many islands, women and young children sleep in one house, men and older boys in another. Men often belong to secret societies and spend a lot of time in their highly decorated clubhouses.

Native beliefs are still important. Many Melanesians worship their ancestors, who they believe still live among them. A significant number of Melanesians were converted to Christianity by missionaries during the early 19th century.

On two island groups—Fiji and New Caledonia—Melanesians have had to share political and economic power with relative newcomers from India and France. This situation has caused severe disruptions in both places.

ECONOMICS

Economically, it will be a struggle for New Caledonia or any of the four independent nations to achieve long-term self-sufficiency. The region's population is expected to double between 1990 and 2020, threatening to wipe out many economic gains. The need for imported machinery, fuel, and even food—New Caledonia must import approximately one-quarter of its food—requires Melanesians to generate more

led to bloody clashes during the 1980s and to a plan that offers the possibility of independence in 1998.

About the size of Massachusetts, New Caledonia sits 682 mi. (1,100 km.) east of Australia. It includes the main island, New Caledonia (also called Grande Terre); the Loyalty Islands; the Isle of Pines; the Bélep Islands; and the uninhabited Chesterfield Islands in the Coral Sea.

The French annexed New Caledonia in 1853. The lure of free land for farming and stockraising drew white settlers, as did major mineral finds. Melanesians ended up with reservations on only 20 percent of the land. Their traditional way of life collapsed, and their numbers fell from an estimated 70,000 before 1853 to about 17,000 in 1921. By 1990, Melanesians' numbers had increased to 68,000, about 44 percent of a total population of 154,000.

After World War II, Melanesians gained French citizenship and rights. Some migrated to the capital city, Nouméa. Yet most chose to remain in rural areas. By 1990, the average family income for Melanesians was about one-third the income enjoyed by Europeans, who made up about 35 percent of the population.

A plan agreed to in 1988 divided the colony into three self-governing provinces. In 1989 elections, Melanesians won control of the Northern and Loyalty Islands provinces. Europeans won control of the Southern Province, which includes Nouméa. After nine years of limited self-rule, islanders will vote on whether to seek greater independence from France.

and more exports. During the 1990s, however, only Papua New Guinea exported enough goods to cover the cost of needed imports.

Still, much about Melanesia's prospects is hopeful. Unlike Micronesia, Melanesia is relatively rich in mineral and timber resources, although the rugged terrain makes them difficult to exploit. It is also blessed with fertile soil, especially on the islands' coastal plains. Most Melanesians are able to raise their own food. This helps them remain free of the need to earn cash in order to pay for costly imports.

HISTORY

Melanesians are thought to be a mix of peoples with roots in Southeast Asia. Their earliest ancestors probably crossed into New Guinea about 50,000 years ago. About 10,000 years ago, Papuan peoples came from Southeast Asia to settle on New Guinea's coasts, forcing those who had arrived before them into the interior. Later still, perhaps around 3000 B.C., a lighter-skinned people arrived from Indonesia and the Philippines and lived among the Papuans. Over the following millennia, the descendants of these peoples sailed east, establishing colonies as far away as New Caledonia and Fiji.

Portuguese seafarers looking for a route to the Spice Islands became the first Westerners to see New Guinea in 1526. Spaniards seeking gold and silver explored its coast in 1568. A short-lived Spanish settlement was set up on Vanuatu in 1606. Abel Tasman, a Dutchman, put Fiji on European maps in 1643. Europeans did not know about New Caledonia until the British navigator James Cook studied it in 1774.

Westerners had little impact on Melanesian cultures until the early 1800s, when American and European whalers stopped by the islands for rest and to take on food and water. Missionaries followed, altering the Melanesians' beliefs and managing to stop such practices as cannibalism and the nearly nonstop warfare.

Soon afterward, the European powers began to divide the region among themselves. France annexed New Caledonia in 1853. In 1884, the British made southeast New Guinea a protectorate; the northeast came under German control in 1899. Germany took over the northern Solomons in 1885, and the British took control of the southern Solomons in 1893. In 1887, the British and French set up a joint commission to protect Vanuatu, and agreed to administer it jointly in 1906. At the start of World War I, Australians replaced Germans in northeast New Guinea and the northern Solomons, which are now part of Papua New Guinea. Melanesia saw much action during World War II.

Independence. Demands for self-government began after World War II. Fiji won its independence in 1970, Papua New Guinea in 1975, and Vanuatu in 1979. The southern Solomons became the independent nation of Solomon Islands in 1978.

Only New Caledonia remains under colonial rule, a fact that led to bloody conflicts between Melanesians and French settlers during the 1980s. On Fiji, fears of Melanesian Fijians that they were losing political power to Indian Fijians triggered another sort of reaction in 1987—the first military coup in the Pacific islands. Melanesian Fijians were later guaranteed a permanent legislative majority. Beginning in 1989 and continuing into the late 1990s, secessionist rebels on the island of Bougainville fought for independence from Papua New Guinea.

Port Moresby, the capital of Papua New Guinea, has a large, well-protected harbor.

PAPUA NEW GUINEA

Papua New Guinea, which lies in the southwest Pacific about 100 mi. (160 km.) northeast of Australia, consists of the eastern half of one huge island, and many smaller islands and island groups. Most of its territory is located in the eastern part of the huge Indonesian archipelago, a chain of thousands of islands that helps form a boundary between the Indian and Pacific oceans.

Over past centuries, these islands served as stepping-stones for numerous migrations of peoples from Asia. Today, Papua New Guinea contains several thousand distinct communities of people, who speak some 650 languages. About 160 of these languages seem totally unrelated to any other, the result of the isolation imposed on Papua New Guineans by the islands' rugged terrain.

THE LAND

Papua New Guinea has a total area of 178,260 sq. mi. (461,693 sq. km.). About 85 percent of its land area lies in the eastern half of the island of New Guinea, the world's second-largest island. The western half of the island, a province of Indonesia, is called Irian Jaya.

Papua New Guinea has four distinct regions: (1) Papua, the southern portion of New Guinea; (2) Momase, the northern portion of New Guinea; (3) the Highlands, the central portion of New Guinea; and (4) the island territories, which lie to the north and east of New Guinea. These include Manus Island, New Ireland, New Britain, and other islands of the Bismarck Archipelago; Bougainville and Buka in the Western Solomons; Woodlark; and the Trobriand, D'Entrecasteaux, and Louisiade island groups.

The most prominent geographical feature is a mountain system, the central cordillera, that extends the length of New Guinea and crosses the boundary between Papua New Guinea and Irian Jaya. The numerous

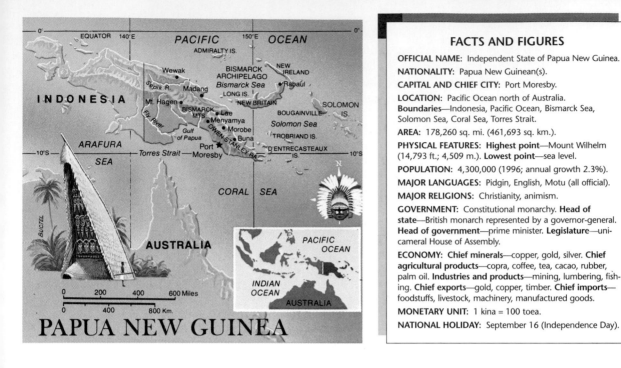

PAPUA NEW GUINEA

FACTS AND FIGURES

OFFICIAL NAME: Independent State of Papua New Guinea.

NATIONALITY: Papua New Guinean(s).

CAPITAL AND CHIEF CITY: Port Moresby.

LOCATION: Pacific Ocean north of Australia. **Boundaries**—Indonesia, Pacific Ocean, Bismarck Sea, Solomon Sea, Coral Sea, Torres Strait.

AREA: 178,260 sq. mi. (461,693 sq. km.).

PHYSICAL FEATURES: Highest point—Mount Wilhelm (14,793 ft.; 4,509 m.). **Lowest point**—sea level.

POPULATION: 4,300,000 (1996; annual growth 2.3%).

MAJOR LANGUAGES: Pidgin, English, Motu (all official).

MAJOR RELIGIONS: Christianity, animism.

GOVERNMENT: Constitutional monarchy. **Head of state**—British monarch represented by a governor-general. **Head of government**—prime minister. **Legislature**—unicameral House of Assembly.

ECONOMY: Chief minerals—copper, gold, silver. **Chief agricultural products**—copra, coffee, tea, cacao, rubber, palm oil. **Industries and products**—mining, lumbering, fishing. **Chief exports**—gold, copper, timber. **Chief imports**—foodstuffs, livestock, machinery, manufactured goods.

MONETARY UNIT: 1 kina = 100 toea.

NATIONAL HOLIDAY: September 16 (Independence Day).

mountain peaks reach as high as 15,000 ft. (4,572 m.). Between the mountain ranges, there are some broad upland valleys, reaching heights of between 5,000 and 10,000 ft. (1,500 to 3,000 m.). Large, swift rivers rise in these mountains and valleys and flow north, east, and south to reach the ocean. The largest, the Fly, begins in the mountains of western Papua and flows more than 700 mi. (1,100 km.) through the southwestern plains.

Luxuriant rain forest covers more than 70 percent of the country. The soil, however, is generally shallow and infertile, in part because extremely heavy rainfall has leached out the nutrients. There is very little highly productive agricultural land, except in the broad lowland valleys of the Markham and Ramu rivers and in some highland valleys.

Mountains—some of them active or dormant volcanoes—cover much of the smaller islands, too. Many of Papua New Guinea's mountains contain rich mineral resources. The copper mines on the island of Bougainville, formerly important sources of revenue, have been closed due to civil strife. The nation contains two of the world's three largest gold deposits, and high-grade oil was discovered there in 1986.

Papua New Guinea's climate is tropical, with average daily temperatures of about 81° F. (27° C.) in most lowland, coastal, and island areas. Daily temperatures in the highlands are cooler, averaging about 61° F. (16° C.) at 6,000 ft. (1,830 m.).

Developing transportation and communications over such rugged terrain is extremely difficult. For this reason, the government must struggle to unite the nation's many communities into a single political, social, and economic group.

THE PEOPLE

The people of Papua New Guinea are a mixture of related and unrelated ethnic and tribal groups. Although there are about a thousand tribes living in thousands of villages and speaking hundreds of different languages, the people can be placed in three main divisions. First are the

Papuans, New Guinea's basic population type, notable for long, thin legs; skin color ranging from dusky to deep brown; and frizzly hair. (The Malay word *papuwah* means "woolly-haired.") A far smaller group consists of Pygmies, people who average 5 ft. (1.5 m.) in height and have skin color that ranges from yellow to black. Melanesians populate the islands north and east of New Guinea and also settled on New Guinea's eastern tip. Foreign residents, more than half from Australia, account for just over 1 percent of the population.

The distribution of the population is extremely uneven. Vast swamplands, mountainous areas, and infertile regions are virtually uninhabited. By contrast, some coastal areas and some interior valleys of greater fertility have high population densities. About 40 percent of the population live in the Highlands.

In recent years, many Papua New Guineans have moved to towns and cities in search of jobs and opportunity. The population of Port Moresby, the capital, more than doubled in the 1980s and continues to increase. Port Moresby has most of the manufacturing and service industries of the country. Lae, a major port, is second in size.

More than half of the people are Christian, including both Roman Catholics and Protestants. Non-Christians maintain traditional religious beliefs, which include the worship of ancestors and spirits.

English, Pidgin, and Motu are official languages, and English is used in the public and missionary schools. Melanesian Pidgin, a simplified form of English, is widely used in the northern part of the country. Police Motu, used in Papua, is being overtaken by Pidgin, which may someday become the national language of Papua New Guinea.

For most Papua New Guineans, life centers around the village. There, men often build houses for their wives, daughters, and younger sons, and separate houses for themselves and their older sons. A longhouse serves one or several villages as a clubhouse and ritual center for men. The symbols of spirits and ancestors are kept in the longhouse, and religious rites are performed there. Older sons, upon reaching a certain age, are allowed entry into the longhouse, where they are initiated into the men's secret cult. Each village also has a rectangular-shaped park, which provides a meeting place for feasts, dances, and various other social activities.

ECONOMY

Papua New Guinea has a two-tiered economy. On one tier, about 70 percent of the people live on a subsistence level, producing their own food, clothing, and shelter. The chief food crops are sago (a starch obtained from a palm tree), taro (an edible root resembling a potato), yams, sweet potatoes, and bananas. This diet is supplemented by various vegetables, wild fruits, nuts, and fish. Meat from pigs, chickens, and wild animals is available in limited supply in some villages.

The second tier is the market economy. Plantations supply copra (dried coconut meat), cacao, coffee, tea, rubber, palm oil, and cattle for export. Mining—especially gold and copper mining—plays an important role in the economy, although the huge Paguna copper mine on Bougainville (which had provided 40 percent of the nation's exports) was closed in 1989 by the activities of separatist rebels on that island. Manufacturing consists mainly of food, wood, and metal processing.

Brightly painted community houses serve as centers of activity for many Papua New Guineans.

Many Papua New Guineans take part in both economic tiers, producing food for themselves and selling any surplus. In some areas, women have set up cooperative moneymaking ventures. One such venture, in a highland village, is a recreation center in which women sell snacks and beer to the men.

HISTORY AND GOVERNMENT

Humans arrived on New Guinea as many as 50,000 years ago, probably from Asia by way of the islands of the Indonesian archipelago. The first people fished, hunted, or gathered edible plants for food. Later arrivals were farmers who introduced various fruits and vegetables as well as domesticated animals such as dogs and pigs.

The first Europeans to visit New Guinea were probably Spanish and Portuguese navigators in the 1500s. In the early 1800s, the Dutch colonized western New Guinea. Later in the century, Germans established themselves in the northeastern part of the island, and the British in the southeast. In 1906, Australia took over British New Guinea and governed it as the Territory of Papua. The Australians occupied German New Guinea at the beginning of World War I. Later, they administered it as the Territory of New Guinea, first under a mandate from the League of Nations and then as a United Nations Trust Territory. In 1949, the two territories were joined as the Territory of Papua and New Guinea.

Papua New Guinea achieved self-government in 1973 and complete independence on September 16, 1975. It is a member of the United Nations and the Commonwealth of Nations.

Papua New Guinea is a parliamentary democracy. Its head of state is the British monarch, who is represented by a governor-general. The prime minister, the head of the government, is the leader of the majority party in the House of Assembly, a single-chamber legislature. The judiciary consists of a supreme court and a national court.

THOMAS FRANK BARTON, Indiana University

SOLOMON ISLANDS

The Solomon Islands remain essentially rural in character. Most people still live in small villages of thatched-roofed huts.

Few places on earth are as fascinating as the Solomon Islands, an archipelago in the southwest Pacific that is occupied mainly by a single independent nation. The islands were named by a Spanish explorer who tried—and failed—to colonize them four centuries ago. He named them after the fabled Isles of Solomon, thought to contain unimaginable wealth as the site of the biblical King Solomon's mines.

Today, these islands are valued not for the precious stones and metals the Spanish explorer sought, but for their rich mix of cultures and for their astonishing range of natural wonders. Solomon Islanders are Melanesian, Polynesian, and Micronesian. They speak nearly 90 languages and live among jungle-clad mountains and cascading waterfalls, active volcanoes and coral reefs, beaches of white and black sand, and more than 230 varieties of wild orchids and other tropical flowers.

THE LAND

The nation of the Solomon Islands lies about 1,200 mi. (1,900 km.) northeast of Australia. The largest island in the Solomons chain, Bougainville, belongs to Papua New Guinea, as does its medium-sized northern neighbor, Buka. The rest of the archipelago belongs to the nation of the Solomon Islands. It stretches 1,116 mi. (1,800 km.) from the Shortland Islands in the northwest to Tikopia and Fataka in the southeast, and nearly 560 mi. (900 km.) from the Ontong Java atoll in the north to Rennell Island in the south.

Most of the nation's major islands are arrayed in roughly two parallel strings that are separated by the New Georgia Sound. From west to east, the six main islands are Choiseul, New Georgia, Santa Isabel, Malaita, Guadalcanal, and San Cristobal. The Santa Cruz group, farthest to the east, contains, among other islands, Nendo, with rich bauxite reserves, and the uninhabited Tinakula Island, the Solomons' most active volcano.

The larger islands are mountainous and covered with dense rain forests. These forests teem with animals, including more than 140 species of birds, 70 species of reptiles, and gorgeous butterflies and moths. The coastal belts, where most Solomon Islanders live, are lined with coconut palms and ringed by reefs.

The smaller islands are low-lying coral atolls. The New Britain Trench, southwest of the archipelago, is the source of frequent earthquakes. Rennell Island, 124 mi. (200 km.) south of Guadalcanal, has 490-ft. (150-m.) sheer limestone cliffs, formed by the upthrust of the Earth's crust; the island is the world's largest raised atoll. Rennell Island's cliffs surround a lake that is dotted by about 200 small islands.

The Solomon Islands' capital, **Honiara,** is on the northeast coast of Guadalcanal, the site of heavy fighting during World War II. Honiara became the Solomons' capital after the war, when British colonial officials decided to make use of the abandoned U.S. facilities. Today, Honiara has more than 30,000 residents, somewhat less than one-tenth of the nation's population.

The weather is generally hot and humid throughout the year, with an average temperature of 80° F. (27° C.). Rainfall is heavy, about 120 in. (305 cm.) a year, and the islands suffer squalls and cyclones from November through April. In May 1986, an unusually late cyclone ravaged the islands. The torrential rains tore out sections of mountains that excessive logging had already made unstable. Tons of soil and mammoth trees washed down the river valleys, snapping bridges, sweeping away houses, and wiping out years of economic gains.

THE PEOPLE AND THE ECONOMY

About 93 percent of the Solomon Islanders are Melanesians, and they live mainly on the six large islands. About 4 percent are Polynesian, living on the outlying islands of Rennell, Bellona, Sikaiana, Ontong Java, Anuta, and Tikopia. Micronesians resettled from the Gilbert Islands, now Kiribati, have lived near Honiara and on the island of Gizo since the 1950s. Small communities of Europeans and Chinese also live on Gizo and Guadalcanal.

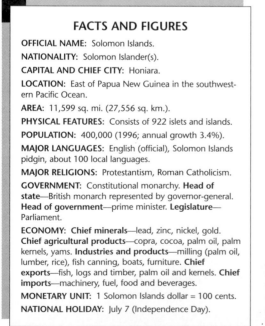

FACTS AND FIGURES

OFFICIAL NAME: Solomon Islands.

NATIONALITY: Solomon Islander(s).

CAPITAL AND CHIEF CITY: Honiara.

LOCATION: East of Papua New Guinea in the southwestern Pacific Ocean.

AREA: 11,599 sq. mi. (27,556 sq. km.).

PHYSICAL FEATURES: Consists of 922 islets and islands.

POPULATION: 400,000 (1996; annual growth 3.4%).

MAJOR LANGUAGES: English (official), Solomon Islands pidgin, about 100 local languages.

MAJOR RELIGIONS: Protestantism, Roman Catholicism.

GOVERNMENT: Constitutional monarchy. **Head of state**—British monarch represented by governor-general. **Head of government**—prime minister. **Legislature**—Parliament.

ECONOMY: Chief minerals—lead, zinc, nickel, gold. **Chief agricultural products**—copra, cocoa, palm oil, palm kernels, yams. **Industries and products**—milling (palm oil, lumber, rice), fish canning, boats, furniture. **Chief exports**—fish, logs and timber, palm oil and kernels. **Chief imports**—machinery, fuel, food and beverages.

MONETARY UNIT: 1 Solomon Islands dollar = 100 cents.

NATIONAL HOLIDAY: July 7 (Independence Day).

THE SOLOMON ISLANDS

In a nation where people speak nearly 90 distinct languages, a simplified form of English called Solomon Islands pidgin enables people from the different groups to communicate. English is the official language, but it is spoken by less than 2 percent of the population. Almost all Solomon Islanders are Christians. Education is not compulsory, although as many as three-quarters of all school-aged children attend some primary school. About 15 percent of Solomon Islanders can read and write.

On the Solomon Islands nearly nine out of 10 people live in small villages, mostly near the shore. There, they farm native vegetables on individual plots and supplement their diets with fish, wild pig, and tropical fruits. On the island of Malaita, where many people live in the rugged interior, small herds of cattle are raised for food.

Most villagers live in thatched houses built on platforms that are raised off the ground. Landownership is important—in fact, it is the major source of an islander's status—and it is passed on by the mother or the father, according to local custom. Only about one in three Solomon Islanders takes part in the cash economy, running a business or working for wages.

Fish, timber, cocoa, copra (dried coconut meat), and palm oil are the major export products. Tuna fishing and fish processing are the most rapidly growing industries. With Japanese help, the Solomon Islands have been able to launch a 40-boat fishing fleet that employs about 1,500 Solomon Islanders. There are deposits of bauxite (aluminum ore), phosphates, and some gold.

Population growth is high, however. Although economic growth outpaced population growth in the 1990s, unemployment remains high, especially around towns such as Honiara, to which young men have gravitated in search of work. Another economic problem involves logging. Far fewer trees are being planted than are being harvested, risking the loss of topsoil, wildlife, and eventually the timber industry itself.

HISTORY AND GOVERNMENT

Archaeologists believe that hunter-gatherers lived on the larger islands at least as far back as 1000 B.C. The European who put the Solomons on the map was the Spanish explorer Alvaro de Mendana y Neyra, who sailed from Peru in 1567. He died of malaria while trying to set up a colony on Nendo in 1595. Other attempts to colonize the islands failed, and Solomon Islanders were left alone for nearly two centuries.

The islands remained isolated until missionaries, traders, and sailors arrived in the 1800s. Germany claimed the northern islands in 1885, while the southern Solomons became a British protectorate in 1893. Some of the German-controlled islands were transferred to Australia following World War I. The northern islands became part of Papua New Guinea in 1975. The British Solomons became self-governing in 1976, and independent as the Solomon Islands on July 7, 1978.

The Solomon Islands are a parliamentary democracy in the British Commonwealth. The British monarch is head of state, and is represented by a governor-general chosen by the nation's 81-member, single-house Parliament. The prime minister, elected by the Parliament, heads the government. All citizens 18 years of age and older have the right to vote.

HAROLD M. ROSS, St. Norbert College

Vanuatu's capital city of Vila is also the main port for the tiny South Pacific nation.

VANUATU

The New Hebrides, islands in the southwest Pacific that were jointly administered by France and Britain for 74 years, became the independent nation of Vanuatu on July 30, 1980. Since then, the people of Vanuatu—the name means "our land"—have moved to develop their economy and forge a national identity out of their many colorful cultures.

THE LAND

Vanuatu is a Y-shaped chain of volcanic and coral islands that stretches from north to south for about 560 mi. (900 km.). Located about 1,200 mi. (1,930 km.) northeast of Australia, it includes 12 large islands and about 70 smaller ones. Efate, an island near the top of the Y's stem, is the site of the young nation's capital city, Vila.

Vanuatu's islands were formed by volcanic activity thousands of years ago, and several volcanoes are still active, including an underwater one near the island of Tongoa. These mountainous islands are densely forested, particularly on their east coasts, which receive the most rain. Their western sides are often tropical woodlands or grasslands, particularly in the south.

The people live mainly along the narrow coastal plains of the larger islands. The most populous islands are Efate, Espiritu Santo, Malekula, and Tanna. Vanuatu's climate is hot and wet. Temperatures range from about 60° to 92° F. (16° to 33° C.), and rainfall averages 91 in. (2,310 mm.) per year.

THE PEOPLE

About 94 percent of the Vanuatuans are Melanesian, representing a wide variety of cultures. About 4 percent are of French descent. The rest are Chinese, Vietnamese, and people from other Pacific islands. The most traditional of the Vanuatuans live in the interior of Malekula and

Espiritu Santo, the two largest islands. Pigs are at the center of these traditional cultures, with tribes and leaders trying to acquire as many as possible.

The impact of the outside world is evident throughout the islands. People who never had use for money now need it to buy consumer goods and to pay the tax that supports local governments. Many have left the countryside in search of jobs and excitement. One in 10 Vanuatuans now lives in Vila.

About 115 languages, most with several dialects, are spoken on the islands. Many Vanuatuans can speak five or six languages, including English and French, the official languages. Vanuatu's national language is Bislama, a form of pidgin English that is spoken by almost everyone.

While education is not compulsory, most children attend primary school. The secondary schools are too few to accommodate all who wish to attend. The island of Tanna, with about 25,000 people, opened its first high school in 1987. Malapoa College, in Vila, offers teacher-training courses, and some students attend colleges elsewhere on scholarships. Slightly more than half of all adult Vanuatuans can read and write.

A number of Christian denominations have substantial followings in Vanuatu, and many people follow traditional animist beliefs. During the 1940s, the people of Tanna invented a new religion—"cargo cults"—built around the legend of John Frum (as in "John from America"). These cults developed during World War II, when American troops brought huge quantities of goods onto the island. Apparently, one of the soldiers, a black man named John, distributed goods to the villagers. Many

FACTS AND FIGURES

OFFICIAL NAME: Republic of Vanuatu.

NATIONALITY: Vanuatuan(s).

CAPITAL AND CHIEF CITY: Vila.

LOCATION: Southwestern Pacific Ocean.

AREA: 5,699 sq. mi. (14,760 sq. km.).

PHYSICAL FEATURES: Volcanic and coral islands.

POPULATION: 200,000 (1996; annual growth 2.9%).

MAJOR LANGUAGES: English, French (both official), Bislama.

MAJOR RELIGION: Christianity.

GOVERNMENT: Republic. **Head of state**—president. **Head of government**—prime minister. **Legislature**—Parliament.

ECONOMY: Chief mineral—manganese. **Chief agricultural products**—copra, cocoa, coffee, livestock, fish. **Industries and products**—fish processing, tourism. **Chief exports**—copra, fish, meat. **Chief imports**—food, metals, oil, machinery, ships, vehicles.

MONETARY UNIT: 1 vatu = 100 centimes.

NATIONAL HOLIDAY: July 30 (Independence Day).

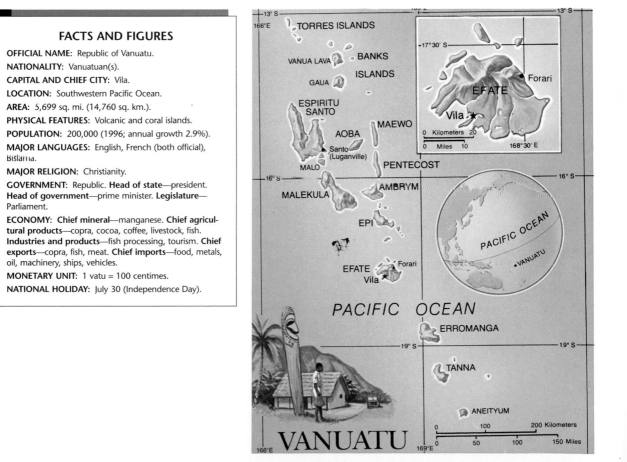

VANUATU

Tannese believe he will return again in a cargo plane or submarine, bringing them food and many good things. Villagers worship John Frum at clearings, where they have set up small red wooden crosses.

THE ECONOMY

Heavily dependent on foreign aid, especially from Australia, Vanuatu is one of the world's least-developed nations. Warm loaves of French bread are sold on Rue Higginson, the main street along Vila's green harbor. But only the well-off can afford it. Most families in Vanuatu grow yams, taros, maniocs, sweet potatoes, and breadfruit on small farms for their own use, and earn little cash.

Coconuts, cacao, and coffee are grown on large plantations for export. Copra (dried coconut meat) is the nation's leading export. Cattle and pigs are raised on the coconut plantations, and their meat is processed for export. A fish-freezing plant on Espiritu Santo prepares tuna, bonito, and other fish for export. A few items, chiefly building materials and beverages, are made locally, but most goods must be imported.

Handicrafts are made for sale to the growing number of tourists who visit the islands each year, attracted by the tropical climate and scenic beauty. Because Vanuatu has no direct taxation, it is growing in importance as an international banking center. The only known mineral is manganese, found on Efate. Though extensive forests are mainly exploited to meet local needs, timber accounts for about 4 percent of the nation's exports.

HISTORY AND GOVERNMENT

Little is known of the early history of Vanuatu. The Portuguese explorer Pedro Fernandes de Queirós established a short-lived settlement there in 1606. After the islands were visited by several French and British explorers late in the 18th century, French and British missionaries, traders, and planters began to settle there.

To protect the lives and property of these settlers, the British and French governments set up a joint naval commission in the area in 1887. Joint British and French administration of the islands was formally established in 1906. Separate schools, churches, hospitals, and police forces were set up for British and French citizens. But little was done for the native people, who had citizenship ties to neither Britain nor France.

Vanuatuan participation in government affairs came slowly. Vanuatuans were not allowed to elect their first representative assembly until 1975. After that, events moved swiftly, and, in 1979, the French and British governments approved a constitution. Shortly before independence, dissident groups on Espiritu Santo and Tanna tried to secede from the rest of the country. The revolts were quickly put down, and independence came in 1980 as scheduled.

Vanuatu has a parliamentary system of government. The 46 members of the one-house legislature are elected for four-year terms by universal suffrage. The leader of the majority party in parliament serves as prime minister and head of the government. Parliament and the leaders of 11 regional councils elect a president to serve for five years as the largely ceremonial head of state. A Council of Chiefs advises the government on the preservation of traditional culture.

HAROLD M. ROSS, St. Norbert College

FIJI

Suva, the Fijian capital, has become an important stop for passenger and cargo ships traveling from Australia to North America.

Once known as the "Cannibal Isles" for a practice its people renounced in the 1850s, Fiji today is a lovely tropical island nation that serves as a communications and transportation hub in the southwest Pacific. Fiji is widely recognized as Oceania's most important island group north of New Zealand. Its name is a corruption of the Tongan word for Viti, which native Fijians call their homeland.

THE LAND

Fiji's 332 islands, of which about a third are occupied, are scattered over some 250,000 sq. mi. (647,500 sq. km.) of ocean. The major islands are strung out in the pattern of an upside-down U, with the Koro Sea in the center. Viti Levu ("Great Fiji"), the largest and most populous island, is on the west, along with many smaller islands. Vanua Levu ("Great Land") and Taveuni, the next largest in size, are in the north. The 57 islands of the Lau Group are on the east. Many smaller islands dot the relatively shallow Koro Sea. About 240 mi. (386 km.) northwest of Vanua Levu is the geographically isolated volcanic island of Rotuma, which was added to the Fiji group in 1881.

Most Fijians live on two islands, Viti Levu and Vanua Levu, which account for half the nation's land area. Composed mostly of volcanic rock, the main islands are generally rugged, but have relatively large areas of flat land where the rivers have formed deltas. Fertile plains are found around the coastlines. The most heavily settled areas are the coastal towns and the river valleys where the land is suitable for farming. Many of the smaller islands are low coral atolls with sandy beaches and stately palms.

Fiji's climate is tropical with an average year-round temperature of 80° F. (27° C.). The southeast sides of the islands, drenched by heavy rains, contain dense rain forests. The northeast sides, which receive less rain, are often dry and treeless.

One-fifth of all Fijians live in **Suva,** Fiji's capital city, on the southeast coast of Viti Levu. Suva is a worldly, exciting port city, with high-rise office buildings, carefully kept parks, and institutions of higher education that include the University of the South Pacific and the Fiji School of Medicine.

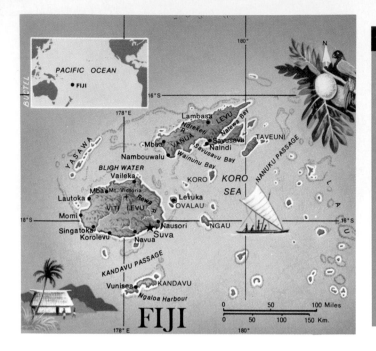

THE PEOPLE

Fiji is the third most populous island group in Oceania, after New Zealand and Hawaii. The population is growing rapidly, creating economic strains, including unemployment.

About 49 percent of Fiji's people are descended from laborers brought to the islands from India to work on the sugar and pineapple plantations between 1879 and 1920. The next largest group, accounting for about 46 percent of the population, comprises people of Fijian origin. The rest are Europeans, part-Europeans, Chinese, and people from other Pacific islands.

Native Fijians and those of Indian origin live largely separate lives. Most native Fijians live much as their ancestors did, in villages of 50 to 400 people led by hereditary chiefs. Schools and radios have brought new ideas to even the remotest villages, and today, 86 percent of all Fijians can read and write. The traditional Fijian house is a thatched log or bamboo structure called a *mbure*. The *mbure*'s mats of woven coconut leaves or reeds can be let down when it rains to keep the house dry. Recently, many villagers have been replacing the wood and thatch with sturdier tin and concrete. Native Fijians grow most of their own food, and few go hungry. According to custom, food and farm tools must be shared with those who ask for them. Virtually all native Fijians are Christians.

About 60 percent of Indian Fijians live on small farms, which they developed on land rented from native Fijians. (Only native Fijians and the government can own land.) Indian Fijians produce sugarcane and other cash crops. In the cities, Indian Fijians run shops and small businesses. Most Indian Fijians follow the Hindu faith. A minority are Muslim.

Fijian and English are the nation's official languages. Native Fijians speak Fijian among themselves, while Indian Fijians speak Hindustani at home. There is very little intermarriage or social mixing between the two groups.

ECONOMY

Native Fijians grow taro, cassava (manioc), yams, bananas, and breadfruit for their own use. Sugar, grown by Fijians of Indian origin on small holdings, and coconuts, grown on large plantations, are the leading commercial crops. Sugar and coconut products have long been important exports. But since Fiji gained its independence, the government has encouraged the growth of small manufacturing industries, the introduction of new crops, and the expansion of the livestock and dairy industries to reduce the country's dependence on the outside world for food and clothing.

Gold mining, traditionally important, is in decline. Other minerals, such as manganese and copper, have begun to take gold's place in the economy. Efforts are also being made to exploit the nation's enormous timber resources. As thousands of acres of trees planted by the Fiji Pine Commission mature in the 1990s, it is expected that timber production and related industries will become important economic activities. Tourism, which has expanded greatly since 1960, is already one of the nation's major revenue producers.

HISTORY AND GOVERNMENT

It is believed that the Fijians' ancestors came from somewhere in Southeast Asia and, over a long period of time, made their way across the islands of the Pacific to Fiji. The first European known to have reached the islands was the Dutch explorer Abel Tasman, in 1643.

There were considerable hazards for the early visitors to the islands, because the Fijians of that time were cannibals. Nevertheless, Americans and Europeans came to plunder the sandalwood resources, which they exhausted entirely in a period of about 10 years. Whalers and other ships called for supplies. Traders sailed through the islands, and some settled there. Missionaries eventually persuaded leading chiefs to abandon cannibalism and become Christians.

To gain favor, missionaries and traders sold or provided firearms to native leaders, intensifying tribal rivalries and enabling Cakobau, chief of the island of Bau, to rule a large portion of Fiji. Faced with defeat in 1854, Cakobau embraced Christianity and gained the support of the missionaries. But he was never able to rule all the people in his realm. In 1874, Fiji became a British colony. It gained independence on October 10, 1970—96 years to the day after it had been ceded to Queen Victoria.

For nearly 17 years, Fiji enjoyed a British-style parliamentary democracy, with 52 members elected to the House of Representatives and 22 appointed to the Senate. Elections in 1987 produced a government dominated by ethnic Indians. Fearing that native Fijians would be frozen out of power, an army officer, Sitiveni Rabuka, took over the government, suspended the constitution, and proclaimed Fiji a republic. Fiji was then ruled by Rabuka's handpicked president and prime minister. A new constitution approved in 1990 called for a 60-member parliament with more than half the seats reserved for native Fijians, prompting thousands of Fijian Indians to leave the country. Parliamentary elections were held in 1992. Rabuka's Fijian Political Party won the largest number of seats, although not a majority, and he was named prime minister. He remained prime minister after new elections held in 1994.

JOHN MILES, Senior Political Affairs Officer, United Nations

At a crafts fair on the island of Tongatapu, villagers shade themselves from the strong tropical sunshine.

POLYNESIA

Polynesia, named after the Greek word for "many islands," is the largest of the Pacific Ocean's three cultural areas. Its patch of the Pacific is roughly triangular in shape, embracing Hawaii in the north, Easter Island in the southeast, and New Zealand in the southwest. The line of the triangle that runs from Hawaii to New Zealand loops out to include the Ellice Islands, which became independent as Tuvalu in 1968.

The Polynesians are thought to have had roots in the Philippines or Indonesia around 5,000 years ago. Their sailing canoes—often rafts made of two or more canoes lashed together—probably carried them to the Bismarck Archipelago. From there, over a period of hundreds of years, they sailed southeast, colonizing Fiji and Tonga, then east to Samoa, the Society Islands, and the Marquesas. From the Societies, ancestors of today's Maori sailed southwest to New Zealand. Other colonists sailed north from the Marquesas to Hawaii and southeast to Easter Island.

The Polynesians established essentially the same sort of society wherever they settled. Over the centuries, distinctive traits emerged. But the shock that would change them all occurred after their discovery by Westerners during the 1600s and 1700s. Besieged by traders, whalers, settlers, and missionaries, all the islands underwent enormous change.

Two of the largest island groups, New Zealand and Hawaii, are now populated predominantly by non-Polynesians. New Zealand (discussed elsewhere in this volume) is an independent nation, and Hawaii (see Volume 5 of LANDS AND PEOPLES) is a U.S. state. The rest grafted Western political systems onto traditional ways of governing themselves.

Today the region's 11 overwhelmingly Polynesian groupings show a good deal of political diversity. They include three independent nations (Tonga, Tuvalu, and Western Samoa), two internally self-governing states (Cook Islands and Niue), two French territories (French Polynesia and Wallis and Futuna), a British colony (Pitcairn), a New Zealand territory (Tokelau), a U.S. territory (American Samoa), and a Chilean province (Easter Island).

THE LAND

Excluding Hawaii and New Zealand, Polynesia's total land area is only 3,259 sq. mi. (8,442 sq. km.), about three times the size of Rhode Island. This land dots an area of the Central and South Pacific that is about 15,000,000 sq. mi. (39,000,000 sq. km.)—more than four times the land area of the United States. The major island groups are Samoa, Tonga, and the five archipelagoes of French Polynesia: the Society, Austral, Tuamotu, Gambier, and Marquesas islands. Tahiti, the largest of the Polynesian islands covered in this section, is one of the Society Islands.

Most Polynesian islands are high and volcanic, some with tall, craggy mountains. Others are of the low coral type, on which coconut palms are the most prominent vegetation. The scarcity of arable land—even in Western Samoa and Tonga, where it is relatively plentiful—has forced many young people to seek work abroad.

Climate. Virtually all of Polynesia is in the tropics, and for the most part the climate is hot and humid. The warmest months south of the equator are November to April. These tend to be the rainiest months, too. Rainfall is heaviest in the mountains of the high volcanic islands, especially on the eastern slopes. From May to October, the islands are cooled by southeast trade winds.

THE PEOPLE

The population of Polynesia, excluding Hawaii and New Zealand, is 632,000 (1996). Nearly 85 percent of the region's people live in French Polynesia (220,000), Western Samoa (200,000), and Tonga (106,000). The other lands range in size from Pitcairn Island's 73 inhabitants to American Samoa's 57,000.

Polynesians are generally tall and golden-skinned, with fine features and straight or wavy hair. The many Polynesian cultures that evolved over thousands of years are closely related. From island to island, close similarities exist between their languages, traditional beliefs, and the way they trace their kinship.

Traditionally, most Polynesian societies were organized around the *ramages*, groups of people related to each other through their mothers or fathers in complicated ways. These relationships determined a person's rank, or social status, within a community. Chiefs inherited their positions from their fathers. They were thought to have *mana*, a sort of invisible power that enabled them to excel. It was *tapu* (taboo) for the most powerful chiefs to come into contact with commoners. Like commoners, however, chiefs fished or grew their own food and did not live off the work of others.

In certain societies, seniority played less of a role. Chiefs in places like Easter Island, the Marquesas, Samoa, and Niue tended to be people who could demonstrate their ability to lead. Other societies, such as

AMERICAN SAMOA

American Samoa, the only U.S. territory south of the equator, boasts one of the finest deepwater harbors in the South Pacific.

The only U.S. territory south of the equator, American Samoa consists of five volcanic islands and two coral atolls. Its administrative center at Utulei, near the village of Pago Pago on the island of Tutuila, oversees one of the best natural deepwater ports in the South Pacific. Jungle-clad mountains are the dominant feature of Tutuila, which covers 53 sq. mi. (137 sq. km.). Rainfall frequently exceeds 100 in. (250 cm.) per year. Nine out of 10 of the territory's 42,000 (1990) people live in 60 villages along Tutuila's coast.

The U.S. annexed Tutuila and Aunuu, a small island off Tutuila's east coast, in

those on Hawaii, Tahiti, and Tonga, developed rigid class systems. A noble class of chiefs sat at the top of this social pyramid, and the highest-ranking among them owned all the land. Lower-ranking chiefs parceled out the land for commoners to use. Vestiges of this system are visible today in the Kingdom of Tonga.

Polynesians worshiped a number of gods, including gods of rain, agriculture, and war. Warfare between competing ramages was common.

Today Polynesians are devout Christians. Chiefs have lost much if not all of their power. In remote islands, however, ramages are still important. Western Samoa, in particular, retains much of its traditional character and social organization.

THE ECONOMY

Most Polynesians raise crops or fish for their food. In French Polynesia, a solid share of the islanders work for the French government or for the tourist industry. U.S. government spending in American Samoa has similarly "Westernized" the local economy.

Coconut products are a major regional export, followed by tropical fruits and fish. Tourism, especially in French Polynesia, generates much-needed income. Revenues from these activities are never enough to meet local needs, however. Foreign aid is a major prop for these island economies. So is money sent home by workers who have jobs abroad, primarily in Australia, New Zealand, New Caledonia, and the U.S.

HISTORY AND GOVERNMENT

Spanish explorers were the first Westerners to visit Polynesia, landing on Tuvalu in 1568, the Marquesas in 1595, and the Tuamotus in 1606. Between 1616 and 1722, the Dutch mapped Futuna, Tonga, Easter Island, and Samoa. British explorers followed, and, between 1765 and 1778, they located Tokelau, Tahiti, Wallis, Pitcairn, the Societies, the Australs, Cook Island, Niue, and Hawaii. Traders and whalers followed.

1900. It added the three volcanic islands in the Manua group—Ofu, Olosega, and Tau—in 1904. Swains Island and the uninhabited Rose Atoll became U.S. possessions during the 1920s.

Like Western Samoans, American Samoans are descendants of people who set up pioneer settlements 3,300 to 3,500 years ago in Fiji, Tonga, and the Samoan island chain. Their language is considered the oldest of the Polynesian tongues. Yet nearly a century of links to the U.S. has weakened the people's commitment to traditional Samoan ways. American Samoans are U.S. nationals but not U.S. citizens—they cannot vote in U.S. elections.

In legal parlance, American Samoa is an "unincorporated territory"—it does not fall under the jurisdiction of the U.S. Constitution. American Samoans prefer it that way. They fear that living under the U.S. Constitution would bring an end to their system of *matai* (chiefs) and communally owned land. Extended families, or *aiga*, own 70 percent of the land. *Matai* assign the land to different family members. Individual Samoans own 25 percent of the land, and the territorial government owns the rest.

The government employs nearly half the work force. Tuna canneries employ one-third. Others are involved in handicrafts, dairy farming, and tourism. At least 85,000 American Samoans live in California, Washington state, Hawaii, and elsewhere in the United States.

Protestant missionaries entered Polynesia in 1797, Roman Catholic missionaries 30 years later. The missionaries translated the Bible into the local languages, for which they created spelling systems, and they taught the islanders to read. They also provided rudimentary health care.

On the larger islands, farmers from Australia, New Zealand, and elsewhere set up plantations. There they grew export crops such as sugar, copra, coffee, cacao, vanilla, fruit, cotton, and rubber. In some cases, they imported labor from India and China.

The Western powers divided up Polynesia among themselves during the second half of the 1800s. France, in control of the Marquesas and Tahiti by 1842, annexed other islands around Tahiti between 1881 and 1887. By 1892, the British had declared protectorates over the Cook, Phoenix, Tokelau, Gilbert, and Ellice islands. The U.S. annexed Hawaii in 1898. Germany and the U.S. divided Samoa between them in 1900, and the British turned both Niue and the Cook Islands over to New Zealand the same year. Britain signed a treaty with Tonga, which gave Britain the right to run the islands' foreign affairs and defense.

New Zealand seized Western Samoa from Germany at the start of World War I. During World War II, Polynesia was generally passed by, although Allied supply bases were set up on Tonga, the Cooks, Tahiti, Wallis, and the Samoan islands.

After the war, the region moved toward self-government. In 1962, Western Samoa became the first Pacific nation to gain its independence. Tonga followed in 1970, Tuvalu in 1978. The Cook Islands became internally self-governing in 1965, leaving New Zealand in charge of foreign relations and defense. Niue and New Zealand worked out a similar arrangement in 1974.

A small independence movement exists in French Polynesia. Elsewhere, however, most islanders have little inclination to break their ties to the Western nations upon whose economic support they have come to depend.

Whitewashed, colonial-style buildings recall Tonga's 70 years as a British protectorate.

TONGA

Citizens of the Kingdom of Tonga—Oceania's only surviving monarchy—are famous for their warmth and gentleness. Captain James Cook, who visited Tonga's islands three times during the 1770s, called them the "Friendly Islands," a name that is sometimes still used.

The Tongan chain consists of 150 islands. The 37 that are inhabited are hospitable places, offering fertile farmland, timber-bearing forests, and mild tropical climates. Tongans are well-educated—93 percent can read and write—and healthy, boasting the world's lowest death rate. Their government, a constitutional monarchy, has been remarkably stable. One reason, perhaps, is that it has confronted Tonga's problems—among them overcrowding, underemployment, and Western culture's challenge to their traditional ways—with wisdom and imagination.

THE LAND

The word *tonga* means "south" in several Polynesian languages. The kingdom is directly south of Western Samoa, whose islands Tongans are thought to have come from about 2,500 years ago. Tonga's 150 islands dot the southwest Pacific Ocean from Niuafo'ou in the north to the Minerva Reefs in the south, a distance of some 575 mi. (925 km.). Basically, however, most of Tonga's islands are clustered in an area about

200 mi. (322 km.) long and 50 mi. (80 km.) wide. These islands fall into three main groups: Vava'u in the north, Ha'apai in the center, and Tongatapu in the south.

Geologically, Tonga consists of two parallel, narrowly separated formations. Both are volcanic in origin. The eastern chain of volcanoes sank, so the islands there are low-lying and coral-covered. The islands in the western chain are high islands with richer volcanic soils.

The basically subtropical climate is hot and humid from December through April. The rest of the year, temperatures rarely rise above a comfortable 80° F. (27° C.).

THE PEOPLE

More than 98 percent of the Tongans are Polynesian. About two out of three live on Tongatapu, the main island and the site of the capital, Nuku'alofa, which means "Abode of Love."

Tongan traditions, along with Christian values and practices, have a profound effect on all Tongans. Outside Nuku'alofa, where Western lifestyles have blended with local ways, life centers around the village and kinship ties.

Land Ownership. An important fixture of village life is Tonga's feudal system. The Crown owns all the land, which is administered by hereditary nobles. Every Tongan male, when he reaches the age of 16, is entitled to rent, for a small fee and for life, 8 1/4 acres (3.4 hectares) of farmland plus a small allotment in town for his house. Tonga's high birthrate and limited resources may soon make this system unworkable. Several thousand landless and jobless Tongans have moved abroad to find wider opportunities.

Religion. Churches are well-attended. About one in three Tongans, including the entire noble class, are Wesleyan Methodists. The rest belong to other Protestant sects or to the Roman Catholic Church. The Sunday Sabbath is observed with great strictness. According to Tonga's constitution, no one can work, play games, or buy or sell anything on Sunday.

The influence of the Christian churches also extends to education. Mission schools provide instruction for three out of 10 primary-school students and nine out of 10 secondary-school students. Tonga has one small private university. Other institutions train teachers, nurses, doctors, and farmers. Education is compulsory for all children aged 6 to 14.

Economy. Most Tongans get their livelihood from subsistence farming and fishing. Tonga has three important exports—coconut products, bananas, and vanilla beans. In order to get the foreign currency it needs to pay for imports—particularly food, machinery, and petroleum—the government of Tonga is encouraging the development of manufacturing and tourism.

HISTORY

According to tradition, *tu'i tongas,* the spiritual kings of Tonga, can be traced back to the 900s. The influence of the *tu'is* seems to have extended to other areas of Polynesia.

Europeans first visited Tonga in 1643, when the Dutch explorer Abel Tasman landed on Tongatapu. English and Spanish sea captains followed. One of them was Captain James Cook. Another well-known visitor was

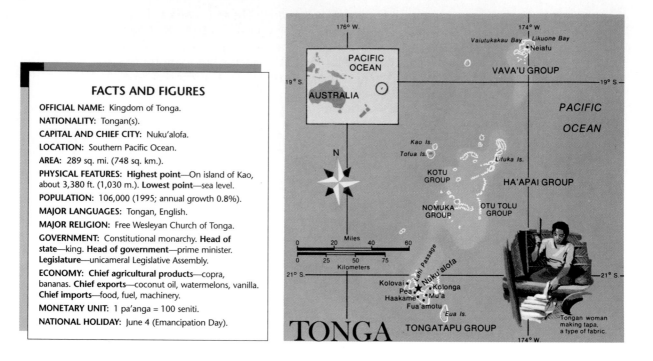

FACTS AND FIGURES

OFFICIAL NAME: Kingdom of Tonga.

NATIONALITY: Tongan(s).

CAPITAL AND CHIEF CITY: Nuku'alofa.

LOCATION: Southern Pacific Ocean.

AREA: 289 sq. mi. (748 sq. km.).

PHYSICAL FEATURES: Highest point—On island of Kao, about 3,380 ft. (1,030 m.). **Lowest point**—sea level.

POPULATION: 106,000 (1995; annual growth 0.8%).

MAJOR LANGUAGES: Tongan, English.

MAJOR RELIGION: Free Wesleyan Church of Tonga.

GOVERNMENT: Constitutional monarchy. **Head of state**—king. **Head of government**—prime minister. **Legislature**—unicameral Legislative Assembly.

ECONOMY: Chief agricultural products—copra, bananas. **Chief exports**—coconut oil, watermelons, vanilla. **Chief imports**—food, fuel, machinery.

MONETARY UNIT: 1 pa'anga = 100 seniti.

NATIONAL HOLIDAY: June 4 (Emancipation Day).

TONGA

Tongan woman making tapa, a type of fabric.

Captain Bligh of the H.M.S. *Bounty*. The famous mutiny took place while the *Bounty* was in Tongan waters.

Christian missionaries made an alliance with a young Tongan chief in the early 1830s. The missionaries supplied the chief with European goods, including arms and ammunition. In return, the chief announced his conversion to Christianity and saw to it that his subjects were similarly converted. With the missionaries' support, the chief became the acknowledged leader, first in his own Ha'apai group, then in the Vava'u group, and finally in the Tongatapu group. In 1845, he became the ruler of all Tonga as King George Tupou I. He later seceded from the Wesleyan, or Methodist, Church and formed his own separate and independent church, the Wesleyan Free Church of Tonga.

The current monarch, King Taufa'ahau Tupou IV, Tonga's first university-educated king, is descended from King George. Under him, Tonga's 70 years as a British-protected state came to an end on June 4, 1970, when Tonga became fully independent.

GOVERNMENT

Tonga's government is a mixture of Polynesian and European elements. The king rules his people on the basis of the 1875 constitution, which combines democracy with the traditional aristocracy of the Polynesians. The principal executive body, appointed by the king, consists of a prime minister and a cabinet. The cabinet is called the Privy Council when the monarch presides over it. The Legislative Assembly consists of the 12 privy councillors; nine Tongan nobles elected by their peers; and nine people's representatives, elected for three-year terms by universal adult suffrage. A Speaker, appointed from among the nobles by the king, presides over the legislature.

JOHN MILES, Senior Political Affairs Officer, United Nations

Most Western Samoans are Christian. On special feast days, pastors lead the children to church.

WESTERN SAMOA

The village's fishermen paddle their dugout canoes in single file, awaiting the order of their *matai,* or chief. At his signal the canoes form a circle, and the paddlers draw it tighter and tighter. Helmsmen slap their paddles against the water to confuse their prey, a school of mackerel; and all at once young men leap from the canoes into the circle, each with a corner of the village's fishnet tied to his toes. The perfectly timed actions bring the village more than a thousand fish.

Somewhere off Western Samoa, this scene has been played out nearly every day for hundreds and perhaps thousands of years. Western Samoans unswervingly follow *fa'a Samoa,* "the Samoan way," despite pressures from the outside world to change.

One source of Western Samoans' pride is the fact that scholars believe that Samoa is the "cradle of Polynesia"—the place that spawned all of Oceania's Polynesians. Archaeological evidence indicates that Southeast Asians migrated to Samoa some 3,000 years ago. A thousand years later, small groups took their distinctive culture east, to places like Tahiti and the Marquesas. That culture remains surprisingly strong in Western Samoa after more than a century and a half of Western contact. Samoa was named for the sacred *(sa)* chicken *(moa)* of Lu, the son of Tagaloa, the God of Creation in the Samoans' traditional religion.

THE LAND

The nine islands of Western Samoa—four of them habitable—are mountainous and of volcanic origin. Of the two main islands, Upolu is the more densely populated and the site of the nation's capital, **Apia** (population 35,000), which has grown into an important commercial and transportation center. Upolu's rich volcanic soil is better suited to agriculture than is that of the larger Savai'i, much of which has been made barren by relatively recent lava flows and porous soil.

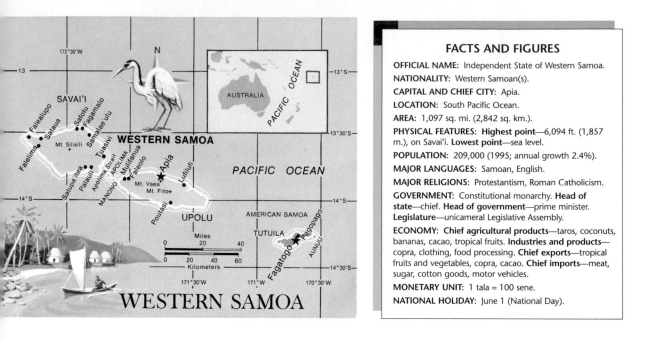

FACTS AND FIGURES

OFFICIAL NAME: Independent State of Western Samoa.

NATIONALITY: Western Samoan(s).

CAPITAL AND CHIEF CITY: Apia.

LOCATION: South Pacific Ocean.

AREA: 1,097 sq. mi. (2,842 sq. km.).

PHYSICAL FEATURES: Highest point—6,094 ft. (1,857 m.), on Savai'i. **Lowest point**—sea level.

POPULATION: 209,000 (1995; annual growth 2.4%).

MAJOR LANGUAGES: Samoan, English.

MAJOR RELIGIONS: Protestantism, Roman Catholicism.

GOVERNMENT: Constitutional monarchy. **Head of state**—chief. **Head of government**—prime minister. **Legislature**—unicameral Legislative Assembly.

ECONOMY: Chief agricultural products—taros, coconuts, bananas, cacao, tropical fruits. **Industries and products**—copra, clothing, food processing. **Chief exports**—tropical fruits and vegetables, copra, cacao. **Chief imports**—meat, sugar, cotton goods, motor vehicles.

MONETARY UNIT: 1 tala = 100 sene.

NATIONAL HOLIDAY: June 1 (National Day).

Western Samoa's mountains are stupendous. Mount Silisili on Savai'i rises to over 6,000 ft. (1,830 m.), and Mount Fito on Upolu rises to over 3,000 ft. (910 m.). Many of the mountains in the interior are covered by dense tropical rain forests. About four-fifths of the lowland forests have been harvested for timber or replaced with plantations.

Besides timber, Western Samoa's main natural resource is fish. The country has no mineral resources. Its climate is tropical. Rainfall is abundant, but there are no large rivers, because water sinks into the porous lava soil. Villagers usually get their water from nearby springs. Rainwater is also captured and stored in tanks.

THE PEOPLE

Although the people of Western Samoa are trying to join their economy to that of the more developed nations, they continue to live simply and with few luxuries. Their homes, called *fales,* are well-suited to the climate. A *fale's* roof is made of thatched leaves, and the sides of the house are left open. For privacy and protection from winds and rain, there are blinds made of coconut-palm leaves. The house's earthen floor is covered with pebbles. Mats are piled up to make seats and beds.

Most Samoans wear plain clothes suited to the warm climate. The *lavalava,* a piece of cloth wrapped around the waist, is worn by men. Women wear a two-piece dress called a *puletasi.*

The basis of the Samoan diet is tropical fruits and vegetables— bananas, coconuts, avocados, papayas, and pineapples, for instance—and poultry, fish, and boar. Foods are still often prepared in a separate cookhouse over an open fire.

Western Samoans are Christian, and most villages have at least one church. Many schools are operated by Protestant or Roman Catholic clergy. About 97 percent of the population can read and write. Some students attend secondary school or universities abroad.

ILLUSTRATION CREDITS

The following list credits, according to page, the sources of illustrations used in volume 2 of LANDS AND PEOPLES. The credits are listed illustration by illustration—top to bottom, left to right. Where necessary, the name of the photographer or artist has been listed with the source, the two separated by a slash. If two or more illustrations appear on the same page, their credits are separated by semicolons.

1 © Nicholas Devore III/Bruce Coleman Inc.
2–3 Jere Donovan
5 George Buctel
6 © Richie/Photo Trends
7 © Bernard P. Wolff/Photo Researchers
8–9 Jeppeson Maps/The H.M. Gousha Co.
10 © C.B. Frith/Bruce Coleman Inc.
12 © Giraudon/Art Resource; © Giraudon/Art Resource
13 © S. Fiore/Shostal-Superstock
14 Phillip Harrington
15 © Manley/Shostal-Superstock
16 © Stephanie Dinkins/Photo Researchers; © Sammy Abboud/FPG Int.; © C.W. Sorensen
17 © Fujihara/Monkmeyer; © Shaskinka Photo Library; © C.W. Sorensen; © Ewing Krainin/Shostal-Superstock
18 John Dominis/© Time Inc.
19 © Raghi Rai/Magnum; © Kalari/Sygma
20 © Richard Todd/InStock
22 Marilyn Silverstone/Magnum Photos
23 © The Granger Collection
24 © Mandel/Ziolo
25 © Cameramann International Ltd.
26 Dankwart Von Knobloch/Lenstour Photos
27 © Santosh Basak/Gamma-Liaison
28 © 1989 Kenneth Jarecke/Contact Press Images
29 © Charlie Cole/Picture Group
30 Christopher Morris/Black Star
31 © Delahaye Luc/Sipa
32 © D. Aubert/Sygma
33 © Wesley Bocxe/Sipa Press
34 © Cameramann International Ltd.
35 Editorial Photocolor Archives, N.Y.
36 Vickie C. Elson/InStock
37 © Robert Nickelsberg/Gamma-Liaison; © Christine Osborne/Photo Researchers
38 Vickie C. Elson/InStock
39 © P. Robert/Sygma
41 Peter Turner
42 © P. Robert/Sygma
43 Frank Schwarz/Lee Ames Studio
44 © M. Attar/Sygma
46 © Luis Villota/The Stock Market
48 Harrison Forman
50 © Art Resource
53 © Ormond Gigli/Rapho Guillemette
54 © Reuters/Bettmann
55 © Abbas/Magnum
56 © John Elk III/Bruce Coleman Inc.
57 © E. Streichan/Shostal-Superstock
58 Scala/Art Resource
59 © Roland & Sabrina Michaud/Woodfin Camp & Assoc.
60 Luis Villota
61 © Damm/Leo de Wys; Doranne Jacobsen/Editorial Photocolor Archives, N.Y.
62 © E. Streichan/Shostal-Superstock; © Carl Purcell/Photo Researchers
63 © William Kaufman/Leo de Wys
64 © Richard Kalvar/Magnum
65 Howard Koslow
66 Anne Bringsjord
68 © Tom Gibson/Envision
69 International Foto File
70 George Buctel
71 © Steve Benbow/Stock, Boston
72 International Foto File
73 © Bersurder/Sipa
74 © Superstock
75 Map by Guenther Vollath; spot art by Howard S. Friedman
77 Both photos: © Dr. Hans Kramarz
78 © Alex Borodulin/Leo de Wys
79 © Tibor Bognar/The Stock Market
80 © Serguei Federov/Woodfin Camp

81 © Lee Day/Black Star
82 Map by Guenther Vollath; spot art by Howard S. Friedman
83 © Fiore/Bavaria Bildagentur
85 © Ken Hawkins/Stock South
86 © Dirk Eiserman/Black Star
87 Map by Guenther Vollath; spot art by Howard S. Friedman
88 Both photos: © Klaus Reisinger/Black Star
90 © Y. Gellie/P. Maitre/Odyssey-Matrix
91 George Buctel
92 © Y. Gellie/P. Maitre/Odyssey-Matrix
94 Lanks/Monkmeyer Press Photo Service
95 © C. Spengler/Sygma
96 Harrison Forman
97 AP/Wide World
98 George Buctel
99 F. & N. Schwitter Library; Herbert Fristedt
101 A. Earle Harrington; F. & N. Schwitter Library
102 © Tamil/Sipa; Roland Neveu/Liaison
103 © Goskun Aral/Sipa
104 © M. Zur/Envision
107 © M. Zur/Envision
108 © M. Zur/Envision
109 © Louis Goldman/Photo Researchers
110 Eric Brown/Monkmeyer Press Photo Service; © Guido Alberto Rossi/The Image Bank
112 © Cindy Charles/Gamma-Liaison
113 © J. Shaul/Sipa
116 © deWildenberg/Sygma
117 George Buctel
118 Jordan Penkower/Editorial Photocolor Archives, N.Y.
119 © F. Sautereau/Rapho-Photo Researchers
120 Luis Villota
122 © W. Eastep/The Stock Market
123 © Dirk Halstead/Gamma-Liaison
124 Courtesy of Aramco; Frank Schwarz/Lee Ames Studio
127 © Mehmet Biber/Photo Researchers
128 © Mehmet Biber/Photo Researchers
130 Brent Brolin
131 Walter Hortens
132 © Lehtikuva/Woodfin Camp & Assoc.
133 © Richard Steedman/The Stock Market
134 Brent Brolin
135 Brian Brake/Rapho Guillemette Pictures
136 © Farida Hanak/Sipa
137 George Buctel
138 © McAllister/Gamma-Liaison
139 Frank Schwarz/Lee Ames Studio
140 © Christine Osborne/Photo Researchers
141 Frank Schwarz/Lee Ames Studio
142 © Raymond Depardon/Gamma-Liaison
143 Frank Schwarz/Lee Ames Studio
144 © Aral/Sipa-Press; © Al Gabas/Sygma
147 © Sebastiao Salgado, Jr./Magnum Photos
149 © de Mulder/Sipa
150 George Buctel
151 © Steve McCurry/Magnum Photos
152 Emil Muench/Ostman Agency
153 Editorial Photocolor Archives, N.Y.
155 © Michael Coyne/The Image Bank
157 George Buctel
158 © J. Guichard/Sygma
160 © John Bryson/The Image Bank
161 © J. Schmitt/The Image Bank
162 Owen Franken
164 © Moradabadi-Reflex/Picture Group
165 © Alan Oddie/Photo Edit
166 Margaret Durrance
168 Wesley McKeown
170 Wesley McKeown
172 Frank Schwarz/Lee Ames Studio
174 © John Elk/Bruce Coleman Inc.
175 George Buctel

176 © Arthur C. Twomey/Photo Researchers; Emil Muench/Ostman Agency
177 S.E. Hedin
179 © Sygma
180 © Fujihara/Monkmeyer
181 © Shostal/Superstock
182 Mulvey-Crump Associates, Inc.
184 © Fujihara/Monkmeyer; © Emil Muench/Lenstour
185 © Alain Dejean/Sygma; J. Alex Langley/DPI
186 © Warren Slater/Monkmeyer
187 © Tim Gibson/Envision
188 © Francis J. Dean/The Image Works
189 © Philippe Gontier/The Image Works
190 © Cyril Letourneur/Sygma
191 © J.P. Laffont/Sygma
192 © D. Aubert/Sygma
195 © S. Vidler/Leo de Wys
196 Jere Donovan
197 © John Elk III/Bruce Coleman Inc.
198 © Richard Todd/InStock
199 © Jonathan T. Wright/Gamma-Liaison
200 © Richard Todd/InStock; © Klaus D. Francke/Peter Arnold Inc.
201 © Richard Todd/InStock
202 S.E. Hedin/Ostman Agency
203 © John Bryson/The Image Bank
205 © Cameramann International Ltd.; © Peter Miller/The Image Bank
206 Robert W. Young/Lenstour Photo Service
207 © Cameramann International Ltd.
208 © Randa Bishop
210 Torben Huss
211 © Jonathan T. Wright/Gamma-Liaison
212 © Mathias Oppersdorff/Photo Researchers
213 © Richard Todd/InStock
214 F. & N. Schwitter Library
215 F. & N. Schwitter Library
216 F. & N. Schwitter Library
217 © Baldev/Sygma
218 © Baldev/Sygma
219 © Paul Slaughter/The Image Bank
220 © Cameramann International Ltd.
221 © Cameramann International Ltd.
222 © Pablo Bartholomew/Gamma-Liaison
223 S.E. Hedin/Ostman Agency
224 © Cameramann International Ltd.
225 © Alan Oddie/Photo Edit
226 F. & N. Schwitter Library
227 © P. & G. Bowater
228 S.E. Hedin
229 © Pablo Bartholomew/Gamma-Liaison
230 Editorial Photocolor Archives, N.Y.
231 George Buctel
233 Margaret Durrance
234 Alan Band
235 George Buctel
237 © Tim Gibson/Envision
238 George Buctel
239 © Chip Hires/Gamma-Liaison
241 © Bruce Thomas/The Stock Market
242 © Bruce Thomas/The Stock Market
244 J. Alex Langley/DPI
245 © Tim Gibson/Envision
246 George Buctel
247 Emil Muench/Ostman Agency
248 A. Earle Harrington
249 A. Earle Harrington
251 © Larry Tackett/Tom Stack & Assoc.
252 George Buctel
253 © Paul Chesley/Photographers Aspen, Inc.
254 Frank Schwarz/Lee Ames Studio; © Paul Chesley/Photographers Aspen, Inc.
255 © R. Ian Lloyd Productions Pte. Ltd.
256 Wesley McKeown
257 © Philip S. Jones/Photo Researchers
258 © D.& J. Heaton/Stock, Boston
259 © Bruce Gordon/Photo Researchers
260 © J. Messerschmidt/Bruce Coleman Inc.; © Ledru/Sygma
261 Lincoln Potter/Liaison
262 © Thomas Ives/The Stock Market
263 © Paul Chesley/Photographers Aspen, Inc.
265 © E.R. Degginger/Bruce Coleman Inc.
266 George Buctel